Character
DEVELOPMENT
IN CHRIST

VOLUME 2
Scripture Guide Study Notes

CHRISTY MORGAN

Character Development in Christ - Volume 2: Scripture Guide Study Notes
Copyright © 2020 by Christy Morgan
Published by Overcoming Publishing, Covington, GA
Contact: christycmorgan@gmail.com

ISBN 978-0-578-75122-1
Printed in the United States of America

Christy Morgan has penned a remarkable work in her *Character Development in Christ* supplemental book. It is filled with powerful revelation that will bring new life to you as you meditate on the expanded truth of God's Word. These *Study Notes* along with the *Personalized Scripture Guide* in *Volume 1*, hits a home run in the life of every believer. I believe this to be the most powerful part of *Character Development in Christ*.

Deanne "Dee" Barnes
Founder, His Wonderful Works, Inc.
CEO, Evans Tool & Die, Inc.
Conyers, Georgia

This supplemental addition is an example of the many years Christy has invested her spiritual life in faithfulness to God's written Word, but also to her time in journaling and listening prayer.

In this time, the Lord spoke directly to her heart to expand new revelation and wisdom of His written Word.

Christy's beautiful character was formed in her vulnerability and humbleness before the Lord. She received more that is true, beautiful, and good forming her renewed identity in Christ Jesus.

We are so blessed by this precious addition of her insights and references which take us deeper into revelations of God's healing Scriptures.

Beverly Gammalo
Christian Prayer Counselor
Stockbridge, Georgia

It is important that Christians build a Scripture based foundation so that our faith is unshakeable. Way too often believers are told to read the Bible. Many have tried and failed having had no direction in their studies. The Scripture Guide Study Notes, this supplemental book for Character Development in Christ, provides a practical, Scriptural guide to building a Biblical foundation. The Notes walk you through the Scriptures that bring healing and maturity in Christ.

While building a firm foundation, those committed to following these instructions will find themselves entering into a more personal relationship with Jesus. This is the ultimate desire of God's heart. He wants a family. Christy gives us a practical way to be part of that intimate circle called family.

The *Notes* help bring greater revelation of the love and power of Jesus. It is a great tool in the hands of a believer.

Eddie Mason
Senior Pastor
Southside Christian Fellowship Church
McDonough, Georgia

I dedicate this book

to my Lord and Savior, Jesus Christ,
who rescued me from myself and restored my soul
from deep-rooted insecurities to a new life in Him.
He has blessed me with a godly husband, Don,
and two beautiful children, Jonathan and Jessica.
This book gives glory to Him and to my heavenly Father
who has made it possible for all of us to live out of
the born-again creation.

CONTENTS

ACKNOWLEDGEMENTS

My special thanks to my husband, Don. You were there for me to read over material and provided the spiritual and mental support I needed throughout this work. Thank you for all the encouraging words and your much-needed strength.

My special thanks to my niece, Lisa Doolittle. You have been an inspiration and my greatest encourager throughout this project. I have called upon you many times for input and you have provided much needed wisdom and insight. You are a treasure.

My special thanks to our long-time friend Robert Moore. You have been so faithful in providing the much-needed technical support throughout the years while writing this book. Your help has been invaluable.

My special thanks to Ellah Mahan who created the beautiful painting that graces the cover of this book. You are a gift from God.

My special thanks to Dr. Su Mason. Along with your common sense and spiritual maturity, I appreciate how you graciously and methodically helped edit this book in its initial stages.

My special thanks to Katie Caron. You helped me by proofreading and making grammar and punctuation corrections where needed in its final stages. You typeset the book, prepared the cover, and all the other details prior to printing. Your professionalism, work ethics, and Christlike character was so refreshing to me and much appreciated.

Christy Morgan

FOREWORD

Never in the history of the church has there been such a need for the whole of Scripture, both Old and New Testaments, to be presented together in one's writing. It has been said, *"the Old Testament is the New Testament concealed: the New Testament is the Old Testament revealed."* Christy Morgan gives balanced biblical foundation in this supplemental book, *Scripture Guide Study Notes*. Here she shows God's amazing wisdom to make known His power given to overcome the strength of the pull of sin, found in *"Who Christ is in you."* Jesus Christ is the same yesterday, today, and forever, therefore it is inaccurate to think Christ is different from one Testament to another.

As Christy presents needed sound doctrine, she shows carefully: that the Divine Nature released in one's inner makeup, does not mean that the Old Testament standard of sin is no longer true and needed. Rather that the overwhelming strength of resurrection ability in Christ, in the New Testament, empowers the born-again believer to walk in the righteousness of that standard by the new life of Christ breaking forth in them. She helps us see the power of Christ's ability surging in one's reborn spirit empowers them to overcome the fallen nature as their mind is renewed. Her writing declares grace, God's pure life in Christ infused into the believer, is the means to experience glorious liberty in secret. This liberty is not about outward freedom seen of men, but in the hidden places of the heart seen by God – *"For he is not a Jew, which is one outwardly; neither is that circumcision, which is outward in the flesh: but he is a Jew, which is one inwardly; and circumcision is that of the heart, in the spirit, and not in the letter; whose praise is not of men, but of God"* (Romans 2:28-29). The blood of Jesus saves us from the penalty of sin and the nature of Christ saves us from the power of sin. Christy shows the practicality of Scripture from both the Old and the New Testament, brings relationship with Christ's very presence to us, as our minds are being renewed. Under His authority and living in this abiding place in Him, who loved us and gave Himself for us, we live by faith.

Chris Strong
Senior Pastor, Christ Fellowship
of Stone Mountain
Stone Mountain, Georgia

INTRODUCTION

This supplemental book includes over 350 pages of **Study Notes** covering each portion of Scripture contained in the **Personalized Scripture Guide - Volume 1**. Throughout these **Study Notes** are personal notes, teachings, and insights. It also contains over 6,000 Scripture quotations, many repetitive, and of those approximately 5,700 quotes are taken from the King James Version. This supplemental book is designed to inform, to encourage, and to help bring spiritual maturity in Christ to many. I also refer to certain chapters throughout the **Notes** (e.g., **My Story – Part One**, **My Story – Part Two**, **A Heart of Thanksgiving**, **Prayers of Repentance**), these can be found in **Character Development in Christ - Volume 1**.

Throughout these **Study Notes**, when quoting Scriptures in the Old Testament, where "LORD" is used, it is referring to *Yahweh (YWHW)*. The name *Yahweh (YHWH)* occurs over 6,500 times in the Old Testament and comes from the Tetragrammaton – meaning four letters – *YHWH* and means "Self-Existing or Eternal." *Jehovah* is used in the King James Version but most Bible scholars do not believe that *Jehovah* is the proper name for *YHWH (Exodus 6:3; Psalm 83:18; Isaiah 12:2; Isaiah 26:4)*. When quoting Scriptures in the Old Testament where "Lord" is used, it is usually referring to the Hebrew name *Adonai*. The name *Adonai* occurs over 400 times in the Old Testament and means "the Lord (used as a proper name of God only): (my) Lord."

Also, included in these **Study Notes** are the Hebrew and Greek definitions for many of the words contained in Scripture. It is important to read these definitions as the Books of the Bible in the Old Testament were originally written in Hebrew and the Books of the Bible in the New Testament were originally written in Greek. Unless otherwise noted, all Hebrew and Greek definitions are taken from the Strong's Exhaustive Concordance.

DIRECTIVES

To use as a study guide, take one portion of Scripture [i.e., 1(a), 1(b), 1(c), 1(d), 1(e)] each week along with the corresponding "words of wisdom" from the Lord (*Heart-to-heart*) from the **Personalized Scripture Guide - Volume 1**. Study, ponder, and pray over the corresponding **Study Notes** and Scriptures.

— or —

Take the liberty to use these **Study Notes** in whatever manner works best for you as you familiarize yourself with the **Personalized Scripture Guide - Volume 1**.

[To use as reference material]

Use the Subject Index and/or the Scripture Index by Subject Matter located in the back of the book, then go to the Contents page in the front of the book to find the page number.

STUDY NOTES - PART ONE

I pray these study notes along with the many Scriptures derived from both the Old and the New Testament will help you gain a greater understanding of (1) your heavenly Father's eternal love, care, and faithfulness toward you, and (2) the importance of casting your cares, anxieties, and distractions upon Him because He cares for you.

"Other seed [of the same kind] fell among thorn plants, and the thistles grew and pressed together and utterly choked and suffocated it, and it yielded no grain." Mark 4:7 (AMPCE)

"And the ones sown among the thorns are others who hear the Word; then the cares and anxieties of the world and distractions of the age, and the pleasure and delight and false glamour and deceitfulness of riches, and the craving and passionate desire for other things creep in and choke and suffocate the Word, and it becomes fruitless." Mark 4:18-19 (AMPCE)

"Likewise, ye younger, submit yourselves unto the elder. Yea, all of you be subject one to another, and be clothed with humility: for God resisteth the proud, and giveth grace to the humble. Humble yourselves therefore under the mighty hand of God, that he may exalt you in due time: casting all your care upon him; for he careth for you. Be sober, be vigilant; because your adversary the devil, as a roaring lion, walketh about, seeking whom he may devour: whom resist stedfast in the faith, knowing that the same afflictions are accomplished in your brethren that are in the world." 1 Peter 5:5-9

1(a) *You are* **Elohim – the Creator God**. *(Ref.: Genesis 1:1; Isaiah 40:28)*

I would like to begin by quoting a passage from the book, *The Broken Image*:

> One of the principal names for our God is *Elohim*, and we find Him thus referred to 2,701 times in the Scriptures. Elohim, a Hebrew word, indicates the relation of God to man as Creator. The healing of man—and his loneliness—has to do with acknowledging himself to be a creature, *created*, and in looking up and away from himself, from self-worship to the worship of Elohim, Creator of all that is: time, space, mass, myself. It is in this worship that our one true face appears, displacing the old false faces. It is in this honest and open speaking relationship that our true self bursts forth, cracking the shell of the old false self; and our old bondages and compulsions fall away with it.
>
> But man would be God. Every inclination of his will, therefore, tends toward self-consciousness and flees from the God who is calling him into dialogue with Himself—into God-consciousness. Thus, from worshiping God as Creator, man worships himself, the creature. Homosexual behavior is merely one of the twisted paths this basic fallen condition in man takes. Truly, to write of the healing of the homosexual is to write of the healing of all men everywhere. We are all fallen, and until we find ourselves in Him, we thrust about for identity in the creature, the created… (Payne, 1996, Page 125).[1]

I was amazed when I read this as it so rang true for me. I desperately tried to find my identity and completion in God's created being, woman. I was a homosexual and I truly believed that I was born that way (for details please refer to **My Story – Part One - Volume 1**). I so thank my Lord Jesus Christ for rescuing me from my pursuit of wholeness through His created, female, instead of Him, my Creator. For in Him we live and move and have our being *(Acts 17:28)*. He has released in me a flow of living water that can only be found in Him, the fountain of living waters *(Jeremiah 17:13)*. I can truly say that I am a new creation in Christ and I am continually growing in this new creation; old things have passed away and behold all things are new and all things are of God *(2 Corinthians 5:16-20)*.

1(b) You are my God. *You made me and You made my world.* (Psalm 118:28-AMPCE) *(Ref.: Psalm 139:14-16)*

If we believe what the Bible says then we know that this statement is true. It is essential that we reprogram our thinking to the truth of God's Word and who He is instead of trusting in our own intellect, emotions, and feelings based on what we think is right *(Romans 12:1-2)*. Proverbs 16:25 reads – "*There is a way that seemeth right unto a man, but the end thereof are the ways of death.*" Satan uses our carnal thought patterns along with our feelings, emotions, and circumstances to deceive us and to blind our minds to the truth of God's Word, thereby keeping us in darkness. It is only through the glorious light of the gospel that darkness is dispelled from within us to give the light of the knowledge of the glory of God in the face of Jesus Christ *(2 Corinthians 4:3-6)*. The carnal or natural man cannot receive the things of God as they are foolishness to him *(1 Corinthians 2:14)*. The Lord has put in every seed the DNA to reproduce after its own kind. He is present to watch the seed bring forth every creature. He is omnipresent *(Jeremiah 23:24; John 1:3)*! He has also put in the seed of His Word the DNA to create and bring forth the new man created in Christ Jesus which Peter describes as the hidden

5

man of the heart *(Ephesians 2:10; 1 Peter 3:4)*.

Below are Scriptures relating to God's creation, forming us in our mother's womb:

Psalm 139:13-16 *(NASB) – For You formed my inward parts; You wove me in my mother's womb. I will give thanks to You, for I am fearfully and wonderfully made; wonderful are Your works, and my soul knows it very well. My frame was not hidden from You, when I was made in secret, and skillfully wrought in the depths of the earth; Your eyes have seen my unformed substance; and in Your book were all written the days that were ordained for me, when as yet there was not one of them.*

References:
Ecclesiastes 11:5 *– As thou knowest not what is the way of the spirit, nor how the bones do grow in the womb of her that is with child: even so thou knowest not the works of God who maketh all.* ***Isaiah 44:24*** *– Thus saith the LORD, thy redeemer, and he that formed you from the womb, "I am the LORD, that maketh all things; that stretcheth forth the heavens alone; that spreadeth abroad the earth by myself…"* ***Jeremiah 1:4-5*** *– Then the word of the LORD came unto me, saying, "Before I formed thee in the belly I knew thee; and before thou camest forth out of the womb I sanctified thee, and I ordained thee a prophet unto the nations."* ***Luke 1:35-44*** *(NIV) – The angel answered, "The Holy Spirit will come on you, and the power of the Most High will overshadow you. So the holy one to be born will be called the Son of God. Even Elizabeth your relative is going to have a child in her old age, and she who was said to be unable to conceive is in her sixth month. For no word from God will ever fail." "I am the Lord's servant," Mary answered. "May your word to me be fulfilled." Then the angel left her. At that time Mary got ready and hurried to a town in the hill country of Judea, where she entered Zechariah's home and greeted Elizabeth. When Elizabeth heard Mary's greeting, the baby leaped in her womb, and Elizabeth was filled with the Holy Spirit. In a loud voice she exclaimed: "Blessed are you among women, and blessed is the child you will bear! But why am I so favored, that the mother of my Lord should come to me? As soon as the sound of your greeting reached my ears, the baby in my womb leaped for joy."* ***Galatians 1:15-17*** *– But when it pleased God, who separated me from my mother's womb, and called me by his grace, to reveal his Son in me, that I might preach him among the heathen; immediately I conferred not with flesh and blood…*

Here are Scriptures relating to God's creation which include mankind and the new creation in Christ: Genesis 1:1,3-28; Job 35:10; Psalm 33:6, 100:3; Isaiah 42:5, 43:5-7, 21, 45:18; 49:1,5, 54:5; Jeremiah 1:5, 27:4-5, 32:17; Zechariah 12:1; John 1:1-3, 12-13, 3:1-9; Acts 17:24; 1 Corinthians 8:6; Ephesians 2:10, 3:8-12, 4:17-24; Colossians 1:12-20; Hebrews 11:1-3; 1 Peter 1:22-25, 2:1-3, 3:1-4; Revelation 4:11.

How can something as awesome as this creation and everything that has breath come into existence in any other way than a Creator who is more magnificent and awesome than the creation! Let's take, for example, one of God's small creatures, the bat. They are nocturnal, the only mammal that flies, and most are found in dark caves. As I was watching the video, *God of Creation*, produced and distributed by Moody Video, Dr. Moon explained how bats avoid obstacles and the other thousands of bats where there is no light:

> Bats are not blind; they have eyes and they can see. The key to the bats' success in avoiding obstacles is not their ability to see. They emit strange cries in flight that can't be picked up by ordinary microphones. They are far beyond the range of the human

ear. A very special high frequency amplifier tuned to 32,000 cycles, for a particular bat was used and translated these inaudible sounds into sounds we can hear. Bats' ears are extremely sensitive to high pitch sounds. The bats' own cries are signals that guide it in flight. Science has proved conclusively that bats are guided in flight by echoes of their signal cries, a kind of radar. Man's radar takes tons of equipment and a crew of men to operate, but a bat carries its radar in its tiny head (Dr. Moon, 1945).[2]

This is just one example of God's awesome work. How could that have just happened?

The most amazing creation since the fall of man is the new birth in Christ! What would this world look like if every member of the body of Christ were walking in the fullness of the born-again creation (the image of God in righteousness and true holiness – *Ephesians 4:22-24*)? Paul said in *Ephesians 5:25-28* that the Lord is coming for a church without spot or wrinkle. The Lord's Word sanctifies and cleanses us on the inside from all that defiles and brings death. It is essential to deal with our heart issues before a holy and loving God and continue to renew the *spirit of our minds* to His truth in order for the new creation (our true self), within the heart of every born-again believer to grow into maturity and strength *(Ephesians 4:20-24; 1 Peter 2:2-3)*. Nicodemus asked Jesus in *John 3:9, "How can these things be?"* It by-passes the human reasoning to think that someone can literally be born again. But God made this possible through the death, burial, and resurrection of our Lord and Savior Jesus Christ. The first step in being born again is to admit before a holy and loving God that you are a sinner and to ask for His forgiveness through His Son Jesus Christ. Then ask the Lord Jesus Christ to come into your life, confessing Him as Lord and Savior. Peter writes,

> *Repent and be baptized, every one of you, in the name of Jesus Christ for the forgiveness of your sins. And you will receive the gift of the Holy Spirit. The promise is for you and your children and for all who are far off—for all whom the Lord our God will call.*
> (Acts 2:38-39, NIV)

Here is how I received the baptism of His Spirit. I asked the Lord to come back into my life in someone's living room late one night after everyone had gone to bed. It was months later at a Christian Conference when Pastor Bob Yandian asked if anyone wanted to receive the baptism of the Holy Spirit that I <u>chose</u> to go up front and he laid his hands on me and I received. The word "receive," in "*receive the gift of the Holy Spirit*" is the Greek word *lambano* meaning "to accept, to take." This Greek word *lambano* is the same word used in *Matthew 26:26* when Jesus took bread, and blessed it, and broke it, and gave it to the disciples, and said, *"Take (lambano), eat; this is my body."* The Holy Spirit is a gift and must be received as a gift. For instance, Jesus said,

> *For everyone who asks receives (lambano); the one who seeks finds, and to the one who knocks, the door will be opened. Which of you fathers, if your son asks for a fish, will give him a snake instead? Or if he asks for an egg, will give him a scorpion? <u>If you then, though you are evil, know how to give good gifts to your children, how much more will your Father in heaven give the Holy Spirit to those who ask him!</u>*
> (Luke 11:10-13, NIV)

I was water baptized twice. First, at the age of eight, when my entire family was water baptized. Then again in my early forties when I had a greater understanding of its meaning.

Below are two passages of Scripture in the book of Acts where people received the baptism of the Holy Spirit:

1. *Acts 8:14-17 – Now when the apostles which were at Jerusalem heard that Samaria had received the word of God, they sent unto them Peter and John: who, when they had come down, prayed for them, that they might receive the Holy Ghost: (For as yet he was fallen upon none of them: only they were baptized in the name of the Lord Jesus.) Then laid they their hands on them, and they received the Holy Ghost.*
2. *Acts 19:1-6 (NKJV) – And it happened, while Apollos was at Corinth, that Paul, having passed through the upper regions, came to Ephesus. And finding some disciples he said to them, "Did you receive the Holy Spirit when you believed?" So they said to him, "We have not so much as heard whether there is a Holy Spirit." And he said to them, "Into what then were you baptized?" So they said, "Into John's baptism." Then Paul said, "John indeed baptized with a baptism of repentance, saying to the people that they should believe on Him who would come after him, that is, on Christ Jesus." When they heard this, they were baptized in the name of the Lord Jesus. And when Paul had laid hands on them, the Holy Spirit came upon them, and they spoke with tongues and prophesied.*

First, I would like to share my own personal experience concerning praying in an unknown tongue or praying in the spirit. Paul writes,

> *Follow after charity (God's love), and desire spiritual gifts, but rather that ye may prophesy. For he that speaketh in an unknown tongue speaketh not unto men, but unto God: for no man understandeth him; howbeit in the spirit he speaketh mysteries.*
> (1 Corinthians 14:1-2)

He goes on to write,

> *For if I pray in an unknown tongue, my spirit prayeth, but my understanding is unfruitful. What is it then? I will pray with the spirit, and I will pray with the understanding also: I will sing with the spirit, and I will sing with the understanding also. Else when thou shalt bless with the spirit, how shall he that occupieth the room of the unlearned say Amen at thy giving of thanks, seeing he understandeth not what thou sayest? For thou verily givest thanks well, but the other is not edified. I thank my God, I speak with tongues more than ye all: yet in the church I had rather speak five words with my understanding, that by my voice I might teach others also, than ten thousand words in an unknown tongue. Brethren, be not children in understanding: howbeit in malice be ye children, but in understanding be men.*
> (1 Corinthians 14:14-20)

Praying in the spirit is a gift from God for every born-again believer. When your spirit prays, you are not speaking to men but to God as no man understands you. This is why it sounds like gibberish to others, unless the Spirit of God moves on you in a church setting to give a tongue and moves on another or yourself to give the interpretation *(1 Corinthians 12:10)*. Paul had a revelation of the importance of speaking in tongues. Let's look again at *verse 2* and *18*, "For he that speaketh in an [unknown] tongue speaketh not unto men, but unto God: for no man understandeth him; howbeit in the spirit he speaketh *mysteries. I thank my God I speak with tongues more than ye all."* This man, Paul, wrote one-third of the New Testament as the mysteries he prayed became revelation to him and then penned them on paper for the benefit of the church. This is why I believe he said to the church in *verse 13*, *"Wherefore let him that speaketh in an unknown tongue pray that he may interpret."* Paul also said, *"I will pray with the spirit, and I will pray with the understanding also: I will sing with the spirit, and I will sing with the understanding also."* Here he is clearly telling the church that we can choose to pray in the spirit just as we choose to pray with our understanding. As I shared earlier, it wasn't too long after I had asked the Lord to come back into my life that I had the opportunity to receive the baptism of His Holy Spirit. A friend and I were at a conference where Pastor Bob Yandian was ministering the Word of God. At the end of his message he asked if anyone wanted to receive Jesus Christ as their Lord and Savior. I knew that I had taken care of that. Then he asked, "Is there anyone who would like to receive the baptism of the Holy Spirit?" I felt something rise up within me, so I stood up and at the same time my friend stood up as well and we were asked to come up front. As we stood before the pastor, he said, "From this day forward you will never be the same," and he prayed that the Lord would baptize us with His Spirit *(John 1:33, Luke 11:9-13)*. Afterwards, we were escorted back to a room where two precious ladies talked with us about what had just happened and then told us that because we had received the baptism of the Holy Spirit, we could now pray in the spirit. They then said that they were going to begin to pray in the spirit (or in tongues) and encouraged us to join with them, however, neither of us joined in as we both felt awkward in doing so. Both ladies understood how we felt, but encouraged us both to exercise the gift. In my desperation to know Christ and to grow closer to Him, the next morning, while I was in my car on my way to work, I said, "Lord, You said, 'If I ask, I shall receive.' I know I received the baptism of Your Holy Spirit last night because I asked, so by faith I'm going to start praying in the spirit" – *Luke 11:9-13*. I then began to speak aloud with an unknown tongue and immediately this thought came to me, "You're crazy! You've lost it!" I said, "I don't have anything to lose!" So I continued to pray in the spirit. Throughout the years I have prayed in the spirit consistently and I have found that it is one of the most powerful things a believer can do. Here is an example of how praying in tongues can help solve problems at a practical level: Back in the day, sometime around 1984-1985, when I was a supervisor at AT&T, one of my responsibilities was the call center. One day, my District Manager approached me and asked if I would come up with a plan to help the call center run more efficiently. As I had no clue or any ideas, while at home and during my prayer time, I asked the Lord for wisdom in this area. I then began to pray in tongues. As my spirit was praying, a plan began to emerge within me. After prayer, I wrote the plan out and presented it to the District Manager the following day. He came to me and said that the plan was exactly what was needed and it was implemented immediately. I also love praying in tongues as there is only so much I can pray with my own understanding and I know that much is being accomplished as my spirit is praying directly to God *(1 Corinthians 14:2)*! I value this gift. Let's look again at what Paul said,

> *Follow after charity (God's love), and desire spiritual gifts, but rather that ye may prophesy. For he that speaketh in an unknown tongue speaketh not unto men, but unto God: for no man understandeth him; howbeit in the spirit he speaketh mysteries. But he that prophesieth speaketh unto men to edification, and exhortation, and comfort. He that speaketh in an unknown tongue edifieth himself; but he that prophesieth edifieth the church. I thank my God, I speak with tongues more than ye all: yet in the church I had rather speak five words with my understanding, that by my voice I might teach others also, than ten thousand words in an unknown tongue. Brethren, be not children in understanding: howbeit in malice be ye children, but in understanding be men.*

The word "edifieth" in the Greek is *oikodomeo* meaning "to be a house-builder, i.e. construct or (figuratively) confirm." Its meaning in the Thayer's Greek Lexicon is "since both a Christian church and individual Christians are likened to a building or temple in which God or the Holy Spirit dwells (1 Corinthians 3:9; 2 Corinthians 6:16; Ephesians 2:21), the erection of which temple will not be completely finished till the return of Christ from heaven, those who, by action, instruction, exhortation, comfort, promote the Christian wisdom of others and help them to live a correspondent life are regarded as taking part in the erection of that building… **to promote growth in Christian wisdom, affection, grace, virtue, holiness, blessedness**: absolutely, Acts 20:32; 1 Corinthians 8:1; 1 Corinthians 10:23; 1 Corinthians 14:4; 1 Thessalonians 5:11." It is a root word for the phrase "building up" and "built up" used in the following passages of Scripture:

1. ***Jude 1:20-21*** *– But ye, beloved, building up yourselves on your most holy faith, praying in the Holy Ghost, keep yourselves in the love of God, looking for the mercy of our Lord Jesus Christ unto eternal life.*
2. ***Colossians 2:6-7*** *– As ye have therefore received Christ Jesus the Lord, so walk ye in him: rooted and built up in him, and stablished in the faith, as ye have been taught, abounding therein with thanksgiving.*

The phrase "building up" and "built up" in the Greek is *epoikodomeo* meaning "to build upon, i.e. (figuratively) to rear up:–build thereon." As we edify and build ourselves up in Christ, through His Word and prayer, we are equipping ourselves to be able to edify and strengthen others in the things of God.

Second, as the Holy Spirit came upon Mary and she conceived Jesus Christ, the Holy Spirit was in Jesus at conception *(Luke 1:35)*. However, Jesus received the fullness of the Holy Spirit when He was baptized by John *(Matthew 3:13-16)*.

> *The next day John saw Jesus coming toward him and said, "Look, the Lamb of God, who takes away the sin of the world! This is the one I meant when I said, 'A man who comes after me has surpassed me because he was before me. I myself did not know him, but the reason I came baptizing with water was that he might be revealed to Israel.'" Then John gave this testimony: "I saw the Spirit come down form heaven as a dove and remain on him. And I myself did not know him, but the one who sent me to baptize with water told me, 'The man on whom you see the Spirit come down and remain is the one who will baptize with the Holy Spirit.' I have seen and testify that this is God's Chosen One."*
>
> (John 1:29-34, NIV)

John also said in *John 3:34 (NKJV) – "For He (Jesus) whom God has sent speaks the words of God, for God does not give the Spirit by measure."* In order to live a victorious, empowered life in Christ one must be baptized with His Holy Spirit and fire *(Matthew 3:10-12)*. It is through His Word and by the power of His Spirit that the born-again creation within grows and matures and brings forth spiritual fruit *(1 Peter 2:2, Galatians 5:22-26)*. If you are not born again and Jesus Christ is not the Lord of your life, I would like for you to consider making the decision to do so right now and then to submit to His Lordship in your life. If this is in your heart to do, you can say your own prayer or here is a prayer you can pray to Him (Romans 10:6-15):

A Prayer to become born again:
"Dear God in Heaven, I believe that Jesus Christ is Lord of Heaven and Earth. I believe that You raised Him from the dead and He is now seated at Your right hand in Heaven. I now choose to make Him Lord of my life by surrendering my life to Him. I confess to You that I am a sinner and I need a Savior to save me from my sin and the punishment of that sin. I ask You, Jesus, to come into my life right now by the power of Your Spirit and to forgive me of my sins. I surrender my life to you and make you Lord. Thank you for receiving me as Your own."

If you asked Jesus to come into your life, welcome to God's family!! I suggest that you tell two or three people that you received Him as your personal Lord and Savior. Ask the Lord to direct you to the church family He would have you to become knit together with, be water baptized in the name of the Lord Jesus—a righteous act—and receive the gift of the Holy Spirit (Acts 2:37-38). Immerse yourself in Christ through prayer and renewing your mind to God's Word in order to grow and mature in Him *(Hebrews 10:25; 1 John 1:7; Matthew 3:13-16; 1 Peter 1:23-2:3; Romans 12:1-2; Ephesians 4:20-24; Colossians 2:6-8)*. I also want to encourage you to be real with your heavenly Father and some mature believers in Christ concerning your heart issues to help you overcome and begin to put to death the old man (i.e., ungodly thought patterns and mindsets as the Lord reveals them to you) *(James 5:16)*.

1(c) *Thank You for all that You have given me. (Ref.: Ephesians 5:20; 1 Thessalonians 5:18; Hebrews 13:15)*

We are created in God's image, after His likeness. How do you feel when you are appreciated? For example, isn't it a blessing when your spouse, children, employer, teacher, etc., gives thanks to you for the things you've done or for who you are as a person. It certainly blesses me! It touches something on the inside of me that brightens my day. On the other hand, how do you feel when you're around someone who is a complainer or seems to never be pleased? As for me, it is grievous and weighs heavy on my heart. Let's consider the children of Israel, as God's intent was to bless them and bring them into the promised land. But because of their continual murmuring and complaining, He was frustrated and angry with them and they ended up dying in the wilderness, with the exception of Joshua and Caleb who were obedient to the Lord and truly trusted in Him *(Numbers 14)*. Jesus said in *Matthew 25:40* — "…*inasmuch as ye have done it unto one of the least of these my brethren, ye have done it unto me.*" When we murmur and complain to others, we murmur and complain to the Lord *(Exodus 16:8)*. When we are thankful and kind toward others we are thankful and kind toward the Lord *(Matthew 25:32-40)*. So with that, below is an example where the Lord helped me to see the importance of giving thanks for my husband:

"The Lord spoke to my heart one day when my husband, Don, and I were in the kitchen. I was sitting at the kitchen table and Don was in the kitchen doing something. I was looking at him and within myself, I was picking at something that he wasn't doing right, not at that particular moment, but just in his character. In other words, I had an evil eye toward him. The Lord immediately arrested that thought and said, *"You're more focused on what he's not doing right than on the things he does do right."* I asked the Lord to forgive me and shortly after that I felt prompted to make a list of the good qualities in my husband and I began using that list to give thanks to the Lord for him during my time of speaking aloud the Lord's truths using the *Personalized Scripture Guide - Volume 1*. Making conscious efforts to give thanks can become a powerful behavior pattern in our lives. It helps to still the enemy's tactics in building strongholds of hate and cynicism. Over the years I have seen amazing results in my heart and changes in my husband's heart too!"

I want to encourage you to use the *Heart of Thanksgiving Prayer Guide - Volume 1*, provided in Chapter 7, to help remind you of the things to give the Lord thanks for (i.e., your family, friends, health, hot and cold water, a roof over your head, clothing, food, provision, sanctification in your heart and in your loved one's too). List the good things concerning your loved ones and others, especially those who are closest to you and offer up prayers with thanksgiving for them. Even to those you may be feeling bitterness and resentment toward, after forgiving them, begin to give thanks to the Lord for them and offer up prayers with thanksgiving (e.g., thanking Him for their salvation and for His will to be done in their lives). It is also important after releasing any bitterness and resentment to the Lord to ask the Lord for a cleansing from all unrighteousness concerning wrong mindsets and attitudes toward others *(Ephesians 5:25-27; 1 John 1:9)*. Allow praise and thanksgiving to flow from your heart to His.

Below are Scriptures relating to giving thanks and praising God:

Psalm 92:1 – *It is a good thing to give thanks unto the LORD, and to sing praises unto thy name, O most High.*

References:
Psalm 118:1, 24, 29 – *O, give thanks unto the LORD; for he is good: because his mercy endureth for ever. This is the day which the LORD hath made; we will rejoice and be glad in it. O give thanks unto the LORD; for he is good: for his mercy endureth for ever.* *Luke 17:11-19* – *And it came to pass, as he went to Jerusalem, that he passed through the midst of Samaria and Galilee. And as he entered a certain village, there met him ten men that were lepers, which stood afar off: and they lifted up their voices, and said, "Jesus, Master, have mercy on us." And when he saw [them], he said unto them, "Go, shew yourselves unto the priests." And it came to pass, that, as they went, they were cleansed. And one of them, when he saw that he was healed, turned back, and with a loud voice glorified God, and fell down on his face at his feet, giving him thanks: and he was a Samaritan. And Jesus answering said, "Were there not ten cleansed? but where [are] the nine? There are not found that returned to give glory to God, save this stranger. And he said unto him, "Arise, go thy way: thy faith has made thee whole."* The Greek word for whole is *sozo* and means "to save, i.e. deliver or protect (literally or figuratively):– heal, preserve, save (self), do well, be (make) whole." I believe it moved Jesus to see the faith and humility of heart in the Samaritan man that chose to return and glorify God, falling down on his face at His feet, giving Him thanks. Jesus told the Samaritan, *"Arise, go thy way: thy faith has made thee whole."* I believe the faith and humility of heart within him would serve as a protective barrier from leprosy. The other nine chose not to give thanks. I believe this was an indication of pride and arrogance in their hearts which could open the door for the disease to return. *Ephesians 5:17-21 (NKJV)* – *Therefore do not be unwise, but understand what the will of the Lord is. And do not be drunk with wine, in which is dissipation; but be filled with the Spirit, speaking to one another in psalms and hymns and spiritual songs, singing and making melody in your heart to the Lord, giving thanks always for all things to God the Father in the name of our Lord Jesus Christ, submitting to one another in the fear of God.* *Colossians 2:6-7* – *As ye have therefore received Christ Jesus the Lord, so walk ye in him: rooted and built up in him, and stablished in the faith, as ye have been taught, abounding therein with*

thanksgiving. **1 Thessalonians 5:18** – *In everything give thanks: for this is the will of God in Christ Jesus concerning you.* (In everything give thanks is a very powerful statement. This means giving thanks in the good times and in the bad times, knowing that all things work together for good to those who love God and are called according to His purpose *[Romans 8:28].* This is the Gospel's Good News! The Greek word for thanks is *eucharisteo* meaning "to be grateful…"). **Hebrews 13:15** *(NKJV)* – *Thereby by Him let us continually offer the sacrifice of praise to God, that is, the fruit of our lips, giving thanks to His name.*

Please refer to **Note 10b** for additional information and Scriptures relating to the importance of giving thanks.

1(d) How precious and weighty also are Your thoughts to me, O God! How vast is the sum of them! If I could count them, they would be more in number than the sand. (Psalm 139:17-18-AMPCE)

The Hebrew word for "precious" is *yaqar* meaning "a primitive root; properly, apparently, to be heavy, i.e. (figuratively) valuable…" Therefore the word precious can mean <u>valuable</u>. In order to gain a better understanding of how vast and infinite His thoughts are toward you, lets look at an illustration from Dr. Moon's classic film, *God of Creation*, where he compares the vastness of the universe with the grains of sand on all the seashores:

> The Milky Way is merely our view of our own galaxy. But ours is just one galaxy. Everywhere we look out in space there are others. How many stars are there? Astronomers tell us that there are at least 100 billion stars in our galaxy. There are 100 million of these galaxies in known space and known space is just one billion of theoretical space. So if we would number the stars we must multiply 100 billion x 100 million x 1,000 million this equals 10 octillion stars or 1028 power (10,000,000,000,000, 000,000,000,000,000). <u>To get an idea of how much that is you would have to count all the grains of sand on all the seashores in the entire world</u> (Dr. Moon, 1945).[3]

Psalm 147:4-5 (NKJV) reads, *"He counts the numbers of the stars; He calls them all by name. Great is our LORD, and mighty in power; His understanding is infinite."* In other words, His understanding is infinite, immeasurable, boundless, incalculable. *Hosea 1:10* reads that the sand of the sea cannot be measured or numbered; and in *Jeremiah 33:22, "As the host of heaven cannot be numbered, neither the sand of the sea measured…"* Our Creator not only can count all the stars but He calls them all by name! Therefore, it is impossible to wrap our brains around just how great and numerous are His loving thoughts toward us!

Only our Creator God has the capacity to have a close intimate relationship with millions of people at the same time!! He is an amazing God! And as you can see, our Father's love for us and His thoughts toward us go much deeper than the mind can comprehend. The way we receive God's love comes by the power of His Holy Spirit through the new birth in Christ. Jesus took away the sin of the world through His obedience unto death, even the death of the cross. Those who receive Jesus Christ as their Lord and Savior will be able to experience this love as they grow in Christ. His thoughts towards us are thoughts of peace (i.e., wholeness in Christ – fullness of joy, hope, faith, love). We rest in His love and the only way we can grasp His love toward us is in our inner man—the hidden man of the heart. Paul writes,

For this reason I bow my knees to the Father, from whom every family in heaven and earth derives its name, that He would grant you, according to the riches of His glory, to be strengthened with power through His Spirit in the <u>inner man</u>, so that Christ may dwell in your hearts through faith; and that you, being rooted and grounded in love, may be able to comprehend with all the saints what is the breadth and length and height and depth, and to know the love of Christ which passes knowledge; that you may be filled up to all the fullness of God.

(Ephesians 3:14-19, NASB)

For I am persuaded, that neither death, nor life, nor angels, nor principalities, nor powers, nor things present, nor things to come, nor height, nor depth, nor any other creature, shall be able to separate us from the love of God which is in Christ Jesus our Lord.

(Romans 8:38-39)

1(e) ...[And the Lord answered], Can a woman forget her nursing child, that she should not have compassion on the son of her womb? Yes, they may forget, yet I will not forget you. (Isaiah 49:15-AMPCE)

Do you feel your heavenly Father has forgotten you? He certainly has not! The depths of His love for you passes knowledge. The Lord says in the following passage of Scripture:

Can a mother forget the baby at her breast and have no compassion on the child she has borne? Though she may forget, I will not forget you! See, I have engraved you on the palms of my hands; your walls are ever before me.

(Isaiah 49:15-16, NIV)

God's love for us sent His only Son as a final sacrifice in order for us to become born again into His family and to be nurtured and developed in His righteousness and holiness where we can truly experience and live out of His love for us, where our true identity resides. We are ever engraved in the palms of His nail-scarred hands where we, individually, will forever be remembered and where His very purpose is to give Himself for us *(Hebrews 7:25)*. After Jesus was crucified, He appeared to His disciples when they were gathered together in an enclosed area. He said, "Peace be with you." <u>He then showed them His hands and His side</u>. And the disciples were glad when they saw the Lord. And Jesus said to them again,

"Peace be with you! As the Father has sent me, I am sending you." And with that he breathed on them and said, "Receive the Holy Spirit. If you forgive anyone's sins, their sins are forgiven; if you do not forgive them, they are not forgiven." Now Thomas (also known as Didymus), one of the Twelve, was not with the disciples when Jesus came. So the other disciples told him, "We have seen the Lord!" But he said to them, "Unless I see the nail marks in his hands and put my finger where the nails were, and put my hand into his side, I will not believe." A week later his disciples were in the house again, and Thomas was with them. Though the doors were locked, Jesus came and stood among them and said, "Peace

be with you!" Then he said to Thomas, "Put your finger here; see my hands. Reach out your hand and put it into my side. Stop doubting and believe." Thomas said to him, "My Lord and my God!" Then Jesus told him, "Because you have seen me, you have believed; blessed are those who have not seen and yet have believed."

(John 20:21-29, NIV)

The Lord's love runs deep and His nail-scarred hands are a sign of His great love!

One evening I was watching a video of an eagle taking care of her young. Every night the eagle would faithfully gather her young under her to protect them and bring comfort and warmth to them. Day after day she would faithfully go search for food and return to provide nourishment to them. Those eaglets would gaze up at their mother and open their mouths as the mother filled them with the nourishment they needed in order to grow. God has put that nurturing quality in His creation concerning their young as this is a small glimpse of His faithfulness toward us in nurturing and developing the new man within every born-again believer.

Another Hebrew name of God is *El-Shaddai (Shadday)* and occurs 48 times in the Old Testament displaying God as Almighty. The passage of Scripture that comes to mind concerning this name is,

He that dwelleth in the secret place of the most High shall abide under the shadow of the Almighty (Shaddai). I will say of the Lord, He is my refuge and my fortress: my God; in him will I trust. Surely he shall deliver thee from the snare of the fowler, and from the noisome pestilence. He shall cover thee with his feathers, and under his wings shalt thou trust: his truth shall be thy shield and buckler.

(Psalm 91:1-4)

God is our Protector, our Covering, our Strength, our Comfort, our Sustainer, our Nurturer, our Healer, our Counsellor, our Constant Companion. Nothing can harm those who choose to dwell in His care. Our will is an amazing gift our Creator has given to us. As born-again believers, we can choose to be nourished by Him and grow into His image to experience abundant life or we can choose to go our own way. In either case, we will all appear before the judgment seat of Christ, to receive the things done in our own body, whether good or bad *(1 Corinthians 5:10; Revelations 22:12-15)*. We choose as the Lord says in the following passage of Scripture:

I call heaven and earth to record this day against you, that I have set before you life and death, blessing and cursing: therefore <u>choose life</u>, that both thou and thy seed (descendants) may live: that thou mayest love the LORD thy God, and that thou mayest obey his voice, and that thou mayest cleave unto him: for he is thy life, and the length of thy days...

(Deuteronomy 30:19-20)

2(a) *You are **El-Olam** – the Everlasting God. (Ref.: Genesis 21:33)*

The meaning of the Hebrew word *El* is "<u>strength</u>; as adjective, <u>mighty; especially the Almighty</u> (but used also of any deity):–<u>God</u> (god), x goodly, x great, idol, might(-y one), <u>power</u>, <u>strong</u>." *Olam* occurs 439 times in the King James Bible and its meaning is "properly **concealed**, <u>i.e. the vanishing point; generally, time out of mind (past or future)</u>, i.e. (practically) <u>eternity</u>; frequentatively, adverbial (especially with prepositional prefix) <u>always:–alway(-s), ancient</u> (time, any more, <u>continuance, eternal</u>, (for, (n-)) <u>ever(-lasting</u>, -more, of old), lasting, long (time), (of) old (time), perpetual, at any time, <u>(beginning of the) world (+ without end)</u>." Paul writes,

> *Now to him that is of power to stablish you according to my gospel, and the preaching of Jesus Christ, according to the revelation of the mystery, which was kept secret since the world began, but now is made manifest, and by the scriptures of the prophets, according to the commandment of the everlasting God, made known to all nations for the obedience of faith: to God only wise, be glory through Jesus Christ for ever. Amen.*
>
> (Romans 16:25-27)

The words "of the everlasting" in the Greek is *aionios* meaning "eternal." It's meaning in the Thayer's Greek Lexicon is "**without beginning or end, that which always has been and always will be:** Romans 16:26." He is the everlasting God and He never changes *(Isaiah 40:28; Malachi 3:6; Hebrews 13:8)*! We also see that ***El-Olam*** can be defined as our mighty, powerful, everlasting, eternal Savior, our Redeemer, as noted in *Isaiah 45:17 (NKJV)* which reads, *"But Israel shall be saved by the LORD with an <u>everlasting (olam) salvation</u>; You shall not be ashamed or disgraced Forever and ever."* The word "salvation" in Hebrew is *teshuwah* meaning "rescue:--deliverance, help, safety, salvation, victory." All those who have been born again are Abraham's seed (the father of Israel) and heirs according to the promise *(Galatians 3:28-29)*. The Lord Jesus Christ never changes; He is the same yesterday, today, and forever *(Hebrews 13:8)*. There is nothing on this earth or in hell that is too mighty or too powerful for the Lord Jesus Christ to save us from, for He came to destroy the works of the devil *(1 John 3:8)*. It's up to us to receive what the Lord did; as He is *"The Christ,"* the power and the wisdom of God *(Matthew 28:18; 1 Corinthians 1:24)*. Below are three passages of Scripture that affirm where our freedom is found, and His name is Jesus:

1. ***John 7:38-39*** *(AMPCE) – He who believes in Me [who cleaves to and trusts in and relies on Me] as the Scripture has said, from his innermost being shall flow [continuously] springs and rivers of living water. But He was speaking here of the Spirit, Whom those who believed (trusted, had faith) in Him were afterward to receive. For the [Holy] Spirit had not yet been given, because Jesus was not yet glorified (raised to honor).*

2. ***John 1:1-5, 14*** *(NIV) – In the beginning was the Word, and the Word was with God, and the Word was God. He was with God in the beginning. Through him all things were made; without him nothing was made that has been made. In him was life, and that life was the light of all mankind. The light shines in the darkness, and the darkness has not overcome it. The Word became flesh and made his dwelling among us. We have seen his glory of the one and only Son, who came from the Father, full of grace and truth.*

3. ***John 8:31-36*** *(NKJV) – Then Jesus said to those Jews who believed Him, "If you abide in My word, you are My disciples indeed. And you shall know the truth, and the truth shall make you free." They answered Him, "We are Abraham's descendants, and have never been in bondage to anyone. How can You say, 'You will be made free'?" Jesus answered them, "Most assuredly, I say to you, whoever commits sin is a slave of sin. And a slave does not abide in the house forever, but a son abides forever. Therefore if the Son makes you free, you shall be free indeed."*

Freedom is not found in doing anything we want to do (e.g., having sex outside of marriage, getting high on drugs and alcohol, being entertained with pornography) or saying anything we want to say (e.g., lying, cursing, gossiping, backbiting, murmuring, complaining) or being anyone we want to be (e.g., an alcoholic, a homosexual, an adulterer, a liar). Partaking in these and other works of the flesh (the old man or false self) leads to bondage to those sins and death *(Proverbs 14:12; Romans 8:1-8; Galatians 2:19-21, 5:19-25)*. True freedom is found in living out of the new creation in Christ, the new man. It is essential that we know Christ *(Philippians 3:8-11; Matthew 24:35; Luke 6:47-49)*. In this freedom, we are able to praise the Lord in unfavorable circumstances because of the freedom operating within us *(2 Corinthians 4:17-18)*. We being rooted and grounded in His love are able to trust Him in every situation and circumstance of life *(Acts 16:19-26; Psalm 46:1-7)*!! He keeps us in perfect peace as our minds are stayed on Him *(Isaiah 26:3-4)*. He is our everlasting strength *(Romans 8:35-39)*!

2(b) Your kingdom is an everlasting kingdom, and Your dominion endures throughout all generations. (Psalm 145:13-AMPCE)

The Lord's kingdom is not of this world,

> *"Am I a Jew?" Pilate replied. "Your own people and chief priests handed you over to me. What is it you have done?" Jesus said, "My kingdom is not of this world. If it were, my servants would fight to prevent my arrest by the Jewish leaders. But now my kingdom is from another place."*
>
> (John 18:35-36, NIV)

If His kingdom is not of this world then where is His kingdom? His kingdom rule is in Heaven, where He resides, and His kingdom rules over all *(Psalm 103:19)*. One day, every soul will know that Jesus Christ is Lord *(Philippians 2:8-11)*. To those who have truly given themselves to Christ, the kingdom of God dwells within them,

> *Now when He (Jesus) was asked by the Pharisees when the kingdom of God would come, He answered them and said, "The kingdom of God does not come with observation; nor will they say, 'See here!' or 'See there!' For indeed, the kingdom of God is within you."*
>
> (Luke 17:20-21, NKJV)

Our life consists of much more than eating, drinking, and the clothes we wear. Jesus describes this in *Luke 12:23-32* which I encourage you to read. The Lord ends this passage of Scripture saying,

> *…For all these things do the nations of the world seek after: and your Father knoweth that ye have need of these things. But rather seek ye the kingdom of God; and all these things shall be added unto you. Fear not, little flock; for it is your Father's good pleasure to give you the kingdom.*
>
> (Luke 12:30-32)

And finally, what does His kingdom produce in those it indwells? The answer is found in *Romans 14:17 (NKJV)* which reads, *"For the kingdom of God is not eating and drinking, but righteousness and peace and joy in the Holy Ghost."*

We are born into God's kingdom through the hidden man of the heart or the new creation in Christ. Christ is not of this world and neither are we who believe, as our citizenship is in Heaven *(John 14:30, 15:19, 17:14-23, 18:36; Romans 12:1-2; Philippians 3:20-21; Hebrews 11:8-10; 1 John 2:15-17)*. We have been delivered from the power of darkness and translated into the kingdom of His dear Son *(Colossians 1:13)* and we are seated together in heavenly places in Christ Jesus *(Ephesians 2:4-7)*. We are called to worship our heavenly Father in spirit and in truth. Jesus said,

> *But the hour is coming, and now is, when the true worshipers will worship the Father in spirit and truth; for the Father is seeking such to worship Him. God is Spirit, and those who worship Him must worship in spirit and truth.*
>
> (John 4:23-24, NKJV)

Worshipping the Father in spirit and in truth has several implications. We first must understand that His Words are spirit and life *(John 6:63)*, therefore, true worshipers feed on His Word and submit to His Word. We are a spirit, we have a soul, and we live in a body. When our spirit becomes born again, we grow by desiring and feeding on the Word of God, submitting our will to the will of our heavenly Father, spending time in His presence, worshipping Him as Lord and Savior, and being real with Him concerning our troubles *(1 Peter 2:1-3; Romans 12:1-2; Ephesians 4:22-24; Psalm 62:8, 142:2)*. This begins the process of putting to death (crucifying) the old man, our self-centered carnal nature *(Romans 6:6; Galatians 2:19-21; Ephesians 4:20-24)*. The Lord's body was broken and His blood shed on the cross in order for His Words, which are full of grace and truth, to go into the depths of the born-again believer's heart to dispel and destroy the works of darkness and to bring purity to the heart from all defilement/pollutants *(Mark 7:1-23; John 1:14; 2 Corinthians 4:6; Hebrews 4:12-13; 1 John 3:8)*. For those who choose to continue to walk in darkness, defiling and deceiving their own hearts, will not inherit the kingdom of God *(1 Corinthians 6:9-11)*. Jesus came to destroy the works of the devil in us – *1 John 3:8 (NKJV)* – *"He who sins is of the devil, for the devil has sinned from the beginning. For this purpose the Son of God was manifested, that He might destroy the works of the devil."*

He has called us to live by faith! Paul writes,

> *I have been crucified with Christ; it is no longer I who live, but Christ lives in me; and the life which I now live in the flesh I live by faith in the Son of God, who loved me and gave Himself for me. I do not set aside the grace of God; for if righteousness comes through the law, then Christ died in vain.*
>
> (Galatians 2:20-21, NKJV)

Whatever is not of faith is sin; and the just shall live by faith *(Romans 14:23; Habakkuk 2:4; Romans 1:17; Galatians 3:11; Hebrews 10:38)*. Many of us are looking for life (e.g., joy, peace, fulfillment) and trying to find wholeness and completion in and through the creation rather than our Creator, the One who gave His life so that *"In Him"* we might have life and that more abundantly *(John 10:10; Acts 17:28; Ephesians 1:8-10)*. I can testify that true life, wholeness, and completion is <u>only</u> found in Jesus Christ as I, too, tried to find it through fulfilling the lust of my flesh and living a homosexual lifestyle until He revealed Himself to me. Jesus said,

> *Enter by the narrow gate; for wide is the gate and broad is the way that leads to destruction, and there are many who go in by it. Because narrow is the gate and difficult is the way*

which leads to life, and there are few who find it.

(Matthew 7:13-14, NKJV)

While on this earth, abundant life can only be found in Him—He is the narrow gate *(John 14:6)*! Let's look at the following passage of Scripture:

> *Open to me the gates of righteousness: I will go through them, and I will praise the LORD. This is the gate of the LORD, through which the righteous shall enter. I will praise You, for you have answered me, and have become my salvation. The stone which the builders rejected has become the chief cornerstone. This was the LORD's doing; it is marvelous in our eyes.*

(Psalm 118:19-23, NKJV)

Jesus is the stone which the builders rejected. It is only through Him that we can walk in true righteousness and holiness *(Matthew 21:32-46)*!

Jesus also said in *John 10:10, "The thief cometh not, but for to steal, and to kill, and to destroy: I am come that they might have life, and that they might have it more abundantly."* Our responsibility is to seek Him and to deal with our own sin and shortcomings before a Holy God:

> *In this the love of God was manifested toward us, that God has sent His only begotten Son into the world, that we might live through Him. In this is love, not that we loved God, but that He loved us and sent His Son to be the propitiation for our sins.*

(1 John 4:9-10, NKJV)

He has equipped us to be more than conquerors in Him, as we are in the world but not of the world *(Romans 8:32-39; 1 John 5:4; John 15:19)*. Where there is a kingdom there is a King and His name is Jesus Christ and He is calling His people to be set apart from the kingdoms of this world, looking for a city whose builder and maker is God *(Matthew 6:33; Hebrews 11:8-10)*. Again, His kingdom dwells within us and faith is the substance that causes His kingdom to become a reality *(Luke 17:20-21; Hebrews 11:1-16)*.

Below are Scriptures relating to the gospel of the kingdom:

Matthew 24:3-14 – The disciples asked Jesus to tell them what would be the sign of His coming and of the end of the world? *And Jesus answered, "…For nation shall rise against nation, and kingdom against kingdom: and there shall be famines, and pestilences, and earthquakes, in divers places. All these are the beginning of sorrows. Then shall they deliver you up to be afflicted, and shall kill you: and ye shall be hated of all nations for my name's sake. And then shall many be offended, and shall betray one another, and shall hate one another. And many false prophets shall rise, and shall deceive many. And because iniquity shall abound, the love of many shall wax cold. But he that shall endure unto the end, the same shall be saved. And this gospel of the kingdom shall be preached in all the world for a witness unto all nations; and then shall the end come."*

References:
Mark 1:14-15 – *Now after John was put in prison, Jesus came into Galilee, preaching the gospel of the kingdom of God, and saying, "The time is fulfilled, and the kingdom of God is at hand: repent ye, and*

*believe the gospel." **Acts 11:15-18** (NIV) – Peter said, "As I began to speak, the Holy Spirit came on them as he had come on us at the beginning. Then I remembered what the Lord had said: 'John baptized with water, but you will be baptized with the Holy Spirit.' So if God gave them the same gift he gave us who believed in the Lord Jesus Christ, who was I to think that I could stand in God's way?" When they heard this, they had no further objections and praised God, saying, "So then, even to Gentiles God has granted repentance that leads to life." **Acts 14:22** – Confirming the souls of the disciples, and exhorting them to continue in the faith, and that we must through much tribulation enter into the kingdom of God. **Romans 1:16-17** – Paul writes, "For I am not ashamed of the gospel of Christ: for it is the power of God unto salvation to everyone that believeth; to the Jew first, and also to the Greek. For therein is the righteousness of God revealed from faith to faith: as it is written, 'The just shall live by faith.' **1 Corinthians 1:18** – Paul writes, "For the preaching of the cross is to them that perish foolishness; but unto us which are saved it is the power of God." **Colossians 2:6-7** – Paul writes, "As ye have therefore received Christ Jesus the Lord, so walk ye in him: rooted and built up in him, and stablished in the faith, as ye have been taught, abounding therein with thanksgiving. Beware lest any man spoil you through philosophy and vain deceit, after the tradition of men, after the rudiments of the world, and not after Christ."*

Please refer to **Note 13b** for additional information and Scriptures relating to the kingdom of God.

3(a) *You are* **Alpha and Omega, the beginning and the ending, the first and the last, the Almighty.** *There* is no God in heaven above or on earth below like You. (Revelations 1:8, 11; 1 Kings 8:23-NKJV)

God is amazing! *Alpha* and *Omega* are the first and last letters of the Greek alphabet meaning He is the Beginning and the End, the First and the Last. It is written,

> *In the beginning was the Word, and the Word was with God, and the Word was God. He was with God in the beginning. Through him all things were made; without him nothing was made that has been made. The Word became flesh and made his dwelling among us. We have seen his glory, the glory of the one and only Son, who came from the Father, full of grace and truth.*
>
> (John 1:1-3, 14, NIV)

His understanding is infinite and unsearchable. It is written in *Psalm 147:4-5 (NIV)* – "He counts the number of the stars; He calls them all by name. Great is our Lord, and mighty in power; His understanding is infinite."

The Hebrew word for "infinite" is *micpar* meaning "a number, def. (arithmetical) or indefinite distance (large, innumerable)." I believe the stars in all the galaxies and the grains of sand on all the seashores in the entire world helps us to understand the vastness of our Creator (**Note 1d**). The Lord also searches all hearts, and understands all the imaginations of the thoughts *(1 Chronicles 28:9)*. There is nothing hidden from Him *(Hebrews 4:12-13)*. What an amazing God!

Another marvel that the Lord created is the sun. Below are some interesting observations about the sun from Moody Science's classic film *God of Creation:*

> - *The sun is 93 million miles from the earth. It's the closest star to the earth.*
> - *It's a fairly typical star in size and temperature. There are other stars so much larger that they make our sun but a speck in comparison. How far away are they? Traveling at the speed of light, 186,000 miles per second, it takes a little over 5 years to reach Alpha Centauri (4.2 light years away), the nearest star out there in space.*
> - *The sun is 1,500,000 times larger than our earth. It's so big that if it were hollow, more than a million planets as large as the earth would fit inside.*
> - *Its surface is 10,000 degrees Fahrenheit to as much as 50,000 degrees Fahrenheit at a distance of 1,000 miles from the sun. The hottest region of the sun is the critical part, or core, 27,000,000 degrees Fahrenheit (Dr. Moon, 1945).*[1]

It is written in *Psalm 19:1 – "The heavens declare the glory of God; and the firmament sheweth His handywork."* How could the sun and all of creation just happen? It couldn't! It's foolish to think that something as awesome as this creation could happen apart from our Wonderful Creator. There is truly no God like our God, the Creator of the universe!

Below are Scriptures relating to our God:

1. ***Psalm 89:6-8*** *(NKJV) – For who in the heavens can be compared to the LORD? Who among the sons of the mighty can be likened to the LORD? God is greatly to be feared in the assembly of the saints, and to be held in reverence by all those around Him. O LORD God of hosts, who is mighty like You, O LORD? Your faithfulness also surrounds You.*

References:
Psalm 72:18-19 *– Blessed be the LORD God, the God of Israel, Who only doeth wondrous things! And blessed be his glorious name for ever: and let the whole earth be filled with his glory; Amen, and Amen.* ***Isaiah 40:25-26, 28-31*** *(NKJV) – To whom then will you liken Me, or to whom shall I be equal?" says the Holy One. Lift up your eyes on high, and see who has created these things, who brings out their host by number; He calls them all by name, by the greatness of His might and the strength of His power; not one is missing. Have you not known? Have you not heard? The everlasting God, the LORD, the Creator of the ends of the earth, neither faints nor is weary. His understanding is unsearchable. He gives power to the weak, and to those who have no might He increases strength. Even the youths shall faint and be weary, and the young men shall utterly fall, but those who wait on the LORD shall renew their strength; they shall mount up with wings like eagles, they shall run and not be weary, they shall walk and not faint.* ***Colossians 1:15-18*** *(NIV) – The Son is the image of the invisible God, the firstborn over all creation. For in him all things were created: things in heaven and on earth, visible and invisible, whether thrones or powers or rulers or authorities; all things have been created through him and for him. He is before all things, and in him all things hold together. And he is the head of the body, the church; he is the beginning and the firstborn from among the dead, so that in everything he might have the supremacy.*

2. ***Hebrews 9:11-14*** *(NKJV) – But Christ came as High Priest of the good things to come, with the greater and more perfect tabernacle not made with hands, that is, not of this creation. Not with the blood of goats and calves, but with His own blood He entered the Most Holy Place once for all, having obtained eternal redemption. For if the blood of bulls and goats and the ashes of a heifer, sprinkling the*

unclean, sanctifies for the purifying of the flesh, how much more shall the blood of Christ, who through the eternal Spirit offered Himself without spot to God, cleanse your conscience from dead works to serve the living God?

References:
Hebrews 13:20-21 *– Now the God of peace, that brought again from the dead our Lord Jesus, that great shepherd of the sheep, through the blood of the everlasting covenant, make you perfect in every good work to do his will, working in you that which is wellpleasing in his sight, through Jesus Christ; to whom be glory for ever and ever. Amen.* ***1 Peter 2:24-25*** *– Who his own self bare our sins in his own body on the tree, that we, being dead to sins, should live unto righteousness: by whose stripes ye were healed. For ye were as sheep going astray; but are now returned unto the Shepherd and Bishop (Overseer) of your souls.*

Here are additional Scriptures relating to our God: 2 Chronicles 16:9; Psalm 47:1-9; Proverbs 15:3; Isaiah 45:5-12, 18-22, 46:9-10, 48:12-13; Jeremiah 10:6-7, 12-13.

3(b) *You are* the author and finisher of *my* faith. (Hebrews 12:2)

The Greek word for "author" is *archegos* meaning "a <u>chief leader:—author, captain, prince</u>." The Lord is our chief leader and the captain of our salvation *(Hebrews 2:10)*! The first thing He does concerning our faith is to call us to repentance. *Acts 11:18* reads, "…*Then hath God also to the Gentiles granted <u>repentance unto life</u>.*" Christ is the Author of the born-again creation (our true self) as He brings this creation forth by the power of His Spirit. Paul said in *Romans 1:17; Galatians 3:11;* and *Hebrews 10:38* that the just shall live by faith. Living by faith is a new way of living and as we mature in Christ we go from faith to faith and as we increase in our walk of faith, the righteousness of God is revealed in us and we truly become a friend of God; just as Abraham, Moses, and the disciples *(Romans 1:17; 2 Corinthians 10:15; Isaiah 41:8; James 2:23; Exodus 33:11; John 15:13-17)*. Jesus said to His disciples,

> *A new commandment I give to you, that you love one another, even as I have loved you, that you also love one another. By this all men will know that you are My disciples, if you have love one for another.*
>
> (John 13:34-35, NASB)

This is, truly, the only way that faith will operate – *Galatians 5:6* – "*For in Jesus Christ neither circumcision availeth any thing, nor uncircumcision; <u>but faith which worketh by love</u>.*" What separates a believer who is a babe in Christ from a disciple who is mature in Christ? Jesus answered that question in *John 8:31-32*, "<u>*If ye continue in my word*</u>, *then are ye my disciples indeed; and ye shall know the truth, and the truth shall make you free.*" His Words are spirit and they are life *(John 6:63)*. Jesus is the Author of our faith as He is the Word of God, full of grace and truth *(John 1:14)*. As we continue in His Words and in submission to His Lordship, the life and the power, contained in His Words, changes us into His image—the firstborn among many brethren *(Romans 8:29)*.

The word "finisher" in the Greek is *teleiotes* meaning "a completer, i.e. consummator–finisher." The root word is *teleioo* meaning "to <u>complete</u>, i.e. (literally) accomplish, or (figuratively) consummate (in character):–consecrate, finish, fulfil, make) perfect." Jesus, through His Word and by His Spirit, brings complete maturity to the born-again creation within. He is the Author and the Finisher of this new creation. Through Jesus Christ, our heavenly Father nurtures us, corrects us, helps us, and never leaves us, nor forsakes us! His desire is for us to grow up in Christ, putting on the new man, so we can truly walk in abundant life!

The word "faith" in the Greek is *pistis* meaning "<u>persuasion</u>, i.e. credence; moral conviction (of religious truth, or the truthfulness of God or a religious teacher), especially reliance upon Christ for salvation; abstractly, constancy in such profession; by extension, the system of religious (Gospel) truth itself:—assurance, belief, believe, faith, fidelity." Growing in faith brings the reality of His divine nature that emanates from the depth of our beings *(John 7:37-39)*. For we are complete in Him, who is the head of all principality and power *(Colossians 2:10)*. Our completeness comes through the born-again creation within us. Jesus begins this process of wholeness and completion through the new birth and continues as we grow in Christ. The author of Hebrews writes,

> *For it was fitting for Him, for whom are all things, and through whom are all things, in bringing many sons to glory, to perfect the author of their salvation through sufferings. For both He who sanctifies and those who are sanctified are all from one Father; for which reason He is not ashamed to call them brethren, saying, "I WILL PROCLAIM YOUR NAME TO MY BRETHREN, IN THE MIDST OF THE CONGREGATION I WILL SING YOUR PRAISE."*

(Hebrews 2:10-12, NASB)

He which has begun a good work in you will complete it until the day of Jesus Christ as we have our fellowship in the gospel. Faithful is He who calls you who also will do it *(Philippians 1:3-6; 1 Thessalonians 5:23-24)*. Let's close with the following passage of Scripture explaining that we too are not exempt from suffering:

> *Be sober, be vigilant; because your adversary the devil, as a roaring lion, walketh about, seeking whom he may devour: whom resist steadfast in the faith, knowing that the same afflictions are accomplished in your brethren that are in the world. But the God of all grace, who hath called us unto his eternal glory by Christ Jesus, after that ye have suffered a while, make you perfect, stablish, strengthen, settle you. To him be glory and dominion for ever and ever. Amen.*

(1 Peter 5:8-11)

God's intent is for us to be able to say, as Jesus said in *John 14:30 – "Hereafter I will not talk much with you: for the prince of this world cometh, and hath nothing in me."*

Here are Scriptures relating to faith: Isaiah 32:17; Matthew 10:22, 17:20-21, 21:21-22; Mark 4:26-32; Luke 17:6; John 16:33; Acts 16:4-5; Romans 1:16-17, 4:4-5, 14-16, 5:1-2, 6:15-17, 10:16-17; 1 Corinthians 13:2, 15:14-28; 2 Corinthians 3:5-9; Galatians 5:5-6, 6:14-15; Ephesians 2:8-10, 6:10-18; Colossians 2:1-3, 6-15; 2 Thessalonians 3:1-3; Philemon 1:4-6; Hebrews 4:1-2; 1 John 3:23-24, 4:9, 5:4-5, 11; Revelation 2:7, 11, 17, 3:5, 21, 21:7.

Please refer to **Notes 11**, **12**, and **37b** for additional information and Scriptures relating to faith.

Ezekiel 48:35 states that the name of the city in which the tribes of Israel possessed is "THE LORD IS THERE" – *Yahweh-Shammah*. The city had twelve gates named after the twelve tribes of Israel (three gates on the north side, three gates on the east side, three gates on the south side, and three gates on the west side). There is also a city in Heaven (the kingdom of God) where the Lord resides, described in *Revelations 21*. There are twelve gates in that city, as well, which are the names of the twelve tribes of Israel: Three gates on the east, three gates on the north, three gates on the south, and three gates on the west. The wall of the city had twelve <u>foundations</u>, and in them the names of the twelve apostles of the Lamb. Paul writes,

> *…having abolished in His flesh the enmity, that is, the law of commandments contained in ordinances, so as to create in Himself one **new man** from the two, thus making peace, and that He might reconcile them both to God in one body through the cross, thereby putting to death the enmity. And He came and preached peace to you who were afar off and to those who were near. For through Him we both have access by one Spirit to the Father. Now, therefore, you are no longer strangers and foreigners, but fellow citizens with the saints and members of the household of God, having been built on the **foundation** of the apostles and prophets, Jesus Christ Himself being the chief cornerstone, in whom the whole building, being fitted together, grows into a holy temple in the Lord, in whom you also are being built together for a dwelling place of God in the Spirit.*
>
> (Ephesians 2:15-22, NKJV)

There are two powerful points that I would like to share concerning this passage of Scripture:

<u>new man</u>
This new man is the born-again creation within. In *John 14:30*, Jesus said to His disciples, "*…for the prince of this world cometh, and hath nothing in me.*" Jesus did not have the carnal nature residing within Him as He was not born of a corruptible seed (the seed of Adam), but of an incorruptible seed, by the Holy Spirit and the power of the Most High *(Luke 1:35)*. As we become born again, by an incorruptible seed, the Word of God, we too have the nature of Christ residing within us *(1 Peter 1:22-25)*. As we, the church, choose to allow that incorruptible seed to grow and mature through the renewal process, our carnal nature loses its strength and therefore Satan, the prince of this world, loses his authority in our lives.

<u>foundation</u>
Inspired by the Holy Spirit, Jesus used His holy apostles and prophets to pen His God-breathed Words of truth within the pages of the Bible *(2 Peter 1:17-21; 2 Timothy 3:16-17 – AMPCE)*. We are His temple and God *(Yahweh-Shammah)* dwells within us and He will never leave us nor forsake us *(1 Corinthians 3:16, 6:19-20; 2 Corinthians 6:16; Luke 17:20-21; Hebrews 13:5)*! It is essential that we allow the Holy Spirit to dig deep into the core of our very being, by the Word of God, to remove ungodly mindsets/beliefs, judgments, etc., that are tied to the carnal sin nature, the old man *(Hebrews 4:12)*. As Jesus instructed us,

> *Whosoever cometh to me, and heareth my sayings, and doeth them, I will shew you to whom*

he is like: he is like a man which built an house, and digged deep, and laid the foundation on a rock: and when the flood arose, the stream beat vehemently upon that house, and could not shake it: for it was founded upon a <u>rock</u>. But he that heareth, and doeth not, is like a man that without a foundation built an house upon the earth; against which the stream did beat vehemently, and immediately it fell; and the ruin of that house was great.

(Luke 6:47-49)

Now let's look at the following passage of Scripture,

When Jesus came into the region of Caesarea Philippi, He asked his disciples, saying, "Whom do men say that I, the Son of Man, am?" So they said, "Some say John the Baptist, some Elijah, and others Jeremiah or one of the prophets." He said to them, "But who do you say that I am?" Simon Peter answered and said, "You are the Christ, the Son of the living God." Jesus answered and said to him, "Blessed are you, Simon Barjonah, for flesh and blood has not revealed this to you, but my Father who is in heaven. And I also say to you that you are Peter, and on this <u>rock</u> I will build My church, and the gates of Hades shall not prevail against it."

(Matthew 16:13-18, NKJV)

The word "rock" in both *Matthew 16:18* and *Luke 6:48* in the Greek is *petra* meaning "a (mass of) rock (literally or figuratively):–rock." Its meaning in the Thayer's Greek Lexicon is "metaphorically, <u>a man like a rock, by reason of his firmness and strength of soul</u>: Matthew 16:18." Peter was one of the Lord's apostles and through the revelations contained in the Scriptures of the Bible written by Peter and the other apostles (i.e., Matthew, Mark, Luke, John, Paul), the church, the body of Christ, is built. Through the firmness and strength of the revelation of who Christ is within each individual member of the body of Christ, the gates of hell cannot prevail against her! This firmness and strength of soul is usually attained through resistance. Let's read *1 Timothy 4:7-8* in order to get a better understanding of this. *"But refuse profane and old wives' fables, and exercise thyself rather unto godliness. For bodily exercise profiteth little: but godliness is profitable unto all things, having promise of the life that now is, and of that which is to come."* The word "exercise" in *1 Timothy 4:7* in the Greek is *gymnazo*. Its meaning in the Thayer's Greek Lexicon is "to exercise vigorously in any way, either in body or the mind: of one who strives earnestly to become godly, 1 Timothy 4:7." God's desire for every member of the body of Christ is to grow in godliness, or in the new man in Christ (e.g., righteousness, holiness, love, joy, perseverance). In order to do this, let's think of someone who uses weights in resistance or strength training. This type of exercise causes muscles to contract against external pressure resulting in a greater strength and firmness. In the same way spiritually, as we equip ourselves with His Word by renewing our minds to it, when the pressures and trials of life come (e.g., temptations, fears, afflictions, hardships) as we choose to resist the natural flow of our carnality (i.e., the old man) and "exercise" godly attributes against the pressures and trials of life, we begin to grow strong and firm in who we are in Christ (the new man). I believe this helps to better understand *Acts 14:22 – "Confirming the souls of the disciples, and exhorting them to continue in the faith, and that we must through much tribulation enter into the kingdom of God."*

4(b) Though I walk through the [deep, sunless] valley of the shadow of death, I will fear or dread no evil, for You are with me. (Psalm 23:4-AMPCE)

In the Old Testament, when the ark of the covenant was present the Lord was there, as you cannot separate the Lord from His Word *(John 1:1)*. After Solomon built the Temple for the Lord, the ark was placed in the inner sanctuary of the temple, in the most holy place *(2 Chronicles 5:1-14; Hebrews 9:1-20)*. Since we are the temple of the Holy Spirit, His Word is placed in the most holy place of our temple, the heart of man *(1 Corinthians 3:16)*. It's not our physical organ but it is in our belly. Jesus said in *John 7:38* – "*He that believeth on me, as the scripture hath said, out of his belly shall flow rivers of living water.*" The word "belly" here in the Greek is *koilia* which means "a cavity, i.e. (especially) the abdomen; by implication, the matrix; figuratively, the heart-belly, womb." Every male and female has a spiritual womb and this is where the life-giving flow of His Spirit, the light of life resides *(John 8:12)*. In the natural, there are times when we wake up in the morning where it's cloudy and stormy weather outside. Though it looks dark and dreary by the cloud cover, the sun is there and will eventually break through the darkness. In the same way, there are times in our own lives when we feel darkness and dreariness on the inside of us. During those times, I want to encourage you that as born-again children of the Most-High God, the Son is there and will eventually break through the darkness and dreariness within as we continue to stay focused on Him. Peter writes,

> We have also a more sure word of prophecy; whereunto ye do well that ye take heed, as unto a light that shineth in a dark place, until the day dawn, and the day star arise in your hearts: knowing this first, that no prophecy of the scripture is of any private interpretation. For the prophecy came not in old time by the will of man: but holy men of God spake as they were moved by the Holy Ghost.
>
> (2 Peter 1:19-21)

Here is an example in my own life where I felt I was in the valley of the shadow of death:

In the latter part of 2013, my husband and I applied for life insurance. The insurance company sent a nurse to draw blood and check our vitals. When my results came back, I was taken aback as it showed that my white blood cell count was too numerous to count! I had not had a physical in five years and during those five years I had no symptoms that anything was wrong, and I was not on any type of prescription medication. I made an appointment in January 2014 with my doctor and had a physical. The same results came back, so she referred me to a urologist. In February 2014, I went to the urologist who had many tests ordered which revealed a large kidney stone in my right kidney and the stone had damaged it. He said that the kidney had to be removed and was not sure if there was cancer or any disease until he went in, removed the kidney, and sent it off to be examined. If there was cancer, he was concerned that it had spread into my lymph nodes. My kidney was removed in June 2014. From the time my results came back at the end of 2013 until July 2014, I felt that I was in the valley of the shadow of death. Some days were a struggle working through thoughts that produced fear and anxiety. But, through it all, I held onto Jesus and His Word. I also knew that I had not finished the work the Lord called me to do and that gave me hope. I give Him much thanks that the test results found no disease or cancer, Hallelujah!! I had come to the conclusion that whether I stayed or whether I went home to be with the Lord, my trust and my life was in Him.

There may be times in your life when you can't seem to go forward, but I want to encourage you to stand strong in the power and love of God. He is faithful to shine His light in any areas of darkness!

Here are Scriptures relating to the Lord being with us through difficult times: 1 Samuel 30:6; Psalm 23, 36:9, 42:5, 56:3-4, 11, 64:1, 108:3-6; Isaiah 50:10; Habakkuk 3:17-19; John 16:33; Hebrews 13:20-21; 1 Peter 2:25.

5(a) *You are* **The Light of the world**. (John 8:12-AMPCE)

Jesus said in *John 8:12, "I am the light of the world: he who followeth me shall not walk in darkness, but shall have the light of life."* You cannot walk in darkness and follow Christ at the same time for in Him there is no darkness *(1 John 1:5-7)*! As we choose to follow Christ, we may feel like we're still in darkness, but He has called us out of darkness and into His marvelous light *(1 Peter 2:9)*. As we continue to follow Him and not give up, we will begin to see the light of life operating within our hearts and souls as He heals our broken hearts and restores our depraved souls *(Isaiah 1:2-6; Psalm 23:1-3)*. Living in habitual sin is living in darkness and brings depravation to our souls. We were not created to live in sin, we were created to live in Him and nothing is hidden from the Lord. *(Psalm 90:8; 1 Corinthians 4:5; Acts 17:28; 1 John 4:9; Hebrews 4:12-13)*. Paul writes,

> *For ye were sometimes darkness, but now are ye light in the Lord: walk as children of light: (for the fruit of the Spirit is in all goodness and righteousness and truth;) proving what is acceptable unto the Lord. Wherefore, he saith, 'Awake thou that sleepest, and arise from the dead, and Christ shall give thee light.*
>
> (Ephesians 5:8-10, 14)

As the fruit of the Spirit is produced in our lives, we are walking in the new man in Christ, and walking in the light of life. For instance, the destiny of an apple seed is to grow into a fruit-bearing apple tree. This happens as the tree becomes deeply rooted in rich soil and matures enough to bear fruit. So too is our destiny in Christ, to walk and live out of the born-again creation, the new man. We, as babes in Christ, must grow in Him in order to become more deeply rooted and founded securely in His Love *(1 Peter 2:1-3; Ephesians 3:17-19)*. It is then that we become spiritually mature enough to bring forth the fruit of the Spirit *(Galatians 5:22-25)*.

The Lord God is the Light of His people:

> *In the beginning was the Word, and the Word was with God, and the Word was God. The same was in the beginning with God. All things were made by him; and without him was not any thing made that was made. And the Word was made flesh, and dwelt among us, (and we beheld his glory, the glory as of the only begotten of the Father,) full of grace and truth.*
>
> (John 1:1-3, 14)

The Lord is the Word and the Word was manifested in the flesh and His name is Jesus Christ, therefore the essence of who He is indwells His Word. In order to clarify this statement, Paul said, in *2 Timothy 3:16-17* – *"All scripture is given by <u>inspiration</u> of God, and is profitable for doctrine, for reproof, for correction, for instruction in righteousness: that the man of God may be perfect, thoroughly furnished unto all good works."* The word "inspiration" in the Greek is *theopneustos* meaning "<u>divinely breathed in</u>: given by inspiration of God." It is from a root word *theos* meaning "a deity, especially the supreme Divinity." You cannot separate God from His Word found in the holy Scriptures of the Bible. I'm reminded of *Genesis 2:7* when God formed man out of the dust of the ground, and <u>breathed</u> into his nostrils <u>the breath of life</u> and man became a living soul. The word "breathed" in Hebrew is *naphach* which is "a primitive root; to puff, in various applications (literally, to inflate, blow hard…):–blow, breath…" The word "breath" in "<u>the breath of life</u>" in Hebrew is *neshamah* meaning "a puff, i.e. wind, angry or vital breath, <u>divine inspiration</u>…" When God breathed the breath of life into Adam, He breathed life into every human being that would ever be born of woman. God has also breathed life into His holy Scriptures. He uses the holy Scriptures and His Holy Spirit to breathe into us the <u>light of life</u>, Jesus Christ *(John 8:12)*. Before the fall, Adam was living out of God's nature in every sense of the word, and because of what Jesus did for us on the cross, we too have the opportunity to live out of God's divine nature in every area of our lives *(Romans 8:29)*.

If you walk in the Spirit, you have put off the old man and put on the new man, and are walking in the <u>light of life</u> as the fruit of the Spirit is in all goodness, righteousness, and truth *(Galatians 5:22-25; Ephesians 5:8-10)*. I believe the Lord's intent for every "believer in Christ" is to allow the written Word of God to become life-giving as it is consumed into the heart through the eye gate, ear gate, and mouth gate. Jesus said in *Matthew 12:34*, *"…out of the abundance of the heart the mouth speaks."* In other words, the heart and the mouth are connected by a small member called the tongue (please read *James 3:6-18*; *Jeremiah 17:9-10*). This is why I believe it is essential for a born-again believer to speak out the Word of God – *Psalm 45:1b* – *"My tongue is the pen of a ready writer."* – *Proverbs 7:3b* – *"…write them on the tablet of your heart."*

> *The night is far spent, the day is at hand: let us therefore cast off the works of darkness, and let us put on the armour of light. Let us walk honestly, as in the day; not in rioting and drunkenness, not in chambering and wantonness, not in strife and envying. <u>But put ye on the Lord Jesus Christ, and make not provision for the flesh, to fulfil the lusts thereof</u>.*
> (Romans 13:12-14)

Below are Scriptures relating to the light of God's Word:

1. **Psalm 119:130** *(NKJV)* – *The entrance of Your words gives light; it gives understanding to the simple.*

References:
Psalm 119:105 (NKJV) – Your word is a lamp to my feet and a light to my path. **Proverbs 4:18** – *But the path of the just is as the shining light, that shineth more and more unto the perfect day.* **Proverbs 6:23** – *For the commandment is a lamp; and the law is light; and reproofs of instruction are the way of life.* **Proverbs 13:9** – *The light of the righteous rejoiceth: but the lamp of the wicked shall be put out.* **Proverbs 15:30** – *The light of the eyes rejoiceth the heart: and a good report maketh the bones fat.* **Proverbs 16:15** – *In the light of the king's countenance is life; and his favour is as a cloud of the latter rain.* **Proverbs 29:13** – *The poor and the deceitful man meet together: the LORD lighteneth both their eyes.* **Isaiah 2:5** – *O house of Jacob, come ye, and let us walk in the light of the LORD.* **John 1:1-4, 14** – *In the beginning was the Word,*

and the Word was with God, and the Word was God. The same was in the beginning with God. All things were made by him; and without him was not anything made that was made. In him was life; and the life was the light of men. And the Word was made flesh, and dwelt among us, (and we beheld his glory, the glory as of the only begotten of the Father,) full of grace and truth. **2 Peter 1:19-21** — *We have also a more sure word of prophecy; whereunto ye do well that ye take heed, as unto a light that shineth in a dark place, until the day dawn, and the day star arise in your hearts: knowing this first, that no prophecy of the scripture is of any private interpretation. For the prophecy came not in old time by the will of man: but holy men of God spake as they were moved by the Holy Ghost.*

2. ***Proverbs 3:1-4*** *(NIV)* — *My son, do not forget my teaching, but keep my commands in your heart, for they will prolong your life many years and bring you peace and prosperity. Let love and faithfulness never leave you; bind them around your neck, <u>write them on the tablet of your heart</u>. Then you will win favor and a good name in the sight of God and man.*

References:
Proverbs 7:1-3 *(NIV)* — *My son, keep my words and store up my commands within you. Keep my commands and you will live; guard my teachings as the apple of your eye. Bind them on your fingers; <u>write them on the tablet of your heart</u>.* **Isaiah 59:21** — *As for me, this is my covenant with them, saith the LORD; "My spirit that is upon thee, and my words which I have put in thy mouth, shall not depart out of thy mouth, nor out of the mouth of thy seed, nor out of the mouth of thy seed's seed," saith the LORD, "from henceforth and for ever."* **Jeremiah 31:33** — *But this shall be the covenant that I will make with the house of Israel; "After those days," saith the LORD, "I will put My law in their inward parts, and write it in their hearts; and will be their God, and they shall be My people.* **Hebrews 4:12** — *For the word of God is quick (living), and powerful, and sharper than any twoedged sword, piercing even to the dividing asunder of soul and spirit, and of the joints and marrow, and is a discerner of the thoughts and intents of the heart.* **Hebrews 8:7-10** *(NKJV)* — *For if that first covenant had been faultless, then no place would have been sought for a second. Because finding fault with them, He says: "Behold, the days are coming," says the LORD, "when I will make a new covenant with the house of Israel and with the house of Judah—not according to the covenant that I made with their fathers in the day when I took them by the hand to lead them out of the land of Egypt; because they did not continue in My covenant, and I disregarded them," says the LORD. "For this is the covenant that I will make with the house of Israel after those days," says the LORD: "I will put My laws in their mind and write them on their hearts; and I will be their God, and they shall be My people..."*

I want to encourage you to allow His Word to be a light in every area of your life in order to produce His character and nature within you.

Here are Scriptures relating to God's light: 2 Samuel 22:28-37; Job 29:1-3, 33:27-30; Psalm 13:3-6, 18:28-30, 27:1, 36:9, 43:3, 44:3, 56:13, 89:15-16, 90:8, 97:11, 104:1-2, 112:4, 118:27, 139:7-12; Isaiah 5:20-21, 8:19-20, 9:2, 42:16, 58:6-11, 60:1-3, 19-20; Daniel 12:3; Micah 7:7-9; Habakkuk 3:3-4; Matthew 4:16, 5:14-16; Luke 1:78-79, 2:29-32, 11:33-36; John 3:19-21, 8:12, 9:5, 11:9-10, 12:35-36, 46; Acts 22:6-11; 1 Corinthians 4:5; 2 Corinthians 4:3-7, 6:14; Philippians 2:14-16; Colossians 1:12-17; 1 Thessalonians 5:5; 1 Timothy 6:13-16; 2 Timothy 1:9-11; James 1:16-18; 1 Peter 2:9; 2 Peter 1:16-21; 1 John 1:5-10, 2:8-11; Revelation 22:1-6.

Please see **Note 26b** for information and Scriptures relating to the Father of lights.

5(b) *You are* my light and my salvation; whom *(or what)* shall I fear? The entrance of *Your* words *gives* light; it *gives* understanding to the simple. Your word is a lamp to my feet and a light to my path. Show me Your ways, O LORD; teach me Your paths. Lead me in Your truth and teach me, for You are the God of my salvation; on You I <u>wait</u> all the day. (Psalm 27:1, 119:130, 105-NKJV, 25:4-5-NKJV) *(Ref.: Romans 8:31-39)*

The Hebrew word for "wait" is *qavah* and its meaning is "to bind together (perhaps by twisting), i.e., collect; (figuratively) <u>to expect</u>:–gather (together), <u>look</u>, <u>patiently</u>, tarry, <u>wait</u> (<u>for</u>, <u>on</u>, <u>upon</u>)." We find our joy and strength in the Lord as we <u>daily fix our hope in Him</u> rather than in what our feelings dictate based on the cares of this life, the deceitfulness of riches, and the lust of other things *(Nehemiah 8:10; Isaiah 40:31; Mark 4:18-19)*. We are deceived if we think we can continue to follow after the dictates of the flesh instead of fixing our hope in Christ, as this choice leads to misery *(Proverbs 14:12; Romans 6:19-23)*. This is why it is essential to renew our minds to God's Word *(Romans 12:2; Ephesians 4:20-24)*. The entrance of His Word enlightens our darkness so we can clearly see the paths of righteousness; for in the way of righteousness is life, and in the pathway thereof there is no death *(Psalm 18:28-30, 119:130; Proverbs 12:28; Ephesians 4:22-24)*. Let's look at the following passage of Scripture concerning the thoughts and ways of God:

> *For My thoughts are not your thoughts, neither are your ways my ways, saith the LORD. For as the heavens are higher than the earth, so are My ways higher that your ways, and My thoughts than your thoughts. For as the rain cometh down, and the snow from heaven, and returneth not thither, but watereth the earth, and maketh it bring forth and bud, that it may give seed to the sower, and bread to the eater: so shall my word be that goeth forth out of my mouth: it shall not return unto me void, but it shall accomplish that which I please, and it shall prosper in the thing whereto I sent it.*
>
> (Isaiah 55:8-11)

Through God's living Word, His thoughts and His ways become a reality within us and reveal any stronghold that is keeping us from experiencing abundant life *(John 10:10; Matthew 7:13-14; 2 Corinthians 10:4-6)*. The Lord said in *Isaiah 65:2 – "I have spread out my hands all the day long unto a rebellious people, which walketh in a way that was not good, after their own thoughts."* The Lord Jesus Christ spread out His hands on the cross and is calling us to forsake our ways and come to Him.

Below are four passages of Scripture relating to the wonders of His great mercy:

1. ***Lamentations 3:22-24*** – <u>*It is of the LORD'S mercies*</u> *that we are not consumed, because his compassions fail not.* <u>*They are new every morning*</u>*: great is thy faithfulness. The LORD is my portion, saith my soul; therefore, will I hope in him.* (The word "new" in Hebrew is *chadash* meaning "new:– <u>fresh, new thing</u>." In other words, every morning the mercies of the Lord are new, never seen before. Every morning His loving-kindness brings a new freshness to those who hope in Him).

2. ***Psalm 36:5-6*** – *Thy mercy, O LORD, is in the heavens; and thy faithfulness reacheth unto the clouds. Thy righteousness is like the great mountains; thy judgments are a great deep: O LORD, thou preserveth man and beast.* (His mercy [lovingkindness] goes beyond what we can see. His mercy and truth go hand in hand – *Psalm 61:7, 85:10, 89:14; Proverbs 3:3, 14:22, 16:6, 20:28.* Without His mercy, His truth would not be able to spring up from within the hearts of born-again believers to bring

forth the new man in Christ – *Psalm 85:10-13*! Hallelujah for Your mercies, O Lord).

3. **Psalm 57:9-10** *(NKJV) – I will praise You, O LORD, among the peoples; I will sing to You among the nations. For Your mercy reaches unto the heavens, and Your truth unto the clouds.*

4. **Psalm 103:11-18** *– For as the heaven is high above the earth, so great is his mercy toward them that fear him. As far as the east is from the west, so far hath he removed our transgressions from us. Like as a father pitieth his children, so the LORD pitieth them that fear him. For he knoweth our frame; he remembereth that we are dust. As for man, his days are as grass: as a flower of the field, so he flourisheth. For the wind passeth over it, and it is gone; and the place thereof shall know it no more. But the mercy of the LORD is from everlasting to everlasting upon them that fear him, and his righteousness unto children's children; to such as keep his covenant, and to those that remember his commandments to do them.*

All of the Lord's paths are mercy and truth. In order to walk in His paths, it is essential that we are obedient to His will through humbleness of mind, renewing the *spirit of our minds* to the truth of His Word, and an intimate relationship with Him through prayer and worship.

Here are Scriptures relating to teaching us His ways: Exodus 33:12-13; Deuteronomy 4:35-36; 1 Samuel 12:23-25; 1 Kings 8:35-36, 57-58; Psalm 32:8-9, 34:9-16, 81:10-14, 86:11, 143:10; Proverbs 4:11; Isaiah 2:3-5, 48:17-18; Jeremiah 7:23; Hosea 14:9; Micah 4:2; Matthew 11:29-30.

Here are Scriptures relating to the paths of life: 1 Samuel 12:23-25; 1 Kings 8:35-36; 2 Chronicles 6:26-27; Psalm 16:11, 17:5, 23:3, 25:4-5, 9-10, 27:11, 32:8-9, 43:3, 65:11, 119:35, 105, 133; Proverbs 2:6-9, 3:6, 13-17, 4:11, 18, 8:17-21, 12:28; Isaiah 2:3-5, 42:16, 48:17-18; Jeremiah 6:16, 18:15-16; Micah 4:2; Matthew 7:13-14; Romans 6:4-7.

Please refer to **Note 34b** for additional information and Scriptures relating to this subject matter.

5(c) *You* lead the humble in what is right and the humble *You teach Your ways.* I clothe *myself* with humility [as the garb of a servant, so that its covering cannot possibly be stripped from *me*, with *freedom from pride and arrogance] toward others. For You set Yourself against the proud*, but *You give* grace to the humble. *As I walk in humility, lowliness of mind and trusting in You, my* life shall be clearer than the noonday and rise above *my misery*; though there be darkness, it shall be as the morning. Light is sown for *me* and strewn along *my* pathway, and joy [the irrepressible joy which comes from consciousness of *Your* favor and protection]. (Psalm 25:9-AMPCE; 1 Peter 5:5-AMPCE; Job 11:17-AMPCE; Psalm 97:11-AMPCE)(*Ref.: Philippians 2:3-13*)

We have a choice to walk in pride (self-centeredness and high-mindedness—trusting in our own wisdom and ability) or to walk in humility (God-centeredness and lowliness of mind—trusting in the Lord's wisdom and ability in us, for He has our best interest at heart). Pride and earthly wisdom (e.g., bitter envying and strife) is the outward expression of our carnal nature. Humility and God's wisdom (e.g., pure, peaceable, and gentle) is the outward expression of our new nature in Christ *(James 3:13-18)*. It is essential that we choose to walk humbly before our God in order to walk in abundant life *(John 10:10)*. While we are growing in Christ, as we yield to His will in humility, the old man looses its strength as we choose to deprive pride of the power to stay in control. We will also see the grace of God in our lives as we continue to go the way of humility and resist walking in pride *(1 Peter 5:5)*.

Below are Scriptures relating to pride vs humility:

1. *Psalm 138:6* – *Though the LORD be high, yet hath he respect unto the lowly: but the proud he knoweth afar off.*

References:
Proverbs 18:12 – *Before destruction the heart of a man is haughty, and <u>before honor is humility</u>.* *Proverbs 22:4* – *By humility and the fear of the LORD are riches, and honour, and life.* *Proverbs 28:13* – *He who covereth his sins shall not prosper: but whoso confesseth and forsaketh them will have mercy.* *Proverbs 29:23* – *A man's pride shall bring him low: but honor shall uphold the humble in spirit.* *Isaiah 57:15* – *For thus saith the high and lofty One that inhabiteth eternity, whose name is Holy; "I dwell in the high and holy place, with him also that is of a contrite and humble spirit, to revive the spirit of the humble, and to revive the heart of the contrite ones."* *Lamentations 3:25-27* – *The LORD is good unto them that wait for him, to the soul that seeketh him. It is good that a man should both hope and quietly wait for the salvation of the LORD. It is good for a man that he bear the yoke in his youth.* *Matthew 23:12* – *Jesus said, "And whosoever shall exalt himself shall be abased (humbled); and he that shall humble himself shall be exalted."* *Mark 10:13-15* – *And they brought young children to him, that he should touch them: and his disciples rebuked those that brought them. But when Jesus saw it, he was much displeased, and said unto them, "Suffer the little children to come unto me, and forbid them not: for of such is the kingdom of God. Verily I say unto you, Whosoever shall not receive the kingdom of God as a little child, he shall not enter therein."*

2. *Proverbs 1:7* – *<u>The fear of the LORD is the beginning of knowledge</u>: but fools despise wisdom and instruction.*

References:
Proverbs 3:34 – *Surely, He scorneth the scorners: <u>but he giveth grace to the lowly (humble)</u>.* *Proverbs 5:12-14 (NKJV)* – *"How I have hated instruction, and my heart despised correction! I have not obeyed the voice of my teachers, nor inclined my ear to those who instructed me! I was on the verge of total ruin…"* *Proverbs 8:13* – *The fear of the LORD is to hate evil: pride, and arrogancy, and the evil way, and the froward (perverse) mouth do I hate.* *Proverbs 11:2* – *When pride cometh, then cometh shame; but with the lowly (humble) is wisdom.* *Proverbs 13:9-10* – *The light of the righteous rejoiceth: but the lamp of the wicked will be put out. Only by pride cometh contention: but with the well advised is wisdom.* *Proverbs 15:16-17, 33* – *Better is little with the fear of the LORD, than great treasure and trouble therewith. Better is a dinner with herbs where love is, than a stalled ox and hatred therewith. The fear of the LORD is the instruction of wisdom; and before honor is humility.* *Proverbs 16:5, 18-19* – *Everyone that is proud in heart is an abomination to the LORD: though hand join in hand, he shall not be unpunished. Pride goeth before destruction, and an haughty spirit before a fall. Better it is to be of an humble spirit with the lowly (humble), than to divide the spoil with the proud.* *Proverbs 17:1* – *Better is a dry morsel, and quietness therewith, than an house full of sacrifices with strife.* *Titus 3:1-2* – *Put them in mind to be subject to principalities and powers, to obey magistrates, to be ready to every good work, to speak evil of no man, to be no brawlers, but gentle, shewing all meekness unto all men.* *1 Peter 5:5* – *Likewise, ye younger, submit yourselves unto the elder. Yea, all of you be subject one to another, and be clothed with humility: for God resisteth the proud, and giveth grace to the humble.*

Here are additional Scriptures relating to pride vs humility: 2 Samuel 22:28-37; 2 Chronicles 7:14, 12:1, 5-7; Psalm 5:5, 32:8-9, 92:12-15, 95:6-11; Proverbs 14:3, 22:17-19, 28:25; Isaiah 38:1-6,

57:15; Jeremiah 7:23-24; Micah 6:6-8; Zephaniah 2:3; Matthew 6:22, 18:1-5, 19:13-15, 20:25-28, 23:11-12; Luke 6:46-49; 12:4-5; Acts 20:19; Romans 12:16; 2 Corinthians 7:6; 1 Timothy 6:3-8; James 4:6-8, 10; 1 Peter 5:5-11.

Please refer to **Notes 34a** and **35** for additional information and Scriptures relating to this subject matter.

> **5(d)** All the days of the desponding and <u>afflicted</u> are made evil [by anxious thoughts and forebodings], <u>but he who has a glad heart has a continual feast [regardless of circumstances]</u>. (Proverbs 15:15-AMPCE)

The Hebrew word for "afflicted" is *aniy* meaning "depressed, in mind or circumstances…" Here is a passage of Scripture that I believe sums up this verse:

> *Therefore we do not lose heart. Even though our outward man is perishing, yet the inward man is being renewed day by day. For our light affliction, which is but for a moment, is working for us a far more exceeding eternal weight of glory, while we do not look at the things which are seen, but at the things which are not seen. For the things which are seen are temporary, but the things which are not seen are eternal.*
>
> (2 Corinthians 4:16-18, NKJV)

For those who choose to walk in humility, lowliness of mind before God, have chosen to trust in Him and the truth of His Word rather than the circumstances of life, knowing that God is in them, with them, and will never leave them nor forsake them *(Hebrews 13:5)*.

> **6(a)** *You are* **LORD** – *You are* **a man of war**. (Exodus 15:3)

"*You are LORD – You are a man of war*" comes from part of a song in *Exodus 15:1-21* where Moses and the children of Israel sang a song to the LORD after they saw the great work He did in delivering them from the hand of the Egyptians and parting the Red Sea. These great works caused the children of Israel to fear the LORD and believe Him and his servant Moses *(Exodus 14:18-31)*: Below is part of the song:

> *…I will sing to the LORD, for He has triumphed gloriously! The horse and its rider He has thrown into the sea! The LORD is my strength and song, and He has become my salvation; He is my God, and I will praise Him; My father's God, and I will exalt Him. <u>The LORD is a man of war; the LORD is His name</u>.*
>
> (Exodus 15:1-3, NKJV)

As you read through the Old Testament, you will see how the Lord fought for Israel, delivering them from their enemies. I want you to know that if you are in Christ then you too are Abraham's seed, who is the father of Israel, and heirs according to the promise *(Galatians 3:29)*. As the Lord fought for Israel, He too fights for you and how much more because of the blood of Jesus *(Hebrews 8:1-10)*:

> *From the end of the earth will I cry unto thee, when my heart is overwhelmed: lead me to the rock (Jesus) that is higher than I. For thou hast been a shelter for me, and a strong tower from the enemy. I will abide in thy tabernacle forever: I will trust in the covert of thy wings. Selah (pause and think about this).*

(Psalm 61:2-4)

He is the same yesterday, today, and forever; He never changes *(Hebrews 13:8; Malachi 3:6)*! The Lord desires for us to walk in victory by living out of the born-again creation in Christ, the new man.

Below are Scriptures relating to the Lord always being the same:

Exodus 3:13-15 *– And Moses said unto God, "Behold, when I come unto the children of Israel, and shall say unto them, The God of your fathers hath sent me unto you; and they shall say to me, 'What is his name?' What shall I say unto them?" And God said unto Moses, "I AM THAT I AM:" and he said, "Thus shalt thou say unto the children of Israel, 'I AM hath sent me unto you.'" And God said moreover unto Moses, "Thus shalt thou say unto the children of Israel, 'The LORD God of your fathers, the God of Abraham, the God of Isaac, and the God of Jacob, hath sent me unto you: this is my name for ever, and this is my memorial unto all generations.'"*

References:
Psalm 135:13 *– Thy name, O LORD, endureth for ever; and thy memorial, O LORD, throughout all generations.* ***Malachi 3:6*** *– For I am the LORD, I change not; therefore ye sons of Jacob are not consumed.* ***John 8:56-58*** *(NIV) – Jesus said to the Jews, "Your father Abraham rejoiced at the thought of seeing my day; he saw it and was glad." "You are not yet fifty years old," they said to him, "and you have seen Abraham!" "Very truly I tell you," Jesus answered, "before Abraham was born, I am!"* ***Hebrews 13:8*** *– Jesus Christ the same yesterday, and to day, and for ever.*

Please refer to **Notes 6b, 16a,** and **16b** for additional information and Scripture references relating to this subject matter.

6(b) The name of the LORD *is* a strong tower: *I run into it and I am safe. You are* my hiding place and my shield; I hope in Your word. *You preserve me from trouble and surround me with songs of deliverance. You* only *are* my rock and my salvation; *You are* my defense; I shall not be moved. I LOVE You, fervently and devotedly, O Lord, my Strength. *You are my God* in Whom I will trust and take refuge. If God be for *me*, who *or what* can be against *me? You are* on my side; I will not fear: what can man do *to* me? (Proverbs 18:10; Psalm 119:114, 62:6, 18:1, 18:2-AMPCE; Romans 8:31; Psalm 118:6-NKJV) *(Ref.: Psalm 32:7; Romans 8:31-39)*

It is important to understand that when we become born again, we become one with Him. Let's look at four passages of Scripture that support this:

1. ***John 17:20-26*** *– As Jesus was praying to the Father He said – "Neither pray I for these alone (His disciples), but for them also which shall believe on me through their word; that they all*

34

may be one; as thou, Father, art in me, and I in thee, that they also may be one in us: that the world may believe that thou hast sent me..."

2. **Acts 17:28** – *For in him (Jesus) we live, and move, and have our being; as certain also of your own poets have said, "for we are also his offspring."*

3. **Romans 12:5** – *So we, being many, are one body in Christ, and every one members one of another.*

4. **Galatians 3:28-29** – *There is neither Jew nor Greek, there is neither bond nor free, there is neither male nor female: for ye are all one in Christ Jesus. And if ye be Christ's, then are ye Abraham's seed, and heirs according to the promise.*

We live in His presence (i.e., His love, His care, His strength, His grace, His wisdom). Paul writes,

> *But God, who is rich in mercy, for his great love wherewith he loved us, even when we were dead in sins, hath quickened us (made us alive) together with Christ, (by grace ye are saved;) and hath raised us up together, and made us sit together in heavenly places in Christ Jesus: that in the ages to come he might shew the exceeding riches of his grace in his kindness toward us through Christ Jesus.*

(Ephesians 2:4-7)

His love is the most powerful force in the universe and our life is hid with Christ in God *(Colossians 3:3)*! He is our protector, our safety, our defense, our strength and He is calling us to grow in Him, rooted and grounded in His love, so we can truly experience His presence, and therefore, when the trials of life come we will not be moved *(Ephesians 3:17; 2 Corinthians 4:16-18)*! Our focus should be on the One who loved us and gave His only Son for us and on the One who gave Himself for us *(John 3:16-17)*. The following passage of Scripture reflects the ones who choose to grow in Christ:

> *Therefore, we do not become discouraged (utterly spiritless, exhausted, and wearied out through fear). Though our outer man is [progressively] decaying and wasting away, yet our inner self (our new man) is being [progressively] renewed day after day. For our light, momentary affliction (this slight distress of the passing hour) is ever more and more abundantly preparing and producing and achieving for us an everlasting weight of glory [beyond all measure, excessively surpassing all comparisons and all calculations, a vast and transcendent glory and blessedness never to cease!] Since we consider and look not to the things that are seen but to the things that are unseen; for the things that are visible are temporal (brief and fleeting), but the things that are invisible are deathless and everlasting.*

(2 Corinthians 4:16-18, AMPCE)

Below are two examples of men of faith who were not moved by the circumstances of life:

The first example is about Stephen, a man full of faith and power who did great wonders and miracles among the people. In *Acts 6-7*, there arose certain men who began to dispute Stephen but they were not able to resist the wisdom and the spirit by which he spoke. And they then had men say that he, Stephen, spoke blasphemous words against Moses and God. This stirred up the people, the elders, and the scribes, so they seized him and brought him before the council, and the high priest asked him if these things were so? Stephen responded by speaking about God's directives to Abraham and to Moses,

"You stiff-necked and uncircumcised in heart and ears! You always resist the Holy Spirit; as your fathers did, so do you. Which of the prophets did your fathers not persecute? And they killed those who foretold the coming of the Just One, of whom you now have become the betrayers and murderers, who have received the law by the direction of angels and have not kept it." When they heard these things, they were cut to the heart, and they gnashed at him with their teeth. But he, being full of the Holy Spirit, gazed into heaven and saw the glory of God, and Jesus standing at the right hand of God, and said, "Look! I see the heavens opened and the Son of Man standing at the right hand of God!" Then they cried out with a loud voice, stopped their ears, and ran at him with one accord; and they cast him out of the city and stoned him. And the witnesses laid down their clothes at the feet of a young man named Saul. And they stoned Stephen as he was calling on God and saying, "Lord Jesus, receive my spirit." Then he knelt down and cried out with a loud voice, "Lord, do not charge them with this sin." And when he had said this, he fell asleep.

(Acts 7:51-60, NKJV)

Notice that Jesus stood to honor and to receive Stephen! Stephen loved the Lord, and Jesus chose to deliver Stephen by allowing him to receive a better resurrection *(Hebrews 11:35).*

The second example is found in *Daniel 3* where three servants of the Lord, Shadrach, Meshach, and Abednego, refused to bow down and worship the gods of Nebuchadnezzar. Nebuchadnezzar gave them another chance to fall down and worship the image which he had made and warned them,

> *...but if ye worship not, ye shall be cast the same hour into the midst of a burning fiery furnace; and who is that God that shall deliver you out of my hands?*

(Daniel 3:15)

And they answered the king,

> *O Nebuchadnezzar, we are not careful to answer thee in this matter. If it be so, our God whom we serve is able to deliver us from the burning fiery furnace, and he will deliver us out of thine hand, O king. But if not, be it known unto thee, O king, that we will not serve thy gods, nor worship the golden image which thou hast set up.*

(Daniel 3:16-18)

Then in *Daniel 3:19-23*, Nebuchadnezzar was full of fury and commanded that they should heat the furnace seven times more than it was usually heated. And he commanded the most mighty men in his army to bind Shadrach, Meshach, and Abednego, and to cast them into the burning fiery furnace. Then,

> *King Nebuchadnezzar was astonished; and he rose in haste and spoke, saying to his counselors, "Did we not cast three men bound into the midst of the fire?" They answered and said to the king, "True, O king." "Look!" he answered, "I see four men loose, walking in the midst of the fire; and they are not hurt, and the form of the fourth is like the Son of God."*

(Daniel 3:24-25, NKJV)

Let's see what happened when Shadrach, Meshach, and Abednego came out of the furnace:

And the satraps, administrators, governors, and the king's counselors gathered together, and they saw these men on whose bodies the fire had no power; the hair of their head was not singed nor were their garments affected, and the smell of fire was not on them.

(Daniel 3:27, NKJV)

God chose to deliver them when they were bound and thrown into the midst of the fire. And what a great deliverance that was!

The one thing that all four of these men had in common (Stephen, Shadrach, Meshach, and Abednego) was that their love and dedication toward God was greater than their love for self. If we are self-centered, we are walking in pride and fear; if we are God-centered, we are walking in humility and faith (the just shall live by faith – *Habakkuk 2:4; Romans 1:17; Galatians 3:11; Hebrews 10:38*). I believe Paul summed it up when he wrote,

… Yes, and I will continue to rejoice, for I know that through your prayers and God's provision of the Spirit of Jesus Christ what has happened to me will turn out for my deliverance. I eagerly expect and hope that I will in no way be ashamed, but will have sufficient courage so that now as always Christ will be exalted in my body, whether by life or by death. For to me, to live is Christ and to die is gain. If I am to go on living in the body, this will mean fruitful labor for me. Yet what shall I choose? I do not know! I am torn between the two: I desire to depart and be with Christ, which is better by far; but it is more necessary for you that I remain in the body. Convinced of this, I know that I will remain, and I will continue with all of you for your progress and joy in the faith, so that through my being with you again your boasting in Christ Jesus will abound on account of me.

(Philippians 1:18-26, NIV)

I want to encourage you to read *Hebrews 11*, the chapter that reports the results of men and women who <u>chose</u> to live by faith.

When we become born again, we are in Christ and the things that we suffer are working in us an eternal weight of glory. He is calling us to a new life in Him by living out of the new man—the born-again nature that we received when we accepted Jesus Christ as our Lord and Savior, and not according to the old man—our carnal/self-centered nature *(Romans 8:1-39)*. We also need to understand that as soon as we receive Jesus Christ as our Lord and Savior we are born into God's family *(1 Corinthians 3:1-7; 1 Peter 2:1-3)*. There is a spiritual growth and maturity that takes place within us as we continue to: feed on the Word of God, pray, and submit to His ways. It is also important to note that His love for His babes is just as great and protecting as His love for those who have matured in Christ! Paul writes,

What shall we then say to these things? If God be for us, who can be against us? He that spared not his own Son, but delivered him up for us all, how shall he not with him also freely give us all things? Who shall lay any thing to the charge of God's elect? It is God that justifieth. Who is he that condemneth? It is Christ that died, yea rather, that is risen again, who is even at the right hand of God, who also maketh intercession for us. <u>Who shall separate us from the love of Christ? Shall tribulation, or distress, or persecution, or famine, or nakedness, or peril, or sword?</u> As it is written, "for thy sake we are killed all the day *long; we are accounted as sheep for the slaughter." Nay, in all these things we are more than conquerors through him that loved us. <u>For I am persuaded, that neither death, nor life, nor angels, nor principalities, nor powers, nor things present, nor things to come, nor height, nor depth, nor any other creature, shall be able to separate us from the love of God, which is in Christ Jesus our Lord.</u>*

(Romans 8:31-39)

Below are Scriptures relating to trusting in the living God:

Psalm 17:8-9 *(NKJV) – Keep me as the apple of Your eye; hide me under the shadow of Your wings, from the wicked who oppress me, from my deadly enemies who surround me.*

References:
Psalm 9:9 *– The LORD also will be a refuge for the oppressed, a refuge in times of trouble.* ***Psalm 37:39-40*** *– But the salvation of the righteous is of the LORD: he is their strength in the time of trouble. And the LORD shall help them, and deliver them: he shall deliver them from the wicked, and save them, because they trust in him.* ***Psalm 56:3-4, 11*** *– What time I am afraid, I will trust in thee. In God I will praise his word, in God I have put my trust; I will not fear what flesh can do unto me. In God have I put my trust: I will not be afraid what man can do unto me.* ***Psalm 57:1-3, 7*** *(NIV) – Have mercy on me, my God, have mercy on me, for in you I take refuge. I will take refuge in the shadow of your wings until the disaster has passed. I cry out to God Most High, to God, who vindicates me. He sends from heaven and saves me, rebuking those who hotly pursue me—God sends forth his love and his faithfulness. My heart, O God, is steadfast, my heart is steadfast; I will sing and make music.* ***Psalm 118:6, 8-9*** *– The LORD is on my side; I will not fear: what can man do unto me? It is better to trust in the LORD than to put confidence in man. It is better to trust in the LORD than to put confidence in princes.* ***Proverbs 29:25*** *– The fear of man bringeth a snare: but whoso putteth his trust in the LORD shall be safe.* ***Isaiah 26:3-4*** *(NKJV) – You will keep him in perfect peace, whose mind is stayed on You, because he trusts in You. Trust in the LORD forever, for in YAH, the LORD, is everlasting strength.* ***2 Thessalonians 2:16-17*** *– Now our Lord Jesus Christ himself, and God, even our Father, which hath loved us, and hath given us everlasting consolation and good hope through grace, comfort your hearts, and stablish you in every good word and work.*

Here are additional Scriptures relating to trusting in the living God: 1 Samuel 30:6; 2 Samuel 22:20-37; 2 Kings 6:14-17; Psalm 1:1-6; 5:11-12, 7:10, 18:19-35, 21:7, 27:1-6, 31:19-21, 33:18-22, 34:8-15, 36:5-7, 42:5, 46:1-5, 62:1-2, 5-8, 64:10, 91:1-16, 94:22, 121:1-2, 5, 128:1-6, 138:1-3, 142:2-7, 144:1-2; Proverbs 14:26-27, 18:10, 30:5; Isaiah 45:17-18, 51:12-13; Jeremiah 17:5-8; Lamentations 3:24-26; Ezekiel 18:21-32; Hosea 13:9; Matthew 10:28; Mark 8:34-38; Luke 6:46-49; 1 Thessalonians 5:5-10; Hebrews 13:5-6; 1 Peter 3:8-17.

Please refer to **Notes 6a**, **16a**, **16b**, and **40** for additional information and Scriptures relating to this subject matter.

7(a) *You are **Abba, Father**. I thank You that I have received Your precious Holy Spirit which <u>produces sonship</u> making You my Father. (Ref.: Romans 8:15; Galatians 4:6-7)*

Below are three passages of Scripture relating to Abba Father:

1. ***Mark 14:36*** – *Jesus said, "Abba, Father, all things are possible unto thee; take away this cup from me: nevertheless not what I will, but what thou wilt."*
2. ***Romans 8:15*** – *Paul said, "For ye have not received the spirit of bondage again to fear; but ye have received the spirit of adoption, whereby we cry, Abba, Father."*
3. ***Galatians 4:6*** – *Paul said, "And because ye are sons, God hath sent forth the Spirit of his Son into your hearts, crying, Abba, Father."*

In the Vine's Expository Dictionary of Old and New Testament Words, the meaning for the word "Abba" is "…'Abba' the word framed by the lips of infants, and <u>betokens unreasoning trust</u>; 'father' expresses an intelligent apprehension of the relationship. The two together express the love and intelligent confidence of the child."[1] In *Mark 14:36* you see that Jesus fully trusted His heavenly Father even unto His death. Paul writes,

> *And being found in fashion as a man, he (Jesus) humbled himself, and became obedient unto death, even the death of the cross. Wherefore God also hath highly exalted him, and given him a name which is above every name: that at the name of Jesus every knee should bow, of things in heaven, and things in earth, and thing under the earth; and that every tongue should confess that Jesus Christ is Lord, to the glory of God the Father.*
>
> (Philippians 2:8-11)

And Jesus said to His disciples,

> <u>*All power is given unto me in heaven and in earth*</u>*. Go ye therefore, and teach all nations, baptizing them in the name of the Father, and of the Son, and of the Holy Ghost: teaching them to observe all things whatsoever I have commanded you: and, lo, I am with you alway, even unto the end of the world. Amen.*
>
> (Matthew 28:18-20)

Our heavenly Father has given to every born-again believer, the spirit of adoption where we can cry, "Abba, Father." He desires for us to trust Him in every situation and circumstance of life, as we have the Spirit of His Son Jesus, abiding within us!

Jesus said to His disciples,

> *If a son asks for bread from any father among you, will he give him a stone? Or if he asks for a fish, will he give him a serpent instead of a fish? Or if he asks for an egg, will he offer him a scorpion? If you then, being evil, know how to give good gifts to your children, how much more will your heavenly Father give the Holy Spirit to those who ask Him!*
>
> (Luke 11:11-13, NKJV)

In *Matthew 7:9-11*, Jesus said the same thing, but instead of saying, "*…how much more will your heavenly Father give the <u>Holy Spirit</u> to those who ask Him?,*" He said, "*…how much more will your Father who is in heaven give <u>good things</u> to those who ask Him.*" We must remember that "*every good gift and every perfect gift is from above, and cometh down from the Father of lights, with whom there is no* *variableness, neither shadow of turning…" (James 1:17-18).* Our heavenly Father's intent is to do good to His children and to give good gifts to us through His Holy Spirit. He has given to His children all things that pertain to life and godliness *(2 Peter 1:3)*. It is also important to remember when He corrects us He's doing it for our profit that we may be partakers of His holiness *(Hebrews 12:10)*.

As relating to sonship, Paul describes it best,

> *For ye are <u>all</u> the children of God by faith in Christ Jesus. For as many of you as have been baptized into Christ have put on Christ. There is neither Jew nor Greek, there is neither bond nor free, there is neither male nor female: for ye are all one in Christ Jesus. And if ye be Christ's, then are ye Abraham's seed, and heirs according to the promise.*
>
> (Galatians 3:26-29)

Christ has called us to put on the new man as we are joint heirs with Him through the born-again creation within *(Ephesians 4:20-24; Colossians 3:1-14; Romans 8:17)*!

Below are Scriptures relating to sonship, His children:

1. ***Matthew 12:47-50*** *(NASB) – Someone said to Him, "Behold, Your mother and Your brothers are standing outside, seeking to speak to You. But Jesus answered the one who was telling Him and said, "Who is My mother and who are My brothers?" And stretching out His hand toward His disciples, He said, "Behold, My mother and My brothers! For whoever does the will of My Father who is in heaven, he is My brother and sister and mother."*

References:
Romans 8:11-21, 28-29 *– But if the Spirit of him that raised up Jesus from the dead dwell in you, he that raised up Christ from the dead shall also quicken (make alive) your mortal bodies by his Spirit that dwelleth in you. Therefore, brethren, we are debtors, not to the flesh, to live after the flesh. For if ye live after the flesh, ye shall die: but if ye through the Spirit do mortify the deeds of the body, ye shall live. For as many as are led by the Spirit of God, they are the sons of God. For ye have not received the spirit of bondage again to fear; but ye have received the Spirit of adoption, whereby we cry Abba, Father. The Spirit itself beareth witness with our spirit, that we are the children of God: and if children, then heirs; heirs of God, and joint-heirs with Christ; if so be that we suffer with him, that we may be also glorified together. For I reckon that the sufferings of this present time are not worthy to be compared with the glory which shall be revealed in us. For the earnest expectation of the creature waiteth for the manifestation of the sons of God. For the creature was made subject to vanity, not willingly, but by reason of him who hath subjected the same in hope, because the creature itself also shall be delivered from the bondage of corruption into the glorious liberty of the children of God. And we know that all things work together for good to them that love God, to them who are the called according to his purpose. For whom he did foreknow, he also did predestinate to be conformed to the image of his Son, that he might be the firstborn among many brethren. **2 Corinthians 6:14-18** (NASB) – Do not be bound together with unbelievers; for what partnership have righteousness and lawlessness, or what fellowship has light with darkness? Or what harmony has Christ with Belial, or what has a believer in common with an unbeliever? Or what agreement has the temple of God with idols? For we are the temple of the living God; just as God said, "I WILL DWELL IN THEM AND WALK AMONG THEM; AND I WILL BE THEIR GOD, AND THEY SHALL BE MY PEOPLE. Therefore, COME OUT FROM THEIR MIDST AND BE SEPARATE," says the Lord. "AND DO NOT TOUCH WHAT IS UNCLEAN; and I will welcome*

you. And I will be a father to you, and you shall be sons and daughters to Me," says the Lord Almighty. **Galatians 4:1-7** (NKJV) – Now I say that the heir, as long as he is a child, does not differ at all from a slave, though he is master of all, but is under guardians and stewards until the time appointed by the father. Even so we, when we were children, were in bondage under the elements of the world. But when the fullness of the time had come, God sent forth His son, born of a woman, born under the law, to redeem those who were under the law, that we might receive the adoption as sons. And because you are sons, God has sent forth the Spirit of His Son into your hearts, crying out, "Abba, Father!" Therefore you are no longer a slave but a son, and if a son, then an heir of God through Christ. **Ephesians 1:3-6** (NASB) – Blessed be the God and Father of our Lord Jesus Christ, who has blessed us with every spiritual blessing in the heavenly places in Christ, just as He chose us in Him before the foundation of the world, that we should be holy and blameless before Him. In love He predestined us to adoption as sons through Jesus Christ to Himself, according to the kind intention of His will, to the praise of the glory of His grace, which He freely bestowed on us in the Beloved. **Ephesians 2:19-22** (NASB) – So then, you are no longer strangers and aliens, but you are fellow citizens with the saints, and are of God's household, having been built on the foundation of the apostles and prophets, Christ Jesus Himself being the corner stone, in whom the whole building, being fitted together, is growing into a holy temple in the Lord, in whom you also are being built together into a dwelling of God in the Spirit. **Ephesians 3:14-21** – For this cause I bow my knees unto the Father of our Lord Jesus Christ, of whom the whole family in heaven and earth is named, that he would grant you, according to the riches of his glory, to be strengthened with might by his Spirit in the inner man; that Christ may dwell in your hearts by faith; that ye, being rooted and grounded in love, may be able to comprehend with all saints what is the breadth, and length, and depth, and height; and to know the love of Christ, which passeth knowledge, that ye might be filled with all the fulness of God. Now unto him that is able to do exceeding abundantly above all that we ask or think, according to the power that worketh in us, unto him be glory in the church by Christ Jesus throughout all ages, world without end. Amen. **Ephesians 5:1-2** (NKJV) – Therefore, be imitators of God as dear children. And walk in love, as Christ also has loved us and given Himself for us, an offering and a sacrifice to God for a sweet-smelling aroma. **1 Thessalonians 5:5-10** – Ye are all the children of light, and the children of the day: we are not of the night, nor of darkness. Therefore let us not sleep, as do others; but let us watch and be sober. For they that sleep sleep in the night; and they that be drunken are drunken in the night. But let us, who are of the day, be sober, putting on the breastplate of faith and love; and for an helmet, the hope of salvation. For God hath not appointed us to wrath, but to obtain salvation by our Lord Jesus Christ, who died for us, that, whether we wake or sleep, we should live together with him. **2 Timothy 2:19** – Nevertheless the foundation of God stands sure, having this seal, "The Lord knoweth them that are his." And, "Let every one that nameth the name of Christ depart from iniquity." **Hebrews 2:10-13** – For it became him, for whom are all things, and by whom are all things, in bringing many sons unto glory, to make the captain of their salvation perfect through sufferings. For both he that sanctifieth and they who are sanctified are all of one: for which cause he is not ashamed to call them brethren, saying, "I will declare thy name unto my brethren, in the midst of the church will I sing praise unto thee." And again, "I will put my trust in him." And again, "Behold I and the children which God hath given me." **1 Peter 1:3-5, 22-25** (NASB) – Blessed be the God and Father of our Lord Jesus Christ, who according to His great mercy has caused us to be born again to a living hope through the resurrection of Jesus Christ from the dead, to obtain an inheritance which is imperishable and undefiled and will not fade away, reserved in heaven for you, who are protected by the power of God through faith for a salvation ready to be revealed in the last time. Since you have in obedience to the truth purified your souls for a sincere love of the brethren, fervently love one another from the heart, for you have been born again, not of seed which is perishable but imperishable, that is, through the living and enduring word of God. For, "ALL FLESH IS LIKE GRASS, AND ALL ITS GLORY LIKE THE FLOWER OF GRASS. THE GRASS WITHERS, AND THE FLOWER FALLS

OFF, BUT THE WORD OF THE LORD ENDURES FOREVER." And this is the word which was preached to you.

2. **1 John 5:20-21** – *And we know that the Son of God is come, and hath given us an understanding, that we may know him that is true, and we are in him that is true, even in his Son Jesus Christ. This is the true God, and eternal life. Little children, keep yourselves from idols. Amen.*

Reference:

John 17:3 – *And this is life eternal, that they might know thee the only true God, and Jesus Christ, whom thou hast sent.* (Every born-again child of God is living in eternal life right now! The Lord desires for us to know Him through His Word and by His Spirit in order to walk in abundant life!).

Please refer to **Note 1b** for information and Scriptures relating to being filled with the Holy Spirit and a prayer to become born again.

> **7(b)** *I can trust that You have my best interest at heart! (Ref.: Jeremiah 29:11, 32:38-41; Hebrews 12:5-11)*

Throughout the New Testament, Jesus continually revealed that your heavenly Father has your best interest at heart. In *Matthew 10:30*, Jesus said that the very hairs of your head are all numbered. I take that to mean that He is concerned about, and desires to be a part of, every detail of your life. David said that the Lord will perfect that which concerns you and Peter said to cast <u>all</u> of your care upon Him because He cares for you *(Psalm 138:8; 1 Peter 5:7)*. Jesus came to destroy the works of the devil in your life *(1 John 3:8)*. Jesus said in *John 10:10, "The thief cometh not, but for to steal, and to kill, and to destroy: I am come that they might have life, and that they might have it more abundantly."* The thief cares about himself and his own gain; Jesus cares about you and your gain and desires for you to live out of His abundant life! Our heavenly Father corrects us because He does have our best interest at heart.

> *Furthermore, we had earthly fathers to discipline us, and we respected them; shall we not much rather be subject to the Father of spirits, and live? For they disciplined us for a short time as seemed best to them, but He disciplines us for our good, so that we may share His holiness.*
>
> (Hebrews 12:9-10, NASB)

His way is the only way that leads to life *(Matthew 7:13-14; John 6:63)*! Our ways may seem right to us, but its end is death *(Proverbs 14:12, 16:25)*. This is why it is essential as born-again believers, to put off the old man and to put on the new man by renewing the *spirit of our minds (Ephesians 4:20-24)*.

Below are Scriptures relating to our heavenly Father's correction:

Nehemiah 9:20 (NASB) – *You gave Your good Spirit to instruct them, Your manna You did not withhold from their mouth, and You gave them water for their thirst.*

References:

Psalm 119:67-68, 71-72 (NASB) – Before I was afflicted, I went astray, but now I keep Your word. You are good and do good; teach me Your statutes. It is good for me that I was afflicted, that I may learn Your statutes. The law of Your mouth is better to me than thousands of gold and silver pieces. **Proverbs 1:23** – *Turn you at my reproof: behold, I will pour out my spirit unto you, I will make known my words unto you.* **Proverbs 3:11-12** – *My son, despise not the chastening of the LORD; neither be weary of his correction: for whom the LORD loveth he correcteth; even as a father the son in whom he delighteth.* **Hebrews 12:3-11** – *For consider him that endured such contradiction of sinners against himself, lest ye be wearied and faint in your minds. Ye have not yet resisted unto blood, striving against sin. And ye have forgotten the exhortation which speaketh unto you as unto children, "My son, despise not thou the chastening of the Lord, nor faint when thou art rebuked of him for whom the Lord loveth he chasteneth, and scourgeth every son whom he receiveth." If ye endure chastening, God dealeth with you as with sons; for what son is he whom the father chasteneth not? But if ye be without chastisement, whereof all are partakers, then are ye bastards, and not sons. Furthermore we have had fathers of our flesh which corrected us, and we gave them reverence: shall we not much rather be in subjection unto the Father of spirits, and live? For they verily for a few days chastened us after their own pleasure; but he for our profit, that we might be partakers of his holiness. Now no chastening for the present seemeth to be joyous, but grievous: nevertheless afterward it yieldeth the peaceable fruit of righteousness unto them which are exercised thereby.* **Revelation 3:19** – *As many as I love, I rebuke and chasten: be zealous therefore, and repent.*

I want to give thanks to the Lord for chastening me concerning the deep-seated ingrained carnal mindsets that were operating within me, rather than leaving me to myself. After walking with Him for twelve years, He caused my environment to become a heated furnace to draw out those impurities and to teach me the importance of renewing my mind to His truths in order to flush them out! It was not joyous at the time, but thank God, now I'm yielding the peaceable fruit of righteousness through living out of the born-again creation (**My Story – Part Two - Volume 1**). It was worth it all *(Hebrews 12:11)*!

7(c) *Just as Jesus cried out to You in the hour of temptation,* "Abba, [which means] Father, everything is possible for You. Take away this cup from Me; yet not what I will, but what You [will]." *I too trust my life to You today, not my will but Your will be done.* (Mark 14:36-AMPCE) *(Ref.: Mark 14:35; 1 Peter 2:21-23)*

Let's begin by looking at the following passage of Scripture:

[You who are] household servants, be submissive to your masters with all [proper] respect, not only to those who are kind and considerate and reasonable, but also to those who are surly (overbearing, unjust, and crooked). For one is regarded favorably (is approved, acceptable, and thankworthy) if, as in the sight of God, he endures the pain of unjust suffering. [After all] what kind of glory [is there in it] if, when you do wrong and are punished for it, you take it patiently? But if you bear patiently with suffering [which results] when you do right and that is undeserved, it is acceptable and pleasing to God. For even to this you have been called [it is inseparable from your vocation]. For Christ also suffered for you, leaving you [His personal] example, so that you should follow in His footsteps. He was guilty of no sin, neither was deceit (guile) ever found on His lips. When He was reviled and insulted, He did not revile or offer insult in return; [when] He was abused and suffered, He made no threats [of vengeance]; but He trusted [Himself and everything] to Him Who judges fairly

(righteously).

(1 Peter 2:18-23, AMPCE)

Why would suffering for doing right be acceptable and pleasing to God? It's certainly not because He takes pleasure in us being hurt or wronged—absolutely not! I believe when He looks upon one of His children who choose to suffer and not retaliate for doing right, He sees that child trusting in his heavenly Father who is the true Judge, as Christ did in His obedience, even unto His death. The key to Christ's victory is that He loved His heavenly Father more than He loved Himself and trusted His Father's perfect love for Him. We, too, are called to love God more than ourselves and to trust His perfect love for us. This is the key to enduring temptation. We must surrender our will and gain the strength to do His will through His Word and prayer.

It is important for us to consider Jesus who endured such hostility from sinners, lest we become weary and discouraged in our souls. We have not yet resisted to bloodshed, striving against sin *(Luke 22:39-46; Hebrews 12:4),*

> *No temptation has overtaken you but such as is common to man; and God is faithful, who will not allow you to be tempted beyond what you are able, but with the temptation will provide the way of escape also, so that you will be able to endure it. Therefore, my beloved, flee from idolatry.*
>
> (1 Corinthians 10:13-14, NASB)

Just as Stephen, Shadrach, Meshach, and Abednego (see **Note 6b**) set their affections on things above, so too our heavenly Father has called us to set our affections on things above and not on the things that are on the earth *(Colossians 3:2)*. In order to trust the Lord in difficult and trying situations, I have found that journaling to the Lord and keeping my mind renewed to the truth of His Word helps me to trust Him. It gives me confidence that He has my cares, my frustrations, my fears, etc. Keeping my mind renewed to the new man helps me to keep my mind stayed on Him – "*You will keep him in perfect peace, whose mind is stayed on You, because he trusts in You. Trust in the LORD forever, for in YAH, the LORD, is everlasting strength*" – Isaiah 26:3-4 (NKJV). Paul writes,

> *Do not be anxious about anything, but in every situation, by prayer and petition, with thanksgiving, present your requests to God. And the peace of God, which transcends all understanding, will guard your hearts and your minds in Christ Jesus. Finally, brothers and sisters, whatever is true, whatever is noble, whatever is right, whatever is pure, whatever is lovely, whatever is admirable—if anything is excellent or praiseworthy—think about such things.*
>
> (Philippians 4:6-8, NIV)

James writes,

> *Blessed is a man who perseveres under trial; for once he has been approved, he will receive the crown of life which the Lord has promised to those who love Him. Let no one say when he is tempted, "I am tempted by God"; for God cannot be tempted by evil, and He Himself does not tempt anyone. But each one is tempted when he is carried away and enticed by his own lusts. Then when lust has conceived, it gives birth to sin; and when sin is accomplished,*

it brings forth death. Do not be deceived, my beloved brethren. Every good thing given and every perfect gift is from above, coming down from the Father of lights, with whom there is no variation or shifting shadow. In the exercise of His will He brought us forth by the word of truth, so that we would be a kind of first fruits among His creatures.

(James 1:12-18, NASB)

Jesus set His affections on things above not on the things of the earth *(John 5:19, 30)* and therefore we can better understand *Hebrews 12:2, "Looking unto Jesus the author and finisher of our faith; who for the joy that was set before him endured the cross, despising the shame, and is set down at the right hand of the throne of God."* What was set before Jesus that brought Him joy? Here are a few things I believe helped Him to endure the cross: (1) His love for His heavenly Father was greater than His love for Himself, (2) the satisfaction of doing the will of His Father and finishing the work He was called to do, (3) through His obedience unto death, He would bring many sons and daughters unto glory *(Hebrews 2:10)*, (4) He would destroy the works of the devil *(1 John 3:8)*. Paul writes,

And being found in appearance as a man, he humbled himself by becoming obedient to death—even death on a cross! Therefore God exalted him to the highest place and gave him the name that is above every name, that at the name of Jesus every knee should bow, in heaven and on earth and under the earth, and every tongue acknowledge that Jesus Christ is Lord, to the glory of God the Father.

(Philippians 2:8-11, NIV)

It is important to note here that God exalts those who walk in humble obedience *(Psalm 75:6-7; Matthew 23:12; 1 Peter 5:6)*!

In the Old Testament, the Hebrew word for "trust" is *batach, chacah,* and *mibtach* and in the New Testament, the Greek word for "trust" is *elpizo*. Below are their meanings and samples of Scripture where these words are found (Note: it is important for us to run to Him and to confide in Him concerning our fears – e.g., our cares, anxieties, frustrations, concerns):

Batach – "figuratively, to trust, be confident or sure:–be bold – (confident, secure, sure)…"
1. *1 Chronicles 5:20 – …for they cried to God in the battle, and He was intreated of them; <u>because they put their trust in Him</u>.*
2. *Psalm 9:10 – <u>And they that know thy name will put their trust in thee</u>: for thou, LORD, hast not forsaken them that seek thee.*
3. *Psalm 22:4-5 – <u>Our fathers trusted in thee: they trusted</u>, and thou didst deliver them. They cried unto thee, and were delivered: <u>they trusted in thee</u>, and were not confounded.*
4. *Psalm 84:12 – O Lord of Hosts, <u>blessed is the man that trusteth in thee</u>.*
5. *Proverbs 3:5-8 – <u>Trust in the Lord with all thine heart</u>; and lean not unto thine own understanding. In all thy ways acknowledge him, and he shall direct thy paths. Be not wise in thine own eyes: fear the LORD, and depart from evil. It shall be health to thy navel, and marrow to thy bones.*

Chacah – "to flee for protection; figuratively, to confide in:–have hope, make refuge, (put) trust."
1. *Psalm 18:28-30 – For thou wilt light my candle: the LORD my God will enlighten my darkness. For by thee I have run through a troop; and by my God have I leaped over a wall. As*

for God, his way is perfect: the word of the LORD is tried: <u>he is a buckler to all those that trust in him</u>.

    2. *Psalm 37:40 – And the LORD shall help them, and deliver them: <u>he shall deliver them from the wicked, and save them, because they trust in him</u>.*

<u>*Mibtach*</u> – "properly, a refuge, i.e. (objective) security, or (subjective) assurance:–confidence, hope, sure, trust."
Proverbs 22:17-19 – Bow down thine ear, and hear the words of the wise, and apply thine heart unto my knowledge. For it is a pleasant thing if thou keep them within thee; they shall withal be fitted in thy lips. <u>That thy trust</u> may be in the LORD, I have made known to thee this day, even to thee.

<u>*Elpizo*</u> – "to expect or confide:–(have, thing) hope(-d) (for), trust."
1 Timothy 4:10 – For therefore we both labor and suffer reproach, because <u>we trust</u> in the living God, who is the Saviour of all men, specially of those that believe.

Below are Scriptures relating to our abiding place:

1. ***Proverbs 15:24*** *– The way of life is above to the wise, that he may depart from hell beneath.*

References:
Proverbs 16:23 *– The heart of the wise teacheth his mouth, and addeth learning to his lips.* ***Ephesians 2:4-7*** *– But God, who is rich in mercy, for his great love wherewith he loved us, even when we were dead in sins, hath quickened us together with Christ, (by grace ye are saved;) and hath raised us up together, and made us sit together in heavenly places in Christ Jesus: that in the ages to come he might shew the exceeding riches of his grace in his kindness toward us through Christ Jesus.* ***Philippians 3:18-21*** *– (For many walk, of whom I have told you often, and now tell you even weeping, that they are the enemies of the cross of Christ: whose end is destruction, whose God is their belly, and whose glory is in their shame, who mind earthly things.) For our conversation (citizenship) is in heaven; from whence also we look for the Saviour, the Lord Jesus Christ: who shall change our vile body, that it may be fashioned like unto his glorious body, according to the working whereby he is able even to subdue all things unto himself.* ***Colossians 3:1-3*** *– If ye then be risen with Christ, seek those things which are above, where Christ sitteth on the right hand of God. Set your affection on things above, not on things on the earth. For ye are dead, and your life is hid with Christ in God.*

2. ***John 12:35-36*** *– Then Jesus said unto them, "Yet a little while is the light with you. Walk while ye have the light, lest darkness come upon you: for he that walketh in darkness knoweth not whither he goeth. While ye have light, believe in the light, that ye may be the children of light."*

References:
1 John 2:9-11 *– He that saith he is in the light, and hateth his brother, is in darkness even until now. He that loveth his brother abideth in the light, and there is none occasion of stumbling in him. But he that hateth his brother is in darkness, and walketh in darkness, and knoweth not whither he goeth, because that darkness hath blinded his eyes.* ***Ephesians 5:8-10, 14, 17*** *– For ye were sometimes darkness, but now are ye light in the Lord: walk as children of light: (for the fruit of the Spirit is in all goodness and righteousness and truth;) proving what is acceptable unto the Lord. Wherefore he saith, "Awake thou that sleepest, and arise from the dead, and Christ shall give thee light. Wherefore be ye not unwise, but understanding what the will of the Lord is.*

3. **Colossians 3:9-11** – *...seeing that ye have put off the old man with his deeds; and have put on the new man, which is renewed in knowledge after the image of him that created him: where there is neither Greek nor Jew, circumcision nor uncircumcision, Barbarian, Scythian, bond nor free: but Christ is all, and in all.*

References:
Romans 12:1-2 – *I beseech you therefore, brethren, by the mercies of God, that ye present your bodies a living sacrifice, holy, acceptable unto God, which is your reasonable service. And do not be conformed to this world: but be ye transformed by the renewing of your mind, that ye may prove what is that good, and acceptable, and perfect, will of God.* **Ephesians 4:21-24** – *If so be that ye have heard him, and have been taught by him, as the truth is in Jesus: that ye put off concerning the former conversation (behavior) the old man, which is corrupt according to the deceitful lusts; and be renewed in the spirit of your mind; and that ye put on the new man, which after God is created in righteousness and true holiness.* **Hebrews 4:12** – *For the word of God is quick (alive), and powerful, and sharper than any twoedged sword, piercing even to the dividing asunder of soul and spirit, and of the joints and marrow, and is a discerner of the thoughts and intents of the heart.*

8(a) *You are **Yahweh-Shalom** – **The Prince of Peace**. (Ref: Isaiah 9:6)*

The Hebrew word *Shalown* (pronunciation: *Shalom*) means wholeness and soundness in Christ (i.e., health, completeness, prosperity, peace, safe, well) and is found in the born-again creation where Christ and His kingdom rule resides. I'm reminded of the passage of Scripture where John said in *3 John 1:2* – *"Beloved, I wish above all things that thou mayest prosper and be in health, even as thy soul prospereth."* In Christ are hid all the treasures of wisdom and knowledge, He is the power and the wisdom of God, and we have this treasure in earthen vessels *(Colossians 2:1-3; 1 Corinthians 1:24; 2 Corinthians 4:7)*. This is why it is essential that we put off the old man and *"renew the spirit of our minds"* and put on the new man in Christ where our true inheritance resides!

8(b) The government shall be upon *Your* shoulder: and *Your name* shall be called Wonderful, Counsellor, The mighty God, The everlasting Father, The Prince of Peace. (Isaiah 9:6)

Let's begin with the following passage of Scripture:

> *For unto us a child is born, unto us a son is given: and the <u>government</u> shall be upon his shoulder: and his name shall be called Wonderful, Counsellor, The Mighty God, The everlasting Father, The Prince of Peace. Of the increase of His <u>government</u> and peace there shall be no end, upon the throne of David, and upon his kingdom, to order it, and to establish it with judgment and with justice from henceforth even for ever. The zeal of the LORD of hosts will perform this.*
>
> (Isaiah 9:6-7)

I believe we need to establish to what government Isaiah is referring. Jesus said in *John 18:36, "My kingdom in not of this world: if my kingdom were of this world, then would my servants fight, that I should not be delivered to the Jews: but now is my kingdom not from hence.*" The government of the kingdom of God is upon His shoulder and we must understand that <u>our citizenship is in Heaven</u>, from which we also eagerly wait for our Savior, the Lord Jesus Christ *(Philippians 3:20)*. In *Philippians 3:20*, the King James Version uses the word conversation instead of citizenship. The word "conversation" in the Greek is *politeuma*. Its meaning in the Thayer's Greek Lexicon is "the constitution of a commonwealth, form of government and the laws by which it is administered, the commonwealth whose citizens we are." Again, this is why it is essential for us to renew the *spirit of our minds* to the truth of God's Word in order for us to live out of His governing rule *(Ephesians 4:22-23)*! Paul writes,

> *I beseech you therefore, brethren, by the mercies of God, that ye present your bodies a living sacrifice, holy, acceptable unto God, which is your reasonable service. And be not conformed to this world: but be ye transformed by the renewing of your mind, that ye may prove what is that good, and acceptable, and perfect, will of God.*
>
> (Romans 12:1-2)

Does this mean that we should not participate in voting in this country? I believe *Romans 13:1-7* clearly states that governing authorities or powers are ordained of God and therefore we should not only pray for those who are in authority, but be part of the process to hopefully put in office those whose policies reflect the will of God in order to help us lead a quiet and peaceable life in all godliness and honesty *(1 Timothy 2:1-4)*. Paul writes,

> *…But every man in his own order: Christ the firstfruits; afterward they that are Christ's at his coming. Then cometh the end, when he shall have delivered up the kingdom to God, even the Father; when he shall have put down all rule and all authority and power. For he must reign, till he hath put all enemies under his feet. The last enemy that shall be destroyed is death.*
>
> (1 Corinthians 15:16-26)

Jesus is preparing a bride for Himself not having spot or wrinkle, who is strong in the Lord and in the power of His might and who proclaims and lives out of the kingdom of God that dwells within her *(Ephesians 5:25-27, 6:10; John 17:20-21)*. *Proverbs 14:34* reads – *"Righteousness exalteth a nation: but sin is a reproach to any people."* *Psalm 33:12* reads – *"Blessed is the nation whose God is the Lord…"* It is written in *Hebrews 13:8* that *"Jesus Christ is the same yesterday, to day, and forever."* He will always be the Prince of Peace. He will always be our Wonderful Counselor – He will always bring us back to the foundation of God, to that which is solid *(Proverbs 19:21; Isaiah 28:29; Jeremiah 32:19; Romans 11:33-36; 16:25-27; Ephesians 1:11; Hebrews 6:17-18)*! He is our Mighty God; He is our everlasting Father *(Isaiah 9:6)*. There is no one like Him. He bore our sins in His own body and by His stripes we are healed because of His love for the Father and His love for us *(1 Peter 2:24-25)*! He is the bright and morning star that rises in our hearts as we choose to surrender our hearts and minds to Him *(2 Peter 1:19; Revelation 22:16)*. He is the Rock of our salvation and upon this Rock (the solid foundation of truth) the gates of hell will not prevail *(Matthew 16:18; Luke 6:48)*. I would like to close with *Isaiah 25:1* – *"O LORD, thou art my God; I will exalt thee, I will praise thy name; for thou hast done wonderful things; <u>thy counsels of old are faithfulness and truth</u>."*

Below are Scriptures relating to the Lord's peace:

1. *Psalm 72:5, 7 – They shall fear thee as long as the sun and moon endure, throughout all generations. In his days shall the righteous flourish; and abundance of peace so long as the moon endureth.*

References:
Isaiah 55:6-12 – Seek ye the LORD while he may be found, call ye upon him while he is near: let the wicked forsake his way, and the unrighteous man his thoughts: and let him return unto the LORD, and he will have mercy upon him; and to our God, for he will abundantly pardon. "For my thoughts are not your thoughts, neither are your ways my ways," saith the LORD. "For as the heavens are higher than the earth, so are my ways higher than your ways, and my thoughts than your thoughts. For as the rain cometh down, and the snow from heaven, and returneth not thither, but watereth the earth, and maketh it bring forth and bud, that it may give seed to the sower, and bread to the eater: so shall my word be that goeth forth out of my mouth: it shall not return unto me void, but it shall accomplish that which I please, and it shall prosper in the thing whereto I sent it. For ye shall go out with joy, and be led forth with peace…" Matthew 11:28-30 – Jesus said, "Come unto me, all ye that labour and are heavy laden, and I will give you rest. Take my yoke upon you, and learn of me; for I am meek and lowly in heart: and ye shall find rest unto your souls. For my yoke is easy, and my burden is light." Luke 21:25-27 – Jesus said, "And there shall be signs in the sun, and in the moon, and in the stars; and upon the earth distress of nations, with perplexity; the sea and the waves roaring; men's hearts failing them for fear, and for looking after those things which are coming on the earth: for the powers of heaven shall be shaken. And then shall they see the Son of man coming in a cloud with power and great glory." (We lose our peace when we look after those things that are coming on the earth rather than keeping our minds stayed on Christ). *Colossians 3:15-16 – And let the peace of God rule in your hearts, to the which also ye are called in one body; and be ye thankful. Let the word of Christ dwell in you richly in all wisdom; teaching and admonishing one another in psalms and hymns and spiritual songs, singing with grace in your hearts to the Lord.*

2. *Psalm 131:2 – Surely I have behaved and quieted myself, as a child that is weaned of his mother: my soul is even as a weaned child.*

Reference:
Ephesians 2:10-16 – For we are his workmanship, created in Christ Jesus unto good works, which God hath before ordained that we should walk in them. Wherefore remember, that ye being in time past Gentiles in the flesh, who are called Uncircumcision by that which is called the Circumcision in the flesh made by hands; that at that time ye were without Christ, being aliens from the commonwealth of Israel, and strangers from the covenants of promise, having no hope, and without God in the world: but now in Christ Jesus ye who sometimes were far off are made nigh by the blood of Christ. For he is our peace, who hath made both one, and hath broken down the middle wall of partition between us; having abolished in his flesh the enmity, even the law of commandments contained in ordinances; for to make in himself of twain one new man, so making peace; and that he might reconcile both unto God in one body by the cross, having slain the enmity thereby: and came and preached peace to you which were afar off, and to them that were nigh. For through him we both have access by one Spirit unto the Father. Now therefore ye are no more strangers and foreigners, but fellow citizens with the saints, and of the household of God; and are built upon the foundation of the apostles and prophets, Jesus Christ himself being the chief cornerstone; in whom all the building fitly framed together groweth unto an holy temple in the Lord: in whom ye also are builded together for an habitation of God through the Spirit.

3. **Romans 14:17-19** – For the kingdom of God is not meat and drink; but righteousness, and peace, and joy in the Holy Ghost.

References:
Romans 10:15 – And how shall they preach, except they be sent? As it is written, "How beautiful are the feet of them that preach the gospel of peace, and bring glad tidings of good things!" **Galatians 5:22-23** – But the fruit of the Spirit is love, joy, peace, longsuffering, gentleness, goodness, faith, meekness, temperance: against such there is no law. **2 John 1:1-4** – The elder unto the elect lady and her children, whom I love in the truth; and not I only, but also all they that have known the truth; for the truth's sake, which dwelleth in us, and shall be with us for ever. Grace be with you, mercy, and peace, from God the Father, and from the Lord Jesus Christ, the Son of the Father, in truth and love. I rejoiced greatly that I found of thy children walking in truth, as we have received a commandment from the Father.

4. **Romans 15:13** – Now the God of hope fill you with all joy and peace in believing, that ye may abound in hope, through the power of the Holy Ghost.

References:
Romans 15:33 – Now the God of peace be with you all. Amen. **Romans 16:20** – And the God of peace shall bruise Satan under your feet shortly. The grace of our Lord Jesus Christ be with you. Amen. **2 Corinthians 13:11** (NIV) – Finally, brothers and sisters, rejoice! Strive for full restoration, encourage one another, be of one mind, live in peace. And the God of love and peace will be with you. **1 Thessalonians 5:15-24** – See that none render evil for evil unto any man; but ever follow that which is good, both among yourselves, and to all men. Rejoice evermore. Pray without ceasing. In everything give thanks: for this is the will of God in Christ Jesus concerning you. Quench not the Spirit. Despise not prophesyings. Prove all things; hold fast that which is good. Abstain from all appearance of evil. And the very God of peace sanctify you wholly; and I pray God your whole spirit and soul and body be preserved blameless unto the coming of our Lord Jesus Christ. Faithful is he that calleth you, who also will do it. **Hebrews 13:20-21** (NIV) – Now may the God of peace, who through the blood of the eternal covenant brought back from the dead our Lord Jesus, that great Shepherd of the sheep, equip you with everything good for doing his will, and may he work in us what is pleasing to him, through Jesus Christ, to whom be glory for ever and ever. Amen.

5. **1 Corinthians 7:14-15** – For the unbelieving husband is sanctified by the wife, and the unbelieving wife is sanctified by the husband: else were your children unclean; but now are they holy. But if the unbelieving depart, let him depart. A brother or a sister is not under bondage in such cases: but God hath called us to peace.

References:
1 Corinthians 14:33 – For God is not the author of confusion (instability or disorder), but of peace, as in all churches of the saints. **Ephesians 4:1-6** – I therefore, the prisoner of the Lord, beseech you that ye walk worthy of the vocation wherewith ye are called, with all lowliness and meekness, with longsuffering, forbearing one another in love; endeavoring to keep the unity of the Spirit in the bond of peace. There is one body, and one Spirit, even as ye are called in one hope of your calling; one Lord, one faith, one baptism, one God and Father of all, who is above all, and through all, and in you all. **Ephesians 6:12-20** – For we wrestle not against flesh and blood, but against principalities, against powers, against the rulers of the darkness of this world, against spiritual wickedness in high places. Wherefore take unto you the whole armour of God, that ye may be able to withstand in the evil day, and having done all, to stand. Stand

therefore, having your loins girt about with truth, and having on the breastplate of righteousness; and your feet shod with the preparation of the gospel of peace; above all, taking the shield of faith, wherewith ye shall be able to quench all the fiery darts of the wicked. And take the helmet of salvation, and the sword of the Spirit, which is the word of God...

6. ***1 Peter 1:1-2*** *– Peter, an apostle of Jesus Christ, to the strangers scattered throughout Pontus, Galatia, Cappadocia, Asia, and Bithynia, elect according to the foreknowledge of God the Father, through sanctification of the Spirit, unto obedience and sprinkling of the blood of Jesus Christ: Grace unto you, and peace, be multiplied.*

References:

2 Peter 1:2-4 *– Grace and peace be multiplied unto you through the knowledge of God, and of Jesus our Lord, according as his divine power hath given unto us all things that pertain unto life and godliness, through the knowledge of him that hath called us to glory and virtue: whereby are given unto us exceeding great and precious promises: that by these ye might be partakers of the divine nature, having escaped the corruption that is in the world through lust.* ***Jude 1:1-2*** *– Jude, the servant of Jesus Christ, and brother of James, to them that are sanctified by God the Father, and preserved in Jesus Christ, and called: Mercy unto you, and peace, and love, be multiplied.*

Please refer to **Notes 8d** and **10a** for additional information and Scriptures relating to the Lord's peace.

8(c) *Jesus, You said,* "In the world you have tribulation and trials and distress and frustration; but be of good cheer [take courage; be confident, certain, undaunted]! For I have overcome the world. [I have deprived it of power to harm you and have conquered it for you.] (John 16:33-AMPCE)

The Greek word for "tribulation" is *thlipsis* meaning "pressure (literally or figuratively):–afflicted- (tion), anguish, burdened, persecution, tribulation, trouble." Its root word is *thlibo* meaning "to crowd (literally or figuratively):--afflict, narrow, throng, suffer tribulation, trouble." The Thayer's Greek Lexicon meaning is "**a compressed way,** i.e. **narrow, straitened, contracted,** Matthew 7:14..." Jesus said,

> *Enter ye in at the strait gate: for wide is the gate, and broad is the way, that leadeth to destruction, and many there be which go in thereat: because strait is the gate, and narrow is the way, which leadeth unto life, and few there be that find it.*
>
> (Matthew 7:13-14)

The Greek word for "narrow" is *thlibo* and is the root word for tribulation. It is important to note here that in *Mark 4*, Jesus gave a parable of the sower sowing seed, the Word of God, into the hearts of men and women. Jesus told of the different types of heart ground where the Word of God was sown. He said,

> *The sower soweth the word. And these are they by the wayside, where the word is sown; but when they have heard, Satan cometh immediately and taketh away the word that was sown in their hearts. And these are they likewise which are sown on stony ground; who, when they have heard the word, immediately receive it with gladness; and have no root in themselves,*

and so endure but for a time: afterward, when <u>affliction</u> or persecution ariseth for the word's sake, immediately they are offended.

(Mark 4:14-17)

The word "affliction" is the same Greek word *thlipsis* meaning tribulation. Notice Jesus said that affliction/tribulation or persecution arises for the Word's sake. Satan uses tribulation in people's lives to try to keep the Word of God from taking root in their hearts. We, as born-again believers, enter into the kingdom through much tribulation (pressure, trouble, anguish) - *Acts 14:22*. It takes time to become deeply rooted in Christ *(Colossians 2:6-7)*! For example, before an oak tree becomes deeply rooted in the earth it's very easy for it to be uprooted from the ground by a strong storm; but once it becomes deeply rooted with its trunk strong from the nourishment of the earth it is almost impossible for any storm to uproot that tree. It is essential for us not to be ignorant of Satan's devices! If you are not rooted in Christ, when tribulation (pressure, trouble, anguish) comes you could be tempted to say, "This stuff doesn't work! Where is God!!" I want to encourage you not to do that! Continue to press into Christ even during the stormy times of life. **Character Development in Christ** is designed to help the born-again believer stay focused on Christ and to gain a deeper connection with God by speaking aloud the Scriptures contained in the **Personalized Scripture Guide - Volume 1**, along with using the **Personal Prayer Journal – From your heart to His - Volume 1**, to deal with circumstances of life that are causing turmoil (e.g., anger, pain, frustration, confusion, insecurities). As you continue in this process you will find it easier to trust Him while going through unpleasant circumstances and will become more and more rooted in Him and mature in the faith! Continuing on with *Mark 4*, Jesus said,

> *And these are they which are sown among thorns; such as hear the word, and the cares of this world, and the deceitfulness of riches, and the lusts of other things entering in, choke the word, and it becometh unfruitful.*

(Mark 4:18-19)

Again, we are talking about the narrow gate here! It is essential to release our cares to the Lord and not to live out of them! In *John 14:6*, Jesus said, *"I am the way, the truth, and the life: no man cometh unto the Father, but by me."* It is also written in *John 1:1, 14*,

> *In the beginning was the Word, and the Word was with God, and the Word was God. And the Word was made flesh, and dwelt among us, (and we beheld his glory, the glory as of the only begotten of the Father,) full of grace and truth.*

You cannot separate Christ from the Word of God! He is the strait gate *(John 14:6)*! Therefore, it is essential to have an eternal perspective, keeping our eyes on the One who came to give us life and that more abundantly *(Colossians 3:1-3; John 10:10)*. Jesus said in *Matthew 6:33*, *"But seek ye first the kingdom of God, and his righteousness; and all these things shall be added unto you."* Remember, Jesus Christ is the same yesterday, today, and forever *(Hebrews 13:8)*. He will always be our Prince of Peace, and tribulation, trials, distress, and frustration will always try to steal His peace from our hearts. It is essential to be aware of this very fact and to stay focused on the One who overcame the world and conquered it for us. Remember, His Spirit is more powerful and greater than the spirit of this world. Paul writes,

And you hath he quickened (made alive), who were dead in trespasses and sins; wherein in time past ye walked according to the course of this world, <u>according to the prince of the power of the air, the spirit that now worketh in the children of disobedience.</u>

(Ephesians 2:1-2)

Jesus is the Prince of Peace and Satan is referred to as the prince of the power of the air and the prince of this world as Jesus stated in *John 14:30 – "Hereafter I will not talk much with you: for <u>the prince of this world cometh, and hath nothing in me."</u>* In order for us to walk in newness of life in Christ, by His Word and through the power of His Spirit, Christ desires to remove those things in us that are rooted in our carnal nature that the enemy uses to define us or to compromise our walk with Him. Remember, because of what Jesus did on the cross, all authority (power) has been given to Him both in heaven and earth *(Matthew 28:18).*

Jesus has made unto us wisdom, redemption, sanctification, and righteousness and in Him are hid all the treasures of wisdom and knowledge *(1 Corinthians 1:30; Colossians 2:3).* Christ is the power of God and the wisdom of God and He is in us and we are in Him *(1 Corinthians 1:22-24; Colossians 1:27; Acts 17:28).* Our life is not fashioned according to the course and dictates of this world, the prince of the power of the air, but our life is fashioned after the ways and purposes of God! Those who are in Christ should look at tribulation, trials, distress, frustration, etc., differently than those who are operating under the influence of this world. Here is an example in the Old Testament:

The LORD directed Moses to send men to spy out the land of Canaan,

> *And the LORD spake unto Moses, saying, "Send thou men, that they may search the land of Canaan, which I give unto the children of Israel: of every tribe of their fathers shall ye send a man, every one a ruler among them."*
>
> (Numbers 13:1-2)

So Moses chose twelve spies representing the twelve tribes of Israel. And told the men,

> *Get you up this way southward, and go up to the mountain: and see the land, what it is; and the people that dwelleth therein, whether they be strong or weak, few or many; and what the land is that they dwell in, whether it be good or bad; and what cities they be that they dwell in, whether in tents, or in strong holds; and what the land is, whether it be fat or lean, whether there be wood therein, or not. And be ye of good courage, and bring of the fruit of the land.*
>
> (Numbers 13:17-20)

So the men went up and spied out the land:

> *And they came unto the brook of Eshcol, and cut down from thence a branch with one cluster of grapes, and they bare it between two upon a staff (pole); and they brought of the pomegranates, and of the figs. And they returned from searching of the land after forty days.*
>
> (Numbers 13:23, 25)

When the spies returned, they gave their report to Moses and Aaron and all the congregation of the

53

children of Israel:

> *We went to the land where you sent us. It truly flows with milk and honey, and this is its fruit. <u>Nevertheless, the people who dwell in the land are strong; the cities are fortified and very large; moreover we saw the descendants of Anak there.</u> The Amalekites dwell in the land of the South; the Hittites, the Jebusites, and the Amorites dwell in the mountains; and the Canaanites dwell by the sea and along the banks of Jordan.*
>
> (Numbers 13:27-29, NKJV)

After the spies' report, the congregation became restless and fearful and in *Numbers 13:30, Caleb stilled the people before Moses, and said,* "<u>Let us go up at once, and possess it; for we are well able to overcome it.</u>" But the men that went up with him said,

> *"We be not able to go up against the people; for they are stronger than we." And they brought up an evil report of the land which they had searched unto the children of Israel, saying, "The land, through which we have gone to search it, is a land that eateth up the inhabitants thereof; and all the people that we saw in it are men of great stature. And there we saw the giants, the sons of Anak, which come of the giants: and we were in our own sight as grasshoppers, and so we were in their sight."*
>
> (Numbers 13:31-33)

So the children of Israel lifted up their voices and cried, and the people wept all night. They murmured and complained against Moses and Aaron and they said to them,

> *"Would God that we had died in the land of Egypt! Or would God we had died in this wilderness! And wherefore hath the LORD brought us unto this land, to fall by the sword, that our wives and our children should be a prey? Were it not better for us to return into Egypt?" And they said one to another, "Let us make a captain, and let us return into Egypt." Then Moses and Aaron fell on their faces before all the assembly of the congregation of the children of Israel. And Joshua the son of Nun, and Caleb the son of Jephunneh, which were of them that searched the land, rent their clothes: and they spake unto the company of the children of Israel, saying, "The land, which we passed through to search it, is an exceeding good land. If the LORD delight in us, then he will bring us into this land, and give it us; a land which floweth with milk and honey. Only rebel not ye against the LORD, neither fear ye the people of the land; for they are bread for us: their defence is departed from them, and the LORD is with us: fear them not." But all the congregation bade stone them with stones. And the glory of the LORD appeared in the tabernacle of the congregation before all the children of Israel. And the LORD said unto Moses, "How long will this people provoke me? And how long will it be ere they believe me, for all the signs which I have shewed among them?"*
>
> (Numbers 14:2-11)

The Lord was angry with the children of Israel and was ready to destroy all of them and to start over with Moses, but Moses interceded for them and the Lord pardoned them *(Numbers 14:12-20)*. However, the Lord said to Moses,

Because all those men which have seen my glory, and my miracles, which I did in Egypt and in the wilderness, and have tempted me now these ten times, and have not hearkened to my voice; surely they shall not see the land which I sware unto their fathers, neither shall any of them that provoked me see it: <u>but my servant Caleb, because he had another spirit with him, and hath followed me fully, him will I bring into the land whereinto he went; and his seed (descendants) shall possess it</u>. Say unto them, "As truly as I live," saith the LORD, "as ye have spoken in mine ears, so will I do to you: your carcasses shall fall in this wilderness; and all that were numbered of you, according to your whole number, from twenty years old and upward, which have murmured against me, doubtless ye shall not come into the land, concerning which I sware to make you dwell therein, <u>save Caleb the son of Jephunneh, and Joshua the son of Nun</u>. But your little ones, which ye said should be a prey, them will I bring in, and they shall know the land which ye have despised. After the number of days in which ye searched the land, even forty days, each day for a year, shall ye bear your iniquities, even forty years, and ye shall know my breach of promise."

(Numbers 14:21-24, 28-31, 34)

Notice that Caleb and Joshua had a different spirit than the other ten spies that came back with an evil report. We too, who are born again, have a different spirit operating within us. Our spirit is born again, made alive in Christ. It is essential for us to understand that we are living under a new covenant where Jesus Christ became the final sacrifice for our sins and because of that we have "The Overcomer" dwelling on the inside of us. John writes in *1 John 4:4 – "Ye are of God, little children, and have overcome them: because greater is He that is in you, than he that is in the world."* Jesus said in *John 16:33 – "These things I have spoken unto you, that in me ye might have peace. In the world ye shall have tribulation: but be of good cheer; I have overcome the world."* The word "overcome" in the Greek is *nikao* meaning "to subdue (literally or figuratively):–conquer, overcome, prevail, get the victory." The root word for "overcome" is *nike* meaning "conquest (abstractly), i.e. (figuratively) the means of success:– victory." It is through faith in Christ that we overcome *(1 John 5:4-6)*! Caleb and Joshua had faith in the Lord and through that faith they were confident that He would subdue their enemies and give them the promised land. Remember, Caleb told the children of Israel in *Numbers 13:30 (NKJV), "Let us go up at once and take possession, for we are well able to overcome it…"* And Joshua said,

The land, which we passed through to search it, is an exceeding good land. If the LORD delight in us, then he will bring us into this land, and give it us; a land which floweth with milk and honey. Only rebel not ye against the LORD, neither fear ye the people of the land; for they are bread for us: their defence is departed from them, and the LORD is with us: fear them not.

(Numbers 14:7-9)

Caleb and Joshua were operating out of an eternal perspective and true faith in the LORD! Their confidence and trust was in the Lord's ability not in their own. Remember, what the other ten spies said,

"We be not able to go up against the people; for they are stronger than we." And they brought up an evil report of the land which they had searched unto the children of Israel, saying, "The land, through which we have gone to search it, is a land that eateth up the inhabitants thereof; and all the people that we saw in it are men of great stature. <u>And there we saw</u>

the giants, the sons of Anak, which come of the giants: and we were in our own sight as grasshoppers, and so we were in their sight."

(Numbers 13:31-33)

These ten spies had a grasshopper mentality, focusing on the way they saw themselves (e.g., low self-esteem, low self-worth, rejected, inadequate, fearful) and thinking others saw them that way too. We, as born-again believers, can also have a grasshopper mentality and never receive all the Lord has for us in this life. This is where the Lord may have you attend a program like *Living Waters* and/or Christian counseling in order to bring healing and/or bring to light any root issues that are hindering you from walking in the new man in Christ. It is essential that we, like Caleb and Joshua, stay focused on the Lord. We are to focus on Him, how He sees us, and His great love for us. In His heart we are valued (so much so that He gave His life for us), we are accepted in Him, and His love for us passes knowledge *(John 3:16; Ephesians 1:6, 3:19)*. We must renew our minds to His truths!

What happened to Caleb and Joshua? Forty years later, after Moses and all of the men that were twenty years old and older had died, the Lord called Joshua to lead the children of Israel into the promised land *(Joshua 1:1-18)*. Let's see what happened to Caleb:

> *Then the children of Judah came unto Joshua in Gilgal: and Caleb the son of Jephunneh the Kenezite said unto him, "Thou knowest the thing that the LORD said unto Moses the man of God concerning me and thee in Kadeshbarnea. Forty years old was I when Moses the servant of the LORD sent me from Kadeshbarnea to espy (spy) out the land; and I brought him word again as it was in mine heart. Nevertheless, my brethren that went up with me made the heart of the people melt: but I wholly followed the LORD my God. And Moses swore on that day, saying, 'Surely the land whereon thy feet have trodden shall be thine inheritance, and thy children's forever, because thou hast wholly followed the LORD my God.' And now, behold, the LORD hath kept me alive, as he said, these forty and five years, even since the LORD spake this word unto Moses, while the children of Israel wandered in the wilderness: and now, lo, I am this day fourscore and five (85) years old. As yet I am as strong this day as I was in the day that Moses sent me: as my strength was then, even so is my strength now, for war, both to go out, and to come in. Now therefore give me this mountain, whereof the LORD spake in that day; for thou heardest in that day how the Anakims were there, and that the cities were great and fenced: if so be the LORD will be with me, then I shall be able to drive them out, as the LORD said." And Joshua blessed him, and gave unto Caleb the son of Jephunneh Hebron for an inheritance. Hebron therefore became the inheritance of Caleb the son of Jephunneh the Kenezite unto this day, because that he wholly followed the LORD God of Israel.*

(Joshua 14:6-14)

Our God is the same yesterday, today, and forever. He never changes *(Hebrews 13:8; Malachi 3:6)*! He is faithful to those who wholly follow Him. Caleb and Joshua entered the promised land as they had a different spirit than those of their generation. Let's follow the Lord wholly that it may go well with us and that we may be overcomers in Christ! John writes,

> *Love not the world, neither the things that are in the world. If any man love the world, the love of the Father is not in him. For all that is in the world, the lust of the flesh, and the*

lust of the eyes, and the pride of life, is not of the Father, but is of the world. And the world passeth away, and the lust thereof: but he that doeth the will of God abideth for ever.

(1 John 2:15-17)

The lust of the flesh, the lust of the eyes, and the pride of life are tied to our carnal nature. Our heavenly Father has delivered us from the power of darkness, which derives its power from our carnal nature, and has translated us into the kingdom of his dear Son *(Colossians 1:13)*. Paul writes,

And we know that God causes all things to work together for good to those who love God, to those who are called according to His purpose. For those whom He foreknew, He also predestined to become conformed to the image of His Son, so that He would be the firstborn among many brethren; and these whom He predestined, He also called; and these whom He called, He also justified; and these whom he justified, He also glorified.

(Romans 8:28-30, NASB)

As the born-again creation within grows and matures we are able to put on Christ, the new man, and live out of His divine nature *(Romans 13:14; Ephesians 4:21-24; Colossians 3:8-10)*. Jesus said,

For God so loved the world, that he gave his only begotten Son, that whosoever believeth in him should not perish, but have everlasting life. For God sent not his Son into the world to condemn the world; but that the world through him might be saved.

(John 3:16-17)

His kingdom dwells within the born-again believer *(Luke 17:20-21)*.

Below are Scriptures relating to overcoming:

1. **Romans 12:19-21** – *Dearly beloved, avenge not yourselves, but rather give place unto wrath: for it is written, "Vengeance is Mine; I will repay," saith the Lord. Therefore, if thine enemy hunger, feed him; if he thirst, give him a drink: for in so doing thou shalt heap coals of fire on his head." Be not overcome of evil, but overcome evil with good.*

Reference:
Matthew 5:43-48 *(NKJV) – Jesus said, "You have heard that it was said, 'You shall love your neighbor and hate your enemy.' But I say to you, love your enemies, bless those who curse you, do good to those who hate you, and pray for those who spitefully use you and persecute you, that you may be sons of your Father in heaven; for He makes His sun rise on the evil and on the good, and sends rain on the just and on the unjust. For if you love those who love you, what reward have you? Do not even the tax collectors do the same? And if you greet your brethren only, what do you do more than others? Do not even the tax collectors do so? Therefore, you shall be perfect, just as your Father in heaven is perfect."*

2. **1 John 2:14** – *I have written unto you, fathers, because ye have known him that is from the beginning. I have written unto you, young men, because ye are strong, and the word of God abideth in you, and ye have overcome the wicked one.*

References:

1 John 4:4 – *Ye are of God, little children, and have overcome them: because greater is he that is in you, than he that is in the world.* *1 John 5:4, 5* – *For whatsoever is born of God overcometh the world: and this is the victory that overcometh the world, even our faith. Who is he that overcometh the world, but he that believeth that Jesus is the Son of God?* *Revelation 2:7, 11, 17, 26* – *He that hath an ear, let him hear what the Spirit saith unto the churches; "To him that overcometh will I give to eat of the tree of life, which is in the midst of the paradise of God." He that hath an ear, let him hear what the Spirit saith unto the churches; "He that overcometh shall not be hurt of the second death." He that hath an ear, let him hear what the Spirit saith unto the churches: "To him that overcometh will I give to eat of the hidden manna, and will give him a white stone, and in the stone a new name written, which no man knoweth saving he that receiveth it." Jesus said, "And he that overcometh, and keepeth my works unto the end, to him will I give power over the nations."* *Revelation 3:5, 12, 21* – *"He that overcometh, the same shall be clothed in white raiment; and I will not blot out his name out of the book of life, but I will confess his name before my Father, and before his angels." "Him that overcometh will I make a pillar in the temple of my God, and he shall go no more out: and I will write upon him the name of my God, and the name of the city of my God, which is new Jerusalem, which cometh down out of heaven from my God: and I will write upon him my new name." "To him that overcometh will I grant to sit with me in my throne, even as I also overcame, and am set down with my Father in his throne."* *Revelation 12:10-12* – *And I heard a loud voice saying in heaven, "Now is come salvation, and strength, and the kingdom of our God, and the power of his Christ: for the accuser of our brethren is cast down, which accused them before our God day and night. And they overcame him by the blood of the Lamb, and by the word of their testimony; and they loved not their lives unto the death. Therefore rejoice, ye heavens, and ye that dwell in them. Woe to the inhabiters of the earth and of the sea! For the devil is come down unto you, having great wrath, because he knoweth that he hath but a short time."* *Revelation 21:7* – *"He that overcometh shall inherit all things; and I will be his God, and he shall be my son."* (God has given great and precious promises to those who overcome in this life! Remember Caleb and Joshua – *Joshua 14:6-14*).

Below are Scriptures relating to the means of success:

Deuteronomy 8:18-20 – Moses said to the children of Israel (Abraham's seed), *"But thou shalt remember the LORD thy God: for it is he that giveth thee power to get wealth, that he may establish his covenant which He sware unto thy fathers, as it is this day. And it shall be, if thou do at all forget the LORD thy God, and walk after other gods, and serve them, and worship them, I testify against you this day that ye shall surely perish. As the nations which the LORD destroyeth before your face, so shall ye perish; because ye would not be obedient unto the voice of the LORD your God."*

References:

Joshua 1:6-8 – The Lord told Joshua, *"Be strong and of a good courage: for unto this people shalt thou divide for an inheritance the land, which I sware unto their fathers to give them. Only be thou strong and very courageous, that thou mayest observe to do according to all the law, which Moses my servant commanded thee: turn not from it to the right hand or to the left, that thou mayest prosper whithersoever thou goest. This book of the law shall not depart out of thy mouth; but thou shalt meditate therein day and night, that thou mayest observe to do according to all that is written therein: for then thou shalt make thy way prosperous, and then thou shalt have good success."* *Psalm 1:1-3* – *Blessed is the man that walketh not in the counsel of the ungodly, nor standeth in the way of sinners, nor sitteth in the seat of the scornful. But his delight is in the law of the LORD; and in his law doth he meditate day and night. And he shall be like a tree planted by the rivers of water, that bringeth forth his fruit in his season; his leaf also shall not wither; and whatsoever he doeth shall prosper.* **Galatians 3:27-29** – *For as many of you as have been baptized into Christ have put on Christ. There is neither Jew nor Greek, there is neither bond nor free, there is neither male nor female: for ye are all one in Christ Jesus. And if ye be Christ's, then are ye Abraham's seed, and heirs according to the promise.* **3 John 1:2** – *Beloved, I wish above all things that thou mayest prosper and be in health, even as thy soul prospereth.* (It is essential that we continue to give ourselves to Christ and His Word in order to fulfill the plan and purpose He has for us – *Jeremiah 29:11-13; Romans 8:28-39; 2 Peter 1:1-11*. We are in the world but not of it, as our citizenship is in Heaven – *Ephesians 2:5-6, 19; Philippians 3:20; Colossians 3:1-3*. The Lord's kingdom is not of this world – *John 18:36*. He has called us to live out of His kingdom that dwells within us and His kingdom is righteousness, peace, and joy in the Holy Ghost – *Luke 17:20-21; Romans 14:17*).

Below are Scriptures relating to God's mercy and comforts:

1. **Deuteronomy 4:29-31** – *But if from thence thou shalt seek the LORD thy God, thou shalt find him, if thou seek him with all thy heart and with all thy soul. When thou art in tribulation, and all these things are come upon thee, even in the latter days, if thou turn to the LORD thy God, and shalt be obedient unto his voice; (for the LORD thy God is a merciful God;) he will not forsake thee, neither destroy thee, nor forget the covenant of thy fathers which he sware unto them.*

References:
Psalm 62:8 – *Trust in Him at all times; ye people; pour out your heart before him: God is a refuge for us. Selah.* **Psalm 84:10** – *For a day in thy courts is better than a thousand. I had rather be a doorkeeper in the house of my God, than to dwell in the tents of wickedness.* **Psalm 94:19** (NKJV) – *In the multitude of my anxieties within me, Your comforts delight my soul.* **Psalm 138:8** – *The LORD will perfect that which concerneth me: thy mercy, O LORD, endureth forever: forsake not the works of thine own hands.* **Luke 18:1-8** – *And he (Jesus) spake a parable unto them to this end, that men ought always to pray, and not to faint; saying, "There was in a city a judge, which feared not God, neither regarded man: and there was a widow in that city; and she came unto him, saying, 'Avenge me of mine adversary.' And he would not for a while: but afterward he said within himself, 'Though I fear not God, nor regard man; yet because this widow troubleth me, I will avenge her, lest by her continual coming she weary me.' And the Lord said, "Hear what the unjust judge saith. And shall not God avenge his own elect, which cry day and night unto him, though he bear long with them? I tell you that he will avenge them speedily nevertheless when the Son of man cometh, shall he find faith on the earth?"* **Romans 11:32-34** – *For God hath concluded them all in unbelief, that he might have mercy upon all. O the depth of the riches both of the wisdom and knowledge of God! How unsearchable are his judgments, and his ways past finding out! For who hath known the mind of the Lord? Or who hath been his counsellor?* **2 Corinthians 1:3-5** – *Blessed be God, even the Father of our Lord Jesus Christ, the Father of mercies, and the God of all comfort; who comforteth us in all our tribulation, that we may be able to comfort them which are in any trouble, by the comfort wherewith we ourselves are comforted of God. For as the sufferings of Christ abound in us, so our consolation also aboundeth by Christ.* **2 Corinthians 7:4** – *…I am filled with comfort. I am exceeding joyful in all our tribulation.* (See **Romans 15:4-6.**)

2. **Psalm 34:19** – *Many are the afflictions of the righteous: but the LORD delivereth him out of them all.*

References:

Psalm 37:23-24 – *The steps of a good man are ordered by the LORD: and he delighteth in his way. Though he fall, he shall not be utterly cast down: for the LORD upholdeth him with his hand.* **Micah 7:8** – *Rejoice not against me, O mine enemy: when I fall, I shall arise; when I sit in darkness, the LORD shall be a light unto me.*

3. **Psalm 46:1-5** (NIV) – *God is our refuge and strength, an ever-present help in trouble. Therefore we will not fear, though the earth give way and the mountains fall into the heart of the sea, though its waters roar and foam and the mountains quake with their surging. There is a river whose streams make glad the city of God, the holy place where the Most High dwells. God is within her, she will not fall; God will help her at break of day.*

References:
Psalm 36:9 – *For with thee is the fountain of life: in thy light shall we see light.* **Proverbs 13:14** – *The law of the wise is a fountain of life, to depart from the snares of death.* **Proverbs 18:4** – *The words of a man's mouth are as deep waters, and the wellspring of wisdom as a flowing brook.* **Isaiah 12:1-2** – *Behold, God is my salvation; I will trust, and not be afraid: for the LORD JEHOVAH is my strength and my song; he also is become my salvation. Therefore with joy shall ye draw water out of the wells of salvation.* **Isaiah 44:2-3** – *Thus saith the LORD that made thee, and formed thee from the womb, which will help thee; "Fear not, O Jacob, my servant; and thou, Jesurun, whom I have chosen. For I will pour water upon him that is thirsty, and floods upon the dry ground: I will pour my spirit upon thy seed, and my blessing upon thine offspring.* **John 4:13-14** – *Jesus answered and said unto her, "Whosoever drinketh of this water shall thirst again: but whosoever drinketh of the water that I shall give him shall never thirst; but the water that I shall give him shall be in him a well of water springing up into everlasting life."* **John 7:37-39** – *In the last day, that great day of the feast, Jesus stood and cried, saying, "If any man thirst, let him come unto me, and drink. He that believeth on me, as the scripture hath said, out of his belly shall flow rivers of living water." (But this spake he of the Spirit, which they that believe on him should receive: for the Holy Ghost was not yet given; because that Jesus was not yet glorified.)*

Below are Scriptures relating to taking up your cross:

Matthew 10:38-39 – *Jesus said, "And he that taketh not his cross, and followeth after me, is not worthy of me. He that findeth his life shall lose it: and he that loseth his life for my sake shall find it."*

References:
Matthew 16:24-26 – *Then said Jesus unto his disciples, "If any man will come after me, let him deny himself, and take up his cross, and follow me. For whosoever will save his life shall lose it: and whosoever will lose his life for my sake shall find it. For what is a man profited, if he shall gain the whole world, and lose his own soul? Or what shall a man give in exchange for his soul?"* **Hebrews 13:20-21** – *Now the God of peace, that brought again from the dead our Lord Jesus, that great shepherd of the sheep, through the blood of the everlasting covenant, make you perfect in every good work to do his will, working in you that which is wellpleasing in his sight, through Jesus Christ; to whom be glory for ever and ever. Amen.* **Philippians 2:12-13** – *Wherefore, my beloved, as ye have always obeyed, not as in my presence only, but now much more in my absence, work out your own salvation with fear and trembling. For it is God which worketh in you both to will and to do of his good pleasure.* **2 Timothy 2:11-13** – *It is a faithful saying: For if we be dead with him, we shall also live with him: if we suffer, we shall also reign with him: if we deny him, he also will deny us: if we believe not, yet he abideth faithful: he cannot deny himself.* **1 Peter 5:10-11** – *But the God of*

all grace, who hath called us unto his eternal glory by Christ Jesus, after that ye have suffered a while, make you perfect, stablish, strengthen, settle you. To him be glory and dominion for ever and ever. Amen.

Below are Scriptures relating to trials and tribulation:

1. ***Matthew 16:13-19*** *– When Jesus came into the coast of Caesarea Philippi, he asked his disciples, saying, "Whom do men say that I the Son of man, am?" And they said, "Some say that thou art John the Baptist: some, Elias; and others, Jeremias, or one of the prophets." He saith unto them, "But whom say ye that I am?" And Simon Peter answered and said, "Thou art the Christ, the Son of the living God." And Jesus answered and said unto him, "Blessed art thou, Simon Barjona: for flesh and blood hath not revealed it unto thee, but my Father which is in heaven. And I say also unto thee, that thou art Peter, and upon this rock I will build my church; and the gates of hell shall not prevail against it. And I will give unto thee the keys of the kingdom of heaven: and whatsoever thou shalt bind on earth shall be bound in heaven: and whatsoever thou shalt loose on earth shall be loosed in heaven."*

References:
Proverbs 24:5, 10, 16 *– A wise man is strong; yea, a man of knowledge increaseth strength. If thou faint in the day of adversity, thy strength is small. For a just man falleth seven times, and riseth up again: but the wicked shall fall into mischief.* ***Proverbs 30:24-28*** *– There be four things which are little upon the earth, but they are exceeding wise: …the conies are but a feeble folk, yet make they their houses in the rocks (a place of refuge)…* ***Luke 6:46-49*** *– Jesus said, "And why call ye me, Lord, Lord, and do not the things which I say? Whosoever cometh to me, and heareth my sayings, and doeth them, I will shew you to whom he is like: He is like a man which built an house, and digged deep, and laid the foundation on a rock: and when the flood arose, the stream beat vehemently upon that house, and could not shake it: for it was founded upon a rock. But He that heareth, and doeth not, is like a man that without a foundation built an house upon the earth; against which the stream did beat vehemently, and immediately it fell; and the ruin of that house was great."* ***John 6:66-68*** *– From that time many of his disciples went back, and walked no more with him. Then said Jesus unto the twelve, "Will ye also go away?" Then Simon Peter answered him, "Lord, to whom shall we go? Thou hast the words of eternal life."*

2. ***Acts 14:21-22*** *– And when they had preached the gospel to that city, and had taught many, they returned again to Lystra, and to Iconium, and Antioch, confirming the souls of the disciples, and exhorting them to continue in the faith, and that we must through much tribulation enter into the kingdom of God.*

References:
Matthew 13:20-21 *– Jesus said, "But he that received the seed into stony places, the same is he that heareth the word, and anon (immediately) with joy receiveth it; yet hath he not root in himself, but dureth for a while: for when tribulation or persecution ariseth because of the word, by and by he is offended."* ***Luke 21:19*** *– Jesus said, "In your patience possess ye your souls."* ***John 15:18-21*** *– Jesus said, "If the world hate you, ye know that it hated me before it hated you. If ye were of the world, the world would love his own: but because ye are not of the world, but I have chosen you out of the world, therefore the world hateth you. Remember the word that I said to you, 'The servant is not greater than his lord.' If they have persecuted me, they will also persecute you; if they have kept My saying, they will keep yours also. But all these things will they do unto you for my name's sake, because they know not him who sent me."* ***Romans 5:1-5*** *– Therefore*

being justified by faith, we have peace with God through our Lord Jesus Christ: by whom also we have access by faith into this grace wherein we stand, and rejoice in hope of the glory of God. And not only so, but we glory in tribulations also: knowing that tribulation worketh patience; and patience, experience; and experience, hope: and hope maketh not ashamed; because the love of God is shed abroad in our hearts by the Holy Ghost which is given unto us. **Romans 8:15-19** *– For ye have not received the spirit of bondage again to fear; but ye have received the Spirit of adoption, whereby we cry, Abba, Father. The Spirit itself beareth witness with our spirit, that we are the children of God and if children, then heirs; heirs of God, and joint-heirs with Christ; if so be that we suffer with him, that we may be also glorified together. For I reckon that the sufferings of this present time are not worthy to be compared with the glory which shall be revealed in us. For the earnest expectation of the creature waiteth for the manifestation of the sons of God.* **Romans 8:35-39** *– Who shall separate us from the love of Christ? Shall tribulation, or distress, or persecution, or famine, or nakedness, or peril, or sword? As it is written: "For thy sake we are killed all the day long; we are accounted as sheep for the slaughter." Nay, in all these things we are more than conquerors through Him that loved us. For I am persuaded, that neither death, nor life, nor angels, nor principalities, nor powers, nor things present, nor things to come, nor height, nor depth, nor any other creature, shall be able to separate us from the love of God which is in Christ Jesus our Lord.* **Romans 12:10-13** *– Be kindly affectioned one to another with brotherly love; in honour preferring one another; not slothful in business; fervent in spirit; serving the Lord; rejoicing in hope; patient in tribulation; continuing instant in prayer; distributing to the necessity of saints; given to hospitality.* How can we do this if we are weighed down with cares, worries, fears, anger, hurts, etc.! It is essential that we release these to the Lord. **1 Corinthians 4:20** *– For the kingdom of God is not in word, but in power.* **2 Corinthians 7:4** *– …I am filled with comfort. I am exceeding joyful in all our tribulation.* **2 Corinthians 12:7-10** *– Paul said, "And lest I should be exalted above measure through the abundance of the revelations, there was given to me a thorn in the flesh, the messenger of Satan to buffet me, lest I should be exalted above measure. For this thing I besought the Lord thrice (three times), that it might depart from me." And he (the Lord) said unto me, "My grace is sufficient for thee: for my strength is made perfect in weakness…" "Therefore, I take pleasure in infirmities, in reproaches, in necessities, in persecutions, in distresses for Christ's sake: for when I am weak, then I am strong.* **1 Thessalonians 3:1-4** *– Wherefore when we could no longer forbear, we thought it good to be left at Athens alone; and sent Timotheus (Timothy), our brother, and minister of God, and our fellowlabourer in the gospel of Christ, to establish you, and to comfort you concerning your faith: that no man should be moved by these afflictions: for yourselves know that we are appointed thereunto. For verily, when we were with you, we told you before that we should suffer tribulation; even as it came to pass, and ye know.* **2 Thessalonians 1:3-8** *– We are bound to thank God always for you, brethren, as it is meet (fitting), because your faith groweth exceedingly, and the charity (God's love) of every one of you all toward each other aboundeth; so that we ourselves glory in you in the churches of God for your patience and faith in all your persecutions and tribulations that you endure: which is a manifest token of the righteous judgment of God, that ye may be counted worthy of the kingdom of God, for which ye also suffer; seeing it is a righteous thing with God to recompense tribulation to them that trouble you; and to you who are troubled rest with us, when the Lord Jesus shall be revealed from heaven with His mighty angels, in flaming fire taking vengeance on them that know not God, and that obey not the gospel of our Lord Jesus Christ.* **2 Timothy 3:10-12** *(NKJV) – But you have carefully followed my doctrine, manner of life, purpose, faith, longsuffering, love, perseverance, persecutions, afflictions, which happened to me at Antioch, at Iconium, at Lystra—what persecutions I endured. And out of them all the Lord delivered me. Yes, and all who desire to live godly in Christ Jesus will suffer persecution.* **Hebrews 6:11-12** *– And we desire that every one of you do shew the same diligence to the full assurance of hope unto the end: that ye be not slothful, but followers of them who through faith and patience inherit the promises.* **James 1:2-4** *– My brethren, count it all joy when ye fall into divers temptations; knowing this, that the trying of your faith* *worketh patience. But let patience have her perfect work, that ye may be perfect and entire, wanting nothing.* ***James 5:9-11*** *(NIV) – Don't grumble against one another, brothers and sisters, or you will be judged. The Judge is standing at the door! Brothers and sisters, as an example of patience in the face of suffering, take the prophets who spoke in the name of the Lord. As you know, we count as blessed those who have persevered. You have heard of Job's perseverance and have seen what the Lord finally brought about. The Lord is full of compassion and mercy.* ***1 Peter 1:6-9*** *(NIV) – In all this you greatly rejoice, though now for a little while you may have had to suffer grief in all kinds of trials. These have come so that the proven genuineness of your faith—of greater worth than gold, which perishes even though refined by fire—may result in praise, glory and honor when Jesus Christ is revealed. Though you have not seen him, you love him; and even though you do not see him now, you believe in him and are filled with an inexpressible and glorious joy for you are receiving the end result of your faith, the salvation of your souls.* ***1 Peter 2:21-23*** *(AMPCE) – For even to this were you called [it is inseparable from your vocation]. For Christ also suffered for you, leaving you [His personal] example, so that you should follow in His footsteps. He was guilty of no sin, neither was deceit (guile) ever found on His lips. When he was reviled and insulted, He did not revile or offer insult in return; [when] He was abused and suffered, He made no threats [of vengeance]; but he trusted [Himself and everything] to Him Who judges fairly (righteously).*

3. ***Colossians 2:15*** *– Having spoiled principalities and powers, he (Jesus) made a shew of them openly, triumphing over them in it.*

References:
Hebrews 2:14-18 *– Forasmuch then as the children are partakers of flesh and blood, he also himself likewise took part of the same; that through death he might destroy him that had the power of death, that is, the devil; and deliver them who through fear of death were all their lifetime subject to bondage. For verily he took not on him the nature of angels; but he took on him the seed of Abraham. Wherefore in all things it behoved him to be made like unto his brethren, that he might be a merciful and faithful high priest in things pertaining to God, to make reconciliation for the sins of the people. For in that he himself hath suffered being tempted, he is able to succour them that are tempted.* ***1 John 3:8*** *– He that committeth sin is of the devil; for the devil sinneth from the beginning. For this purpose, the Son of God was manifested, that he might destroy the works of the devil.* (God desires to destroy the works of the devil, who gains access through our carnal nature, in every man, woman, and child on the face of this earth).

8(d) Peace I leave with you; My [own] peace I now give and bequeath to you. Not as the world gives do I give to you. Do not let your *heart* be troubled, neither let *it* be afraid. [Stop allowing *yourself* to be agitated and disturbed; and do not permit *yourself* to be fearful and intimidated and cowardly and unsettled.]" (John 14:27-AMPCE)

Paul writes,

> *For to be carnally minded is death; but to be spiritually minded is life and peace. Because the carnal mind is enmity against God: for it is not subject to the law of God, neither indeed can be. So then they that are in the flesh cannot please God.*
>
> (Romans 8:6-8)

It is impossible for our carnal nature, the old man, to receive and live out of God's peace. Those who are carnally minded, or babes in Christ, are governed by their carnal nature (i.e., ungodly thought patterns along with the feelings and emotions associated with those thoughts—anger, rage, anxieties, fears, forebodings, jealousy, envy, strife – *1 Corinthians 3:1-3*). The Lord desires for us to release to Him the circumstances of life and the ungodly thought patterns that produce these feelings and emotions as they arise. Below are four passages of Scripture as it relates to releasing our cares, fears, frustrations, etc., to Him:

1. ***Psalm 62:8*** – *Trust in Him at all times; ye people, pour out your heart before him: God is a refuge for us.*
2. ***Psalm 142:2*** *(NKJV) – I pour out my complaint before Him; I declare before Him my trouble.*
3. ***1 Peter 5:5-11*** – *Likewise, ye younger, submit yourselves unto the elder. Yea, all of you be subject one to another, and be clothed with humility: for God resisteth the proud, and giveth grace to the humble. Humble yourselves therefore under the mighty hand of God, that he may exalt you in due time:* <u>casting all your care upon him; for he careth for you.</u> *Be sober, be vigilant; because your adversary the devil, as a roaring lion, walketh about, seeking whom he may devour: whom resist stedfast in the faith, knowing that the same afflictions are accomplished in your brethren that are in the world. But the God of all grace, who hath called us unto his eternal glory by Christ Jesus, after that ye have suffered a while, make you perfect, stablish, strengthen, settle you. To him be glory and dominion for ever and ever. Amen.*
4. ***Philippians 4:6-8*** – *Be careful (anxious) for nothing; but in every thing by prayer and supplication with thanksgiving let your requests be made known unto God. And the peace of God, which passeth all understanding, shall keep your hearts and minds through Christ Jesus. Finally, brethren, whatsoever things are true, whatsoever things are honest, whatsoever things are just, whatsoever things are pure, whatsoever things are lovely, whatsoever things are of good report; if there be any virtue, and if there be any praise, think on these things.*

Our Lord is a covenant keeping God! After the flood that took place in *Genesis 7*, God told Noah,

This is the token of the covenant which I make between me and you and every living creature that is with you, for perpetual generations: I do set my bow in the cloud, and it shall be for a token of a covenant between me and the earth. And it shall come to pass, when I bring a cloud over the earth, that the bow shall be seen in the cloud: and I will remember my covenant, which is between me and you and every living creature of all flesh; and the waters shall no more become a flood to destroy all flesh. <u>And the bow shall be in the cloud; and I will look upon it, that I may remember the everlasting covenant between God and every living creature of all flesh that is upon the earth.</u>

(Genesis 9:12-16)

Concerning the waters of Noah, the Lord, our Redeemer also said,

"For thy Maker is thine husband; the LORD of hosts is his name; and thy Redeemer the Holy One of Israel; the God of the whole earth shall he be called. For the LORD hath called thee as a woman forsaken and grieved in spirit, and a wife of youth, when thou wast refused," saith thy God. "For a small moment have I forsaken thee; but with great

mercies will I gather thee. In a little wrath I hid my face from thee for a moment; but with everlasting kindness will I have mercy on thee," saith the LORD thy Redeemer. "For this is as the waters of Noah unto me: for as I have sworn that the waters of Noah should no more go over the earth; so have I sworn that I would not be wroth with thee, nor rebuke thee. For the mountains shall depart, and the hills be removed; but my kindness shall not depart from thee,' saith the LORD that hath mercy on thee."

(Isaiah 54:5-10)

He has given unto us His covenant of peace that shall not be removed just as the waters of Noah will no longer flood the earth. The Lord revealed to me years ago that as our heavenly Father sees the rainbow and remembers His covenant with Noah and every living creature of all flesh, He also looks at Jesus, seated at His right hand, and remembers the new everlasting covenant He has made with Him and all those who are in Him through His shed blood on the cross *(Ephesians 1:17-23; Colossians 3:1-4; Hebrews 1:3; 1 Peter 3:22; Romans 12:1-5; 1 Corinthians 1:2-3, 30-31, 15:22; Colossians 1:20)*. Jesus is the mediator of this new covenant *(Hebrews 8:6-13)*. He certainly is for us and not against us *(Romans 8:31-39)*!

Please refer to **Notes 8b** and **10a** for additional information and Scripture references relating to the Lord's peace.

---

9. *So, Lord, I respond to You right now by giving You all of **my cares**, **my concerns**, and **my fears** which include situations and circumstances that have caused me to **feel anxious**, **worried**, **depressed**, **hurt**, **disappointed**, **insecure**, **intimidated**, or **threatened** because You care for me. I also give You the things that **agitate**, **anger**, **disturb**, or **frustrate** me, and **the things that I am unsettled with**. I realize that these thoughts and feelings are the very things that keep me from living in Your peace and operating in clarity of mind and heart, so I choose to be specific as I pour out my heart to You. (Ref.: Psalm 62:8, 142:2; 1 Peter 5:5-7; John 14:27)*

Meditating on the "what ifs" in life (e.g., worries, cares, fears) produces a war zone within our minds and keeps us from enjoying the life and peace Jesus died to give to us. If you are dealing with any of the feelings or emotions listed above, it is important to be real with your heavenly Father about them as this helps to put off the old man. Please refer to the ***Personal Prayer Journal – From your heart to His – Details and Instructions - Volume 1***. Part One is designed to encourage you to cast your cares, concerns, and/or fears upon Him. If you feel you need to be real (honest) with the Lord concerning these issues such as: insecurities, depression, anger, agitation, frustration, things you are unsettled with, please go to Part Three. If we choose not to release these feelings to the Lord by being real (honest) with Him, these suppressed feelings and emotions can build within us and, like a volcano, can erupt onto others. Therefore, releasing our cares, fears, concerns, frustrations, etc., to the Lord helps to relieve the pressure from within us knowing that He has it; and as we continue to renew our minds to the truth of His Word concerning the new man, keeps us free and at peace to love others well (please see the ***Personalized Scripture Guide - Volume 1***).

Below is a powerful prayer:

My life dissolves and weeps itself away for heaviness; raise me up and strengthen me according to [the promises of] Your word. Remove from me the way of falsehood and unfaithfulness [to You], and graciously impart Your law to me. I have chosen the way of truth and faithfulness; Your ordinances have I set before me. I cleave to Your testimonies; O Lord, put me not to shame! I will [not merely walk, but] run the way of Your commandments, when You give me a heart that is willing.

(Psalm 119:28-32, AMPCE)

Below are Scriptures relating to releasing our cares, fears, frustrations, etc., to Him:

1. ***2 Samuel 22:7*** – *In my distress I called upon the LORD, and cried to my God: and he did hear my voice out of his temple, and my cry did enter into his ears.*

References:
Psalm 25:1-2 – *A Psalm of David. Unto thee, O LORD, do I lift up my soul. O my God, I trust in thee: let me not be ashamed, let not mine enemies* (e.g., fear, insecurities, doubt, unbelief) *triumph over me.* ***Psalm 55:22*** – *Cast thy burden upon the LORD, and he shall sustain thee; he shall never suffer the righteous to be moved.* ***Psalm 61:1-2*** – *[[To the chief Musician upon Neginah, A psalm of David.]] Hear my cry, O God; attend unto my prayer. From the end of the earth will I cry unto thee, when my heart is overwhelmed: lead me to the rock that is higher than I.* ***Psalm 62:8*** – *Trust in him at all times; ye people, <u>pour out your heart before him</u>: God is a refuge for us.* ***Psalm 94:19*** – *In the multitude of my thoughts within me thy comforts delight my soul.* ***Psalm 119:26*** – *I have declared my ways, and thou heardest me: teach me your statutes.* ***Psalm 139:23-24*** – *Search me, O God, and know my heart: try me, and know my thoughts: and see if there be any wicked way in me, and lead me in the way everlasting.* ***Psalm 142:2*** – <u>*I pour out my complaint before him; I shewed (declared) before Him my trouble.*</u> ***Proverbs 3:5-6*** – *Trust in the LORD with all thine heart; and lean not unto thine own understanding. <u>In all thy ways acknowledge him</u>, and he shall direct thy paths.* ***Proverbs 4:23-24*** – *Keep thy heart with all diligence; for out of it are the issues of life. Put away from thee a froward mouth, and perverse lips put far from thee.* ***1 Peter 5:6-10*** – *Humble yourselves therefore under the mighty hand of God, that he may exalt you in due time: <u>casting all your care upon him; for he careth for you</u>. Be sober, be vigilant; because your adversary the devil, as a roaring lion, walketh about, seeking whom he may devour: whom resist stedfast in the faith, knowing that the same afflictions are accomplished in your brethren that are in the world. But the God of all grace, who hath called us unto his eternal glory by Christ Jesus, after that ye have suffered a while, make you perfect, stablish, strengthen, settle you.*

2. ***Psalm 27:13-14*** – *I had fainted, unless I had believed to see the goodness of the LORD in the land of the living. Wait on the LORD: be of good courage, and he shall strengthen thine heart: wait, I say, on the LORD.*

References:
Psalm 62:5-8 *(NKJV)* – *My soul, wait silently for God alone, for my expectation is from Him. He only is my rock and my salvation; He is my defense; I shall not be moved. In God is my salvation and my glory; the rock of my strength, and my refuge, is in God. Trust in Him at all times, you people; pour out your heart before Him; God is a refuge for us.* ***Psalm 138:8*** – *The LORD will perfect that which concerneth me: thy mercy, O LORD, endureth for ever: forsake not the works of thine own hands.* ***Matthew 6:27-34*** – *Jesus said, "Which of you by taking thought can add one cubit unto his stature? And why take ye thought for raiment (clothing)? Consider the lilies of the field, how they grow; they toil not, neither do they spin: and yet*

I say unto you, that even Solomon in is all his glory was not arrayed like one of these. Wherefore, if God so clothe the grass of the field, which today is, and tomorrow is cast into the oven, shall he not much more clothe you, O ye of little faith? Therefore, take no thought, saying, 'What shall we eat?' or, 'What shall we drink?' or, 'Wherewithal shall we be clothed?' (For after all these things do the Gentiles seek:) for your heavenly Father knoweth that ye have need of all these things. But seek ye first the kingdom of God, and his righteousness; and all these things shall be added unto you. Take therefore no thought for the morrow: for the morrow shall take thought for the things of itself. Sufficient unto the day is the evil thereof."

3. **Proverbs 12:25** *(NASB) – Anxiety in a man's heart weighs it down, but a good word makes it glad.*

References:
Proverbs 22:5 *– Thorns and snares are in the way of the froward (perverse); he that doth keep his soul shall be far from them.* **Proverbs 23:7** *– For as he thinketh in his heart, so is he…* **Luke 21:26, 34** *– Jesus said, "…Men's hearts failing them for fear, and for looking after those things which are coming on the earth: for the powers of heaven shall be shaken. And take heed to yourselves, lest at any time your hearts be overcharged with surfeiting, and drunkenness, and cares of this life, and so that day come upon you unawares.* **2 Corinthians 10:3-6** *– For though we walk in the flesh, we do not war after the flesh: (for the weapons of our warfare are not carnal, but mighty through God to the pulling down of strong holds;) casting down imaginations, and every high thing that exalteth itself against the knowledge of God, and bringing into captivity every thought to the obedience of Christ; and having in a readiness to revenge all disobedience, when your obedience is fulfilled.*

Below are Scriptures relating to the tongue:

1. **Psalm 34:12-19** *– What man is he that desireth life, and loveth many days, that he may see good? Keep thy tongue from evil, and thy lips from speaking guile. Depart from evil, and do good; seek peace, and pursue it. The eyes of the LORD are upon the righteous, and his ears are open unto their cry. The face of the LORD is against them that do evil, to cut off the remembrance of them from the earth. The righteous cry, and the LORD heareth, and delivereth them out of all their troubles. The LORD is nigh unto them that are of a broken heart; and saveth such as be of a contrite spirit. Many are the afflictions of the righteous: but the LORD delivereth him out of them all.*

References:
Psalm 37:5, 8 *– Commit thy way unto the LORD; trust also in him; and he shall bring it to pass. Cease from anger, and forsake wrath: fret not thyself in any wise to do evil.* **James 1:18-27** *– Of his own will begat he us with the word of truth, that we should be a kind of firstfruits of his creatures. Wherefore, my beloved brethren, let every man be swift to hear, slow to speak, slow to wrath: for the wrath of man worketh not the righteousness of God. Wherefore lay apart all filthiness and superfluity of naughtiness, and receive with meekness the engrafted word, which is able to save your souls. But be ye doers of the word, and not hearers only, deceiving your own selves. For if any be a hearer of the word, and not a doer, he is like unto a man beholding his natural face in a glass: for he beholdeth himself, and goeth his way, and straightway forgetteth what manner of man he was. But whoso looketh into the perfect law of liberty, and continueth therein, he being not a forgetful hearer, but a doer of the work, this man shall be blessed in his deed. If any man among you seem to be religious, and bridleth not his tongue, but deceiveth his own heart, this man's religion is vain. Pure religion and undefiled before God and the Father is this, to visit the fatherless and widows in their affliction, and to keep himself unspotted from the world.* **James 3:3-18** *– Behold, we put bits in the horses'*

*mouths, that they may obey us; and we turn about their whole body. Behold also the ships, which though they be so great, and are driven of fierce winds, yet are they turned about with a very small helm (rudder), whithersoever the governor (helmsman) listeth (impulse). Even so the tongue is a little member, and boasteth great things. Behold, how great a matter a little fire kindleth! And the tongue is a fire, a world of iniquity: so is the tongue among our members, that it defileth the whole body, and setteth on fire the course of nature; and it is set on fire of hell. For every kind of beasts, and of birds, and of serpents, and of things in the sea, is tamed, and hath been tamed of mankind: but the tongue can no man tame; it is an unruly evil, full of deadly poison. Therewith bless we God, even the Father; and therewith curse we men, which are made after the similitude of God. Out of the same mouth proceedeth blessing and cursing. My brethren, these things ought not so to be. Doth a fountain send forth at the same place sweet water and bitter? Can the fig tree, my brethren, bear olive berries? Either a vine, figs? So can no fountain both yield salt water and fresh. Who is a wise man endued with knowledge among you? Let him shew out of a good conversation (behavior) his works with meekness of wisdom. But if ye have bitter envying and strife in your hearts, glory not, and lie not against the truth. This wisdom descendeth not from above, but is earthly, sensual, devilish. For where envying and strife is, there is confusion and every evil work. But the wisdom that is from above is first pure, then peaceable, gentle, and easy to be intreated, full of mercy and good fruits, without partiality, and without hypocrisy. And the fruit of righteousness is sown in peace of them that make peace. **1 Peter 3:8-12** – Finally, be ye all of one mind, having compassion one of another, love as brethren, be pitiful, be courteous: not rendering evil for evil, or railing for railing: but contrariwise blessing; knowing that ye are thereunto called, that ye should inherit a blessing. For he that will love life, and see good days, let him refrain his tongue from evil, and his lips that they speak no guile: let him eschew (avoid) evil, and do good; let him seek peace, and ensue (pursue) it. For the eyes of the Lord are over the righteous, and his ears are open unto their prayers: but the face of the Lord is against them that do evil.*

10(a) *I* let the peace (soul harmony which comes) from Christ rule (act as umpire continually) in *my heart* [deciding and settling with finality all questions that arise in my *mind*, in that peaceful state] to which as a [member of Christ's] one body *I have been* called [to live]. (Colossians 3:15-AMPCE)

The word peace in the Greek is *eirene*. Its meaning in the Thayer's Greek Lexicon is "according to a conception distinctly peculiar to Christianity, **the tranquil state of a soul assured of its salvation through Christ, and so fearing nothing from God and content with its earthly lot, of whatsoever sort that is.**" Renewing our minds to the truth of God's Word is essential for the rule of Christ to be active within us. If we don't know the Word of His truth how can we walk in His peace and enjoy the fruits of His righteousness? One who does not operate in the truth of God's Word—His righteousness, cannot experience the true peace of God. Below are five passages of Scripture where righteousness and peace go hand in hand:

1. **Psalm 85:10** – *Mercy and truth are met together; righteousness and peace have kissed each other.*
2. **Isaiah 32:17** – *And the work of righteousness shall be peace; and the effect of righteousness quietness and assurance for ever.*
3. **Isaiah 48:18** – *O that thou hadst hearkened to my commandments! Then had thy peace been as a river, and thy righteousness as the waves of the sea.*

4. *Romans 14:17* – For the kingdom of God is not meat and drink; but righteousness, and peace, and joy in the Holy Ghost.
5. *James 3:18* – And the fruit of righteousness is sown in peace of them that make peace.

Let His Word rule in you so you may continually experience His peace and wisdom in righteousness and true holiness which comes from the new man.

Below are six passages of Scripture relating to God's peace and wisdom flowing together:

1. *Proverbs 3:13-18* – Happy is the man that findeth wisdom, and the man that getteth understanding. For the merchandise of it is better than the merchandise of silver, and the gain thereof than fine gold. She is more precious than rubies: and all the things thou canst desire are not to be compared unto her. Length of days is in her right hand; and in her left hand riches and honour. Her ways are ways of pleasantness, and all her paths are peace. She is a tree of life to them that lay hold upon her: and happy is every one that retaineth her.
2. *Romans 8:5-6* – For they that are after the flesh do mind the things of the flesh; but they that are after the Spirit the things of the Spirit. For to be carnally minded is death; but to be spiritually minded is life and peace.
3. *Galatians 6:14-16* – But God forbid that I should glory, save in the cross of our Lord Jesus Christ, by whom the world is crucified unto me, and I unto the world. For in Christ Jesus neither circumcision availeth any thing, nor uncircumcision, but a new creature. And as many as walk according to this rule, peace be on them, and mercy, and upon the Israel of God.
4. *James 3:16-18* – For where envying and strife is, there is confusion and every evil work. But the wisdom that is from above is first pure, then peaceable, gentle, and easy to be intreated, full of mercy and good fruits, without partiality, and without hypocrisy. And the fruit of righteousness is sown in peace of them that make peace.
5. *1 Peter 3:10-11* – For he that will love life, and see good days, let him refrain his tongue from evil, and his lips that they speak no guile: let him eschew (avoid) evil, and do good; let him seek peace, and ensue (pursue) it.
6. *2 Peter 1:2-4* – Grace and peace be multiplied unto you through the knowledge of God, and of Jesus our Lord, according as his divine power hath given unto us all things that pertain unto life and godliness, through the knowledge of him that hath called us to glory and virtue: whereby are given unto us exceeding great and precious promises: that by these ye might be partakers of the divine nature, having escaped the corruption that is in the world through lust.

Below are additional Scriptures relating to God's peace and wisdom:

Peace
Numbers 6:22-26 – And the Lord spake unto Moses, saying, "Speak unto Aaron and unto his sons, saying, 'On this wise ye shall bless the children of Israel, saying unto them, "The LORD bless thee, and keep thee: the LORD make his face shine upon thee, and be gracious unto thee: the LORD lift up his countenance upon thee, and give thee peace.'"

References:
Psalm 4:8 – I will both lay me down in peace, and sleep: for thou, LORD, only makest me dwell in safety.
Psalm 29:11 – The LORD will give strength to His people; the LORD will bless His people with peace.

Psalm 37:11 – *But the meek shall inherit the earth; and shall delight themselves in the abundance of peace.* *Psalm 85:8-13* – *I will hear what God the LORD will speak: for he will speak peace unto his people and to his saints: but let them not turn again to folly. Surely his salvation is nigh them that fear him; that glory may dwell in our land. Mercy and truth are met together; righteousness and peace have kissed each other. Truth shall spring out of the earth; and righteousness shall look down from heaven. Yea, the LORD shall give that which is good; and our land shall yield her increase. Righteousness shall go before him; and shall set us in the way of his steps.* *Psalm 119:165* – *Great peace have they which love thy law: and nothing shall offend them.* *Psalm 145:18* – *The LORD is nigh unto all them that call upon him, to all that call upon him in truth.* *Isaiah 26:3-4 (NKJV)* – *You will keep him in perfect peace, whose mind is stayed on You, because he trusts in You. Trust in the Lord forever, for in Yah, the Lord, is everlasting strength.* *Isaiah 40:28-31* – *Hast thou not known? Hast thou not heard, that the everlasting God, the LORD, the Creator of the ends of the earth, fainteth not, neither is weary? There is no searching of his understanding. He giveth power to the faint; and to them that have no might he increaseth strength. Even the youths shall faint and be weary, and the young men shall utterly fall: but they that wait upon the LORD shall renew their strength; they shall mount up with wings as eagles; they shall run, and not be weary; and they shall walk and not faint.* *Isaiah 57:19-21* – *"I create the fruit of the lips; Peace, peace to him that is far off, and to him that is near," saith the LORD; "and I will heal him. But the wicked are like the troubled sea, when it cannot rest, whose waters cast up mire and dirt. There is no peace," saith my God, "to the wicked."* *Jeremiah 29:11-13* – *"For I know the thoughts that I think toward you," saith the LORD, "thoughts of peace, and not of evil, to give you an expected end. Then shall ye call upon me, and ye shall go and pray unto me, and I will hearken unto you. And ye shall seek me, and find me, when ye shall search for me with all your heart."* *John 16:33* – *"These things I have spoken unto you, that in me ye might have peace. In the world ye shall have tribulation: but be of good cheer; I have overcome the world.* *Romans 5:1-2* – *Therefore being justified by faith, we have peace with God through our Lord Jesus Christ: By whom also we have access by faith into this grace wherein we stand, and rejoice in hope of the glory of God.* *Ephesians 2:14-16* – *For he (Jesus) is our peace, who hath made both one, and hath broken down the middle wall of partition between us; having abolished in his flesh the enmity, even the law of commandments contained in ordinances; for to make in himself of twain one new man, so making peace; and that he might reconcile both unto God in one body by the cross, having slain the enmity thereby.* *Colossians 1:20* – *And, having made peace through the blood of his cross, by him to reconcile all things unto himself; by him, I say, whether they be things in earth, or things in heaven.* *2 Thessalonians 3:16* – *Now may the Lord of peace himself give you peace always by all means. The Lord be with you all.* *2 Timothy 2:22* – *Flee also youthful lusts: but follow righteousness, faith, charity (God's love), peace, with them that call on the Lord out of a pure heart.* *Hebrews 12:14-15* – *Follow peace with all men, and holiness, without which no man shall see the Lord: looking diligently lest any man fail of the grace of God; lest any root of bitterness springing up trouble you, and thereby many be defiled.* *1 Peter 3:4* – *But let it be the hidden man of the heart, in that which is not corruptible, even the ornament of a meek and quiet spirit, which is in the sight of God of great price.* *1 Peter 5:14* – *Greet ye one another with a kiss of charity (God's love). Peace be with you all that are in Christ Jesus. Amen.*

Wisdom
1. *1 Corinthians 1:23-24* – *But we preach Christ crucified, unto the Jews a stumblingblock, and unto the Greeks foolishness; but unto them which are called, both Jews and Greeks, <u>Christ the power of God, and the wisdom of God</u>.*

References:
Proverbs 4:5-9 – *Get wisdom, get understanding: forget it not; neither decline from the words of my mouth.*

Forsake her not, and she shall preserve thee: love her, and she shall keep thee. Wisdom is the principal thing; therefore, get wisdom: and with all thy getting get understanding. Exalt her, and she shall promote thee: she shall bring thee to honour, when thou doest embrace her. She shall give to thine head an ornament of grace: a crown of glory shall she deliver to thee. **Proverbs 19:8** *– He that getteth wisdom loveth his own soul: he that keepeth understanding shall find good.* **1 Corinthians 1:30-31** *–* <u>*But of him are ye in Christ Jesus, who of God is made unto us wisdom, and righteousness, and sanctification, and redemption:*</u> *that, according as it is written, "He that glorieth, let him glory in the Lord."* **Colossians 1:25-27** *– Paul said, "Whereof I am made a minister, according to the dispensation of God which is given to me for you, to fulfil the word of God; even the mystery which hath been hid from ages and from generations, but now is made manifest to his saints: to whom God would make known what is the riches of the glory of this mystery among the Gentiles;* <u>*which is Christ in you, the hope of glory.*</u>*"* **Colossians 2:2-3** *– …to the acknowledgement of the mystery of God, and of the Father, and of Christ;* <u>*in whom are hid all the treasures of wisdom and knowledge.*</u>

2. **John 4:24** *– Jesus said, "God is a Spirit: and they that worship him must worship him in spirit and in truth."*

References:
Matthew 16:13-19 *– When Jesus came into the coast of Caesarea Philippi, he asked his disciples, saying, "Whom do men say that I, the Son of man am?" And they said, "Some say that thou art John the Baptist: some, Elias; and others, Jeremias, or one of the prophets." He saith unto them, "But whom say ye that I am?" And Simon Peter answered and said, "Thou art the Christ, the Son of the living God." And Jesus answered and said unto him, "Blessed art thou, Simon Barjona: for flesh and blood hath not revealed it unto thee, but my Father which is in heaven. And I say also unto thee, that thou art Peter, and upon this rock (of revelation knowledge) I will build my church; and the gates of hell shall not prevail against it. And I will give unto thee the keys of the kingdom of heaven: and whatsoever thou shalt bind on earth shall be bound in heaven: and whatsoever thou shalt loose on earth shall be loosed in heaven."* **Luke 6:46-49** *– Jesus said, "And why call ye me, 'Lord, Lord,' and do not the things which I say? Whosoever cometh to me, and heareth my sayings, and doeth them, I will shew you to whom he is like: He is like a man which built an house, and digged deep, and laid the foundation on a rock: and when the flood arose, the stream beat vehemently upon that house, and could not shake it: for it was founded upon a rock. But He that heareth, and doeth not, is like a man that without a foundation built an house upon the earth; against which the stream did beat vehemently, and immediately it fell; and the ruin of that house was great."* **James 1:5-8** *– If any of you lack wisdom, let him ask of God, that giveth to all men liberally, and upbraideth not; and it shall be given him. But let him ask in faith, nothing wavering. For he that wavereth is like a wave of the sea driven with the wind and tossed. For let not that man think that he shall receive any thing of the Lord. A double minded man is unstable in all his ways.* **1 Peter 1:22-23** *– Seeing ye have purified your souls in obeying the truth through the Spirit unto unfeigned love of the brethren, see that ye love one another with a pure heart fervently: being born again, not of corruptible seed, but of incorruptible, by the word of God, which liveth and abideth forever.*

3. **Psalm 34:11-14** *– Come, ye children, hearken unto me: I will teach you the fear of the LORD. Who is the man that desireth life, and loveth many days, that he may see good? Keep thy tongue from evil, and thy lips from speaking guile. Depart from evil, and do good; seek peace, and pursue it.*

Reference:
Psalm 111:10 *– The fear of the LORD is the beginning of wisdom: a good understanding have all they that do his commandments: his praise endureth forever.*

4. **Romans 12:17-20** – *Recompense to no man evil for evil. Provide things honest in the sight of all men. If it be possible, as much as lieth in you, live peaceably with all men. Dearly beloved, avenge not yourselves, but rather give place unto wrath: for it is written, "Vengeance is mine; I will repay," saith the Lord. Therefore, if thine enemy hunger, feed him; if he thirst, give him drink: for in so doing thou shalt heap coals of fire on his head.*

Please refer to **Note 8b** and **8d** for additional information and Scriptures relating to the Lord's peace.

10(b) *I am* thankful (appreciative), [giving praise to *You* always] – making melody to *You* with [*Your*] grace in *my heart.* (Colossians 3:15-16-AMPCE)

Giving thanks and singing and making melody to the Lord is a powerful force! Paul said in *1 Thessalonians 5:18 – "In every thing give thanks: for this is the will of God in Christ Jesus concerning you."* In everything give thanks is a very powerful statement! The Greek word for "thanks" is *eucharisteo* meaning "to be grateful, i.e. (actively) to express gratitude (towards); specially, to say grace at a meal:– (give) thank(-ful,-s)." As the Word of Christ dwells in us richly, we can't help but give thanks! Paul writes,

> *So there remains a Sabbath rest for the people of God. For the one who has entered His rest has himself also rested from his works, as God did from His. Therefore, let us be diligent to enter that rest, so that no one will fall, through following the same example of disobedience. For the word of God is living and active and sharper than any two-edged sword, and piercing as far as the division of soul and spirit, of both joints and marrow, and able to judge the thoughts and intentions of the heart.*
>
> (Hebrews 4:9-12, NASB)

God uses His Word and His Spirit to work in us both to will and to do His good pleasure, including a humble heart of thanksgiving *(Philippians 2:13)*. As we become rooted in Christ, we begin to look not at the things that are seen which are temporary but the things that are unseen, the eternal things of God—walking by faith and not by sight *(2 Corinthians 4:18, 5:7)*. It's easy to give thanks when things are going well and things are going our way. When we are met with trials, tribulation, and persecution, or when things are not going our way, we are able to see how deeply rooted we are in Christ by how we respond *(Luke 8:5-6, 13)*. An example of this is when Paul and Silas were cast into prison:

> *And it came to pass, as we went to prayer, a certain damsel possessed with a spirit of divination met us, which brought her masters much gain by soothsaying: the same followed Paul and us, and cried, saying, "These men are the servants of the most high God, which shew unto us the way of salvation." And this did she many days. But Paul, being grieved, turned and said to the spirit, "I command thee in the name of Jesus Christ to come out of her." And he came out the same hour. And when her masters saw that the hope of their gains was gone, they caught Paul and Silas, and drew them into the marketplace unto the rulers, and brought them to the magistrates, saying, "These men, being Jews, do exceedingly trouble our city, and teach customs, which are not lawful for us to receive, neither to observe, being Romans." And the multitude rose up together against them: and the magistrates rent off their clothes,*

and commanded to beat them. And when they had laid many stripes upon them, they cast them into prison, charging the jailor to keep them safely: who, having received such a charge, thrust them into the inner prison, and made their feet fast in the stocks. And at midnight Paul and Silas prayed, and sang praises unto God: and the prisoners heard them. And suddenly there was a great earthquake, so that the foundations of the prison were shaken: and immediately all the doors were opened, and every one's bands were loosed.

(Acts 16:16-26)

If Paul and Silas can pray and sing praises to God in this environment, how much more should we in our unfavorable circumstances. Praise is a powerful weapon. It takes our focus off our circumstance and onto the one who helps us obtain victory in and through it.

Below are Scriptures relating to giving thanks and praising God:

1 Chronicles 16:8-11 – Give thanks unto the LORD, call upon his name, make known his deeds among the people. Sing unto him, sing psalms unto him, talk ye of all his wondrous works. Glory ye in his holy name: let the heart of them rejoice that seek the LORD. Seek the LORD and his strength, seek his face continually.

References:

Psalm 34:1-4 – I will bless the LORD at all times: his praise shall continually be in my mouth. My soul shall make her boast in the LORD: the humble shall hear thereof, and be glad. O magnify the LORD with me, and let us exalt his name together. I sought the LORD, and he heard me, and delivered me from all my fears. Psalm 66:8-9 – O bless our God, ye people, and make the voice of his praise to be heard: which holdeth our soul in life, and suffereth not our feet to be moved. Psalm 67:5-7 – Let the people praise thee, O God; Let all the people praise thee. Then shall the earth yield her increase; and God, even our own God, shall bless us. God shall bless us; and all the ends of the earth shall fear him. Psalm 68:3-4 (NKJV) – But let the righteous be glad; let them rejoice before God; yes, let them rejoice exceedingly. Sing to God, sing praises to His name; extol Him who rides on the clouds, by His name YAH, and rejoice before Him. Psalm 100:4-5 – Enter into his gates with thanksgiving, and into his courts with praise: be thankful unto him, and bless his name. For the LORD is good; his mercy is everlasting; and his truth endureth to all generations. Psalm 103:1-5 – Bless the LORD, O my soul: and all that is within me, bless his holy name. Bless the LORD, O my soul, and forget not all his benefits: who forgiveth all thine iniquities; who healeth all thy diseases; who redeemeth thy life from destruction; who crowneth thee with lovingkindness and tender mercies; who satisfieth thy mouth with good things; so that thy youth is renewed like the eagle's. Psalm 104:33-34 – I will sing unto the LORD as long as I live: I will sing praise to my God while I have my being. My meditation of him shall be sweet: I will be glad in the LORD. Psalm 107:8-9 – Oh that men would praise the LORD for his goodness, and for his wonderful works to the children of men! For he satisfieth the longing soul, and filleth the hungry soul with goodness. Psalm 113:1-3 – Praise ye the LORD. Praise, O ye servants of the LORD, praise the name of the LORD. Blessed be the name of the LORD from this time forth and for evermore. From the rising of the sun unto the going down of the same the LORD'S name is to be praised. Psalm 117:1-2 – O praise the LORD, all ye nations: praise him, all ye people. For his merciful kindness is great toward us: and the truth of the LORD endureth forever. Praise ye the LORD. Psalm 145:21 – My mouth shall speak the praise of the LORD: and let all flesh bless his holy name for ever and ever. Psalm 146:1-2 – Praise ye the LORD. Praise the LORD, O my soul. While I live will I praise the LORD: I will sing praises unto my God while I have any being. Psalm 147:1 – Praise ye the LORD: for it is good to sing praises unto our God; for it is pleasant, and praise is comely (beautiful). Psalm 149:1-4 – Praise ye the LORD! Sing unto the LORD *a new song, and his praise in the congregation of saints. Let Israel rejoice in him that made him: let the children of Zion be joyful in their King. Let them praise his name in the dance: let them sing praises unto him with the timbrel and harp. For the LORD taketh pleasure in his people: he will beautify the meek with salvation. **Psalm 150:6** – Let every thing that hath breath praise the LORD. Praise ye the LORD! **Romans 12:12** – Rejoicing in hope; patient in tribulation; continuing instant in prayer. **Philippians 4:4** – Rejoice in the Lord alway: and again I say, Rejoice. **Colossians 4:2** – Continue in prayer, and watch in the same with thanksgiving. **1 Thessalonians 5:16-18** – Rejoice evermore. Pray without ceasing. In every thing give thanks: for this is the will of God in Christ Jesus concerning you. **Hebrews 13:15** – By him (Christ) therefore let us offer the sacrifice of praise to God continually, that is, the fruit of our lips giving thanks to his name.*

I want to encourage you to use the **Heart of Thanksgiving Prayer Guide - Volume 1**, please see **Note 1c** for details.

I believe the following passage of Scripture sums up **Notes 9** and **10**:

> *Rejoice in the Lord always. Again, I will say rejoice! Let your gentleness be known to all men. The Lord is at hand. Be anxious for nothing, but in everything by prayer and supplication, with thanksgiving, let your requests be made known to God; and the peace of God, which surpasses all understanding, will guard your hearts and minds through Christ Jesus. Finally, brethren, whatever things are true, whatever things are noble, whatever things are just, whatever things are pure, whatever things are lovely, whatever things are of good report, if there is any virtue and if there is anything praiseworthy—meditate on these things. The things which you learned and received and heard and saw in me, these do, and the God of peace will be with you.*

> (Philippians 4:4-9, NKJV)

Here are additional Scriptures relating to giving thanks and praising God: Psalm 105:1-5, 148:1-14.

Please refer **Note 1c** for additional information and Scriptures relating to the importance of giving thanks.

---

11. *I understand that* whatsoever is born of God *overcomes* the world: and this is the victory that *overcomes* the world, even *my* faith. (1 John 5:4.)

This is why it's essential to put off the old man and to put on the new man in Christ. Paul said in *Romans 13:14 – "But put ye on the Lord Jesus Christ, and make not provision for the flesh, to fulfill the lusts thereof."* Paul also said in *Galatians 3:27 – "For as many of you as have been baptized into Christ have put on Christ!"* Jesus Christ is the one that has overcome the world and has conquered it for us. Jesus said in *John 16:33 – "These things I have spoken unto you, that in me ye might have peace. In the world ye shall have <u>tribulation</u>: but be of good cheer; <u>I have overcome the world</u>."* The root word for "tribulation" is *thlipsis* meaning "pressure (literally or figuratively):–afflicted(-tion), anguish, burdened, persecution, tribulation, trouble." It's only by faith in Him and through Him that we are victorious over the things that are in the world. It is written in *1 John 2:15-17,*

> *Love not the world, neither the things that are in the world. If any man love the world, the love of the Father is not in him. For all that is in the world, the lust of the flesh, and the lust of the eyes, and the pride of life, is not of the Father, but is of the world. And the world passeth away, and the lust thereof: but he that doeth the will of God abideth forever.*

In order to overcome the lust of the flesh, the lust of the eyes, and the pride of life we must grow up in Christ. Paul writes in *Galatians 5:16* – "*This I say then, <u>walk in the Spirit, and ye shall not fulfil the lust of the flesh.</u>*" There may be times when fasting is required in order to do this. Paul also writes in *Galatians 5:6* that faith works by love. This is not an emotional surface love, this is God's unconditional love, the most powerful force in the universe brought forth by the Spirit of God within our hearts (see **Notes 28c**, **29a**, **29b**, **29c**, **30**, and **31** for information and Scripture references concerning God's love). In *John 8:31-32*, Jesus said to the Jews who believed in Him, "*If ye continue in my word, then are ye my disciples indeed; and ye shall know the truth, and the truth shall make you free.*" He also said in *John 6:63*, "*It is the spirit that quickeneth (gives life); the flesh profiteth nothing: the words that I speak unto you, they are spirit, and they are life.*"

Just as a fruit-bearing tree becomes mature enough to bear fruit, so too as we learn to function in the love of God, by continuing in His Word and putting on the new man, faith is produced, seen, and enjoyed. Paul writes,

> *And I, brethren, could not speak unto you as unto spiritual, but as unto carnal, even as unto babes in Christ. I have fed you with milk, and not with meat: for hitherto ye were not able to bear it, neither yet now are ye able. For ye are yet carnal: for whereas there is among you envying, and strife, and divisions, are ye not carnal, and walk as men?*
>
> (1 Corinthians 3:1-3)

It is also written,

> *For every one that useth milk is unskilful in the word of righteousness: for he is a babe. But strong meat belongeth to them that are of full age, even those who by reason of use have their senses exercised to discern both good and evil.*
>
> (Hebrews 5:13-14)

Below are Scriptures concerning the Word of His power:

1. *Joshua 1:1-9 – Now after the death of Moses the servant of the LORD it came to pass that the LORD spake unto Joshua the son of Nun, Moses' minister, saying, "Moses my servant is dead; now therefore arise, go over this Jordan, thou, and all this people, unto the land which I do give to them, even to the children of Israel. Every place that the sole of your foot shall tread upon, that have I given unto you, as I said unto Moses. From the wilderness and this Lebanon even unto the great river, the river Euphrates, all the land of the Hittites, and unto the great sea toward the going down of the sun, shall be your coast. There shall not any man be able to stand before thee all the days of thy life: as I was with Moses, so I will be with thee: I will not fail thee, nor forsake thee. Be strong and of a good courage: for unto this people shalt thou divide for an inheritance the land, which I sware unto their fathers to give them.*

Only be thou strong and very courageous, that thou mayest observe to do according to all the law, which Moses my servant commanded thee: turn not from it to the right hand or to the left, that thou mayest prosper whithersoever thou goest. This book of the law shall not depart out of thy mouth; but thou shalt meditate therein day and night, that thou mayest observe to do according to all that is written therein: for then thou shalt make thy way prosperous, and then thou shalt have good success. Have not I commanded thee? Be strong and of a good courage; be not afraid, neither be thou dismayed: for the LORD thy God is with thee whithersoever thou goest."

References:
Proverbs 24:5, 10, 16 *– A wise man is strong; yea, a man of knowledge increaseth strength. If thou faint in the day of adversity, thy strength is small. For a just man falleth seven times, and riseth up again: but the wicked shall fall into mischief.* ***Proverbs 30:24-28*** *– There be four things which are little upon the earth, but they are exceeding wise: …the conies are but a feeble folk, yet make they their houses in the rocks (a place of refuge);…* ***Matthew 7:21-27*** *– Jesus said, "Not every one that saith unto me, 'Lord, Lord,' shall enter into the kingdom of heaven; but he that doeth the will of my Father which is in heaven. Many will say to me in that day, 'Lord, Lord, have we not prophesied in thy name? And in thy name have cast out devils? And in thy name done many wonderful works?' And then will I profess unto them, 'I never knew you: depart from me, ye that work iniquity.' Therefore whosoever heareth these sayings of mine, and doeth them, I will liken him unto a wise man, which built his house upon a rock: and the rain descended, and the floods came, and the winds blew, and beat upon that house; and it fell not: for it was founded upon a rock. And every one that heareth these sayings of mine, and doeth them not, shall be likened unto a foolish man, which built his house upon the sand: and the rain descended, and the floods came, and the winds blew, and beat upon that house; and it fell: and great was the fall of it."* ***Acts 6:7*** *– And the word of God increased; and the number of the disciples multiplied in Jerusalem greatly; and a great company of the priests were obedient to the faith.* ***Acts 12:24*** *– But the word of God grew and multiplied.* ***Acts 19:20*** *– So mightily grew the word of God and prevailed.* ***Acts 20:32*** *– and now, brethren, I commend you to God, and to the word of his <u>grace</u>, which is able to build you up, and to give you an inheritance among all them which are sanctified.* Please Note: The word grace in the Greek is *charis* meaning "…espec. the divine influence upon the heart, and its reflection in the life; including gratitude…" ***Acts 26:17-18*** *(NKJV) – Jesus said to Paul, "I will deliver you from the Jewish people, as well as from the Gentiles, to whom I now send you, to open their eyes, in order to turn them from darkness to light, and from the power of Satan to God, that they may receive forgiveness of sins and an inheritance among those who are sanctified by faith in Me."* ***Romans 10:17*** *– So then faith cometh by hearing, and hearing by the word of God.* ***Ephesians 3:8-12, 20-21*** *– Paul said, "Unto me, who am less than the least of all saints, is this grace given, that I should preach among the Gentiles the unsearchable riches of Christ, and to make all men see what is the fellowship of the mystery, which from the beginning of the world hath been hid in God who created all things by Christ Jesus: to the intent that now unto the principalities and powers in heavenly places might be known by the church the manifold wisdom of God, according to the eternal purpose which he purposed in Christ Jesus our Lord: in whom we have boldness and access with confidence by the faith of him. Now unto him that is able to do exceeding abundantly above all that we ask or think, according to the power that worketh in us, unto him be glory in the church by Christ Jesus throughout all ages, world without end. Amen.* (God's desire is for His Word to grow mightily and prevail within you – *Isaiah 55:7-11* and *Mark 4:14,20*).

2. ***Romans 12:1-2*** *– I beseech you therefore, brethren, by the mercies of God, that ye present your bodies a living sacrifice, holy, acceptable unto God, which is your reasonable service. And be not conformed to this world: but be ye transformed by the renewing of your mind, that ye may prove what is that good,*

76

and acceptable, and perfect, will of God.

References:

2 Corinthians 3:17-18 *– Now the Lord is that Spirit: and where the Spirit of the Lord is, there is liberty. But we all, with open face beholding as in a glass the glory of the Lord, are changed into the same image from glory to glory, even as by the Spirit of the Lord.* ***Ephesians 4:22-23*** *– That ye put off concerning the former conversation (behavior) the old man, which is corrupt according to the deceitful lusts; and be renewed in the spirit of your mind; and that ye put on the new man, which after God is created in righteousness and true holiness.* ***Ephesians 6:10-13*** *– Finally, my brethren, be strong in the Lord, and in the power of his might. Put on the whole armour of God, that ye may be able to stand against the wiles of the devil. For we wrestle not against flesh and blood, but against principalities, against powers, against the rulers of the darkness of this world, against spiritual wickedness in high places. Wherefore take unto you the whole armour of God, that ye may be able to withstand in the evil day, and having done all, to stand.* Please Note: As we put on the new man, we are putting on the armour of God! ***Colossians 1:25-27*** *– Paul said, "Whereof I am made a minister, according to the dispensation of God which is given to me for you, to fulfil the word of God; even the mystery which hath been hid from ages and from generations, but now is made manifest (apparent) to his saints: to whom God would make known what is the riches of the glory of this mystery among the Gentiles; which is Christ in you, the hope of glory."* ***Colossians 3:9-11*** *– …seeing that ye have put off the old man with his deeds; and have put on the new man, which is renewed in knowledge after the image of him that created him: where there is neither Greek nor Jew, circumcision nor uncircumcision, Barbarian, Scythian, bond nor free: but Christ is all, and in all.* ***James 1:22-25*** *– But be ye doers of the word, and not hearers only, deceiving your own selves. For if any be a hearer of the word, and not a doer, he is like unto a man beholding his natural face in a glass: for he beholdeth himself, and goeth his way, and straightway forgetteth what manner of man he was. But whoso looketh into the perfect law of liberty, and continueth therein, he being not a forgetful hearer, but a doer of the work, this man shall be blessed in his deed.* ***1 John 4:4*** *– Ye are of God, little children, and have overcome them: because greater is he (Christ) that is in you, than he that is in the world.*

3. ***John 1:1-4, 14*** *– In the beginning was the Word, and the Word was with God, and the Word was God. The same was in the beginning with God. All things were made by him; and without him was not any thing made that was made. In him was life; and the life was the light of men. And the Word was made flesh, and dwelt among us, (and we beheld his glory, the glory as of the only begotten of the Father,) full of grace and truth.*

References:

1 Corinthians 1:20-25 *– Where is the wise? Where is the scribe? Where is the disputer of this world? For after that in the wisdom of God the world by wisdom knew not God, it pleased God by the foolishness of preaching to save them that believe. For the Jews require a sign, and the Greeks seek after wisdom: but we preach Christ crucified, unto the Jews a stumbling block, and unto the Greeks foolishness; but unto them which are called, both Jews and Greeks, Christ the power of God, and the wisdom of God. Because the foolishness of God is wiser than men; and the weakness of God is stronger than men.* ***1 Corinthians 1:30-31*** *– But of him are ye in Christ Jesus, who of God is made unto us wisdom, and righteousness, and sanctification, and redemption: that, according as it is written, "He that glorieth, let him glory in the Lord."* ***2 Corinthians 10:3-6*** *– For though we walk in the flesh, we do not war after the flesh: (For the weapons of our warfare are not carnal, but mighty through God to the pulling down of strong holds;) casting down imaginations, and every high thing that exalteth itself against the knowledge of God, and bringing into* *captivity every thought to the obedience of Christ; and having in a readiness to revenge all disobedience, when your obedience is fulfilled.* **Hebrews 1:1-4** *(NKJV) – God, who at various times and in various ways spoke in time past to the fathers by the prophets, has in these last days spoken to us by His Son, whom He has appointed heir of all things, through whom also He made the worlds; who being the brightness of His glory and the express image of His person, and upholding all things by the word of His power, when He had by Himself purged our sins, sat down at the right hand of the Majesty on high, having become so much better than the angels, as He has by inheritance obtained a more excellent name than they.* **Hebrews 4:11-16** *– Let us labour therefore to enter into that rest, lest any man fall after the same example of unbelief. For the word of God is quick (alive), and powerful, and sharper than any twoedged sword, piercing even to the dividing asunder of soul and spirit, and of the joints and marrow, and is a discerner of the thoughts and intents of the heart. Neither is there any creature that is not manifest in his sight: but all things are naked and opened unto the eyes of him with whom we have to do. Seeing then that we have a great high priest, that is passed into the heavens, Jesus the Son of God, let us hold fast our profession (confession). For we have not an high priest which cannot be touched with the feelings of our infirmities; but was in all points tempted like as we are, yet without sin. Let us therefore come boldly unto the throne of grace, that we may obtain mercy and find grace to help in time of need.* **Hebrews 10:23** *– Let us hold fast the profession (confession) of our faith without wavering; (for he is faithful that promised.)*

4. **Hebrews 2:14-15** *– Forasmuch then as the children are partakers of flesh and blood, he (Jesus) also himself likewise took part of the same; that through death he might destroy him that had the power of death, that is, the devil; and deliver them who through fear of death were all their lifetime subject to bondage.*

References:
Luke 10:19 *– Jesus said to His disciples, "Behold, I give unto you power to tread on serpents and scorpions, and over all the power of the enemy: and nothing shall by any means hurt you."* **1 John 3:8** *– He that committeth sin is of the devil; for the devil sinneth from the beginning. For this purpose, the Son of God was manifested, that he might destroy the works of the devil.*

Below are Scriptures relating to faith:

1. **Habakkuk 2:4** *– …the just shall live by his faith.*

References:
Psalm 116:10 *– I believed, therefore have I spoken…* **John 6:63** *– Jesus said, "It is the spirit that quickeneth (gives life); the flesh profiteth nothing: the words that I speak unto you, they are spirit, and they are life."* **Romans 1:17** *– For therein is the righteousness of God revealed from faith to faith: as it is written, "The just shall live by faith."* **Romans 14:23** *– …for whatsoever is not of faith is sin.* **2 Corinthians 4:13-14** *– We having the same spirit of faith, according as it is written, "I believed, and therefore have I spoken;" we also believe, and therefore speak; knowing that he which raised up the Lord Jesus shall raise up us also by Jesus, and shall present us with you.* **2 Corinthians 5:6-7** *– Therefore we are always confident, knowing that, whilst we are at home in the body, we are absent from the Lord: (For we walk by faith, not by sight:).* **Galatians 2:20** *– Paul said, "I am crucified with Christ: nevertheless I live; yet not I, but Christ liveth in me: and the life which I now live in the flesh I live by the faith of the Son of God, who loved me, and gave himself for me."* **1 Timothy 6:12** *– Fight the good fight of faith, lay hold on eternal life…* **Hebrews 10:38-39** *– Now the just shall live by faith: but if any man draw back, my soul shall have no pleasure in*

*him. But we are not of them who draw back unto perdition; but of them that believe to the saving of the soul. **1 Peter 1:23-2:2** – Being born again, not of corruptible seed, but of incorruptible, by the word of God, which liveth and abideth forever. For all flesh is as grass, and all the glory of man as the flower of grass. The grass withereth, and the flower thereof falleth away: but the word of the Lord endureth for ever. And this is the word which by the gospel is preached unto you. Wherefore laying aside all malice, and all guile, and hypocrisies, and envies, and all evil speakings, as newborn babes, desire the sincere milk of the word, that ye may grow thereby.*

2. **Romans 4:16-25** – *Therefore it is of faith, that it might be by grace; to the end the promise might be sure to all the seed; not to that only which is of the law, but to that also which is of the faith of Abraham; who is the father of us all, (as it is written, "I have made thee a father of many nations,") before him whom he believed, even God, who quickeneth (makes alive) the dead, and calleth those things which be not as though they were. Who against hope believed in hope, that he might become the father of many nations, according to that which was spoken, "So shall thy seed be." And being not weak in faith, he considered not his own body now dead, when he was about an hundred years old, neither yet the deadness of Sara's womb: he staggered not at the promise of God through unbelief; but was strong in faith, giving glory to God; and being fully persuaded that, what he had promised, he was able also to perform. And therefore, it was imputed to him for righteousness. Now it was not written for his sake alone, that it was imputed to him; but for us also, to whom it shall be imputed, if we believe on him that raised up Jesus our Lord from the dead; who was delivered for our offences, and was raised again for our justification.*

References:

John 3:36 – *He that believeth on the Son hath everlasting life: and he that believeth not the Son shall not see life; but the wrath of God abideth on him.* ***Galatians 3:5-7, 9, 11*** – *He therefore that ministereth to you the Spirit, and worketh miracles among you, doeth he it by the works of the law, or by the hearing of faith? Even as Abraham believed God, and it was accounted to him for righteousness. Know ye therefore that they which are of faith, the same are the children of Abraham. So then they which be of faith are blessed with faithful Abraham. But that no man is justified by the law in the sight of God, it is evident: for, the just shall live by faith.* ***Galatians 5:6*** – *For in Jesus Christ neither circumcision availeth anything, nor uncircumcision; but faith which worketh by love.* ***2 Thessalonians 1:3-4*** – *We are bound to thank God always for you, brethren, as it is meet, because that your faith groweth exceedingly, and the charity (God's love) of every one of you all toward each other aboundeth; so that we ourselves glory in you in the churches of God for your patience and faith in all your persecutions and tribulations that ye endure.* ***James 2:14-26*** – *What doth it profit, my brethren, though a man say he hath faith, and have not works? Can faith save him? If a brother or sister be naked, and destitute of daily food, and one of you say unto them, "Depart in peace, be ye warmed and filled;" notwithstanding ye give them not those things which are needful to the body; what doeth it profit? Even so faith, if it hath not works, is dead, being alone. Yea, a man may say, "Thou hast faith, and I have works:" shew me thy faith without thy works, and I will shew thee my faith by my works. Thou believest that there is one God; thou doest well: the devils also believe, and tremble. But wilt thou know, O vain man, that faith without works is dead? Was not Abraham our father justified by works, when he had offered Isaac his son upon the altar? Seest thou how faith wrought with his works, and by works was faith made perfect? And the scripture was fulfilled which saith, "Abraham believed God, and it was imputed unto him for righteousness: and he was called the Friend of God." Ye see then how that by works a man is justified, and not by faith only. Likewise, also was not Rahab the harlot justified by works, when she had received the messengers, and had sent them out another way? For as the body without the spirit is dead, so faith without* *works is dead also.*

3. ***Romans 8:24-25*** *– For we are saved by hope: but hope that is seen is not hope: for what a man seeth, why doth he yet hope for? But if we hope for that we see not, then do we with patience wait for it.*

References:
Luke 11:27-28 *– and it came to pass, as he (Jesus) spake these things, a certain woman of the company lifted up her voice, and said unto him, "Blessed is the womb that bare the, and the paps which thou hast sucked." But he said, "Yea rather, blessed are they that hear the word of God, and keep it."* ***Romans 10:17*** *– So then faith cometh by hearing, and hearing by the word of God.* ***2 Corinthians 4:17-18*** *– For our light affliction, which is but for a moment, worketh for us a far more exceeding and eternal weight of glory; while we look not at the things which are seen, but at the things which are not seen: for the things which are seen are temporal; but the things which are not seen are eternal.* ***Hebrews 11:1, 3, 6*** *– Now faith is the substance of things hoped for, the evidence of things not seen. Through faith we understand that the worlds were framed by the word of God, so that things which are seen were not made of things which do appear. But without faith it is impossible to please him: for he that cometh to God must believe that he is, and that he is a rewarder of them that diligently seek him.*

4. ***2 Corinthians 1:24*** *– Not for that we have dominion over your faith, but are helpers of your joy: for by faith ye stand.*

References:
Acts 14:21-22 *– And when they had preached the gospel to that city, and had taught many, they returned again to Lystra, and to Iconium, and Antioch, confirming the souls of the disciples, and exhorting them to continue in the faith, and that we must through much tribulation enter into the kingdom of God.* ***1 Corinthians 15:1-2*** *– Moreover, brethren, I declare unto you the gospel which I preached unto you, which also ye have received, and wherein ye stand; by which also ye are saved…* ***Colossians 1:3-6, 21-23*** *– We give thanks to God and the Father of our Lord Jesus Christ, praying always for you, since we heard of your faith in Christ Jesus, and of the love which ye have to all the saints, for the hope which is laid up for you in heaven, whereof ye heard before in the word of the truth of the gospel; which is come unto you, as it is in all the world; and bringeth forth fruit, as it doth also in you, since the day ye heard of it, and knew the grace of God in truth. And you, that were sometime alienated and enemies in your mind by wicked works, yet now hath he reconciled in the body of his flesh through death, to present you holy and unblameable and unreproveable in his sight: if ye continue in the faith grounded and settled, and be not moved away from the hope of the gospel, which ye have heard, and which was preached to every creature which is under heaven; whereof I Paul am made a minister.* ***2 Peter 1:1-9*** *– Simon Peter, a servant and an apostle of Jesus Christ, to them that have obtained like precious faith with us through the righteousness of God and our Saviour Jesus Christ: Grace and peace be multiplied unto you through the knowledge of God, and of Jesus our Lord, according as his divine power hath given unto us all things that pertain unto life and godliness, through the knowledge of him that hath called us to glory and virtue: whereby are given unto us exceeding great and precious promises: that by these ye might be partakers of the divine nature, having escaped the corruption that is in the world through lust. And beside this, giving all diligence, add to your faith virtue; and to virtue knowledge; and to knowledge temperance; and to temperance patience; and to patience godliness; and to godliness brotherly kindness; and to brotherly kindness charity (God's love). For if these things be in you, and abound, they make you that ye shall neither be barren nor unfruitful in the knowledge of our Lord Jesus Christ. But he that lacketh these things is blind, and cannot see afar off, and hath forgotten that he was purged from his old sins.*

5. *James 1:2-4* — *My brethren, count it all joy when ye fall into divers temptations; knowing this, that the trying of your faith worketh patience. But let patience have her perfect work, that ye may be perfect and entire, wanting nothing.*

References:
Hebrews 6:12 — *That ye be not slothful, but followers of them who through faith and patience inherit the promises.* ***1 Peter 1:3-9 (NKJV)*** — *Blessed be the God and Father of our Lord Jesus Christ, who according to His abundant mercy has begotten us again to a living hope through the resurrection of Jesus Christ from the dead, to an inheritance incorruptible and undefiled and that does not fade away, reserved in heaven for you, who are kept by the power of God through faith for salvation ready to be revealed in the last time. In this you greatly rejoice, though now for a little while, if need be, you have been grieved by various trials, that the genuineness of your faith, being much more precious than gold that perishes, though it is tested by fire, may be found to praise, honor, and glory at the revelation of Jesus Christ, whom having not seen, you love. Though now you do not see Him, yet believing, you rejoice with joy inexpressible and full of glory, receiving the end of your faith—the salvation of your souls.* ***1 Peter 5:8-11*** — *Be sober, be vigilant; because your adversary the devil, as a roaring lion, walketh about, seeking whom he may devour: whom resist stedfast in the faith, knowing that the same afflictions are accomplished in your brethren that are in the world. But the God of all grace, who hath called us unto his eternal glory by Christ Jesus, after that ye have suffered a while, make you perfect, stablish, strengthen, settle you. To him be glory and dominion for ever and ever. Amen.* ***Jude 1:3*** — *Beloved, when I gave all diligence to write unto you of the common salvation, it was needful for me to write unto you, and exhort you that ye should earnestly contend for the faith which was once for all delivered unto the saints.*

Please refer to **Notes 3b, 8c,** and **12** for additional information relating to this subject matter and Scriptures relating to trials and tribulation.

Please refer to **Notes 37a** and **37b** for additional information and Scriptures relating to overcoming the old man through crucifying the flesh.

---

12. *I thank You, Lord, that* all authority (all power of rule) in heaven and on earth has been given to *You. You have destroyed* the works of the devil *and I am in You and You are in me. I thank You for Your faithfulness in my life. I choose to look* away [from all that will distract] to, *You,* Jesus. *My focus is on You today!* (Matthew 28:18-AMPCE; 1 John 3:8; Hebrews 12:2-AMPCE) *(Ref.: Hebrews 2:11; Acts 17:28; 1 Peter 4:19; Hebrews 12:2)*

Hebrews 12:2 in the King James Version reads, "*Looking* unto Jesus the author and finisher of our faith…" The Greek word for "looking" is *aphorao*. Its meaning in the Thayer's Greek Lexicon is "to turn the eyes away from other things and fix them on something. Tropically, to turn one's mind to: Hebrews 12:2." It is essential that we stay focused on Jesus. How do we look away from all that will distract, and look to Jesus? Let's look at a passage of Scripture that will help answer this question:

> *And when the disciples saw him walking on the sea, they were troubled, saying, "It is a spirit;" and they cried out for fear. But straightway Jesus spake unto them, saying, "Be of*

good cheer; it is I; be not afraid." And Peter answered him and said, "Lord, if it be thou, bid me come unto thee on the water." And he said, "Come." And when Peter was come down out of the ship, he walked on the water, to go to Jesus. But when he saw the wind boisterous, he was afraid; and beginning to sink, he cried, saying, "Lord, save me." And immediately Jesus stretched forth his hand, and caught him, and said unto him, "O thou of little faith, wherefore didst thou doubt?"

(Matthew 14:26-31)

The word "come" spoken by the Lord to Peter was the solid ground by which Peter could walk on water. As long as he kept his eyes focused on Jesus he literally walked on the water. But as soon as he took his eyes off of Jesus and fixed them on the boisterous winds (strong and powerful), fear struck his heart and mind and he began to sink. His immediate response was, *"Lord, save me!"* And Jesus was faithful to do so with a question to Peter, *"O you of little faith, why did you doubt?"* Jesus is a <u>brilliant</u> and a <u>patient</u> teacher! He is the Author and the Finisher of our faith *(Hebrews 12:2)*. He helps us, just as he helped Peter. Jesus is no longer in the flesh, as He was with Peter and the other disciples, but He is in us which is much better. Jesus said to His disciples in *John 16:7 – "Nevertheless I tell you the truth; it is expedient for you that I go away: for if I go not away, the Comforter (Holy Spirit) will not come unto you; but if I depart, I will send him unto you."* Isaiah 26:3-4 (NKJV) gives us the key on how to stay focused on Jesus, *"You will keep him in perfect peace, <u>whose mind is stayed on You</u>, because he trusts in You. Trust in the LORD forever, for in Yah, the LORD, is everlasting strength."* As we keep our minds renewed to His Words of truth instead of focusing on the temporary circumstances of life, our focus stays on Him keeping us in a place of peace. Part of staying focused on Christ is releasing our fears (e.g., anxieties, worries, hurts, concerns) to Him, by being real (honest) with Him. As Peter cried out to the Lord in fear and Jesus rescued him, so too as we cry out to the Lord, He rescues us and continues to teach and strengthen us in His truth and peace through our humble submission to Him.

Below are Scriptures relating to staying focused on Christ and trusting in Him:

1. *Joshua 1:8 – This book of the law shall not depart out of thy mouth; but thou shalt meditate therein day and night, that thou mayest observe to do according to all that is written therein: for then thou shalt make thy way prosperous, and then thou shalt have good success.*

References:
Psalm 1:1-3 – Blessed is the man that walketh not in the counsel of the ungodly, nor standeth in the way of sinners, nor sitteth in the seat of the scornful. But his delight is in the law of the LORD; and in his law doth he meditate day and night. And he shall be like a tree planted by the rivers of water, that bringeth forth his fruit in his season; his leaf also shall not wither; and whatsoever he doeth shall prosper. John 10:7-11 – Then said Jesus unto them again, "Verily, verily, I say unto you, I am the door of the sheep. All that ever came before me are thieves and robbers: but the sheep did not hear them. I am the door: by me if any man enter in, he shall be saved, and shall go in and out, and find pasture. The thief cometh not, but for to steal, and to kill, and to destroy: I am come that they might have life, and that they might have it more abundantly. I am the good shepherd: the good shepherd giveth his life for the sheep." John 14:6 – Jesus saith to him, "I am the way, the truth, and the life: no man cometh unto the Father, but by me." John 17:3 – And this is life eternal, that they might know thee the only true God, and Jesus Christ, whom thou hast sent. Acts 17:28 – For in him we live, and move, and have our being; as certain also of your own poets have said, "For we are also his offspring." Romans 12:1-2 – I beseech you therefore, brethren, by the mercies of God, that ye

present your bodies a living sacrifice, holy, acceptable unto God, which is your reasonable service. And be not conformed to this world: but be ye transformed by the renewing of your mind, that ye may prove what is that good, and acceptable, and perfect, will of God. **2 Corinthians 1:20-22** – *For all the promises of God in him are yea, and in him Amen, unto the glory of God by us. Now he which stablisheth us with you in Christ, and hath anointed us, is God. Who hath sealed us, and given the earnest of the Spirit in our hearts.* **Ephesians 4:22-23** – *That ye put off concerning the former conversation (behavior) the old man, which is corrupt according to the deceitful lusts; and be renewed in the spirit of your mind; and that ye put on the new man, which after God is created in righteousness and true holiness.* **Colossians 3:1-4, 9-11** – *If ye then be risen with Christ, seek those things which are above, where Christ sitteth on the right hand of God. Set your affection on things above, not on things on the earth. For ye are dead, and your life is hid with Christ in God. When Christ, who is our life, shall appear, then shall ye also appear with him in glory. …seeing that ye have put off the old man with his deeds; and have put on the new man, which is renewed in knowledge after the image of him that created him: where there is neither Greek nor Jew, circumcision nor uncircumcision, Barbarian, Scythian, bond nor free: but Christ is all, and in all.* **Hebrews 6:17-20** – *Wherein God, willing more abundantly to shew unto the heirs of promise the immutability of his counsel, confirmed it by an oath: that by two immutable things, in which it was impossible for God to lie, we might have a strong consolation, who have fled for refuge to lay hold upon the hope set before us: which hope we have as an anchor of the soul, both sure and stedfast, and which entereth into that within the veil; whither the forerunner is for us entered, even Jesus, made an high priest for ever after the order of Melchisedec*

2. **2 Chronicles 20:12, 20** – *Jehoshaphat said "O our God, wilt thou not judge them? For we have no might against this great company that cometh against us; neither know we what to do: but our eyes are upon thee. …Believe in the LORD your God, so shall ye be established; believe his prophets, so shall ye prosper."*

References:
Psalm 25:15 – *Mine eyes are ever toward the LORD; for he shall pluck my feet out of the net.* **Psalm 121:1-2** – *I will lift up mine eyes unto the hills, from whence cometh my help. My help cometh from the LORD, which made heaven and earth.* **Psalm 141:8** – *But mine eyes are unto thee, O GOD the Lord: in thee is my trust; leave not my soul destitute.*

3. **Psalm 145:18** – *The LORD is nigh unto all them that call upon him, to all that call upon him in truth.*

References:
Hosea 12:6 – *Therefore turn thou to thy God: keep mercy and judgment, and wait on thy God continually.* **Luke 11:34** – *Jesus said, "The light of the body is the eye: therefore when thine eye is single, thy whole body also is full of light; but when thine eye is evil, thy body also is full of darkness."* **John 1:1-4, 14** – *In the beginning was the Word, and the Word was with God, and the Word was God. The same was in the beginning with God. All things were made by him; and without him was not any thing made that was made. In him was life; and the life was the light of men. And the Word was made flesh, and dwelt among us, (and we beheld his glory, the glory as of the only begotten of the Father,) full of grace and truth.* **Romans 14:7-8** – *For none of us liveth to himself, and no man dieth to himself. For whether we live, we live unto the Lord; and whether we die, we die unto the Lord: whether we live therefore, or die, we are the Lord's.* **1 Corinthians 15:31** – *Paul said, "…I die daily."* **2 Corinthians 4:17-18** – *For our light affliction, which is but for a moment, worketh for us a far more exceeding and eternal weight of glory; while we look not at*

the things which are seen, but at the things which are not seen: for the things which are seen are temporal; but the things which are not seen are eternal. **Galatians 1:3-5** *– Grace be to you and peace from God the Father, and from our Lord Jesus Christ, who gave himself for our sins, that he might deliver us from this present evil world, according to the will of God and our Father: to whom be glory for ever and ever. Amen.* **Galatians 2:20** *– Paul said, "I am crucified with Christ: nevertheless, I live; yet not I, but Christ liveth in me: and the life which I now live in the flesh I live by the faith of the Son of God, who loved me, and gave himself for me."* **James 1:27** *– Pure religion and undefiled before God and the Father is this, to visit the fatherless and widows in their affliction, and to keep himself unspotted from the world.* **2 Peter 1:19-21** *– We have also a more sure word of prophecy; whereunto ye do well that ye take heed, as unto a light that shineth in a dark place, until the day dawn, and the day star arise in your hearts: knowing this first, that no prophecy of the scripture is of any private interpretation. For the prophecy came not in old time by the will of man: but holy men of God spake as they were moved by the Holy Ghost.* **1 John 2:14-17** *– I have written unto you, fathers, because ye have known him that is from the beginning. I have written unto you, young men, because ye are strong, and the word of God abideth in you, and ye have overcome the wicked one. Love not the world, neither the things that are in the world. If any man love the world, the love of the Father is not in him. For all that is in the world, the lust of the flesh, and the lust of the eyes, and the pride of life, is not of the Father, but is of the world. And the world passeth away, and the lust thereof: but he that doeth the will of God abideth forever.*

Please refer to **Notes 3b**, **11**, and **37b** for additional information and Scriptures relating to this subject matter.

STUDY NOTES - PART TWO

I pray these study notes along with the many Scriptures derived from both the Old and the New Testament will help you gain a greater understanding of (1) your heavenly Father's eternal love, care, and faithfulness toward you, and (2) the importance of keeping your mind stayed on Him and refraining from idolatrous acts originating from the old man.

"Other seed [of the same kind] fell on ground full of rocks, where it had not much soil; and at once it sprang up, because it had no depth of soil; and when the sun came up, it was scorched, and because it had not taken root, it withered away." Mark 4:5-6 (AMPCE)

"And in the same way the ones sown upon stony ground are those who, when they hear the Word, at once receive and accept and welcome it with joy; and they have no real root in themselves, and so they endure for a little while; then when trouble or persecution arises on account of the Word, they immediately are offended (become displeased, indignant, resentful) and they stumble and fall away. And the ones sown among the thorns are others who hear the Word; then the cares and anxieties of the world and distractions of the age, and the pleasure and delight and false glamour and deceitfulness of riches, and the craving and passionate desire for other things creep in and choke and suffocate the Word, and it becomes fruitless." Mark 4:16-19 (AMPCE)

13(a) *You are **Yeshua**, my salvation. You sent Moses to deliver Israel from Egypt, You raised up judges to deliver Israel from their enemies, and You've sent Jesus to deliver me from my sin. (Ref.: Exodus 15:2; Exodus 3:1-10; Judges 2:16; John 1:29)*

The word *yeshuwah* (pronunciation: *yeshua*) is the Hebrew word for God's salvation meaning "something saved, i.e. (abstractly) deliverance; hence, aid, victory, prosperity:–deliverance, health, help(-ing), salvation, save, saving (health), welfare." God so loved the world that He gave His only begotten Son, Jesus, that whosoever believes on Him should not perish, but have everlasting life *(John 3:16)*. When John the baptist saw Jesus he said, *"Behold the Lamb of God which takes away the sin of the world" (John 1:29)*. God called Moses to deliver the children of Israel out of Egypt, using him to work mighty wonders until Pharoah finally said, "Go!" *(Exodus 12:31)*. When Moses lifted his rod and stretched forth his hand over the Red Sea, the Lord caused the sea to go back by a strong east wind all that night so the children of Israel could pass over on dry ground, but when Pharaoh's army began to go through the Red Sea, on dry ground, the Lord caused the sea to come down upon them and they drowned *(Exodus 14:10-31)*. This is not to be compared with what Jesus Christ did for us though His obedience unto death! He literally bore our sins in His own body and took the penalty for our sins and paid the price for us; therefore, those who receive Jesus as their Lord and Savior will be saved. Those who choose not to receive Jesus Christ as their Lord and Savior will have to pay the penalty for their own sin which is to be eternally separated from God! He bore the sin of all mankind: past, present, and future in His own body. This is why, when Jesus was dying on the cross, He said in *Matthew 27:46* and *Mark 15:34, "My God, My God, why have You forsaken Me?"* God is holy and there is no darkness nor unrighteousness in Him *(1 John 1:5; Psalm 92:15)*. Christ is separate from sinners and because He was made to be sin who knew no sin, He became separated from God for us *(Hebrews 7:26)*! Therefore, those who receive His sacrifice are in Him and have passed from death to life *(John 5:24; 1 John 3:14)*. More good news is that we now have a place to take our sins, our failures, our pain, our struggles, and His name is Jesus. Hallelujah! He is the Shepherd and Bishop of our souls and has come to make us free from the law of sin and death through the law of the Spirit of life in Christ Jesus *(1 Peter 2:25; Romans 8:2)*. Jesus said in *John 14:6, "I am the way, the truth, and the life: no man cometh unto the Father, but by me."* It is only through Jesus Christ that we can be washed and cleansed from our sins and become born again to walk in newness of life in Him *(Ephesians 5:26; 1 John 1:9; Romans 6:4)*. He is the One who died for you and paid the price for your sin which separates you from God. Muhammad did not die for you. Buddha did not die for you. Allah did not die for you. No other god died for you and took your sins; those that serve other gods are in for a rude awakening when they die and face the One who loved them enough to die for them. Don't allow that to happen to you. Receive Jesus Christ as your Lord and Savior. He will give you new life! Please refer to **Note 1b** for "**A prayer to become born again**."

Around the year 2000, the Lord gave me some additional lyrics, where underlined, to go along with the song, "Awesome God" by Rich Mullins:

My God, You are an Awesome God, You reign from Heaven above, with wisdom and with power and with love my God You are an Awesome God. <u>And I will bow before Your Holy Throne, I will praise You, yes, all the day long. I thank You, Lord, for Your love toward me and how you have set me free.</u> My God, You are an Awesome God! <u>Oh, Lord, I've seen in the days of old Your glory which You so graciously bestowed, how You used Moses to set Your</u>

people free and gave them the victory. My God, You are an Awesome God! And now, through the shed blood of Jesus Christ, Your glory is being revealed with great wonder and might not to be compared to the days of old for greater works than those are about to unfold. My God, You are an Awesome God.

Below are Scriptures relating to Jesus, our Savior:

1. ***Psalm 130:3-8*** *– If thou, LORD, shouldest mark iniquities, O LORD, who shall stand? But there is forgiveness with thee, that thou mayest be feared. I wait for the LORD, my soul doth wait, and in his word do I hope. My soul waiteth for the LORD more than they that watch for the morning: I say, more than they that watch for the morning. Let Israel hope in the LORD: for with the LORD there is mercy, and with him is plenteous redemption. And He shall redeem Israel from all his iniquities.*

References:
Isaiah 43:1, 3, 10-11 *– But now thus saith the LORD that created thee, O Jacob, and he that formed thee, O Israel, "Fear not: for I have redeemed thee, I have called thee by thy name; thou art mine. For I am the LORD thy God, the Holy One of Israel, thy Saviour…" "Ye are my witnesses," saith the LORD, "and my servant whom I have chosen: that ye may know and believe me, and understand that I am he: before me there was no God formed, neither shall there be after me. I, even I, am the LORD; and beside me there is no saviour.* ***Isaiah 45:21-23*** *– "…and there is no God else beside me; a just God and a Saviour; there is none beside me. Look unto me, and be ye saved, all the ends of the earth: for I am God, and there is none else. I have sworn by myself, the word is gone out of my mouth in righteousness, and shall not return, that unto me every knee shall bow, every tongue shall swear."* ***John 1:1-5, 14*** *– In the beginning was the Word, and the Word was with God, and the Word was God. The same was in the beginning with God. All things were made by him; and without him was not any thing made that was made. In him was life; and the life was the light of men. And the light shineth in darkness; and the darkness comprehended it not. And the Word was made flesh, and dwelt among us, (and we beheld his glory, the glory as of the only begotten of the Father,) full of grace and truth.* ***John 8:56-58*** *– Jesus said to the Jews, "Your father Abraham rejoiced to see my day: and he saw it, and was glad." Then said the Jews unto him, "Thou art not yet fifty years old, and hast thou seen Abraham?" Jesus said unto them, "Verily, verily, I say unto you, before Abraham was, I am."*

2. ***Matthew 1:18-21*** *– Now the birth of Jesus Christ was on this wise: when as his mother Mary was espoused to Joseph, before they came together, she was found with child of the Holy Ghost. Then Joseph her husband, being a just man, and not willing to make her a publick (public) example, was minded to put her away privily (secretly). But while he thought on these things, behold, the angel of the Lord appeared unto him in a dream, saying, "Joseph, thou son of David, fear not to take unto thee Mary thy wife: for that which is conceived in her is of the Holy Ghost. And she shall bring forth a son, and thou shalt call his name JESUS: for he shall save his people from their sins."*

References:
John 1:29 *– The next day John seeth Jesus coming unto him, and saith, "Behold the Lamb of God, which taketh away the sin of the world."* ***John 10:7-9*** *– Then said Jesus unto them again, "Verily, verily, I say unto you, I am the door of the sheep. All that ever came before me are thieves and robbers: but the sheep did not hear them. I am the door: by me if any man enter in, he shall be saved, and shall go in and out, and find pasture."* ***Acts 4:10, 12*** *– Be it known unto you all, and to all the people of Israel, that by the name of Jesus Christ of Nazareth, whom ye crucified, whom God raised from the dead, even by him doth this man stand*

here before you whole. Neither is there salvation in any other: for there is none other name under heaven given among men, whereby we must be saved. **Acts 5:30-32** – *The God of our fathers raised up Jesus, whom ye slew and hanged on a tree. Him hath God exalted with his right hand to be a Prince and a Saviour, for to give repentance to Israel, and forgiveness of sins. And we are his witnesses of these things; and so is also the Holy Ghost, whom God hath given to them that obey him. (See Luke 24:39-47).* **Romans 5:6-10** – *For when we were yet without strength, in due time Christ died for the ungodly. For scarcely for a righteous man will one die: yet peradventure for a good man some would even dare to die. But God commendeth his love toward us, in that, while we were yet sinners, Christ died for us. Much more then, being now justified by his blood, we shall be saved from wrath through him. For if, when we were enemies, we were reconciled to God by the death of his Son, much more, being reconciled, we shall be saved by his life.* **Hebrews 1:1-4** – *God, who at sundry times and in divers manners spake in time past unto the fathers by the prophets, hath in these last days spoken unto us by his Son, whom he hath appointed heir of all things, by whom also he made the worlds; who being the brightness of his glory, and the express image of his person, and upholding all things by the word of his power, when he had by himself purged our sins, sat down on the right hand of the Majesty on high; being made so much better than the angels, as he hath by inheritance obtained a more excellent name than they.* **Hebrews 2:1-4** – *Therefore we ought to give the more earnest heed to the things which we have heard, lest at any time we should let them slip. For if the word spoken by angels was stedfast, and every transgression and disobedience received a just recompence of reward; how shall we escape, if we neglect so great salvation; which at the first began to be spoken by the Lord, and was confirmed unto us by them that heard him; God also bearing them witness, both with signs and wonders, and with divers (various) miracles, and gifts of the Holy Ghost, according to his own will?* **Hebrews 5:7-10** – *Who in the days of his flesh, when he had offered up prayers and supplications with strong crying and tears unto him that was able to save him from death, and was heard in that he feared;* <u>*though he were a Son, yet learned he obedience by the things which he suffered*</u>*; and being made perfect, he became the author of eternal salvation unto all them* <u>*that obey him*</u>*. Called of God an high priest after the order of Melchisedec.* **Hebrews 9:11-14** – *But Christ being come an high priest of good things to come, by a greater and more perfect tabernacle, not made with hands, that is to say, not of this building; neither by the blood of goats and calves, but by his own blood he entered in once into the holy place, having obtained eternal redemption for us. For if the blood of bulls and of goats, and the ashes of an heifer sprinkling the unclean, sanctifieth to the purifying of the flesh: how much more shall the blood of Christ, who through the eternal Spirit offered himself without spot to God, purge your conscience from dead works to serve the living God?* **Hebrews 9:27-28** – *And as it is appointed unto men once to die, but after this the judgment: so Christ was once offered to bear the sins of many; and unto them that look for him shall he appear the second time without sin unto salvation.* **1 John 1:5-9** – *This then is the message which we have heard of him, and declare unto you, that God is light, and in him is no darkness at all. If we say that we have fellowship with him, and walk in darkness, we lie, and do not the truth: but if we walk in the light, as he is in the light, we have fellowship one with another, and the blood of Jesus Christ his Son cleanseth us from all sin. If we say that we have no sin, we deceive ourselves, and the truth is not in us. If we confess our sins, he is faithful and just to forgive us our sins, and to cleanse us from all unrighteousness.* **1 John 4:14-19** – *And we have seen and do testify that the Father sent the Son to be the Saviour of the world. Whosoever shall confess that Jesus is the Son of God, God dwelleth in him, and he in God. And we have known and believed the love that God hath to us. God is love; and he that dwelleth in love dwelleth in God, and God in him. Herein is our love made perfect, that we may have boldness in the day of judgment: because as he is, so are we in this world. There is no fear in love; but perfect love casteth out fear: because fear hath torment. He that feareth is not made perfect in love. We love him, because he first loved us.* **Jude 1:25** – *To the only wise God our Saviour, be glory and majesty, dominion and power, both now and ever. Amen.* **Revelation 1:5-6** – *And from Jesus Christ, who is the faithful witness, and the first* *begotten of the dead, and the prince of the kings of the earth. Unto him that loved us, and washed us from our sins in his own blood, and hath made us kings and priests unto God and his Father; to him be glory and dominion for ever and ever. Amen.*

3. **Mark 2:16-17** – *And when the scribes and Pharisees saw him eat with publicans and sinners, they said unto his disciples, "How is it that he eateth and drinketh with publicans and sinners?" When Jesus heard it, he saith unto them, "They that are whole have no need of the physician, but they that are sick: I came not to call the righteous, but sinners to repentance."*

References:
2 Corinthians 5:14-15 – *For the love of Christ constraineth us; because we thus judge, that if one died for all, then were all dead: and that he died for all, that they which live should not henceforth live unto themselves, but unto him which died for them, and rose again.* **Galatians 2:20-21** – *Paul said, "I am crucified with Christ: nevertheless I live; yet not I, but Christ liveth in me: and the life which I now live in the flesh I live by the faith of the Son of God, who loved me, and gave himself for me. I do not frustrate the grace of God: for if righteousness come by the law, then Christ is dead in vain."* **1 Timothy 1:15-17** – *Paul said, "This is a faithful saying, and worthy of all acceptation, that Christ Jesus came into the world to save sinners; of whom I am chief. Howbeit for this cause I obtained mercy, that in me first Jesus Christ might shew forth all longsuffering, for a pattern to them which should hereafter believe on him to life everlasting. Now unto the King eternal, immortal, invisible, the only wise God, be honour and glory for ever and ever. Amen.*

13(b) *Continue to lead the way, Lord, and I will follow You to the promised land, the kingdom of God that dwells within my heart! (Ref.: Luke 17:21, 6:46-49)*

When God was taking the Israelites into the promised land, Moses said,

> *When the LORD thy God shall bring thee into the land whither thou goest to possess it, and hath cast out many nations before thee, the Hittites, and the Girgashites, and the Amorites, and the Canaanites, and the Perizzites, and the Hivites, and the Jebusites, seven nations greater and mightier than thou; and when the LORD thy God shall deliver them before thee; thou shalt smite them and utterly destroy them; thou shalt make no covenant with them, nor shew mercy unto them.*
>
> (Deuteronomy 7:1-2)

Notice that all of these nations were greater and mightier than the children of Israel, so therefore, looking at this situation in the natural could produce much fear and anxiety. However, because they had wandered in the wilderness for forty years due to their parent's unbelief, they were humbled and learned to trust God and the one(s) the Lord raised up to lead them. The Lord called Joshua to lead the Israelites into the promised land. The Lord spoke to Joshua saying,

> *Be strong and of a good courage: for unto this people shalt thou divide for an inheritance the land, which I sware unto their fathers to give them. Only be thou strong and very courageous, that thou mayest observe to do according to all the law, which Moses my servant commanded thee: turn not from it to the right hand or to the left, that thou mayest prosper whithersoever thou goest. This book of the law shall not depart out of thy mouth;*

but thou shalt meditate therein day and night, that thou mayest observe to do according to
all that is written therein: for then thou shalt make thy way prosperous, and then thou shalt
have good success.

(Joshua 1:6-8)

Now, in the New Testament, our promised land is the kingdom of God and Jesus leads us to that promised land which dwells within us! Jesus said in *Luke 12:32 – "Fear not, little flock; for it is your Father's good pleasure to give you the kingdom."* In *Luke 17:20-21* the Pharisees demanded Jesus to tell them when the kingdom of God should come. Jesus responded, *"The kingdom of God cometh not with observation: neither shall they say, 'Lo here! or, lo there!' For, behold, the kingdom of God is within you."* Paul writes in *Philippians 3:20 – "For our conversation (citizenship) is in heaven; from whence also we look for the Saviour, the Lord Jesus Christ."* The word "conversation" in the Greek is *politeuma*. Its meaning in the Thayer's Greek Lexicon is "a state, commonwealth, the commonwealth whose citizens we are." In order to truly enjoy the fruits of living as a citizen in God's kingdom we must renew our minds to the truth of His Word, so that we are able to cast down imaginations and every high thing that exalts itself against the knowledge of God in obedience to Christ. It is through this practice that God is able to pull down the strongholds in our lives that keep us bound to the old man, our carnal nature, and thus keeps us from truly living out of His kingdom—righteousness, peace, and joy in the Holy Spirit *(Romans 14:17)*. Paul writes,

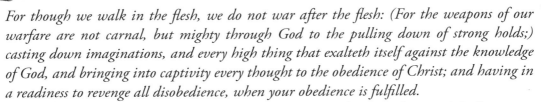

> *For though we walk in the flesh, we do not war after the flesh: (For the weapons of our warfare are not carnal, but mighty through God to the pulling down of strong holds;) casting down imaginations, and every high thing that exalteth itself against the knowledge of God, and bringing into captivity every thought to the obedience of Christ; and having in a readiness to revenge all disobedience, when your obedience is fulfilled.*

(2 Corinthians 10:3-6)

The Greek word for "stronghold" is *ochyroma* and means "(to fortify, through the idea of holding safely); a castle (figuratively, argument):–stronghold." Its meaning in the Thayer's Greek Lexicon is "tropically, **anything on which one relies:** in 2 Corinthians 10:4 of the arguments and reasonings by which a disputant endeavors to fortify his opinion and defend it against his opponent." These mental strongholds can be formed through hurts/woundings, fears, childhood trauma and/or how we internalize certain behaviors from significant others, especially parents, etc., which can form a protective barrier within us to keep us from being hurt. It can also cause ingrained carnal mindsets to form concerning what we think about ourselves, God, and others. The word "ingrained" means "1. (of a habit, belief or attitude) firmly fixed or established; difficult to change. 2. (of dirt or a stain) deeply embedded and thus difficult to remove."[1] These are the areas of our lives that keep us from experiencing the kingdom of God through the born-again creation within us. This is why it is essential to renew the *spirit of our minds*, or the governing *spirit of our minds*, to the new creation – see the ***Personalized Scripture Guide – Details and Directives - Volume 1***, for more information on this subject matter *(Ephesians 4:22-23)*. The writer of Hebrews describes what the Word of God does in conjunction with the Holy Spirit within us as we choose to renew our minds to the truth of His Word:

> *For the word of God is quick (living), and powerful, and sharper than any twoedged sword,*
> *piercing even to the dividing asunder of soul and spirit, and of the joints and marrow, and*
> *is a discerner of the thoughts and intents of the heart.*

(Hebrews 4:12)

The Word of God begins to demolish these strongholds within us. This is very important as Paul writes in *Romans 8:6*, *"For to be carnally minded is death; but to be spiritually minded is life and peace."* He continues with,

Because the carnal mind is enmity against God: for it is not subject to the law of God, neither indeed can be. So then they that are in the flesh cannot please God. …But if the Spirit of him that raised up Jesus from the dead dwell in you, he that raised up Christ from the dead shall also quicken (give life to) your mortal bodies by his Spirit that dwelleth in you. Therefore, brethren, we are debtors, not to the flesh, to live after the flesh. For if ye live after the flesh, ye will die: but if ye through the Spirit do mortify the deeds of the body, ye shall live. For as many as are led by the Spirit of God, they are the sons of God. For ye have not received the spirit of bondage again to fear; but ye have received the Spirit of adoption, whereby we cry, Abba, Father.

(Romans 8:7-15)

Let's look at the following passage of Scripture:

There is a river, the streams whereof shall make glad the city of God, the holy place of the tabernacles of the most High. God is in the midst of her; she shall not be moved: God shall help her, and that right early.

(Psalm 46:4-5)

This river makes glad those who dwell in the city of God. This river is what Jesus was proclaiming,

In the last day, that great day of the feast, Jesus stood and cried, saying, 'If any man thirst, let him come unto me, and drink. He that believeth on me, as the scripture hath said, out of his belly shall flow rivers of living water.' (But this spake he of the Spirit, which they that believe on him should receive: for the Holy Ghost was not yet given; because that Jesus was not yet glorified.)

(John 7:37-39)

The kingdom of God is righteousness, peace, and joy in the Holy Ghost – *Romans 14:17*. In *John 4*, Jesus came into the city of Samaria called Sychar, which was near the plot of ground that Jacob gave to his son Joseph, and Jacob's well was there. Jesus' disciples had gone away into the city to purchase food and Jesus was wearied from his journey and sat on Jacob's well. There was a woman of Samaria who had come to draw water and Jesus asked her to give Him a drink. After a lengthy dialogue between Him and the woman, in *John 4:13-14*, Jesus told the woman of Samaria,

Whosoever drinketh of this water shall thirst again: but whosoever drinketh of the water that I shall give him shall never thirst; but the water that I shall give him shall be in him a well of water springing up into everlasting life.

(John 4:13-14)

When the woman asked Him to give her a drink of that living water Jesus said to her in *John 4:16*, *"Go, call thy husband, and come hither."* In *John 4:17-18*, The woman responded with, *"I have no husband."* Jesus said, *"This is true! For you have had five husbands; and he whom you now have is not your husband."* I believe, at that moment, Jesus was going to the deep need within her with His living water! This woman had been trying to find happiness and fulfillment through other men, but true fulfillment can only come through His living water (the Holy Spirit) which comes through Christ.

In the Old Testament, Isaac (Abraham's son), I believe, was a type and shadow of Jesus. Let's look at the following passage of Scripture:

> *And the man (Isaac) waxed great, and went forward, and grew until he became very great: for he had possession of flocks, and possession of herds, and great store of servants: and the Philistines envied him. <u>For all the wells which his father's servants had digged in the days of Abraham his father, the Philistines had stopped them, and filled them with earth</u>. And Isaac digged again the wells of water, which they had digged in the days of Abraham his father; for the Philistines had stopped them after the death of Abraham: and he called their names after the names by which his father had called them. And Isaac's servants digged in the valley, and found there a well of springing water.*
>
> (Genesis 26:13-15, 18-19)

But, because of contention concerning the water between the herdsmen of Gerar and Isaac's herdsmen,

> *He (Isaac) removed from thence, and digged another well; and for that they strove not: and he called the name of it Rehoboth; and he said, "For now the LORD hath made room for us, and <u>we shall be fruitful in the land</u>."*
>
> (Genesis 26:22)

I believe the Philistines were a type and shadow of our adversary, the devil *(1 Peter 5:8-9)*. As the Philistines filled the wells with earth to stop the flow of the well spring of water, I also believe, our adversary, the devil, desires to fill our "earthen vessel" with earthy substance in order to stop the flow of His living water within us (e.g., ingrained carnal mindsets, cares and anxieties of this world, lust of other things, deceitfulness of riches – *2 Corinthians 4:7; John 7:38-39; Mark 4:14-20*)! The Lord's desire is for us to draw from the wells of salvation and to live out of His kingdom (righteousness, peace, and joy in the Holy Ghost), the eternal things of God *(Isaiah 12:2-3; 2 Corinthians 4:18)*. As we submit to His Lordship, Jesus, the Word of God, by His Spirit removes the ingrained carnal mindsets and thought patterns that run deep within us, as well as other hindrances, in order to tap into the living water within—the rivers which make glad the city of God *(John 1:1-4, 14; Psalm 46:4)*!

In *John 2:1-5*, Jesus and his disciples were called to a wedding. When they had run out of wine, Jesus' mother said to Him, *"They have no wine."* She then said to the servants, *"Whatsoever he saith unto you, do it."* There were six water pots of stone that held about twenty or thirty gallons each and in *John 2:7*, Jesus told the servants, *"Fill the waterpots with water."* And they filled them to the brim. In *John 2:8*, Jesus said to them, *"Draw out now, and bear unto the governor of the feast."* When the governor tasted the water that was made into wine and had no idea where it came from, he went to the bridegroom and said in *John 2:10*, *"Every man at the beginning doth set forth good wine; and when men have well drunk, then that which is worse: but thou hast kept the good wine until now."* Paul writes,

For ye were sometimes darkness, but now are ye light in the Lord: walk as children of light: (for the fruit of the Spirit is in all goodness and righteousness and truth;) proving what is acceptable unto the Lord. Wherefore be ye not unwise, but understanding what the will of the Lord is. And be not drunk with wine, wherein is excess; but be filled with the Spirit; speaking to yourselves in psalms and hymns and spiritual songs, singing and making melody in your heart to the Lord; giving thanks always for all things unto God and the Father in the name of our Lord Jesus Christ; submitting yourselves one to another in the fear of God.

(Ephesians 5:8-10, 17-21)

Living in the kingdom of God brings gladness and fruitfulness within us. Just as Isaac said in *Genesis 26:22*, "...*For now the LORD hath made room for us, and we shall be fruitful in the land.*" So are we fruitful in His kingdom through His Word and by His Spirit (living water) within us as we mature in Christ. This is the grace of God!

The kingdom of God can also be compared with sowing seed in the earth. In *Mark 4:1-20*, Jesus talks about sowing the Word of God into the hearts of men. He talked of the different heart grounds (i.e., a heart ground that is stony – not rooted in Christ, a heart ground full of thorns – cares and anxieties of this world, deceitfulness of riches, and lust of other things, which choke the Word of God and it becomes unfruitful, and a heart ground that is good ground, which brings forth fruit, with patience - *Luke 8:15*). Christ then compared the kingdom of God as when a man cast seed into the ground:

So is the kingdom of God, as if a man should cast seed into the ground; and should sleep, and rise night and day, and the seed should spring and grow up, he knoweth not how. For the earth bringeth forth fruit of herself; first the blade, then the ear, after that the full corn in the ear. But when the fruit is brought forth, immediately he putteth in the sickle, because the harvest is come. Whereunto shall we liken the kingdom of God? Or with what comparison shall we compare it? It is like a grain of mustard seed, which, when it is sown in the earth, is less than all the seeds that be in the earth: but when it is sown, it groweth up, and becometh greater than all herbs, and shooteth out great branches; so that the fowls of the air may lodge under the shadow of it.

(Mark 4:26-32)

It takes time to see the fulfillment of His kingdom in our lives so don't get weary in well doing for you will reap if you faint not *(Galatians 6:9)*. Let's look at three passages of Scripture relating to patience:

1. **Luke 8:15** – Jesus said "*But that on good ground are they, which in an honest and good heart, having heard the word, keep it, and bring forth fruit with patience.*"
2. **Luke 21:19** – Jesus said, "*In your patience possess ye your souls.*"
3. **Romans 5:3** – ...*but we glory in tribulations also: knowing that tribulation worketh patience...*

The word "patience" in these passages of Scripture in the Greek is *hypomone*. Its meaning in the Thayer's Greek Lexicon is "steadfastness, constancy, endurance; in the N. T. the characteristic of a man who is unswerved from his deliberate purpose and his loyalty to faith and piety by even the greatest trials and sufferings." Its root word, is *hypomeno*. Its meaning in the Thayer's Greek Lexicon is "to persevere:

absolutely and emphatically, under misfortunes and trials to hold fast to one's faith in Christ." This Greek word is found in *Romans 12:12*, "*... patient in tribulation.*" Remember, *Acts 14:21-22 – "... confirming the souls of the disciples, and exhorting them to continue in the faith, <u>and that we must through much tribulation enter into the kingdom of God.</u>*"

Below are Scriptures relating to God's kingdom and its foundation:

1. ***Romans 8:16-18*** *– Paul writes, "The Spirit itself beareth witness with our spirit, that we are the children of God: and if children, then heirs; heirs of God, and joint-heirs with Christ; if so be that we suffer with him, that we may be also glorified together. For I reckon that the sufferings of this present time are not worthy to be compared with the glory which shall be revealed in us."*

Reference:
2 Corinthians 4:6-11 *– Paul writes, "For God, who commanded the light to shine out of darkness, hath shined in our hearts, to give the light of the knowledge of the glory of God in the face of Jesus Christ. But we have this treasure in earthen vessels, that the excellency of the power may be of God, and not of us. We are troubled on every side, yet not distressed; we are perplexed, but not in despair; persecuted, but not forsaken; cast down, but not destroyed; always bearing about in the body the dying of the Lord Jesus, that the life also of Jesus might be made manifest in our body. For we which live are alway delivered unto death for Jesus' sake, that the life also of Jesus might be made manifest in our mortal flesh."*

2. ***Psalm 103:19*** *– The LORD hath prepared his throne in the heavens; and his kingdom ruleth over all.*

References:
Proverbs 10:25 *– As the whirlwind passeth, so is the wicked no more: but the righteous is an everlasting foundation.* ***Matthew 24:35*** *– Jesus said, "Heaven and earth shall pass away, but my words shall not pass away."* ***Luke 6:47-49*** *– Jesus said, "Whosoever cometh to me, and heareth my sayings, and doeth them, I will shew you to whom he is like: he is like a man which built an house, and digged deep, and laid the foundation on a rock: and when the flood arose, the stream beat vehemently upon that house, and could not shake it: for it was founded upon a rock. But he that heareth, and doeth not, is like a man that without a foundation built an house upon the earth; against which the stream did beat vehemently, and immediately it fell; and the ruin of that house was great."* ***John 1:1-2, 14*** *– In the beginning was the Word, and the Word was with God, and the Word was God. The same was in the beginning with God. And the Word was made flesh, and dwelt among us, (and we beheld his glory, the glory as of the only begotten of the Father,) full of grace and truth.* ***John 14:5-6*** *– Thomas saith unto him, "Lord, we know not whither thou goest; and how can we know the way?" Jesus saith unto him, "I am the way, the truth, and the life: no man cometh unto the Father, but by me."* ***Hebrews 12:27-29*** *– And this word, "Yet once more," signifieth the removing of those things that are shaken, as of things that are made, that those things which cannot be shaken may remain. Wherefore we receiving a kingdom which cannot be moved, let us have grace, whereby we may serve God acceptably with reverence and godly fear: for our God is a consuming fire.* ***Revelations 11:15*** *– And the seventh angel sounded; and there were great voices in heaven, saying, "The kingdoms of this world are become the kingdoms of our Lord, and of his Christ; and he shall reign for ever and ever."*

3. ***Matthew 6:24-33*** *– Jesus said, "No man can serve two masters: for either he will hate the one, and love the other; or else he will hold to the one, and despise the other. Ye cannot serve God and mammon. Therefore I say unto you, take no thought for your life, what ye shall eat, or what ye shall drink; nor yet*

for your body, what ye shall put on. Is not the life more than meat, and the body than raiment? Behold the fowls of the air: for they sow not, neither do they reap, nor gather into barns; yet your heavenly Father feedeth them. Are ye not much better than they? Which of you by taking thought can add one cubit unto his stature? And why take ye thought for raiment? Consider the lilies of the field, how they grow; they toil not, neither do they spin: and yet I say unto you, that even Solomon in all his glory was not arrayed like one of these. Wherefore, if God so clothe the grass of the field, which to day is, and to morrow is cast into the oven, shall he not much more clothe you, O ye of little faith? Therefore, take no thought, saying, 'What shall we eat?' or, 'What shall we drink?' or, 'wherewithal shall we be clothed?' (For after all these things do the Gentiles seek:) for your heavenly Father knoweth that ye have need of all these things. <u>But seek ye first the kingdom of God, and his righteousness; and all these things shall be added unto you.</u>"

References:

Proverbs 15:15 *(AMPCE) – All the days of the desponding and afflicted are made evil [by anxious thoughts and forebodings], but he who has a glad heart has a continual feast [regardless of circumstances].* **Matthew 13:44** *– Jesus said, "Again, the kingdom of heaven is like unto treasure hid in a field; the which when a man hath found, he hideth, and for joy thereof goeth and selleth all that he hath, and buyeth that field."* **Luke 12:32** *– Jesus said, "Fear not, little flock; for it is your Father's good pleasure to give you the kingdom."* **Romans 14:17** *– For the kingdom of God is not meat and drink; but righteousness, and peace, and joy in the Holy Ghost.* **Acts 14:21-22** *– …confirming the souls of the disciples, and exhorting them to continue in the faith, and that we must through much tribulation enter into the kingdom of God.* **2 Corinthians 4:17-18** *– For our light affliction, which is but for a moment, worketh for us a far more exceeding and eternal weight of glory; while we look not at the things which are seen, but at the things which are not seen: for the things which are seen are temporal; but the things which are not seen are eternal.* **2 Peter 1:2-11** *– Peter writes, "Grace and peace be multiplied unto you through the knowledge of God, and of Jesus our Lord, according as his divine power hath given unto us all things that pertain unto life and godliness, through the knowledge of him that hath called us to glory and virtue: whereby are given unto us exceeding great and precious promises: that by these ye might be partakers of the divine nature, having escaped the corruption that is in the world through lust. And beside this, giving all diligence, add to your faith virtue; and to virtue knowledge; and to knowledge temperance; and to temperance patience; and to patience godliness; and to godliness brotherly kindness; and to brotherly kindness charity (God's love). For if these things be in you, and abound, they make you that ye shall neither be barren nor unfruitful in the knowledge of our Lord Jesus Christ. But he that lacketh these things is blind, and cannot see afar off, and hath forgotten that he was purged from his old sins. Wherefore the rather, brethren, give diligence to make your calling and election sure: for if ye do these things, ye shall never fall: for so an entrance shall be ministered unto you abundantly into the everlasting kingdom of our Lord and Saviour Jesus Christ.* (Peter is speaking here of nurturing and developing the born-again creation, the new man—the divine nature in Christ. The new man is the one who is blessed and able to see and to walk in the kingdom of our Lord and Savior Jesus Christ!).

Please refer to **Notes 2b** for additional information and Scriptures relating to the kingdom of God and the gospel of the kingdom.

Please refer to **Note 4a** for important information relating to exercising godliness – resistance training.

Throughout this Note Section, when quoting Scriptures in the Old Testament, where "Lord" is used it is usually referring to the Hebrew name *Adonai* and when "LORD" is used it is referring to *YHWH*. The Hebrew word *Adonai (Adonay)* occurs approximately 400 times in the Old Testament. For example, when David said in *Psalm 68:19, "Blessed be the Lord, who daily loadeth us with benefits, even the God of our salvation. Selah."* Its meaning in the Hebrew is "an emphatic form of *Adown;* the Lord (used as a proper name of God only):–(my) Lord." The meaning of *Adown* is "from an unused root (meaning to rule); sovereign, i.e. controller (human or divine): lord, master, owner." This meaning implies a personal relationship with the Lord, an understanding of His Lordship in every area of one's life. For example, the Hebrew word *Adown* is found in *Psalm 110:1* when David said, *"The LORD said unto my Lord,"* *'Sit thou at my right hand, until I make thine enemies thy footstool.'"* Another example of this Hebrew name *Adown* is found in *Genesis 18:12* when Sarah laughed within herself when she heard the LORD tell Abraham that she was going to have a child. She was well past her time of childbearing and said, *"After I am waxed old shall I have pleasure, my lord being old also?"* She called her husband, Abraham, lord. Peter refers to this when he is exhorting married women to be submissive to their husbands:

> *But let it be the hidden man of the heart, in that which is not corruptible, even the ornament of a meek and quiet spirit, which is in the sight of God of great price. For after this manner in the old time the holy women also, who trusted in God, adorned themselves, being in subjection (submissive) unto their own husbands: even as Sara obeyed Abraham, calling him lord: whose daughters ye are, as long as ye do well, and are not afraid with any amazement (alarm).*

> (1 Peter 3:4-6)

The key to submission is "trusting in God!" There is a security and strength seen in a godly woman whose trust is in her personal relationship with her Lord *(Adonai)*, living out of the hidden man of the heart. Therefore, she can submit as she is confident that God's will supersedes her husband's will, her employer's will, her father's will. As her heart is surrendered to the Lord's will she doesn't have to protect herself. He is her protector and defender, and can change hearts when needed *(Proverbs 21:1)*. Through the hidden man of the heart the wisdom and strength of God resonates. This not only refers to women but to men, as well, as the hidden man of the heart is the new man in Christ dwelling in every born-again believer. Scripture tells us that Moses was very meek, above all the men which were upon the face of the earth *(Numbers 12:3)*. The Creator of the universe wants to have a personal relationship with every man, woman, and child on the face of this earth. The question is, will you allow Him to be your personal Lord?

When referring to Jesus Christ as our husband, Paul is comparing the relationship of husband and wife to Christ and His church:

> *Husbands, love your wives, even as Christ also loved the church, and gave himself for it; that he might sanctify and cleanse it with the washing of water by the word, that he might present it to himself a glorious church, not having spot, or wrinkle, or any such thing; but that it should be holy and without blemish. So ought men to love their wives as their own*

bodies. He that loveth his wife loveth himself. For no man ever yet hated his own flesh; but nourisheth and cherisheth it, even as the Lord the church: for we are members of his body, of his flesh, and of his bones. For this cause shall a man leave his father and mother, and shall be joined unto his wife, and they two shall be one flesh. This is a great mystery: but I speak concerning Christ and the church. Nevertheless, let every one of you in particular so love his wife even as himself; and the wife see that she reverence her husband.

(Ephesians 5:25-33)

It is important to understand that when compared to God we are all feminine, meaning His authority supersedes what we think is right. For there is a way that seems right to a man but the end thereof is death *(Proverbs 14:12)*. Just as our Lord and Savior Jesus Christ is submissive to God in every area of His life, so too we are called to the same. His Lordship, at a personal level in our lives, develops over time as our relationship with Him grows and our minds are renewed to the authority of His Word.

Please refer to **Notes 39**, **40**, **44a**, and **44b** for additional information and Scriptures relating to this subject matter.

14(b) You are my Lord; I have no good beside or beyond You. (Psalm 16:2-AMPCE)

In *Mark 10:17-18* – *"…there came one running, and kneeled to him (Jesus), and asked him, 'Good Master, what shall I do that I may inherit eternal life?' And Jesus said unto him, <u>'Why callest me good? There is none good but one, that is, God.</u>'"* Paul confirmed this when he said in *Romans 7:18* – *"For I know that in me (that is, in my flesh,) dwelleth no good thing…"* John 1:14 reads, *"And the Word was made flesh, and dwelt among us, (and we beheld his glory, the glory as of the only begotten of the Father,) full of grace and truth."* The word "grace" here in the Greek is *charis* meaning "the divine influence upon the heart, and its reflection in the life…" When pertaining to this particular passage of Scripture *(John 1:14)*, its meaning in the Thayer's Greek Lexicon is "the merciful kindness by which God, exerting his holy influence upon souls, turns them to Christ, keeps, strengthens, increases them in Christian faith, knowledge, affection, and kindles them to the exercise of the Christian virtues." Only through Christ and His Word can our hearts truly reflect the goodness of God. Jesus said,

> *A good man out of the good treasure of his heart bringeth forth that which is good; and an evil man out of the evil treasure of his heart bringeth forth that which is evil: for of the abundance of the heart his mouth speaketh.*

(Luke 6:45)

Jesus is clearly saying here that goodness comes from the heart of man and apart from the grace and truth of God's Word influencing our hearts, our hearts are deceitful and wicked as noted in the following passage of Scripture:

> <u>*The heart is deceitful above all things, and desperately wicked*</u>*; who can know it? I the Lord search the heart, I try the reins (mind), even to give every man according to his ways, and according to the fruit of his doings.*

(Jeremiah 17:9-10)

Jesus also said,

> But those things which proceed out of the mouth come forth from the heart; and they defile the man. For out of the heart proceed evil thoughts, murders, adulteries, fornications, thefts, false witness, blasphemies: these are the things which defile a man: but to eat with unwashen hands defileth not a man.
>
> (Matthew 15:18-20)

This verse emphasizes the fear of the Lord as God has given to each of us a free will to do whatever we so choose. We can choose to go our own way fulfilling our own selfish desires—which leads to destruction or we can choose to surrender to the Lordship of Jesus Christ and go His way—which leads to abundant life *(Matthew 7:13-14; John 10:10)*. Paul writes,

> For we must all appear before the judgment seat of Christ; that every one may receive the things done in his body, according to that he hath done, whether it be good or bad. Knowing therefore the terror of the Lord, we persuade men; but we are made manifest unto God; and I trust also are made manifest in your consciences.
>
> (2 Corinthians 5:10-11)

The fruit of the Spirit springing forth from the heart of man is the manifestation of the goodness of God and truly reveals to us that goodness can only come from Him! Let's look at what Paul writes in the following three passages of Scripture relating to the fruit of the Spirit:

1. ***Galatians 5:22-24*** *– But the fruit of the Spirit is love, joy, peace, longsuffering, gentleness, goodness, faith, meekness, temperance: against such there is no law. And they that are Christ's have crucified the flesh with the affections and lusts.*
2. ***Ephesians 5:8-10*** *– For ye were sometimes darkness, but now are ye light in the Lord: walk as children of light: (for the fruit of the Spirit is in all goodness and righteousness and truth;) proving what is acceptable unto the Lord.*
3. ***Colossians 1:10-18*** *– ...that ye might walk worthy of the Lord unto all pleasing, being fruitful in every good work, and increasing in the knowledge of God; strengthened with all might, according to his glorious power, unto all patience and longsuffering with joyfulness; giving thanks unto the Father, which hath made us meet (able) to be partakers of the inheritance of the saints in light: who hath delivered us from the power of darkness, and hath translated us into the kingdom of his dear Son...*

Please note that as we bear spiritual fruit we are living out of the new man in Christ, as the Lordship of Jesus Christ has full reign in our lives. Operating out of the works of the flesh (e.g., adultery, fornication, hatred, idolatry, strife, murder, envy, drunkenness) opens the door to Satan, the enemy of our souls, to wreak havoc in our lives producing turmoil within. Operating out of the born-again creation produces the fruit of the Spirit which is the evidence of true righteousness and holiness resulting in <u>peace and confident trust in Him</u> *(Isaiah 32:17; Ephesians 4:24)*. Peter writes,

> For he that will love life, and see good days, let him refrain his tongue from evil, and his lips that they speak no guile (deceit): let him eschew (turn away from) evil, and do good; let him seek peace, and ensue (pursue) it. For the eyes of the Lord are over the righteous, and his ears

are open unto their prayers: but the face of the Lord is against them that do evil. And who is he that will harm you, if ye be followers of that which is good?

(1 Peter 3:10-13)

We must also remember and understand that apart from the breath of God, we are nothing but dirt:

And the LORD God formed man of the dust of the ground, and breathed into his nostrils the breath of life; and man became a living soul. The LORD God said to Adam, "…In the sweat of thy face shalt thou eat bread, till thou return unto the ground; for out of it wast thou taken: for dust thou art, and unto dust shalt thou return.

(Genesis 2:7, 3:17-19)

Paul writes,

And so it is written, "The first man Adam was made a living soul; the last Adam was made a quickening (life-giving) spirit." Howbeit that was not first which is spiritual, but that which is natural; and afterward that which is spiritual. The first man is of the earth, earthy: the second man is the Lord from heaven. As is the earthy, such are they also that are earthy: and as is the heavenly, such are they also that are heavenly. And as we have borne the image of the earthy, we shall also bear the image of the heavenly.

(1 Corinthians 15:45-49)

As God breathed into Adam the breath of life and he became a living soul; the Word of God—God-breathed—is full of grace and truth, and when planted within the heart and soul of the believer, nourishes, develops, and supports the born-again creation within—the hidden man of the heart, as Paul writes in *2 Timothy 3:16-17 – "All scripture is given <u>by inspiration (divinely breathed) of God</u>, and is profitable for doctrine, for reproof, for correction, for instruction in righteousness: that the man of God may be perfect, thoroughly furnished unto all good works."*

Below are Scriptures relating to the goodness of God:

1. **Psalm 52:1** – …*the goodness of God endureth continually.*

References:
Psalm 31:19-20 (NKJV) – *Oh, how great is Your goodness, which you have laid up for those who fear You, which You have prepared for those who trust in You in the presence of the sons of men!* ***Psalm 143:10*** – *Teach me to do thy will; for thou art my God: thy spirit is good; lead me into the land of uprightness.* ***Nahum 1:7*** – *The LORD is good, a strong hold in the day of trouble; and he knoweth them that trust in him.* ***Romans 2:4-11*** – *Or despisest thou the riches of his goodness and forbearance and longsuffering; not knowing that the goodness of God leadeth thee to repentance? But after thy hardness and impenitent heart treasurest up unto thyself wrath against the day of wrath and revelation of the righteous judgment of God; who will render to every man according to his deeds: to them who by patient continuance in well doing seek for glory and honour and immortality, eternal life: but unto them that are contentious, and do not obey the truth, but obey unrighteousness, indignation and wrath, tribulation and anguish, upon every soul of man that doeth evil, of the Jew first, and also of the Gentile; but glory, honour, and peace, to every man that*

worketh good, to the Jew first, and also to the Gentile: for their is no respect of persons with God. **Romans 11:22** *– Behold therefore the goodness and severity of God: on them which fell, severity; but toward thee, goodness, if thou continue in his goodness: otherwise thou also shalt be cut off.*

2. **Psalm 112:1, 5-8** *– Praise ye the LORD. Blessed is the man that feareth the LORD, that delighteth greatly in his commandments. A good man sheweth favour, and lendeth: he will guide his affairs with discretion. Surely, he shall not be moved for ever: the righteous shall be in everlasting remembrance. He shall not be afraid of evil tidings: his heart is fixed, trusting in the LORD. His heart is established…*

References:
Proverbs 14:14 *(NKJV) – The backslider in heart will be filled with his own ways, but a good man will be satisfied from above.* **John 15:4-5** *– Jesus said, "Abide in me, and I in you. As the branch cannot bear fruit of itself, except it abide in the vine; no more can ye, except ye abide in me. I am the vine, ye are the branches: he that abideth in me, and I in him, the same bringeth forth much fruit: for without me ye can do nothing."* **Romans 12:9** *– Let love be without dissimulation. Abhor that which is evil; cleave to that which is good.* **Romans 15:14** *– And I myself also am persuaded of you, my brethren, that ye also are full of goodness, filled with all knowledge, able also to admonish one another.* **2 Corinthians 3:5** *– Not that we are sufficient of ourselves to think any thing as of ourselves; but our sufficiency (ability) is of God. but our sufficiency (ability) is of God.* **Galatians 5:22-24** *– But the fruit of the Spirit is love, joy, peace, longsuffering, gentleness, goodness, faith, meekness, temperance: against such there is no law. And they that are Christ's have crucified the flesh with the affections and lusts.* **Philemon 1:6** *– That the communication of thy faith may become effectual by the acknowledging of every good thing which is in you in Christ Jesus.*

3. **Proverbs 20:6** *(NKJV) – Most men will proclaim each his own goodness, but who can find a faithful man?*

Reference:
Luke 18:10-14 *– Jesus spoke a parable saying, "Two men went up into the temple to pray; the one a Pharisee, and the other a publican. The Pharisee stood and prayed thus with himself, 'God, I thank thee, that I am not as other men are, extortioners, unjust, adulterers, or even as this publican. I fast twice in the week, I give tithes of all that I possess.' And the publican, standing afar off, would not lift up so much as his eyes unto heaven, but smote upon his breast, saying, 'God be merciful to me a sinner.' I tell you, this man went down to his house justified rather than the other: for every one that exalteth himself shall be abased (humbled); and he that humbleth himself shall be exalted."*

15(a) *You are* **Qanna – Jealous**. For *I will* worship no other god: for the LORD, whose name *is* Jealous, *is* a jealous God. (Exodus 34:14) *(Ref.: Exodus 34:14)*

The ten commandments are recorded in *Exodus 20:1-17* and *Deuteronomy 5:16-21.* The first two commandments relate to not putting other gods before Him. The LORD said,

1. **Exodus 20:3** *(NKJV) – You shall have no other gods before Me.*
2. **Exodus 20:4-6** *(NKJV) – You shall not make for yourself a carved image (or idol)—any*

likeness of anything that is in heaven above, or that is in the earth beneath, or that is in the water under the earth; you shall not bow down to them nor serve them. For I, the LORD your God, am a jealous God, visiting the iniquity of the fathers upon the children to the third and fourth generations of those who hate Me, but showing mercy to thousands, to those who love Me and keep My commandments.

The Lord is jealous over you! Making idols in one's heart to try and fill the longings of the heart is very dangerous and is grievous to Him. Paul writes,

So kill (deaden, deprive of power) the evil desire lurking in your members [those animal impulses and all that is earthly in you that is employed in sin]: sexual vice, impurity, sensual appetites, unholy desires, and all greed and covetousness, for that is idolatry (the deifying of self and other created things instead of God). It is on account of these [very sins] that the [holy] anger of God is ever coming upon the sons of disobedience (those who are obstinately opposed to the divine will), among whom you also once walked, when you were living in and addicted to [such practices].

(Colossians 3:5-7, AMPCE)

He also writes,

Ye cannot drink of the cup of the Lord, and the cup of devils: ye cannot be partakers of the Lord's table and of the table of devils. Do we provoke the Lord to jealousy? Are we stronger than he?

(1 Corinthians 10:21-22)

The Lord created all things for His pleasure:

1. ***Colossians 1:16-17*** – Paul writes, "For by him were all things created, that are in heaven, and that are in earth, visible and invisible, whether they be thrones, or dominions, or principalities, or powers: all things were created by him, and for him: and he is before all things, and by him all things consist."
2. ***Revelation 4:9-11*** – John writes, "And when those beasts give glory and honour and thanks to him that sat on the throne, who liveth for ever and ever, the four and twenty elders fall down before him that sat on the throne, and worship him that liveth for ever and ever, and cast their crowns before the throne, saying, 'Thou art worthy, O Lord, to receive glory and honour and power: for thou hast created all things, and for thy pleasure they are and were created.'"

In the beginning God created male and female because He wanted a family. He gave them their own will so they could choose whether they wanted to yield to His Lordship which produces life and peace or to yield to their own ways and desires which produces destruction (see **Note 18b**). Adam and Eve chose to go their own way by disobeying God and eating from the tree of the knowledge of good and evil. This act of disobedience caused God's glory to depart from them and their offspring, therefore causing much evil in the earth:

And GOD saw that the wickedness of man was great in the earth, and that every imagination of the thoughts of his heart was only evil continually. And it repented the LORD that he had made man on the earth, and it grieved him at his heart. And the LORD said, "I will destroy man whom I have created from the face of the earth; both man, and beast, and the creeping thing, and the fowls of the air; for it repenteth me that I have made them." But Noah found grace in the eyes of the LORD.

(Genesis 6:5-8)

Thank God for Noah! He found grace in the LORD's sight or you and I would not be here today!

Those who receive Jesus Christ as their Lord and Savior have become members of Christ. This is very precious and valuable to God and He takes this very seriously. He is committed to you and requires your commitment to Him. Paul writes,

Know ye not that your bodies are the members of Christ? Shall I then take the members of Christ, and make them the members of an harlot? God forbid. What? Know ye not that he which is joined to an harlot is one body? "For two," saith he, "shall be one flesh." But he that is joined unto the Lord is one spirit. Flee fornication. Every sin that a man doeth is without the body; but he that committeth fornication sinneth against his own body. What? Know ye not that your body is the temple of the Holy Ghost which is in you, which ye have of God, and ye are not your own? For ye are bought with a price: therefore, glorify God in your body, and in your spirit, which are God's.

(1 Corinthians 6:15-20)

Concerning sexual immorality, anything outside of the marriage bed between a man and a woman defiles—makes unclean or pollutes, as written in *Hebrews 13:4 – "Marriage is honorable in all, and the bed undefiled: but whoremongers and adulterers God will judge."* Let's examine the word "defile" by first looking at the following passage of Scripture where Jesus said,

But those things which proceed out of the mouth come forth from the heart; and they defile the man. For out of the heart proceed evil thoughts, murders, adulteries, fornications, thefts, false witness, blasphemies: these are the things which defile a man.

(Matthew 15:18-20)

The Greek word for "defile" is *koinoo* meaning to "call common, defile, <u>pollute</u>, unclean." It is impossible for the born-again creation within to come to full maturity if our heart ground is polluted. Repentance and cleansing from defilement must take place within us in order for the incorruptible seed of the Word of God to grow and produce fruit *(1 John 1:9; Ephesians 5:25-27; Mark 4:3-32; Galatians 5:21-25).*

In the following passage of Scripture, Paul compares the relationship between a husband and a wife to the relationship between Christ and His church:

Husbands, love your wives, even as Christ also loved the church, and gave himself for it; that he might sanctify and cleanse it with the washing of water by the word, that he might present it to himself a glorious church, not having spot, or wrinkle, or any such thing; but that it should be holy and without blemish. So ought men to love their wives as their own bodies. He that loveth his wife loveth himself. For no man ever yet hated his own flesh; but

103

nourisheth and cherisheth it, even as the Lord the church: for we are members of his body, of his flesh, and of his bones. For this cause shall a man leave his father and mother, and shall be joined unto his wife, and they two shall be one flesh. This is a great mystery: but I speak concerning Christ and the church. Nevertheless, let every one of you in particular so love his wife even as himself; and the wife see that she reverence her husband.

(Ephesians 5:25-33)

When a husband and wife give themselves to each other in every way do you not think jealousy would be aroused if one of them chose to commit adultery against the other? Well, we are created in God's image and those who are born again are one with Him *(John 17:11, 20-21; Acts 17:28)*. He too becomes jealous over us if we choose to give ourselves to another (i.e., the world):

1. ***Jeremiah 3:20-22*** – *"Surely as a wife treacherously departeth from her husband, so have ye dealt treacherously with me, O house of Israel," saith the LORD. A voice was heard upon the high places, weeping and supplications of the children of Israel: for they have perverted their way, and they have forgotten the LORD their God. "Return, ye backsliding children, and I will heal your backslidings…"*
2. ***James 4:4-8*** *(NKJV) – Adulterers and adulteresses! Do you not know that friendship with the world is enmity with God? Whoever therefore wants to be a friend of the world makes himself an enemy of God. Or do you think that the Scripture says in vain, "The Spirit who dwells in us yearns jealously?" But He gives more grace. Therefore, He says: "God resists the proud, but gives grace to the humble." Therefore, submit to God. Resist the devil and he will flee from you. Draw near to God and He will draw near to you. Cleanse your hands, you sinners; and purify your hearts, you double-minded.*

It is also essential to understand the longsuffering, goodness, and forbearance of our God; for it is His goodness that leads us to repentance *(Romans 2:4)*. He suffers long with us and I'm a prime example of His longsuffering as I walked away from Him for six years, thinking that true life was found in doing what I wanted to do, fulfilling the lust of my flesh. After giving myself to the lust of my flesh for six years, I came to the end of myself. He was merciful and revealed Himself to me. I asked Him to forgive me and to come back into my life. I did suffer consequences from my wrong decisions but He has restored my soul and the living water flowing within me has brought me the true riches of life *(Galatians 6:7-8; John 7:37-39)*. I give Him much thanks! See ***My Story – Part One*** and ***Part Two - Volume 1*** for details. I can testify to the fact that He is a patient, merciful, and gracious God. As Satan deceived me into thinking that life would be dull and boring if I continued to follow after Christ, I believe he deceives many into believing this lie which is far from the truth! God gives us all things richly to enjoy. He has given us all things that pertain to life and godliness, and He truly came to give us life and that more abundantly *(1 Timothy 6:17; 2 Peter 1:3; John 10:10)*. Here is a passage of Scripture in Nehemiah that describes His mercy and longsuffering toward His people:

But after they had rest, they again did evil before You. Therefore, You left them in the hand of their enemies, so that they had dominion over them; yet when they returned and cried out to You, You heard from heaven; and many times You delivered them according to Your mercies, and testified against them, that You might bring them back to Your law. Yet they acted proudly, and did not heed your commandments, but sinned against Your judgments,

"Which if a man does, he shall live by them." And they shrugged their shoulders, stiffened their necks, and would not hear. Yet for many years You had patience with them, and testified against them by Your Spirit in Your prophets. Yet they would not listen; therefore, you gave them into the hand of the peoples of the lands. Nevertheless in Your great mercy You did not utterly consume them nor forsake them; for you are God, gracious and merciful.

(Nehemiah 9:28-31, NKJV)

Below are Scriptures relating to God's jealousy and holy anger:

1. ***Exodus 20:1-6*** – *And God spake all these words, saying, "I am the LORD thy God, which have brought thee out of the land of Egypt, out of the house of bondage. Thou shalt have no other gods before me. Thou shalt not make unto thee any graven image, or any likeness of any thing that is in heaven above, or that is in the earth beneath, or that is in the water under the earth: thou shalt not bow down thyself to them, nor serve them: for I the LORD thy God am a jealous God, visiting the iniquity of the fathers upon the children unto the third and fourth generation of them that hate me; and shewing mercy unto thousands of them that love me, and keep my commandments."*

References:
Numbers 14:18, 26-33 – *The Lord is longsuffering, and of great mercy, forgiving iniquity and transgression, and by no means clearing the guilty, visiting the iniquity of the fathers upon the children unto the third and fourth generation. And the Lord spake unto Moses and unto Aaron, saying, "How long shall I bear with this evil congregation, which murmur against me? I have heard the murmurings of the children of Israel, which they murmur against me. Say unto them, 'As truly as I live,' saith the LORD, 'as ye have spoken in mine ears, so will I do to you: your carcasses shall fall in this wilderness; and all that were numbered of you, according to your whole number, from twenty years old and upward, which have murmured against me, doubtless ye shall not come into the land, concerning which I sware to make you dwell therein, save Caleb the son of Jephunneh, and Joshua the son of Nun. But your little ones, which ye said should be a prey, them will I bring in, and they shall know the land which ye have despised. But as for you, your carcasses, they shall fall in this wilderness. And your children shall wander in the wilderness forty years, and bear your whoredoms, until your carcasses be wasted in the wilderness.'"* ***1 Samuel 12:20-25*** – *And Samuel said unto the people, "Fear not: ye have done all this wickedness: yet turn not aside from following the LORD, but serve the LORD with all your heart; and turn ye not aside: for then should ye go after vain things, which cannot profit nor deliver; for they are vain. For the LORD will not forsake his people for his great name's sake: because it hath pleased the LORD to make you his people. Moreover as for me, God forbid that I should sin against the LORD in ceasing to pray for you: but I will teach you the good and the right way: only fear the LORD, and serve him in truth with all your heart: for consider how great things he hath done for you. But if ye shall still do wickedly, ye shall be consumed, both ye and your king."* ***Matthew 21:12-13*** – *And Jesus went into the temple of God, and cast out all them that sold and bought in the temple, and overthrew the tables of the moneychangers, and seats of them that sold doves, and said unto them, "It is written, 'My house shall be called a house of prayer;' but ye have made it a den of thieves."* ***Romans 14:7-9*** – *For none of us liveth to himself, and no man dieth to himself. For whether we live, we live unto the Lord; and whether we die, we die unto the Lord: whether we live therefore, or die, we are the Lord's. For to this end Christ both died, and rose, and revived, that he might be Lord both of the dead and living.* ***1 Corinthians 6:9-11*** – *Know ye not that the unrighteous shall not inherit the kingdom of God? Be not deceived: neither fornicators, nor idolaters, nor adulterers, nor effeminate, nor abusers of themselves with mankind, nor thieves, nor covetous, nor drunkards, nor revilers, nor extortioners, shall inherit the kingdom of God. And such were some of you:*

but ye were washed, but ye are sanctified, but ye are justified in the name of the Lord Jesus, and by the Spirit of our God. **2 Corinthians 6:15-18** *– And what concord hath Christ with Belial? Or what part hath he that believeth with an infidel? And what agreement hath the temple of God with idols? For ye are the temple of the living God; as God hath said, "I will dwell in them, and walk in them; and I will be their God, and they shall be my people. Wherefore come out from among them, and be ye separate", saith the Lord, "and touch not the unclean thing; and I will receive you, and will be a Father unto you, and ye shall be my sons and daughters, saith the Lord Almighty."* **Colossians 3:5-7** *(AMPCE) – So kill (deaden, deprive of power) the evil desire lurking in your members [those animal impulses and all that is earthly in you that is employed in sin]: sexual vice, impurity, sensual appetites, unholy desires, and all greed and covetousness, for that is idolatry (the deifying of self and other created things instead of God). It is on account of these [very sins] that the [holy] anger of God is ever coming upon the sons of disobedience (those who are obstinately opposed to the divine will), among whom you also once walked, when you were living in and addicted to [such practices].* **2 Thessalonians 2:9-12** *– Even him, whose coming is after the working of Satan with all power and signs and lying wonders, and with all deceivableness of unrighteousness in them that perish; because they received not the love of the truth, that they might be saved. And for this cause God shall send them strong delusion, that they should believe a lie: that they all might be damned who believed not the truth, but had pleasure in unrighteousness.* **Hebrews 10:26 -30** *– For if we sin willfully after that we have received the knowledge of the truth, there remaineth no more sacrifice for sins, but a certain fearful looking for of judgment and fiery indignation, which shall devour the adversaries. He that despised Moses' law died without mercy under two or three witnesses: of how much sorer punishment, suppose ye, shall he be thought worthy, who hath trodden underfoot the Son of God, and hath counted the blood of the covenant, wherewith he was sanctified, an unholy thing, and hath done despite unto the Spirit of grace? For we know him that hath said, "Vengeance belongeth unto me, I will recompense," saith the Lord. And again, "The Lord shall judge his people."* **1 Peter 4:17-19** *– for the time is come that judgment must begin at the house of God: and if it first begin at us, what shall the end be of them that obey not the gospel of God? And if the righteous scarcely be saved, where shall the ungodly and the sinner appear? Wherefore let them that suffer according to the will of God commit the keeping of their souls to him in well doing, as unto a faithful Creator.* **2 Peter 2:20-22** *– For if after they have escaped the pollutions of the world through the knowledge of the Lord and Saviour Jesus Christ, they are again entangled therein, and overcome, the latter end is worse with them than the beginning. For it had been better for them not to have known the way of righteousness, than, after they have known it, to turn from the holy commandment delivered unto them. But it is happened unto them according to the true proverb, "The dog is turned to his own vomit again; and the sow that was washed to her wallowing in the mire."* **1 John 2:15-17** *– Love not the world, neither the things that are in the world. If any man love the world, the love of the Father is not in him. For all that is in the world, the lust of the flesh, and the lust of the eyes, and the pride of life, is not of the Father, but is of the world. And the world passeth away, and the lust thereof: but he that doeth the will of God abideth forever.* **Revelation 3:5** *– Jesus said, "He that overcometh, the same shall be clothed in white raiment; and I will not blot out his name out of the book of life, but I will confess his name before my Father, and before his angels."*

2. **Deuteronomy 4:23-24** *– Moses said, "Take heed unto yourselves, lest ye forget the covenant of the LORD your God which He made with you, and make you a graven image, or the likeness of any thing, which the LORD thy God hath forbidden thee. For the LORD thy God is a consuming fire, even a jealous God."*

References:
Hebrews 12:25-29 *– See that ye refuse not him that speaketh. For if they escaped not who refused him that*

spake on earth, much more shall not we escape, if we turn away from him that speaketh from heaven: whose voice then shook the earth: but now he hath promised, saying, "Yet once more I shake not the earth only, but also heaven." and this word, "Yet once more," signifieth the removing of those things that are shaken, as of things that are made, that those things which cannot be shaken may remain. Wherefore we receiving a kingdom which cannot be moved, let us have grace, whereby we may serve God acceptable with reverence and godly fear: for our God is a consuming fire.

3. **Malachi 3:6** – *"For I am the Lord I change not…"*

References:
Matthew 5:17-18 *– Jesus said, "Think not that I am come to destroy the law, or the prophets: I am not come to destroy, but to fulfil. For verily I say unto you, till heaven and earth pass, one jot or one tittle shall in no wise pass from the law, till all be fulfilled.* ***Hebrews 13:8*** *– Jesus Christ the same yesterday, and to day, and for ever.*

Please refer to **Notes 15b**, **17b**, and **18a** for additional information and Scriptures relating to this subject matter.

15(b) *I choose to* keep *myself* from idols (false gods) – [from anything and everything that would occupy the place in *my* heart due to *You*, from any sort of substitute for *You* that would take first place in *my* life]. *Help me to see and remove anything in my heart that is taking Your rightful place as my God.* (1 John 5:21-AMPCE) *(Ref.: Hebrews 4:12-13; Philippians 2:12-13)*

There is pleasure in sin for only a season, *Hebrews 11:24-26 – "…than to enjoy the pleasures of sin for a season…"* but afterwards it brings forth death:

> *Blessed is the man that endureth temptation: for when he is tried, he shall receive the crown of life, which the Lord hath promised to them that love him. Let no man say when he is tempted, "I am tempted of God": for God cannot be tempted with evil, neither tempteth he any man: but every man is tempted, when he is drawn away of his own lust, and enticed. Then when lust hath conceived, it bringeth forth sin: and sin, when it is finished, bringeth forth death. Do not err, my beloved brethren. Every good gift and every perfect gift is from above, and cometh down from the Father of lights, with whom is no variableness, neither shadow of turning. Of his own will begot he us with the word of truth, that we should be a kind of first fruits of his creatures.*

> (James 1:12-18)

The word "death" in the Greek is *thanatos*. Its meaning in the Thayer's Greek Lexicon is "metaphorically, the loss of that life which alone is worthy of the name, i.e. 'the misery of soul arising from sin, which begins on earth but lasts and increases after the death of the body': 2 Corinthians 3:7; James 1:15."

If Satan was able to tempt and deceive Eve who was living in a perfect environment how much more can we be enticed and deceived to go after those things of the world that would keep us from experiencing the vastness, goodness, and love of our heavenly Father through our Lord and Savior Jesus Christ. Remember, *"every good and perfect gift comes from the Father of lights with whom there is no variation or shadow of turning" (James 1:17).* John writes,

> *But if we walk in the light, as he is in the light, we have fellowship one with another, and the blood of Jesus Christ his Son cleanseth us from all sin. If we say that we have no sin, we deceive ourselves, and the truth is not in us. If we confess our sins, he is faithful and just to forgive us our sins, and to cleanse us from all unrighteousness. If we say that we have not sinned, we make him a liar, and his word is not in us.*

(1 John 1:7-10)

The Lord is not calling us to be perfect, He is calling us to have relationship with Him and through that relationship, submission to Him and to His will. He is faithful to bring forth the new creation within us as we continue to yield ourselves to Him. His desire is for us to invest our lives in Him and not in our flesh:

> *Be not deceived; God is not mocked: for whatsoever a man soweth, that shall he also reap. For he that soweth to his flesh shall of the flesh reap corruption; but he that soweth to the Spirit shall of the Spirit reap life everlasting. And let us not be weary in well doing: for in due season we shall reap, if we faint not.*

(Galatians 6:7-9)

Please read *Galatians 5:16-26* to see the works of the flesh and the fruit of the Spirit.

Below are Scriptures relating to the importance of obedience:

1. ***Psalm 18:19-21*** *– He brought me forth also into a large place; he delivered me, because he delighted in me. The LORD rewarded me according to my righteousness; according to the cleanness of my hands hath he recompensed me. For I have kept the ways of the LORD, and have not wickedly departed from my God.*

Reference:
2 Corinthians 5:10-11 *– For we must all appear before the judgment seat of Christ; that every one may receive the things done in his body, according to that he hath done, whether it be good or bad. Knowing therefore the terror of the Lord, we persuade men...*

2. ***Luke 6:46-49*** *– Jesus said, "And why call ye me, 'Lord, Lord,' and do not the things which I say? Whosoever cometh to me, and heareth my sayings, and doeth them, I will shew you to whom he is like: he is like a man which built an house, and digged deep, and laid the foundation on a rock: and when the flood arose, the stream beat vehemently upon that house, and could not shake it: for it was founded upon a rock. But he that heareth, and doeth not, is like a man that without a foundation built an house upon the earth; against which the stream did beat vehemently, and immediately it fell; and the ruin of that house was great."*

3. ***Luke 12:15-21*** *– Jesus said, "Take heed, and beware of covetousness: for a man's life consisteth not in the abundance of the things which he possesseth." And he spake a parable unto them, saying, "The ground of a certain rich man brought forth plentifully: and he thought within himself, saying, 'What shall I do, because I have no room where to bestow my fruits?' and he said, 'This will I do: I will pull*

down my barns, and build greater; and there will I bestow all my fruits and my goods. And I will say to my soul, "Soul, thou hast much goods laid up for many years; take thine ease, eat, drink, and be merry."' But God said unto him, 'Thou fool, this night thy soul shall be required of thee: then whose shall those things be, which thou hast provided?' "So is he that layeth up treasure for himself, and is not rich toward God."

References:

Mark 8:34-36 — And when he (Jesus) had called the people unto him with his disciples also, he said unto them, "Whosoever will come after me, let him deny himself, and take up his cross, and follow me. For whosoever will save his life shall lose it; but whosoever shall lose his life for my sake and the gospel's, the same shall save it. For what shall it profit a man, if he shall gain the whole world, and lose his own soul?"

4. *Hebrews 9:13-14 — For if the blood of bulls and of goats, and the ashes of an heifer sprinkling the unclean, sanctifieth to the purifying of the flesh: how much more shall the blood of Christ, who through the eternal Spirit offered himself without spot to God, purge your conscience from dead works to serve the living God?*

Please refer to **Notes 15a**, **17b**, and **18a** for additional information and Scriptures relating to this subject matter.

16(a) *You are **Yahweh-Sabaoth – the LORD of Hosts**. Hosts in Hebrew means a mass of persons organized for war. O LORD God of hosts, Who is mighty like You? (Ref.: Psalm 89:8-NKJV)*

Sabaoth is the Greek form of the Hebrew word *Tsebaoth*. Below are the two passages of Scripture referring to the Lord of *Sabaoth*:

1. *Romans 9:29 — And as Esaias (Isaiah) said before: Except the Lord of Sabaoth had left us a seed, we had been as Sodoma (Sodom), and been made like unto Gomorrah.*
2. *James 5:4 — Behold, the hire of the labourers who have reaped down your fields, which is of you kept back by fraud, crieth: and the cries of them which have reaped are entered into the ears of the Lord of sabaoth.*

The Greek meaning for *Sabaoth* is "of Hebrew origin; armies; sabaoth (i.e. tsebaoth), a military epithet of God:–sabaoth." In *Romans 9:29* Paul is referring to *Isaiah 1:9* – "*Except the <u>LORD of hosts</u> had left unto us a very small remnant, we should have been as Sodom, and we should have been like unto Gomorrah.*" "LORD of Hosts" in Hebrew is *Yahweh-tsaba*. It is a title of might, power, and strength referring to "a mass of persons organized for war (an army)." Much of the time our warfare is within our own selves concerning the areas of our lives where we have not surrendered to the Lordship of Jesus Christ and/or where we have not renewed the *spirit of our minds* to the truth of His Word. The Spirit of God moves mightily through His Word to bring His will to pass in the hearts and minds of His people. It is written in *Hebrews 4:12-13* – "*For the word of God is quick (alive), and powerful, and sharper than any twoedged sword, piercing even to the dividing asunder of soul and spirit, and of the joints and marrow, and is a discerner of the thoughts and intents of the heart. Neither is there any creature that is* *not manifest in his sight: but all things are naked and opened unto the eyes of him with whom we have to do.*" The Greek word for "quick" is *zao* meaning "a primary verb; to live (literally or figuratively):–life (-time), (a-)live(-ly), quick." The Greek word for "powerful" is *energes* meaning "active, operative:– effectual, powerful." His Word is incorruptible seed and when planted in good heart ground, produces <u>power</u> to become the sons and daughters of God, <u>strength</u> to walk in the ways of God, and <u>might</u> to pull down the strongholds that keep God's promises and the fruit of His nature from becoming a reality within us *(1 Peter 1:23; Mark 4:14-32; 2 Corinthians 10:3-6)*. As we allow the Spirit of God and His Word to nurture, develop, and support the born-again creation within, we become stronger and better able to resist the wiles of the devil. We are more than conquerors through Him who loves us *(Romans 8:37)*. Let's look at an example in David's life where the Lord worked through him to defeat the enemy of Israel:

David was instructed by his father to take grain, loaves, and cheese to the Valley of Elah where Saul, the king of Israel, and the army of Israel were setting up battle against the Philistines. David's father wanted him to see how his three other sons were doing and to report back to him. When David arrived, the army of Israel was perplexed because there was a champion of the Philistines named Goliath whose height was a little over 9 feet. David was a very young man, loved the Lord, and spent much time with Him. First, let's see what Goliath had to say to the ranks of Israel:

> *Goliath stood and shouted to the ranks of Israel, "Why do you come out and line up for battle? Am I not a Philistine, and are you not the servants of Saul? Choose a man and have him come down to me. If he is able to fight and kill me, we will become your subjects; but if I overcome him and kill him, you will become our subjects and serve us." Then the Philistine said, "This day I defy the armies of Israel! Give me a man and let us fight each other." On hearing the Philistine's words, Saul and all the Israelites were dismayed and terrified.*
>
> (1 Samuel 17:8-11, NIV)

So, when David arrived, the men of Israel said to David,

> *Do you see how this man keeps coming out? He comes out to defy Israel. The king will give great wealth to the man who kills him. He will also give him his daughter in marriage and will exempt his family from taxes in Israel.*
>
> (1 Samuel 17:25, 27 NIV)

Now let's see what David said to King Saul about this matter:

> *"Let no one lose heart on account of this Philistine; your servant will go and fight him." Saul replied, "You are not able to go out against this Philistine and fight him; you are only a young man, and he has been a warrior from his youth." But David said to Saul, "Your servant has been keeping his father's sheep. When a lion or a bear came and carried off a sheep from the flock, I went after it, struck it and rescued the sheep from its mouth. When it turned on me, I seized it by its hair, struck it and killed it. Your servant has killed both the lion and the bear; this uncircumcised Philistine will be like one of them, because he has defied the armies of the living God. The LORD who rescued me from the paw of the lion and paw of the bear will rescue me from the hand of this Philistine." Saul said to David, "Go, and the LORD be with you."*

(1 Samuel 17:32-37, NIV)

David had a history with God and he was confident in His God and knew that God would give him the victory! So David went out to meet Goliath and said to him,

> *You come against me with sword and spear and javelin, but I come against you in the name of the LORD Almighty, the God of the armies of Israel, whom you have defied. This day the LORD will deliver you into my hands, and I'll strike you down and cut off your head. This very day I will give the carcasses of the Philistine army to the birds and wild animals, and the whole world will know that there is a God in Israel. All those gathered here will know that it is not by sword or spear that the LORD saves; for the battle is the LORD's, and he will give all of you into our hands.*
>
> (1 Samuel 17:45-47, NIV)

David defeated Goliath with a sling and a stone *(1 Samuel 7:49-50)*.

This story is important because God desires to defeat the enemy of your soul through your faith in Him. Peter exhorts us,

> *Be sober, be vigilant; because your adversary the devil, as a roaring lion, walketh about, seeking whom he may devour: whom resist stedfast in the faith, knowing that the same afflictions are accomplished in your brethren that are in the world. But the God of all grace, who hath called us unto his eternal glory by Christ Jesus, after that ye have suffered a while, make you perfect, stablish, strengthen, settle you. To him be glory and dominion for ever and ever. Amen.*
>
> (1 Peter 5:8-11)

Be assured that as you stay focused on the Lord—being single-minded through trials, tribulation, and temptations—He is faithful to make you strong and firm in Him, established in the faith.

Below are Scriptures relating to the LORD of Hosts:

1. *2 Samuel 6:2 – And David arose, and went with all the people that were with him from Baale of Judah, to bring up from thence the ark of God, whose name is called by the name of the LORD of hosts that dwelleth between the cherubims.*

References:
2 Kings 6:15-17 – And when the servant of the man of God was risen early, and gone forth, behold, an host compassed the city both with horses and chariots. And his servant said unto him (Elisha), "Alas, my master! How shall we do?" And he answered, "Fear not: for they that be with us are more than they that be with them." And Elisha prayed, and said, "LORD, I pray thee, open his eyes, that he may see." And the LORD opened the eyes of the young man; and he saw: and, behold, the mountain was full of horses and chariots of fire round about Elisha. **1 Chronicles 11:9** *– So David waxed greater and greater: for the LORD of hosts was with him.* **2 Chronicles 32:7-8** *– Be strong and courageous, be not afraid nor dismayed for the king of Assyria, nor for all the multitude that is with him: for there be more with us than with him: with him is an arm of flesh; but with us is the LORD our God to help us, and to fight our battles. And the people rested*

themselves upon the words of Hezekiah king of Judah. (The Lord is with you to fight your battles – i.e., anger, rage, lust, hurts, and pains – You are not alone! He said, "I will never leave you nor forsake you!" Pour your heart out to Him and trust His love for you). ***Psalm 24:7-10*** *– Lift up your heads, O ye gates; and be ye lift up, ye everlasting doors; and the King of glory shall come in. Who is this King of glory? The LORD strong and mighty, the LORD mighty in battle. Lift up your heads, O ye gates; even lift them up, ye everlasting doors; and the King of glory shall come in. Who is this King of glory? The LORD of hosts, he is the King of glory. Selah (pause and think about this).* ***Psalm 33:4-22*** *(NIV) – For the word of the LORD is right and true; he is faithful in all he does. The LORD loves righteousness and justice; the earth is full of his unfailing love. By the word of the LORD were the heavens made, their starry host by the breath of his mouth. He gathers the waters of the sea into jars; he puts the deep into storehouses. Let all the earth fear the LORD; let all the people of the world revere him. For he spoke, and it came to be; he commanded, and it stood firm. The LORD foils the plans of the nations; he thwarts the purposes of the peoples. But the plans of the LORD stand firm forever, the purposes of his heart through all generations. Blessed is the nation whose God is the LORD, the people he chose for his inheritance. From heaven the LORD looks down and sees all mankind; from his dwelling place he watches all who live on earth—he who forms the hearts of all, who considers everything they do. No king is saved by the size of his army; no warrior escapes by his great strength. A horse is a vain hope for deliverance; despite all its great strength it cannot save. But the eyes of the LORD are on those who fear him, on those whose hope is in his unfailing love, to deliver them from death and keep them alive in famine. We wait in hope for the LORD; he is our help and our shield. In him our hearts rejoice, for we trust in his holy name. May your unfailing love rest upon us, LORD, even as we put our hope in you.* ***Psalm 46:7, 10-11*** *– The LORD of hosts is with us; the God of Jacob is our refuge. Selah (pause and think about that). Be still, and know that I am God: I will be exalted among the heathen, I will be exalted in the earth. The LORD of hosts is with us; the God of Jacob is our refuge. Selah (pause and think about that).* ***Proverbs 21:31*** *– The horse is prepared against the day of battle: but safety is of the LORD.* ***Isaiah 6:3*** *– And one cried unto another, and said: "Holy, holy, holy, is the LORD of hosts: the whole earth is full of his glory."* ***Isaiah 8:13*** *– Sanctify the LORD of hosts himself; and let him be your fear, and let him be your dread.* ***Jeremiah 31:35*** *– Thus saith the LORD, which giveth the sun for a light by day, and the ordinances of the moon and of the stars for a light by night, which divideth the sea when the waves thereof roar; The LORD of hosts is his name.* ***Amos 4:13*** *– For, lo, he that formeth the mountains, and createth the wind, and declareth unto man what is his thought, that maketh the morning darkness, and treadeth upon the high places of the earth, The Lord, The God of hosts, is his name.* ***Amos 5:14-15*** *– Seek good, and not evil, that ye may live: and so the LORD, the God of hosts, shall be with you, as ye have spoken. Hate the evil, love the good, and establish judgment in the gate: it may be that the LORD God of hosts will be gracious unto the remnant of Joseph.* ***Hebrews 13:5-6*** *– Let your conversation (character) be without covetousness; and be content with such things as ye have: for he hath said, "I will never leave thee, nor forsake thee." So that we may boldly say, "The Lord is my helper, and I will not fear what man shall do unto me."*

2. ***Jeremiah 50:33-34*** *– Thus saith the LORD of hosts; "… Their Redeemer is strong; the LORD of hosts is his name…"*

References:

Isaiah 47:4 *– As for our redeemer, the LORD of hosts is His name, the Holy One of Israel.* (Your Redeemer, Jesus Christ, gave Himself for you that He might redeem you from all your iniquities and purify you unto Himself. You are a new creation in Him produced by an incorruptible seed, the Word of God).
Romans 8:29-39 *– For whom he did foreknow, he also did predestinate to be conformed to the image of his Son, that he might be the firstborn among many brethren. Moreover, whom he did predestinate, them*

he also called: and whom he called, them he also justified: and whom he justified, them he also glorified. What shall we then say to these things? If God be for us, who can be against us? He that spared not his own Son, but delivered him up for us all, how shall he not with him also freely give us all things? Who shall lay any thing to the charge of God's elect? It is God that justifieth. Who is he that condemneth? It is Christ that died, yea rather, that is risen again, who is even at the right hand of God, who also maketh intercession for us. Who shall separate us from the love of Christ? Shall tribulation, or distress, or persecution, or famine, or nakedness, or peril, or sword? As it is written, "for thy sake we are killed all the day long; we are accounted as sheep for the slaughter." Nay, in all these things we are more than conquerors through him that loved us. For I am persuaded, that neither death, nor life, nor angels, nor principalities, nor powers, nor things present, nor things to come, nor height, nor depth, nor any other creature, shall be able to separate us from the love of God, which is in Christ Jesus our Lord. **1 Corinthians 15:55-57** *(NIV) – "Where, O death, is your victory? Where, O death, is your sting?" The sting of death is sin, and the power of sin is the law. But thanks be to God! He gives us the victory through our Lord Jesus Christ.* **Titus 2:11-14** *(NKJV) – …looking for the blessed hope and glorious appearing of our great God and Saviour Jesus Christ, who gave Himself for us, that He might redeem us from every lawless deed and purify for Himself His own special people, zealous for good works.* **1 Peter 1:23** *– Being born again, not of corruptible seed, but of incorruptible, by the word of God, which liveth and abideth forever.* **1 John 3:8** *– He that committeth sin is of the devil; for the devil sinneth from the beginning. For this purpose, the Son of God was manifested, that he might destroy the works of the devil.*

Please refer to **Notes 6a**, **6b**, and **16b** for additional information and Scriptures relating to this subject matter.

16(b) Your faithfulness also surrounds You. *I trust Your might and Your faithfulness in my life to free me from all things that keep me from being like You.* (Psalm 89:8-NKJV) *(Ref.: Hebrews 4:12-13; Philippians 2:12-13; Romans 8:29-30)*

The Lord's faithfulness reaches to the clouds *(Psalm 36:5)*. He knows when we sit down and when we rise up and He is mighty in that He knows our thoughts even before we speak them *(Psalm 139:2; Matthew 9:4)*. Think about how many people are on this earth, and God who is Almighty knows everyone's thoughts and He knows all men and what is in man *(John 2:24-25)*. Trust His love for you to accomplish His will in your life as you continue to submit to His Lordship.

Below are Scriptures relating to God's faithfulness:

1. **Psalm 40:10** *(NIV) – David said, "I do not hide your righteousness in my heart; I speak of your faithfulness and your saving help. I do not conceal your love and your faithfulness from the great assembly."*

References:
Psalm 36:5 *– Thy mercy, O LORD, is in the heavens; and thy faithfulness reacheth unto the clouds.* **Psalm 89:1** *– I will sing of the mercies of the LORD forever: with my mouth will I make known thy faithfulness to all generations.* **Psalm 92:1-2** *– It is a good thing to give thanks unto the LORD, and to sing praises unto thy name, O most High: to shew forth thy lovingkindness in the morning, and thy faithfulness every night.* **Psalm 119:90** *– Thy faithfulness is unto all generations: thou hast established the earth, and it*

abideth. **Isaiah 25:1** – *O LORD, thou art my God; I will exalt thee, I will praise thy name; for thou hast done wonderful things; thy counsels of old are faithfulness and truth.* **Lamentations 3:22-23** – *It is of the LORD'S mercies that we are not consumed, because his compassions fail not. They are new every morning: great is thy faithfulness.*

2. **1 Corinthians 1:4-9** – *I thank my God always on your behalf, for the grace of God which is given you by Jesus Christ; that in everything ye are enriched by him, in all utterance, and in all knowledge; even as the testimony of Christ was confirmed in you: so that ye come behind in no gift; waiting for the coming of our Lord Jesus Christ: who shall also confirm you unto the end, that ye may be blameless in the day of our Lord Jesus Christ. God is faithful, by whom ye were called unto the fellowship of his Son Jesus Christ our Lord.*

References:
1 Corinthians 10:13-14 – *There hath no temptation taken you but such as is common to man: but God is faithful, who will not suffer you to be tempted above that ye are able; but will with the temptation also make a way to escape, that ye may be able to bear it. Wherefore, my dearly beloved, flee from idolatry.* **1 Thessalonians 5:23-24** – *And the very God of peace sanctify you wholly; and I pray God your whole spirit and soul and body be preserved blameless unto the coming of our Lord Jesus Christ. Faithful is he that calleth you, who also will do it.* **2 Thessalonians 3:1-3** – *Finally, brethren, pray for us, that the word of the Lord may have free course, and be glorified, even as it is with you: and that we may be delivered from unreasonable and wicked men: for all men have not faith. But the Lord is faithful, who shall stablish you, and keep you from evil.* **1 Peter 4:17-19** – *For the time is come that judgment must begin at the house of God: and if it first begin at us, what shall the end be of them that obey not the gospel of God? And if the righteous scarcely be saved, where shall the ungodly and the sinner appear? Wherefore let them that suffer according to the will of God commit the keeping of their souls to him in well doing, as unto a faithful Creator.* **1 John 1:9** – *If we confess our sins, he is faithful and just to forgive us our sins, and to cleanse us from all unrighteousness.* **Revelation 19:11** – *And I saw heaven opened, and behold a white horse; and he that sat upon him was called Faithful and True, and in righteousness he doth judge and make war.*

Please refer to **Notes 6a, 6b,** and **16a** for additional information and Scriptures relating to this subject matter.

17(a) If then *I* have been raised with Christ [to a new life, thus sharing His resurrection from the dead], *I* aim at and seek the [rich, eternal treasures] that are above, where Christ is, seated at the right hand of God. And *I set my mind and keep it set on what is above (the higher things), not on the things that are on the earth. For [as far as this world is concerned] I have died, and my [new, real] life is hidden with Christ in God. When Christ, Who is my life, appears, then I also will appear with Him in [the splendor of His] glory.* (Colossians 3:1-4-AMPCE)

We have been raised with Christ to a new life as a new creation in Him *(Galatians 6:15)*. In Christ are hid all the treasures of wisdom and knowledge *(Colossians 2:3)* and these true riches reside within us. Paul writes,

For God, who commanded the light to shine out of darkness, hath shined in our hearts, to give the light of the knowledge of the glory of God in the face of Jesus Christ. But we have this treasure in earthen vessels, that the excellency of the power may be of God, and not of us.

(2 Corinthians 4:6-7)

We are in Him and He is in us *(John 17:20-23; Acts 17:28)*. At the moment we receive Jesus Christ as our Lord and Savior we are His babes and are beginning a journey of a new life in Him as God loves, covers, and protects His own *(1 Peter 2:2)*. Jesus said in *John 10:10 – "The thief cometh not, but for to steal, and to kill, and to destroy: I am come that they might have life, and that they might have it more abundantly."* The enemy of our soul, Satan, does not want us to grow and mature into strong believers in Christ as we then become a threat to his kingdom. He wants us to continue to live out of our carnal nature (e.g., the strongholds that are within us rooted in lies, deception, insecurities, fears, anxieties) – *Matthew 12:25-26*. Therefore, as born-again believers, it is essential that we choose to seek those things that are above by renewing the *spirit of our minds* to the truth of God's Word in order to grow and mature in Christ.

As babes in Christ, we still live out of our carnal nature, governed by our feelings and emotions, and are self-centered—focusing primarily on "me," "myself," and "I" (e.g., what "I" feel and what "I" think is right). Let's look at two passages of Scripture that confirm this statement:

1. *1 Corinthians 3:1-3 – And I, brethren, could not speak unto you as unto spiritual, but as unto carnal, even as unto babes in Christ. I have fed you with milk, and not with meat: for hitherto ye were not able to bear it, neither yet now are ye able. For ye are yet carnal: for whereas there is among you envying, and strife, and divisions, are ye not carnal, and walk as men?*

2. *Hebrews 5:13-14 – For everyone that useth milk is unskillful in the word of righteousness: for he is a babe. But strong meat belongeth to them that are of full age, even those who by reason of use have their senses exercised to discern both good and evil.*

The Lord helped me to see in my own life that anytime I would get upset, frustrated, disturbed, etc., there was one common denominator, "ME!" When I began to renew the *spirit of my mind* to the truth of God's Word concerning the born-again creation within (i.e., the *Personalized Scripture Guide - Volume 1*), I found myself more heavenly minded. I began to function in a place of peace and security in Christ as the life-giving flow of His Spirit and the grace and truth contained in His Words began to dispel the lies and deceptions of the devil. Therefore, I was not moved by situations and circumstances, where in the past they would have caused an eruption of bad feelings and emotions because of my own insecurities, fears, and anxieties (please see *My Story – Part Two - Volume 1* for details).

The *Personalized Scripture Guide*, the heart of *Character Development in Christ*, is designed to help you exercise and become skillful in the word of righteousness at a heart level, working in you to help nurture, develop, and support the born-again creation within, the hidden man of the heart. It is written,

For the word of God is quick (alive), and powerful, and sharper than any twoedged sword, piercing even to the dividing asunder of soul and spirit, and of the joints and marrow, and

[handwritten margin note: "The anger of men is about us - mostly"]

115

is a discerner of the thoughts and intents of the heart.

(Hebrews 4:12)

When Jesus was in the wilderness and being tempted by the devil the weapon that He used against Satan was the Word of God, *"It is written…!"* The Word of God and submission to His Word is the only weapon that can defeat Satan in your own life *(Ephesians 6:17)!*

Below are Scriptures relating to seeking God:

Psalm 105:3-4 – Glory ye in his holy name: let the heart of them rejoice that seek the LORD. Seek the LORD, and his strength: seek his face evermore.

References:
*Deuteronomy 4:29 – But if from thence thou shalt seek the LORD thy God, thou shalt find him, if thou seek him with all thy heart and with all thy soul. **Joshua 1:8** – The Lord said to Joshua, "This book of the law shall not depart out of thy mouth; but thou shalt meditate therein day and night, that thou mayest observe to do according to all that is written therein: for then thou shalt make thy way prosperous, and then thou shalt have good success." **1 Chronicles 16:10-11** – Glory ye in his holy name: let the heart of them rejoice that seek the LORD. Seek the LORD and his strength, seek his face continually. **2 Chronicles 12:13-14** – …And he did evil, because he prepared not his heart to seek the LORD. **Psalm 1:1-3** – Blessed is the man that walketh not in the counsel of the ungodly, nor standeth in the way of sinners, nor sitteth in the seat of the scornful. But his delight is in the law of the LORD; and in his law doth he meditate day and night. And he shall be like a tree planted by the rivers of water, that bringeth forth his fruit in his season; his leaf also shall not wither; and whatsoever he doeth shall prosper. **Psalm 9:10** – And they that know thy name will put their trust in thee: for thou, LORD, hast not forsaken them that seek thee. **Psalm 14:1-2** – The fool hath said in his heart, "There is no God." They are corrupt, they have done abominable works, there is none that doeth good. The LORD looked down from heaven upon the children of men, to see if there were any that did understand, and seek God. **Psalm 22:26** – the meek shall eat and be satisfied: they shall praise the LORD that seek him: your heart shall live for ever. **Psalm 34:10** – The young lions do lack, and suffer hunger: but they that seek the LORD shall not want any good thing. **Psalm 119:2** – Blessed are they that keep his testimonies, and that seek him with the whole heart. **Proverbs 15:24** – The way of life is above to the wise, that he may depart from hell beneath. **Proverbs 16:23** – The heart of the wise teacheth his mouth, and addeth learning to his lips. **Proverbs 19:8, 19-21, 23** – He that getteth wisdom loveth his own soul: he that keepeth understanding shall find good. A man of great wrath shall suffer punishment: for if thou deliver him, yet thou must do it again. Hear counsel, and receive instruction, that thou mayest be wise in thy latter end. There are many devices in a man's heart; nevertheless the counsel of the LORD, that shall stand. The fear of the LORD tendeth to life: and he that hath it shall abide satisfied; he shall not be visited with evil. **Proverbs 28:5** – Evil men understand not judgment: but they that seek the LORD understand all things. **Jeremiah 29:11-13** – "For I know the thoughts that I think toward you," saith the LORD, "thoughts of peace, and not of evil, to give you an expected end. Then shall ye call upon me, and ye shall go and pray unto me, and I will hearken unto you. And ye shall seek me, and find me, when ye shall search for me with all your heart. **Matthew 6:24-33** – Jesus said, "…But seek ye first the kingdom of God, and his righteousness; and all these things shall be added unto you." **John 7:16-18** (NKJV) – Jesus answered them and said, "My doctrine is not Mine, but His who sent Me. If anyone wills to do His will, he shall know concerning the doctrine, whether it is from God or whether I speak on My own authority. He who speaks from himself seeks his own glory; but He who seeks the glory of the One who sent Him is true, and no unrighteousness is in*

*Him." **John 17:3** – And this is life eternal, that they might know thee the only true God, and Jesus Christ, whom thou hast sent. **Philippians 3:7-11** – Paul said, "But what things were gain to me, those I counted loss for Christ. Yea doubtless, and I count all things but loss for the excellency of the knowledge of Christ Jesus my Lord: for whom I have suffered the loss of all things, and do count them but dung, that I may win Christ, and be found in him, not having mine own righteousness, which is of the law, but that which is through the faith of Christ, the righteousness which is of God by faith: that I may know him, and the power of his resurrection, and the fellowship of his sufferings, being made conformable unto his death; if by any means I might attain unto the resurrection of the dead."*

Below are Scriptures relating to living in Christ:

1. ***Romans 14:6-9*** *– He that regardeth the day, regardeth it unto the Lord; and he that regardeth not the day, to the Lord he doeth not regard it. He that eateth, eateth to the Lord, for he giveth God thanks; and he that eateth not, to the Lord he eateth not, and giveth God thanks. For none of us liveth to himself, and no man dieth to himself. For whether we live, we live unto the Lord; and whether we die, we die unto the Lord: whether we live therefore, or die, we are the Lord's. For to this end Christ both died, and rose, and revived, that he might be Lord both of the dead and living.*

Reference:
2 Corinthians 5:14-15 *– For the love of Christ constraineth us; because we thus judge, that if one died for all, then were all dead: and that he died for all, that they which live should not henceforth live unto themselves, but unto him which died for them, and rose again.*

2. ***1 Corinthians 15:45-49*** *(NIV) – So it is written: "The first man Adam became a living being"; the last Adam, a life-giving spirit. The spiritual did not come first, but the natural, and after that the spiritual. The first man (Adam) was of the dust of the earth; the second man (Jesus) is of heaven. As was the earthly man, so are those who are of the earth; and as is the heavenly man, so also are those who are of heaven. And just as we have borne the image of the earthly man, so shall we bear the image of the heavenly man.*

References:
Isaiah 55:6-11 *(NIV) – Seek the LORD while he may be found; call on him while he is near. Let the wicked forsake their ways and the unrighteous their thoughts. Let them turn to the LORD, and he will have mercy on them, and to our God, for he will freely pardon. "For my thoughts are not your thoughts, neither are your ways my ways," declares the LORD. "As the heavens are higher than the earth, so are my ways higher than your ways and my thoughts than your thoughts. As the rain and the snow come down from heaven, and do not return to it without watering the earth and making it bud and flourish, so that it yields seed for the sower and bread for the eater, so is my word that goes out from my mouth: it will not return to me empty, but will accomplish what I desire and achieve the purpose for which I sent it. **John 1:1-5, 14** – In the beginning was the Word, and the Word was with God, and the Word was God. The same was in the beginning with God. All things were made by him; and without him was not any thing made that was made. In him was life; and the life was the light of men. And the light shineth in darkness; and the darkness comprehended it not. And the Word was made flesh, and dwelt among us, (and we beheld his glory, the glory as of the only begotten of the Father,) full of grace and truth. **John 15:1-8** – Jesus said, "I am the true vine, and my Father is the husbandman. Every branch in me that beareth not fruit he taketh away: and every branch that beareth fruit, he purgeth it, that it may bring forth more fruit. Now ye are clean through the word which I have*

spoken unto you. Abide in me, and I in you. As the branch cannot bear fruit of itself, except it abide in the vine; no more can ye, except ye abide in me. I am the vine, ye are the branches: He that abideth in me, and I in him, the same bringeth forth much fruit: for without me ye can do nothing. If a man abide not in me, he is cast forth as a branch, and is withered; and men gather them, and cast them into the fire, and they are burned. If ye abide in me, and my words abide in you, ye shall ask what ye will, and it shall be done unto you. Herein is my Father glorified, that ye bear much fruit; so shall ye be my disciples. **2 Corinthians 3:17-18** *– Now the Lord is that Spirit: and where the Spirit of the Lord is, there is liberty. But we all, with open face beholding as in a glass the glory of the Lord, are changed into the same image from glory to glory, even as by the Spirit of the Lord.* **James 1:22-25** *– But be ye doers of the word, and not hearers only, deceiving your own selves. For if any be a hearer of the word, and not a doer, he is like unto a man beholding his natural face in a glass: for he beholdeth himself, and goeth his way, and straightway forgetteth what manner of man he was. But whoso looketh into the perfect law of liberty, and continueth therein, he being not a forgetful hearer, but a doer of the work, this man shall be blessed in his deed.*

3. **Ephesians 2:1-10, 19-22** *– And you hath he quickened (made alive), who were dead in trespasses and sins; wherein in time past ye walked according to the course of this world, according to the prince of the power of the air, the spirit that now worketh in the children of disobedience: among whom also we all had our conversation (behavior) in times past in the lusts of our flesh, fulfilling the desires of the flesh and of the mind; and were by nature the children of wrath, even as others. But God, who is rich in mercy, for his great love wherewith he loved us, even when we were dead in sins, hath quickened (made us alive) together with Christ, (by grace ye are saved;) and hath raised us up together, and made us sit together in heavenly places in Christ Jesus: that in the ages to come he might shew the exceeding riches of his grace in his kindness toward us through Christ Jesus. For by grace are ye saved through faith; and that not of yourselves: it is the gift of God: not of works, lest any man should boast. For we are his workmanship, created in Christ Jesus unto good works, which God hath before ordained that we should walk in them. Now therefore ye are no more strangers and foreigners, but fellow citizens with the saints, and of the household of God; and are built upon the foundation of the apostles and prophets, Jesus Christ himself being the chief corner stone; in whom all the building fitly framed together groweth unto an holy temple in the Lord: in whom ye also are builded together for an habitation of God through the Spirit.*

References:
Psalm 27:5-6 *– For in the time of trouble he shall hide me in his pavilion: in the secret of his tabernacle shall he hide me; he shall set me up upon a rock. And now shall mine head be lifted up above mine enemies round about me: therefore will I offer in his tabernacle sacrifices of joy; I will sing, yea, I will sing praises unto the LORD.* **Acts 17:28-30** *– For in him (Christ) we live, and move, and have our being; as certain also of your own poets have said, for we are also his offspring. Forasmuch then as we are the offspring of God, we ought not to think that the Godhead is like unto gold, or silver, or stone, graven by art and man's device. And the times of this ignorance God winked at; but now commandeth all men every where to repent…* **Romans 8:11** *(NIV) – And if the Spirit of him who raised Jesus from the dead is living in you, he who raised Christ from the dead will also give life to your mortal bodies because of his Spirit who lives in you.* **Philippians 3:18-21** *– (For many walk, of whom I have told you often, and now tell you even weeping, that they are the enemies of the cross of Christ: whose end is destruction, whose God is their belly, and whose glory is in their shame, who mind earthly things.) For our conversation (citizenship) is in heaven; from whence also we look for the Saviour, the Lord Jesus Christ: who shall change our vile body, that it may be fashioned like unto his glorious body, according to the working whereby he is able even to subdue all things unto himself.*

Colossians 2:12-15 (NIV) – *Having been buried with him in baptism, in which you were also raised with him through your faith in the working of God, who raised him from the dead. When you were dead in your sins and in the uncircumcision of your flesh, God made you alive with Christ. He forgave us all our sins, having canceled the charge of our legal indebtedness, which stood against us and condemned us; he has taken it away, nailing it to the cross. And having disarmed the powers and authorities, he made a public spectacle of them, triumphing over them by the cross.* **Hebrews 12:22-24** – *But ye have come to Mount Sion (Zion), and unto the city of the living God, the heavenly Jerusalem, and to an innumerable company of angels, to the general assembly and church of the firstborn, which are written in heaven, and to God the Judge of all, and to the spirits of just men made perfect, and to Jesus the mediator of the new covenant, and to the blood of sprinkling, that speaketh better things than that of Abel.*

4. **Hebrews 9:14** – *How much more shall the blood of Christ, who through the eternal Spirit offered himself without spot to God, purge your conscience from dead works to serve the living God?*

References:
Luke 1:74-75 – *That he would grant unto us, that we being delivered out of the hand of our enemies might serve him without fear, in holiness and righteousness before him, all the days of our life.* **John 3:3 (NIV)** – *Jesus replied, "Very truly I tell you, no one can see the kingdom of God unless they are born again."* **Romans 13:13-14** – *Let us walk honestly, as in the day; not in rioting and drunkenness, not in chambering and wantonness, not in strife and envying. But put ye on the Lord Jesus Christ, and make not provision for the flesh, to fulfil the lusts thereof.* **Romans 12:1-2** – *I beseech you therefore, brethren, by the mercies of God, that ye present your bodies a living sacrifice, holy, acceptable unto God, which is your reasonable service. And be not conformed to this world: but be ye transformed by the renewing of your mind, that ye may prove what is that good, and acceptable, and perfect, will of God.* **Galatians 3:26-29** – *For ye are all the children of God by faith in Christ Jesus. For as many of you as have been baptized into Christ have put on Christ. There is neither Jew nor Greek, there is neither bond nor free, there is neither male nor female: for ye are all one in Christ Jesus. And if ye be Christ's, then are ye Abraham's seed, and heirs according to the promise.* **Galatians 6:15** – *For in Christ Jesus neither circumcision availeth any thing, nor uncircumcision, but a new creature.* **Ephesians 4:20-24** – *but ye have not so learned Christ; if so be that ye have heard him, and have been taught by him, as the truth is in Jesus: that ye put off concerning the former conversation (behavior) the old man, which is corrupt according to the deceitful lusts; and be renewed in the spirit of your mind; and that ye put on the new man, which after God is created in righteousness and true holiness.*

Here are some additional Scriptures relating to living in Christ: Romans 8:1-6; 1 Corinthians 1:24; Ephesians 1:3-23, 5:8-10, 14-17; Philippians 3:13-21; Hebrews 11:12-16; 1 Peter 1:13-16, 23-25; 2 Peter 1:17-21; 1 John 5:11-12, 20-21; 3 John 1:2.

Please refer to **Note 36a** for additional Scriptures relating to seeking God.

> **17(b)** *Therefore, I put off the old man by putting to death (depriving of power)* the evil desire lurking in my members [those animal impulses and all that is earthly in *me* that is employed in sin]: sexual vice, impurity, sensual appetites, unholy desires, and all greed and covetousness, for that is idolatry (the deifying of self and other created things instead of God). It is on account of these [very sins] that the [holy] anger of God is ever coming upon the sons of disobedience (those who are obstinately opposed to the divine will). (Colossians 3:5-6-AMPCE) *(Ref.: Colossians 3:5, 9)*

There are two parts to the old man. The first is found here in *Colossians 3:5* where in our own self-centeredness and self-seeking—independence from God—we try to fulfill and satisfy the cravings of the flesh derived from our carnal nature. The second part is found in *Colossians 3:8* (**Note 27a**). Let's look at *Colossians 3:5* in the King James Version – *"Mortify therefore your members which are upon the earth; fornication, uncleanness, inordinate affection, evil concupiscence, and covetousness, which is idolatry."* The word "mortify" in the Greek is *nekroo*. Its meaning in the Thayer's Greek Lexicon is "**to deprive of power, destroy the strength of:** i.e. the evil desire lurking in the members (of the body), Colossians 3:5." Let's look at the following words described in **17b** along with the corresponding word used in the King James Version and the Greek meaning in the Thayer's Greek Lexicon:

AMPCE	KJV	Greek Word and Meaning
- sexual vice	fornication	*porneia* – "properly, of illicit sexual intercourse in general."
- impurity	uncleanness	*akatharsia* – "in a moral sense, the impurity of lustful, luxurious, profligate living."
- sensual appetites	inordinate affection	*pathos* – "a feeling which the mind suffers, an affection of the mind, emotion, passion; passionate desire. In the N. T. in a bad sense, depraved passion."
- unholy	evil	*kakos* – "(morally, i.e.) of a mode of thinking, feeling, acting; base, wrong, wicked: of persons."
- desires	concupiscence	*epithymia* – "desire, craving, longing: specifically, desire for what is forbidden, lust."
- covetousness	covetousness	*pleonexia* – "greedy desire to have more, covetousness, avarice."

Again, the Greek word for "concupiscence," or as the *AMPCE* reads "desires" is *epithymia*. This Greek word is used in *Ephesians 4:22-24* where Paul is telling us,

> *...put off concerning the former conversation (behavior) the old man, which is corrupt according to the deceitful <u>lusts</u>; and be renewed in the spirit of your mind; and that ye put on the new man, which after God if created in righteousness and true holiness.*

Paul said, *"Walk in the Spirit, and ye shall not fulfil the lust of the flesh"* (Galatians 5:16). The word "lust" is the same Greek word *epithymia*. He also said, *"For to be carnally minded is death; but to be spiritually minded is life and peace"* (Romans 8:6). In order to walk in the Spirit, it is essential that we set our minds on things above by renewing the *spirit of our minds*. As we choose to fill our *inmost mind* with the purity, power, and life-giving flow of the Word of God, it begins to flush out the ingrained carnal beliefs and mindsets that hold us captive to the old man. The Greek word for "deceitful" in *Ephesians*

4:24, is *apate*. Its meaning in the Thayer's Greek Lexicon is "the lusts excited by deceit, i.e. by deceitful influences seducing to sin." Both *apate* (deceitful) and *epithymia* (concupiscence/lust) are used in *Mark 4:19* in the parable of the sower sowing the seed (the Word of God). Why is it so important to kill and deprive of power these acts? Jesus answers that question in this parable. In *Mark 4:7 – Jesus said, "And some (seed) fell among thorns, and the thorns grew up, and choked it, and it yielded no fruit."* He revealed the meaning of this part of the parable in *Mark 4:18-19*, where He said, *"And these are they which are sown among thorns; such as hear the word, and the cares of this world, and the* <u>*deceitfulness*</u> *of riches, and the* <u>*lusts*</u> *of other things entering in, choke the word, and it becometh unfruitful."* In this parable, the heart of man is the ground where the Word of God is sown. When our hearts are consumed with the cares of this world, deceitfulness of riches, and/or lust of other things we are consumed with ourselves causing our hearts to become defiled/polluted *(Mark 7:14-23)*. When this occurs, the only thing that grows in our heart ground are thorn plants that are hurtful to us and to anyone that tries to interfere with our self-consumption. Only through repentance before a holy God can the defilement be removed from our hearts through the cleansing blood of Christ and renewing our *inmost minds* to His truth *(1 John 1:7-9; Ephesians 5:25-27; 4:20-24)*.

These acts are manifestations of the old man—our self-centered carnal nature! We partake of these sins in order to fulfil the deep longings of our hearts and to gratify one thing—"ME," "MYSELF," and "I." It is deceptive to think that this type of grasping behavior can ever fulfill the deep longings of our hearts. I have found that the more I give into my flesh, the more it wants! It is only through the infilling of His Holy Spirit—His rivers of living water, renewing our minds to His truth, and true intimacy with the Lord (through prayer and surrender to His will), that the deep places of need and deprivation can be satisfied. It is only through our Creator's presence and His Words of truth that wholeness can come *(John 7:37-39; Romans 12:1-2; John 14:23, 17:17)*. God gives us richly all things to enjoy. He has given us all things that pertain to life and godliness, and He truly came to give us life and that more abundantly *(1 Timothy 6:17; 2 Peter 1:3; John 10:10)*. As we renew our minds to the truth of God's Word, it is essential that we guard our hearts from the cares of this world, the deceitfulness of riches, and lusts of other things in order for His Word to have full reign in our lives. Jesus said in *Luke 12:15 – "Take heed, and beware of covetousness: for a man's life consisteth not in the abundance of the things which he possesseth."* Colossians 3:5 in the Amplified Version helps us to see what idolatry truly is. *"It is the deifying of self and other created things instead of God."* It's putting ourselves, others, or things first place in our hearts and minds rather than our commitment and devotion to Him. Therefore, it is essential that we take an honest look at our lives and the things that we have built our lives upon to see exactly where our true love and devotion lies.

Let's look at several passages of Scripture to better understand God's view concerning this behavior. We will begin with *Luke 4:5-8* as a foundational Scripture where Satan tempted Jesus in the wilderness along with several references relating to idolatry:

Luke 4:5-8 – And the devil, taking him (Jesus) up into an high mountain, shewed unto him all the kingdoms of the world in a moment of time. And the devil said unto him, "All this power will I give thee, and the glory of them: for that is delivered unto me; and to whomsoever I will I give it. If thou therefore wilt worship me, all shall be thine." And Jesus answered and said unto him, "Get thee behind me, Satan: for it is written, 'Thou shalt worship the Lord thy God, and him only shalt thou serve.'"

References:

Deuteronomy 6:13 – Thou shalt fear the LORD thy God, and serve him… Deuteronomy 10:20 – Thou shalt fear the LORD thy God; him shalt thou serve, and to him shalt thou cleave… Joshua 24:14 – Now therefore fear the LORD, and serve him in sincerity and in truth: and put away the gods which your fathers served on the other side of the flood, and in Egypt; and serve ye the LORD. 1 Samuel 7:3 – And Samuel spake unto all the house of Israel, saying, "If ye do return unto the LORD with all your hearts, then put away the strange gods and Ashtaroth from among you, and prepare your hearts unto the LORD, and serve him only: and he will deliver you out of the hand of the Philistines." 1 Samuel 12:24 – Only fear the LORD, and serve him in truth with all your heart: for consider how great things he hath done for you.

Notice Jesus said in *Luke 4:8 – "Get thee behind me, Satan: for it is written, 'Thou shalt worship the Lord thy God, and him only shalt thou serve.'"* However in the other Scripture references, instead of using the phrase *"worship the Lord and serve Him"* the phrase *"fear the Lord and serve Him"* is used. This is important because when we reverence the Lord by turning away from our idolatrous behavior, we are truly worshipping Him.

The story that I eluded to in **Note 13b** goes along with this subject matter. Let's look at it again, a little closer, to better understand God's perspective on true worship. In *John 4*, Jesus revealed to the woman of Samaria His desire to bring fulfillment and satisfaction to the deep longings of her heart:

> *Now Jacob's well was there. Jesus therefore, being wearied from His journey, sat thus by the well. It was about the sixth hour. A woman of Samaria came to draw water. Jesus said to her, "Give Me a drink." For His disciples had gone away into the city to buy food. Then the woman of Samaria said to Him, "How is it that You, being a Jew, ask a drink from me, a Samaritan woman?" For Jews have no dealings with Samaritans. Jesus answered and said to her, "If you knew the gift of God, and who it is who says to you, 'Give Me a drink,' you would have asked Him, and He would have given you living water." The woman said to Him, "Sir, You have nothing to draw with, and the well is deep. Where then do You get that living water? Are You greater than our father Jacob, who gave us the well, and drank from it himself, as well as his sons and his livestock?" Jesus answered and said to her, "Whoever drinks of this water will thirst again, but whoever drinks of the water that I shall give him will never thirst. But the water that I shall give him will become in him a fountain of water springing up into everlasting life." The woman said to Him, "Sir, give me this water, that I may not thirst, nor come here to draw." Jesus said to her, "Go, call your husband, and come here." The woman answered and said, "I have no husband." Jesus said to her, "You have well said, 'I have no husband,' for you have had five husbands, and the one whom you now have is not your husband; in that you spoke truly."*
>
> (John 4:6-18, NKJV)

When the woman asked Jesus for this living water, Jesus went to the point of her need. He asked her to go call her husband and come to Him. Jesus knew that she was living with a man who was not her husband and prior to this, she had five husbands. There was a deep need in this woman to be loved, as with all of us, and she was trying to satisfy this need through a man, God's creation, instead of her Creator. Let's be clear—substance abuse, sexual vice, fame, fortune, etc., can never satisfy the deep longings of the human heart and soul. The story goes on:

The woman said to Him, "Sir, I perceive that you are a prophet. Our fathers worshiped on this mountain, and you Jews say that in Jerusalem is the place where one ought to worship." Jesus said to her, "Woman, believe Me, the hour is coming when you will neither on this mountain, nor in Jerusalem, worship the Father. You worship what you do not know; we know what we worship, for salvation is of the Jews. But the hour is coming, and now is, when the true worshipers will worship the Father in spirit and truth; for the Father is seeking such to worship Him. God is Spirit, and those who worship Him must worship in spirit and truth."

(John 4:19-24, NKJV)

Because of what Jesus did on the cross, being a true worshipper of God is putting off the old man and putting on the new man in Christ, by renewing the *spirit of our minds*. What Jesus is offering to "whosoever" is not religion but a true relationship with Him, the Creator of the universe and our personal Creator! The law cannot fulfill the deep longings of the heart, as it is an external commandment that can never get to the heart of the matter. Only Jesus, the Word of God, through the power of His Holy Spirit, His living water, which is the true source of life—can go into the depths of our being to bring righteousness, true holiness, joy, and peace to our hearts and souls—freeing us from all the cravings of the flesh. Jesus has made it possible for us to live out of this new creation, to become born again and to put on the new man in Christ. How glorious is that? He knows the deep longings and deprivations of the heart and soul that we try to fill through our own carnality. The fear of the Lord is healthy! The fear of the Lord is clean and enduring! It keeps us in a place of reverence and honor toward the One who loved us so much that He gave His only Son and toward the One who loved us so much that He gave His own life! Jesus paid the ultimate price in order for us to be free from sin and its penalty, restoring us back to His original intent.

His kingdom that dwells within us is righteousness, peace, and joy in the Holy Ghost *(Romans 14:17)*. His joy within us produces His strength day by day and moment by moment *(Nehemiah 8:10)*. We must understand that we are deceived if we think that living out of our sensual appetites will bring fulfillment and satisfaction. We will always come up empty and will continue to thirst for that which only Christ, our Creator, can give. Understand that there is pleasure in sin for a season but afterwards it brings death *(Hebrews 11:23-26; James 1:13-18)*. As I shared in **Note 15b**, let's look again at the following passage of Scripture in order to understand the origin of temptation:

Let no man say when he is tempted, "I am tempted of God": for God cannot be tempted with evil, neither tempteth he any man: but every man is tempted, when he is drawn away of his own lust, and enticed. Then when lust hath conceived, it bringeth forth sin: and sin, when it is finished, bringeth forth death. Do not err, my beloved brethren. Every good gift and every perfect gift is from above, and cometh down from the Father of lights, with whom is no variableness, neither shadow of turning. Of his own will begat he us with the word of truth, that we should be a kind of firstfruits of his creatures.

(James 1:13-18)

The word "death" in the Greek is *thanatos* and its meaning in the Thayer's Greek Lexicon is "metaphorically, the loss of that life which alone is worthy of the name, i.e. 'the misery of soul arising from sin, which begins on earth but lasts and increases after the death of the body.'"

I am well aware of the finished product of sin in my own life; sin had damaged my soul to the point where I thought I was going to have a nervous breakdown as everything that I had built my life upon was crumbling around me. My main sin was living a lifestyle of homosexuality, thinking I was born that way, and therefore trying to fill the deep longings of my heart through another woman. I indulged in this lifestyle for thirteen years, from the age of thirteen until the age of twenty-six, until my world began crashing around me and I felt there was nothing left. Paul writes in the book of Romans,

> *Professing themselves to be wise, they became fools, and changed the glory of the uncorruptible God into an image made like to corruptible man, and to birds, and four-footed beasts, and creeping things. Wherefore God also gave them up to uncleanness through the lusts of their own hearts, to dishonour their own bodies between themselves: who changed the truth of God into a lie, and worshipped and served the creature more than the Creator, who is blessed for ever. Amen. For this cause God gave them up unto vile affections: for even their women did change the natural use into that which is against nature: and likewise also the men, leaving the natural use of the woman, burned in their lust one toward another; men with men working that which is unseemly, and receiving in themselves that recompence of their error which was meet. And even as they did not like to retain God in their knowledge, God gave them over to a reprobate mind, to do those things which are not convenient; being filled with all unrighteousness, fornication, wickedness, covetousness, maliciousness; full of envy, murder, debate, deceit, malignity; whisperers, backbiters, haters of God, despiteful, proud, boasters, inventors of evil things, disobedient to parents, without understanding, covenantbreakers, without natural affection, implacable, unmerciful.*
>
> (Romans 1:22-31)

This was me! In **My Story – Part One - Volume 1**, I share how at the age of eighteen I turned to the Lord, but only for a brief time and then went back into the homosexual lifestyle. My selfish behavior began to intensify and *Ephesians 2:1-5* describes exactly what was going on within me as there was no restraint on my flesh. I conducted myself in the passions of my flesh; my behavior was governed by my corrupt and sensual nature, obeying the impulses and deep cravings of the flesh and thoughts of my mind. I was controlled by the prince of the power of the air, the demon spirit that works in the sons and daughters of disobedience. I was a selfish mess! I had come to a place where I didn't even want the Lord's name mentioned in my presence. On several occasions, random people whom I had never met approached me to share Jesus and I would say, "I don't want to hear it!" There was one guy that tried to share Jesus with me and I literally began pushing him away and telling him to be quiet and to leave me alone! I didn't understand then, but God had given me over to a reprobate mind. He had given me over to my own sin and the consequences of that sin. During that time, while at a gay bar one evening, I was talking to a girlfriend of mine (who was bisexual, attracted to both men and women) and I distinctly remember telling her, "You can leave this lifestyle, I can't!" I was imprisoned to my own sin! At the age of twenty-six, a few months after I had asked the Lord to come back into my life, He showed me in Scripture exactly my state-of-being:

> *For the LORD hath spoken "… Why should ye be stricken any more? Ye will revolt more and more: the whole head is sick, and the whole heart faint. From the sole of the foot even unto the head there is no soundness in it; but wounds, and bruises, and putrifying sores: they have not been closed, neither bound up, neither mollified with ointment."*
>
> (Isaiah 1:2-6)

The Lord began to restore my soul, bringing healing and wholeness to my broken and sick heart. I have found that only Jesus Christ, my Creator, can satisfy the deep longings of my heart through the life giving flow of His Spirit *(John 4:10-18, 7:37-39)*! Please read **My Story – Part One - Volume 1** for details.

As we choose to renew our minds to God's Word, we will be equipped to kill those evil desires lurking in our members. For it is through this renewal process that we become spiritually minded, producing life and peace within us. Thank God Jesus paid the penalty for our sin and He is faithful to deliver us from our sin if we cry out to Him in true repentance. Jesus ever lives to make intercession for us and He is the <u>mediator</u> between God and man *(Romans 8:34; Hebrews 7:22-25; 1 Timothy 2:5)*. The Greek word for "mediator" is *mesites* and its meaning in the Thayer's Greek Lexicon is "one who intervenes between two, either in order to make or restore peace and friendship, or form a compact or for ratifying a covenant. Christ, interposed by his death and restored the harmony between God and man which human sin had broken." He is also our advocate – *1 John 2:1* – *"My little children, these things write I unto you, that ye sin not. And if any man sin, we have an advocate with the Father, Jesus Christ the righteous."* The Greek word for "advocate" is *parakletos* and is also used in *John 14:16, 26, 15:26* and *16:7* when referring to the Holy Spirit as our Comforter. Its meanings in the Thayer's Greek Lexicon is "universally, one who pleads another's cause with one, an intercessor: so of Christ, in his exaltation at God's right hand, pleading with God the Father for the pardon of our sins, 1 John 2:1. In the widest sense, a helper, succorer, aider, assistant; so of the Holy Spirit destined to take the place of Christ with the apostles (after his ascension to the Father), to lead them to a deeper knowledge of the gospel truth, and give them divine strength needed to enable them to undergo trials and persecutions on behalf of the divine kingdom: John 14:16, 26; John 15:26; John 16:7."

If you are struggling with sin, I want to encourage you to begin to renew the *spirit of your mind* to the truth of God's Word (**Personalized Scipture Guide - Volume 1**) and to be real with the Lord by going to **A Personal Prayer Journal – From your heart to His – Part Two - Volume 1**. Part Two is designed to help you work through any idolatrous sins of the old man that is hindering your relationship with Christ (e.g., the love for money and/or fame, gluttony, alcohol, drugs, pornography, sex outside of God's design for marriage, emotional dependency, control, manipulation, covetousness). After completing Part Two, if any of these sins you have listed have become a stronghold in your life you would then go to Part Three in order to be specific and real with the Lord (i.e., journaling the circumstance/situation and/or thought process that causes us to go after others and/or things instead of Christ). After being real with the Lord and confessing your sins to Him, I recommend that you prayerfully consider having an accountability partner, a mature Christian, who can help you walk through any areas of difficulty. Confessing your transgressions to another, after having confessed them to the Lord, will help you work through some of these areas in your life as you bring them to the light and receive prayer *(James 5:16)*. If you are still having difficulty, I recommend that you prayerfully consider attending a program like *Living Waters* and/or Christian counseling (one who understands that Jesus is the only true healer) where the Lord can bring to light and set you free from any strongholds or root issues (e.g., areas in your life that may have taken place in your childhood that helped form core beliefs/strongholds that are keeping you bound to the old man). Confession, forgiveness, and healing prayer with members of the body of Christ helps to bring healing to your heart and soul. (Please see **Support and Help**.)

The Lord's desire is to restore us back to true innocence. Jesus said in *Mark 10:14 – "Suffer the little children to come unto me, and forbid them not: for of such is the kingdom of God."* Let's also look at a passage of Scripture where Jesus reveals to us who is the greatest in His kingdom:

> *At the same time came the disciples unto Jesus, saying, "Who is the greatest in the kingdom of heaven?" And Jesus called a little child unto him, and set him in the midst of them, and said, "Verily I say unto you, except ye be converted, and become as little children, ye shall not enter into the kingdom of heaven. Whosoever therefore shall humble himself as this little child, the same is greatest in the kingdom of heaven."*
>
> (Matthew 18:1-4)

It is also important to understand that God does not have a problem with someone who is wealthy. There were many men and women of God in the Bible who were wealthy. Paul writes,

> *Charge them that are rich in this world, that they be not highminded, nor trust in uncertain riches, but in the living God, who giveth us richly all things to enjoy; that they do good, that they be rich in good works, ready to distribute, willing to communicate (share); laying up in store for themselves a good foundation against the time to come, that they may lay hold on eternal life.*
>
> (1 Timothy 6:17-19)

It is God who gives us richly all things to enjoy! Money is not the root of all evil, the <u>love</u> of money is the root of all evil *(1 Timothy 6:10)*. Jesus said in *John 10:10 – "…I am come that they might have life, and that they might have it more abundantly."* Jesus is our Shepherd and the lover and the anchor of our souls *(Psalm 23; 1 Peter 2:25; Romans 8:35-39; Hebrews 6:19)*. He desires to meet our needs by His presence and to feed, direct, and guide us by His Word through the power of His Spirit, for He is our Counselor (He will always be our Counselor; as He will always bring us back to the foundation of God; to that which is solid, the Gospel truth – *Proverbs 19:21; Isaiah 28:29; Jeremiah 18:15, 32:19; Luke 6:47-49; Romans 11:33-36; 16:25-27; Ephesians 1:11; Hebrews 6:17-20)*. I share more about the topic of wealth in **Note 43**.

In closing and to recap, He has given us His Holy Spirit in order to lead us into a deeper knowledge of the Gospel truth and to provide divine strength for us to undergo our own personal trials, tribulation, and temptations as we seek to do His will. He is good and nothing this world has to offer compares to His goodness! Here is a passage of Scripture where the "wisdom of God" confirms this statement:

> *All the words of my mouth are in righteousness; there is nothing froward or perverse in them. They are all plain to him that understandeth, and right to them that find knowledge. Receive my instruction, and not silver; and knowledge rather than choice gold. For wisdom is better than rubies; and all the things that may be desired are not to be compared to it. The fear of the LORD is the beginning of wisdom: and the knowledge of the holy is understanding. For by me thy days shall be multiplied, and the years of thy life shall be increased.*
>
> (Proverbs 8:8-11, 9:10-11)

As we choose to turn away from our sensual appetites and turn to Him, we are choosing to walk in the fear of the Lord which opens the door to His wisdom in our lives. We enjoy the fruits of His wisdom as we choose to renew our minds to the truth of His Word. Solomon, whom God gave wisdom and exceedingly much understanding, and largeness of heart like the sand on the seashore *(1 Kings 4:29),* said it best,

> *All has been heard; the end of the matter is: Fear God [revere and worship Him, knowing that He is] and keep His commandments, for this is the whole of man [the full, original purpose of his creation, the object of God's providence, the root of character, the foundation of all happiness, the adjustment to all inharmonious circumstances and conditions under the sun] and the whole [duty] for every man. For God shall bring every work into judgment, with every secret thing, whether it is good or evil.*
>
> (Ecclesiastes 12:13-14, AMPCE)

In the New Testament, this is referring to putting on the new man in Christ.

Below are Scriptures relating to idolatry and the importance of walking in His ways:

1. ***Deuteronomy 28:13-14*** *– And the LORD shall make thee the head, and not the tail; and thou shalt be above only, and thou shalt not be beneath; if that thou hearken unto the commandments of the LORD thy God, which I command thee this day, to observe and to do them: and thou shalt not go aside from any of the words which I command thee this day, to the right hand, or to the left, to go after other gods to serve them.*

References:

Joshua 7:10-26 – And the LORD said unto Joshua, "Get thee up; wherefore liest thou thus upon thy face? Israel has sinned, and they have also transgressed my covenant which I commanded them: for they have even taken of the accursed thing, and have also stolen, and dissembled also, and they have put it even among their own stuff. Therefore, the children of Israel could not stand before their enemies, but turned their backs before their enemies, because they were accursed: neither will I be with you any more, except ye destroy the accursed from among you. Up, sanctify the people, and say, 'Sanctify yourselves against tomorrow:' for thus saith the LORD God of Israel, 'There is an accursed thing in the midst of thee, O Israel: thou canst not stand before thine enemies, until ye take away the accursed thing from among you. In the morning therefore ye shall be brought according to your tribes: and it shall be, that the tribe which the LORD taketh shall come according to the families thereof; and the family which the LORD shall take shall come by households; and the household which the LORD shall take shall come man by man. And it shall be, that he that is taken with the accursed thing shall be burnt with fire, he and all that he hath: because he hath transgressed the covenant of the LORD, and because he hath wrought folly in Israel.'" So Joshua rose up early in the morning, and brought Israel by their tribes; and the tribe of Judah was taken: and he brought the family of Judah; and he took the family of the Zarhites: and he brought the family of the Zarhites man by man; and Zabdi was taken: and he brought his household man by man; and Achan, the son of Carmi, the son of Zabdi, the son of Zerah, of the tribe of Judah, was taken. And Joshua said unto Achan, "My son, give, I pray thee, glory to the LORD God of Israel, and make confession unto him; and tell me now what thou hast done; hide it not from me." And Achan answered Joshua, and said, "Indeed I have sinned against the LORD God of Israel, and thus and thus have I done: when I saw among the spoils a goodly Babylonish garment, and two hundred shekels of silver, and a wedge of gold of fifty shekels weight, then I coveted them, and took them; and, behold, they are hid in the earth in the midst of my tent, and the silver under it." So Joshua sent messengers, and they ran unto the tent; and, behold, it was hid in his tent, and the silver under it. And they *took them out of the midst of the tent, and brought them unto Joshua, and unto all the children of Israel, and laid them out before the LORD. And Joshua, and all Israel with him, took Achan the son of Zerah, and the silver, and the garment, and the wedge of gold, and his sons, and his daughters, and his oxen, and his asses, and his sheep, and his tent, and all that he had: and they brought them unto the **valley of Achor**. And Joshua said, "Why hast thou troubled us? The LORD shall trouble thee this day." And all Israel stoned him with stones, and burned them with fire, after they had stoned them with stones. And they raised over him a great heap of stones unto this day. So the LORD turned from the fierceness of his anger. Wherefore the name of the place was called, the **valley of Achor**, unto this day. **Psalm 32:5** – I acknowledged my sin unto thee, and mine iniquity have I not hid. I said, "I will confess my transgressions unto the LORD;" and thou forgavest the iniquity of my sin. **Proverbs 28:13-14, 16** – He that covereth his sins shall not prosper: but whoso confesseth and forsaketh them shall have mercy. Happy is the man that feareth alway: but he that hardeneth his heart shall fall into mischief. …he that hateth covetousness shall prolong his days. **Jeremiah 3:12-13** – Go and proclaim these words toward the north, and say, 'Return, thou backsliding Israel, saith the LORD; 'and I will not cause mine anger to fall upon you: for I am merciful,' saith the LORD, 'and I will not keep anger for ever. Only acknowledge thine iniquity, that thou hast transgressed against the LORD thy God…' **Jeremiah 31:34** – "And they shall teach no more every man his neighbour, and every man his brother, saying, 'Know the LORD': for they shall all know me, from the least of them unto the greatest of them," saith the LORD. "For I will forgive their iniquity, and I will remember their sin no more." **Hosea 2:15** – I will give her her vineyards from thence, and the **valley of Achor** for a door of hope… (Where the **valley of Achor** was a "valley of trouble" for Achan, even though he confessed his sin. Because he troubled Israel the LORD troubled him and his family by destroying them. Now, because of the blood of Jesus, the LORD transformed the **valley of Achor** or "trouble" into a door of hope for us, as we humble ourselves and confess our sins). **Ephesians 2:1-7** – And you hath he quickened (made alive), who were dead in trespasses and sins; wherein in time past ye walked according to the course of this world, according to the prince of the power of the air, the spirit that now worketh in the children of disobedience: among whom also we all had our conversation (behavior) in times past in the lusts of our flesh, fulfilling the desires of the flesh and of the mind; and were by nature the children of wrath, even as others. But God, who is rich in mercy, for his great love wherewith he loved us, even when we were dead in sins, hath quickened us (made us alive) together with Christ, (by grace ye are saved;) and hath raised us up together, and made us sit together in heavenly places in Christ Jesus: that in the ages to come he might shew the exceeding riches of his grace in his kindness toward us through Christ Jesus. **1 Thessalonians 1:9-10** – …and how ye turned to God from idols to serve the living and true God… **James 5:16** – Confess your faults (falls, offences, sins, trespasses) one to another, and pray one for another, that ye may be healed. The effectual fervent prayer of a righteous man availeth much. (This is why it's not good to confess your trespasses to just anyone. After having confessed your sins to the Lord, when confessing your faults to another, it is important that you confess them to a mature believer in Christ whose prayers avail much). **Hebrews 11:13-16** – These all died in faith, not having received the promises, but having seen them afar off, and were persuaded of them, and embraced them, and confessed that they were strangers and pilgrims on the earth. For they that say such things declare plainly that they seek a (heavenly) country… **1 Peter 2:11** – Dearly beloved, I beseech (exhort) you as strangers and pilgrims, abstain from fleshly lusts, which war against the soul. **1 Peter 2:24-25 (NIV)** – "He himself bore our sins" in his body on the cross, so that we might die to sins and live for righteousness; "by his wounds you have been healed." For "you were like sheep going astray," but now you have returned to the Shepherd and Overseer of your souls. **1 Peter 4:1-5** – Forasmuch then as Christ hath suffered for us in the flesh, arm yourselves likewise with the same mind: for he that hath suffered in the flesh hath ceased from sin; that he no longer should live the rest of his time in the flesh to the lusts of men, but to the will of God. For the time past of our life may suffice us to have wrought the will of the Gentiles, when we* *walked in lasciviousness, lusts, excess of wine, revellings, banquetings, and abominable idolatries: wherein they think it strange that ye run not with them to the same excess of riot, speaking evil of you: who shall give account to him that is ready to judge the quick (living) and the dead.*

2. ***Psalm 103:10-19*** *– He hath not dealt with us after our sins; nor rewarded us according to our iniquities. For as the heaven is high above the earth, so great is his mercy toward them that fear him. As far as the east is from the west, so far hath he removed our transgressions from us. Like as a father pitieth his children, so the LORD pitieth them that fear him. For he knoweth our frame; he remembereth that we are dust. As for man, his days are as grass: as a flower of the field, so he flourisheth. For the wind passeth over it, and it is gone; and the place thereof shall know it no more. But the mercy of the LORD is from everlasting to everlasting upon them that fear him, and his righteousness unto children's children; to such as keep his covenant and to those that remember his commandments to do them. The LORD hath prepared his throne in the heavens; and his kingdom ruleth over all.*

References:
Psalm 119:36-38 *(AMPCE) – Incline my heart to Your testimonies and not to covetousness (robbery, sensuality, unworthy riches). Turn away my eyes from beholding vanity (idols and idolatry); and restore me to vigorous life and health in Your ways. Establish Your word and confirm Your promise to Your servant, which is for those who reverently fear and devotedly worship You.* ***Proverbs 16:6*** *– By mercy and truth iniquity is purged: and by the fear of the LORD men depart from evil.* ***Proverbs 22:5*** *– Thorns and snares are in the way of the froward (perverse): he that doth keep his soul shall be far from them.* ***James 1:22-27*** *– But be ye doers of the word, and not hearers only, deceiving your own selves. For if any be a hearer of the word, and not a doer, he is like unto a man beholding his natural face in a glass: for he beholdeth himself, and goeth his way, and straightway forgetteth what manner of man he was. But whoso looketh into the perfect law of liberty, and continueth therein, he being not a forgetful hearer, but a doer of the work, this man shall be blessed in his deed. If any man among you seem to be religious, and bridleth not his tongue, but deceiveth his own heart, this man's religion is vain. Pure religion and undefiled before God and the Father is this, to visit the fatherless and widows in their affliction, and to keep himself unspotted from the world.*

3. ***Psalm 119:1-3, 9, 11*** *– Blessed are the undefiled in the way, who walk in the law of the LORD. Blessed are they that keep his testimonies, and that seek him with the whole heart. They also do no iniquity: they walk in his ways. Wherewithal shall a young man cleanse his way? By taking heed thereto according to thy word. Thy word have I hid in mine heart, that I might not sin against thee.*

References:
Proverbs 13:15 *– Good understanding giveth favour: but the way of transgressors is hard.* ***Mark 7:20-23*** *– And Jesus said, "that which cometh out of the man, that defileth the man. For from within, out of the heart of men, proceed evil thoughts, adulteries, fornications, murders, thefts, covetousness, wickedness, deceit, lasciviousness, an evil eye, blasphemy, pride, foolishness: all these evil things come from within, and defile the man."* ***Luke 12:13-21*** *– And one of the company said unto him, "Master, speak to my brother, that he divide the inheritance with me. And he (Jesus) said unto him, "Man, who made me a judge or a divider over you?" And he said unto them, "Take heed, and beware of covetousness: for a man's life consisteth not in the abundance of the things which he possesseth." And he spake a parable unto them, saying, "The ground of a certain rich man brought forth plentifully: and he thought within himself, saying, 'What shall I do, because I have no room where to bestow my fruits?' and he said, 'This will I do: I will pull down my barns, and build*

*greater; and there will I bestow all my fruits and my goods.' And I will say to my soul, 'Soul, thou hast much goods laid up for many years; take thine ease, eat, drink, and be merry.' But God said unto him, 'Thou fool, this night thy soul shall be required of thee: then whose shall those things be, which thou hast provided?' "So is he that layeth up treasure for himself, and is not rich toward God." **Romans 6:1-4** (NIV) – What shall we say, then? Shall we go on sinning so that grace may increase? By no means! We are those who have died to sin; how can we live in it any longer? Or don't you know that all of us who were baptized into Christ Jesus were baptized into his death? We were therefore buried with him through baptism into death in order that, just as Christ was raised from the dead through the glory of the Father, we too may live a new life.*

Here are some additional Scriptures relating to idolatry and the importance of walking in His ways: 1 Samuel 15:22-23; Proverbs 6:32-33; Jeremiah 7:23; Daniel 4:27; John 5:1-15; John 8:10-12; Acts 17:30-31; Romans 2:4-6, 5:6-11, 6:13-23, 7:4-8:7, 13:11-14; 1 Corinthians 6:9-20, 10:1-22; Ephesians 5:1-17; 1 Thessalonians 1:9-10, 4:1-8; 2 Timothy 2:19; Titus 2:11-14; Hebrews 12:14-29, 13:5-6; James 1:13-18; 1 Peter 1:22-25; 1 John 1:5-10, 5:20-21.

Please refer to **Notes 15a**, **15b**, and **18a** for additional information and Scriptures relating to this subject matter.

Please refer to **Note 43** for additional information and Scriptures relating to wealth.

Please refer again to **Notes 16a** and **16b** for additional information and Scriptures relating to His strength and faithfulness.

Please refer to **Note 26b** for additional information relating to the Holy Spirit, His living water.

18(a) For if *I* live according to [the dictates of] the flesh, *I* will surely die. But if through the power of the [Holy] Spirit *I am* [habitually] putting to death (making extinct, deadening) the [evil] deeds prompted by the body, *I* shall [really and genuinely] live forever. For all who are led by the Spirit of God are sons of God. Search me, O God, and know my heart: try me, and know my thoughts: and see if *there be any* wicked way in me, and lead me in the way everlasting. (Romans 8:13-14-AMPCE; Psalm 139:23-24)

The word "wicked" in Hebrew is *otseb* meaning "<u>an idol</u> (as fashioned); also pain (bodily or mental):–idol, sorrow, x wicked." (Please read **Note 17b**.) One way idolatry can find its roots in our lives is through the way we internalize things that happened to us, especially as a young child (e.g., woundings, hurts, offenses, trauma that produced fear). These roots become buried within us producing protective vows, judgments, strongholds, and/or unforgiveness which can produce ungodly behavior patterns that are contrary to God's will for us. It is only by His Word and through the power of His Spirit that these roots can be revealed and removed *(Luke 3:8-9; Hebrews 4:12-13)*. Much of the time, the Lord chooses to use mature members of His body to help bring His healing to others *(James 5:16-17)*. In the King James Version, *Romans 8:13* reads, *"For if ye live after the flesh, ye shall die..."* The word "after" is the Greek word *kata*. Its meaning in the Thayer's Greek Lexicon is "according to anything as a standard, agreeably to." Therefore, this passage of Scripture doesn't apply to someone who occasionally slips up or is truly seeking the Lord's freedom from a particular stronghold. This applies to someone who repeatedly or habitually lives after their carnal nature as a standard or normal way of life. The word "die" in the Greek is *apothnesko* and its meaning in the Thayer's Greek Lexicon is "of eternal death, as it is called, i.e. to be subject to eternal misery, and that, too, already beginning on earth." What a sobering statement! In order to better understand this it is important to look back at what happened to Adam and Eve:

> *Now the serpent was more subtle than any beast of the field which the Lord God had made. And he said unto the woman, "Yea, hath God said, 'Ye shall not eat of every tree of the garden?'" And the woman said unto the serpent, "We may eat of the fruit of the trees of the garden: but of the fruit of the tree which is in the midst of the garden, God hath said, 'Ye shall not eat of it, neither shall ye touch it, lest ye die.'" And the serpent said unto the woman, "Ye shall not surely die: For God doth know that in the day ye eat thereof, then your eyes shall be opened, and ye shall be as gods, knowing good and evil." And when the woman saw that the tree was good for food, and that it was pleasant to the eyes, and a tree to be desired to make one wise, she took of the fruit thereof, and did eat, and gave also unto her husband with her; and he did eat. And the eyes of them both were opened, and they knew that they were naked; and they sewed fig leaves together, and made themselves aprons.*
>
> (Genesis 3:1-7)

Satan is also referred to as the serpent in the book of Revelation:

> *And I saw an angel come down from heaven, having the key of the bottomless pit and a great chain in his hand. And he laid hold on the dragon, that old serpent, which is the Devil, and Satan, and bound him a thousand years.*
>
> (Revelation 20:1-3)

Before Eve was created, when God put Adam in the garden of Eden, He commanded him, saying,

> *"Of every tree of the garden thou mayest freely eat: but of the tree of the knowledge of good and evil, thou shalt not eat of it: for in the day that thou eatest thereof thou shalt surely die." And the Lord God said, "It is not good that the man should be alone; I will make him an help meet for him."*
>
> (Genesis 2:16-18)

The word "die" in the Hebrew is *muwth* meaning "to die (literally or figuratively); …(put to, worthy of) death, destroy(-er), cause to, be like to, must) die…" Satan, the serpent, deceived Eve into eating from the tree of the knowledge of good and evil and she, in turn, gave the fruit to Adam and he ate and the eyes of them both were opened and they saw that they were naked… In partaking of this fruit, they lost their spiritual authority and began to function out of a different nature, the carnal nature. The carnal mind is enmity against God, and therefore, those who are in the flesh cannot please Him *(Romans 8:7-8)*. Notice Adam did not physically die when he ate from the tree of the knowledge of good and evil, he physically died when he was 930 years old. Both Adam and Eve died spiritually as soon as they ate from the tree and therefore began to see things from a different perspective by living out of a different nature, independent from God. They were no longer in union and in oneness with God, as the glory of God was removed from within them. They became their own gods, determining their own destiny, and were subject to Satan's power and craftiness. Let's look at the following passage of Scripture that reveals the result of Satan's power and craftiness in the heart and soul of man:

> *And God saw that the wickedness of man was great in the earth, and that every imagination of the thoughts of his heart was only evil continually. And it repented the LORD that he had made man on the earth, and it grieved him at his heart. And the LORD said, "I will destroy man whom I have created from the face of the earth; both man, and beast, and the creeping thing, and the fowls of the air; for it repenteth me that I have made them." But Noah found grace in the eyes of the LORD.*

> (Genesis 6:5-8)

Thank God for Noah or we wouldn't be here!

Remember when Satan was tempting Jesus in the wilderness?

> *...And the devil, taking him up into an high mountain, shewed unto him all the kingdoms of the world in a moment of time. And the devil said unto him, "All this power will I give thee, and the glory of them: for that is delivered unto me; and to whomsoever I will I give it. If thou therefore wilt worship me, all shall be thine." And Jesus answered and said unto him, "Get thee behind me, Satan: for it is written, 'Thou shalt worship the Lord thy God, and him only shalt thou serve...'"*

> (Luke 4:1-12)

Jesus successfully conquered death, hell, and the grave by continuing to ward off Satan's temptations with, "*It is written...*,"something Adam failed to do in the garden. He could have said something like, "God said not to eat of the tree of the knowledge of good and evil, so I'm not going to do it!" The good news for us is that Jesus came to take back that which was taken from the first Adam through his disobedience. Paul wrote,

> *For as in Adam all die, even so in Christ shall all be made alive. And so it is written, "The first man Adam was made a living soul;" the last Adam was made a quickening (life-giving) spirit. Howbeit that was not first which is spiritual, but that which is natural; and afterward that which is spiritual. The first man is of the earth, earthy: the second man is the Lord from heaven. As is the earthy, such are they also that are earthy: and as is the heavenly, such are they also that are heavenly. And as we have borne the image of the earthy, we shall also bear the image of the heavenly. Now this I say, brethren, that flesh and blood cannot inherit the kingdom of God; neither doth corruption inherit incorruption.*

> (1 Corinthians 15:22, 45-50)

This is why it is essential to become born again, not of a corruptible seed but of an incorruptible seed, by the Word of God, which lives and abides forever. This born-again creation restores us back to God's original intent for mankind *(1 Peter 1:23)*. Jesus said in *John 3:3* that except a man be born again, he cannot see the kingdom of God! When God sentenced the serpent, He foretold of the coming of Jesus Christ to free us from our carnal nature through the new birth in order to become partakers of His divine nature, restoring us back in union and oneness with God in Christ Jesus *(John 17:11, 20-26)*. The key to living out of the reality of this new nature is to deprive of power the carnal impulses of the flesh by putting on the new man in Christ *(1 Peter 1:22-2:3; Ephesians 4:20-24)*. Paul writes,

> *Now unto him that is able to do exceeding abundantly above all that we ask or think, according to the power that worketh in us, unto him be glory in the church by Christ Jesus throughout all ages, world without end. Amen.*

(Ephesians 3:20-21)

This is very important! Paul, in *Romans 7* was very aware of this dilemma:

> *For when we were in the flesh, the motions of sins, which were by the law, did work in our members to bring forth fruit unto death. But now we are delivered from the law, that being dead wherein we were held; that we should serve in newness of spirit, and not in the oldness of the letter. What shall we say then? Is the law sin? God forbid. Nay, I had not known sin, but by the law: for I had not known lust, except the law had said, 'Thou shalt not covet.' But sin, taking occasion by the commandment, wrought (produced) in me all manner of concupiscence (evil desire). For without the law sin was dead. For I was alive without the law once: but when the commandment came, sin revived, and I died. And the commandment, which was ordained to life, I found to be unto death. For sin, taking occasion by the commandment, deceived me, and by it slew me. Wherefore the law is holy, and the commandment holy, and just, and good. Was then that which is good made death unto me? God forbid. But sin, that it might appear sin, working death in me by that which is good; that sin by the commandment might become exceeding sinful. <u>For we know that the law is spiritual: but I am carnal, sold under sin.</u> For that which I do I allow not: for what I would, that do I not; but what I hate, that do I. If then I do that which I would not, I consent unto the law that it is good. Now then it is no more I that do it, but sin that dwelleth in me. For I know that in me (that is, in my flesh,) dwelleth no good thing: for to will is present with me; but how to perform that which is good I find not. For the good that I would I do not: but the evil which I would not, that I do. Now if I do that I would not, it is no more I that do it, but sin that dwelleth in me. I find then a law, that, when I would do good, evil is present with me. For I delight in the law of God after the inward man (the born-again creation): but I see another law in my members, <u>warring against the law of my mind</u>, and bringing me into captivity to the law of sin which is in my members. O wretched man that I am! Who shall deliver me from the body of this death? I thank God through Jesus Christ our Lord. So then with the mind I myself serve the law of God; but with the flesh the law of sin.*

(Romans 7:5-25)

Paul continues on and explains the key to our freedom in Christ,

> *There is therefore now no condemnation to them which are in Christ Jesus, who walk not after the flesh, but after the Spirit. For the law of the Spirit of life in Christ Jesus hath made me free from the law of sin and death. For what the law could not do, in that it was weak through the flesh, God sending his own Son in the likeness of sinful flesh, and for sin, condemned sin in the flesh: that the righteousness of the law might be fulfilled in us, who walk not after the flesh, but after the Spirit. For they that are after the flesh do mind the things of the flesh; but they that are after the Spirit the things of the Spirit. <u>For to be carnally</u>*

minded is death; but to be spiritually minded is life and peace. Because the carnal mind is enmity against God: for it is not subject to the law of God, neither indeed can be. So then they that are in the flesh cannot please God.

(Romans 8:1-8)

This passage of Scripture is very powerful, revealing to us why God sent His only Son, to condemn sin in the flesh. The law given by Moses, the old covenant, could not make a person holy or righteous; if there could have been a law to make us righteous then Christ would not have had to come *(Galatians 2:21)*. Again, the law is spiritual and holy, but because we are carnal, sold under sin, the law could not break through that carnality and free us from sin! (See **Note 18b**.) This is the reason God sent His Son in the likeness of sinful flesh to condemn sin in the flesh that the righteousness of the "law" might be fulfilled in those who walk not after the flesh, but after the Spirit. Jesus took away the sin of the world and His sacrifice is available to all who will receive it *(John 1:29; John 3:16-17)*! Let's look again at the following passage of Scripture:

For they that are after the flesh do mind the things of the flesh; but they that are after the Spirit the things of the Spirit. <u>For to be carnally minded is death; but to be spiritually minded is life and peace</u>. Because the carnal mind is enmity against God: for it is not subject to the law of God, neither indeed can be. So then they that are in the flesh cannot please God.

(Romans 8:5-8)

This goes back again to the importance of renewing the *spirit of your mind* or your *inmost mind* to the born-again creation within *(Ephesians 4:22-24)*. We please God by living out of this new birth, producing the fruit of the Spirit in our lives *(Galatians 5:22-25)*. Paul confirmed this when he wrote,

For this ye know, that no whoremonger, nor unclean person, nor covetous man, who is an idolater, hath any inheritance in the kingdom of Christ and of God. Let no man deceive you with vain words: for because of these things cometh the wrath of God upon the children of disobedience. Be not ye therefore partakers with them. For ye were sometimes darkness, but now are ye light in the Lord: walk as children of light: (for the fruit of the Spirit is in all goodness and righteousness and truth;) proving what is acceptable unto the Lord.

(Ephesians 5:5-10)

Our responsibility is to bring our sin to the Lord, those hidden things of the heart that we do not want exposed. It is very important that we come out from hiding and be real with the Lord (He already knows anyway – *Psalm 139:1-2*). If after confessing your sin to Him you are still struggling, you may need to confess it to a specific other, a mature believer in the body of Christ, and have an accountability partner. As we are faithful to do this, it's like turning on a light switch in a dark room causing the strength of that darkness to disappear.

Confess to one another therefore your faults (your slips, your false steps, your offenses, your sins) and pray [also] for one another, that you may be healed and restored [to a spiritual tone of mind and heart]. The earnest (heartfelt, continued) prayer of a righteous man makes tremendous power available [dynamic in its working].

(James 5:16, AMPCE)

Why do we confess to specific others—mature believers in the body of Christ? Below are five very important reasons:

1. Christ works through His body.
2. It helps to dismantle pride.
3. It provides a place of power that is needed for deliverance and healing.
4. It dispels the power of darkness by bringing it out into the light.
5. A mature believer in Christ will not disclose your sin to others.

Below are five additional passages of Scripture concerning confession:

1. ***Psalm 32:5*** *– I acknowledged my sin unto thee, and mine iniquity have I not hid. I said, I will confess my transgressions unto the LORD; and thou forgavest the iniquity of my sin.*
2. ***Proverbs 28:13 (NIV)*** *– Whoever conceals their sins does not prosper, but the one who confesses and renounces them finds mercy.*
3. ***Matthew 3:4-6*** *– And the same John had his raiment (clothing) of camel's hair, and a leathern girdle about his loins; and his meat was locust and wild honey. Then went out to him Jerusalem, and all Judaea, and all the region round about Jordan, and were baptized of him in Jordan, confessing their sins.*
4. ***Acts 19:18-20*** *– And many that believed came, and confessed, and shewed their deeds. Many of them also which used curious arts brought their books together, and burned them before all men: and they counted the price of them, and found it fifty thousand pieces of silver. So mightily grew the word of God and prevailed.*
5. ***1 John 1:9*** *– If we confess our sins, he is faithful and just to forgive us our sins, and to cleanse us from all unrighteousness.*

The Lord was made to be sin for us so that we might be made the righteousness of God in Him *(2 Corinthians 5:21)*. Paul writes,

> *Christ hath redeemed us from the curse of the law, being made a curse for us: for it is written, 'Cursed is every one that hangeth on a tree': that the blessing of Abraham might come on the Gentiles through Jesus Christ; that we might receive the promise of the Spirit through faith. And if ye be Christ's, then are ye Abraham's seed, and heirs according to the promise.*
>
> (Galatians 3:13-14, 29)

Always remember that <u>Jesus came to save the world not to condemn it</u> as noted in the two Scripture references below:

1. ***John 3:16-17*** *– Jesus Said, "For God so loved the world, that he gave his only begotten Son, that whosoever believeth in him should not perish, but have everlasting life. For God sent not his Son into the world to condemn the world; but that the world through him might be saved."*
2. ***Matthew 9:10-13*** *– And it came to pass, as Jesus sat at meat in the house, behold, many publicans and sinners came and sat down with him and his disciples. And when the Pharisees saw it, they said unto his disciples, 'Why eateth your Master with publicans and sinners?" But*

when Jesus heard that, he said unto them, "They that be whole need not a physician, but they that are sick. But go ye and learn what that meaneth, I will have mercy, and not sacrifice: for I am not come to call the righteous, but sinners to repentance."

Below are Scriptures relating to God's "all knowing" presence and our carnality:

1. ***1 Samuel 16:6-7*** – *And it came to pass, when they were come, that he (Samuel) looked on Eliab, and said, "Surely the LORD's anointed is before him." But the Lord said unto Samuel, "Look not on his countenance, or on the height of his stature; because I have refused him: for the LORD seeth not as man seeth; for man looketh on the outward appearance, but the LORD looketh on the heart."*

Reference:
1 Samuel 17:28-29 *(NASB)* This passage of Scripture gives us a clue as to what the Lord was seeing in Eliab's heart – *Now Eliab his oldest brother heard when he spoke to the men; and Eliab's anger burned against David and he said, "Why have you come down? And with whom have you left those few sheep in the wilderness? I know your insolence and the wickedness of your heart; for you have come down in order to see the battle." But David said, "What have I done now?"* (Evidently, Eliab was constantly badgering David and what Eliab was accusing David of is exactly what was working in his own heart! The Lord resists the proud but gives grace to the humble – *1 Peter 5:5*).

2. ***Psalm 33:15*** *(NIV)* – *He who forms the hearts of all, who considers everything they do.*

References:
1 Chronicles 28:9 – *David said to his son Solomon, "And thou, Solomon my son, know thou the God of thy father, and serve him with a perfect heart and with a willing mind: for the LORD searcheth all hearts, and understandeth all the imaginations of the thoughts..."* ***Psalm 94:11-12*** – *The LORD knoweth the thoughts of man, that they are vanity. Blessed is the man whom thou chastenest, O LORD, and teachest out of thy law.* ***Psalm 139:1-4*** – *A Psalm of David. O LORD, thou hast searched me, and known me. Thou knowest my downsitting and mine uprising, thou understandeth my thought afar off. Thou compassest my path and my lying down, and art acquainted with all my ways. For there is not a word in my tongue, but, lo, O LORD, thou knowest it altogether.* ***Matthew 9:4*** – *And Jesus knowing their thoughts said, "Wherefore think ye evil in your hearts?"* ***John 2:24-25*** – *But Jesus did not commit himself unto them, because he knew all men, and needed not that any should testify of man: for he knew what was in man.* ***Hebrews 4:12-13*** – *For the word of God is quick (alive), and powerful, and sharper than any twoedged sword, piercing even to the dividing asunder of soul and spirit, and of the joints and marrow, and is a discerner of the thoughts and intents of the heart. Neither is there any creature that is not manifest in his sight: but all things are naked and opened unto the eyes of him with whom we have to do.* ***Hebrews 8:10*** – *"For this is the covenant that I will make with the house of Israel after those days," saith the Lord; "I will put my laws into their mind, and write them in their hearts: and I will be to them a God, and they shall be to me a people."*

3. ***Proverbs 15:32-33*** – *He that refuseth instruction despiseth his own soul: but he that heareth reproof getteth understanding. The fear of the LORD is the instruction of wisdom; and before honour is humility.*

References:

Job 5:17 – *Behold, happy is the man whom God correcteth: therefore, despise not thou the chastening of the Almighty.* **Psalm 25:7-14** – *Remember not the sins of my youth, nor my transgressions: according to thy mercy remember me for thy goodness' sake, O LORD. Good and upright is the LORD: therefore will he teach sinners in the way. The meek will he guide in judgment: and the meek will he teach his way. All the paths of the LORD are mercy and truth unto such as keep his covenant and his testimonies. For thy name's sake, O LORD, pardon mine iniquity; for it is great. What man is he that feareth the LORD? Him shall he teach in the way that he shall choose. His soul shall dwell at ease; and his seed shall inherit the earth. The secret of the LORD is with them that fear him; and he will shew them his covenant.* **1 Corinthians 11:26-32** *(NIV) – For whenever you eat this bread and drink this cup, you proclaim the Lord's death until he comes. So then, whoever eats the bread or drinks the cup of the Lord in an unworthy manner will be guilty of sinning against the body and blood of the Lord. Everyone ought to examine themselves before they eat of the bread and drink from the cup. For those who eat and drink without discerning the body of Christ eat and drink judgment on themselves. That is why many among you are weak and sick, and a number of you have fallen asleep. But if we were more discerning with regard to ourselves, we would not come under such judgment. Nevertheless, when we are judged in this way by the Lord, we are being disciplined so that we will not be finally condemned with the world.* **Hebrews 12:5-10** *(NKJV) – And you have forgotten the exhortation which speaks to you as to sons: "My son, do not despise the chastening of the LORD, nor be discouraged when you are rebuked by Him; for whom the LORD loves He chastens, and scourges every son whom He receives." If you endure chastening, God deals with you as with sons; for what son is there whom a father does not chasten? But if you are without chastening, of which all have become partakers, then you are illegitimate and not sons. Furthermore, we have had human fathers who corrected us, and we paid them respect. Shall we not much more readily be in subjection to the Father of spirits and live? For they indeed for a few days chastened us as seemed best to them, but He for our profit, that we may be partakers of His holiness.*

4. **Isaiah 48:17-19, 22** – *Thus saith the LORD, thy Redeemer, the Holy one of Israel; "…O that thou hadst hearkened to my commandments! Then had thy peace been as a river, and thy righteousness as the waves of the sea… There is no peace," saith the LORD, "unto the wicked."*

References:
Isaiah 57:19-21 – *"I create the fruit of the lips; Peace, peace to him that is far off, and to him that is near," saith the Lord; "and I will heal him. But the wicked are like the troubled sea, when it cannot rest, whose waters cast up mire and dirt. "There is no peace," says the LORD, "to the wicked."* **James 1:1-8** *(NIV) – … But when you ask, you must believe and not doubt, because the one who doubts is like a wave of the sea, blown and tossed by the wind. That person should not expect to receive anything from the Lord. Such a person is double-minded and unstable in all they do.* (God considers the wicked as those whose hearts are not toward Him, who mind earthly things) – **Philippians 3:17-20** – *Brethren, be followers together of me, and mark them which walk so as ye have us for an ensample (pattern). (For many walk, of whom I have told you often, and now tell you even weeping, that they are the enemies of the cross of Christ: whose end is destruction, whose God is their belly, and whose glory is in their shame, who mind earthly things.) for our conversation (citizenship) is in heaven; from whence also we look for the Saviour, the Lord Jesus Christ.*

5. **Ezekiel 18:30-32** – *"Therefore I will judge you, O house of Israel, every one according to his ways," saith the Lord GOD. "Repent, and turn yourselves from all your transgressions; so iniquity shall not be your ruin. Cast away from you all your transgressions, whereby ye have transgressed; and make you a new heart and a new spirit: for why will ye die, O house of Israel? For I have no pleasure in the death of him that dieth," saith the Lord GOD: "wherefore turn yourselves, and live ye."*

References:

Psalm 32:5 – *I acknowledged my sin unto thee, and mine iniquity have I not hid. I said, I will confess my transgressions unto the LORD; and thou forgavest the iniquity of my sin. Selah (pause and think about it).*
Proverbs 14:14, 16 (NKJV) – *The backslider in heart will be filled with his own ways, but a good man will be satisfied from above. A wise man fears and departs from evil, but a fool rages and is self-confident.*
Proverbs 16:6, 25 – *By mercy and truth iniquity is purged: and by the fear of the LORD men depart from evil. There is a way that seemeth right unto a man, but the end thereof are the ways of death.* **Proverbs 19:16, 27** *(NKJV)* – *He who keeps the commandment keeps his soul, but he who is careless of conduct will die. Cease listening to instruction, my son, and you will stray from the words of knowledge.* **Proverbs 28:13-14, 26** – *He that covereth his sins shall not prosper: but whoso confesseth and forsaketh them shall have mercy. Happy is the man that feareth alway: but he that hardeneth his heart shall fall into mischief. He that trusteth in his own heart is a fool: but whoso walketh wisely, he shall be delivered.* **Isaiah 1:18-19** – *"Come now, and let us reason together," saith the LORD: "Though your sins be as scarlet, they shall be as white as snow; though they be red like crimson, they shall be as wool. If ye be willing and obedient, ye shall eat the good of the land.* **Micah 7:18-19** – *Who is a God like unto thee, that pardoneth iniquity, and passeth by the transgression of the remnant of his heritage? He retaineth not his anger for ever, because he delighteth in mercy. He will turn again, he will have compassion upon us; he will subdue our iniquities; and thou wilt cast all their sins into the depths of the sea.* **Romans 6:17-23** – *But God be thanked, that ye were the servants of sin, but ye have obeyed from the heart that form of doctrine which was delivered you. Being then made free from sin, ye became the servants of righteousness. I speak after the manner of men because of the infirmity (weakness) of your flesh: for as ye have yielded your members servants to uncleanness and to iniquity unto iniquity; even so now yield your members servants to righteousness unto holiness. For when ye were the servants of sin, ye were free from righteousness. What fruit had ye then in those things whereof ye are now ashamed? For the end of those things is death. But now being made free from sin, and become servants to God, ye have your fruit unto holiness, and the end everlasting life. For the wages of sin is death; but the gift of God is eternal life through Jesus Christ our Lord.*

Here are some additional Scriptures relating to God's "all knowing" presence and our carnality: 2 Chronicles 27:6; Psalm 62:12; Proverbs 13:13-15, 21, 14:30; 22:8, 24:12; Jeremiah 17:10; Matthew 3:2, 7:21-27, 12:34-37, 16:27; Romans 2:4-10, 7:5-6, 14:7-12; 2 Corinthians 4:3-4, 5:10, 10:3-6; Galatians 5:19-25, 6:7-10; 1 Thessalonians 5:22; 1 Timothy 1:9-11; Titus 2:11-14; Hebrews 2:18, 9:14; 1 Peter 4:1-5; Revelation 2:23.

Please refer to **Notes 15a**, **15b**, and **17b** for additional information and Scriptures relating to this subject matter.

18(b) *For* the thief comes only in order to steal and kill and destroy. *You* came that *I* may have and enjoy life, and have it in abundance (to the full, till it overflows). (John 10:10-AMPCE)

It is written in *Hebrews 13:8*, *"Jesus Christ the same yesterday, and to day, and for ever."* He never changes! Paul writes in *Colossians 3:1 (NASB)* – *"Therefore if you have been raised up with Christ, keep seeking the things above, where Christ is, seated at the right hand of God."* Jesus Christ came that we might have life and that more abundantly! This abundant life can only be found in Him (*John 10:10*). David writes in *Psalm 16:11 (NASB)* – *"You will make known to me the path of life; in Your presence is fullness of joy; in Your right hand there are pleasures forever."* This path of life and fullness of joy can only be found in Christ! It is only through the Lord's obedience unto death that we can truly experience this abundant life and fullness of joy. Through His obedience, the kingdom of God dwells within us—righteousness, peace, and joy in the Holy Ghost *(Luke 17:20-21; Romans 14:17)*. In Him we live and move and have our being *(Acts 17:28)*.

It is important to look at the following four passages of Scripture relating to Satan, the god of falsehood and evil, as it relates to this world and to God's creation, male and female!

1. ***2 Corinthians 4:3-4*** *– But if our gospel be hid, it is hid to them that are lost: in whom the god of this world hath blinded the minds of them which believe not, lest the light of the glorious gospel of Christ, who is the image of God, should shine unto them.*

2. ***Ephesians 2:1-3*** *– And you hath he quickened (made alive), who were dead in trespasses and sins; wherein in time past ye walked according to the course of this world, according to the prince of the power of the air, the spirit that now worketh in the children of disobedience: among whom also we all had our conversation (behavior) in times past in the lusts of our flesh, fulfilling the desires of the flesh and of the mind; and were by nature the children of wrath, even as others.*

3. ***1 John 2:16-17*** *– For all that is in the world, the lust of the flesh, and the lust of the eyes, and the pride of life, is not of the Father, but is of the world. And the world passeth away, and the lust thereof: but he that doeth the will of God abideth forever.*

4. ***1 John 5:19*** *– And we know that we are of God, and the whole world lieth in wickedness.*

Now let's look again at what took place with Adam and Eve to see how Satan deceived Eve in order to take Adam's God-given authority:

Now the serpent was more subtle than any beast of the field which the Lord God had made. And he said unto the woman, "Yea, hath God said, 'Ye shall not eat of every tree of the garden?'" And the woman said unto the serpent, "We may eat of the fruit of the trees of the garden: but of the fruit of the tree which is in the midst of the garden, God hath said, 'Ye shall not eat of it, neither shall ye touch it, lest ye die.'" And the serpent said unto the woman, "Ye shall not surely die: For God doth know that in the day ye eat thereof, then your eyes shall be opened, and ye shall be as gods, knowing good and evil." And when the woman saw that the tree was good for food, and that it was pleasant to the eyes, and a tree to be desired to make one wise, she took of the fruit thereof, and did eat, and gave also unto her husband with her; and he did eat. And the eyes of them both were opened, and they knew that they were naked; and they sewed fig leaves together, and made themselves aprons.

(Genesis 3:1-7)

In this passage of Scripture, the serpent, who is called the prince of the power of the air in *Ephesians 2:1-2*, tempted Eve to partake of the tree of the knowledge of good and evil. He tempted her with the lust of the flesh *(when Eve saw that the tree was good for food)*, the lust of the eyes *(when Eve saw that the tree was pleasant to the eyes)*, and the pride of life *(when Eve perceived that the tree was desirable to make one wise; to be as gods)*. Satan used the same tactic when he tempted Jesus in the wilderness *(Matthew 4:1-10)*. He uses the same tactic on us as John explains,

Love not the world, neither the things that are in the world. If any man love the world, the love of the Father is not in him. For all that is in the world, <u>the lust of the flesh</u>, and <u>the lust of the eyes</u>, and <u>the pride of life</u>, is not of the Father, but is of the world. And the world passeth away, and the lust thereof: but he that doeth the will of God abideth for ever.

(1 John 2:15-17)

Again, as explained in **Note 18a**, as soon as Adam ate of the forbidden fruit, it didn't take long for Satan's power and craftiness to begin to rule through man's carnal nature:

And God saw that the wickedness of man was great in the earth, and that every imagination of the thoughts of his heart was only evil continually. And it repented the LORD that he had made man on the earth, and it grieved him at his heart. And the LORD said, "I will destroy man whom I have created from the face of the earth; both man, and beast, and the creeping thing, and the fowls of the air; for it repenteth me that I have made them." But Noah found grace in the eyes of the LORD.

(Genesis 6:5-8)

In the following passage of Scripture, God commanded Adam:

"Of every tree of the garden thou mayest freely eat: but of the tree of the knowledge of good and evil, thou shalt not eat of it: for in the day that thou eatest thereof thou shalt surely die." And the LORD God said, "It is not good that the man should be alone; I will make him an help meet for him."

(Genesis 2:16-18)

God commanded Adam not Eve! The moment Eve ate of the fruit, before she gave the fruit to Adam, her eyes were not opened – *Genesis 3:6-7 – "…she took of the fruit thereof and did eat, and gave also unto her husband with her; and he did eat. <u>And the eyes of them both were opened</u>, and they knew that they were naked…"* Adam was Eve's covering and protector and as long as he chose not to eat of that fruit, Eve was covered. Also, we must remember that the life of the flesh is in the blood which comes from the seed of man *(Leviticus 17:11)*. The man's seed or sperm gives life to the egg within the woman. Woman then becomes the carrier of that life within her. Before Adam ate of the fruit of the knowledge of the tree of good and evil his seed was pure and incorruptible. At that point, Adam's offspring, born after him, would not have been tainted by sin and death! However, after Adam ate of the fruit his seed became impure and corruptible and we are the product of that seed. Mary became the carrier of Jesus Christ, the last Adam, who was the Son of God. The seed that impregnated her was pure and incorruptible as it came from the power of the Most High God. In the same way, if only Eve had partaken of the fruit of the tree of the knowledge of good and evil, and not Adam, Adam's pure and incorruptible seed would have produced pure and holy offspring. Therefore, I believe, if Eve alone had partaken of the forbidden fruit there would not have been life altering consequences *(1 Corinthians 15:45; Luke 1:30-35)*. What God intended in the beginning for mankind is still His plan!

Jesus Christ came that we might have life and that more abundantly! Christ has redeemed us, but we are not exempt from Satan's craftiness to keep us from God's best by detouring us to what we think, in our wisdom, will bring us life *(Ephesians 6:10-12)*. Remember, Eve was in a perfect environment and she was deceived. How much more can we be deceived and drawn away from God's best by Satan's craftiness! As Paul said in *2 Corinthians 11:3, AMPCE, "But [now] I am fearful, lest that even as the serpent beguiled Eve by his cunning, so your minds may be corrupted and seduced from wholehearted and sincere and pure devotion to Christ."* Through a twisted lie, Satan (the serpent) deceived Eve to rebel against God's will in the hopes that when she offered the fruit to Adam he would also partake. In Adam's disobedience, Satan's desire was achieved causing both Adam and Eve and their seed after them to operate and function out of a carnal nature—independent from God, produced by a corruptible seed *(Isaiah 14:12-15; Genesis 3:1-4)*. This is why the law given by Moses could not make us perfect, because of this carnal nature. This is why Jesus came in order for a spiritual circumcision to take place within our hearts to strip away the whole corrupt flesh life (our carnal nature) from within us so that we can walk in an entirely new nature, His divine nature within—the born-again creation or hidden man of the heart, our true selves!

What God intended in the beginning for mankind is still His plan! Let's see how He chose to restore us back to His original intent. Paul writes,

> *Wherefore, as by one man sin entered into the world, and death by sin; and so death passed upon all men, for that all have sinned: (For until the law sin was in the world: but sin is not imputed when there is no law. Nevertheless, death reigned from Adam to Moses, even over them that had not sinned after the similitude (likeness) of Adam's transgression, who is the figure of him that was to come. But not as the offence, so also is the free gift. For if through the offence of one many be dead, much more the grace of God, and the gift by grace, which is by one man, Jesus Christ, hath abounded unto many. And not as it was by one that sinned, so is the gift: for the judgment was by one to condemnation, but the free gift is of many offences unto justification. For if one man's offence death reigned by one; much more they which receive abundance of grace and of the gift of righteousness shall reign in life by one, Jesus Christ.) Therefore as by the offence of one judgment came upon all men to condemnation; even so by the righteousness of one the free gift came upon all men unto justification of life. For as by one man's disobedience many were made sinners, so by the obedience of one shall many be made righteous. Moreover the law entered, that the offence might abound. But where sin abounded, grace did much more abound: that as sin hath reigned unto death, even so might grace reign through righteousness unto eternal life by Jesus Christ our Lord.*
>
> (Romans 5:12-21)

Paul also writes,

> *And so it is written, "The first man Adam was made a living soul; the last Adam was made a quickening spirit." Howbeit that was not first which is spiritual, but that which is natural; and afterward that which is spiritual. The first man is of the earth, earthy: the second man is the Lord from heaven. As is the earthy, such are they also that are earthy: and as is the heavenly, such are they also that are heavenly. And as we have borne the image of the earthy, we shall also bear the image of the heavenly.*
>
> (1 Corinthians 15:45-49)

This is why we must be born again, produced by an incorruptible seed from above *(1 Peter 1:22-25)*! Peter writes,

Seeing ye have purified your souls in obeying the truth through the Spirit unto unfeigned love of the brethren, see that ye love one another with a pure heart fervently: being born again, not of corruptible seed, but of incorruptible, by the word of God, which liveth and abideth forever. For all flesh is as grass, and all the glory of man as the flower of grass. The grass withereth, and the flower thereof falleth away: but the word of the Lord endureth for ever. And this is the word which by the gospel is preached unto you. Wherefore laying aside all malice, and all guile, and hypocrisies, and envies, and all evil speakings, as newborn babes, desire the sincere milk of the word, that ye may grow thereby: if so be ye have tasted that the Lord is gracious.

(1 Peter 1:22-2:3)

Paul writes,

In Him also you were circumcised with a circumcision not made with hands, but in a [spiritual] circumcision [performed by] Christ by stripping off the body of the flesh [the whole corrupt, carnal nature with its passions and lusts].

(Colossians 2:11, AMPCE)

Paul also writes in the book of Romans,

We know that our old (unrenewed) self was nailed to the cross with Him in order that [our] body [which is the instrument] of sin might be made ineffective and inactive for evil, that we might no longer be the slaves of sin.

(Romans 6:6, AMPCE)

Again, Jesus came that we might have life and that more abundantly! Our carnal nature produces death and must be crucified. Satan cannot be everywhere at the same time—his rule is through our carnal nature *(Romans 8:5-8; James 3:14-18)*. After Adam and Eve ate from the tree of the knowledge of good and evil, God said to the serpent,

Because thou hast done this, thou art cursed above all cattle, and above every beast of the field; upon thy belly shalt thou go, and dust shalt thou eat all the days of thy life: <u>and I will put enmity between thee and the woman, and between thy seed and her seed; it shall bruise thy head, and thou shalt bruise his heel</u>.   HE

(Genesis 3:14-15)

When referring to the woman, I believe God was declaring to the serpent or Satan the following: The "incorruptible seed" of Jesus Christ (the last Adam) which produces the new creation, His bride—the church, will bruise or overwhelm the head or the authority of carnality produced by the "corruptible seed" which came through Adam's disobedience.

It is also very important that when we come to God and receive Jesus Christ as our Lord and Savior and are enlightened through His Word that we turn not away from Him. If we choose to walk away from Him, God forbid, we open ourselves up to the enemy of our soul who comes only to steal from us, to deceive us into giving up, and to destroy what God intends for us to have *(John 10:10; 1 Peter 5:8-10)*. I am a prime example of this. I received Jesus Christ as my Lord and Savior at the age of

eighteen and sought Him diligently for two years. At the age of twenty I made the foolish decision to walk away from Him! When I made that decision, I said to Him, "Lord, I can't serve You and do what I want to do so I'm going to have to leave." Below are two regretful consequences that took place in my life because of this decision. Please read *My Story – Part One - Volume 1* for details:

1. This decision opened the door to the enemy of my soul, Satan, and I was given a protective covering from him that kept the born-again creation within me hidden for twenty years after I came back to the Lord at the age of twenty-six. This covering was removed from me at the age of forty-six. (Please see *My Story – Part Two - Volume 1* for details.)

2. During those six years, from the age of twenty to twenty-six, I was running so hard to fulfill the cravings of my flesh, as deep within me I saw myself as a reject. My whole existence was to try to gain happiness and I thought that finding the right woman would do just that; but in my futile search, along with drinking alcohol and partaking in other drugs to help ease my pain, I found that God's creation "woman" could not fill the deep longings of my heart and soul. At the end of those six years, there was no soundness left in me, I was full of wounds and had absolutely no peace (*Isaiah 1:4-7; Galatians 6:7-8*). This originated from deception and led to demonic oppression which had a strong influence over my thoughts, feelings, and actions.

Thank God for His restoration in my life! Jesus Christ is an amazing and wonderful Lord and Savior!

In lieu of this, I would like for us to look at the following passage of Scripture:

> *Be sober, be vigilant; because your adversary the devil, as a roaring lion, walketh about, seeking whom he may devour: whom resist steadfast in the faith, knowing that the same afflictions are accomplished in your brethren that are in the world. But the God of all grace, who hath called us unto his eternal glory by Christ Jesus, after that ye have suffered a while, make you perfect, stablish, strengthen, settle you.*
>
> (1 Peter 5:8-10)

Notice that Peter said, "*after you have suffered a while*" and *Acts 14:22* reads "*...and that we must through much tribulation enter into the kingdom of God!*" The key to endure suffering is to be rooted in Christ in the same way a mature oak tree is rooted in the ground which requires patience. If we allow patience to have her perfect work, we will become strong believers in Christ and whole, wanting nothing, as we will be totally fulfilled in Him (*James 1:2-4*). When the storms come to a deeply rooted oak tree, it is virtually impossible to pull that tree out of the ground because of the strength of its root system. In using this analogy, babes in Christ who <u>are not</u> deeply rooted in Him when the storms of life come, some may turn away from the Lord thinking that the Word of God does not work. In *Luke 8*, Jesus spoke a parable comparing the Word of God to seed that is sown in the ground; the ground being compared to the heart of man. *Luke 8:5-6 – "A sower went out to sow his seed: ...and some fell upon a rock; and as soon as it was sprung up, it withered away, because it lacked moisture."* He then gave the understanding of the parable:

> *Now the parable is this: the seed is the word of God. They on the rock are they, which, when they hear, receive the word with joy; and these have no root, which for a while believe, and in time of temptation fall away.*

(Luke 8:11, 13)

As babes in Christ, the Lord's will is for us, as born-again believers, to desire the sincere milk of the Word that we may grow in the things of God and trust Him through the trials of life. Through relationship with Him—rooted and built up in Him and established in the faith, the trials and pressures of life then become part of our resistance, or strength training, in order for us to become stronger in Him *(Ephesians 3:17; Colossians 2:7)*. See **Note 4a** for details. The following passage of Scripture is the result of a mature believer in Christ:

> *For our light, momentary affliction (this slight distress of the passing hour) is ever more and more abundantly preparing and producing and achieving for us an everlasting weight of glory [beyond all measure, excessively surpassing all comparisons and all calculations, a vast and transcendent glory and blessedness never to cease!], since we consider and look not to the things that are seen but to the things that are unseen; for the things that are visible are temporal (brief and fleeting), but the things that are invisible are deathless and everlasting.*
>
> (2 Corinthians 4:17-18, AMPCE)

God so loves us that He gave His only begotten Son so that when we receive Him as our Lord and Savior and choose to live out of His nature within us, we can walk in newness of life *(John 3:16; Romans 6:4)*. Jesus destroyed the works of the devil. John writes in *1 John 3:8 – "He that committeth sin is of the devil; for the devil sinneth from the beginning. For this purpose, the Son of God was manifested, that he might destroy the works of the devil."* This is why Jesus said in *John 14:30, "…the prince of this world cometh, and hath nothing in me."* Satan rules through our carnal sin nature. Jesus did not have this nature within Him as He was born of a virgin, conceived by an incorruptible seed by the power of the Holy Spirit. Again, this is why it is essential that we become born again by an incorruptible seed, the Word of God that lives and abides forever. It is also essential to renew the *spirit of our minds* or *inmost mind* to the truth of God's Word in order to grow up in Christ and put on the new man *(1 Peter 1:23; Ephesians 4:22-24)*. He has given us all things that pertain to life and godliness. Peter writes,

> *According as his divine power hath given unto us all things that pertain unto life and godliness, through the knowledge of him that hath called us to glory and virtue: whereby are given unto us exceeding great and precious promises: that by these ye might be partakers of the divine nature, having escaped the corruption that is in the world through lust.*
>
> (2 Peter 1:3-4)

Below are Scriptures relating to abundant life and eternal life in Christ:

1. ***Proverbs 8:35** – For whoso findeth me (wisdom) findeth life, and shall obtain favour of the LORD.*

References:
*1 Corinthians 1:24 – But unto them which are called, both Jews and Greeks, Christ the power of God, and the wisdom of God. **Luke 6:46-49** – Jesus said, "And why call ye me, 'Lord, Lord,' and do not the things which I say? Whosoever cometh to me, and heareth my sayings, and doeth them, I will shew you to whom he is like: he is like a man which built an house, and digged deep, and laid the foundation on a rock: and when the flood arose, the stream beat vehemently upon that house, and could not shake it: for it was founded upon a rock. But he that heareth, and doeth not, is like a man that without a foundation built an house upon the*

*earth; against which the stream did beat vehemently, and immediately it fell; and the ruin of that house was great." **1 Timothy 6:6-12** – But godliness with contentment is great gain. For we brought nothing into this world, and it is certain we can carry nothing out. And having food and raiment let us be therewith content. But they that will be rich fall into temptation and a snare, and into many foolish and hurtful lusts, which drown men in destruction and perdition. For the love of money is the root of all evil: which while some coveted after, they have erred from the faith, and pierced themselves through with many sorrows. But thou, O man of God, flee these things; and follow after righteousness, godliness, faith, love, patience, meekness. Fight the good fight of faith, lay hold on eternal life, whereunto thou art also called...* (Only the righteousness that comes through Jesus Christ leads to life!).

2. ***John 16:5-15*** *(NKJV)* – *"But now I go away to Him who sent Me, and none of you asks Me, 'Where are You going?' But because I have said these things to you, sorrow has filled your heart. Nevertheless, I tell you the truth. It is to your advantage that I go away; for if I do not go away, the Helper will not come to you; but if I depart, I will send Him to you. And when He has come, He will convict the world of sin, and of righteousness, and of judgment: of sin, because they do not believe in Me; of righteousness, because I go to My Father and you see Me no more; of judgment, because the ruler of this world is judged. I still have many things to say to you, but you cannot hear them now. However, when He, the Spirit of truth, has come, He will guide you into all truth; for He will not speak on His own authority, but whatever He hears He will speak; and He will tell you things to come. He will glorify Me, for He will take of what is Mine and declare it to you. All things that the Father has are Mine. Therefore, I said that He will take of Mine and declare it to you."*

3. ***John 17:1-3*** – *These words spake Jesus, and lifted up his eyes to heaven, and said, "Father, the hour is come; glorify thy Son, that thy Son also may glorify thee: as thou hast given him power over all flesh, that he should give eternal life to as many as thou hast given him. And this is life eternal, that they might know thee the only true God, and Jesus Christ, whom thou hast sent."*

References:
2 Peter 1:2-4 – *Grace and peace be multiplied unto you through the knowledge of God, and of Jesus our Lord, according as his divine power hath given unto us all things that pertain unto life and godliness, through the knowledge of him that hath called us to glory and virtue: whereby are given unto us exceeding great and precious promises: that by these ye might be partakers of the divine nature, having escaped the corruption that is in the world through lust.* ***1 John 1:1-10*** – *That which was from the beginning, which we have heard, which we have seen with our eyes, which we have looked upon, and our hands have handled, of the Word of life; (for the life was manifested, and we have seen it, and bear witness, and shew unto you that eternal life, which was with the Father, and was manifested unto us;) that which we have seen and heard declare we unto you, that ye also may have fellowship with us: and truly our fellowship is with the Father, and with his son Jesus Christ. And these things write we unto you, that your joy may be full. This then is the message which we have heard of him, and declare unto you, that God is light, and in him is no darkness at all. If we say that we have fellowship with him, and walk in darkness, we lie, and do not the truth: but if we walk in the light, as he is in the light, we have fellowship one with another, and the blood of Jesus Christ his Son cleanseth us from all sin. If we say that we have no sin, we deceive ourselves, and the truth is not in us. If we confess our sins, he is faithful and just to forgive us our sins, and to cleanse us from all unrighteousness. If we say that we have not sinned, we make him a liar, and his word is not in us.* ***1 John 4:9*** – *In this was manifested the love of God toward us, because that God sent his only begotten Son into the world, that we might live through him.* ***1 John 5:11-13, 20-21*** – *And this is the record, that God hath given to us eternal*

life, and this life is in his Son. He that hath the Son hath life; and he that hath not the Son of God hath not life. These things have I written unto you that believe on the name of the Son of God; the ye may know that ye have eternal life, and that ye may believe on the name of the Son of God. And we know that the Son of God is come, and hath given us an understanding, that we may know him that is true, and we are in him that is true, even in his Son Jesus Christ. This is the true God, and eternal life. Little children, keep yourselves from idols. Amen. **Jude 1:21** *– Keep yourselves in the love of God, looking for the mercy of our Lord Jesus Christ unto eternal life.*

4. ***Ephesians 2:1-10*** *– And you hath he quickened (made alive), who were dead in trespasses and sins; wherein in time past ye walked according to the course of this world, according to the prince of the power of the air, the spirit that now worketh in the children of disobedience: among whom also we all had our conversation (behavior) in times past in the lusts of our flesh, fulfilling the desires of the flesh and of the mind; and were by nature the children of wrath, even as others. But God, who is rich in mercy, for his great love wherewith he loved us, even when we were dead in sins, hath quickened us (made us alive) together with Christ, (by grace ye are saved;) and hath raised us up together, and made us sit together in heavenly places in Christ Jesus: that in the ages to come he might shew the exceeding riches of his grace in his kindness toward us through Christ Jesus. For by grace are ye saved through faith; and that not of yourselves: it is the gift of God: not of works, lest any man should boast. For we are his workmanship, created in Christ Jesus unto good works, which God hath before ordained that we should walk in them.*

References:

John 1:1, 4, 14 *– In the beginning was the Word, and the Word was with God, and the Word was God. In him was life; and the life was the light of men. And the Word was made flesh, and dwelt among us, (and we beheld his glory, the glory as of the only begotten of the Father,) full of grace and truth.* **1 Timothy 4:8** *– For bodily exercise profiteth little: but godliness is profitable unto all things, having promise of the life that now is, and of that which is to come.* **2 Timothy 1:1, 9-10** *– Paul, an apostle of Jesus Christ by the will of God, according to the promise of life which is in Christ Jesus. Who hath saved us, and called us with an holy calling, not according to our works, but according to his own purpose and grace, which was given us in Christ Jesus before the world began, but is now made manifest by the appearing of our Saviour Jesus Christ, who hath abolished death, and hath brought life and immortality to light through the gospel.* **Titus 1:1-3** *– Paul, a servant of God, and an apostle of Jesus Christ, according to the faith of God's elect, and the acknowledging of the truth which is after godliness; in hope of eternal life, which God, that cannot lie, promised before the world began; but hath in due times manifested his word through preaching, which is committed unto me according to the commandment of God our Saviour.* **Hebrews 5:9** *– And being made perfect, he (Jesus) became the author of eternal salvation unto all them that obey him.*

5. ***James 1:13-18*** *– Let no man say when he is tempted, "I am tempted of God:" for God cannot be tempted with evil, neither tempteth he any man: but every man is tempted, when he is drawn away of his own lust, and enticed. Then when lust hath conceived, it bringeth forth sin: and sin, when it is finished, bringeth forth death. Do not err, my beloved brethren. Every good gift and every perfect gift is from above, and cometh down from the Father of lights, with whom is no variableness, neither shadow of turning. Of his own will begat he us with the word of truth, that we should be a kind of firstfruits of his creatures.*

STUDY GUIDE - PART THREE

I pray these study notes along with the many Scriptures derived from both the Old and the New Testament will help you gain a greater understanding of (1) your heavenly Father's eternal love, care, and faithfulness toward you, (2) the carnal behavior patterns and mindsets of the old man, and (3) the new man in Christ. This is very important, as victory in Christ is obtained as we choose to put off the old man, be renewed in the *spirit of our minds*, and put on the new man which after God is created in righteousness and true holiness.

"This I say therefore, and testify in the Lord, that ye henceforth walk not as other Gentiles walk, in the vanity of their mind, having the understanding darkened, being alienated from the life of God through the ignorance that is in them, because of the blindness of their heart: who being past feeling have given themselves over unto lasciviousness, to work all uncleanness and greediness. But ye have not so learned Christ; if so be that ye have heard him, and have been taught by him, as the truth is in Jesus: that ye put off concerning the former conversation (behavior) the old man, which is corrupt according to the deceitful lusts; and be renewed in the spirit of your mind; and that ye put on the new man, which after God is created in righteousness and true holiness." (Ephesians 4:17-24)

"But be ye doers of the word, and not hearers only, deceiving your own selves. For if any be a hearer of the word, and not a doer, he is like unto a man beholding his natural face in a glass: for he beholdeth himself, and goeth his way, and straightway forgetteth what manner of man he was. But whoso looketh into the perfect law of liberty, and continueth therein, he being not a forgetful hearer, but a doer of the work, this man shall be blessed in his deed." (James 1:22-25)

"For whatsoever is born of God overcometh the world: and this is the victory that overcometh the world, even our faith." (1 John 5:4)

19(a) *You are **Yahweh – LORD**. I understand that You are the LORD. Before You there was no God formed, neither shall there be after You. (Ref.: Isaiah 43:10)*

Throughout these study notes, when quoting Scriptures in the Old Testament where "LORD" is used, it is referring to *Yahweh (YHWH)*. The name *Yahweh (YHWH)* occurs over 6,500 times in the Old Testament and is derived from the Tetragrammaton – meaning four letters – *YHWH* and means "Self-Existing or Eternal." *Jehovah* is used in the King James Version but most Bible scholars do not believe that *Jehovah* is the proper name for *YHWH (Exodus 6:3; Psalm 83:18; Isaiah 12:2; Isaiah 26:4)*. When quoting Scriptures in the Old Testament where "Lord" is used, it is usually referring to the Hebrew name *Adonai (Adonay)*. The name *Adonai* occurs over 400 times in the Old Testament and means "the Lord (used as a proper name of God only): (my) Lord." For more information on the Hebrew name *Adonai*, please see **Note 14a**.

When referring to LORD (*YHWH*), let's look at a passage of Scripture in Exodus that describes a redemptive relationship between God and His people:

> *And God said unto Moses, "I AM THAT I AM": and he said, "Thus shalt thou say unto the children of Israel, 'I AM hath sent me unto you.'" And God said moreover unto Moses, "Thus shalt thou say unto the children of Israel, <u>'The LORD (YHWH) God of your fathers, the God of Abraham, the God of Isaac, and the God of Jacob, hath sent me unto you: this is my name for ever, and this is my memorial unto all generations.'"</u>*
> (Exodus 3:14-15)

Also, when referring to LORD (*YHWH*) in *Psalm 23*, He is described as our Shepherd who restores us and leads us in the paths of righteousness, who delivers us from the fear of evil, and comforts us in our time of need. The Self-Existing and Eternal God desires to reveal Himself to those who choose to seek Him *(Philippians 3:7-15)*. He has given us His Holy Spirit that we might know Him and understand the things He has freely given to us *(Matthew 16:13-17; Luke 10:22; Luke 12:32; Romans 1:16-17, 8:14-18; 1 Corinthians 2:7-14; Galatians 1:15-16; Ephesians 3:1-11, 14-19; Hebrews 8:11; 1 John 2:24-27)*.

Only God is Self-Existent and Eternal. No one formed Him, fashioned Him, or shaped Him! He imparts His nature to us through His redemptive qualities (e.g., virtue, joy, strength, life, wisdom, power, might, excellence) without the help of outside influences. His desire is to reveal Himself and to integrate who He is into oneness with us! Our true worth and value is found in Him and whether some believe it or not, we "all" need Him as He is our Creator and knows our innerworkings better than we do *(Colossians 1:12-18; Acts 17:28; John 3:16; Ephesians 2:1-7; Psalm 139:1-2)*! We begin to tap into the wealth of His glory as we surrender our lives to Him and walk in obedience to His will.

> *For our light, momentary affliction (this slight distress of the passing hour) is ever more and more abundantly preparing and producing and achieving for us an everlasting weight of glory [beyond all measure, excessively surpassing all comparisons and all calculations, a vast and transcendent glory and blessedness never to cease!], since we consider and look not to the things that are seen but to the things that are unseen; for the things that are visible are temporal (brief and fleeting), but the things that are invisible are deathless and everlasting.*

Below are Scriptures relating to God's eternal greatness:

1. ***Exodus 34:5-7*** – *And the LORD descended in the cloud, and stood with him (Moses) there, and proclaimed the name of the LORD. And the LORD passed by before him (Moses), and proclaimed, "The LORD, The LORD God, merciful and gracious, longsuffering, and abundant in goodness and truth, keeping mercy for thousands, forgiving iniquity and transgression and sin, and that will by no means clear the guilty; visiting the iniquity of the fathers upon the children, and upon the children's children, unto the third and to the fourth generation."*

References:
Deuteronomy 10:17 *(NKJV)* – *For the LORD your God is God of gods and Lord of lords, the great God, mighty and awesome, who shows no partiality nor takes a bribe.* ***2 Samuel 7:22*** – *David said, "Wherefore thou art great, O LORD God: for there is none like thee, neither is there any God beside thee, according to all that we have heard with our ears."* ***2 Samuel 22:47*** – *The LORD liveth; and blessed be my rock; and exalted be the God of the rock of my salvation.* ***1 Chronicles 29:10-12*** – *Wherefore David blessed the LORD before all the congregation: and David said, "Blessed be thou, LORD God of Israel our father, for ever and ever. Thine, O LORD, is the greatness, and the power, and the glory, and the victory, and the majesty: for all that is in the heaven and in the earth is thine; thine is the kingdom, O LORD, and thou art exalted as head above all. Both riches and honour come of thee, and thou reignest over all; and in thine hand is power and might; and in thine hand it is to make great, and to give strength unto all."* ***Psalm 18:2*** – *The LORD is my rock, and my fortress, and my deliverer; my God, my strength, in whom I will trust; my buckler, and the horn of my salvation, and my high tower.* ***Psalm 18:30-36*** – *As for God, his way is perfect: the word of the LORD is tried: he is a buckler to all those that trust in him. For who is God save the LORD? Or who is a rock save our God? It is God that girdeth me with strength, and maketh my way perfect. He maketh my feet like hinds' feet, and setteth me upon my high places. He teacheth my hands to war, so that a bow of steel is broken by mine arms. Thou hast also given me the shield of thy salvation: and thy right hand hath holden me up, and thy gentleness hath made me great. Thou hast enlarged my steps under me, that my feet did not slip.* ***Psalm 18:46*** – *The LORD liveth; and blessed be my rock; and let the God of my salvation be exalted.* ***Psalm 57:10-11*** – *For thy mercy is great unto the heavens, and thy truth unto the clouds. Be thou exalted, O God, above the heavens: let thy glory be above all the earth.* ***Psalm 83:18*** *(NKJV)* – *That they may know that You, whose name alone is the LORD, are the Most High over all the earth.* ***Psalm 105:1-7*** – *O give thanks unto the LORD; call upon his name: make known his deeds among the people. Sing unto him, sing psalms unto him: talk ye of all his wondrous works. Glory ye in his holy name: let the heart of them rejoice that seek the LORD. Seek the LORD, and his strength: seek his face evermore. Remember his marvelous works that he hath done; his wonders, and the judgments of his mouth; O ye seed (descendants) of Abraham his servant, ye children of Jacob his chosen. He is the LORD our God: his judgments are in all the earth.* ***Psalm 146:3-10*** – *Put not your trust in princes, nor in the son of man, in whom there is no help. His breath goeth forth, he returneth to his earth; in that very day his thoughts perish. Happy is he that hath the God of Jacob for his help, whose hope is in the LORD his God: which made heaven, and earth, the sea, and all that therein is: which keepeth truth for ever: which executeth judgment for the oppressed: which giveth food to the hungry. The LORD looseth the prisoners: the LORD openeth the eyes of the blind: the LORD raiseth them that are bowed down: the LORD loveth the righteous: the LORD preserveth the strangers; he relieveth the fatherless and widow: but the way of the wicked he turneth upside down. The LORD shall reign forever, even thy God, O Zion, unto all generations. Praise ye the LORD.* ***Isaiah 44:6, 8*** – *Thus saith the LORD*

the King of Israel, and his redeemer the LORD of hosts; "I am the first, and I am the last; beside me there is no God. ...Is there a God beside me? Yea, there is no God; I know not any."

2. ***Isaiah 26:3-4 (NKJV)*** *– You will keep him in perfect peace, whose mind is stayed on You, because he trusts in You. Trust in the LORD forever, for in YAH, the LORD, is everlasting strength.*

References:
Luke 6:46-49 *– Jesus said, "And why call ye me, 'Lord, Lord,' and do not the things which I say? Whosoever cometh to me, and heareth my sayings, and doeth them, I will shew you to whom he is like: he is like a man which built an house, and digged deep, and laid the foundation on a rock: and when the flood arose, the stream beat vehemently upon that house, and could not shake it: for it was founded upon a rock. But he that heareth, and doeth not, is like a man that without a foundation built an house upon the earth; against which the stream did beat vehemently, and immediately it fell; and the ruin of that house was great."*
Hebrews 12:25-29 *– See that ye refuse not him that speaketh. For if they escaped not who refused him that spake on earth, much more shall not we escape, if we turn away from him that speaketh from heaven: whose voice then shook the earth: but now he hath promised, saying, "Yet once more I shake not the earth only, but also heaven." And this word, "Yet once more," signifieth the removing of those things that are shaken, as of things that are made, that those things which cannot be shaken may remain. Wherefore we receiving a kingdom which cannot be moved, let us have grace, whereby we may serve God acceptably with reverence and godly fear: for our God is a consuming fire.* (It is only by building our house – our hearts and minds – on the Rock, Jesus Christ, that we cannot be shaken! Jesus Christ is the Alpha and the Omega, the First and the Last, Beginning and the End – *Revelation 1:11-17, 2:8, 22:13*).

3. ***Hebrews 13:8*** *– Jesus Christ the same yesterday, and to day, and for ever.*

References:
Malachi 3:6 *– "For I am the LORD, I change not; therefore ye sons of Jacob are not consumed."* ***John 8:58*** *(NKJV) – Jesus said to them, "Most assuredly, I say to you, before Abraham was, I AM."*

19(b) *Besides You there is no savior. (Ref.: Isaiah 43:11)*

The LORD is Israel's Savior. He saved them from their enemies, giving them the victory. The LORD made a covenant with His friend Abraham *(Genesis 15)*. God said to Abram,

> *Know for certain that your descendants will be strangers in a land that is not theirs, where they will be enslaved and oppressed four hundred years. But I will also judge the nation whom they will serve, and afterward they will come out with many possessions.*
> (Genesis 15:13-14, NASB)

After four hundred thirty years, the LORD used Moses to deliver Abraham's descendants from the land of Egypt and the hand of Pharoah *(Exodus 12)*. According to *Exodus 12:37*, there were 600,000 young men besides women, children, and old men. Therefore, if you include women, children, and old men, the estimated number of Abraham's descendants who were delivered out of Egypt could have been over 2 million people! Because of their disobedience, they wandered in the wilderness for forty years and the LORD then used Joshua to take them into the promised land *(Joshua 1)*. It's important to note what Paul writes,

> *There is neither Jew nor Greek, there is neither bond nor free, there is neither male nor female: for ye are all one in Christ Jesus. And if ye be Christ's, then are ye Abraham's seed (descendants), and heirs according to the promise.*
>
> (Galatians 3:28-29)

The mature believer in Christ is walking in the new man in Christ, where there are no gender or racial divides, cultural issues, etc., for we are all one in Christ. The Lord Jesus Christ is the Savior of the world. John said in *1 John 4:14-15 – "And we have seen and do testify that the Father sent the Son to be the Saviour of the world. Whosoever shall confess that Jesus is the Son of God, God dwelleth in him, and he in God."* In the book of Matthew, an angel of the Lord appeared to Joseph in a dream, saying,

> *"Joseph, thou son of David, fear not to take unto thee Mary thy wife: for that which is conceived in her is of the Holy Ghost. And she shall bring forth a son, and thou shalt call his name JESUS: for he shall save his people from their sins." Now all this was done, that it might be fulfilled which was spoken of the Lord by the prophet, saying, "Behold, a virgin shall be with child, and shall bring forth a son, and they shall call his name Emmanuel, which being interpreted is, 'God with us.'"*
>
> (Matthew 1:20-23)

The Greek word for "Jesus" is *Iesous*. The meaning in the Thayer's Greek Lexicon is "Jesus, the Son of God, the Saviour of mankind." In *John 8:58 (NKJV) – Jesus said to them, "Most assuredly, I say to you, before Abraham was, I AM."* Notice the Lord revealed Himself as *I AM* just as God revealed Himself to Moses in *Exodus 3:14-15* saying, *"I AM THAT I AM:…"* This name describes a redemptive relationship between God and His people. After Jesus talked to a man who could not follow Him because he had great possessions, He told His disciples,

> *"Verily I say unto you, That a rich man shall hardly enter into the kingdom of heaven. And again I say unto you, It is easier for a camel to go through the eye of a needle, than for a rich man to enter into the kingdom of God." When his disciples heard it, they were exceedingly amazed, saying, "Who then can be saved?" But Jesus beheld them, and said unto them, "With men this is impossible; but with God all things are possible."*
>
> (Matthew 19:23-26)

Jesus has redeemed us from the curse of the law being made a curse for us, that the blessing of Abraham might come on the Gentiles through Jesus Christ, that we might receive the promise of the Spirit through faith *(Galatians 3:13-14)*. He is our Savior and nothing is impossible for Him—He is the Great *I AM*! Hebrews 13:8 reads – *"Jesus Christ the same yesterday, and to day, and for ever."* Jesus is God:

> *In the beginning was the Word, and the Word was with God, and the Word was God. The same was in the beginning with God. All things were made by him; and without him was not any thing made that was made. In him was life; and the life was the light of men. And the Word was made flesh, and dwelt among us, (and we beheld his glory, the glory as of the only begotten of the Father,) full of grace and truth.*

Below are Scriptures relating to Jesus, our source of life and Savior:

<u>Jesus, our Source of Life</u>

Psalm 36:9 – *For with thee is the fountain of life: in thy light shall we see light.*

References:
Proverbs 13:13-14 – *Whoso despiseth the word shall be destroyed: but he that feareth the commandment shall be rewarded. The law of the wise is a fountain of life, to depart from the snares of death.* ***Proverbs 14:26-27*** – *In the fear of the LORD is strong confidence: and his children shall have a place of refuge. The fear of the LORD is a fountain of life, to depart from the snares of death.* ***Proverbs 18:4*** – *The words of a man's mouth are as deep waters, and the wellspring of wisdom as a flowing brook.* ***Isaiah 12:3*** – *Therefore with joy shall ye draw water out of the wells of salvation.* ***Isaiah 44:2-3*** – *Thus saith the LORD that made thee, and formed thee from the womb, which will help thee; "Fear not, O Jacob, my servant; and thou, Jesurun, whom I have chosen. For I will pour water upon him that is thirsty, and floods upon the dry ground: I will pour my spirit upon thy seed, and my blessing upon thine offspring."* ***Jeremiah 2:13*** – *For my people have committed two evils; they have forsaken me the fountain of living waters, and hewed them out cisterns, broken cisterns, that can hold no water.* ***Jeremiah 17:13*** – *O LORD, the hope of Israel, all that forsake thee shall be ashamed, and they that depart from me shall be written in the earth, because they have forsaken the LORD, the fountain of living waters.* ***Zechariah 13:1*** – *In that day there shall be a fountain opened to the house of David and to the inhabitants of Jerusalem for sin and for uncleanness.* ***John 4:13-14*** – *Jesus answered and said to her, "Whosoever drinketh of this water shall thirst again: but whosoever drinketh of the water that I shall give him shall never thirst; but the water that I shall give him shall be in him a well of water springing up into everlasting life."* ***John 7:38-39*** – *Jesus said, "He that believeth on me, as the scripture hath said, out of his belly shall flow rivers of living water. (But this spake he of the Spirit, which they that believe on him should receive: for the Holy Ghost was not yet given; because that Jesus was not yet glorified).*

<u>Jesus, our Savior</u>

Hosea 13:4 – *Yet I am the LORD thy God from the land of Egypt, and thou shalt know no god but me: for there is no saviour beside me.*

References:
John 1:29 – *The next day John seeth Jesus coming unto him, and saith, "Behold the Lamb of God, which taketh away the sin of the world."* ***Acts 4:10-12*** – *Be it known unto you all, and to all the people of Israel, that by the name of Jesus Christ of Nazareth, whom ye crucified, whom God raised from the dead, even by him doth this man stand here before you whole. This is the stone which was set at nought of you builders, which is become the head of the corner. Neither is there salvation in any other: for there is none other name under heaven given among men, whereby we must be saved.* ***Philippians 2:8-11*** – *And being found in fashion as a man, he humbled himself, and became obedient unto death, even the death of the cross. Wherefore God also hath highly exalted him, and given him a name which is above every name: that at the name of Jesus every knee should bow, of things in heaven, and things in earth, and things under the earth;*

and that every tongue should confess that Jesus Christ is Lord, to the glory of God the Father. **1 Timothy 1:15-17** – Paul said, *"This is a faithful saying, and worthy of all acceptation, that Christ Jesus came into the world to save sinners; of whom I am chief. Howbeit for this cause I obtained mercy, that in me first Jesus Christ might shew forth all longsuffering, for a pattern to them which should hereafter believe on him to life everlasting. Now unto the King eternal, immortal, invisible, the only wise God, be honour and glory for ever and ever. Amen."* **1 Timothy 2:5-7** – Paul said, *"For there is one God, and one mediator between God and men, the man Christ Jesus; who gave himself a ransom for all, to be testified in due time. Whereunto I am ordained a preacher, and an apostle, (I speak the truth in Christ, and lie not;) a teacher of the Gentiles in faith and verity (truth)."* **Hebrews 5:8-10** – *Though he were a Son, yet learned he obedience by the things which he suffered; and being made perfect, he became the author of eternal salvation unto all them that obey him...* **Hebrews 9:11-12** – *But Christ being come an high priest of good things to come, by a greater and more perfect tabernacle, not made with hands, that is to say, not of this building; neither by the blood of goats and calves, but by his own blood he entered in once into the holy place, having obtained eternal redemption for us.* **Jude 1:24-25** – *Now unto him that is able to keep you from falling, and to present you faultless before the presence of his glory with exceeding joy, to the only wise God our Saviour, be glory and majesty, dominion and power, both now and ever. Amen.* **Revelation 5:11-14** – *And I beheld, and I heard the voice of many angels round about the throne and the beasts and the elders: and the number of them was ten thousand times ten thousand, and thousands of thousands; saying with a loud voice, "Worthy is the Lamb (Jesus) that was slain to receive power, and riches, and wisdom, and strength, and honour, and glory, and blessing." And every creature which is in heaven, and on the earth, and under the earth, and such as are in the sea, and all that are in them, heard I saying, "Blessing, and honour, and glory, and power, be unto him that sitteth upon the throne, and unto the Lamb for ever and ever." And the four beasts said, "Amen." And the four and twenty elders fell down and worshipped him that liveth for ever and ever.*

20(a) *You are* **El-Elyon – the Most High God.** *You are supreme, the number one Ruler in the universe. (Ref.: Genesis 14:19-20; Psalm 83:18; Daniel 4:31-32)*

The Hebrew word for "God" is *El* meaning "strength; as adjective, mighty; especially the Almighty (but used also of any deity): God (god), x goodly, x great, idol, might (-y one), power, strong." The Hebrew word for "Most High" is *Elyown* (pronunciation: *Elyon),* meaning "an elevation, i.e. (adj.) lofty (comparison); as title, <u>the Supreme</u>: (Most, on) high(-er, -est), upper(-most)." (Note: In *Daniel 4* the word "Most High" is the Hebrew word *illay*. The Strong's definition is "(Aramaic) supreme (i.e. God):– (most) high." *Illay* occurs 10 times in the book of Daniel and is the Aramaic equivalent for *El Elyon).* In *Daniel 4:1-37,* God reveals Himself to Nebuchadnezzar, the king of Babylon, as "The Most-High" God who rules in the kingdom of men. It begins in *Daniel 4,* when Nebuchadnezzar had a dream and none of the wise men, magicians, Chaldeans, or soothsayers were able to make known to the king the interpretation of the dream. Last of all, Daniel came before him. When Nebuchadnezzar told Daniel the dream, Daniel's thoughts troubled him for one hour. Afterwards, Daniel revealed the interpretation to Nebuchadnezzar. Here is the interpretation:

> *The tree that you saw, which became large and grew strong, whose height reached to the sky and was visible to all the earth and whose foliage was beautiful and its fruit abundant, and in which was food for all, under which the beasts of the field dwelt and in whose branches*

the birds of the sky lodged—it is you, O king; for you have become great and grown strong, and your majesty has become great and reached to the sky and your dominion to the end of the earth. In that the king saw an angelic watcher, a holy one, descending from heaven and saying, "Chop down the tree and destroy it; yet leave the stump with its roots in the ground, but with a band of iron and bronze around it in the new grass of the field, and let him be drenched with the dew of heaven, and let him share with the beasts of the field until seven periods of time pass over him, this is the interpretation, O king, and this is the decree of the Most High, which has come upon my lord the king: that you be driven away from mankind and your dwelling place be with the beasts of the field, and you be given grass to eat like cattle and be drenched with the dew of heaven; and seven periods of time will pass over you, until you recognize that the Most High is ruler over the realm of mankind and bestows it on whomever He wishes. And in that it was commanded to leave the stump with the roots of the tree, your kingdom will be assured to you after you recognize that it is Heaven that rules.

(Daniel 4:20-26, NASB)

A year later, Nebuchadnezzar was walking in the palace of the kingdom of Babylon when the interpretation of the dream came to pass:

The king reflected and said, "Is this not Babylon the great, which I myself have built as a royal residence by the might of my power and for the glory of my majesty?" While the word was in the king's mouth, a voice came from heaven, saying, "King Nebuchadnezzar, to you it is declared: sovereignty has been removed from you, and you will be driven away from mankind, and your dwelling place will be with the beasts of the field. You will be given grass to eat like cattle, and seven periods of time will pass over you until you recognize that the Most High is ruler over the realm of mankind and bestows it on whomever He wishes." Immediately the word concerning Nebuchadnezzar was fulfilled; and he was driven away from mankind and began eating grass like cattle, and his body was drenched with the dew of heaven until his hair had grown like eagles' feathers and his nails like birds' claws. "But at the end of that period, I, Nebuchadnezzar, raised my eyes toward heaven and my reason (understanding) returned to me, and I blessed the Most High and praised and honored Him who lives forever; For His dominion is an everlasting dominion, and His kingdom endures from generation to generation. All the inhabitants of the earth are accounted as nothing, but He does according to His will in the host of heaven and among the inhabitants of earth; and no one can ward off His hand or say to Him, 'What have You done?' At that time my reason returned to me. And my majesty and splendor were restored to me for the glory of my kingdom, and my counselors and my nobles began seeking me out; so I was reestablished in my sovereignty, and surpassing greatness was added to me. Now I, Nebuchadnezzar, praise, exalt and honor the King of heaven, for all His works are true and His ways just, and He is able to humble those who walk in pride."

(Daniel 4:30-37, NASB)

Only the Most High God knows how to get our attention to help us to see who He truly is and to worship Him as the only true and living God!

God resists the proud but gives grace to the humble *(1 Peter 5:5)*. Pride is the outward expression of our carnal nature! Before Satan fell, his name was Lucifer and he was an anointed cherub, perfect in all his ways from the day he was created, until iniquity was found in him *(Ezekiel 28:14-15)*. Let's look at a passage of Scripture in Isaiah that shows us the iniquity that caused his unredeemable fall:

> *How you have fallen from heaven, O star of the morning, son of the dawn! You have been cut down to the earth, you who have weakened the nations! But you said in your heart, "I will ascend to heaven; I will raise my throne above the stars of God, and I will sit on the mount of assembly in the recesses of the north. I will ascend above the heights of the clouds; I will make myself like the Most High." Nevertheless you will be thrust down to Sheol, to the recesses of the pit.*
>
> (Isaiah 14:12-15, NASB)

Pride is the iniquity that caused Lucifer to fall. Pride goes before destruction and a haughty spirit before a fall *(Proverbs 16:18)*. Therefore, we must always remember to clothe ourselves with humility as Peter describes:

> *…Clothe (apron) yourselves, all of you, with humility [as the garb of a servant, so that its covering cannot possibly be stripped from you, with freedom from pride and arrogance] toward one another. For God sets Himself against the proud (the insolent, the overbearing, the disdainful, the presumptuous, the boastful)-[and He opposes, frustrates, and defeats them], but gives grace (favor, blessing) to the humble.*
>
> (1 Peter 5:5, AMPCE)

Below are eleven promises from the Bible found in *Psalm 91:1-16* for those who choose to dwell in the secret place of the Most High (*Elyon*):

1. They will abide under the shadow of the Almighty.
2. The LORD will be their refuge and fortress, their covering. He will be their shield and buckler.
3. The LORD will be with them in trouble and will deliver them and honor them.
4. They will not be afraid.
5. No evil will befall them.
6. No plague will come near their dwelling.
7. He will give His angels charge over them, to keep them in all their ways.
8. They will walk in His authority over the enemy.
9. The LORD will exalt them.
10. They will call upon the LORD, and He will answer them.
11. With long life the LORD will satisfy them and show them His salvation.

These are wonderful promises from a faithful God who loves you! Remember the Most High rules! The key to dwelling in the secret place is setting your love upon Him *(Psalm 91:14)*. How do you set your love upon Him? The answer is found in the following passage of Scripture:

> *Judas (not Iscariot) said to Him, "Lord, what then has happened that You are going to disclose Yourself to us and not to the world?" Jesus answered and said to him, "If anyone loves Me, he will keep My word; and My Father will love him, and we will come to him and make Our abode with him. He who does not love Me does not keep My words; and the*

word which you hear is not Mine, but the Father's who sent Me."
(John 14:22-24, NASB)

Humble yourself, therefore, before the Lord and surrender your life to Him. Seek Him with all of your heart through His Word and prayer. His Words must be first place in the life of a Christian. It takes more than just believing there is a God and believing that Jesus Christ is the Son of God. Even the devils believe and tremble *(James 2:19)*. This is a life commitment to be God-centered and not self-centered. The New Testament reveals the "secret place" of the Father—Jesus Christ. Those who choose to live in Him are living in the "secret place" and have found the true meaning of life! Paul affirms this in the following passages of Scripture:

1. ***Galatians 2:20*** – *I am crucified with Christ: nevertheless I live; yet not I, but Christ liveth in me: and the life which I now live in the flesh I live by the faith of the Son of God, who loved me, and gave himself for me.*
2. ***Galatians 6:14*** – *But God forbid that I should glory, save (except) in the cross of our Lord Jesus Christ, by whom the world is crucified unto me, and I unto the world.*
3. ***Ephesians 3:8-11*** – *Unto me, who am less than the least of all saints, is this grace given, that I should preach among the Gentiles the unsearchable riches of Christ; and to make all men see what is the fellowship of the mystery, which from the beginning of the world hath been hid in God, who created all things by Jesus Christ: to the intent that now unto the principalities and powers in heavenly places might be known by the church the manifold wisdom of God, according to the eternal purpose which he purposed in Christ Jesus our Lord.*
4. ***Colossians 3:3*** – *For ye are dead, and your life is hid with Christ in God.*

It is in Christ that we live and move and have our being *(Acts 17:28)*!

Below are Scriptures relating to the Most High God:

Psalm 47:1-2 – *O clap your hands, all ye people; shout unto God with a voice of triumph. For the LORD most high (Elyon) is terrible (to be feared); he is a great King over all the earth.*

References:
Psalm 83:18 (NKJV) – *That they may know that You, whose name alone is the LORD, are the Most High (Elyon) over all the earth.* ***Psalm 91:1*** – *He that dwelleth in the secret place of the Most High (Elyon) shall abide under the shadow of the Almighty.* ***Psalm 97:9*** – *For thou, LORD, art high above (Elyon) all the earth: thou art exalted far above all gods.* ***Proverbs 21:30*** – *There is no wisdom nor understanding nor counsel against the LORD.* ***Revelation 11:15*** – *And the seventh angel sounded; and there were great voices in heaven, saying, "The kingdoms of this world are become the kingdoms of our Lord, and of his Christ; and he shall reign for ever and ever."*

20(b) *and with You there is no partiality. (Ref.: Colossians 3:23-25; 1 Peter 2:23; Romans 2:11)*

God does not have favorites! He doesn't like one over the other because of personality or good looks. He is, however, a respecter of obedience and a respecter of disobedience. God is love and His love for us is real; He proved His love by giving His Son to die on the cross so whosoever believes in Him shall not perish but have everlasting life *(John 3:16)*. He is the Most High God, the ruler of the universe. God is not partial, but He is righteous in His judgments. We will all stand before the judgment seat of Christ to give an account before Him. Below are three passages of Scripture that confirm this:

1. **Romans 14:10-12** *(NASB) – But you, why do you judge your brother? Or you again, why do you regard your brother with contempt? For we will all stand before the judgment seat of God. For it is written, "AS I LIVE, SAYS THE LORD, EVERY KNEE SHALL BOW TO ME, AND EVERY TONGUE SHALL GIVE PRAISE TO GOD." So then each one of us will give an account of himself to God.*

2. **Romans 2:5-6** *(NASB) – But because of your stubbornness and unrepentant heart you are storing up wrath for yourself in the day of wrath and revelation of the righteous judgment of God, who WILL RENDER TO EACH PERSON ACCORDING TO HIS DEEDS: to those who by perseverance in doing good seek for glory and honor and immortality, eternal life; but to those who are selfishly ambitious and do not obey the truth, but obey unrighteousness, wrath and indignation. There will be tribulation and distress for every soul of man who does evil, of the Jew first and also of the Greek, but glory and honor and peace to everyone who does good, to the Jew first and also to the Greek. For there is no partiality with God.*

3. **1 Peter 1:17-19** *(NASB) – If you address as Father the One who impartially judges according to each one's work, conduct yourselves in fear during the time of your stay on earth; knowing that you were not redeemed with perishable things like silver or gold from your futile way of life inherited from your forefathers, but with precious blood, as of a lamb unblemished and spotless, the blood of Christ.*

The Greek word for "work" in *1 Peter 1:17* is *ergon* and its meaning in the Thayer's Greek Lexicon is "an act, deed, thing done: the genitive of person and subjunctive, his whole way of feeling and acting, his aims and endeavors." The true works of God originate from the born-again creation whose origin is from God, birthed by His Word and the power of His Holy Spirit. This born-again creation lives by faith and grows in grace, operating from a place of trust and obedience to his/her heavenly Father. Jesus was made to be sin for us that we might become the righteousness of God in Him *(2 Corinthians 5:21)*. Some may say, "Oh I believe in Jesus Christ! I believe He died for my sins!" However, their lifestyle and their behavior are contrary to the truth of God's Word. Beware! Even the devils believe and tremble *(James 2:19)*! God is calling us to live out of a new life in Christ. We have been bought with a price and we are to glorify Him in our bodies and in our spirits, which are His *(1 Corinthians 6:20)*. God has a call on each of our lives (e.g., a husband, a father, a mother, a housewife, a minister of the gospel, a businessman or woman, an employee, an employer, a house cleaner, a janitor, a waitress/waiter) and whatever the call, He is looking for us to put off the old man and put on the new man in Christ. Our true destiny in this life is to be conformed to the image of His Son *(Romans 8:29)*. Let's close with the following passage of Scripture:

And so faith, hope, love abide [faith-conviction and belief respecting man's relation to God and divine things; hope-joyful and confident expectation of eternal salvation; love-true affection for God and man, growing out of God's love for and in us], these three; but the greatest of these is love. Eagerly pursue and seek to acquire [this] love [make it your aim, your great quest]…

(1 Corinthians 13:13-14:1, AMPCE)

Below are Scriptures relating to God's impartial judgments:

2 Corinthians 5:7-10 – *(For we walk by faith, not by sight:) we are confident, I say, and willing rather to be absent from the body, and to be present with the Lord. Wherefore we labour, that, whether present or absent, we may be accepted of him. For we must all appear before the judgment seat of Christ; that every one may receive the things done in his body, according to that he hath done, whether it be good or bad.*

References:

Leviticus 19:15 – *The Lord spoke to Moses, "Ye shall do no unrighteousness in judgment: thou shalt not respect the person of the poor, nor honour the person of the mighty: but in righteousness shalt thou judge thy neighbour.* ***Psalm 62:11-12*** *(NASB) – Once God has spoken; twice I have heard this: that power belongs to God; and lovingkindness is Yours, O Lord, for you recompense a man according to his work.* ***Proverbs 24:12, 23*** *(NASB) – If you say, "See, we did not know this," does He not consider it who weighs the hearts? And does He not know it who keeps your soul? And will He not render to man according to his work? These also are sayings of the wise. To show partiality in judgment is not good.* ***Ecclesiastes 12:13-14*** *– Let us hear the conclusion of the whole matter: Fear God, and keep his commandments: for this is the whole duty of man. For God shall bring every work into judgment, with every secret thing, whether it be good, or whether it be evil.* ***Jeremiah 17:10*** *– I the LORD search the heart, I try the reins (mind), even to give every man according to his ways, and according to the fruit of his doings.* ***Acts 10:34-36*** *– Then Peter opened his mouth, and said, "Of a truth I perceive that God is no respecter of persons (shows no partiality): but in every nation he that feareth him, and worketh righteousness, is accepted with him. The word which God sent unto the children of Israel, preaching peace by Jesus Christ: (he is Lord of all).* ***Galatians 6:7*** *– Be not deceived; God is not mocked: for whatsoever a man soweth, that shall he also reap.* ***James 2:1-5*** *– My brethren, have not the faith of our Lord Jesus Christ, the Lord of glory, with respect of persons (with partiality)…*

Please refer to **Note 38b** for additional information and Scriptures relating to this subject matter.

21(a) *You are **Yahweh-Tsidkenu – THE LORD MY RIGHTEOUSNESS.** (Ref.: Jeremiah 23:5-6)*

Below are the two passages of Scripture where *Yahweh-Tsidkenu* occurs in the Old Testament:

1. ***Jeremiah 23:5-6*** *– "Behold, the days come," saith the LORD, "that I will raise unto David a righteous Branch, and a King shall reign and prosper, and shall execute judgment and justice in the earth. In his days Judah shall be saved, and Israel shall dwell safely:* <u>and this is his name whereby he shall be called, THE LORD OUR RIGHTEOUSNESS."</u>
2. ***Jeremiah 33:14-16*** *– "Behold, the days come," saith the LORD, "that I will perform that good thing which I have promised unto the house of Israel and to the house of Judah. In those days, and at that time, will I cause the Branch of righteousness to grow up unto David; and he shall execute judgment and righteousness in the land. In those days shall Judah be saved, and Jerusalem shall dwell safely:* <u>and this is the name wherewith she shall be called, The LORD our righteousness."</u>

Notice *Jeremiah 23:6* reads, *"…and this is his name whereby he shall be called, THE LORD OUR*

RIGHTEOUSNESS" – referring to Jesus Christ. And *Jeremiah 33:16* reads, *"…and this is the name wherewith she shall be called, The LORD our righteousness"* – referring to His bride, the church. He has given us His name and we are one with Him and we are complete in Him. The Hebrew meaning for *Tsidqenuw* is "Jehovah (is) our right; Jehovah-Tsidkenu, a symbolical epithet of the Messiah and of Jerusalem:–the Lord our righteousness." Let's look at the following passage of Scripture:

> *Those that be planted in the house of the LORD shall flourish in the courts of our God. They shall still bring forth fruit in old age; they shall be fat and flourishing; to shew that the LORD is upright: he is my rock, and there is no unrighteousness in him.*
>
> (Psalm 92:13-15)

There is no perverseness in Him, there is no injustice in Him, there is no evil in Him, there is no iniquity in Him, there is no wickedness in Him. He is pure, holy, and undefiled, and it is only through the new man in Christ that we can walk in this kind of righteousness and true holiness (*Ephesians 4:20-24*). Our righteousness apart from Christ are as filthy rags (*Isaiah 64:6*). I am reminded of the following passage of Scripture where Jesus said,

> *Enter ye in at the strait gate: for wide is the gate, and broad is the way, that leadeth to destruction, and many there be which go in thereat: because strait is the gate, and narrow is the way, which leadeth unto life, and few there be that find it.*
>
> (Matthew 7:13-14)

Crucifying the flesh is not easy! Taking up our cross daily and following Him, at times, is not easy! But those who choose to overcome the flesh and walk in the born-again creation (the new man in Christ) will find abundant life (*Psalm 118:19-23; John 10:10*)!!

Below are Scriptures relating to the righteousness of God:

1. ***Psalm 11:7*** – *For the righteous LORD loveth righteousness; his countenance doth behold the upright.*

References:
Psalm 9:7-8 – *But the LORD shall endure forever: he hath prepared his throne for judgment. And he shall judge the world in righteousness, he shall minister judgment to the people in uprightness.* ***Psalm 96:12-13*** – *Let the field be joyful, and all that is therein: then shall all the trees of the wood rejoice before the LORD: for he cometh, for he cometh to judge the earth: he shall judge the world with righteousness, and the people with his truth.* ***Psalm 119:142*** – *Thy righteousness is an everlasting righteousness, and thy law is truth.* ***Proverbs 19:29*** – *Judgments are prepared for scorners, and stripes for the back of fools.* (At the cross, Jesus took upon Himself the scorner's judgments and the fool's stripes in order for them to walk in newness of life in Him, in His righteousness and holiness. See *Romans 5:6-11* below). ***Proverbs 26:11*** – *As a dog returneth to his vomit, so a fool returneth to his folly.* ***Isaiah 45:18-19*** – *"…I am the LORD; and there is none else. I have not spoken in secret, in a dark place of the earth: I said not unto the seed of Jacob, 'Seek ye me in vain'; I the LORD speak righteousness, I declare things that are right."* ***Jeremiah 4:1-4*** *(NKJV)* – *"If you will return, O Israel," says the LORD, "Return to Me; and if you will put away your abominations out of My sight, then you shall not be moved. And you shall swear, 'The LORD lives,' in truth, in judgment, and in righteousness; the nations shall bless themselves in Him, and in Him they shall glory." For thus says the LORD to the men of Judah and Jerusalem: "Break up your fallow ground, and do*

not sow among thorns. Circumcise yourselves to the LORD, and take away the foreskins of your hearts, you men of Judah and inhabitants of Jerusalem, lest My fury come forth like fire, and burn so that no one can quench it, because of the evil of your doings." ***Zechariah 8:7-8*** – Thus saith the LORD of hosts; "Behold, I will save my people from the east country, and from the west country; and I will bring them, and they shall dwell in the midst of Jerusalem: and they shall be my people, and I will be their God, in truth and in righteousness." ***Romans 5:6-11, 19-21*** – For when we were yet without strength, in due time Christ died for the ungodly. For scarcely for a righteous man will one die: yet peradventure for a good man some would even dare to die. But God commendeth his love toward us, in that, while we were yet sinners, Christ died for us. Much more then, being now justified (made righteous) by his blood, we shall be saved from wrath through him. For if, when we were enemies, we were reconciled to God by the death of his Son, much more, being reconciled, we shall be saved by his life. And not only so, but we also joy in God through our Lord Jesus Christ, by whom we have now received the atonement. For as by one man's (Adam's) disobedience many were made sinners, so by the obedience of one (Jesus Christ) shall many be made righteous. Moreover the law entered, that the offence might abound. But where sin abounded, grace did much more abound: that as sin hath reigned unto death, even so might grace reign through righteousness unto eternal life by Jesus Christ our Lord. ***1 Corinthians 1:27-31*** – But God hath chosen the foolish things of the world to confound the wise; and God hath chosen the weak things of the world to confound the things which are mighty; and base things of the world, and things which are despised, hath God chosen, yea, and things which are not, to bring to nought (nothing) things that are: that no flesh should glory in his presence. But of him are ye in Christ Jesus, who of God is made unto us wisdom, and righteousness, and sanctification, and redemption: that, according as it is written, He that glorieth, let him glory in the Lord. ***Galatians 1:1-5*** – Paul, an apostle, (not of men, neither by man, but by Jesus Christ, and God the Father, who raised him from the dead;) and all the brethren which are with me, unto the churches of Galatia: "Grace be to you and peace from God the Father, and from our Lord Jesus Christ, who gave himself for our sins, that he might deliver us from this present evil world, according to the will of God and our Father: to whom be glory for ever and ever. Amen. ***Ephesians 4:21-24*** – If so be the ye have heard him, and have been taught by him, as the truth is in Jesus: that ye put off concerning the former conversation (behavior) the old man, which is corrupt according to the deceitful lusts; and be renewed in the spirit of your mind; and that ye put on the new man, which after God is created in righteousness and true holiness. ***1 John 3:5-10*** – And ye know that he (Jesus) was manifested to take away our sins; and in him is no sin. Whosoever abideth in him sinneth not: whosoever sinneth hath not seen him, neither known him. Little children, let no man deceive you: he that doeth righteousness is righteous, even as he (Jesus) is righteous. He that committeth sin is of the devil; for the devil sinneth from the beginning. For this purpose the Son of God was manifested, that he might destroy the works of the devil. Whosoever is born of God doth not commit sin; for his seed remaineth in him: and he cannot sin, because he is born of God. In this the children of God are manifest, and the children of the devil: whosoever doeth not righteousness is not of God, neither he that loveth not his brother.

2. ***Hebrews 7:14-16, 24-28*** – For it is evident that our Lord sprang out of Juda (Judah); of which tribe Moses spake nothing concerning priesthood. And it is yet far more evident: for that after the similitude (likeness) of Melchisidec there ariseth another priest, who is made, not after the law of a carnal commandment, but after the power of an endless life. But this man (Jesus), because he continueth ever, hath an unchangeable priesthood. Wherefore he is able also to save them to the uttermost that come unto God by him, seeing he ever liveth to make intercession for them. For such an high priest became us, who is holy, harmless, undefiled, separate from sinners, and made higher than the heavens; who needeth not daily, as those high priests, to offer up sacrifice, first for his own sins, and then for the people's: for this he did once, when he offered up himself. For the law maketh men high priests which have infirmity; but

the word of the oath, which was since the law, maketh the Son, who is consecrated for evermore.

Reference:
Hebrews 9:26-28 – *For then must he (Jesus) often have suffered since the foundation of the world: but now once in the end of the world hath he appeared to put away sin by the sacrifice of himself. And as it is appointed unto men once to die, but after this the judgment: so Christ was once offered to bear the sins of many; and unto them that look for him shall he appear the second time without sin unto salvation.*

Please refer to **Note 21b** for additional Scriptures relating to the righteousness of God.

21(b) *Jesus, I thank You that You were made* to be sin Who knew no sin, that in and through *You I* might become [endued with, viewed as being in, and *an example* of] the righteousness of God [what *I* ought to be, approved and acceptable and in right relationship with You, by Your goodness]. (2 Corinthians 5:21-AMPCE)

The great exchange took place the day Jesus Christ died on the cross! He bore our sins in His own body on the tree that we being dead to sin should live unto righteousness *(1 Peter 2:24)*. The Lord Jesus Christ chose to humble Himself and became obedient unto death, even the death of the cross, becoming the final sacrifice for our sins in order to give to us abundant life *(Philippians 2:8; John 10:10)*. He made it possible for us to walk in newness of life that can only be found in Him *(Romans 6:4)*. The reality of this "newness of life" comes as we choose to renew the *spirit of our minds* or *inmost mind* and put on the new man which after God is created in righteousness and true holiness *(Ephesians 4:20-24)*. In the way of His righteousness is life; and in the pathway thereof there is no death *(Proverbs 12:28)*! He did what the law could not do *(Romans 8:3)*. Again, as stated in **Note 20b**, God has a call on each of our lives (e.g., a husband, a father, a mother, a housewife, a minister of the gospel, a businessman or woman, an employee, an employer, a house cleaner, a janitor, a waitress/waiter) and whatever the call, He is looking for us to put off the old man and put on the new man in Christ. Our true destiny in this life is to be conformed to the image of His Son *(Romans 8:29)*!

Renewing the *spirit of our minds* or *inmost mind* to the truth of God's Word concerning the new man in Christ is the key to putting on the new man, producing life and peace *(Ephesians 4:20-24)*. For in doing that, His Word works in us to unearth the old man (our carnal nature), bringing it to the light so we can faithfully confess and repent of those things before the Lord *(Hebrews 4:12-13)*. Remember, going about to establish our own righteousness is to God as filthy rags *(Isaiah 64:6)*. Righteousness is a gift from God through the death, burial, and resurrection of His Son, Jesus Christ. Righteousness and holiness go hand in hand. His Righteousness paves the way within us to become holy through sanctification *(Romans 6:19)*. Paul writes,

Therefore, if any man be in Christ, he is a new creature: old things are passed away; behold, all things are become new. And all things are of God, who hath reconciled us to himself by Jesus Christ, and hath given unto us the ministry of reconciliation; to wit, that God was in Christ, reconciling the world unto himself, not imputing their trespasses unto them; and hath committed unto us the word of reconciliation. Now then we are ambassadors for Christ, as though God did beseech you by us: we pray you in Christ's stead, be ye reconciled to God. For he hath made him to be sin for us, who knew no sin; that we

162

might be made the righteousness of God in him.

(2 Corinthians 5:17-21)

Below are additional Scriptures relating to the righteousness of God:

1. **Psalm 103:12** – *As far as the east is from the west, so far hath he removed our transgressions from us.*

References:
Psalm 37:3-6, 37-40 – *Trust in the LORD, and do good; so shalt thou dwell in the land, and verily thou shalt be fed. Delight thyself also in the LORD; and he shall give thee the desires of thine heart. Commit thy way unto the LORD; trust also in him; and he shall bring it to pass. And he shall bring forth thy righteousness as the light, and thy judgment as the noonday. Mark the perfect (undefiled) man, and behold the upright: for the end of that man is peace. But the transgressors shall be destroyed together: the end of the wicked shall be cut off. But the salvation of the righteous is of the LORD: he is their strength in the time of trouble. And the LORD shall help them, and deliver them: he shall deliver them from the wicked, and save them, because they trust in him.* **Isaiah 32:17** *(AMPCE) – And the effect of righteousness will be peace [internal and external], and the result of righteousness will be quietness and confident trust forever.* **Isaiah 43:25** – *I, even I, am he that blotteth out thy transgressions for mine own sake, and will not remember thy sins.* **2 Corinthians 3:5-9** – *Not that we are sufficient of ourselves to think any thing as of ourselves; but our sufficiency is of God; who also hath made us able ministers of the new testament (new covenant); not of the letter, but of the spirit: for the letter killeth, but the spirit giveth life. But if the ministration of death, written and engraven in stones, was glorious, so that the children of Israel could not steadfastly behold the face of Moses for the glory of his countenance; which glory was to be done away: how shall not the ministration of the spirit be rather glorious? For if the ministration of condemnation be glory, much more doth the ministration of righteousness exceed in glory.* **Hebrews 8:12-13** – *"For I will be merciful to their unrighteousness, and their sins and their iniquities will I remember no more." In that he saith, "A new covenant," he hath made the first old. Now that which decayeth and waxeth old is ready to vanish away.* **Hebrews 10:16-17** – *"This is the covenant that I will make with them after those days," saith the Lord, "I will put my laws into their hearts, and in their minds will I write them; and their sins and iniquities will I remember no more.*

2. **Proverbs 12:3, 5, 7, 12-14, 17-19, 28** – *A man shall not be established by wickedness: but the root of the righteous shall not be moved. The thoughts of the righteous are right: but the counsels of the wicked are deceit. The wicked are overthrown, and are not: but the house of the righteous shall stand (see Luke 6:46-49). The wicked desireth the net of evil men: but the root of the righteous yieldeth fruit (see Galatians 5:22-24). The wicked is snared by the transgression of his lips: but the just shall come out of trouble. A man shall be satisfied with good by the fruit of his mouth: and the recompence of a man's hands shall be rendered unto him. He that speaketh truth sheweth forth righteousness: but a false witness deceit. There is that speaketh like the piercings of a sword: but the tongue of the wise is health. The lip of truth shall be established for ever: but a lying tongue is but for a moment. In the way of righteousness is life; and in the pathway thereof there is no death.*

References:
Psalm 55:22 – *Cast thy burden upon the LORD, and he shall sustain thee: he shall never suffer the righteous to be moved.* **Proverbs 10:2-3, 11, 20** – *Treasures of wickedness profit nothing: but righteousness delivereth from death. The Lord will not suffer the soul of the righteous to famish... the mouth of a righteous man is a well of life: but violence covereth the mouth of the wicked. The tongue of the just is as choice*

silver: the heart of the wicked is little worth. **Proverbs 11:5-6, 8, 18-19, 30-31** – *The righteousness of the perfect (undefiled) shall direct his way: but the wicked shall fall by his own wickedness. The righteousness of the upright shall deliver them: but transgressors shall be taken in their own naughtiness. The righteous is delivered out of trouble, and the wicked cometh in his stead. The wicked worketh a deceitful work: but to him that soweth righteousness shall be a sure reward. As righteousness tendeth to life: so he that pursueth evil pursueth it to his own death. The fruit of the righteous is a tree of life; and he that winneth souls is wise. Behold, the righteous shall be recompensed in the earth: much more the wicked and the sinner.* **Isaiah 61:1-3** – *The Spirit of the Lord GOD is upon me; because the LORD hath anointed me to preach good tidings unto the meek; he hath sent me to bind up the brokenhearted, to proclaim liberty to the captives, and the opening of the prison to them that are bound; to proclaim the acceptable year of the LORD, and the day of vengeance of our God; to comfort all that mourn; to appoint unto them that mourn in Zion, to give unto them beauty for ashes, the oil of joy for mourning, the garment of praise for the spirit of heaviness; that they might be called trees of righteousness, the planting of the LORD, that he might be glorified.* **Galatians 5:22-24** – *But the fruit of the Spirit is love, joy, peace, longsuffering, gentleness, goodness, faith, meekness, temperance: against such there is no law. And they that are Christ's have crucified the flesh with the affections and lusts.* **Galatians 6:7-8** – *Be not deceived; God is not mocked: for whatsoever a man soweth, that shall he also reap. For he that soweth to his flesh shall of the flesh reap corruption; but he that soweth to the Spirit shall of the Spirit reap life everlasting.* **Philippians 1:6, 9-11** – *Being confident of this very thing, that he which hath begun a good work in you will perform it until the day of Jesus Christ. And this I pray, that your love may abound yet more and more in knowledge and in all judgment; that ye may approve things that are excellent; that ye may be sincere and without offence till the day of Christ; being filled with the fruits of righteousness, which are by Jesus Christ, unto the glory and praise of God.*

3. **Proverbs 15:6, 9, 19, 28-29** – *In the house of the righteous is much treasure: but in the revenues of the wicked is trouble. The way of the wicked is an abomination unto the LORD: but he loveth him that followeth after righteousness. The way of the slothful man is as an hedge of thorns: but the way of the righteous is made plain. The heart of the righteous studieth to answer: but the mouth of the wicked poureth out evil things. The LORD is far from the wicked: but he heareth the prayer of the righteous.*

References:
Psalm 118:19-23 (NKJV) – *Open to me the gates of righteousness: I will go through them, and I will praise the LORD. This is the gate of the LORD, through which the righteous shall enter. I will praise You, for you have answered me, and have become my salvation. The stone which the builders rejected has become the chief cornerstone. This was the LORD's doing; it is marvelous in our eyes.* **Proverbs 13:6, 21** – *Righteousness keepeth him that is upright in the way: but wickedness overthroweth the sinner. Evil pursueth sinners: but to the righteous good shall be repaid.* **Proverbs 14:9** – *Fools make a mock at sin: but among the righteous there is favour.* **Proverbs 21:21** – *He that followeth after righteousness and mercy findeth life, righteousness, and honour.* **2 Corinthians 6:14-16** – *Be ye not unequally yoked together with unbelievers: for what fellowship hath righteousness with unrighteousness? And what communion hath light with darkness? And what concord hath Christ with Belial? Or what part hath he that believeth with an infidel? And what agreement hath the temple of God with idols? For ye are the temple of the living God; as God hath said, "I will dwell in them, and walk in them; and I will be their God, and they shall be my people."* **1 Timothy 6:11-12** – *But thou, O man of God, flee these things; and follow after righteousness, godliness, faith, love, patience, meekness. Fight the good fight of faith, lay hold on eternal life, whereunto thou art also called...* **1 John 2:28-29** – *And now, little children, abide in him (Jesus); that, when he shall appear, we may have confidence, and not be ashamed before him at his coming. If ye know that he is righteous, ye know that every one that doeth*

righteousness is born of him.

4. ***Ephesians 6:12-18*** *— For we wrestle not against flesh and blood, but against principalities, against powers, against the rulers of the darkness of this world, against spiritual wickedness in high places. Wherefore take unto you the whole armour of God, that ye may be able to withstand in the evil day, and having done all, to stand. Stand therefore, having your loins girt about with truth, and having on the breastplate of righteousness…*

Reference:
1 Thessalonians 5:8 *— But let us, who are of the day, be sober, putting on the breastplate of faith and love; and for an helmet, the hope of salvation.* (Note: the breastplate of faith and love is the same as the breastplate of righteousness.)

5. ***Isaiah 53:5-6*** *— But he (Jesus) was wounded for our transgressions, he was bruised for our iniquities: the chastisement of our peace was upon him; and with his stripes we are healed. All we like sheep have gone astray; we have turned every one to his own way; and the LORD hath laid on him the iniquity of us all.*

References:
1 Peter 2:21-25 *— …who his own self (Jesus) bare our sins in his own body on the tree, that we, being dead to sins, should live unto righteousness: by whose stripes ye were healed. For ye were as sheep going astray; but are now returned unto the Shepherd and Bishop of your souls.* ***2 Peter 2:20-22*** *— For if after they have escaped the pollutions of the world through the knowledge of the Lord and Saviour Jesus Christ, they are again entangled therein, and overcome, the latter end is worse with them than the beginning. For it had been better for them not to have known the way of righteousness, than, after they have known it, to turn from the holy commandment delivered unto them. But it is happened unto them according to the true proverb, "The dog is turned to his own vomit again; and the sow that was washed to her wallowing in the mire."*

Here are more Scriptures relating to the righteousness of God: Deuteronomy 30:11-15; 2 Samuel 22:21-31; Psalm 1:1-6, 15:1-5, 34:17,19, 119:172; Proverbs 2:20-22, 10:16, 25, 28-32, 12:10, 16:13; Isaiah 55:6-13, 61:11; Hosea 10:12-13; Matthew 5:6, 6:24-34; Luke 6:43-49; Romans 1:16-17, 3:19-31, 4:1-25, 6:1-4, 15-23, 7:14-25, 8:10, 9:30-33, 10:3-13, 12:1-2; 1 Corinthians 15:34; Galatians 3:5-14, 19-29; Ephesians 4:9-16, 5:8-10; 1 Timothy 4:7-8; 2 Timothy 3:16-17; 1 Peter 3:12.

Please refer to **Note 21a** for additional Scriptures relating to the righteousness of God.

22(a) *You are **Yahweh-M'Kaddesh – You are the LORD who sanctifies**. (Ref.: Exodus 31:13; Leviticus 20:7-8; Hebrews 2:11, 9:11-18)*

M'Kaddesh is derived from the Hebrew word *qadash* which occurs over 150 times in the King James Version. The meaning of *qadash* is "to be (causatively, <u>make, pronounce or observe as) clean (ceremonially or morally)</u>…" To bring wholeness within. There is no one like God in all of creation! The amazing thing is that our heavenly Father gave His only begotten Son, Jesus Christ, so that we can

165

live out of His righteousness and holiness. He alone sanctifies us by the truth of His Word and through the power of His Holy Spirit. This sanctification can only be found in the born-again creation, the new man *(John 17:17; Romans 15:16; Ephesians 4:23-24)*. This is why Paul speaks of the importance of sanctification to the church at Corinth,

> *And I, brethren, could not speak unto you as unto spiritual, but as unto carnal, even as unto babes in Christ. I have fed you with milk, and not with meat: for hitherto ye were not able to bear it, neither yet now are ye able. For ye are yet carnal: for whereas there is among you envying, and strife, and divisions, are ye not carnal, and walk as men?*
>
> (1 Corinthians 3:1-3)

God is calling us to "grow up" in Christ in order to experience His goodness, His glory, His life-giving presence within us and to express His image in all the earth. *(Ephesians 4:15; Hebrews 6:1; 1 Peter 2:2, 5:10; 2 Peter 3:18)*. Paul writes,

> *And the very God of peace sanctify you wholly; and I pray God your whole spirit and soul and body be preserved blameless unto the coming of our Lord Jesus Christ. Faithful is he that calleth you, who also will do it.*
>
> (1 Thessalonians 5:23-24)

The word "sanctify" in the Greek is *hagiazo* meaning "to make holy, i.e. (ceremonially) purify or consecrate; (mentally) to venerate: hallow, be holy, sanctify." Its meaning in the Thayer's Greek Lexicon is "to purify internally by reformation of the soul: John 17:17, 19 (through knowledge of the truth, cf. John 8:32); 1 Thessalonians 5:23; 1 Corinthians 1:2…" The word sanctify comes from the root word *hagios* meaning "…(most) holy (one, thing), saint." Below is a passage of Scripture containing the Greek word *hagios*:

> *But as he which hath called you is holy (hagios), so be ye holy (hagios) in all manner of conversation (behavior); because it is written, "Be ye holy (hagios); for I am holy (hagios)." And if ye call on the Father, who without respect of persons judgeth according to every man's work, pass the time of your sojourning here in fear: for as much as ye know that ye were not redeemed with corruptible things, as silver and gold, from your vain conversation (behavior) received by tradition from your fathers; but with the precious blood of Christ, as of a lamb without blemish and without spot.*
>
> (1 Peter 1:15-19)

Below are Scriptures relating to sanctification:

1. ***Hebrews 2:9-12*** *– But we see Jesus, who was made a little lower than the angels for the suffering of death, crowned with glory and honour; that he by the grace of God should taste death for every man. For it became him, for whom are all things, and by whom are all things, in bringing many sons unto glory, to make the captain of their salvation perfect through sufferings. For both he that sanctifieth and they who are sanctified are all of one: for which cause he is not ashamed to call them brethren, saying, "I will declare thy name unto my brethren, in the midst of the church will I sing praise unto thee."*

References:

Proverbs 17:3 – *The fining pot is for silver, and the furnace for gold: but the LORD trieth (examines) the hearts.* ***Isaiah 1:24-26*** – *Therefore saith the Lord, the LORD of hosts, the mighty One of Israel, "Ah, I will ease me of mine adversaries, and avenge me of mine enemies: and I will turn my hand upon thee, and purely purge away thy dross, and take away all thy tin: and I will restore thy judges as at the first, and thy counsellors as at the beginning: afterward thou shalt be called, The city of righteousness, the faithful city."* ***Malachi 3:1-3*** – *"Behold, I will send my messenger, and he shall prepare the way before me: and the Lord, whom ye seek, shall suddenly come to his temple, even the messenger of the covenant, whom ye delight in: behold, he shall come," saith the LORD of hosts. "But who may abide the day of his coming? And who shall stand when he appeareth? For he is like a refiner's fire, and like fullers' soap: and he shall sit as a refiner and purifier of silver: and he shall purify the sons of Levi, and purge them as gold and silver, that they may offer unto the LORD an offering in righteousness."*

2. ***Hebrews 10:8-14*** – *Above when he said, "Sacrifice and offering and burnt offerings and offering for sin thou wouldest not, neither hadst pleasure therein;" which are offered by the law; then he said, "Lo, I come to do thy will, O God." He taketh away the first, that he may establish the second. By the which will we are sanctified through the offering of the body of Jesus Christ once for all. And every priest standeth daily ministering and offering oftentimes the same sacrifices, which can never take away sins: but this man, after he had offered one sacrifice for sins forever, sat down on the right hand of God; from henceforth expecting till his enemies be made his footstool. For by one offering he hath perfected for ever them that are sanctified.*

References:

John 17:17-19 – *Jesus said, "Sanctify them through thy truth: Thy word is truth. As thou hast sent me into the world, even so have I also sent them into the world. And for their sakes I sanctify myself, that they also might be sanctified through the truth."* ***Romans 1:1-4*** – *Paul, a servant of Jesus Christ, called to be an apostle, separated unto the gospel of God, (which he had promised afore by his prophets in the holy scriptures,) concerning his Son Jesus Christ our Lord, which was made of the seed of David according to the flesh; and declared to be the Son of God with power, according to the spirit of holiness, by the resurrection from the dead.* ***Acts 26:17-18 (NKJV)*** – *Jesus said to Paul, "I will deliver you from the Jewish people, as well as from the Gentiles, to whom I now send you, to open their eyes, in order to turn them from darkness to light, and from the power of Satan to God, that they may receive forgiveness of sins and an inheritance among those who are sanctified by faith in Me."* ***1 Corinthians 1:2, 30-31*** – *Unto the church of God which is at Corinth, to them that are sanctified in Christ Jesus, called to be saints, with all that in every place call upon the name of Jesus Christ our Lord, both theirs and ours. But of him are ye in Christ Jesus, who of God is made unto us wisdom, and righteousness, and sanctification, and redemption: that, according as it is written, "He that glorieth, let him glory in the Lord."* ***2 Thessalonians 2:13*** – *But we are bound to give thanks alway to God for you, brethren beloved of the Lord, because God hath from the beginning chosen you to salvation through sanctification of the Spirit and belief of the truth.* ***1 Timothy 4:7-8*** – *But refuse profane and old wives' fables, and exercise thyself rather unto godliness. For bodily exercise profiteth little: but godliness is profitable unto all things, having promise of the life that now is, and of that which is to come.* ***Hebrews 9:13-14*** – *For if the blood of bulls and of goats, and the ashes of an heifer sprinkling the unclean, sanctifieth to the purifying of the flesh: how much more shall the blood of Christ, who through the eternal Spirit offered himself without spot to God, purge your conscience from dead works to serve the living God?* ***1 Peter 1:2*** – *Elect according to the foreknowledge of God the Father, through sanctification of the Spirit, unto obedience and sprinkling of the blood of Jesus Christ: Grace unto you, and peace, be multiplied.*

3. *1 Corinthians 6:9-11 – Know ye not that the unrighteous shall not inherit the kingdom of God? Be not deceived: neither fornicators, nor idolaters, nor adulterers, nor effeminate, nor abusers of themselves with mankind, nor thieves, nor covetous, nor drunkards, nor revilers, nor extortioners, shall inherit the kingdom of God. And such were some of you: but ye are washed, but ye are sanctified, but ye are justified in the name of the Lord Jesus, and by the Spirit of our God.*

References:

1 Corinthians 7:1-2 – Now concerning the things whereof ye wrote unto me: it is good for a man not to touch a woman. Nevertheless, to avoid fornication, let every man have his own wife, and let every woman have her own husband. (Scripture is clear that marriage is honorable and the marriage bed is undefiled – *Hebrews 13:4*. Marriage, according to God's design, is only between a man and a woman. Therefore, in God's eyes any sexual act outside of His design is sexual immorality. Do not be deceived, just because the government or the courts choose to make a ruling that same sex marriage is legal, it will NEVER be acceptable nor pleasing to God). *1 Thessalonians 4:1-8 – Furthermore then we beseech you, brethren, and exhort you by the Lord Jesus, that as ye have received of us how ye ought to walk and to please God, so ye would abound more and more. For ye know what commandments we gave you by the Lord Jesus. For this is the will of God, even your sanctification, that ye should abstain from fornication: that every one of you should know how to possess his vessel in sanctification and honour; not in the lust of <u>concupiscence</u>, even as the Gentiles which know not God: that no man go beyond and defraud his brother in any matter: because that the Lord is the avenger of all such, as we also have forewarned you and testified. For God hath not called us unto uncleanness, but unto holiness. He therefore that despiseth, despiseth not man, but God, who hath also given unto us his holy Spirit.* The Greek word for concupiscence is *epithymia* which means "a longing (especially for what is forbidden):– concupiscence, desire, lust (after)." The root word is *epithymeo* which means "to set the heart upon, i.e. long for (rightfully or otherwise):–covet, desire, would fain, lust (after)."

22(b) *You* sanctify [purify, consecrate, separate *me* for Yourself, *You* make *me* holy] by the Truth; Your Word is Truth. The sum of Your word is truth. (John 17:17-AMPCE; Psalm 119:160-AMPCE)

My definition of "truth" is defined as "*the reality of life based on the Word of God.*" Again, the word "sanctify" in the Greek is *hagiazo* meaning "<u>to make holy</u>, i.e. (ceremonially) purify or consecrate; (mentally) to venerate:–hallow, be holy, sanctify." Those who believe and trust in the Lord Jesus Christ have been given His Holy Spirit which is the divine essence and carrier of His holiness. Only the Word of God through the power of His "Holy" Spirit can make one holy or set apart for Him. Sanctification is a process of cleansing and removing the pollutants from the heart and mind. In my own life, the Lord did a major tempering work within me that lasted seven years by putting me in an environmental furnace. This furnace was fueled by the ingrained carnal mindsets that were holding me captive to the old man (please see **My Story – Part Two - Volume 1** for details). In the beginning of *Matthew 15*, the scribes and the Pharisees came to Jesus and asked Him why his disciples transgressed the traditions of the elders by not washing their hands when eating bread? Jesus upbraided them and then called the multitudes and said to them in *Matthew 15:11*, "*Not that which goeth into the mouth defileth a man; but that which cometh out of the mouth, this defileth a man.*" In *verse 15*, Peter asked Jesus to explain the parable to them (His disciples). So Jesus said,

Are you also still without understanding? Do you not yet understand that whatever enters

the mouth goes into the stomach and is eliminated? But those things which proceed out of the mouth come from the heart, and they defile a man. For out of the heart proceed evil thoughts, murders, adulteries, fornications, thefts, false witness, blasphemies. These are the things which defile a man, but to eat with unwashed hands does not defile a man.

(Matthew 15:16-20, NKJV)

The Greek word for "defile" is *koinoo* which means "to make (or consider) profane (ceremonially):— call common, defile, <u>pollute</u>, <u>unclean</u>." It comes from the root word *koinos* which means "common, i.e. (literally) shared by all or several, or (ceremonially) profane:—common, defiled, <u>unclean</u>, <u>unholy</u>." Sanctification is God's will for every born-again believer in Christ *(1 Thessalonians 4:3-4)*. He desires to get to the depths of our carnality through the Word of His power to bring sanctification and purity of heart and mind. It is written in the book of Hebrews,

For the word of God is quick (living), and powerful, and sharper than any twoedged sword, piercing even to the dividing asunder of soul and spirit, and of the joints and marrow, and is a discerner of the thoughts and intents of the heart. Neither is there any creature that is not manifest in his sight: but all things are naked and opened unto the eyes of him with whom we have to do.

(Hebrews 4:12-13)

Paul also writes about the sanctifying power of the Word of God,

Husbands, love your wives, even as Christ also loved the church, and gave himself for it; that he might sanctify and cleanse it with the washing of water by the word, that he might present it to himself a glorious church, not having spot, or wrinkle, or any such thing; but that it should be holy and without blemish.

(Ephesians 5:25-27)

We cannot make ourselves holy! I believe it is important to share again, the correlation between the kidneys and the *inmost mind*, as I shared in **Understanding Its Importance** and **My Story – Part Two - Volume 1**. It is essential and important to renew the *spirit of your mind* or your *inmost mind* to the power, purity, and life of God's Word. Let's look at the following passages of Scripture:

- *Psalm 26:2 – David said, "Examine me, O LORD, and prove me; try my reins and my heart."*
- *Jeremiah 17:10 – I the LORD search the heart, I try the reins, even to give every man according to his ways, and according to the fruit of his doings.*
- *Revelation 2:23 – Jesus said, "…and all the churches shall know that I am he which searcheth the reins and hearts: and I will give unto every one of you according to your works."*

The word "reins" in Hebrew is *kilyah* which means "(only in the plural): a kidney (as an essential organ); figuratively, the mind (as the interior self):—kidneys, reins." The word "reins" in Greek is *nephros* which means "a kidney (plural), i.e. (figuratively) <u>the inmost mind</u>:—reins." In looking up the synonyms for "inmost mind," two words stuck out to me—subconscious and spirit. This, I believe, is what Paul is referring to in *Ephesians 4:23*, "be renewed in the *spirit of your mind* or your *inmost mind*." One correlation between the kidneys and the *inmost mind* is that the kidneys are located deep within the body and the *inmost mind* is located deep within the soul. As explained in **My Story – Part**

Two - Volume 1, as the Lord had me personalize certain portions of Scripture (now contained in the *Personalized Scripture Guide - Volume 1*) regarding His eternal love, care, and faithfulness toward me and Scriptures regarding putting off the old man and putting on the new man, a change began to take place on the inside of me! As I began speaking them aloud for six months, "and receiving them as my own," the power, purity, and life of His Word began to consistently flow into my *inmost mind*. As the kidneys remove toxic waste from the blood to keep the body healthy, in the same way, the *inmost mind*, as the life of His Word became a consistent flow, began to filter and flush out ingrained carnal core beliefs and mindsets or toxic waste (e.g., rebellion, pride, insecurities, rejection), the primary source of the old man. *(Leviticus 17:11; Psalm 119:9; John 6:63; Ephesians 5:25-27; 1 Peter 1:22-2:3, 3:1-4).* This is true sanctification producing His righteousness, holiness, and the fruit of the Spirit *(Ephesians 4:22-24; Galatians 5:22-24).*

When God chooses people to do great things for Him, His sanctification process runs deep and is essential in order for His work to be accomplished according to His will. Unfortunately, too many times when God puts a dream or a work in the hearts and minds of His children, some tend to want to bypass the sanctification process and begin to try fulfilling the dream or the work within them due to their own excitement. When we get ahead of God by trying to fulfill the call in our own strength, before the sanctification process is complete, it can end up in disaster and extreme disappointment, and therefore, we can easily become discouraged and disillusioned.

One example in the Old Testament is Joseph who had a dream from God and was called to do a great work for Him. Joseph's father was Jacob (Israel). He favored Joseph above his other children and made him a coat of many colors. When the brothers saw that their father loved Joseph more than them, they hated Joseph. When Joseph was seventeen, he had a dream and shared it with his brothers who after hearing the dream, hated him even more. The dream depicted that Joseph would reign over them. One day, the eleven sons were in Dothan taking care of the flocks and Joseph went to find them. When the brothers saw Joseph afar off, they wanted to kill him. But one of his brothers, Reuben, delivered Joseph out of their hands by saying, "*Let us not kill him. Shed no blood, but cast him into this pit that is in the wilderness, and lay no hand upon him.*" Reuben wanted to bring him back to his father. So they stripped the coat of many colors off of Joseph and cast him into a pit and then sat down to eat bread. While the brothers were eating, they looked and saw a company of Ishmaelites coming from Gilead with their camels bearing spices, balm, and myrrh to take to Egypt. Judah then suggested to his brothers that instead of killing Joseph they should sell him to the Ishmaelites for twenty pieces of silver and they agreed. Then as the Midianite merchantmen passed by, the brothers drew Joseph out of the pit and sold him to the Ishmaelites for twenty pieces of silver. Evidently, Reuben had gone away from his brothers when they sold him, and when Reuben returned to the pit to check on Joseph, he was not there and he tore his clothes. He then went back to his brothers and said that he was gone! So they took Joseph's coat, killed a kid of a goat and dipped the coat in the blood, and brought it to their father; and said, "*This have we found: know now whether it be your son's coat or not.*" So, Jacob, his father, thought Joseph was killed *(Genesis 37)*. Joseph was brought down to Egypt; and Potiphar, an officer of Pharaoh, bought him from the Ishmaelites. And it is written in *Genesis 39:2-16*,

> *And the LORD was with Joseph, and he was a prosperous man; and he was in the house of his master the Egyptian. And his master saw that the LORD was with him, and that the LORD made all that he did to prosper in his hand. And Joseph found grace in his sight, and he served him: and he made him overseer over his house, and all that he had he put into his*

hand. And it came to pass from the time that he had made him overseer in his house, and over all that he had, that the LORD blessed the Egyptian's house for Joseph's sake; and the blessing of the LORD was upon all that he had in the house, and in the field. And he left all that he had in Joseph's hand; and he knew not ought he had, save the bread which he did eat. And Joseph was a goodly person, and well favoured. And it came to pass after these things, that his master's wife cast her eyes upon Joseph; and she said, "Lie with me." But he refused, and said unto his master's wife, "Behold, my master wotteth not (does not know) what is with me in the house, and he hath committed all that he hath to my hand; there is none greater in this house than I; neither hath he kept back any thing from me but thee, because thou art his wife: how then can I do this great wickedness, and sin against God?" And it came to pass, as she spake to Joseph day by day, that he hearkened not unto her, to lie by her, or to be with her. And it came to pass about this time, that Joseph went into the house to do his business; and there was none of the men of the house there within. And she caught him by his garment, saying, "Lie with me": and he left his garment in her hand, and fled, and got him out. And it came to pass, when she saw that he had left his garment in her hand, and was fled forth, that she called unto the men of the house, and spake unto them, saying, "See, he hath brought in an Hebrew unto us to mock us; he came in unto me to lie with me, and I cried with a loud voice: and it came to pass, when he heard that I lifted up my voice and cried, that he left his garment with me, and fled, and got him out." And she laid up his garment by her, until his lord came home.

Potiphar's wife then told her husband the same lie. When Joseph's master, Potiphar, heard this, his anger was kindled. He took Joseph and put him into the prison, a place where the king's prisoners were bound. And in *Genesis 39:21-23,*

> *But the LORD was with Joseph, and shewed him mercy, and gave him favour in the sight of the keeper of the prison. And the keeper of the prison committed to Joseph's hand all the prisoners that were in the prison; and whatsoever they did there, he was the doer of it. The keeper of the prison looked not to any thing that was under his hand; because the LORD was with him, and that which he did, the LORD made it to prosper.*

Let's recap. At the age of seventeen, Joseph was sold to the Ishmaelites for twenty pieces of silver and then taken to Egypt. Potiphar, an officer of Pharoah, bought Joseph and he served Potiphar in Potiphar's house until his wife falsely accused him of trying to lie with her after she had continually tried to seduce him to lie with her and he continued to say no. Because of her false accusation, her husband, Potiphar, had Joseph put into prison. It is not clear how long he was in prison, but he was probably there for at least ten years. Scripture reveals that the Lord was with Joseph both in Potiphar's house and in prison, as everything Joseph did, the Lord made to prosper. He had great favor! However, this did not keep Joseph from being sold into slavery, tempted to lie with Potiphar's wife, falsely accused by Potiphar's wife, and put into prison for possibly ten years. This is assuming that he served in Potiphar's house for three years as he was seventeen years old when his brothers sold him to the Ishmaelites, and by the time he was released from prison he was thirty years old. The Lord used all of this to sanctify Joseph as *Psalm 105:16-22* reads:

> *Moreover He called for a famine upon the land: He brake the whole staff of bread (destroyed the provision). He sent a man before them, even Joseph, who was sold for a servant: whose*

feet they hurt with fetters: he was laid in iron: until the time that His word came: the word
of the LORD <u>tried</u> him. The king sent and loosed him; even the ruler of the people, and let
him go free. He made him lord of his house, and ruler of all his substance: to bind his princes
at his pleasure; and teach his senators wisdom.

The word "tried" in Hebrew is *tsaraph* meaning "a primitive root; to fuse (metal), <u>i.e. refine (literally</u> <u>or figuratively</u>):–<u>cast</u>, <u>(re-) fine(-er)</u>, founder, <u>goldsmith</u>, melt, <u>pure</u>, <u>purge away</u>, try." As I shared earlier, about the correlation between the kidney and the *inmost mind*, this same word is used in *Psalm 26:2* where David prayed, *"Examine me, O LORD, and prove me; <u>try my reins</u> and my heart."* His sanctification in us is very important! God released Joseph from prison when God's refining process was complete. Joseph's dream literally came to pass (please read *Genesis 40-47*). In the same way, when the Lord has a work for you to accomplish, you may feel you're in a prison or heated furnace, but know that God is using that prison or furnace to bring sanctification to your *inmost mind* and heart in order for the born-again creation to come forth and His work to be accomplished within you.

Right before Joseph's father, Jacob, died, he called his sons to him and in *Genesis 49:1* he said, *"Gather yourselves together, that I may tell you that which shall befall you in the last days."* When Jacob came to Joseph he said:

> <u>*Joseph is a fruitful bough, even a fruitful bough by a well: whose branches run over the wall*</u>:
> *the archers have sorely grieved him, and shot at him, and hated him: but his bow abode*
> *in strength, and the arms of his hands were made strong by the hands of the mighty God of*
> *Jacob; (from thence is the shepherd, the stone of Israel:) even by the God of thy father, who*
> *shall help thee; and by the Almighty, who shall bless thee with blessings of heaven above,*
> *blessings of the deep that lieth under, blessings of the breasts, and of the womb: the blessings*
> *of thy father have prevailed above the blessings of my progenitors (ancestors) unto the utmost*
> *bound of the everlasting hills: they shall be on the head of Joseph, and on the crown of the*
> *head of him that was separate from his brethren.*
>
> (Genesis 49:22-26)

Joseph was a man of great character through all his trials. His character portrayed humbleness of mind, faith, hope, patience, steadfastness, integrity, honor, goodness, peace, perseverance, and trust in God. In the same way that Jacob called Joseph *"a fruitful bough by a well: whose branches run over the wall"* we too become fruitful as we choose to surrender our will to the Lordship of Jesus Christ and renew the *spirit of our minds* to the power, purity, and life of God's Word. In doing this, the wellspring of life provides the needful spiritual nourishment and strength to the hidden man of the heart in order to grow and mature, bringing forth the fruit of the Spirit *(1 Peter 1:22-2:3; Proverbs 16:22; John 4:14, 7:38-39; Galatians 5:22-24)*. This maturity helps us to endure the trials of life with great character and trust in our heavenly Father.

Below are Scriptures relating to the importance of yielding to His truth:

1. **Proverbs 1:29-33** – *For that they hated knowledge, and did not choose the fear of the LORD: they would none of my counsel: they despised all my reproof. Therefore shall they eat of the fruit of their own way, and be filled with their own devices. For the turning away of the simple shall slay them, and the prosperity of fools shall destroy them. But whoso hearkeneth unto me shall dwell safely, and shall be*

quiet from fear of evil.

References:

Job 5:17 *– Behold, happy is the man whom God correcteth: therefore, despise not thou the chastening of the Almighty.* ***Psalm 94:12-13*** *(NKJV) – Blessed is the man whom You instruct, O LORD, and teach out of Your law, that You may give him rest from the days of adversity, until the pit is dug for the wicked.* ***Psalm 107:17*** *– Fools because of their transgression, and because of their iniquities, are afflicted.* ***Proverbs 3:1-2, 11-12*** *– My son, forget not my law; but let thine heart keep my commandments: for length of days, and long life, and peace, shall they add to thee. My son, despise not the chastening of the LORD; neither be weary of his correction: for whom the LORD loveth he correcteth; even as a father the son in whom he delighteth.* ***Proverbs 15:5*** *– A fool despiseth his father's instruction: but he that regardeth reproof (correction) is prudent.* ***Matthew 7:21-27*** *– Jesus said, "Not every one that saith unto me, 'Lord, Lord,' shall enter into the kingdom of heaven: but he that doeth the will of my Father which is in heaven. Many will say to me in that day, 'Lord, Lord, have we not prophesied in thy name? And in thy name have cast out devils? And in thy name done many wonderful works?' And then will I profess unto them, 'I never knew you: depart from me, ye that work iniquity.' Therefore whosoever heareth these sayings of mine, and doeth them, I will liken him unto a wise man, which built his house upon a rock: and the rain descended, and the floods came, and the winds blew, and beat upon that house; and it fell not: for it was founded upon a rock. And every one that heareth these sayings of mine, and doeth them not, shall be likened unto a foolish man, which built his house upon the sand: and the rain descended, and the floods came, and the winds blew, and beat upon that house; and it fell: and great was the fall of it."* ***Hebrews 12:1-11*** *(NKJV) – Therefore we also, since we are surrounded by so great a cloud of witnesses, let us lay aside every weight, and the sin which so easily ensnares us, and let us run with endurance the race that is set before us, looking unto Jesus, the author and finisher of our faith, who for the joy that was set before Him endured the cross, despising the shame, and has sat down at the right hand of the throne of God. For consider Him who endured such hostility from sinners against Himself, lest you become weary and discouraged in your souls. You have not yet resisted to bloodshed, striving against sin. And you have forgotten the exhortation which speaks to you as to sons: "My son, do not despise the chastening of the Lord, nor be discouraged when you are rebuked by Him; for whom the Lord loves He chastens, and scourges every son whom He receives." If you endure chastening, God deals with you as with sons; for what son is there whom a father does not chasten? But if you are without chastening, of which all have become partakers, then you are illegitimate and not sons. Furthermore, we have had human fathers who corrected us, and we paid them respect. Shall we not much more readily be in subjection to the Father of spirits and live? For they indeed for a few days chastened us as seemed best to them, but He for our profit, that we may be partakers of His holiness. Now no chastening seems to be joyful for the present, but painful; nevertheless, afterward it yields the peaceable fruit of righteousness to those who have been trained by it.*

2. ***Psalm 12:6*** *– The words of the LORD are pure words: as silver tried in a furnace of earth, purified seven times.*

References:

Psalm 119:142, 160 *(NKJV) – Your righteousness is an everlasting righteousness, and Your law is truth. The entirety of your word is truth, and every one of Your righteous judgments endures forever.* ***Proverbs 7:1-3*** *– My son, keep my words, and lay up my commandments with thee. Keep my commandments, and live; and my law as the apple of thine eye. Bind them upon thy fingers, write them upon the table of thine heart.* (How do you write God's law – His words – on the table of your heart? By using your tongue – *Psalm 45:1 – …my tongue is the pen of a ready writer.*) ***Proverbs 30:5*** *– Every word of God is pure: he is a shield* *unto them that put their trust in him.* **Matthew 5:43-48** *— Jesus said, "Ye have heard that it hath been said, 'Thou shalt love thy neighbour, and hate thine enemy.' But I say unto you, love your enemies, bless them that curse you, do good to them that hate you, and pray for them which despitefully use you, and persecute you; that ye may be the children of your Father which is in heaven: for he maketh his sun to rise on the evil and on the good, and sendeth rain on the just and on the unjust. For if ye love them which love you, what reward have ye? Do not even the publicans the same? And if ye salute your brethren only, what do ye more than others? Do not even the publicans so? Be ye therefore perfect, even as your Father which is in heaven is perfect."* (The Greek word for perfect is *teleios* which means "complete (in various applications of labor, growth, mental and moral character, etc.); completeness:–of full age, man, perfect." Completion happens by the power of His Spirit and through the transforming power of the Word of God: becoming Christlike in mind and therefore in character – *Romans 12:1-2; 2 Corinthians 3:17-18; Ephesians 4:20-24; James 1:23-25, 3:2*). **John 1:14, 17** *— And the Word was made flesh, and dwelt among us, (and we beheld his glory, the glory as of the only begotten of the Father,) full of grace and truth. For the law was given by Moses, but grace and truth came by Jesus Christ.* **John 4:23-24** *— Jesus said, But the hour cometh, and now is, when the true worshippers shall worship the Father in spirit and in truth: for the Father seeketh such to worship him. God is a Spirit: and they that worship him must worship him in spirit and in truth."* **John 6:63** *— Jesus said, "It is the spirit that quickeneth (gives life); the flesh profiteth nothing: the words that I speak unto you, they are spirit, and they are life."* **John 8:31-32** *— Then said Jesus to those Jews which believed on him, "If ye continue in my word, then are ye my disciples indeed; and ye shall know the truth, and the truth shall make you free."* **John 14:6** *— Jesus saith unto him, "I am the way, the truth, and the life: no man cometh unto the Father, but by me."* **John 17:1-17** *— These words spake Jesus, and lifted up his eyes to heaven, and said, "Father, the hour is come; glorify thy Son, that thy son also may glorify thee: …Sanctify them through thy truth; thy word is truth."* **Acts 20:32** *— And now, brethren, I commend you to God, and to the word of his grace, which is able to build you up, and to give you an inheritance among all them which are sanctified.* **1 Peter 1:21-25** *— "…seeing ye have purified your souls in obeying the truth through the Spirit unto unfeigned love of the brethren, see that ye love one another with a pure heart fervently: being born again, not of corruptible seed, but of incorruptible, by the word of God, which liveth and abideth for ever. For all flesh is as grass, and all the glory of man as the flower of grass. The grass withereth, and the flower thereof falleth away: but the word of the Lord endureth for ever. And this is the word which by the gospel is preached unto you.*

23(a) *You are* **Holy**. Holy is *Your* name, inspiring awe, reverence, and godly fear. (Psalm 111:9-AMPCE) *(Ref.: 1 Peter 1:16)*

Psalm 111:9 reads in the King James Version – *"…holy and <u>reverend</u> is his name."* The word "reverend" in Hebrew is *yare'* which means "to fear; <u>morally to revere</u>;… <u>reverence</u>…" This Hebrew word occurs over 300 times in the Old Testament. Throughout these passages of Scripture this Hebrew word is used to denote the fear of man, the fear of circumstances, the fear of evil tidings, the fear of God, etc. The Lord's desire is for us to revere Him and Him alone. His desire is for us to be rooted and built up in Him and established in the faith *(Colossians 2:6-10; Ephesians 3:17-21)*. In so doing, we gain a deeper understanding of the reverential fear of the Lord. He alone holds the keys of hell and of death *(Revelation 1:18)*. It is written in *Proverbs 23:17-18 – Let not thine heart envy sinners: but be thou in the fear of the LORD all the day long. For surely there is an end; and thine expectation shall not be cut* *off.* It is important for us to understand that compared to eternity (a life that is never-ending) our life here is as a vapor (an average of seventy to eighty years), for it appears only for a little time and then vanishes away *(James 4:14-17).* When we become born again, our spirit man is one with the Lord. As our spirit man grows into the fullness of Christ we begin to experience eternal life while we are on earth *(Philippians 3:10-11 – AMPCE; 2 Corinthians 4:18 – AMPCE).* The Lord's desire for us is to partake of eternal life while we are living here. Living a life of obedience through reverential godly fear before a holy God helps us to obtain this gift *(Romans 6:23)*!

Let's look at Jesus as our example concerning obedience and godly fear:

> *So also Christ glorified not himself to be made an high priest; but he that said unto him, "Thou art my Son, to day have I begotten thee." As he saith also in another place, "Thou art a priest for ever after the order of Melchisedec." <u>Who in the days of his (Jesus') flesh, when he had offered up prayers and supplications with strong crying and tears unto him that was able to save him from death, and was heard in that he feared; though he were a Son, yet learned he obedience by the things which he suffered; and being made perfect, he became the author of eternal salvation unto all them that obey him</u>; called of God an hight priest after the order of Melchisedec.*
>
> (Hebrews 5:5-10)

The word "feared" in the Greek is *eulabeia.* Its meaning in the Thayer's Greek Lexicon is "simply reverence toward God, godly fear, piety." This word is only found one other place in the New Testament:

> *See that ye refuse not him that speaketh. For if they escaped not who refused him that spake on earth, much more shall not we escape, if we turn away from him that speaketh from heaven: whose voice then shook the earth: but now he hath promised, saying, 'Yet once more I shake not the earth only, but also heaven.' And this word, "Yet once more," signifieth the removing of those things that are shaken, as of things that are made, that those things which cannot be shaken may remain. <u>Wherefore we receiving a kingdom which cannot be moved, let us have grace, whereby we may serve God acceptably with reverence and godly fear: for our God is a consuming fire.</u>*
>
> (Hebrews 12:25-29)

The reverential fear of the Lord and loving God go hand in hand *(Deuteronomy 10:12; Psalm 145:19-20).* If you truly love God, you will fear (be in awe, reverence, and respect) Him. You also cannot separate God from His Word, as the outward manifestation of the fear of God and the love for God is obedience, walking in His ways. Jesus said,

> *"He that hath my commandments, and keepeth them, he it is that loveth me: and he that loveth me shall be loved of my Father, and I will love him, and will manifest myself to him." Judas saith unto him, not Iscariot, "Lord, how is it that thou wilt manifest thyself unto us, and not unto the world?" Jesus answered and said unto him, "If a man love me, he will keep my words: and my Father will love him, and we will come unto him, and make our abode with him. He that loveth me not keepeth not my sayings: and the word which ye hear is not mine, but the Father's which sent me."*
>
> (John 14:21-24)

Below are Scriptures revealing promises and truths from the Old Testament for those who choose to walk in the fear of the LORD:

1. ***Job 28:28*** – *And unto man he said, "Behold, the fear of the Lord, that is wisdom; and to depart from evil is understanding.*

References:
Psalm 111:10 – *The fear of the LORD is the beginning of wisdom: a good understanding have all they that do his commandments: his praise endureth for ever.* ***Proverbs 1:7*** – *The fear of the LORD is the beginning of knowledge: but fools despise wisdom and instruction.* ***Proverbs 9:10-11*** – *The fear of the LORD is the beginning of wisdom: and the knowledge of the holy is understanding. For by me thy days shall be multiplied, and the years of thy life shall be increased.* ***Proverbs 115:33*** – *The fear of the LORD is the instruction of wisdom; and before honour is humility.* (For more information about God's wisdom, please read *Proverbs 8*).

2. ***Psalm 25:12-14*** – *What man is he that feareth the LORD? Him shall he teach in the way that he shall choose. His soul shall dwell at ease; and his seed shall inherit the earth. The secret of the LORD is with them that fear him; and he will shew them his covenant.*

3. ***Psalm 31:19-20*** – *Oh how great is thy goodness, which thou hast laid up for them that fear thee; which thou hast wrought for them that trust in thee before the sons of men! Thou shalt hide them in the secret of thy presence from the pride of man: thou shalt keep them secretly in a pavillion from the strife of tongues.*

4. ***Psalm 33:18-19*** – *Behold, the eye of the LORD is upon them that fear him, upon them that hope in his mercy; to deliver their soul from death, and to keep them alive in famine.*

5. ***Psalm 34:7*** – *The angel of the LORD encampeth round about them that fear him, and delivereth them.*

6. ***Psalm 103:11, 13*** – *For as the heaven is high above the earth, so great is his mercy toward them that fear him. Like as a father pitieth his children, so the LORD pitieth them that fear him.*

7. ***Psalm 112:1-3*** – *Praise ye the LORD. Blessed is the man that feareth the LORD, that delighteth greatly in his commandments. His seed shall be mighty upon earth: the generation of the upright shall be blessed. Wealth and riches shall be in his house: and his righteousness endureth for ever.*

8. ***Psalm 128:1-4*** – *Blessed is every one that feareth the LORD; that walketh in his ways. For thou shalt eat the labour of thine hands: happy shalt thou be, and it shall be well with thee. Thy wife shall be as a fruitful vine by the sides of thine house: thy children like olive plants round about thy table. Behold, that thus shall the man be blessed that feareth the LORD.*

References:
Proverbs 28:14 – *Happy is the man that feareth alway: but he that hardeneth his heart shall fall into mischief.* ***Ecclesiastes 8:12-13*** – *Though a sinner do evil an hundred times, and his days be prolonged, yet surely I know that it shall be well with them that fear God, which fear before him.*

9. ***Psalm 145:19-21*** – *He will fulfil the desire of them that fear him: he also will hear their cry, and will save them. The LORD perserveth all them that love him: but all the wicked will he destroy. My mouth shall speak the praise of the LORD: and let all flesh bless his holy name for ever and ever.*

10. ***Psalm 147:11*** – *The LORD taketh pleasure in them that fear him, in those that hope in his mercy.*

11. ***Proverbs 14:26*** – *In the fear of the LORD is strong confidence: and his children shall have a place of refuge.*

12. ***Proverbs 14:27*** – *The fear of the LORD is a fountain of life, to depart from the snares of death.*

Reference:
Psalm 36:9 – *For with thee is the fountain of life: in thy light shall we see light.* ***Proverbs 13:14*** – *The law of the wise is a fountain of life, to depart from the snares of death.* ***Jeremiah 2:13*** – *For my people have committed two evils; they have forsaken me the fountain of living waters, and hewed them out cisterns, broken cisterns, that can hold no water.* ***Jeremiah 17:13*** – *O LORD, the hope of Israel, all that forsake thee shall be ashamed, and they that depart from me shall be written in the earth, because they have forsaken the LORD, the fountain of living waters.* ***John 7:38-39*** – *Jesus said, "He that believeth on me, as the scripture hath said, out of his belly shall flow rivers of living water." (But this spake he of the Spirit, which they that believe on him should receive: for the Holy Ghost was not yet given; because that Jesus was not yet glorified.)* ***Revelation 21:6*** – *And he said unto me, "It is done. I am Alpha and Omega, the beginning and the end. I will give unto him that is athirst of the fountain of the water of life."*

13. ***Proverbs 16:6*** – *By mercy and truth iniquity is purged: and by the fear of the LORD men depart from evil.*

14. ***Proverbs 19:23*** – *The fear of the LORD tendeth to life: and he that hath it shall abide satisfied; he shall not be visited with evil.*

15. ***Proverbs 22:4*** – *By humility and the fear of the LORD are riches, and honour, and life.*

16. ***Isaiah 33:6*** – *And wisdom and knowledge shall be the stability of thy times, and strength of salvation: the fear of the LORD is his treasure.*

Reference:
2 Corinthians 4:6-7 – *For God, who commanded the light to shine out of darkness, hath shined in our hearts, to give the light of the knowledge of the glory of God in the face of Jesus Christ. But we have this treasure in earthen vessels, that the excellency of the power may be of God, and not of us.*

17. ***Malachi 4:2*** – *But unto you that fear my name shall the Sun of righteousness arise with healing in his wings; and ye shall go forth, and grow up as calves of the stall.*

I believe the following passage of Scripture best sums up these promises and truths. (Remember God never changes. He is the same yesterday, today and forever – *Malachi 3:6; Hebrews 13:8*):

And they shall be my people, and I will be their God: and I will give them one heart, and one way, that they may fear me for ever, for the good of them, and of their children after them: and I will make an everlasting covenant with them, that I will not turn away from them, to do them good; but I will put my fear in their hearts, that they shall not depart from me. Yea, I will rejoice over them to do them good, and I will plant them in this land assuredly with my whole heart and with my whole soul.

(Jeremiah 32:38-41)

What amazing promises and truths to those who choose to walk in the fear of the LORD. These are wonderful promises and truths from a faithful God who loves us! Therefore, humble yourself before Him and surrender your life to Him. Seek Him with all of your heart through His Word and prayer. His Words must be first place in the life of a Christian. It takes more than just believing there is a God and believing that Jesus Christ is the Son of God, even the devils believe and tremble *(James 2:19)*. This is a life commitment to be God-centered and not self-centered. We love Him because He first loved us *(1 John 4:19)*!

Holiness is the very essence of God! He is separate from sinners and there is no unrighteousness in Him *(Psalm 92:15)*. It is amazing to think of God's great love for us in that He sent His only Son, Jesus Christ, to take away the sin of the world. Paul writes,

Therefore if any man be in Christ, he is a new creature: old things are passed away; behold, all things are become new. And all things are of God, who hath reconciled us to himself by Jesus Christ, and hath given to us the ministry of reconciliation; to wit, that God was in Christ, reconciling the world unto himself, not imputing their trespasses unto them; and hath committed unto us the word of reconciliation. Now then we are ambassadors for Christ, as though God did beseech you by us: we pray you in Christ's stead, be ye reconciled to God. For he hath made him to be sin for us, who knew no sin; that we might be made the righteousness of God in him.

(2 Corinthians 5:17-21)

When Jesus was on the cross, all the sin of mankind was put upon Him. God made Jesus who knew no sin to be sin for us! Right before Jesus died, He cried out, *"My God, My God, why hast thou forsaken me?" (Matthew 27:46-50)*. God abandoned Jesus because He cannot look upon sin; He is separate from all that defiles! This demonstrates His great love for us! Now Jesus can come into the depth of our carnality and depravity to make us the <u>new creation</u> that has been in God's heart since the beginning of time. His holiness does inspire awe, reverence, and godly fear – *Psalm 111:9 (AMPCE)* – *"He has sent redemption to His people; He has commanded His covenant to be forever; holy is His name, inspiring awe, reverence and godly fear."*

There are consequences to not walking in the fear of God, as His way is the only way that leads to life! God is pure, mighty, posesses all wisdom and knowledge, loves us with a pure love, and truly has our best interest at heart. Walking in the fear of God motivates us to do His will. His will and His ways are much higher and greater than ours *(Isaiah 55:6-13)*. Surrendering to His will, not being conformed to this world but transformed by the renewing of our minds, is essential for us to walk in His righteousness and holiness *(Romans 12:1-2; Ephesians 4:22-24)*. Sin will rob us of our inheritance and open ourselves up to all types of problems. An example is found in *John 5:1-14:*

Jesus went to Jerusalem and there in Jerusalem was a pool, which was called in Hebrew Bethesda, where many disabled people – blind, lame, and paralyzed were there waiting on the moving of the water. For at a certain season an angel would come and trouble the water and the first one who stepped into the moving water would be healed of their disease. Jesus saw a certain man that was there which had an infirmity thirty-eight years. Jesus asked him if he wanted to be made well? The man responded that when the water was troubled someone would enter into the water before him. Then Jesus said to him, "Rise, take up your bed and walk." And immediately the man was made whole and took up his bed and walked. Later, Jesus found him in the temple, and said to him, "<u>Look, you are well. Sin no more lest a worse thing come upon you.</u>"

Isaiah 40:25 reads – *"To whom then will ye liken me, or shall I be equal?" saith the Holy One.* God is the only One who can sanctify us and make us holy as He is our Holy Creator. Only He can fill the deep longings of our hearts!

Below are additional Scriptures relating to the fear of the Lord:

1. ***Psalm 96:9*** – *O worship the LORD in the beauty of holiness: fear before him, all the earth.*

References:
Psalm 33:4-12 – *For the word of the LORD is right; and all his works are done in truth. He loveth righteousness and judgment: the earth is full of the goodness of the LORD. By the word of the LORD were the heavens made; and all the host of them by the breath of his mouth. He gathereth the waters of the sea together as an heap: he layeth up the depth in storehouses. Let all the earth fear the LORD: let all the inhabitants of the world stand in awe of him. For he spake, and it was done; he commanded, and it stood fast. The LORD bringeth the counsel of the heathen to nought (nothing): he maketh the devices of the people of none effect. The counsel of the LORD standeth for ever, the thoughts of his heart to all generations. Blessed is the nation whose God is the LORD; and the people whom he hath chosen for his own inheritance.* ***Proverbs 14:2, 16*** *– He that walketh in his uprightness feareth the LORD: but he that is perverse in his ways despiseth him. A wise man feareth, and departeth from evil: but the fool rageth, and is confident.* ***Proverbs 15:16*** *– Better is little with the fear of the LORD than great treasure and trouble therewith.* ***Acts 10:34-35*** *– Then Peter opened his mouth, and said, "Of a truth I perceive that God is no respecter of persons (shows no partiality): but in every nation he that feareth him, and worketh righteousness, is accepted with him."* ***Revelation 15:4*** *– Who shall not fear thee, O Lord, and glorify thy name? For thou only art holy: for all nations shall come and worship before thee; for thy judgments are made manifest.*

2. ***Psalm 34:11-15*** – *Come, ye children, hearken unto me: I will teach you the fear of the LORD. What man is he that desireth life, and loveth many days, that he may see good? Keep thy tongue from evil, and thy lips from speaking guile. Depart from evil, and do good; seek peace, and pursue it. The eyes of the LORD are upon the righteous, and his ears are open unto their cry.*

References:
Psalm 119:10-11 – *With my whole heart have I sought thee: O let me not wander from thy commandments. Thy word have I hid in mine heart, that I might not sin against thee.* ***Proverbs 12:15*** *– The way of a fool is right in his own eyes: but he that hearkeneth unto counsel is wise.* ***Proverbs 14:12*** *– There is a way which seemeth right unto a man, but the end thereof are the ways of death.* ***Proverbs 22:5*** *– Thorns and snares*

are in the way of the froward: he that doth keep his soul shall be far from them. **Malachi 3:16-18** – *Then they that feared the LORD spake often one to another: and the LORD hearkened, and heard it, and a book of remembrance was written before him for them that feared the LORD, and that thought upon his name. "And they shall be mine," saith the LORD of hosts, "in the day when I make up my jewels; and I will spare them, as a man spareth his own son that serveth him."*

Please refer to **Notes 22a** and **22b** for information and Scriptures relating to sanctification.

23(b) As the One Who called *me* is holy, *I choose to* be holy in all *my* conduct and manner of living, *by yielding to Your Word.* For it is written, "You shall be holy, for I am holy." (1 Peter 1:15-16-AMPCE)

The Greek word for "holy" is *hagios* meaning "sacred (physically, pure, morally blameless or religious, ceremonially, consecrated):–(most) holy (one, thing), saint." During the time I was seeking the Lord as a teenager, before I walked away from Him, I remember asking a question to a friend of mine who I respected, who was also living in the homosexual lifestyle: "What do you think God thinks of those living a homosexual lifestyle?" Out of all she said to me the one thing that really caught my attention was, "How can a loving God send someone to Hell?" I am fully aware of God's love and how He loved me when I deeply believed that there wasn't anything in me worth loving. But what I've realized within my own self over the years, in my surrender and search for Him, is that God does not send anyone to Hell. Our own choices in life send us to Hell—it's not His will that any should perish *(2 Peter 3:9)*. He's already chosen His will for us but He will not force us to surrender and submit to Him. Through my surrender and submission to His will, His holiness has reached deep within my deprivation and wantonness bringing a wholeness and a purity deep within me. This is His desire and His call for all those who call upon His Name. God's holiness cleanses and purifies the heart and soul of a man to innocence, which sin seeks to destroy. Thank God for His holiness! I believe the word "innocence" is the best way to describe what the Holy Spirit does in the hearts and minds of believers. An example of this is found in the man Daniel of the Old Testament who is described as having an excellent spirit in him *(Daniel 5:12, 6:3)*. He was a man who loved the Lord and was highly exalted by King Belshazzar to be the third ruler in his kingdom. To give a little history let's read *Daniel 5:1-12*:

> *Belshazzar the king made a great feast to a thousand of his lords, and drank wine before the thousand. Belshazzar, whiles he tasted the wine, commanded to bring the golden and silver vessels which his father Nebuchadnezzar had taken out of the temple which was in Jerusalem; that the king, and his princes, his wives, and his concubines might drink therein. Then they brought the golden vessels that were taken out of the temple of the house of God which was at Jerusalem; and the king, and his princes, his wives, and his concubines, drank in them. They drank wine, and praised the gods of gold, and of silver, of brass, of iron, of wood, and of stone. In the same hour came forth fingers of a man's hand, and wrote over against the candlestick upon the plaster of the wall of the king's palace: and the king saw the part of the hand that wrote. Then the king's countenance was changed, and his thoughts troubled him, so that the joints of his loins were loosed, and his knees smote one against another. The king cried aloud to bring in the astrologers, the Chaldeans, and the soothsayers. And the king spake, and said to the wise men of Babylon, "Whosoever shall read this writing, and shew me the interpretation thereof, shall be clothed with scarlet, and have*

a chain of gold about his neck, and shall be the third ruler in the kingdom." Then came in all the king's wise men: but they could not read the writing, nor make known to the king the interpretation thereof. Then was King Belahazzar greatly troubled, and his countenance was changed in him, and his lords were astonied (astonished). Now the queen, by reason of the words of the king and his lords, came into the banquet house: and the queen spake and said, "O king, live for ever: let not thy thoughts trouble thee, nor let thy countenance be changed: there is a man in thy kingdom, in whom is the spirit of the holy gods; and in the days of thy father light and understanding and wisdom, like the wisdom of the gods, was found in him; whom the King Nebuchadnezzar thy father, the king, I say, thy father, made (Daniel) master of the magicians, astrologers, Chaldeans, and soothsayers; forasmuch as an excellent spirit, and knowledge, and understanding, interpreting of dreams, and shewing of hard sentences, and dissolving of doubts, were found in the same Daniel, whom the king named Belteshazzar: now let Daniel be called, and he will shew the interpretation."

In *Daniel 5:13-21*, Daniel was called. The king told Daniel that he would be clothed with scarlet, a gold chain would be put around his neck, and he would be given the third highest position in the kingdom if he could read the writing on the wall and make known to him the interpretation. Daniel told the king he would read the writing on the wall and give the king the interpretation, but to keep his gifts and to give his rewards to someone else. After Daniel reminded the king of what happened to his father, Nebuchadnezzar, when his heart was lifted up and hardened in pride (see **Note 20a**), he said:

And thou his son, O Belshazzar, hast not humbled thine heart, though thou knewest all this (about his father); but hast lifted up thyself against the Lord of heaven; and they have brought the vessels of his house before thee, and thou, and thy lords, thy wives, and thy concubines, have drunk wine in them; and thou hast praised the gods of silver, and gold, of brass, iron, wood, and stone, which see not, nor hear, nor know: and the God in whose hand thy breath is, and whose are all thy ways, hast thou not glorified: then was the part of the hand sent from him; and this writing was written. And this is the writing that was written, MENE, MENE, TEKEL, UPHARSIN. This is the interpretation of the thing: MENE; God hath numbered thy kingdom, and finished it. TEKEL; Thou art weighed in the balances, and art found wanting. PERES; Thy kingdom is divided, and given to the Medes and Persians.

(Daniel 5:22-28)

Even though Daniel told the king to keep his gifts, King Belshazzar commanded that they clothe Daniel with scarlet. They put a chain of gold about his neck, and made a proclamation concerning him that he should be the third ruler in the kingdom. That very night, King Belshazzar was slain and Darius the Mede took the kingdom *(Daniel 5:29-31)*.

It pleased Darius to set over the kingdom an hundred and twenty princes, which should be over the whole kingdom; and over these three presidents; of whom Daniel was first: that the princes might give accounts unto them, and the king should have no damage. Then this Daniel was preferred above the presidents and princes, because an excellent spirit was in him; and the king thought to set him over the whole realm.

(Daniel 6:1-3)

The presidents and princes were jealous of Daniel so they tried to find some charge against him, but found no error or fault in him *(Daniel 6:4)*. They came to the conclusion that they would have to come up with some kind of law against him concerning the law of his God. So they convinced King Darius to make a decree that no one could petition any god or man except for King Darius for thirty days or they would be thrown into the lion's den *(Daniel 6:7)*. Now when Daniel heard that King Darius had signed the decree, he went to his house and continued to do what he had been doing which was to kneel down on his knees three times a day to pray and give thanks to his God. When these men found Daniel praying, they went before King Darius and reminded him of the decree he had signed and told him that Daniel was found making petition before his God. King Darius was very upset with himself and tried to deliver Daniel from having to go into the lion's den but found no way *(Daniel 6:10-15)*. Therefore, Daniel was taken to the lion's den and King Darius spoke to Daniel and said, *"The God you serve continually will deliver you" (Daniel 6:16)*. The king could not sleep and spent the night fasting *(Daniel 6:18)*. The next morning, the king ran to the lion's den and with a lamenting voice cried out in *Daniel 6:20* – *"O Daniel, servant of the living God, is thy God, whom thou servest continually, able to deliver thee from the lions?"* Daniel answered the king,

> *O king, live for ever. My God hath sent his angel, and hath shut the lions' mouths, that they have not hurt me: forasmuch as before him* <u>*innonency*</u> *was found in me; and also before thee, O king, have I done no hurt.*
>
> (Daniel 6:21-22)

The word "innocency" in Aramaic is *zakuw* and means "purity:– innocency." As born-again believers, the same Spirit that raised Jesus Christ from the dead dwells in us, and we too have an excellent spirit! How much more will His Holy Spirit that dwells within us make us pure and holy before Him, restoring innocence to us, as we yield ourselves to Him and renew our minds to His Word *(Romans 8:11, 12:1-2)*. The Holy Spirit is sent to us in order to bring forth the new creation within (the hidden man of the heart) as only the new man can walk in His righteousness and holiness—true innocence before Him—as the *spirit of the mind* or *inmost mind* is renewed *(Ephesians 4:22-24)*.

Below are Scriptures relating to God's holiness:

1. ***Leviticus 19:1-2*** *– And the LORD spake unto Moses, saying, "Speak unto all the congregation of the children of Israel, and say unto them, 'Ye shall be holy: for I the LORD your God am holy.'*

References:
Leviticus 20:26 *– "And ye shall be holy unto me: for I the LORD am holy, and have severed you from other people, that ye should be mine."* ***Psalm 4:3*** *– But know that the LORD hath set apart him that is godly for himself: the LORD will hear when I call unto him.* ***Psalm 26:6-7*** *– I will wash mine hands in innocency: so will I compass thine altar, O LORD: that I may publish with the voice of thanksgiving, and tell of all thy wondrous works.* ***Romans 1:1-6*** *– Paul, a servant of Jesus Christ, called to be an apostle, separated unto the gospel of God, (which he had promised afore by his prophets in the holy scriptures,) concerning his Son Jesus Christ our Lord, which was made of the seed of David according to the flesh; and declared to be the Son of God with power, according to the spirit of holiness, by the resurrection from the dead...* ***Romans 6:17-19*** *– But God be thanked, that ye were the servants of sin, but ye have obeyed from the heart that form of doctrine which was delivered you. Being then made free from sin, ye became the servants of righteousness. I speak after the manner of men because of the infirmity of your flesh: for as ye have yielded your members servants*

to uncleanness and to iniquity unto iniquity; even so now yield your members servants to righteousness unto holiness. **1 Corinthians 2:15-16** – *But he that is spiritual judgeth all things, yet he himself is judged of no man. For who hath known the mind of the Lord, that he may instruct him? But we have the mind of Christ.* **2 Corinthians 7:1** – *Having therefore these promises, dearly beloved, let us cleanse ourselves from all filthiness of the flesh and spirit, perfecting holiness in the fear of God.* **1 Thessalonians 3:12-13** – *And the Lord make you to increase and abound in love one toward another, and toward all men, even as we do toward you: to the end he may stablish your hearts unblameable in holiness before God, even our Father, at the coming of our Lord Jesus Christ with all his saints.* **1 Timothy 1:5-7** – *Now the end of the commandment is charity (God's love) out of a pure heart, and of a good conscience, and of faith unfeigned.* **1 Timothy 3:16** – *And without controversy great is the mystery of godliness: God was manifest in the flesh, justified in the Spirit, seen of angels, preached unto the Gentiles, believed on in the world, received up into glory.* **1 Timothy 4:7-8** – *But refuse profane and old wives' fables, and exercise thyself rather unto godliness. For bodily exercise profiteth little: but godliness is profitable unto all things, having promise of the life that now is, and of that which is to come.* **Titus 2:11-14** – *For the grace of God that bringeth salvation hath appeared to all men, teaching us that, denying ungodliness and worldly lusts, we should live soberly, righteously, and godly, in this present world; looking for that blessed hope, and the glorious appearing of the great God and our Saviour Jesus Christ; who gave himself for us, that he might redeem us from all iniquity, and purify unto himself a peculiar people, zealous of good works.* **Hebrews 12:14-17** – *Follow peace with all men, and holiness, without which no man shall see the Lord: looking diligently lest any man fail of the grace of God; lest any root of bitterness springing up trouble you, and thereby many be defiled; lest there be any fornicator, or profane person, as Esau, who for one morsel of meat sold his birthright. For ye know how that afterward, when he would have inherited the blessing, he was rejected: for he found no place of repentance, though he sought it carefully with tears.* (See *Genesis 25:30-34; 27:1-38*). **1 Peter 1:15-21** – *But as he which hath called you is holy, so be ye holy in all manner of conversation (behavior); because it is written, "Be ye holy; for I am holy." and if ye call on the Father, who without respect of persons judgeth according to every man's work, pass the time of your sojourning here in fear: for as much as ye know that ye were not redeemed with corruptible things, as silver and gold, from your vain conversation (behavior) received by tradition from your fathers; but with the precious blood of Christ, as of a lamb without blemish and without spot: who verily was foreordained before the foundation of the world, but was manifest in these last times for you, who by him do believe in God, that raised him up from the dead, and gave him glory; that your faith and hope might be in God.*

2. **Psalm 99:3, 5, 9** – *Let them praise thy great and terrible name; for it is holy. Exalt ye the LORD our God, and worship at his footstool; for he is holy. Exalt the LORD our God, and worship at his holy hill; for the LORD our God is holy.*

Reference:
Isaiah 57:15 – *For thus saith the high and lofty One that inhabiteth eternity, whose name is Holy; "I dwell in the high and holy place, with him also that is of a contrite and humble spirit, to revive the spirit of the humble, and to revive the heart of the contrite ones."*

Below are Scriptures relating to God's Word:

1. **Joshua 1:1-8** – *Now after the death of Moses the servant of the LORD it came to pass, that the LORD spake unto Joshua the son of Nun, Moses' minister, saying, "…This book of the law shall not depart out of thy mouth; but thou shalt meditate therein day and night, that thou mayest observe to do according*

to all that is written therein: for then thou shalt make thy way prosperous, and then thou shalt have good success."

References:

Psalm 1:1-6 – *Blessed is the man that walketh not in the counsel of the ungodly, nor standeth in the way of sinners, nor sitteth in the seat of the scornful. But his delight is in the law of the LORD; and in his law doeth he meditate day and night. And he shall be like a tree planted by the rivers of water, that bringeth forth his fruit in his season; his leaf also shall not wither; and whatsoever he doeth shall prosper. The ungodly are not so: but are like the chaff which the wind driveth away. Therefore the ungodly shall not stand in the judgment, nor the sinners in the congregation of the righteous. For the LORD knoweth the way of the righteous: but the way of the ungodly shall perish.* **Psalm 57:10** – *For thy mercy is great unto the heavens, and thy truth unto the clouds.* **Psalm 119:89, 130** – *For ever, O LORD, thy word is settled in heaven. The entrance of thy words giveth light; it giveth understanding unto the simple.* **Proverbs 16:6** – *By mercy and truth iniquity is purged: and by the fear of the LORD men depart from evil.* **Isaiah 40:6-8** – *The voice said, "Cry." And he said, "What shall I cry?" "All flesh is grass, and all the goodliness thereof is as the flower of the field: the grass withereth, the flower fadeth: because the spirit of the LORD bloweth upon it: surely the people is grass. The grass withereth, the flower fadeth: but the word of our God shall stand for ever."* **Matthew 7:21-27** – *Jesus said, "Not every one that saith unto me, 'Lord, Lord,' shall enter into the kingdom of heaven; but he that doeth the will of my Father which is in heaven. Many will say to me in that day, 'Lord, Lord, have we not prophesied in thy name? And in thy name have cast out devils? And in thy name done many wonderful works?' And then will I profess unto them, 'I never knew you: depart from me, ye that work iniquity.' Therefore whosoever heareth these sayings of mine, and doeth them, I will liken him unto a wise man, which built his house upon a rock: and the rain descended, and the floods came, and the winds blew, and beat upon that house; and it fell not: for it was founded upon a rock. And every one that heareth these sayings of mine, and doeth them not, shall be likened unto a foolish man, which built his house upon the sand: and the rain descended, and the floods came, and the winds blew, and beat upon that house; and it fell: and great was the fall of it."* (See Matthew 25:32-46, Luke 13:23-28). **Mark 4:1-19** – *Jesus said, "… And these are they which are sown among thorns; such as hear the word, and the cares of this world, and the deceitfulness of riches, and the lusts of other things entering in, choke the word, and it becometh unfruitful."* **John 6:63** – *Jesus said, "It is the spirit that quickeneth (gives life); the flesh profiteth nothing: the words that I speak unto you, they are spirit, and they are life."* **John 8:31-32** – *Then said Jesus to those Jews which believed on him, "If ye continue in my word, then are ye my disciples indeed; and ye shall know the truth, and the truth shall make you free."* **John 17:17** – *Jesus said, "Sanctify them through thy truth: thy word is truth."* **Acts 7:37-53** – *Stephen answered the high priest and addressed the council, "This is that Moses, which said unto the children of Israel, 'A prophet shall the Lord your God raise up unto you of your brethren, like unto me; him shall ye hear.' This is he, that was in the church in the wilderness with the angel which spake to him in the Mount Sina, and with our fathers: who received the lively oracles to give unto us: to whom our fathers would not obey, but thrust him from them, and in their hearts turned back again into Egypt…"* **Ephesians 4:20-24** – *But ye have not so learned Christ; if so be that ye have heard him, and have been taught by him, as the truth is in Jesus: that ye put off concerning the former conversation (behavior) the old man, which is corrupt according to the deceitful lusts; and be renewed in the spirit of your mind; and that ye put on the new man, which after God is created in righteousness and true holiness.* **Hebrews 4:12-13** – *For the word of God is quick (living), and powerful, and sharper than any twoedged sword, piercing even to the dividing asunder of soul and spirit, and of the joints and marrow, and is a discerner of the thoughts and intents of the heart. Neither is there any creature that is not manifest in his sight: but all things are naked and opened unto the eyes of him with whom we have to do.* **Hebrews 5:12-14** – *For when the time ye ought* *to be teachers, ye have need that one teach you again which be the first principles of the oracles of God; and are become such as have need of milk, and not of strong meat. For every one that useth milk is unskilful in the word of righteousness: for he is a babe. But strong meat belongeth to them that are of full age, even those who by reason of use have their senses exercised to discern both good and evil. **1 Peter 1:23-25** – Being born again, not of corruptible seed, but of incorruptible, by the word of God, which liveth and abideth for ever. For all flesh is as grass, and all the glory of man as the flower of grass. The grass withereth, and the flower thereof falleth away: but the word of the Lord endureth for ever. And this is the word which by the gospel is preached unto you.*

2. **1 Peter 5:8-11** – *Be sober, be vigilant; because your adversary the devil, as a roaring lion, walketh about, seeking whom he may devour: whom resist stedfast in the faith, knowing that the same afflictions are accomplished in your brethren that are in the world. But the God of all grace, who hath called us unto his eternal glory by Christ Jesus, after that ye have suffered a while, make you perfect, stablish, strengthen, settle you. To him be glory and dominion for ever and ever. Amen.*

References:
Romans 10:17 – *So then faith cometh by hearing, and hearing by the word of God.* (Jesus overcame the temptations from the devil in the wilderness by saying, *"It is written…"* – see *Matthew 4:1-11*. We too overcome the devil in our own lives by submitting ourselves to God and speaking the reality of His Words of truth, born within our own hearts, during our times of suffering and temptations). **James 1:2-4** – *My brethren, count it all joy when ye fall into divers temptations; knowing this, that the trying of your faith worketh patience. But let patience have her perfect work, that ye may be perfect and entire, wanting nothing.*

Here are additional Scriptures relating to God's holiness: Genesis 17:1-2; Leviticus 11:44; 2 Samuel 22:20-25; Matthew 5:43-48; Romans 6:14-23; 1 Corinthians 1:2-10; 2 Corinthians 6:14-7:1; Ephesians 1:4-10; Philippians 2:15, 3:6; Colossians 1:1-29, 4:12; 1 Thessalonians 4:3-8, 5:15-24; 2 Thessalonians 2:7-13; 2 Timothy 2:19, 3:10-17; Titus 1:1-2; 2 Peter 1:1-21, 3:10-14.

Here are additional Scriptures relating to God's word: Psalm 25:5, 33:6, 138:2; Proverbs 4:4, 20-27; Luke 11:27-28; John 15:26; 2 Timothy 2:15-16, 3:10-17; James 1:21-27; 1 Peter 1:13-25; 2 Peter 1:1-21, 2 John 1:1-6.

23(c) *I* cheerfully submit to, *You,* the Father of spirits, *so I may* [truly] live. For *You* discipline *me* for *my* certain good, that *I* may become a *partaker* of *Your* holiness. (Hebrews 12:9-10-AMPCE) (*Ref.: Ephesians 4:22-24*)

In order to submit to God we must submit to His Word, as you cannot separate the two. His Words are spirit and they are life *(John 1:1-5,14, 6:63)*. To better understand this verse, let's look at the following passage of Scripture:

> *Wherefore seeing we also are compassed about with so great a cloud of witnesses, let us lay aside every weight, and the sin which doth so easily beset us, and let us run with patience the race that is set before us, looking unto Jesus the author and finisher of our faith; who for the joy that was set before him endured the cross, despising the shame, and is set down at*

the right hand of the throne of God. For consider him that endured such contradiction of sinners against himself, lest ye be wearied and faint in your minds. Ye have not yet resisted unto blood, striving against sin. And ye have forgotten the exhortation which speaketh unto you as unto children, "My son, despise not thou the chastening of the Lord, nor faint when thou art rebuked of him: for whom the Lord loveth he chasteneth, and scourgeth every son whom he receiveth." If ye endure chastening, God dealeth with you as with sons; for what son is he whom the father chasteneth not? But if ye be without chastisement, whereof all are partakers, then are ye bastards (illegitimate), and not sons. Furthermore we have had fathers of our flesh which corrected us, and we gave them reverence: shall we not much rather be in subjection unto the Father of spirits, and live? For they verily for a few days chastened us after their own pleasure; but he for our profit, that we might be partakers of his holiness. Now no chastening for the present seemeth to be joyous, but grievous: nevertheless afterward it yieldeth the peaceable fruit of righteousness unto them which are exercised thereby.

(Hebrews 12:1-11)

God's intent for chastening us is for our good, that we might be partakers of His holiness! His desire for us is to be in line with His will and purpose, as He does have our best interest at heart. He knows that sin will destroy our lives and this is why Christ came to abolish sin within us, to give us life and that more abundantly *(1 John 3:8; John 10:10)*. The same Spirit that raised Jesus from the dead dwells in us *(Romans 8:11)*. Paul writes,

If ye then be risen with Christ, seek those things which are above, where Christ sitteth on the right hand of God. Set your affection (mind) on things above, not on things on the earth. For ye are dead, and your life is hid with Christ in God.

(Colossians 3:1-2)

God has called us to be dead to sin and alive to righteousness *(Romans 6:11-18)*. His Spirit satisfies the deep longings of our hearts, and therefore, we no longer desire to find pleasure in sin *(John 7:37-39; 2 Thessalonians 2:12; Hebrews 11:24-25)*! Do not despise the chastening or correction of the Lord. Again, He corrects us for our profit that we may be partakers of His holiness, His divine nature (i.e., His purity, His goodness, His righteousness), to operate and function out of the mind of Christ *(Romans 11:33-34; 1 Corinthians 2:16; Philippians 2:5-13; 1 Peter 1:13-19)*. God teaches and instructs us through His Word and by His Spirit as Paul said in *2 Timothy 3:16-17 – "All scripture is given by inspiration of God, and is profitable for doctrine, for reproof, for correction, for instruction in righteousness: that the man of God may be perfect, throughly furnished unto all good works."* And as Jesus said in *John 16:13 – "Howbeit when he, the Spirit of truth, is come, he will guide you into all truth…"* He also puts us in situations and circumstances and/or uses others (e.g., our spouse, our employer, and/or people who are unpleasant to be around) to unearth ungodly thought processes, etc., that need to be removed from us so that He may be seen more clearly in us, as He sits as a refiner's fire *(2 Corinthians 3:18; Hebrews 12:25-29; James 1:1-27; Malachi 3:1-3)*.

Jesus baptizes us with His Holy Spirit and with fire. John the baptist said,

I indeed baptize you with water unto repentance: but he (Jesus) that cometh after me is mightier than I, whose shoes I am not worthy to bear: he shall baptize you with the Holy Ghost, and with fire: whose fan is in his hand, and he will throughly purge his floor, and

gather his wheat into the garner; but he will burn up the chaff with unquenchable fire.
(Matthew 3:11-12)

It is Christ's desire to thoroughly cleanse His temple (we are the temple of His Holy Spirit—the living God *(1 Corinthians 6:19-20; 2 Corinthians 6:16)*. He has come to cleanse us thoroughly and to flush out the fleshly worthless debris (e.g., ingrained carnal mindsets) within us, again, in order for His image to be seen more clearly in us. Jesus said,

He that believeth on me, as the scripture hath said, out of his belly shall flow rivers of living
water. (But this spake he of the Spirit, which they that believe on him should receive: for the
Holy Ghost was not yet given; because that Jesus was not yet glorified.)
(John 7:38-39)

The word "belly" in the Greek is *koilia* meaning "a cavity, i.e. (especially) the abdomen; by implication, the matrix; figuratively, the heart:–belly, womb." Its meaning in the Thayer's Greek Lexicon is "the innermost part of man, the soul, heart, as the seat of thought, feeling, choice." Concerning the innermost part of man in the Old Testament, listed below are four Scripture references:

1. ***Proverbs 18:8, 26:22*** – *The words of a talebearer are as wounds, and they go down into the "innermost parts" of the belly.*
2. ***Proverbs 20:27, 30*** – *The spirit of man is the candle of the LORD, searching all the "inward parts" of the belly. The blueness of a wound cleanseth away evil: so do stripes the "inward parts" of the belly.*
3. ***Proverbs 24:3-4*** – *Through wisdom is an house builded; and by understanding it is established: and by knowledge shall the chambers (innermost part) be filled with all precious and pleasant riches.*

The Hebrew word for "inward parts" of the belly, "innermost parts" of the belly and "chambers" is the word *cheder* meaning "an inner chamber. An apartment." Missler describes in detail the correlation between the temple that Solomon built in the Old Testament which housed the Ark of the Covenant in the Holy of Holies and our temple where God lives. Missler shares about the Hebrew word *cheder* used to describe our subconscious, as there is no mention of the word subconscious in the Bible. In describing these secret chambers:

"One definition for these secret chambers might be: *a hidden reservoir of mostly untrue beliefs and assumptions, which strongly influence how we evaluate all that happens to us in the present and upon which we make our choices. These choices then determine our actions* (p. 216)."[1]

In looking again at *Proverbs 20:30 – The blueness of a wound cleanseth away evil: so do stripes the "inward parts" of the belly.* Because of what Jesus did on the cross, He is able to go into the depths of our innermost being to totally remove our iniquity, bringing healing and restoration. It is written in Isaiah:

Surely he hath borne our griefs, and carried our sorrows: yet we did esteem him stricken,
smitten of God, and afflicted. But he was wounded for our transgressions, he was bruised for
our iniquities: the chastisement of our peace was upon him; and with his stripes we are healed.
(Isaiah 53:4-5)

Here, Isaiah prophesied that Jesus would die for the sins of the world. Because of His sacrifice (i.e., His woundings, His bruising, His stripes, His death), the Holy Spirit is released from the Father to go into the innermost parts of our belly to unearth and to remove the old man (e.g., our ingrained carnal beliefs and mindsets, woundings, defilement from sin) in order for the new creation within us, the hidden man of the heart, to develop and mature and to enjoy the precious and pleasant riches of Christ *(John 7:38-39; 1 Peter 3:4; Proverbs 24:3-4; Ephesians 3:8)*. Paul writes,

> *For God, who commanded the light to shine out of darkness, hath shined in our hearts, to give the light of the knowledge of the glory of God in the face of Jesus Christ. But we have this treasure in earthen vessels, that the excellency of the power may be of God, and not of us.*
> (2 Corinthians 4:6-7)

Therefore, <u>I want to encourage you to not hold onto that old man</u> by living out of your carnal nature. Instead, be renewed in the *spirit of your mind* and allow the Word of God by the power of His Holy Spirit to unearth and wash away any and all internalized life experiences that have identified you wrongfully (e.g., hurts, vows, judgments, ungodly beliefs) and put on the new man which is created after God in righteousness and true holiness *(Ephesians 4:22-24)*.

Below are additional Scriptures relating to God's correction:

1. ***Deuteronomy 8:2-6*** *— And thou shalt remember all the way which the LORD thy God led thee these forty years in the wilderness, to humble thee, and to prove thee, to know what was in thine heart, whether thou wouldest keep his commandments, or no. And he humbled thee, and suffered thee to hunger, and fed thee with manna, which thou knewest not, neither did thy fathers know; that he might make thee know that man doth not live by bread only, but by every word that proceedeth out of the mouth of the LORD doth man live. Thy raiment (clothing) waxed not old upon thee, neither did thy foot swell, these forty years. Thou shalt also consider in thine heart, that, as a man chasteneth his son, so the LORD thy God chasteneth thee. Therefore thou shalt keep the commandments of the LORD thy God, to walk in his ways, and to fear him.*

References:
Job 5:17 *— Behold, happy is the man whom God correcteth: therefore despise not thou the chastening of the Almighty.* ***Psalm 94:12-13*** *— Blessed is the man whom thou chastenest, O LORD, and teachest him out of thy law; that thou mayest give him rest from the days of adversity, until the pit be digged for the wicked.* ***Proverbs 17:3*** *— the fining pot is for silver, and the furnace for gold: but the LORD trieth the hearts.* ***Proverbs 25:4*** *— Take away the dross from the silver, and there shall come forth a vessel for the finer.* ***Jeremiah 17:9-10*** *— The heart is deceitful above all things, and desperately wicked: who can know it? I the LORD search the heart, I try the reins (mind), even to give every man according to his ways, and according to the fruit of his doings.* ***Hebrews 12:25-29*** *— See that ye refuse not him that speaketh. For if they escaped not who refused him that spake on earth, much more shall not we escape, if we turn away from him that speaketh from heaven: whose voice then shook the earth: but now he hath promised, saying, "Yet once more I shake not the earth only, but also heaven. And this word, "Yet once more," signifieth the removing of those things that are shaken, as of things that are made, that those things which cannot be shaken may remain. Wherefore we receiving a kingdom which cannot be moved, let us have grace, whereby we may serve God acceptably with reverence and godly fear: for our God is a consuming fire.*

2. **Psalm 25:4-5** – *Shew me thy ways, O LORD; teach me thy paths. Lead me in thy truth, and teach me: for thou art the God of my salvation; on thee do I wait all the day.*

References:

Psalm 94:12-13 – *Blessed is the man whom thou chastenest, O LORD, and teachest him out of thy law; that thou mayest give him rest from the days of adversity, until the pit be digged for the wicked.* **Proverbs 1:33** – *God's wisdom speaks, "But whoso hearkeneth unto me shall dwell safely, and shall be quiet from fear of evil."* **Proverbs 3:1-4** – *My son, forget not my law; but let thine heart keep my commandments: for length of days, and long life, and peace, shall they add to thee. Let not mercy and truth forsake thee: bind them about thy neck; write them upon the table of thine heart: so shalt thou find favour and good understanding in the sight of God and man.* **Proverbs 10:17** – *He is in the way of life that keepeth instruction: but he that refuseth reproof erreth.* **Proverbs 12:1** – *Whoso loveth instruction loveth knowledge: but he that hateth reproof is brutish (stupid).* **Proverbs 13:13-15, 18** – *Whoso despiseth the word shall be destroyed: but he that feareth the commandment shall be rewarded. The law of the wise is a fountain of life, to depart from the snares of death. Good understanding giveth favour: but the way of the transgressors is hard. Poverty and shame shall be to him that refuseth instruction: but he that regardeth reproof shall be honoured.* **Proverbs 15:10-11, 31-33** – *Correction is grievous unto him that forsaketh the way: and he that hateth reproof shall die. Hell and destruction are before the LORD: how much more then the hearts of the children of men? The ear that heareth the reproof of life abideth among the wise. He that refuseth instruction despiseth his own soul: but he that heareth reproof getteth understanding. The fear of the LORD is the instruction of wisdom; and before honour is humility.* **Proverbs 29:1** – *He, that being often reproved hardeneth his neck (or refuses to turn from his ways), shall suddenly be destroyed, and that without remedy.* **James 5:19-20** – *Brethren, if any of you do err (goes astray) from the truth, and one convert him; let him know, that he which converteth the sinner from the error of his way shall save a soul from death, and shall hide (or cover) a multitude of sins.*

24(a) *You are* **Love.** *(Ref.: 1 John 4:8)*

John writes in *1 John 4:8* – *"He that loveth not knoweth not God; for God is love."* The Greek word for "love" is *agape* meaning "love, i.e. affection or benevolence; specially (plural) a love-feast.–feast of) charity(-ably), dear, love." Its definition in the Thayer's Greek Lexicon is "God is wholly love, his nature is summed up in love." Love is the essence of who God is and was revealed through the sacrifice of His only Son for the entire world so that whosoever believes in Him should not perish but have everlasting life *(John 3:16)*. He goes on to say *"For God sent not his Son into the world to condemn the world; but that the world through him might be saved" (John 3:17)*. The Greek word for "condemn" is *krino* meaning "to distinguish i.e. decide (mentally or judicially); by implication, to try, condemn, punish…" No, He did not come to condemn or to punish us for our sins but rather to reveal the Father's heart of love to His beloved creation and to free us from our sins. It is sin itself that brings harm to us and uses God's law to condemn us. *1 Corinthians 13* describes God's love in detail. Therefore, below I will insert "God in me" where the Greek word *agape* is found using the *AMPCE Version*:

Verse 4: *God in me endures long (longsuffering) and is patient and kind.*
Verse 6: *God in me rejoices in the truth.*
Verse 7: *God in me bears all things. It is a safe place for others.*

Verse 7: <u>*God in me*</u> *is ever ready to believe the best of every person.*
Verse 7: <u>*God in me*</u> *hopes under all circumstances.*
Verse 7: <u>*God in me*</u> *endures everything [without weakening].*
Verse 8: <u>*God in me*</u> *never fails!*

The love of God is the most powerful force in the universe! The love of God worked in Christ to give sight to the blind, heal the sick, give life to the dead, and to become the sacrificial Lamb to take away the sin of the world; God's love raised Him from the dead. Hallelujah! Paul had a revelation of God's love in his own life and shared this with us,

> *And we know that all things work together for good to them that love God, to them who are the called according to his purpose. For whom he did foreknow, he also did predestinate to be conformed to the image of his Son, that he might be the firstborn among many brethren. Moreover whom he did predestinate them he also called: and whom he called, them he also justified: and whom he justified, them he also glorified. What shall we then say to these things? If God be for us, who can be against us? He that spared not his own Son, but delivered him up for us all, how shall he not with him also freely give us all things? Who shall lay any thing to the charge of God's elect? It is God that justifieth. Who is he that condemneth? It is Christ that died, yea rather, that is risen again, who is even at the right hand of God, who also maketh intercession for us. <u>Who shall separate us from the love of Christ? Shall tribulation, or distress, or persecution, or famine, or nakedness, or peril, or sword? As it is written, "For thy sake we are killed all the day long; we are accounted as sheep for the slaughter." Nay, in all these things we are more than conquerors through him that loved us. For I am persuaded, that neither death, nor life, nor angels, nor principalities, nor powers, nor things present, nor things to come, nor height, nor depth, nor any other creature, shall be able to separate us from the love of God, which is in Christ Jesus our Lord.</u>*
>
> (Romans 8:28-39)

Below are Scriptures relating to God's love:

1. ***John 15:10, 12-13*** *– Jesus said, If ye keep my commandments, ye shall abide in my love; even as I have kept my Father's commandments, and abide in his love. This is my commandment, that ye love one another, as I have loved you. Greater love hath no man than this, that a man lay down his life for his friends. (Only God's love in us can love others well)!*

References:
2 Corinthians 13:11 *– Finally, brethren, farewell. Be perfect, be of good comfort, be of one mind, live in peace; and the God of love and peace shall be with you.* ***Galatians 5:6, 22*** *– For in Jesus Christ neither circumcision availeth any thing, nor uncircumcision; but faith which worketh by love. But the fruit of the Spirit is love, joy, peace, longsuffering, gentleness, goodness, faith, meekness, temperance: against such there is no law. (See 1 Corinthians 13:1-13).* ***2 Thessalonians 3:5*** *– And the Lord direct your hearts into the love of God, and into the patient waiting for Christ.* ***2 Timothy 1:13*** *– Hold fast the form of sound words, which thou hast heard of me, in faith and love which is in Christ Jesus.* ***1 John 2:5, 15-17*** *– But whoso keepeth his word, in him verily is the love of God perfected: hereby know we that we are in him. Love not the world, neither the things that are in the world. If any man love the world, the love of the Father is not in him. For all that is in the world, the lust of the flesh, and the lust of the eyes, and the pride of life, is not of*

the Father, but is of the world. And the world passeth away, and the lust thereof: but he that doeth the will of God abideth for ever. **1 John 4:7-8, 12, 16, 20** *– Beloved, let us love one another: for love is of God; and every one that loveth is born of God, and knoweth God. He that loveth not knoweth not God; for God is love. No man hath seen God at any time. If we love one another, God dwelleth in us, and his love is perfected in us. And we have known and believed the love that God hath to us. God is love; and he that dwelleth in love dwelleth in God, and God in him. If a man say, "I love God," and hateth his brother, he is a liar: for he that loveth not his brother whom he hath seen, how can he love God whom he hath not seen?* **1 John 5:3-4, 19-21** *– For this is the love of God, that we keep his commandments: and his commandments are not grievous. For whatsoever is born of God overcometh the world: and this is the victory that overcometh the world, even our faith. And we know that we are of God, and the whole world lieth in wickedness. And we know that the Son of God is come, and hath given us an understanding, that we may know him that is true, and we are in him that is true, even in his Son Jesus Christ. This is the true God, and eternal life. Little children, keep yourselves from idols. Amen.* **Jude 1:21** *– Keep yourselves in the love of God, looking for the mercy of our Lord Jesus Christ unto eternal life.*

2. **1 Timothy 1:12-17** *– Paul said, "And I thank Christ Jesus our Lord, who hath enabled me, for that he counted me faithful, putting me into the ministry; who was before a blasphemer, and a persecutor, and injurious: but I obtained mercy, because I did it ignorantly in unbelief. And the grace of our Lord was exceeding abundant with faith and love which is in Christ Jesus. This is a faithful saying, and worthy of all acceptation, that Christ Jesus came into the world to save sinners; of whom I am chief. Howbeit for this cause I obtained mercy, that in me first Jesus Christ might shew forth all longsuffering, for a pattern to them which should hereafter believe on him to life everlasting. Now unto the King eternal, immortal, invisible, the only wise God, be honour and glory for ever and ever. Amen.*

Reference:
2 Peter 3:9 *– The Lord is not slack concerning his promise, as some men count slackness; but is longsuffering to usward, not willing that any should perish, but that all should come to repentance.*

Please refer to **Notes 24b, 28c, 29a, 29b, 29c, 30, 32a,** and **32b** for additional information and/or Scriptures relating to God's love.

24(b) *Your love is given freely without any consideration of the merit or object of the person. Thank You that Your love for me is great! (Ref.: John 3:16; Ephesians 2:1-10)*

His love is unconditional! Paul writes,

But God, who is rich in mercy, for his great love wherewith he loved us, even when we were dead in sins, hath quickened us together with Christ, (by grace ye are saved;) and hath raised us up together, and made us sit together in heavenly places in Christ Jesus: that in the ages to come he might shew the exceeding riches of his grace in his kindness toward us through Christ Jesus. For by grace are ye saved through faith; and that not of yourselves: it is the gift of God: not of works, lest any man should boast. For we are his workmanship, created in Christ Jesus unto good works, which God hath before ordained that we should walk in them.

(Ephesians 2:4-10)

This passage of Scripture helps us to see that His love for us goes deeper than our faults, shortcomings, and sin! He is passionately in love with us and He always will be. It is not His will that any should perish but for all to come to repentance. Peter writes,

> *But, beloved, be not ignorant of this one thing, that one day is with the Lord as a thousand years, and a thousand years as one day. The Lord is not slack concerning his promise, as some men count slackness; but is longsuffering to usward, not willing that any should perish, but that all should come to repentance.*
>
> (2 Peter 3:8-9)

The Father can draw us to Jesus, but it is up to us to receive Jesus Christ as our Lord and Savior as God has given us the power of choice *(John 6:44)*. I want to spend some time on this very important phrase "the power of choice" or "our free will." I believe if God would have intervened in someone's will, it would have been in the case of Adam and Eve not to eat the fruit of the knowledge of the tree of good and evil. He told Adam not to eat the fruit and the consequences if he did eat, but He left the choice and the consequences of that choice to him, and He does not interfere with our choices either. He has given us Jesus in order for us to be able to live in the power of a new covenant in order to receive forgiveness of sins and to walk in abundant life, but the choice is ours *(Hebrews 8:6-13, 12:18-29)*. Unfortunately, we can choose to be an abusive parent, a slothful employee, a hateful person, a gossiper, a liar, and the list goes on and on, as Paul describes the works of the flesh in *Galatians 5:19-21*. On the other hand, we can choose to surrender our will to His and begin to renew our minds to His truths to live in newness of life in Christ! God desires to bring the church back to His original intent before Adam and Eve ate of the fruit of the knowledge of the tree of good and evil. But the choice is ours. Paul said in *Philippians 2:12-13*:

> *Wherefore, my beloved, as ye have always obeyed, not as in my presence only, but now much more in my absence, work out your own salvation with fear and trembling. For it is God which worketh in you both to will and to do his good pleasure.*

The phrase "work out" in the Greek is *katergazomai*. Its meaning in the Thayer's Greek Lexicon is "to work out, i.e. to do that from which something results; of man: make every effort to obtain salvation, Philippians 2:12; of things…" The word "salvation" in the Greek is *soteria* meaning "rescue or safety (physically or morally):–deliver, health, salvation, save, saving." The way we work out our salvation is to put off the old man and be renewed in the *spirit of our minds* and put on the new man *(Romans 12:1-2; Ephesians 4:20-24)*! As we renew our minds to the new man in Christ His Word works in us both to will and to do His good pleasure. His Word which is living and powerful begins to flush out ingrained carnal beliefs and mindsets within us that keep us bound to the old man *(Hebrews 4:12-13; Ephesians 5:25-27; Titus 3:4-7)*. I believe this goes along with what Paul says in *1 Timothy 4:7-8* when he encourages us to exercise or work out:

> *But refuse profane and old wives' fables, and exercise thyself rather unto godliness. For bodily exercise profiteth little: but godliness is profitable unto all things, having promise of the life that now is, and of that which is to come.*

The word "exercise" in the Greek is *gymnazo*. Its meaning in the Thayer's Greek Lexicon is "to exercise vigorously, in any way, either the body or the mind: of one who strives earnestly to become godly."

Jesus ever lives to make intercession for us *(Romans 8:34; Hebrews 7:25)*. Prayer and intercession for loved ones who have not received Jesus Christ as their Lord and Savior is so important in order for the blinders to be removed from their eyes (or understanding). Below are two passages of Scripture that support this statement:

1. *Matthew 16:19* – Jesus said, *"And I will give unto thee the keys of the kingdom of heaven: and whatsoever thou shalt bind on earth shall be bound in heaven: and whatsoever thou shalt loose on earth shall be loosed in heaven."*
2. *2 Corinthians 4:3-4* – *But if our gospel be hid, it is hid to them that are lost: in whom the god of this world (Satan) hath blinded the minds of them which believe not, lest the light of the glorious gospel of Christ, who is the image of God, should shine unto them.*

As we pray for our loved ones who are not born again, we have the authority through Jesus to bind away from them the powers of darkness that blind their minds from believing the Gospel of Christ, and to loose the power of the Spirit of God to draw them to Jesus and to loose laborers into their path to share the good news of the Gospel of Christ unto repentance *(John 6:44)*. Let's look at the following passage of Scripture regarding salvation:

And, behold, one came and said unto him, "Good Master, what good thing shall I do, that I may have eternal life?" And he said unto him, "Why callest thou me good? There is none good but one, that is, God: but if thou wilt enter into life, keep the commandments." He saith unto him, "Which?" Jesus said, "Thou shalt do no murder, Thou shalt not commit adultery, Thou shalt not steal, Thou shalt not bear false witness, Honour thy father and thy mother: and, Thou shalt love thy neighbour as thyself." The young man saith unto him, "All these things have I kept from my youth up: what lack I yet?" Jesus said unto him, "If thou wilt be perfect, go and sell that thou hast, and give to the poor, and thou shalt have treasure in heaven: and come and follow me." But when the young man heard that saying, he went away sorrowful: for he had great possessions. Then said Jesus unto his disciples, "Verily I say unto you, that a rich man shall hardly enter into the kingdom of heaven. And again I say unto you, it is easier for a camel to go through the eye of a needle, than for a rich man to enter into the kingdom of God." When the disciples heard it, they were exceedingly amazed, saying, "Who then can be saved?" But Jesus beheld them, and said unto them, "With men this is impossible; but with God all things are possible."

(Matthew 19:16-26)

Based on this passage of Scripture, even though we have our own will and can choose, when praying for our loved ones who are not born again or who have gone astray, I want to encourage you to trust in the fact that with God all things are possible! Also, Paul writes,

And the servant of the Lord must not strive; but be gentle unto all men, apt to teach, patient, in meekness instructing those that oppose themselves; if God peradventure will give them repentance to the acknowledging of the truth; and that they may recover themselves out of the snare of the devil, who are taken captive by him at his will.

(2 Timothy 2:24-26)

Below are additional Scriptures relating to God's love:

1. ***John 17:1-3, 6-11, 20-26*** *(NKJV) – Jesus spoke these words, lifted up His eyes to heaven, and said: "Father, the hour has come. Glorify Your Son, that Your Son also may glorify You, as you have given Him authority over all flesh, that He should give eternal life to as many as You have given Him. And this is eternal life, that they may know You, the only true God, and Jesus Christ whom You have sent. I have manifested Your name to the men whom You have given Me out of the world. They were Yours, You gave them to Me, and they have kept Your word. Now they have known that all things which You have given Me are from You. For I have given to them the words which You have given Me; and they have received them, and have known surely that I came forth from You; and they have believed that You sent Me. I pray for them. I do not pray for the world but for those whom You have given Me, for they are Yours. And all Mine are Yours, and Yours are Mine, and I am glorified in them. Now I am no longer in the world, but these are in the world, and I come to You. Holy Father, keep through Your name those whom You have given Me, that they may be one as We are. I do not pray for these alone, but also for those who will believe in Me through their word; that they all may be one, as You, Father, are in Me, and I in You; that they also may be one in Us, that the world may believe that You sent Me. And the glory which You gave Me I have given them, that they may be one just as We are one: I in them, and You in Me; that they may be made perfect in one, and that the world may know that You have sent Me, and have loved them as You have loved Me. Father, I desire that they also whom You gave Me may be with Me where I am, that they may behold My glory which You have given Me; for You loved Me before the foundation of the world. O righteous Father! The world has not known You, but I have known You; and these have known that You sent Me. And I have declared to them Your name, and will declare it, that the love with which You loved Me may be in them, and I in them."*

References:
Psalm 108:4 *– For thy mercy is great above the heavens: and thy truth reacheth unto the clouds.*
Psalm 138:2 *– I will worship toward thy holy temple, and praise thy name for thy lovingkindness and for thy truth: for thou hast magnified thy word above all thy name.* ***Ephesians 3:14-21*** *– Paul said, "For this cause I bow my knees unto the Father of our Lord Jesus Christ, of whom the whole family in heaven and earth is named, that he would grant you, according to the riches of his glory, to be strengthened with might by his Spirit in the inner man; that Christ may dwell in your hearts by faith; that ye, being rooted and grounded in love, may be able to comprehend with all saints what is the breadth, and length, and depth, and height; and to know the love of Christ, which passeth knowledge, that ye might be filled with all the fullness of God. Now unto him that is able to do exceeding abundantly above all that we ask or think, according to the power that worketh in us, unto him be glory in the church by Christ Jesus throughout all ages, world without end. Amen."*

2. ***Matthew 9:10-13*** *– And it came to pass, as Jesus sat at meat in the house, behold, many publicans and sinners came and sat down with him and his disciples. And when the Pharisees saw it, they said unto his disciples, "Why eateth your Master with publicans and sinners?" But when Jesus heard that, he said unto them, "They that be whole need not a physician, but they that are sick. But go ye and learn what that meaneth, I will have mercy, and not sacrifice: for I am not come to call the righteous, but sinners to repentance."*

References:
Romans 5:6-11 *– For when we were yet without strength, in due time Christ died for the ungodly. For*

scarcely for a righteous man will one die: yet peradventure for a good man some would even dare to die. But God commendeth his love toward us, in that, while we were yet sinners, Christ died for us. Much more then, being now justified by his blood, we shall be saved from wrath through him. For if, when we were enemies, we were reconciled to God by the death of his Son, much more, being reconciled, we shall be saved by his life. And not only so, but we also joy in God through our Lord Jesus Christ, by whom we have now received the atonement.

3. ***Ephesians 5:1-2*** *– Be ye therefore followers of God, as dear children; and walk in love, as Christ also hath loved us, and hath given himself for us an offering and a sacrifice to God for a sweetsmelling savour.*

References:

John 3:16-17 *– For God so loved the world, that he gave his only begotten Son, that whosoever believeth in him should not perish, but have everlasting life. For God sent not his Son into the world to condemn the world; but that the world through him might be saved.* ***2 Timothy 1:7*** *– For God hath not given us the spirit of fear; but of power, and of love, and of a sound mind.* ***1 John 3:1, 16*** *– Behold, what manner of love the Father hath bestowed upon us, that we should be called the sons of God: therefore the world knoweth us not, because it knew him not. Hereby perceive we the love of God, because he laid down his life for us: and we ought to lay down our lives for the brethren.* ***1 John 4:9-10, 18*** *– In this was manifested the love of God toward us, because that God sent his only begotten Son into the world, that we might live through him. Herein is love, not that we loved God, but that he loved us, and sent his Son to be the propitiation for our sins. There is no fear in love; but perfect love casteth out fear: because fear hath torment. He that feareth is not made perfect in love.*

Please refer to **Notes 24a, 28c, 29a, 29b, 29c, 30, 32a,** and **32b** for additional information and/or Scriptures relating to God's love.

25(a) *You prove Your love to me by being:* **Yahweh-Nissi – The LORD my banner.** *You are the standard of my victory in life's conflicts.* Just as Moses lifted up the serpent in the desert [on a pole], so must the Son of Man be lifted up [on the cross], in order that everyone who believes in *You* [who cleaves to *You*, trusts *You*, and relies on *You*] may not perish, but have eternal life and [actually] live forever! (*John 3:14-15-AMPCE*) (*Ref: Exodus 17:15; Isaiah 59:19; Numbers 21:1-9; Song of Solomon 2:4; Psalm 60:4-5, 111:7-9*)

Jehovahnissi is used only once in the Old Testament in the King James Version and is found in *Exodus 17:15.* The Hebrew word for "*Jehovahnissi*" is *Yehovah nicciy* meaning "Jehovah (is) my banner; Jehovah-Nissi, a symbolical name of an altar in the Desert." *Nec,* from which "nissi" is derived, means "a flag; also a sail; by implication, a flagstaff; generally a signal; figuratively, a token:–<u>banner</u>, <u>pole</u>, sail, (en-)<u>sign</u>, standard." In *Exodus 17:15-16*, Moses recognized that the Lord was Israel's banner under which they defeated the Amalekites, so He built an altar and called the name of it Jehovahnissi or The-LORD-IS-My-Banner: For he said in *Exodus 17:16, "Because the LORD hath sworn that the LORD will have war with Amalek from generation to generation."* God never changes (*Malachi 3:6; Hebrews 13:18*). God's power to defeat the Amalekites, the enemy of Israel, is available to defeat the enemy of your soul, the devil *(1 Peter 5:8; 1 John 3:8)*. When I think of a pole I think of what Jesus said,

> *And as Moses lifted up the serpent in the wilderness, even so must the Son of man be lifted up: that whosoever believeth in him should not perish, but have eternal life.* For God so loved the world, that he gave his only begotten Son, that whosoever believeth in him should not perish, but have everlasting life. For God sent not his Son into the world to condemn the world; but that the world through him might be saved.
>
> (John 3:14-17)

Let's read this passage of Scripture in Numbers to see why Moses lifted up the serpent in the wilderness:

> *And when King Arad the Canaanite, which dwelt in the south, heard tell that Israel came by the way of the spies; then he fought against Israel and took some prisoners. And Israel vowed a vow unto the LORD, and said, "If thou wilt indeed deliver this people into my hand, then I will utterly destroy their cities." And the LORD hearkened to the voice of Israel, and delivered up the Canaanites; and they utterly destroyed them and their cities: and he called the name of the place Hormah. And they journeyed from mount Hor by the way of the Red sea, to compass the land of Edom: and the soul of the people was much discouraged because of the way. And the people spake against God, and against Moses, "Wherefore have ye brought us up out of Egypt to die in the wilderness? For there is no bread, neither is there any water; and our soul loatheth this light (insubstantial) bread."*
>
> (Numbers 21:1-5)

The children of Israel were so full of their own carnality "self-centeredness" that they continued to murmur and complain against God and Moses when things did not go their way. Had they truly believed that the Lord would provide the necessary provisions for them, they would have already entered into the promised land. Let's continue:

> *And the LORD sent fiery serpents among the people, and they bit the people; and much people of Israel died. Therefore the people came to Moses, and said, "We have sinned, for we have spoken against the LORD, and against thee; pray unto the LORD, that he take away the serpents from us." And Moses prayed for the people. And the LORD said unto Moses, "Make thee a fiery serpent, and set it upon a pole: and it shall come to pass, that every one that is bitten, when he looketh upon it, shall live." And Moses made a serpent of brass, and put it upon a pole, and it came to pass, that if a serpent had bitten any man, when he beheld the serpent of brass, he lived.*
>
> (Numbers 21:6-9)

(Note: hardness of heart, grumbling, and complaining can lead to lots of problems. Repentance brings healing and deliverance). The word "pole" is the Hebrew word *Nec* the root word for *nissi* as noted above. Therefore, when Jesus said in *John 3:14 – "And as Moses lifted up the serpent in the wilderness, even so must the Son of man be lifted up: that whosoever believeth in him should not perish, but have eternal life."* He is saying that as born-again believers, our focus must be on the One who was made to be sin for us. Christ literally took upon Himself our carnal nature, the source of sin. This work on the cross reached all the way back to Adam and Eve who ate the fruit of the knowledge of the tree of good and evil, falling prey to the serpent's (Satan's) domain which separated Adam and Eve and us from God, bringing forth death *(Genesis 3)*. This is why in *Mark 15:34 (NIV)* Jesus cried out in a loud voice, *"Eloi, Eloi, lema sabachthani?"* which means *"My God, my God, why have You forsaken me?"* He had never been forsaken by His Father and at that moment He truly understood what it was like to be totally separated from Him, and the darkness and death associated with that separation. As He went into the depths of our darkness and death, He made it possible for us to be reconciled to God and to live out of His divine nature and the light of His Word though the power of His Holy Spirit. Jesus destroyed the works of the devil and desires to destroy the works of the devil in our own individual lives *(Hebrews 2:14; 1 John 3:8)*. It is essential for us to stay focused on Him and His life within us as He truly is our Healer, our Deliverer, our Redeemer, our Restorer in life's conflicts, and our Wonderful Counselor! Paul said in *Colossians 3:1-3* to seek those things above, where Christ is, not on the things that are on the earth, for we have died and our real life is hidden with Christ in God. Let's set aside every weight and sin that so easily besets us and let us run with patience the race set before us, looking unto Jesus the author and finisher of our faith *(Hebrews 12:1-2)*. Pilate put the following insignia on the cross on which Jesus was crucified, "JESUS OF NAZARETH THE KING OF THE JEWS":

> *Then delivered he him therefore unto them to be crucified. And they took Jesus, and led him away. And he bearing his cross went forth into a place called the place of a skull, which is called in the Hebrew Golgotha: where they crucified him, and two other with him, on either side one, and Jesus in the midst. And Pilate wrote a title, and put it on the cross. And the writing was, JESUS OF NAZARETH THE KING OF THE JEWS. This title then read many of the Jews: for the place where Jesus was crucified was nigh to the city: and it was written in Hebrew, and Greek, and Latin.*
>
> (John 19:16-20)

The word "cross" in the Greek is *stauros* which means "a stake or <u>post</u> (as set upright), i.e. (specially), a <u>pole</u> or cross (as an instrument of capital punishment); figuratively, exposure to death, i.e. self denial; by implication, the atonement of Christ:–cross." He took the penalty of our sin, which is death, so that in Him we have eternal life. You might say, "Well, I'm not a Jew so that doesn't apply to me." Scripture clearly states that if we are Christ's, we are Abraham's seed (who is the origin of the Jewish nation), and heirs according to the promise *(Galatians 3:29)*. Scripture also states that he is not a Jew, which is one outwardly; neither is circumcision outward in the flesh: but he is a Jew, which is one inwardly; and circumcision is that of the heart, in the spirit *(Romans 2:28-29)*. Thank you, Lord, for your unconditional love toward us! Paul writes,

> *But God commendeth his love toward us, in that, while we were yet sinners, Christ died for us. Much more then, being now justified by his blood, we shall be saved from wrath through him. For if, when we were enemies, we were reconciled to God by the death of his Son, much more, being reconciled, we shall be saved by his life.*
>
> (Romans 5:8-10)

Below are Scriptures relating to God's salvation:

1. ***Psalm 33:16-22** (NIV) – No king is saved by the size of his army; no warrior escapes by his great strength. A horse is a vain hope for deliverance; despite all its great strength it cannot save. But the eyes of the LORD are on those who fear him, on those whose hope is in his unfailing*

love, to deliver them from death and keep them alive in famine. We wait in hope for the LORD; he is our help and our shield. In him our hearts rejoice, for we trust in his holy name. May your unfailing love be with us, LORD, even as we put our hope in you.

References:

Psalm 37:39-40 – But the salvation of the righteous is of the LORD: he is their strength in the time of trouble. And the LORD shall help them, and deliver them: he shall deliver them from the wicked, and save them, because they trust in him. *Psalm 46:11 – The LORD of hosts is with us; the God of Jacob is our refuge. Selah (Pause and think about it).* *Proverbs 29:25 – The fear of man bringeth a snare: but whoso putteth his trust in the LORD shall be safe.* *Matthew 28:18-20 – And Jesus came and spake unto them, saying, "All power is given unto me in heaven and in earth. Go ye therefore, and teach all nations, baptizing them in the name of the Father, and of the Son, and of the Holy Ghost: teaching them to observe all things whatsoever I have commanded you: and, lo, I am with you alway, even unto the end of the world." Amen.* *John 14:27 – Jesus said, "Peace I leave with you, my peace I give unto you: not as the world giveth, give I unto you. Let not you heart be troubled, neither let it be afraid."* *John 16:33 – Jesus said, "These things I have spoken unto you, that in me ye might have peace. In the world ye shall have tribulation: but be of good cheer; I have overcome the world."* *Acts 5:34-39 – Then stood there up one in the council, a Pharisee, named Gamaliel, a doctor of the law, had in reputation among all the people, and commanded to put the apostles forth a little space; and said unto them, "…Refrain from these men, and let them alone: for if this counsel or this work be of men, it will come to nought (nothing): but if it be of God, ye cannot overthrow it; lest haply ye be found even to fight against God."* *1 Corinthians 15:56-57 – The sting of death is sin; and the strength of sin is the law. But thanks be to God, which giveth us the victory through our Lord Jesus Christ.* *Hebrews 2:14 – Forasmuch then as the children are partakers of flesh and blood, he (Jesus) also himself likewise took part of the same; that through death he might destroy him that had the power of death, that is, the devil; and deliver them who through fear of death were all their lifetime subject to bondage.* *1 John 5:4 – For whatsoever is born of God overcometh the world: and this is the victory that overcometh the world, even our faith.*

2. *Proverbs 20:30 – The blueness of a wound cleanseth away evil: so do stripes the inward parts of the belly.*

References:

Isaiah 53:5 – But he (Jesus) was wounded for our transgressions, he was bruised for our iniquities: the chastisement of our peace was upon him; and with his stripes we are healed. *Titus 3:4-7 – But after that the kindness and love of God our Saviour toward man appeared, not by works of righteousness which we have done, but according to his mercy he saved us, by the washing of regeneration, and renewing of the Holy Ghost; which he shed on us abundantly through Jesus Christ our Saviour; that being justified by his grace, we should be made heirs according to the hope of eternal life.* *1 Peter 2:24-25 – Who his own self bare our sins in his own body on the tree, that we, being dead to sins, should live unto righteousness: by whose stripes ye were healed. For ye were as sheep going astray; but are now returned unto the Shepherd and Bishop of your souls.* *2 Peter 3:9 – The Lord is not slack concerning his promise, as some men count slackness; but is longsuffering to usward, not willing that any should perish, but that all should come to repentance.* *1 John 2:1-2 – My little children, these things write I unto you, that ye sin not. And if any man sin, we have an advocate with the Father, Jesus Christ the righteous: and he is the propitiation for our sins: and not for ours only, but also for the sins of the whole world.*

3. **Romans 4:19-25** – *And being not weak in faith, he (Abraham) considered not his own body now dead, when he was about an hundred years old, neither yet the deadness of Sara's womb: he staggered not at the promise of God through unbelief; but was strong in faith, giving glory to God; and being fully persuaded that, what he had promised, he was able also to perform. And therefore it was imputed to him for righteousness. Now it was not written for his sake alone, that it was imputed to him; but for us also, to whom it shall be imputed, if we believe on him that raised up Jesus our Lord from the dead; who was delivered for our offences, and was raised again for our justification.*

References:

John 17:1-3 (NIV) – *After Jesus said this, he looked toward heaven and prayed: "Father, the hour has come. Glorify your Son, that your Son may glorify you. For you granted him authority over all people that he might give eternal life to all those you have given him. Now this is eternal life: that they know you, the only true God, and Jesus Christ, whom you have sent."* ***1 John 5:9-15*** – *If we receive the witness of men, the witness of God is greater: for this is the witness of God which he hath testified of his Son. He that believeth on the Son of God hath the witness in himself: he that believeth not God hath made him a liar; because he believeth not the record that God gave of his Son. And this is the record, that God hath given to us eternal life, and this life is in his Son. He that hath the Son hath life; and he that hath not the Son hath not life. These things have I written unto you that believe on the name of the Son of God; that ye may know that ye have eternal life, and that ye may believe on the name of the Son of God. And this is the confidence that we have in him, that, if we ask any thing according to his will, he heareth us: and if we know that he hear us, whatsoever we ask, we know that we have the petitions that we desired of him.*

Here are additional Scriptures relating to God's salvation: Psalm 33:11-22; Acts 13:26-39; 1 Corinthians 15:51-58; 2 Corinthians 5:14-21; Ephesians 1:1-23, 2:14-22; Hebrews 10:1-25.

Please refer to **Notes 24a, 24b, 28c, 29a, 29b, 29c, 30, 32a, 32b** for information and Scriptures relating to God's love.

Please refer to **Note 25b** for more information relating to the cross of Christ as our banner.

25(b) *The cross of Christ is my banner of God's mighty power of redemption and is also the banner of my warfare, death to the old man – the false self. (Ref.: Psalm 130:7-8; Galatians 6:14)*

Let's first look at "*The cross of Christ as our banner of God's mighty power of redemption*" by looking at three passages of Scripture where Paul describes Christ's redemptive work on the cross:

1. **Galatians 3:13-14** – *Christ hath redeemed us from the curse of the law, being made a curse for us: for it is written, 'Cursed is everyone that hangeth on a tree:' that the blessing of Abraham might come on the Gentiles through Jesus Christ; that we might receive the promise of the Spirit through faith.*

2. **Colossians 1:12-17** – *Giving thanks unto the Father, which hath made us meet (able) to be partakers of the inheritance of the saints in light: who hath delivered us from the power of darkness, and hath translated us into the kingdom of his dear Son: in whom we have redemption through his blood, even the forgiveness of sins: who is the image of the invisible*

God, the firstborn of every creature: for by him were all things created, that are in heaven, and that are in earth, visible and invisible, whether they be thrones, or dominions, or principalities, or powers: all things were created by him, and for him: and he is before all things, and by him all things consist.

3. **Colossians 2:8-9, 13-15** – *Beware lest any man spoil you through philosophy and vain deceit, after the rudiments of the world, and not after Christ. For in him dwelleth all the fulness of the Godhead bodily. And you, being dead in your sins and the uncircumcision of your flesh, hath he quickened together with him, having forgiven you all trespasses; blotting out the handwriting of ordinances that was against us, which was contrary to us, and took it out of the way, nailing it to his cross; and having spoiled principalities and powers, he made a shew of them openly, triumphing over them in it.*

The Greek word for "redemption" in *Colossians 1:14* is *apolytrosis* meaning "(the act) ransom in full, i.e. (figuratively) riddance, or (specially) Christian salvation:–deliverance, redemption." Jesus said in *Mark 10:45* – *"For even the Son of man came not to be ministered unto, but to minister, and to give his life a ransom for many."* The Greek word for "ransom" is *lytron* meaning "something to loosen with, i.e. a redemption price (figuratively, atonement):–ransom." Jesus became our ransom in order to release (redeem) us from Satan's power in our lives—from sin and its consequences. Jesus came to destroy the works of the devil – *1 John 3:8* – *"He that committeth sin is of the devil; for the devil sinneth from the beginning. For this purpose the Son of God was manifested, that he might destroy the works of the devil."* (He came to redeem us back to the Most High God, our heavenly Father. Satan, as the serpent, was there in the Garden of Eden to take God's creation from Him – *Genesis 3:1-24; Luke 4:5-7*). Peter said in *1 Peter 2:21-24* – *"…who his own self bare our sins in his own body on the tree, that we, being dead to sins, should live unto righteousness: by whose stripes ye were healed."* Christ took upon Himself the judgments for scorners and the stripes for fools in order for us to walk in His righteousness and holiness – *Proverbs 19:29; Ephesians 4:1-24.*

When we choose to receive Jesus Christ as our Lord and Savior we become adopted by Him:

Even so we, when we were children, were in bondage under the elements of the world: but when the fulness of the time was come, God sent forth his Son, made of a woman, made under the law, to redeem them that were under the law, that we might receive the adoption of sons. And because ye are sons, God hath sent forth the Spirit of his Son into your hearts, crying, Abba, Father.

(Galatians 4:3-6)

The law came because of sin and reveals God's holiness. Paul said, *"For I would not know lust except the law said, 'You shall not covet…'"* (see *Romans 7*). The same Holy Spirit that raised Christ from the dead dwells in every born-again believer *(Romans 8:11)*! It is also that same Holy Spirit in *Genesis 1* that moved upon the face of the waters and, according to God's command, caused light to come forth out of darkness and life to come forth upon the earth.

Let's look at *"the cross of Christ as our banner of warfare, death to the old man – the false self."* Again, in *Exodus 17:15-16 (NKJV)* – *"And Moses built an altar and called its name, The-LORD-Is-My-Banner; for he said, 'Because the LORD has sworn: the LORD will have war with Amalek from generation to generation.'"* In the Old Testament, the warfare concerning the Israelites, God's chosen people, was fought in the flesh such as with the Amalekites. When God was taking the Israelites into the promised land, Moses said,

> *When the LORD thy God shall bring thee into the land whither thou goest to possess it, and hath cast out many nations before thee, the Hittites, and the Girgashites, and the Amorites, and the Canaanites, and the Perizzites, and the Hivites, and the Jebusites, seven nations greater and mightier than thou; and when the LORD thy God shall deliver them before thee; thou shalt smite them, and utterly destroy them; thou shalt make no covenant with them, nor shew mercy unto them.*
>
> (Deuteronomy 7:1-2)

After being in the wilderness for forty years, the Lord used Joshua to lead the Israelites to defeat their enemies in order to inherit the promised land. The LORD spoke to Joshua:

> *…Be strong and of a good courage: for unto this people shalt thou divide for an inheritance the land, which I sware unto their fathers to give them. Only be thou strong and very courageous, that thou mayest observe to do according to all the law, which Moses my servant commanded thee: turn not from it to the right hand or to the left, that thou mayest prosper whithersoever thou goest. This book of the law shall not depart out of thy mouth; but thou shalt meditate therein day and night, that thou mayest observe to do according to all that is written therein: for then thou shalt make thy way prosperous, and then thou shalt have good success.*
>
> (Joshua 1:1-8)

In the New Testament, our promised land is the kingdom of God and Jesus leads us to that promised land! Jesus said in *Luke 12:32 – "Fear not, little flock; for it is your Father's good pleasure to give you the kingdom."* In *Luke 17:20-21*, when Jesus was demanded of the Pharisees, when the kingdom of God should come, He answered, *"The kingdom of God cometh not with observation: neither shall they say, 'Lo here! Or, lo there!' For, behold, the kingdom of God is within you."*

As we choose to submit to the Lordship of Jesus Christ, by allowing His Words entrance into our innermost being by renewing the *spirit of our minds*, through the power of His Spirit, the lies of the enemy are exposed and we are then able to walk in the light of His grace and truth. Paul writes,

> *For though we walk in the flesh, we do not war after the flesh: (For the weapons of our warfare are not carnal, but mighty through God to the pulling down of strong holds;) casting down imaginations, and every high thing that exalteth itself against the knowledge of God, and bringing into captivity every thought to the obedience of Christ; and having in a readiness to revenge all disobedience, when your obedience is fulfilled.*
>
> (2 Corinthians 10:3-6)

The Greek word for "stronghold" is *ochyroma* which means "(meaning to fortify, through the idea of holding safely); a castle (figuratively, argument):–stronghold." These mental strongholds or lies that we believe to be true can be formed within us through hurts/woundings, fears, childhood trauma, and/or how, at a young age, we internalize certain behavior patterns from significant others, especially parents, which can form a protective barrier within us to keep us from being hurt and also can produce ungodly beliefs concerning what we think about ourselves, God, and others. These are the areas of our lives that keep us from experiencing the kingdom of God through the born-again creation within us. These mental strongholds can be deep-seated within us and therefore difficult to change, because their causes have been there for a long time. This is why it is essential to renew the *spirit of our minds*, to the new creation *(Ephesians 4:22-23)*. It is written in Hebrews, what the Word of God does in the heart, mind, will, and emotions of the believer:

> *For the word of God is quick (living), and powerful, and sharper than any twoedged sword, piercing even to the dividing asunder of soul and spirit, and of the joints and marrow, and is a discerner of the thoughts and intents of the heart.*
>
> (Hebrews 4:12)

The Word of God demolishes strongholds within us. Paul writes,

> *For the law of the Spirit of life in Christ Jesus hath made us free from the law of sin and death. For what the law could not do, in that it was weak through the flesh, God sending his own Son in the likeness of sinful flesh, and for sin, condemned sin in the flesh: that the righteousness of the law might be fulfilled in us, who walk not after the flesh, but after the Spirit. For they that are after the flesh do mind the things of the flesh; but they that are after the Spirit the things of the Spirit. For to be carnally minded is death; but to be spiritually minded is life and peace.*
>
> (Romans 8:2-6)

He continues with,

> *But if the Spirit of him that raised up Jesus from the dead dwell in you, he that raised up Christ from the dead shall also quicken (give life to) your mortal bodies by his Spirit that dwelleth in you. Therefore, brethren, we are debtors, not to the flesh, to live after the flesh. For if ye live after the flesh, ye shall die: but if ye through the Spirit do mortify the deeds of the body, ye shall live. For as many as are led by the Spirit of God, they are the sons of God. For ye have not received the spirit of bondage again to fear; but ye have received the Spirit of adoption, whereby we cry, Abba, Father.*
>
> (Romans 8:11-15)

Renewing our minds to the truth of God's Word is essential in experiencing the transforming power of a new life in Christ. Peter writes,

> *Seeing ye have purified your souls in obeying the truth through the Spirit unto unfeigned love of the brethren, see that ye love one another with a pure heart fervently: being born again, not of corruptible seed, but of incorruptible, by the word of God, which liveth and abideth for ever. For all flesh is as grass, and all the glory of man as the flower of grass. The grass withereth, and the flower thereof falleth away: but the word of the Lord endureth for ever. And this is the word which by the gospel is preached to you. Wherefore laying aside all malice, and all guile, and hypocrisies, and envies, and all evil speakings, as newborn babes, desire the sincere milk of the word, that ye may grow thereby: if so be ye have tasted that the Lord is gracious.*
>
> (1 Peter 1:22-2:3)

This passage of Scripture is very powerful! Peter is saying that the born-again creation, the new man, is born of incorruptible seed by the Word of God that lives and abides forever. He said, as "newborn babes," desire the sincere milk of the word that you may "grow." We do not grow apart from feeding on the Word of God. Paul writes,

And I, brethren, could not speak unto you as unto spiritual, but as unto carnal, even as unto babes in Christ. I have fed you with milk, and not with meat: for hitherto ye were not able to bear it, neither yet now are ye able. For ye are yet carnal: for whereas there is among you envying, and strife, and divisions, are ye not carnal, and walk as men?

(1 Corinthians 3:1-3)

A Christian who is operating in envy, strife, and division is still considered a "babe in Christ" and is not operating out of the new man because he or she is not mature enough to do so. To better understand how this works, let's look at a fruit-bearing tree. It is only when this tree becomes mature or full grown, being deeply rooted in fertile ground, that it can produce fruit. Even so, only a mature Christian can produce the fruit of the Spirit (i.e., love, joy, peace, longsuffering, gentleness, goodness, faith, meekness, temperance), against this fruit there is no law *(Galatians 5:22-23)*! As I describe in detail about the correlation between the *inmost mind* and the kidney in **Note 22b**, it's essential for us to personalize Scriptures and repetitively speak them aloud, receiving them as our own, in order for the power, purity, and life of God's Word to become a consistent flow into our *inmost mind*. As the kidneys remove toxic waste from the blood to keep the body healthy; so too as His Word consistently flows into our *inmost mind*, it begins to flush out ingrained carnal beliefs and mindsets or toxic waste (e.g., rebellion, pride, insecurities, rejection), which is the primary source of the old man. In doing this, we become more deeply rooted and grounded in the love of God. Paul writes,

For this cause I bow my knees unto the Father of our Lord Jesus Christ, of whom the whole family in heaven and earth is named, that he would grant you, according to the riches of his glory, to be strengthened with might by his Spirit in the inner man; that Christ may dwell in your hearts by faith; that ye, being rooted and grounded in love, may be able to comprehend with all the saints what is the breadth, and length, and depth, and height; and to know the love of Christ, which passeth knowledge, that ye might be filled with all the fullness of God. Now unto him that is able to do exceeding abundantly above all that we ask or think, according to the power that worketh in us unto him be glory in the church by Christ Jesus throughout all ages, world without end. Amen.

(Ephesians 3:14-21)

In *Galatians 5:19-21*, Paul reveals to us the works of the flesh and informs us that those who practice these things will not inherit the kingdom of God: adultery, fornication, uncleanness, lasciviousness, idolatry, witchcraft, hatred, variance, emulations, wrath, strife seditions, heresies, envyings, murders, drunkenness, revellings, and such like. In *verses 22-23*, He reveals to us the fruit of the Spirit (love, joy, peace, longsuffering, gentleness, goodness, faith, meekness, temperance: against such there is no law). He then tells us in *verse 24* what we do with the works of the flesh, *"...and they that are Christ's have crucified the flesh with the affections and lusts."* The cross of Christ is our banner of warfare, death to the old man—the false self! For more detailed information on this subject matter please refer to the **Introduction, Understanding Its Importance**, and **My Story – Part Two - Volume 1**.

Below are Scriptures relating to defeating the works of the devil:

Acts 2:34-36 – For David is not ascended into the heavens: but he saith himself, 'The LORD said unto my Lord, "Sit thou on my right hand, until I make thy foes (enemies) thy footstool."' Therefore let all the house of Israel know assuredly, that God hath made that same Jesus, whom ye have crucified, both Lord and Christ.

References:
Romans 7:14-25 – Paul said, "For we know that the law is spiritual: but I am carnal, sold under sin. For that which I do I allow not: for what I would, that do I not; but what I hate, that do I. If then I do that which I would not, I consent unto the law that it is good. Now then it is no more I that do it, but sin that dwelleth in me. For I know that in me (that is, in my flesh) dwelleth no good thing: for to will is present with me; but how to perform that which is good I find not. For the good that I would I do not: but the evil which I would not, that I do. Now if I do that I would not, it is no more I that do it, but sin that dwelleth in me. I find then a law, that, when I would do good, evil is present with me. For I delight in the law of God after the inward man: but I see another law in my members, warring against the law of my mind, and bringing me into captivity to the law of sin which is in my members. O wretched man that I am! Who shall deliver me from the body of this death? I thank God through Jesus Christ our Lord. So then with the mind I myself serve the law of God; but with the flesh the law of sin." Romans 16:19-20 – For your obedience is come abroad unto all men. I am glad therefore on your behalf: but yet I would have you wise unto that which is good, and simple concerning evil. And the God of peace shall bruise Satan under your feet shortly. The grace of our Lord Jesus Christ be with you. Amen. 1 Corinthians 1:21-24 – For after that in the wisdom of God the world by wisdom knew not God, it pleased God by the foolishness of preaching to save them that believe. For the Jews require a sign, and the Greeks seek after wisdom: but we preach Christ crucified, unto the Jews a stumblingblock, and unto the Greeks foolishness; but unto them which are called, both Jews and Greeks, Christ the power of God, and the wisdom of God. 1 Corinthians 15:22-26 – For as in Adam all die, even so in Christ shall all be made alive. But every man in his own order: Christ the firstfruits; afterward they that are Christ's at his coming. Then cometh the end, when he shall have delivered up the kingdom to God, even the Father; when he shall have put down all rule and all authority and power. For he must reign, till he hath put all enemies under his feet. The last enemy that shall be destroyed is death. Ephesians 2:1-7 – And you hath he quickened, who were dead in trespasses and sins; wherein in time past ye walked according to the course of this world, according to the prince of the power of the air, the spirit that now worketh in the children of disobedience: among whom also we all had our conversation (behavior) in times past in the lusts of our flesh, fulfilling the desires of the flesh and of the mind; and were by nature the children of wrath, even as others. But God, who is rich in mercy, for his great love wherewith he loved us, even when we were dead in sins, hath quickened us (made us alive) together with Christ, (by grace ye are saved;) and hath raised us up together, and made us sit together in heavenly places in Christ Jesus: that in the ages to come he might shew the exceeding riches of his grace in his kindness toward us through Christ Jesus. Hebrews 2:14 – Forasmuch then as the children are partakers of flesh and blood, he (Jesus) also himself likewise took part of the same; that through death he might destroy him that had the power of death, that is, the devil; and deliver them who through fear of death were all their lifetime subject to bondage. 1 Peter 3:19-22 (NIV) – After being made alive, he (Jesus) went and made proclamation to the imprisoned spirits—to those who were disobedient long ago when God waited patiently in the days of Noah while the ark was being built. In it only a few people, eight in all, were saved through water, and this water symbolizes baptism that now saves you also— not the removal of dirt from the body but the pledge of a clear conscience toward God. It saves you by the resurrection of Jesus Christ, who has gone into heaven and is at God's right hand—with angels, authorities and powers in submission to him. 1 John 3:8 – He that committeth sin is of the devil; for the devil sinneth

from the beginning. For this purpose the Son of God was manifested, that he might destroy the works of the devil.

Below are Scriptures relating to defeating the works of the devil by putting on the new man:

Galatians 6:14-15 *– Paul said, "But God forbid that I should glory, save in the cross of our Lord Jesus Christ, by whom the world is crucified unto me, and I unto the world. For in Christ Jesus neither circumcision availeth any thing, nor uncircumcision, but a new creature."*

References:
Romans 12:1-2 *– I beseech you therefore, brethren, by the mercies of God that ye present your bodies a living sacrifice, holy, acceptable unto God, which is your reasonable service. And be not conformed to this world: but be ye transformed by the renewing of your mind, that ye may prove what is that good, and acceptable, and perfect, will of God.* ***Romans 13:13-14*** *(NIV) – Let us behave decently, as in the daytime, not in carousing and drunkenness, not in sexual immorality and debauchery, not in dissension and jealousy. Rather, clothe yourselves with the Lord Jesus Christ, and do not think about how to gratify the desires of the flesh.* ***1 Corinthians 2:6-12*** *– Howbeit we speak wisdom among them that are perfect: yet not the wisdom of this world, nor of the princes of this world, that come to nought: but we speak the wisdom of God in a mystery, even the hidden wisdom, which God ordained before the world unto our glory: which none of the princes of this world knew: for had they known it, they would not have crucified the Lord of glory. But as it is written, "Eye hath not seen, nor ear heard, neither have entered into the heart of man, the things which God hath prepared for them that love him." But God hath revealed them unto us by his Spirit: for the Spirit searcheth all things, yea, the deep things of God. For what man knoweth the things of a man, save the spirit of man which is in him? Even so the things of God knoweth no man, but the Spirit of God. Now we have received, not the spirit of the world, but the spirit which is of God; that we might know the things that are freely given to us of God.* ***2 Corinthians 3:17-18*** *– Now the Lord is that Spirit: and where the Spirit of the Lord is, there is liberty. But we all, with open face beholding as in a glass the glory of the Lord, are changed into the same image from glory to glory, even as by the Spirit of the Lord.* ***2 Corinthians 5:17-21*** *– Therefore if any man be in Christ, he is a new creature: old things are passed away; behold, all things are become new. And all things are of God, who hath reconciled us unto himself by Jesus Christ…* ***Galatians 3:27-29*** *– For as many of you as have been baptized into Christ have put on Christ. There is neither Jew nor Greek, there is neither bond nor free, there is neither male nor female: for ye are all one in Christ Jesus. And if ye be Christ's, then are ye Abraham's seed, and heirs according to the promise.* ***Ephesians 2:15*** *– Having abolished in his flesh the enmity, even the law of commandments contained in ordinances; for to make in himself of twain (two) one new man, so making peace.* ***Ephesians 4:20-24*** *– But ye have not so learned Christ; if so be that ye have heard him, and have been taught by him, as the truth is in Jesus: that ye put off concerning the former conversation (behavior) the old man, which is corrupt according to the deceitful lusts; and be renewed in the spirit of your mind; and that ye put on the new man, which after God is created in righteousness and true holiness.* ***Ephesians 5:8-10*** *– For ye were sometimes darkness, but now are ye light in the Lord: walk as children of light: (for the fruit of the Spirit is in all goodness and righteousness and truth;) proving what is acceptable unto the Lord.* ***Colossians 3:8-11*** *– But now ye also put off all these; anger, wrath, malice, blasphemy, filthy communication out of your mouth. Lie not one to another, seeing that ye have put off the old man with his deeds; and have put on the new man, which is renewed in knowledge after the image of him that created him: where there is neither Greek nor Jew, circumcision nor uncircumcision, Barbarian, Scythian, bond nor free: but Christ is all, and in all.* ***1 Peter 3:4*** *– But let it be the hidden man of the heart, in that which is not corruptible, even the ornament of a meek and quiet spirit, which is in the sight of God*

of great price. **1 John 5:4** – *For whatsoever is born of God overcometh the world: and this is the victory that overcometh the world, even our faith.*

Please refer to **Note 25a** for more information relating to the cross of Christ.

26(a) *You are* the **Ancient of Days [God, the eternal Father]**. (Daniel 7:9-AMPCE)

In *Daniel 7*, in the first year of Belshazar king of Babylon, Daniel had a dream and visions passed through his head while he was in his bed. He wrote down the dream and told the sum of the matter. And Daniel said, *"I saw in my vision by night, and, behold, the four winds of the heaven strove upon the great sea. And four great beasts came up from the sea, diverse one from another"* (Daniel 7:1-2). After describing the four beasts, he went on to say in *verses 7:9-10, 13-14*:

> *I beheld till the thrones were cast down, and the <u>Ancient of days</u> did sit, whose garment was white as snow, and the hair of his head like the pure wool: his throne was like the fiery flame, and his wheels as burning fire. A fiery stream issued and came forth from before him: thousand thousands ministered unto him, and ten thousand times ten thousand stood before him: the judgment was set, and the books were opened. I saw in the night visions, and, behold, one like the Son of man came with clouds of heaven, and came to the Ancient of days, and they brought him near before him. And there was given him dominion, and glory, and a kingdom, that all people, nations, and languages, should serve him: his dominion is an everlasting dominion, which shall not pass away, and his kingdom that which shall not be destroyed.*

In this passage of Scripture, the Ancient of Days is the Most High God, our eternal Father, and the Judge of all. Jesus Christ is the Son of man that came with the clouds of heaven, and came to the Ancient of Days and there was given Him dominion, glory, and a kingdom, that all people, nations, and languages, should serve Him. His dominion is an everlasting dominion and His kingdom will never be destroyed. In *Psalm 90:1-17*, [[*A prayer of Moses the man of God.*]] *"Lord, thou hast been our dwelling place in all generations. Before the mountains were brought forth, or ever thou hadst formed the earth and the world, even from everlasting to everlasting, thou art God..."* And in *Proverbs 8*, wisdom is talking throughout the entire chapter,

> *The LORD possessed me in the beginning of his way, before his works of old. I was set up from everlasting, from the beginning, or ever the earth was. When there were no depths, I was brought forth; when there were no fountains abounding with water. Before the mountains were settled, before the hills was I brought forth: while as yet he had not made the earth, nor the fields, nor the highest part of the dust of the world. When he prepared the heavens, I was there: when he set a compass upon the face of the depth: when he established the clouds above: when he strengthened the fountains of the deep: when he gave to the sea his decree, that the waters should not pass his commandment: when he appointed the foundations of the earth: then I was by him, as one brought up with him: and I was daily his delight,*

206

rejoicing always before him; rejoicing in the habitable part of his earth; and my delights were with the sons of men. Now therefore hearken unto me, O ye children: for blessed are they that keep my ways. Hear instruction, and be wise, and refuse it not. Blessed is the man that heareth me, watching daily at my gates, waiting at the posts of my doors. For whoso findeth me findeth life, and shall obtain favour of the LORD. But he that sinneth against me wrongeth his own soul: all they that hate me love death.

(Proverbs 8:22-36)

This wisdom is found in the person of Jesus Christ! Jesus said,

The queen of the south shall rise up in the judgment with the men of this generation, and condemn them: for she came from the utmost parts of the earth to hear the wisdom of Solomon; and, behold, a greater than Solomon is here.

(Luke 11:31)

Jesus Christ is the same yesterday, today, and forever and God does not change (*Hebrews 13:8; Malachi 3:6*). This is why Christ is called our Counselor *(Isaiah 9:6)* as He will always lead us to the ancient paths where we find life, peace, and fulfillment:

1. ***Proverbs 22:28*** – *Remove not the ancient landmark, which thy fathers have set.*
2. ***Jeremiah 18:15*** *(NKJV) – The LORD said, "Because My people have forgotten Me, they have burned incense to worthless idols. And they have caused themselves to stumble in their ways, from the* ancient paths, *to walk in pathways and not on a highway."*

The Hebrew word for "ancient" in these two passages of Scripture is *owlam* (*olam*) and means "… ancient (time), any more, continuance, eternity; …(beginning of the) world (+ without end)." He is *El-Olam*, the Everlasting One. Therefore, do not be deceived! You will never be able to find true joy, peace, and completeness apart from the Ancient of Days, our eternal Father, as true fulfillment only comes through Him. Following after this world's wisdom may temporarily satisfy the longings of the flesh, but the end result is death *(Hebrews 11:25; 1 John 2:15-17; James 1:13-15)*. It's only through God, in intimate fellowship with Him, that the deep longings of our hearts are truly satisfied. Please refer to **Note 2a** for more information on *El-olam*.

Paul writes,

For the preaching of the cross is to them that perish foolishness; but unto us which are saved it is the power of God. For it is written, "I will destroy the wisdom of the wise, and will bring to nothing the understanding of the prudent." Where is the wise? Where is the scribe? Where is the disputer of this world? Hath not God made foolish the wisdom of this world? For after that in the wisdom of God the world by wisdom knew not God, it pleased God by the foolishness of preaching to save them that believe. For the Jews require a sign, and the Greeks seek after wisdom: but we preach Christ crucified, unto the Jews a stumblingblock, and unto the Greeks foolishness; but unto them which are called, both Jews and Greeks, Christ the power of God, and the wisdom of God.

(1 Corinthians 1:18-24)

And Peter writes in *1 Peter 2:25*, "*For ye were as sheep going astray; but are now returned unto the Shepherd and Bishop of your souls.*" Christ is our protector and guide, His wisdom keeps us safe! God's wisdom is found in His Word as the truth is in Christ *(Ephesians 4:21)*. Seek after Him, follow after Him! For whosoever finds wisdom finds life and shall obtain favor of the Lord *(Proverbs 8:35; John 10:10)*. Let's also remember that all Scripture is given by inspiration of God:

> *All scripture is given by inspiration of God, and is profitable for doctrine, for reproof, for correction, for instruction in righteousness: that the man of God may be perfect, throughly furnished unto all good works.*

> (2 Timothy 3:16)

Below are Scriptures relating to the light and wisdom of His Words:

John 1:1-4, 14 – *In the beginning was the Word, and the Word was with God, and the Word was God. The same was in the beginning with God. All things were made by him; and without him was not any thing made that was made. In him was life; and the life was the light of men. And the Word was made flesh, and dwelt among us, (and we beheld his glory, the glory as of the only begotten of the Father,) full of grace and truth.*

References:
Psalm 119:130 – *The entrance of thy words giveth light; it giveth understanding unto the simple.* ***Matthew 7:22-27*** – *Jesus said, "Many will say to me in that day, 'Lord, Lord, have we not prophesied in thy name? And in thy name have cast out devils? And in thy name done many wonderful works?' And then will I profess unto them, I never knew you: depart from me, ye that work iniquity. Therefore whosoever heareth these sayings of mine, and doeth them, I will liken him unto a wise man, which built his house upon a rock: and the rain descended, and the floods came, and the winds blew, and beat upon that house; and it fell not: for it was founded upon a rock. And every one that heareth these sayings of mine, and doeth them not, shall be likened unto a foolish man, which built his house upon the sand: and the rain descended, and the floods came, and the winds blew, and beat upon that house; and it fell: and great was the fall of it."* ***Luke 11:27-28*** – *And it came to pass, as he (Jesus) spake these things, a certain woman of the company lifted up her voice, and said unto him, "Blessed is the womb that bare thee, and the paps (breast) which thou hast sucked." But he said, "Yea rather, blessed are they that hear the word of God, and keep it."* ***John 8:12*** – *Jesus said, "I am the light of the world: he who follows me shall not walk in darkness but have the light of life."* ***2 Corinthians 3:17-18*** – *Now the Lord is that Spirit: and where the Spirit of the Lord is, there is liberty. But we all, with open face beholding as in a glass the glory of the Lord, are changed into the same image from glory to glory, even as by the Spirit of the Lord.* ***James 1:22-25*** – *But be ye doers of the word, and not hearers only, deceiving your own selves. For if any be a hearer of the word, and not a doer, he is like unto a man beholding his natural face in a glass: for he beholdeth himself, and goeth his way, and straightway forgetteth what manner of man he was. But whoso looketh into the perfect law of liberty, and continueth therein, he being not a forgetful hearer, but a doer of the work, this man shall be blessed in his deed.* ***James 3:13-18*** – *Who is a wise man and endued with knowledge among you? Let him shew out of a good conversation (behavior) his works with meekness of wisdom. But if ye have bitter envying and strife in your hearts, glory not, and lie not against the truth. This wisdom descendeth not from above, but is earthly, sensual, devilish. For where envying and strife is, there is confusion and every evil work. But the wisdom that is from above is first pure, then peaceable, gentle, and easy to be intreated, full of mercy and good fruits, without partiality, and without hypocrisy. And the fruit of righteousness is sown in peace of them that make peace.* ***1 Peter***

1:22-25 – Seeing ye have purified your souls in obeying the truth through the Spirit unto unfeigned love of the brethren, see that ye love one another with a pure heart fervently: being born again, not of corruptible seed, but of incorruptible, by the word of God, which liveth and abideth for ever. For all flesh is as grass, and all the glory of man as the flower of grass. The grass withereth, and the flower thereof falleth away: but the word of the Lord endureth for ever. And this is the word which by the gospel is preached unto you.

Please refer to **Notes 7a**, **7b**, and **7c** for additional information and Scriptures relating to our eternal Abba Father.

Please refer to **Note 26b** for Scriptures relating to walking in the light of His Word.

26(b) *You are the **Father of lights**. Every good gift and every perfect gift is from above; it comes down from You, the Father of all [that gives] light. (James 1:17-AMPCE) (Ref: James 1:17)*

Let's begin by looking at *James 1:12-18:*

> *Blessed is the man that endureth temptation: for when he is tried, he shall receive the crown of life, which the Lord hath promised to them that love him. Let no man say when he is tempted, I am tempted of God: for God cannot be tempted with evil, neither tempteth he any man: but every man is tempted, when he is drawn away of his own lust, and enticed. Then when lust hath conceived, it bringeth forth sin: and sin, when it is finished, bringeth forth death. Do not err, my beloved brethren. <u>Every good gift and every perfect gift is from above, and cometh down from the Father of lights, with whom is no variableness, neither shadow of turning.</u> Of his own will begat he (gave birth to) us with the word of truth, that we should be a kind of firstfruits of his creatures.*

All good and perfect gifts come from the Father of lights, with whom there is no change or shadow of turning and His gifts and callings are irrevocable *(Romans 11:29)*! The most powerful and amazing gift our heavenly Father has given to us is His Holy Spirit through the obedience of His Son, Jesus Christ. Jesus was made to be sin for us that we might be made the righteousness of God in Him *(2 Corinthians 5:21)*. Through our Lord's death, burial, and resurrection, the Father has given His Holy Spirit to those who repent and are baptized in the name of Jesus Christ for the remission of sins *(Acts 2:38)*. (Please see **Note 1b** for more information on the baptism of the Holy Spirit.) Below are four passages of Scripture concerning this:

1. ***Luke 11:9-13*** *– Jesus said, "…For every one that asketh receiveth; and he that seeketh findeth; and to him that knocketh it shall be opened. If a son shall ask bread of any of you that is a father, will he give him a stone? Or if he ask a fish, will he for a fish give him a serpent? Or if he shall ask for an egg, will he offer him a scorpion? <u>If ye then, being evil, know how to give good gifts unto your children: how much more shall your heavenly Father give the Holy Spirit to them that ask him?</u>"*
2. ***John 7:38-39*** *– Jesus said, "He that believeth on me, as the scripture hath said, out of his belly shall flow rivers of living water." (But this spake he of the Spirit, which they that believe on him should receive: for the Holy Ghost was not yet given; because that Jesus was not yet glorified.)*

3. ***1 Corinthians 12:4-11*** – *Now there are diversities of gifts, but the same Spirit. And there are differences of administrations, but the same Lord. And there are diversities of operations, but it is the same God which worketh all in all. But the manifestation of the Spirit is given to every man to profit withal. For to one is given by the Spirit the word of wisdom; to another the word of knowledge by the same Spirit; to another faith by the same Spirit; to another gifts of healing by the same Spirit; to another the working of miracles; to another prophecy; to another discerning of spirits; to another divers kinds of tongues; to another the interpretation of tongues: but all these worketh that one and the selfsame Spirit, dividing to every man severally as he will.*

4. ***Hebrews 2:4*** *(NKJV)* – *God also bearing witness both with signs and wonders, with various miracles, and gifts of the Holy Spirit, according to His own will?*

In *John 7:38-39*, Jesus describes the Holy Spirit as rivers of living water. In the natural, in order to bring forth a wellspring of water from the earth, you must dig deep to tap into water. Let's look at Genesis 26:12-19:

> *Then Isaac (Abraham's son, the son of promise) sowed in that land, and received in the same year an hundredfold: and the LORD blessed him. And the man waxed great, and went forward, and grew until he became very great: For he had possession of flocks, and possession of herds, and great store of servants: and <u>the Philistines envied him. For all the wells which his father's servants had digged in the days of Abraham his father, the Philistines had stopped them, and filled them with earth.</u> And Abimelech said unto Isaac, "Go from us; for thou art much mightier than we." And Isaac departed thence, and pitched his tent in the valley of Gerar, and dwelt there. <u>And Isaac digged again the wells of water, which they had digged in the days of Abraham his father; for the Philistines had stopped them after the death of Abraham: and he called their names after the names by which his father had called them. And Isaac's servants digged in the valley, and found there a well of springing water.</u>*

Israel (God's people) seemed to always be at war with the Philistines *(1 Samuel 4, 7:13-14; 2 Kings 18:5-8)*. In the New Testament, *Ephesians 6:12* reveals to us who we wrestle against and it's not flesh and blood: *"For we wrestle not against flesh and blood, but against principalities, against powers, against the rulers of the darkness of this world, against spiritual wickedness in high places."* The devil or Satan is the real enemy. In the New Testament, "devil" in the Greek is *diabolos* and occurs 38 times and "Satan" in the Greek is *Satanas* and occurs 36 times. He is also called the prince of the power of the air, the god of this world, the father of lies, and the thief *(Ephesians 2:1-3; 2 Corinthians 4:3-4; John 8:44, 10:10)*. Peter exhorts us in *1 Peter 5:8,*

> *<u>Be sober, be vigilant;</u> because your adversary the devil, as a roaring lion, walketh about, seeking whom he may devour: whom resist stedfast in the faith, knowing that the same afflictions are accomplished in your brethren that are in the world.*

Satan does not want born-again believers in Christ to tap into the wellspring of living water that dwells within their hearts so he will do whatever he can to keep that from happening. In my case, because of a deep-seated root of rebellion operating within me, I believed the lies about myself and the feelings associated with those lies. I believed that I could drink from the well of self-gratification and intimacy with other women to satisfy the deep longings and deprivations of my heart instead of trusting Christ to bring healing and wholeness to me. I looked to "earthly" things to fill those deep needs, but I always came up short and stayed thirsty and wanting. Because I chose to walk away from the Lord at the age of twenty, the enemy of my soul (Satan) dropped an earthly protective covering on the inside of me. He thought this would totally keep the wellspring of water (the Holy Spirit) from truly flowing and functioning within me. For twenty years after coming back to the Lord at the age of twenty-six, this protective covering did keep His Spirit from truly flowing in my life. This kept me in a place of immaturity in Christ, and therefore kept me from producing the fruit of the Spirit and from being a greater witness for Him. At the age of forty-six, along with continuing to be real (honest) with the Lord concerning issues of the heart, the Lord called me to begin skillfully speaking aloud personalized Scriptures concerning putting off the old man and putting on the new man in Christ four times a week for six months and by doing so, a picture of the born-again creation began to form within me. Four months into this exercise, by His Word and through the power of His Spirit, the Lord removed that protective covering from me! Since that time, the wellspring of His living water has brought wholeness and completion to me and has produced much fruit in my life. I give God much thanks for the gift of His Spirit (see *My Story – Part One* and *Part Two - Volume 1* for details). Please refer to **Note 17b** for more information on Christ's living water, the gift of the Holy Spirit.

Satan also uses the cares of this world, the lust of other things, and the deceitfulness of riches to choke the Word of God within us in order to keep His Word from becoming fruitful in our lives and to keep us from becoming deeply rooted in Him *(Mark 4:1-20)*. Jesus said,

> *And why call ye me, 'Lord, Lord,' and do not the things which I say? Whosoever cometh to me, and heareth my sayings, and doeth them, I will shew you to whom he is like: he is like a man which built an house, <u>and digged deep</u>, and laid the foundation on a rock: and when the flood arose, the stream beat vehemently upon that house, and could not shake it: for it was founded upon a rock. But he that heareth, and doeth not, is like a man that without a foundation built an house upon the earth; against which the stream did beat vehemently, and immediately it fell; and the ruin of that house was great.*
>
> (Luke 6:46-49)

The way we dig deep within this earthen vessel is to be real with the Lord about those things that we struggle with and to allow His Word to have full reign in our hearts and minds to expose and dismantle ingrained carnal beliefs and mindsets (e.g., judgments, prejudices, falsehoods, lustful thoughts), that greatly influence our will and emotions.

God freely gives Himself to us and through the gift of His Holy Spirit, we have been given all things that pertain to life and godliness *(2 Peter 1:3)*. Below are four passages of Scripture concerning this:

1. ***1 Corinthians 2:9-12*** *– But as it is written, "Eye hath not seen, nor ear heard, neither have entered into the heart of man, the things which God hath prepared for them that love him." But God hath revealed them unto us by his Spirit: for the Spirit searcheth all things, yea, the deep things of God. For what man knoweth the things of a man, save the spirit of man which is in him? Even so the things of God knoweth no man, but the Spirit of God. Now we have received, not the spirit of the world, but the spirit which is of God; that we might know the things that are freely given to us of God.* (Because of what Jesus did for us, we literally have God dwelling in us through His Spirit and it is that same Spirit that raised Christ from

the dead—what a powerful and amazing gift – *2 Corinthians 6:16; Romans 8:11*)!

2. ***2 Corinthians 3:17-18*** – *Now the Lord is that Spirit: and where the Spirit of the Lord is, there is liberty. But we all, with open face beholding as in a glass the glory of the Lord, are changed into the same image from glory to glory, even as by the Spirit of the Lord.*

3. ***2 Corinthians 4:6-7*** – *For God, who commanded the light to shine out of darkness, hath shined in our hearts, to give the light of the knowledge of the glory of God in the face of Jesus Christ. But we have this treasure in earthen vessels, that the excellency of the power may be of God, and not of us.*

4. ***2 Peter 1:3-4*** – *According as his divine power hath given unto us all things that pertain unto life and godliness, through the knowledge of him that hath called us to glory and virtue: whereby are given unto us exceeding great and precious promises: that by these ye might be partakers of the divine nature, having escaped the corruption that is in the world through lust.* (As His Spirit reveals to us the knowledge of God we walk in the things that pertain to life and godliness. Again, what an amazing gift)!

Our heavenly Father is love, He is perfect, He is pure, and He is holy—He is a consuming fire! He is light and in Him there is no darkness, neither is there any unrighteousness in Him (*Hebrews 12:29; 1 John 1:5; Psalm 92:15*). His desire for His children is to walk in the light as He is in the light by walking in the revelation or understanding of the truth of His Word. The entrance of His Word <u>gives light</u>; it <u>gives understanding</u> to the simple (*1 John 1:7; Psalm 119:130*). Let's look at the following passage of Scripture:

> *For he received from God the Father honour and glory, when there came such a voice to him from the excellent glory, "This is my beloved Son, in whom I am well pleased." And this voice which came from heaven we heard, when we were with him in the holy mount. We have also a more sure word of prophecy; whereunto ye do well that ye take heed, as unto a light that shineth in a dark place, until the day dawn, and the day star arise in your hearts: knowing this first, that no prophecy of the scripture is of any private interpretation. For the prophecy came not in old time by the will of man: but holy men of God spake as they were moved by the Holy Ghost.*
>
> (2 Peter 1:17-21)

I believe Peter is letting us know that as we choose to focus our attention on the truth of God's Word, we may not see or understand everything that the Lord is doing, but eventually the day (light) will dawn within us and we will be able to see clearly what He is doing and the changes that are being made within us. Here is an example in the natural of how my understanding was darkened and eventually the light came on within me to understand. I took shorthand in my junior and senior year of high school and even though I had a good teacher, both years I barely passed with a "D" because my understanding was not enlightened. However, I did not give up! After high school, I went to Dekalb Technical School and took shorthand again. After a couple of weeks in that class, the "light" came on and I understood it and made an "A" in that class. A few months later, I heard from a friend that AT&T was hiring people who knew shorthand and typing. I went to AT&T and filled out the application and was given a test to see how fast I could take shorthand and type. I was able to write 100 words a minute in shorthand and type 80 words a minute, and I was hired that same day. I am so thankful I did not give up! Concerning spiritual things, sometimes it takes time for understanding to come, but it will come as we continue to press into Him and not give up. Let's look at two passages of Scripture that relate to this:

1. **Mark 4:26-29** – *Jesus said, "So is the kingdom of God, as if a man should cast seed into the ground; and should sleep, and rise night and day, and the seed should spring and grow up, he knoweth not how. For the earth bringeth forth fruit of herself; first the blade, then the ear, after that the full corn in the ear. But when the fruit is brought forth, immediately he putteth in the sickle, because the harvest is come."*
2. **Luke 8:15** – *Jesus said, "But that on the good ground are they, which in an honest and good heart, having heard the word, keep it, and bring forth fruit <u>with patience</u>."*

Peter writes,

> *Nevertheless we, according to his promise, look for new heavens and a new earth, wherein dwelleth righteousness. Wherefore, beloved, seeing that ye look for such things, be diligent that ye may be found of him in peace, without spot, and blameless. And account that the longsuffering of our Lord is salvation; even as our beloved brother Paul also according to the wisdom given unto him hath written unto you; as also in all his epistles, speaking in them of these things; in which are some things hard to be understood, which they that are unlearned and unstable wrest (twist), as they do also the other scriptures, unto their own destruction.*
>
> (2 Peter 3:13-16)

Just because we might not understand certain Scriptures, we need to be encouraged not to "twist" Scriptures to make them conform to our carnal ways of thinking, but to continue to trust the Lord and seek Him for the "light" or "understanding," remembering that there is no darkness or unrighteousness in Him. When we live out of the born-again creation, we are walking in the light of Christ:

> *For ye were sometimes darkness, but now are ye light in the Lord: walk as children of light: (for the fruit of the Spirit is in all goodness and righteousness and truth;) proving what is acceptable unto the Lord.*
>
> (Ephesians 5:8-10)

It takes time for the born-again creation to grow and mature in order to produce the fruit of the Spirit (i.e., love, joy, peace, longsuffering, kindness, goodness, faithfulness, gentleness, self-control – *Galatians 5:22-24*). Jesus said in *John 8:12* – *"I am the light of the world: he that followeth me shall not walk in darkness, but shall have the light of life."*

Below are Scriptures relating to walking in the light of His Word:

Psalm 56:13 – *For thou hast delivered my soul from death: wilt not thou deliver my feet from falling, that I may walk before God in the light of the living?*

References:
Psalm 89:15 – *Blessed is the people that know the joyful sound: they shall walk, O LORD, in the light of thy countenance.* **Ecclesiastes 2:13** – *Then I saw that wisdom excelleth folly, as far as light excelleth darkness.* **Isaiah 2:5** – *O house of Jacob, come ye, and let us walk in the light of the LORD.* **John 1:6-9** – *There was a man sent from God, whose name was John. The same came for a witness to bear witness of the Light, that all men through him might believe. He was not that Light, but was sent to bear witness of that Light. That was*

*the true Light, which lighteth every man that cometh into the world. **John 3:17-21** — For God sent not his Son into the world to condemn the world; but that the world through him might be saved. He that believeth on him is not condemned: but he that believeth not is condemned already, because he hath not believed in the name of the only begotten Son of God. And this is the condemnation, that light is come into the world, and men loved darkness rather than light because their deeds were evil. For everyone that doeth evil hateth the light, neither cometh to the light, lest his deeds should be reproved. But he that doeth truth cometh to the light, that his deeds may be made manifest, that they are wrought in God. **John 11:9-10** — Jesus answered, "Are there not twelve hours in the day? If any man walk in the day, he stumbleth not, because he seeth the light of this world. But if a man walk in the night, he stumbleth, because there is no light in him." **2 Corinthians 4:3-7** — But if our gospel be hid, it is hid to them that are lost: in whom the god of this world hath blinded the minds of them which believe not, lest the light of the glorious gospel of Christ, who is the image of God, should shine unto them. For we preach not ourselves, but Christ Jesus the Lord; and ourselves your servants for Jesus' sake. For God, who commanded the light to shine out of darkness, hath shined in our hearts, to give the light of the knowledge of the glory of God in the face of Jesus Christ. But we have this treasure in earthen vessels, that the excellency of the power may be of God, and not of us. **Ephesians 5:5-14** — For this ye know, that no whoremonger, nor unclean person, nor covetous man, who is an idolater, hath any inheritance in the kingdom of Christ and of God. Let no man deceive you with vain words: for because of these things cometh the wrath of God upon the children of disobedience. Be not ye therefore partakers with them. For ye were sometimes darkness, but now are ye light in the Lord: walk as children of light: (for the fruit of the Spirit is in all goodness and righteousness and truth:) proving what is acceptable unto the Lord. And have no fellowship with the unfruitful works of darkness, but rather reprove (expose) them. For it is a shame even to speak of those things which are done of them in secret. But all things that are reproved are made manifest by the light: for whatsoever doth make manifest is light. Wherefore he saith, "Awake, thou that sleepest, and arise from the dead, and Christ shall give thee light." **Colossians 1:12-15** — Giving thanks unto the Father, which hath made us meet (able) to be partakers of the inheritance of the saints in light: who hath delivered us from the power of darkness, and hath translated us into the kingdom of his dear Son: in whom we have redemption through his blood, even the forgiveness of sins: who is the image of the invisible God, the firstborn of every creature. **Colossians 2:2-3** — That their hearts might be comforted, being knit together in love, and unto all riches of the full assurance of understanding, to the acknowledgement of the mystery of God, and of the Father, and of Christ; in whom are hid all the treasure of wisdom and knowledge. **1 Timothy 6:13-16** — I give thee charge in the sight of God, who quickeneth (gives life to) all things, and before Christ Jesus, who before Pontius Pilate witnessed a good confession; that thou keep this commandment without spot, unrebukeable, until the appearing of our Lord Jesus Christ: which in his times he shall shew, who is the blessed and only Potentate, the King of kings, and Lord of lords; who only hath immortality, dwelling in the light which no man can approach unto; whom no man hath seen, nor can see: to whom be honour and power everlasting. Amen. **2 Timothy 1:10** — But is now made manifest by the appearing of our Saviour Jesus Christ, who hath abolished death, and hath brought life and immortality to light through the gospel. **2 Peter 1:1-11** — Simon Peter, a servant and an apostle of Jesus Christ, to them that have obtained like precious faith with us through the righteousness of God and our Saviour Jesus Christ: grace and peace be multiplied unto you through the knowledge of God, and of Jesus our Lord, according as his divine power hath given unto us all things that pertain unto life and godliness, through the knowledge of him that hath called us to glory and virtue: whereby are given unto us exceeding great and precious promises: that by these ye might be partakers of the divine nature, having escaped the corruption that is in the world through lust. And beside this, giving all diligence, add to your faith virtue; and to virtue knowledge; and to knowledge temperance; and to temperance patience; and to patience godliness; and to godliness brotherly kindness; and to brotherly kindness charity (God's love). For if these things be in you, and abound, they make you that ye* *shall neither be barren nor unfruitful in the knowledge of our Lord Jesus Christ. But he that lacketh these things is blind, and cannot see afar off, and hath forgotten that he was purged from his old sins. Wherefore the rather, brethren, give diligence to make your calling and election sure: for if ye do these things, ye shall never fall: for so an entrance shall be ministered unto you abundantly into the everlasting kingdom of our Lord and Saviour Jesus Christ. 1 John 2:10-11 – He that loveth his brother abideth in the light, and there is none occasion of stumbling in him. But he that hateth his brother is in darkness, and walketh in darkness, and knoweth not whither he goeth, because that darkness hath blinded his eyes.*

Please refer to **Notes 5a** and **5b** for information and Scriptures relating to Jesus being the Light of the world and His light within us.

Please refer to **Note 26a** and **32b** for Scriptures relating to the light and wisdom of His Words.

26(c) It is impossible for *You* ever to prove false or deceive *me*. (Hebrews 6:18-AMPCE)

Based on everything we covered in **Notes 26a** and **26b** we can easily come to the conclusion that it is impossible for the Lord to ever prove false or deceive us as He is the One who brings light or understanding to us in order to walk in His truth and abundant life. There is one deceiver, Satan, who operates in darkness. Paul writes,

> *But I fear, lest by any means, as the serpent beguiled (deceived) Eve through his subtlety (trickery or craftiness), so your minds should be corrupted from the simplicity that is in Christ… For such are false apostles, deceitful workers, transforming themselves into the apostles of Christ. And no marvel; for Satan himself is transformed into an angel of light. Therefore it is no great thing if his ministers also be transformed as the ministers of righteousness; whose end shall be according to their works.*
>
> (2 Corinthians 11:3-15)

Jesus said,

> *If God were your Father, ye would love me: for I proceeded forth and came from God; neither came I of myself, but he sent me. Why do ye not understand my speech? Even because ye cannot hear my word. Ye are of your father the devil, and the lusts of your father ye will do. He was a murderer from the beginning, and abode not in the truth, because there is no truth in him. When he speaketh a lie, he speaketh of his own: for he is a liar, and the father of it.*
>
> (John 8:42-44)

We have to do more than believe! Scripture tells us that even the devils believe and tremble. We must not only be hearers of the Word but doers also *(James 2:14-20)*. We are a chosen generation, a royal priesthood, a holy nation, a peculiar people who should proclaim praises to Him who has called us out of darkness, Satan's domain, into His marvellous light *(1 Peter 2:9)*.

Below are Scriptures relating to God's character:

Titus 1:1-2 – *Paul, a servant of God, and an apostle of Jesus Christ, according to the faith of God's elect, and the acknowledging of the truth which is after godliness; in hope of eternal life, which God, that cannot lie, promised before the world began.*

References:
Exodus 33:18-19, 34:5-7 – *And he (Moses) said, "I beseech thee, shew me thy glory." And he said, "I will make all my goodness pass before thee, and I will proclaim the name of the LORD before thee; and will be gracious to whom I will be gracious, and will shew mercy on whom I will shew mercy." And the LORD descended in the cloud, and stood with him (Moses) there, and proclaimed the name of the LORD. And the LORD passed by before him, and proclaimed, "The LORD, The LORD God, merciful and gracious, longsuffering, and abundant in goodness and truth, keeping mercy for thousands, forgiving iniquity and transgression and sin, and that will by no means clear the guilty; visiting the iniquity of the fathers upon the children, and upon the children's children, unto the third and to the forth generation." Psalm 145:8 – "The LORD is gracious, and full of compassion; slow to anger, and of great mercy. Malachi 3:6 – For I am the LORD, I change not; therefore ye sons of Jacob are not consumed. Hebrews 6:13-20 – For when God made promise to Abraham, because he could swear by no greater, he sware by himself, saying, "Surely blessing I will bless thee, and multiplying I will multiply thee." And so, after he had patiently endured, he obtained the promise. For men verily swear by the greater: and an oath for confirmation is to them an end of all strife. Wherein God, willing more abundantly to shew unto the heirs of promise the immutability of his counsel, confirmed it by an oath: that by two immutable things, in which it was impossible for God to lie, we might have a strong consolation, who have fled for refuge to lay hold upon the hope set before us: which hope we have as an anchor of the soul, both sure and stedfast, and which entereth into that within the veil; whither the forerunner is for us entered, even Jesus, made an high priest for ever after the order of Melchisedec. Hebrews 13:8 – Jesus Christ the same yesterday, and to day, and for ever. 1 Peter 1:15-16 – But as he which hath called you is holy, so be ye holy in all manner of conversation (behavior); because it is written, "Be ye holy; for I am holy." 1 John 4:16 – And we have known and believed the love that God hath to us. God is love; and he that dwelleth in love dwelleth in God, and God in him.*

27(a) I put away and rid *myself* [completely] of all these things: anger, rage, bad feeling toward others, curses and slander, and foulmouthed abuse and shameful utterances from my lips, *and I do not lie to others.* For I have stripped off the old (unregenerate) self *(the old man)* with its evil practices, (Colossians 3:8-9-AMPCE) *(Ref.: Ephesians 4:20-22)*

There are two parts to the old man, the first is found in *Colossians 3:5* (please see **Note 17b**) and the second is found here in *Colossians 3:8*. This part consists of behavior patterns and mindsets derived from our carnal nature, produced by the corruptible seed from our first birth. These behavior patterns and mindsets do not and cannot reflect Christ's divine nature. Only through the new birth, being born again by an incorruptible seed from above, can we truly experience His nature within us and bear spiritual fruit through its maturity. Let's look at the following words described above along with the corresponding word used in the King James Version and its Greek meaning in the Thayer's Greek Lexicon:

AMPCE	KJV	Greek Word and Meaning
- anger	anger	*orge* – anger, "the natural disposition, temper, character; movement or agitation of soul, impulse, desire, any violent emotion," but especially (and chiefly in Attic) anger. In Biblical Greek anger, wrath, indignation.
- rage	wrath	*thymos* – passion, angry heat, anger forthwith boiling up and soon subsiding again…
- bad feelings toward others	malice	*kakia* – malignity, malice, ill-will, desire to injure.
- curses and slander	blasphemy	*blasphemia* – universally, slander, detraction, speech injurious to another's good name.
- Foul-mouthed abuse and shameful utterances	filthy communication	*aischrologia* – foul speaking, low and obscene speech, [R. V. shameful speaking].

The reason I underlined this portion of Scripture, is because when the Lord moved in my heart to begin speaking aloud the Scriptures in the ***Personalized Scripture Guide - Volume 1***, I found it foreign as my carnal defense mechanisms were so ingrained within me, I could not see how I could be free from them.

The Lord began to dismantle these defense mechanisms back in 2001, when as usual I was brewing about something, and out of the blue He spoke to me and said, "You have a deep-seated root of rebellion." The word deep-seated is defined as "existing for a long time and very difficult to change: firmly established."[1] The Lord began to open my eyes/understanding to see that my carnal behavior (e.g., anger, rage, bad feelings toward others, shameful utterances from my lips) was so ingrained or firmly established at a profound level that as hard as I tried to change these character traits by fasting, praying, and seeking God through His Word, I continued to struggle with this carnal behavior. In October 2002, He spoke to my heart and said, "I want four mornings a week for six months." It was during this time, He began to direct me to personalize Scriptures relating to the new man in Christ and to speak them aloud. These Scriptures are now contained in the ***Personalized Scripture Guide - Volume 1***. In speaking aloud these personalized Scriptures, making them my own, four times a week for six months, I began renewing my mind to this new creation. When I would come to this part of my confession, I could not see how I could ever be able to overcome anger, rage, and strife as these emotions were so much a part of who I was! As I began to confess these Scriptures at a personal level, I realized that I was not as "spiritually mature" as I thought I was and I began to repent before the Lord. It wasn't until February 2003 after communing with the Lord four mornings a week for four months that a true and enduring change took place within me through the transformation or metamorphosis of my mind and the removal of a protective covering, which came from the deep-seated root of rebellion. It was such a transformation that it was like a caterpillar who instinctively wraps itself in its cocoon and through a secret process called metamorphosis comes out as a butterfly! Only through the renewal process can we overcome the carnal nature within us and its behavior patterns – *Jeremiah 13:23 – "Can the Ethiopian change his skin, or the leopard his spots? Then may ye also do good, that are accustomed to do evil."* In February 2003, four months into this exercise, something amazing happened. This protective covering was removed and I have not been the same since. The removal of this protective covering allowed His living water (His Holy Spirit) to flow within me in a way that I had never experienced before! What I could not do to change my behavior patterns, the Lord did, by His Word and through the power of His Spirit, as revealed in the following two passages of Scripture:

1. *Hebrews 4:12-13 – For the word of God is quick (living), and powerful, and sharper than any twoedged sword, piercing even to the dividing asunder of soul and spirit, and of the joints and marrow, and is a discerner of the thoughts and intents of the heart. Neither is there any creature that is not manifest in his sight: but all things are naked and opened unto the eyes of him with whom we have to do.*
2. *2 Corinthians 3:2-3 – …Forasmuch as ye are manifestly declared to be the epistle of Christ ministered by us, written not with ink, but with the Spirit of the living God; not in tables of stone, but in fleshy tables of the heart.*

This is why it is so important to renew the *spirit of our minds* in order to walk in the life that is ours in Christ Jesus! Paul writes,

For what the law could not do, in that it was weak through the flesh, God sending his own Son in the likeness of sinful flesh, and for sin, condemned sin in the flesh: that the righteousness of the law might be fulfilled in us, who walk not after the flesh, but after the Spirit. For they that are after the flesh do mind the things of the flesh; but they that are after the Spirit the things of the Spirit. For to be carnally minded is death; but to be spiritually minded is life and peace.

(Romans 8:3-6)

Since that time, the Lord has revealed other things within me that have caused anger and bad feelings to erupt on the inside of me such as judgments toward others and other carnal thought patterns that I needed to repent of and release to Him. Here is an example that took place in 2018:

One Saturday afternoon, Don and I and our grown children, Jonathan and Jessica, had planned to go to Piedmont Park to walk and enjoy the day together. We had just finished lunch and I was at the kitchen sink washing up a few dishes and thinking that we were about ready to leave for the park, when Don said he wanted to do something before we left. Immediately after he said that, bad feelings and ungodly thoughts about him began to erupt within me. I did not direct those thoughts and feelings toward him but was very concerned as to where they were coming from. It was like they were coming from a place that I had no control over. The next day I journaled my concern to the Lord, journaling what took place and confessing to the Lord how sorry I was about my bad feelings and ungodly thoughts toward Don. Afterwards, I went about my day and later that afternoon, as I was going into the kitchen, the Lord spoke to me and said, "This came out of an existing judgment." The next morning I began, again, journaling to the Lord, asking Him to please reveal the judgment in me that caused those bad feelings and ungodly thoughts to erupt? Two days later, He opened me up to see the judgment that had been there for a very long time. He revealed to me that as a child, I had judged my mother of being hateful and selfish. As a child, I knew my mom loved me and my sister (e.g., a stay-at-home mom, prepared our meals, kept a clean environment in our home, rarely left us with a babysitter, did not drink alcohol or partake in other drugs). However, on many occasions, throughout my childhood, there were times when I saw her as hateful and selfish (e.g., she was hard to please, had the final say in our home, and at times her behavior was harsh). But I never thought of it as a judgment, and therefore, never repented of it nor renounced it. When the Lord revealed this to me I went out on the sunporch, where I do most of my praying, got on my knees, and began to weep deeply before Him in true repentance. A couple of weeks later, I went to Don and told him what had happened and the harsh judgment that had formed within me and asked him to forgive me for including him in that judgment and he graciously did.

As the Lord shone the light on this dark place within my heart and repentance took place within me, I became free from this judgment! The Lord also helped me to see that most judgments concerning myself and/or others stemmed from my childhood (e.g., comparing myself to others, the influence of home life and social interaction, internalized behavior patterns from significant others). Jesus said in *Matthew 7:1-2 – "Judge not, that ye be not judged. For with what judgment ye judge, ye shall be judged: and with what measure ye mete, it shall be measured to you again."* The Greek word for "judge" is *krino*. Its meaning in the Thayer's Greek Lexicon is "to pronounce judgment; to subject to censure; of those who act the part of judges or arbiters in the matters of common life, or pass judgment on the deeds and words of others: universally, and without case. of those who judge severely (unfairly), <u>finding fault with this or that in others</u>." In looking back at my own life, before I came back to the Lord at the age of twenty-six, I was a very hateful and selfish person revealing the truth that with the same measure I judged my mother it was measured back to me! I give God much thanks for His great mercy and longsuffering toward me and toward all! Paul writes,

> *For I know nothing by myself; yet am I not hereby justified: but he that judgeth me is the Lord. Therefore judge nothing before the time, until the Lord come, who both will bring to light the hidden things of darkness, and will make manifest the counsels of the hearts: and then shall every man have praise of God.*
>
> (1 Corinthians 4:4-5)

God is faithful to continue to bring to light the dark places within us and make manifest the counsels of our hearts in order for His image to be seen more clearly within us *(Psalm 119:130; 2 Corinthians 3:18; 2 Peter 1:17-21)*. Our transformation is a life long journey throughout our time here in these earthen vessels as we go from faith to faith and glory to glory.

It is also important to note that anger in itself is not sin. Paul writes in *Ephesians 4:26-27 - "Be ye angry, and sin not: let not the sun go down upon your wrath: neither give place to the devil."* Jesus got angry and God knows that living in an unjust world and surrounded by flesh, including our own, we all have a tendency to become angry with ourselves and/or others. Jesus, Himself, got angry *(John 2:13-16; Mark 3:5)*. The key is not to sin in our anger! If we stay focused on Christ, when anger comes His wisdom and grace will be with us to help us through this emotion and to deal with the situation properly. It is important that we do not brew over the situation by allowing our thoughts to take us deeper into the anger; instead, it is important to be real with the Lord about it. Journaling to Him helps us to be specific and to stay focused. It is very important to release the anger and the person you are angry with to the Lord. Jesus said,

> *But I say unto you, that whosoever is angry with his brother without a cause shall be in danger of the judgment: And whosoever shall say to his brother, "Raca" (worthless, empty*

headed) shall be in danger of the council: but whosoever shall say "Thou fool," (dull or stupid, blockhead) shall be in danger of hell fire. <u>Therefore if thou bring thy gift to the altar, and there rememberest that thy brother hath ought (something) against thee; leave there thy gift before the altar, and go thy way; first be reconciled to thy brother, and then come and offer thy gift</u>.

(Matthew 5:22-24)

Concerning this passage of Scripture, it is also important to restore a friendship or to settle or resolve an issue with a brother or sister in Christ who has something against you. Paul writes,

> *To whom ye forgive any thing, I forgive also: for if I forgave any thing, to whom I forgave it, for your sakes forgave I it in the person of Christ; lest Satan should get an advantage of us: for we are not ignorant of his devices.*

(2 Corinthians 2:10-11)

Unforgiveness is a device Satan uses that keeps us bound to the old man and unable to walk in the grace and forgiveness of the Father *(Matthew 6:9-15)*. I also recommend the book *When Good Men Get Angry* by Bill Perkins.

In order to overcome the works of the flesh, we must be born again and grow in grace and spiritual maturity. John gives an account in *John 3:1-6:*

> *There was a man of the Pharisees, named Nicodemus, a ruler of the Jews: the same came to Jesus by night and said unto him, "Rabbi, we know that thou art a teacher come from God: for no man can do these miracles that thou doest, except God be with him." Jesus answered and said unto him, "Verily, verily, I say unto thee, except a man be born again, he cannot see the kingdom of God." Nicodemus saith unto him, "How can a man be born when he is old? Can he enter the second time into his mother's womb, and be born?" Jesus answered, "Verily, verily, I say unto thee, except a man be born of water and of the Spirit, he cannot enter into the kingdom of God. That which is born of the flesh is flesh; and that which is born of the Spirit is spirit."*

There is no way we can walk in newness of life except through the born-again creation. We are born again of an incorruptible seed by the Word of God and Peter tells us to desire the sincere milk of the Word in order to <u>grow</u> in His grace *(Acts 20:32; 1 Peter 1:22-2:2)*. Just as we go through stages in the natural as we grow from babes – to adolescents – to adults, our born-again creation grows from the milk of the Word to the meat of the Word. Paul writes,

> *And I, brethren, could not speak unto you as unto spiritual, but as unto carnal, even as unto babes in Christ. I have fed you with milk, and not with meat: for hitherto ye were not able to bear it, neither yet now are ye able. For ye are yet carnal: for whereas there is among you envying, and strife, and divisions, are ye not carnal, and walk as men?*

(1 Corinthians 3:1-3)

If we are born again and are continually functioning out of our carnal nature (i.e., anger, envy, strife, division, pride), we are babes in Christ! We have not yet allowed the Word of God to consistently flow

220

within our *inmost mind* to flush out our ingrained carnal beliefs and mindsets.

Below are Scriptures relating to anger, wrath, and strife:

1. ***Proverbs 14:3, 14, 17, 29*** *– In the mouth of the foolish is a rod of pride: but the lips of the wise shall preserve them. The backslider in heart shall be filled with his own ways: and a good man shall be satisfied from himself. He that is soon angry dealeth foolishly: and a man of wicked devices is hated. He that is slow to wrath is of great understanding: but he that is hasty of spirit exalteth folly.*

References:
Psalm 36:1 *– [[To the chief Musician, A Psalm of David the servant of the LORD.]] The transgression of the wicked saith within my heart, that there is no fear of God before his eyes.* ***Psalm 37:8-9*** *– Cease from anger, and forsake wrath: fret not thyself in any wise to do evil. For evildoers shall be cut off: but those that wait upon the LORD, they shall inherit the earth.* ***Proverbs 6:16-19*** *– These six things doth the LORD hate: yea, seven are an abomination unto him: a proud look, a lying tongue, and hands that shed innocent blood, an heart that deviseth wicked imaginations, feet that be swift in running to mischief, a false witness that speaketh lies, and he that soweth discord among the brethren.* ***Proverbs 12:13, 17*** *– The wicked is snared by the transgression of his lips: but the just shall come out of trouble. He that speaketh truth sheweth forth righteousness: but a false witness deceit.* ***Proverbs 13:10, 15*** *– Only by pride cometh contention: but with the well advised is wisdom. Good understanding giveth favour: but the way of transgressors is hard.* ***Proverbs 15:17, 18*** *– Better is a dinner of herbs where love is, than a stalled ox and hatred therewith. A wrathful man stirreth up strife: but he that is slow to anger appeaseth strife.* ***Proverbs 16:25, 32*** *– There is a way that seemeth right unto a man, but the end thereof are the ways of death. He that is slow to anger is better than the mighty; and he that ruleth his spirit than he that taketh a city.* ***Proverbs 17:1, 14, 19*** *– Better is a dry morsel, and quietness therewith, than an house full of sacrifices with strife. The beginning of strife is as when one letteth out water: therefore leave off contention, before it be meddled with. He loveth transgression that loveth strife...* ***Proverbs 18:19*** *– A brother offended is harder to be won than a strong city: and their contentions are like the bars of a castle.* ***Proverbs 19:11, 19*** *– The discretion of a man deferreth his anger; and it is his glory to pass over a transgression. A man of great wrath shall suffer punishment: for if thou deliver him, yet thou must do it again.* ***Proverbs 20:3*** *– It is an honour for a man to cease from strife: but every fool will be meddling.* ***Proverbs 22:24-25*** *– Make no friendship with an angry man; and with a furious man thou shalt not go: lest thou learn his ways, and get a snare to thy soul.* ***Proverbs 25:28*** *– He that hath no rule over his own spirit is like a city that is broken down, and without walls.* ***Proverbs 27:3-4*** *– A stone is heavy, and the sand weighty; but a fool's wrath is heavier than them both. Wrath is cruel, and anger is outrageous...* ***Proverbs 28:13-14, 25*** *– He that covereth his sins shall not prosper: but whoso confesseth and forsaketh them shall have mercy. Happy is the man that feareth alway: but he that hardeneth his heart shall fall into mischief. He that is of a proud heart stirreth up strife: but he that putteth his trust in the LORD shall be made fat.* ***Proverbs 29:8, 22-23*** *– ...wise men turn away wrath. An angry man stirreth up strife, and a furious man aboundeth in transgression. A man's pride shall bring him low: but honour shall uphold the humble in spirit.* ***Proverbs 30:33*** *– Surely the churning of milk bringeth forth butter, and the wringing of the nose bringeth forth blood: so the forcing of wrath bringeth forth strife.* ***Ecclesiastes 7:8-9*** *– Better is the end of a thing than the beginning thereof: and the patient in spirit is better than the proud in spirit. Be not hasty in thy spirit to be angry: for anger resteth in the bosom of fools.* ***1 Corinthians 14:20*** *– Brethren, be not children in understanding: howbeit in malice be ye children, but in understanding be men.* ***Ephesians 4:31-32*** *– Let all bitterness, and wrath, and anger, and clamour, and evil speaking, be put away from you, with all malice: and be ye kind one to another, tenderhearted, forgiving one another, even*

as God for Christ's sake hath forgiven you. **Hebrews 12:14-15** – *Follow peace with all men, and holiness, without which no man shall see the Lord: looking diligently lest any man fail of the grace of God; lest any root of bitterness springing up trouble you, and thereby many be defiled.* **James 3:12-18** – *Can the fig tree, my brethren, bear olive berries? Either a vine, figs? So can no fountain both yield salt water and fresh. Who is a wise man endued with knowledge among you? Let him shew out of a good conversation (behavior) his works with meekness of wisdom. But if ye have bitter envying and strife in your hearts, glory not, and lie not against the truth. This wisdom descendeth not from above, but is earthly, sensual, devilish. For where envying and strife is, there is confusion and every evil work. But the wisdom that is from above is first pure, then peaceable, gentle, and easy to be intreated, full of mercy and good fruits, without partiality, and without hypocrisy. And the fruit of righteousness is sown in peace of them that make peace.* **1 Peter 2:1-3** – *Wherefore laying aside all malice, and all guile, and hypocrisies, and envies, and all evil speakings, as newborn babes, desire the sincere milk of the word, that ye may grow thereby: if so be ye have tasted that the Lord is gracious.*

2. **Proverbs 16:23, 27-30** – *The heart of the wise teacheth his mouth, and addeth learning to his lips. An ungodly man diggeth up evil: and in his lips there is as a burning fire. A froward man soweth strife: and a whisperer separateth chief friends. A violent man enticeth his neighbour, and leadeth him into the way that is not good. He shutteth his eyes to devise froward things: moving his lips he bringeth evil to pass.*

References:
Psalm 34:12-15 – *What man is he that desireth life, and loveth many days, that he may see good? Keep thy tongue from evil, and thy lips from speaking guile. Depart from evil, and do good; seek peace, and pursue it. The eyes of the LORD are upon the righteous, and his ears are open unto their cry.* **Proverbs 11:9** – *An hypocrite with his mouth destroyeth his neighbour: but through knowledge shall the just be delivered.* **Proverbs 18:7, 20-21** – *A fool's mouth is his destruction, and his lips are the snare of his soul. A man's belly shall be satisfied with the fruit of his mouth; and with the increase of his lips shall he be filled. Death and life are in the power of the tongue: and they that love it shall eat the fruit thereof.* **Proverbs 26:20-21** – *Where no wood is, there the fire goeth out: so where there is no talebearer, the strife ceaseth. As coals are to burning coals, and wood to fire; so is a contentious man to kindle strife.* **James 1:18-21** – *Of his (God's) own will begat he us with the word of truth, that we should be a kind of firstfruits of his creatures. Wherefore, my beloved brethren, let every man be swift to hear, slow to speak, slow to wrath: for the wrath of man worketh not the righteousness of God. Wherefore lay apart all filthiness and superfluity of naughtiness, and receive with meekness the engrafted word, which is able to save your souls.* **James 3:3-12** – *Behold, we put bits in the horses' mouths, that they may obey us; and we turn about their whole body. Behold also the ships, which though they be so great, and are driven of fierce winds, yet are they turned about with a very small helm, whithersoever the governor (steersman's) listeth (impulse). Even so the tongue is a little member, and boasteth great things. Behold, how great a matter a little fire kindleth! And the tongue is a fire, a world of iniquity: so is the tongue among our members, that it defileth the whole body, and setteth on fire the course of nature; and it is set on fire of hell. For every kind of beasts, and of birds, and of serpents, and of things in the sea, is tamed, and hath been tamed of mankind: but the tongue can no man tame; it is an unruly evil, full of deadly poison. Therewith bless we God, even the Father; and therewith curse we men, which are made after the similitude (likeness) of God. Out of the same mouth proceedeth blessing and cursing. My brethren, these things ought not so be. Doth a fountain send forth at the same place sweet water and bitter? Can the fig tree, my brethren, bear olive berries? Either a vine, figs? So can no fountain both yield salt water and fresh.* (The word "defile" in the Greek is *spiloo* meaning "to stain or spoil (literally or figuratively):–defile, spot." Its root word is *spilos* meaning "a stain or blemish, i.e. (figuratively) defect, disgrace:–spot." Jesus said

222

in *Matthew 12:34* that out of the abundance of the heart the mouth speaks. Only the living Word of God through the power of His Spirit can sanctify and cleanse us from the effects of an uncircumcised heart – *Romans 2:28-29; Hebrews 4:12-13*. The Greek word *spilos* is used twice in the New Testament, *Ephesians 5:25-27 – ...not having <u>spot</u>, or wrinkle...)* and *2 Peter 2:13 – <u>Spots</u> they are and blemishes...).*

Please refer to **Note 5c** for information and Scriptures relating to pride and humility.

> **27(b)** and have clothed *myself* with the new [spiritual self] *(the new man)*, which is [ever in the process of being] renewed and remolded into [fuller and more perfect knowledge upon] knowledge after the image (the likeness) of Him Who created it. (Colossians 3:10-AMPCE) *(Ref.: Ephesians 4:23-24)*

The word "renewed" in the Greek is *anakainoo* meaning "to renovate:–renew." Its meaning in the Thayer's Greek Lexicon is "to cause to grow up new, to make new, to be changed into a new kind of life, opposed to the former corrupt state." It is used one other time in the New Testament where Paul writes,

> *...but though our outward man perish, yet the inward man is <u>renewed</u> day by day. For our light affliction, which is but for a moment, worketh for us a far more exceeding and eternal weight of glory; while we look not at the things which are seen, but at the things which are not seen: for the things which are seen are temporal; but the things which are not seen are eternal.*
>
> (2 Corinthians 4:16-18)

Again, we have been born again not of a corruptible seed but an incorruptible seed, by the Word of God, which lives and abides forever *(1 Peter 1:23)*! The corruptible seed came from Adam, the carnal nature, and as Paul said in *Ephesians 2:2-10*,

> *Wherein in time past ye walked according to the course of this world, according to the prince of the power of the air, the spirit that now worketh in the children of disobedience: among whom also we all had our conversation (behavior) in times past in the lust of our flesh, fulfilling the desires of the flesh and of the mind; and were by nature the children of wrath even as others. But God, who is rich in mercy, for his great love wherewith he loved us, even when we were dead in sins, hath quickened us together with Christ, (by grace ye are saved;) and hath raised us up together, and made us sit together in heavenly places in Christ Jesus: that in the ages to come he might shew the exceeding riches of his grace in his kindness toward us through Christ Jesus. For by grace are ye saved through faith; and that not of yourselves: it is the gift of God: not of works, lest any man should boast. For we are his workmanship, created in Christ Jesus unto good works, which God hath before ordained that we should walk in them.*

The incorruptible seed comes from Jesus and produces the born-again spiritual self, the new man, and in this new creation the life-giving flow of His Spirit resides. Homosexuality or any other sexual vice outside of God's design for marriage comes from our carnal nature, the old man. Pride, arrogance, covetousness, greed, the fear of man, self-centered anger, rage, or any works of the flesh are all indicative of our carnal nature, the old man.

Let's look at four passages of Scripture. These explain the disobedience of the first man, Adam, and the consequences of that disobedience, and the obedience of the last Adam, Jesus Christ, and the fruit and blessings that take place as: (1) Christ recaptures us through the new birth, and (2) as we continue to be renewed in knowledge according to the image of Him who created us, we grow in grace and blessings and bear the fruit of that maturity:

1. **Romans 5:12-21** – *Wherefore, as by one man (Adam) sin entered into the world, and death by sin; and so death passed upon all men, for that all have sinned: (For until the law sin was in the world: but sin is not imputed when there is no law. Nevertheless death reigned from Adam to Moses, even over them that had not sinned after the similitude (likeness) of Adam's transgression, who is the figure of him that was to come. But not as the offence, so also is the free gift. For if through the offence of one (Adam) many be dead, much more the grace of God, and the gift by grace, which is by one man, Jesus Christ, hath abounded unto many. And not as it was by one that sinned, so is the gift: for the judgment was by one to condemnation, but the free gift is of many offences unto justification. For it by one man's offence death reigned by one; much more they which receive abundance of grace and of the gift of righteousness shall reign in life by one, Jesus Christ.) Therefore as by the offence of one judgment came upon all men to condemnation; even so by the righteousness of one the free gift came upon all men unto justification of life. For as by one man's disobedience many were made sinners, so by the obedience of one shall many be made righteous. Moreover the law entered, that the offence might abound. But where sin abounded, grace did much more abound: that as sin hath reigned unto death, even so might grace reign through righteousness unto eternal life by Jesus Christ our Lord.*

2. **1 Corinthians 15:45-49** – *and so it is written, "The first man Adam was made a living soul; the last Adam (Jesus) was made a quickening (life-giving) spirit." Howbeit that was not first which is spiritual, but that which is natural; and afterward that which is spiritual. The first man is of the earth, earthy: the second man is the Lord from heaven. As is the earthy, such are they also that are earthy: and as is the heavenly, such are they also that are heavenly. And as we have borne the image of the earthy, we shall also bear the image of the heavenly.*

3. **Galatians 5:18-24** – *But if ye be led of the Spirit, ye are not under the law. Now the works of the flesh are manifest, which are these; adultery, fornication, uncleanness, lasciviousness, idolatry, witchcraft, hatred, variance (contentions), emulations (jealousy), wrath, strife, seditions (dissension, division), heresies, envyings, murders, drunkenness, revellings, and such like: of the which I tell you before, as I have also told you in time past, that they which do such things shall not inherit the kingdom of God. But the fruit of the Spirit is love, joy, peace, longsuffering, gentleness, goodness, faith, meekness, temperance: against such there is no law. And they that are Christ's have crucified the flesh with the affections and lusts.*

4. **2 Peter 1:2-9** – *Grace and peace be multiplied unto you through the knowledge of God, and of Jesus our Lord, according as his divine power hath given unto us all things that pertain unto life and godliness, through the knowledge of him that hath called us to glory and virtue: whereby are given unto us exceeding great and precious promises: that by these ye might be partakers of the divine nature, having escaped the corruption that is in the world through lust. And beside this, giving all diligence, add to your faith virtue; and to virtue knowledge; and to knowledge temperance; and to temperance patience; and to patience godliness; and to godliness*

brotherly kindness; and to brotherly kindness charity (God's love). For if these things be in you, and abound, they make you that ye shall neither be barren nor unfruitful in the knowledge of our Lord Jesus Christ. But he that lacketh these things is blind, and cannot see afar off, and hath forgotten the he was purged from his old sins.

We must remember that living out of our own righteousness, in the sight of God, is as filthy rags *(Isaiah 64:6)*. True righteousness and holiness is only found in the new man where Satan has no authority *(Ephesians 4:20-24; Philippians 3:5-9; 1 John 3:8)*! For the law of the Spirit of life in Christ Jesus has made us free from the law of sin and death *(Romans 8:2)*. For to be carnally minded is death; but to be spiritually minded is life and peace *(Romans 8:6)*.

Don't give up sowing to the Spirit *(Matthew 13:6, 21)*! Allow the Lord, by His Word and through the power of His Spirit, to take you deeper in Him—rooted and grounded in Christ *(Hebrews 4:12-13; Ephesians 3:14-21; Colossians 2:6-7)*. Just as it takes time for an oak tree to become deeply rooted in the ground and to grow strong and firm, it takes time for the born-again creation within us to become rooted and grounded in Christ, growing strong and firm in Him. As we choose to renew the *spirit of our minds*, we are transformed (or changed) into His image *(Isaiah 61:1-3; Ephesians 4:22-24; Romans 12:1-2)*. You are not alone in this transformation process:

1. *It is God working in you both to will and to do His good pleasure (Philippians 2:13).*
2. *He will never leave you nor forsake you (Hebrews 13:5).*

Living out of the new man in Christ is God's will for every born-again believer in Christ! The process of renewing our minds to the truth of God's Word is essential in revealing to the world His good, perfect, and acceptable will. Below are four passages of Scripture that confirm this statement:

1. **Romans 12:1-2** – *I beseech you, therefore, brethren, by the mercies of God, that ye present your bodies a living sacrifice, holy, acceptable unto God, which is your reasonable service. And be not conformed to this world: but be ye transformed by the renewing of your mind, that ye may prove what is that good, and acceptable, and perfect, will of God.*
2. **Ephesians 4:22-24** – *That ye put off concerning the former conversation (behavior) the old man, which is corrupt according to the deceitful lusts; and be renewed in the spirit of your mind; and that ye put on the new man, which after God is created in righteousness and true holiness.*
3. **Ephesians 5:5-10** *(NKJV)* – *For this you know, that no fornicator, unclean person, nor covetous man, who is an idolater, has any inheritance in the kingdom of Christ and God. Let no one deceive you with empty words, for because of these things the wrath of God comes upon the sons of disobedience. Therefore do not be partakers with them. For you were once darkness, but now you are light in the Lord. Walk as children of light (for the fruit of the Spirit is in all goodness, righteousness, and truth), finding out what is acceptable to the Lord. (See Galatians 5:16-25).*
4. **Colossians 3:1-15** – *If ye then be risen with Christ, seek those things which are above, where Christ sitteth on the right hand of God. Set your affection (mind) on things above, not on things on the earth. For ye are dead, and your life is hid with Christ in God. When Christ, who is our life, shall appear, then shall ye also appear with him in glory. Mortify therefore your members which are upon the earth; fornication, uncleanness, inordinate affection, evil*

concupiscence, and covetousness, which is idolatry: for which things' sake the wrath of God cometh on the children of disobedience: in the which ye also walked some time, when ye lived in them. But now ye also put off all these; anger, wrath, malice, blasphemy, filthy communication out of your mouth. Lie not one to another, seeing the ye have put off the old man with his deeds; and have put on the new man, which is renewed in knowledge after the image of him that created him…

Below is a revelation the Lord revealed to me in the Old Testament as it relates to Christ and His bride, the church, and her struggle in bringing forth the born-again creation within her:

I believe Abraham to be a type and shadow of our heavenly Father; his son, Isaac, a type and shadow of Jesus Christ (as Abraham offered his son, Isaac, as a burnt offering to God); and Rebekah, Isaac's wife, as a type and shadow of the church *(Genesis 17:15-22, 22:2-18, 25:20-23)*. Let's read *Genesis 25:20-23 (AMPCE)*:

Isaac was forty years old when he married Rebekah, the daughter of Bethuel the Aramean of Padan-aram, the sister of Laban the Aramean. And Isaac prayed much to the Lord for his wife because she was unable to bear children; and the Lord granted his prayer, and Rebekah his wife became pregnant. [Two] children struggled together within her, and she said, "If it is so [that the Lord has heard our prayer], why am I like this?" And she went to inquire of the Lord. The Lord said to her, "[The founders of] two nations are in your womb, and the separation of two peoples has begun in your body; the one people shall be stronger than the other, and the elder shall serve the younger."

I believe this prophecy goes much deeper in the heart of the Father than Esau and Jacob, Isaac and Rebekah's twin children, which is this:

As there was a struggle between the two children within Rebekah (a type and shadow of the church), I believe there is a struggle within every born-again believer in Christ, who has the incorruptible seed of the new man, the second birth. This struggle happens in each individual believer as the new birth in Christ is growing within and maturing. This growth and maturity occurs as we choose to crucify the flesh and renew the *spirit of our minds* to His truth *(Galatians 5:16-26; 1 Peter 1:22-2:3; Romans 12:1-2; Ephesians 4:20-24; Colossians 3:1-15)*. Before maturity, we as newborn babes, struggle to serve the Lord in areas of our lives as our carnal nature, fueled by ingrained carnal mindsets, self-centeredness, and lustful desires, is stronger than our new nature in Him *(Galatians 5:16-26)*. The Lord's true focus is to circumcise our hearts and to bring forth the new man and for our soul, which comes from the first birth, to serve this new nature *(Deuteronomy 30:6; Romans 8:1-29; Colossians 2:10-11)*. As the Lord told Rebekah that the elder shall serve the younger, I believe the Lord is calling our soul (the essence of who we are, including our will and emotions), that came from our first birth, *the first Adam – Genesis 2:7*, to no longer serve our carnal nature but to serve the younger, the new man in Christ, *the last Adam – 1 Corinthians 15:45*! As this happens, we truly begin to see strength of character, perseverance, faith, and the life-giving flow of His Spirit within us, as our soul is immersed in Him. The enemy has his way in the earth when we choose to continue to live out of our carnality. This is why I believe this prophecy goes much deeper as He was speaking of when Jesus would pay the price for sin and His Spirit could then come into the hearts of men, women, and children to cause a "new birth" and circumcision of the heart in order to walk in this born-again creation, newness of life in Christ *(Romans 2:28-29)*!

I'm thinking about Adam and Eve, God's original intent for man in the beginning. He has not changed His mind! *(Malachi 3:6; Hebrews 13:8)*. Again, let's look at the following passage of Scripture where Paul writes,

> *And so it is written, "The first man Adam was made a living soul; the last Adam (Jesus) was made a quickening (life-giving) spirit." Howbeit that was not first which is spiritual, but that which is natural; and afterward that which is spiritual. The first man is of the earth, earthy: the second man is the Lord from heaven. As is the earthy, such are they also that are earthy: and as is the heavenly, such are they also that are heavenly. And as we have borne the image of the earthy, we shall also bear the image of the heavenly.*
>
> (1 Corinthians 15:45-50)

Let's look at another passage of Scripture that goes along with this subject matter:

> *Now there was a certain man among the Pharisees named Nicodemus, a ruler (a leader, an authority) among the Jews, who came to Jesus at night and said to Him, "Rabbi, we know and are certain that You have come from God [as] a Teacher; for no one can do these signs (these wonderworks, these miracles—and produce the proofs) that You do unless God is with him." Jesus answered him, "I assure you, most solemnly I tell you, that unless a person is born again (anew, from above), he cannot ever see (know, be acquainted with, and experience) the kingdom of God." Nicodemus said to Him, "How can a man be born when he is old? Can he enter his mother's womb again and be born?" Jesus answered, "I assure you, most solemnly I tell you, unless a man is born of water and [even] the Spirit, he cannot [ever] enter the kingdom of God. What is born of [from] the flesh is flesh [of the physical is physical]; and what is born of the Spirit is spirit."*
>
> (John 3:1-6, AMPCE)

I am convinced that there are two natures within us because of my own walk with the Lord. The struggle that I have had on the inside of me between my flesh and my spirit is living proof that there are two. Please see ***My Story – Parts One*** and ***Two - Volume 1*** for details. In *Romans 7:4-25*, you will see that Paul struggled with this too! Just as Saul, the king of Israel, was changed into another man *(1 Samuel 10:1-6 – Then Samuel took a vial of oil, and poured it upon his (Saul's) head, and kissed him, and said, "… And the Spirit of the LORD will come upon thee, and thou shalt prophesy with them, and shalt be turned into another man."* (For the entire story please read *1 Samuel 8-10.*) How much more, by the Spirit of the Lord, will He transform us into His image, the new man, as we choose to renew the *spirit of our minds* to the truth of His Word! We truly experience strength, endurance, Christlike character, and the life-giving flow of His Spirit, as our souls become immersed in Him.

Below are Scriptures relating to the born-again creation, the new man in Christ:

1. ***Psalm 36:7-9*** *– How excellent is thy lovingkindness, O God! Therefore the children of men put their trust under the shadow of thy wings. They shall be abundantly satisfied with the fatness of thy house; and thou shalt make them drink of the river of thy pleasures. For with thee is the fountain of life: in thy light shall we see light.*

References:

Proverbs 13:14 – *The law of the wise is a fountain of life, to depart from the snares of death.* ***Proverbs 28:26*** – *He who trusteth in his own heart is a fool: but whoso walketh wisely, he shall be delivered.* ***John 4:13-14*** – *Jesus answered and said unto her, "Whosoever drinketh of this water shall thirst again: but whosoever drinketh of the water that I shall give him shall never thirst; but the water that I shall give him shall be in him a well (fountain) of water springing up into everlasting life.* ***John 7:38-39*** – *Jesus said, He that believeth on me, as the scripture hath said, out of his belly shall flow rivers of living water. (But this spake he of the Spirit, which they that believe on him should receive: for the Holy Ghost was not yet given; because that Jesus was not yet glorified.)*

2. ***Isaiah 26:2-4*** *(NKJV) – Open the gates, that the righteous nation which keeps the truth may enter in. You will keep him in perfect peace, whose mind is stayed on You, because he trusts in You. Trust in the LORD forever, for in YAH, the LORD, is everlasting strength.*

References:

Proverbs 11:18-19 – *The wicked worketh a deceitful work: but to him that soweth righteousness shall be a sure reward. As righteousness tendeth to life: so he that pursueth evil pursueth it to his own death.* ***Romans 8:1-8, 29-30*** – *There is therefore now no condemnation to them which are in Christ Jesus, who walk not after the flesh (the old man – our carnal nature), but after the Spirit (the new man in Christ – His divine nature). For the law of the Spirit of life in Christ Jesus hath made me free from the law of sin and death. For what the law could not do, in that it was weak through the flesh, God sending his own Son in the likeness of sinful flesh, and for sin, condemned sin in the flesh: that the righteousness of the law might be fulfilled in us, who walk not after the flesh (the old man – our carnal nature), but after the Spirit (the new man in Christ – His divine nature). For they that are after the flesh do mind the things of the flesh; but they that are after the Spirit the things of the Spirit. For to be carnally minded is death; but to be spiritually minded is life and peace. Because the carnal mind is enmity against God: for it is not subject to the law of God, neither indeed can be. So then they that are in the flesh (the old man) cannot please God. For whom he did foreknow, he also did predestinate to be conformed to the image of his Son, that he might be the firstborn among many brethren. Moreover whom he did predestinate, them he also called: and whom he called, them he also justified: and whom he justified, them he also glorified.* ***1 Corinthians 14:20*** – *Brethren, be not children in understanding: howbeit in malice be ye children (innocent), but in understanding be men (mature in Christ).* ***2 Corinthians 10:3-5*** – *For though we walk in the flesh we do not war after the flesh: (for the weapons of our warfare are not carnal, but mighty through God to the pulling down of strong holds;) casting down imaginations, and every high thing that exalteth itself against the knowledge of God...* ***Galatians 6:7-9*** – *Be not deceived; God is not mocked: for whatsoever a man soweth, that shall he also reap. For he that soweth to his flesh shall of the flesh reap corruption; but he that soweth to the Spirit shall of the Spirit reap life everlasting. And let us not be weary in well doing: for in due season we shall reap, if we faint not.* ***Ephesians 4:20-24*** – *...and be renewed in the spirit of your mind; and that ye put on the new man, which after God is created in righteousness and true holiness.* ***James 1:8*** – *a double minded man is unstable in all his ways.* ***Revelation 3:14-16*** – *And unto the angel of the church of the Laodiceans write; These things saith the Amen, the faithful and true witness, the beginning of the creation of God; "I know thy works, that thou art neither cold nor hot: I would thou wert cold or hot. So then because thou art lukewarm, and neither cold nor hot, I will spue thee out of my mouth."* (The Greek word for "lukewarm" is *chiliaros.* Its meaning in the Thayer's Greek Lexicon is "tepid, lukewarm: metaphorically, of the condition of a soul wretchedly fluctuating between a torpor and a fervour of love." This is someone who has a form of godliness but denies the power of a changed life! This person may possibly go to church on a regular basis, occasionally read the Bible, and possibly pray for others but is content to live out of his or her carnal nature. This is very grievous to the Lord).

3. *James 1:18-25 – Of his (God's) own will begat he us with the word of truth, that we should be a kind of firstfruits of his creatures. Wherefore, my beloved brethren, let every man be swift to hear, slow to speak, slow to wrath: for the wrath of man worketh not the righteousness of God. Wherefore lay apart all filthiness and superfluity of naughtiness, and receive with meekness the engrafted word, which is able to save your souls. But be ye doers of the word, and not hearers only, deceiving your own selves. For if any be a hearer of the word, and not a doer, he is like unto a man beholding his natural face in a glass (mirror): for he beholdeth himself, and goeth his way, and straightway forgetteth what manner of man he was. But whoso looketh into the perfect law of liberty, and continueth therein, he being not a forgetful hearer, but a doer of the work, this man shall be blessed in his deed.*

References:
Luke 8:19-21 – Then came to him (Jesus) his mother and his brethren, and could not come at him for the press. And it was told him by certain which said, "Thy mother and thy brethren stand without, desiring to see thee. And he answered and said unto them, "My mother and my brethren are these which hear the word of God, and do it." **Romans 12:1-2** *– I beseech you therefore, brethren, by the mercies of God, that ye present your bodies a living sacrifice, holy, acceptable unto God, which is your reasonable service. And be not conformed to this world: but be ye transformed by the renewing of your mind, that ye may prove what is that good, and acceptable, and perfect, will of God.* **Romans 13:12-14** *– The night is far spent, the day is at hand: let us therefore cast off the works of darkness, and let us put on the armour of light. Let us walk honestly, as in the day; not in rioting and drunkenness, not in chambering and wantonness, not is strife and envying. But put ye on the Lord Jesus Christ, and make not provision for the flesh, to fulfil the lusts thereof.* **1 Corinthians 2:15-16** *– But he that is spiritual judgeth all things, yet he himself is judged of no man. For who hath known the mind of the Lord, that he may instruct him? But we have the mind of Christ.* **2 Corinthians 3:17-18** *– Now the Lord is that Spirit: and where the Spirit of the Lord is, there is liberty. But we all, with open face beholding as in a glass (mirror) the glory of the Lord, are changed (transformed) into the same image from glory to glory, even as by the Spirit of the Lord.* **Galatians 3:26-29** *– For ye are all children of God by faith in Christ Jesus. For as many of you as have been baptized into Christ have put on Christ. There is neither Jew nor Greek, there is neither bond nor free, there is neither male nor female: for ye are all one in Christ Jesus. And if ye be Christ's, then are ye Abraham's seed, and heirs according to the promise.* **Ephesians 4:22-24** *– That ye put off concerning the former conversation (behavior) the old man, which is corrupt according to the deceitful lusts; and be renewed in the spirit of your mind; and that ye put on the new man, which after God is created in righteousness and true holiness.* **Colossians 3:1-10** *– … And have put on the new man, which is renewed in knowledge after the image of him that created him.* **1 Timothy 4:7-8** *– But refuse profane and old wives' fables, and exercise thyself rather unto godliness. For bodily exercise profiteth little: but godliness is profitable unto all things, having promise of the life that now is, and of that which is to come.* **Titus 3:4-8** *– But after that the kindness and love of God our Saviour toward man appeared, not by works of righteousness which we have done, but according to his mercy he saved us, by the washing of regeneration, and renewing of the Holy Ghost; which he shed on us abundantly through Jesus Christ our Saviour; that being justified by his grace, we should be made heirs according to the hope of eternal life. This is a faithful saying, and these things I will that thou affirm constantly, that they which have believed in God might be careful to maintain good works. These things are good and profitable unto men.* (see **Note 28a**). **Hebrews 5:13-14** *– For every one that useth milk is unskilful in the word of righteousness: for he is a babe (see 1 Peter 2:2). But strong meat belongeth to them that are of full age, even those who by*

reason of use have their senses exercised to discern both good and evil (see 1 Peter 2:2).

Here are additional Scriptures relating to the born again creation, the new man: 2 Chronicles 16:9; Proverbs 4:20-27, 10:25, 11:5-6, 30, 16:6-7, 21:21-22, 23:12, 19, 28:5; Isaiah 32:17; Matthew 6:19-34, 7:21-27; John 15:5-7, 17:17-23; 1 Corinthians 4:15-16; Galatians 4:19; Ephesians 2:1-22; 2 Timothy 2:3-4, 15-22; 1 Peter 2:2-3, 3:1-12.

28(a) *I* clothe *myself* therefore, as *one of* God's own chosen ones (*one of* His own picked representatives), [who are] purified and holy and well-beloved [by God Himself, <u>by putting on behavior marked by] tenderhearted pity and mercy, kind feeling,</u> *humbleness of mind,* <u>gentle ways, [and] patience [which is tireless and long-suffering, and has the power to endure whatever comes, with good temper]</u>. (Colossians 3:12-AMPCE) *(Ref.: Colossians 3:12)*

The reason I underlined this portion of Scripture, is when the Lord moved upon my heart to begin speaking aloud these passages of Scripture contained in the ***Personalized Scripture Guide - Volume 1,*** for my own strength of character in Christ, I found it foreign as the old man was so ingrained within me that it was difficult to see how I could behave any other way (see **Notes 17a** and **27a**). To me it seemed as difficult for my behavior to change as it would be for a leopard to change its spots *(Jeremiah 13:23)*. After the Lord did an internal work within me I realized that truly there was a new man, the born-again creation in Christ, operating on the inside of me that was the total opposite of the old man, the carnal nature. This continual transformation, the reality of walking in the new man, can only occur through the washing of regeneration and renewing of the Holy Spirit as Paul writes,

> *For we ourselves also were sometimes foolish, disobedient, deceived, serving divers lusts and pleasures, living in malice and envy, hateful, and hating one another. But after that the kindness and love of God our Saviour toward man appeared, not by works of righteousness which we have done, but according to his mercy he saved us, by the washing of regeneration, and renewing of the Holy Ghost; which he shed on us abundantly through Jesus Christ our Saviour; that being justified by his grace, we should be made heirs according to the hope of eternal life. This is a faithful saying, and these things I will that thou affirm constantly, that they which have believed in God might be careful to maintain good works. These things are good and profitable unto men.*
>
> (Titus 3:3-8)

The word "washing" in the Greek is *loutron* meaning "a bath, i.e. (figuratively), baptism:–washing." This Greek word is mentioned one other time in the New Testament, *Ephesians 5:26, "That he (Jesus) might sanctify and cleanse it (the church) with the <u>washing</u> of water by the word that he might present it to himself a glorious church, not having spot, or wrinkle, or any such thing; but that it should be holy and without blemish."* The word "regeneration" in the Greek is *paliggenesia* meaning "(spiritual) rebirth (the state or the act), i.e. (figuratively) <u>spiritual renovation</u>; specially, Messianic restoration:—regeneration." Its meaning in the Thayer's Greek Lexicon is "**new birth, reproduction, renewal, recreation**..., hence, 'moral renovation, regeneration, <u>the production of a new life consecrated to God, a radical change of mind for the better</u>.'" The "washing of regeneration" is renewing the inmost mind with a consistent flow of the "water of His Word" in order to flush out all the impurities of the old man. The word "renewing" in "renewing of the Holy Ghost" in the Greek is *anakainosis*. Its meaning in the Thayer's Greek Lexicon is "a renewal, renovation, complete change for the better." This Greek word is mentioned one other time in the New Testament, *Romans 12:2, "And be not conformed to this world: but be ye transformed by the <u>renewing</u> of your mind, that ye may prove what is that good, and acceptable, and perfect, will of God."* The "renewing of the Holy Ghost" reveals that the same Spirit that caused light to shine out of darkness, as God commanded in *Genesis 1:1-3*, has shined in our hearts, to give the light of the knowledge of the glory of God in the face of Jesus Christ. But we have this treasure in earthen vessels, that the excellency of the power may be of God, and not of us *(2 Corinthians 4:6-7)*. We are changed into His image as we renew our minds to His truths. Paul said,

> *Now the Lord is that Spirit: and where the Spirit of the Lord is, there is liberty. But we all, with open face beholding as in a glass the glory of the Lord, are changed into the same image from glory to glory, even as by the Spirit of the Lord.*
>
> (2 Corinthians 3:17-18)

Our part is to get the Word of God on the inside of us, to renew our *inmost mind* to His truths. This allows His Word and the power of His Spirit to do a complete mental renovation and renewal, changing us from the inside out. As born-again believers, we are God's own picked representatives, to reveal Christ to a lost and dying world. This is why it is important for us to grow in Christ in order for His character and nature to be seen in us. Paul writes,

> *Therefore if any man be in Christ, he is a new creature: old things are passed away; behold, all things are become new. And all things are of God, who hath reconciled us to himself by Jesus Christ, and hath given to us the ministry of reconciliation; to wit, that God was in Christ, reconciling the world unto himself, not imputing their trespasses unto them; and hath committed unto us the word of reconciliation. Now then we are ambassadors for Christ, as though God did beseech you by us: we pray you in Christ's stead, be ye reconciled to God. For he hath made him to be sin for us, who knew no sin; that we might be made the righteousness of God in him.*
>
> (2 Corinthians 5:17-21)

The Greek word for "ambassador" is *presbeuo* meaning "<u>to be a senior</u>, i.e. (by implication) act as a representative (figuratively, preacher):–be an ambassador." Clothing ourselves with Christ reveals a maturity, a senior in Christ, not a babe. The Spirit of the Living God is the power source or energy source of this born-again creation. It is the Lord's grace that infuses the born-again creation with the strength and power to walk in newness of life. And as God's ambassadors, we have the backing of Heaven. These Christian attributes (e.g., tenderhearted pity and mercy, kindness, humbleness of mind, gentle ways [and] patience) are a direct reflection of those whose hope and trust is in Jesus Christ and not in their ownselves and/or others.

Why do you think Paul and Silas were able to pray and praise God after having their clothes torn off of them, and having been beaten with many stripes, and cast into an inner prison with their feet shackled? They were able to see in a new dimension through the strength and power of the Holy Spirit infused within the born-again creation within them. Therefore, at midnight while they were in the inner prison, instead of getting angry with God for letting this happen or having a pity party, the born-again creation within them rose up and began to pray and praise God to the point where all the prisoners heard them. Suddenly there was a great earthquake so that the foundations of the prison were shaken and immediately all the doors were opened, and everyone's bands were loosed (please read *Acts 16* for all the details of the story)! This is an excellent example of how the behavior of the born-again creation infused by the power of the Holy Spirit, is tireless, longsuffering, and has the power to endure whatever comes with good temper! We can bring this home to how we live our lives on a daily basis (e.g., whether we are working outside the home facing day-to-day challenges, dealing with a spouse who is overbearing and hard to live with, dealing with difficult situations as a stay-at-home mom, struggling with studies as a college student). Instead of murmuring or complaining to others about the difficult situation or circumstance, it is important to stay focused on Christ by keeping our minds renewed to His truth and putting Him first place by releasing the difficult situation or circumstance to Him. In turn, His grace helps us and causes us to be more than conquerors in any situation or circumstance we face (*Psalm 142:2; Acts 20:32; 2 Corinthians 10:3-6; Ephesians 4:20-24; Colossians 1:9-17; 1 Peter 5:6-10*). After releasing the difficult situation or circumstance to Him, if there is still turmoil within, I want to encourage you to call a mature believer in Christ to share the difficulty and receive prayer to help bring peace and calm, as we need Christ in one another (*James 5:16*). Paul writes,

> *Who shall separate us from the love of Christ? Shall tribulation, or distress, or persecution, or famine, or nakedness, or peril, or sword? As it is written, "For thy sake we are killed all the day long; we are accounted as sheep for the slaughter." Nay, in all these things we are more than conquerors through him that loved us. For I am persuaded, that neither death, nor life, nor angels, nor principalities, nor powers, nor things present, nor things to come, nor height, nor depth, nor any other creature, shall be able to separate us from the love of God, which is in Christ Jesus our Lord.*
>
> (Romans 8:35-39)

Below are Scriptures relating to putting on the new man:

1. ***Ephesians 4:22-24*** *– That ye put off concerning the former conversation (behavior) the old man, which is corrupt according to the deceitful lusts; and be renewed in the spirit of your mind; and that ye put on the new man, which after God is created in righteousness and true holiness.*

References:
Psalm 15:1-5 *– [[A Psalm of David.]] LORD, who shall abide in thy tabernacle? Who shall dwell in thy holy hill? He that walketh uprightly, and worketh righteousness, and speaketh the truth in his heart. He that backbiteth not with his tongue, nor doeth evil to his neighbour, nor taketh up a reproach against his neighbour. In whose eyes a vile person is contemned; but he honoureth them that fear the LORD. He that sweareth to his own hurt, and changeth not. He that putteth not out his money to usury, nor taketh reward against the innocent. He that doeth these thing shall never be moved.* ***Psalm 26:6-7*** *– I will wash mine hands in innocency: so will I compass thine altar, O LORD: that I may publish with the voice of thanksgiving, and tell of all thy wondrous works.* ***Psalm 50:23*** *– The LORD said, "Whoso offereth praise glorifieth me: and to him that ordereth his conversation (course of life or mode of action) aright will I shew the salvation of God."* ***Psalm 106:3*** *– Blessed are they that keep judgment, and he that doeth righteousness at all times.* ***Isaiah 61:10-11*** *– I will greatly rejoice in the LORD, my soul shall be joyful in my God; for he hath clothed me with the garments of salvation, he hath covered me with the robe of righteousness, as a bridegroom decketh himself with ornaments, and as a bride adorneth herself with jewels. For as the*

*earth bringeth forth her bud, and as the garden causeth the things that are sown in it to spring forth; so the Lord GOD will cause righteousness and praise to spring forth before all nations. **Romans 13:12-14** – The night is far spent, the day is at hand: let us therefore cast off the works of darkness, and let us put on the armour of light. Let us walk honestly, as in the day; not in rioting and drunkenness, not in chambering and wantonness, not in strife and envying. But put ye on the Lord Jesus Christ, and make not provision for the flesh, to fulfil the lusts thereof. **2 Corinthians 3:2-3** – …Forasmuch as ye are manifestly declared to be the epistle of Christ ministered by us, written not with ink, but with the Spirit of the living God; not in tables of stone, but in fleshy tables of the heart. **2 Corinthians 5:17-21** – Therefore if any man be in Christ, he is a new creature: old things are passed away; behold, all things are become new. And all things are of God, who hath reconciled us to himself by Jesus Christ, and hath given to us the ministry of reconciliation; to wit, that God was in Christ, reconciling the world unto himself, not imputing their trespasses unto them; and hath committed unto us the word of reconciliation. Now then we are ambassadors for Christ, as though God did beseech you by us: we pray you in Christ's stead, be ye reconciled to God. For he hath made him to be sin for us, who knew no sin; that we might be made the righteousness of God in him. **Galatians 3:27-29** – For as many of you as have been baptized into Christ have put on Christ. There is neither Jew nor Greek, there is neither bond nor free, there is neither male nor female: for ye are all one in Christ Jesus. And if ye be Christ's, then are ye Abraham's seed, and heirs according to the promise. **Ephesians 6:10-20** – Paul said, "Finally, my brethren, be strong in the Lord, and in the power of his might. Put on the whole armour of God, that ye may be able to stand against the wiles of the devil. For we wrestle not against flesh and blood, but against principalities, against powers, against the rulers of the darkness of this world, against spiritual wickedness in high places. Wherefore take unto you the whole armour of God, that ye may be able to withstand in the evil day, and having done all, to stand. Stand therefore, having your loins girt about with truth, and having on the breastplate of righteousness; and your feet shod with the preparation of the gospel of peace; above all, taking the shield of faith, wherewith ye shall be able to quench all the fiery darts of the wicked. And take the helmet of salvation, and the sword of the Spirit, which is the word of God: praying always with all prayer and supplication in the Spirit, and watching thereunto with all perseverance and supplication for the saints; and for me, that utterance may be given unto me, that I may open my mouth boldly, to make known the mystery of the gospel, for which I am an ambassador in bonds: that therein I may speak boldly, as I ought to speak." **Colossians 2:6-15** – As ye have therefore received Christ Jesus the Lord, so walk ye in him: rooted and built up in him, and stablished in the faith, as ye have been taught, abounding therein with thanksgiving. Beware lest any man spoil you through philosophy and vain deceit, after the tradition of men, after the rudiments of the world, and not after Christ. For in him dwelleth all the fulness of the Godhead bodily. And ye are complete in him, which is the head of all principality and power… **2 Timothy 3:10-17** – Paul said, "But thou hast fully known my doctrine, manner of life, purpose, faith, longsuffering, charity (God's love), patience, persecutions, afflictions, which came unto me at Antioch, at Iconium, at Lystra; what persecutions I endured: but out of them all the Lord delivered me. Yea, and all that will live godly in Christ Jesus shall suffer persecution. But evil men and seducers shall wax (grow) worse and worse, deceiving, and being deceived. But continue thou in the things which thou hast learned and hast been assured of, knowing of whom thou hast learned them; and that from a child thou hast known the holy scriptures, which are able to make thee wise unto salvation through faith which is in Christ Jesus. All scripture is given by inspiration of God, and is profitable for doctrine, for reproof, for correction, for instruction in righteousness: that the man of God may be perfect (complete), throughly furnished unto all good works."*

2. ***Luke 21:19*** *– Jesus said, "In your patience possess ye your souls."*

References:

Romans 5:1-5 – *Paul said, "Therefore being justified by faith, we have peace with God through our Lord Jesus Christ: by whom also we have access by faith into this grace wherein we stand, and rejoice in hope of the glory of God. And not only so, but we glory in tribulations also: knowing that tribulation worketh patience; and patience, experience; and experience, hope: and hope maketh not ashamed; because the love of God is shed abroad in our hearts by the Holy Ghost which is given unto us."* ***1 James 1:1-4*** – *James, a servant of God and of the Lord Jesus Christ, to the twelve tribes which are scattered abroad, greeting. My brethren, count it all joy when ye fall into divers temptations; knowing this, that the trying of your faith worketh patience. But let patience have her perfect work, that ye may be perfect (complete) and entire (perfectly sound, whole), wanting nothing.* ***1 Peter 5:6-11*** – *Humble yourselves therefore under the mighty hand of God, that he may exalt you in due time: casting all your care upon him; for he careth for you. Be sober, be vigilant; because your adversary the devil, as a roaring lion, walketh about, seeking whom he may devour: whom resist stedfast in the faith, knowing that the same afflictions are accomplished in your brethren that are in the world. But the God of all grace, who hath called us unto his eternal glory by Christ Jesus, after that ye have suffered a while, make you perfect (complete), stablish, strengthen, settle you. To him be glory and dominion for ever and ever. Amen.*

3. ***James 3:12-18*** – *Can the fig tree, my brethren, bear olive berries? Either a vine, figs? So can no fountain both yield salt water and fresh. Who is a wise man endued with knowledge among you? Let him shew out of a good conversation (behavior) his works with meekness of wisdom. But if ye have bitter envying and strife in your hearts, glory not, and lie not against the truth. This wisdom descendeth not from above, but is earthly, sensual, devilish. For where envying and strife is, there is confusion and every evil work. But the wisdom that is from above is first pure, then peaceable, gentle, and easy to be intreated, full of mercy and good fruits, without partiality, and without hypocrisy. And the fruit of righteousness is sown in peace of them that make peace.*

References:

Proverbs 16:23 – *The heart of the wise teacheth his mouth, and addeth learning to his lips.* ***Proverbs 24:3-6*** – *Through wisdom is an house builded; and by understanding it is established: and by knowledge shall the chambers be filled with all precious and pleasant riches. A wise man is strong; yea, a man of knowledge increaseth strength. For by wise counsel thou shalt make thy war: and in multitude of counsellors there is safety.*

Here are additional Scriptures relating to putting on the new man: Psalm 37:11, 25-31, 37, 39-40; Matthew 7:7-14, 25:31-46; Romans 12:10; Galatians 6:12-16; Ephesians 4:1-16, 29-32; 1 Timothy 6:3-12; 1 Peter 3:1-18.

28(b) *I am* gentle and forbearing with *others* and, if *I have* a difference (a grievance or complaint) against another, readily pardoning; even as *You, Lord, have* [freely] forgiven *me*, so must *I* also [forgive]. (Colossians 3:13-AMPCE)

The word "forbearing" in the Greek is *anecho* meaning "to hold oneself up against, i.e. (figuratively <u>put up with</u>:–bear with, endure, forbear, suffer." The Lord used Paul to show us His longsuffering as a pattern for us:

234

And I thank Christ Jesus our Lord, who hath enabled me, for that he counted me faithful, putting me into the ministry; who was before a blasphemer, and a persecutor, and injurious: but I obtained mercy, because I did it ignorantly in unbelief. And the grace of our Lord was exceeding abundant with faith and love which is in Christ Jesus. This is a faithful saying, and worthy of all acceptation, that Christ Jesus came into the world to save sinners; of whom I am chief. Howbeit for this cause I obtained mercy, that in me first Jesus Christ might shew forth all longsuffering, for a pattern to them which should hereafter believe on him to life everlasting. Now unto the King eternal, immortal, invisible, the only wise God, be honour and glory for ever and ever. Amen.

(1 Timothy 1:12-17)

The word "longsuffering" in the Greek is *makrothymia*. Its meaning in the Thayer's Greek Lexicon is "patience, <u>forbearance</u>, long-suffering, slowness in avenging wrongs." Just as the Lord is longsuffering with us, He is calling us to be longsuffering toward one another. As you read ***My Story – Part One - Volume 1***, you will clearly see the longsuffering of the Lord toward me and since the time of Paul, there are multitudes that can testify to His longsuffering in their own personal lives. Paul also writes in *Ephesians 4:21, "…the truth is in Jesus."* I am reminded of the following passage of Scripture:

In the beginning was the Word (Jesus), and the Word was with God, and the Word was God. The same was in the beginning with God. And <u>the Word was made flesh, and dwelt among us, (and we beheld his glory, the glory as of the only begotten of the Father,) full of grace and truth</u>.

(John 1:1-2, 14)

The Greek word for "grace" is *charis* meaning "…especially the divine influence upon the heart, and its reflection in the life…" In the Thayer's Greek Lexicon one meaning is "is used of 'the merciful kindness by which God, exerting his holy influence upon souls, turns them to Christ, keeps, strengthens, increases them in Christian faith, knowledge, affection, and kindles them to the exercise of the Christian virtues': 2 Corinthians 4:15, 6:1; 2 Thessalonians 1:12." The Lord's grace kindles us to exercise these Christian virtues, strengthening the born-again creation within us. As His offspring, the Lord is gentle and forbearing with us, and therefore, we are to be gentle and forbearing with others. As Paul and Timothy prayed for the saints and the faithful brethren in Christ at Colossae when they heard of their faith in Christ Jesus and their love toward all the saints, we too who walk in faith and love toward the saints can also receive the benefits of this prayer,

For this cause we also, since the day we heard it, do not cease to pray for you, and to desire that ye might be filled with the knowledge of His will in all wisdom and spiritual understanding; that ye might walk worthy of the Lord unto all pleasing, being fruitful in every good work, and increasing in the knowledge of God; <u>strengthened with all might, according to his glorious power, unto all patience and longsuffering with joyfulness</u>; giving thanks unto the Father, which hath made us meet (able) to be partakers of the inheritance of the saints in light: who hath delivered us from the power of darkness, and hath translated us into the kingdom of his dear Son. To whom God would make known what is the riches of the glory of this mystery among the Gentiles; which is Christ in you, the hope of glory.

(Colossians 1:9-13, 27)

The word "knowledge" in the Greek is *epignosis*. Its meaning in the Thayer's Greek Lexicon is "… with the genitive of the person known; — of God, especially the knowledge of his holy will and of the blessings which he has bestowed and constantly bestows on men through Christ: Ephesians 1:17; Colossians 1:10; 2 Peter 1:2; of Christ, i.e. the true knowledge of Christ's nature, dignity, benefits: Ephesians 4:13; 2 Peter 1:8; 2 Peter 2:20…" In order to get the full context, let's take a look at *2 Peter 1:3-8*:

> *According as his divine power hath given unto us all things that pertain unto life and godliness, <u>through the knowledge of him that hath called us to glory and virtue</u>: whereby are given unto us exceeding great and precious promises: that by these ye might be partakers of the divine nature, having escaped the corruption that is in the world through lust. And beside this, giving all diligence, add to your faith virtue; and to virtue knowledge; and to knowledge temperance; and to temperance patience; and to patience godliness; and to godliness brotherly kindness; and to brotherly kindness charity (God's love). For if these things be in you, and abound, they make you that ye shall neither be barren nor unfruitful in the knowledge of our Lord Jesus Christ.*

It is through "knowing Him" that we can put off the old man and put on the new man (*Colossians 3:10*).

Forgiving one another and forgiving ourselves for our own wrong doings is essential in walking in righteousness, peace, and joy in the Holy Ghost which is the kingdom of God *(Romans 14:17)*! Jesus revealed to us the importance of forgiveness in the following two passages of Scripture:

1. ***Matthew 6:9-15*** – *Jesus said, "After this manner therefore pray ye: Our Father which art in heaven, hallowed be thy name. Thy kingdom come. Thy will be done in earth, as it is in heaven. Give us this day our daily bread. And forgive us our debts, as we forgive our debtors. And lead us not into temptation but deliver us from evil: for thine is the kingdom, and the power, and the glory, for ever. Amen. For if ye forgive men their trespasses, your heavenly Father will also forgive you: but if ye forgive not men their trespasses, neither will your Father forgive your trespasses."*
2. ***Matthew 5:22-26*** – *Jesus said, "… Therefore if thou bring thy gift to the altar, and there rememberest that thy brother hath ought (something) against thee; leave there thy gift before the altar, and go thy way; first be reconciled to thy brother, and then come and offer thy gift…"*

It is vital that we forgive others or our heavenly Father will not forgive us! Satan uses unforgiveness as a tactic to get to us. Therefore do no be ignorant of his devices *(2 Corinthians 2:10-11)*. There is no way that the joy and peace of the Lord can penetrate our unwillingness to forgive. The Lord is faithful to reveal any unforgiveness that is working in us. Here is an example in my own life:

One day while I was walking on my treadmill, I began to have bad feelings toward my husband, Don, and I thought within myself, "Where is this coming from?" I realized that I felt deep within myself that he owed me something, and more than an apology. I felt he owed me more sensitivity of his heart, more gentleness, more kindness. As I pondered these thoughts and feelings I realized that I had unforgiveness toward him for not meeting my expectations as a husband and how I thought a husband should behave. I immediately began to pray and proclaim, to the Lord, forgiveness over my husband for not meeting my expectations and released those expectations to Him. Over time, the Lord began to open my eyes to all the good things about Don and the importance of thinking on those things.

It is the wellspring of living water within the born-again believer that brings forth righteousness, peace, and joy; it is NOT dependent on people's behavior or life's circumstances. An example of this is when Peter was addressing wives, he exhorted them,

> *Likewise, ye wives, be in subjection to your own husbands; that, if any obey not the word, they also may without the word be won by the conversation (behavior) of the wives; while they behold your chaste (innocent, perfect, clean, pure) conversation (behavior) coupled with fear. Whose adorning let it not be that outward adorning of plaiting the hair, and of wearing of gold, or of putting on of apparel; but let it be the hidden man of the heart, in that which is not corruptible, even the ornament of a meek and quiet spirit, which is in the sight of God of great price.*
>
> (1 Peter 3:1-4)

Peter had a revelation of the power available to those who choose to live out of the hidden man of the heart, the new man, toward those who are closest to us. The reality of *"Christ in you, the hope of glory,"* is displayed through a meek and quiet spirit which is in the sight of God of great price! When a husband observes this type of behavior in his wife it can have a significant impact on him, drawing him to Christ as he observes her sincere trust in God. The Lord is calling His people not to look on the things which are seen (e.g., unpleasant circumstances, fleshly behavior), but at the things which are not seen (e.g., His truth, His faithfulness, His love), the eternal, deathless, and everlasting things of God *(2 Corinthians 4:18)*. In order to live out of the hidden man of the heart, the new man in Christ and its eternal perspective, a true and sincere relationship with the Lord must be in place and the *inmost mind* or the *spirit of our minds* must be renewed to the knowledge of the true nature of Christ and His love for us, and this takes time *(Ephesians 4:23)*!

Below are Scriptures relating to forgiveness:

Proverbs 25:15 – *By long forbearing is a prince persuaded, and a soft tongue breaketh the bone.* (A soft tongue calms anger and reduces tension).

References:
Proverbs 4:20-23 – *My son, attend to my words; incline thine ear unto my sayings. Let them not depart from thine eyes; keep them in the midst of thine heart. For they are life unto those that find them, and health to all their flesh. Keep thy heart with all diligence; for out of it are the issues of life.* ***Matthew 6:14-15*** – *Jesus said, "For if ye forgive men their trespasses, your heavenly Father will also forgive you: But if ye forgive not men their trespasses, neither will your Father forgive your trespasses."* ***Matthew 18:21-35*** – *Then came Peter to him, and said, "Lord, how oft (often) shall my brother sin against me, and I forgive him? Till seven times?" Jesus saith unto him, "I say not unto thee, until seven times: but, until seventy times seven. Therefore is the kingdom of heaven likened unto a certain king, which would take account of his servants. And when he had begun to reckon, one was brought unto him, which owed him ten thousand talents. But forasmuch as he had not to pay, his lord commanded him to be sold, and his wife, and children, and all that he had, and payment to be made. The servant therefore fell down, and worshipped him, saying, 'Lord, have patience with me, and I will pay thee all.' Then the lord of that servant was moved with compassion, and loosed him,*

and forgave him the debt. But the same servant went out, and found one of his fellowservants, which owed him an hundred pence: and he laid hands on him, and took him by the throat, saying, 'Pay me that thou owest.' And his fellowservant fell down at his feet, and besought him, saying, 'Have patience with me, and I will pay thee all.' And he would not: but went and cast him into prison, till he should pay the debt. So when his fellowservants saw what was done, they were very sorry, and came and told unto their lord all that was done. Then his lord, after that he had called him, said unto him, 'O thou wicked servant, I forgave thee all that debt, because thou desiredst me: shouldest not thou also have had compassion on thy fellowservant, even as I had pity on thee?' And his lord was wroth (provoked, enraged, i.e. became exasperated. Angry), and delivered him to the tormentors, till he should pay all that was due unto him. So likewise shall my heavenly Father do also unto you, if ye from your hearts forgive not every one his brother their trespasses." **Mark 11:25-26** *– Jesus said, "And when ye stand praying, forgive, if ye have ought (anything) against any: that your Father also which is in heaven may forgive you your trespasses. But if ye do not forgive, neither will your Father which is in heaven forgive your trespasses."* **Luke 6:37** *– Jesus said, "Judge not and ye shall not be judged: condemn not, and ye shall not be condemned: forgive, and ye shall be forgiven."* **Luke 11:2-4** *– Jesus said, "When ye pray, say, "…And forgive us our sins; for we also forgive everyone that is indebted to us…"* **Luke 17:3-5** *– Jesus said, "Take heed to yourselves: if thy brother <u>trespass</u> against thee, rebuke him; and if he repent, forgive him. And if he trespass against thee seven times in a day, and seven times in a day turn again to thee, saying, 'I repent;' thou shalt forgive him." And the apostles said unto the Lord, "Increase our faith."* **1 John 1:9** *– If we confess our sins, he (Jesus) is faithful and just to forgive us our sins, and to cleanse us from all unrighteousness.*

In *Luke 17:3-5*, the word "trespass" in the Greek is *hamartano* meaning "properly, to miss the mark (and so not share in the prize), i.e. (figuratively) to err, especially (morally) to sin:–for your faults, offend, sin, trespass." The word "rebuke" in the Greek is *epitimao* meaning "to tax upon, i.e. censure or admonish; by implication, forbid:–(straitly) charge, rebuke." We have every right to rebuke someone who trespasses against us. However, as I have found in my own personal life, once a believer becomes more deeply rooted in God's love, in most cases, they will pay no attention to a suffered wrong as they are no longer easily offended *(1 Corinthians 13:1-8; Psalm 119:165)*. I also believe the reason the disciples asked the Lord to increase their faith is because they could not "see" how someone could forgive the same person for trespassing against them over and over again. To me, this is called "forbearance." Jesus wanted them to be aware of the consequences of unforgiveness in whatever form it may take. We must always guard ourselves against unforgiveness as it can subtly harden our hearts and thus block the flow of the wellspring of life (His Holy Spirit).

In closing, Paul writes,

> *I therefore, the prisoner of the Lord, beseech you that ye walk worthy of the vocation wherewith ye are called, with all lowliness and meekness, with longsuffering, forbearing one another in love; endeavouring to keep the unity of the Spirit in the bond of peace. There is one body, and one Spirit, even as ye are called in one hope of your calling; one Lord, one faith, one baptism, one God and Father of all, who is above all, and through all, and in you all. Let no corrupt communication proceed out of your mouth, but that which is good to the use of edifying, that it may minister grace unto the hearers. And grieve not the Holy Spirit of God, whereby ye are sealed unto the day of redemption. Let all bitterness, and wrath, and anger, and clamour, and evil speaking, be put away from you, with all malice: and be ye kind one to another, tenderhearted, forgiving one another, even as God for Christ's sake*

hath forgiven you.

(Ephesians 4:1-6, 29-32)

28(c) Above all these things *I* put on *love*, which is the bond of perfectness. *And I* let the word of Christ dwell in *me* richly in all wisdom... (Colossians 3:14, 16)

Why above all, put on love? Paul explains the importance of putting on love,

> *Though I speak with the tongues of men and of angels, and have not charity (God's love), I am become as sounding brass, or a tinkling cymbal. And though I have the gift of prophecy, and understand all mysteries, and all knowledge; and though I have all faith, so that I could remove mountains, and have not charity (God's love), I am nothing. And though I bestow all my goods to feed the poor, and though I give my body to be burned, and have not charity (God's love), it profiteth me nothing.*

(1 Corinthians 13:1-3)

He then goes on to describe in *1 Corinthians 13:4-8* what love is and is not. Walking in this kind of love is the perfection/maturity of the born-again believer. Now let's go back to *Colossians 3:14*, the word "perfectness" in the Greek is *teleiotes* meaning "(the state) completeness (mentally or morally):– perfection(-ness)." The character traits of someone walking in the love of God is humility, lowliness of mind, and trusting in Him—perceiving that as He laid down His life for us, we should lay down our lives for the brethren *(1 John 3:16)*. This way of living keeps us in His light in order to see clearly. Below are three passages of Scripture that confirm this truth:

1. *2 Peter 1:3-11* – *According as his divine power hath given unto us all things that pertain unto life and godliness, through the knowledge of him that hath called us to glory and virtue: whereby are given unto us exceeding great and precious promises: that by these ye might be partakers of the divine nature, having escaped the corruption that is in the world through lust. And beside this, giving all diligence, add to your faith virtue; and to virtue knowledge; and to knowledge temperance; and to temperance patience; and to patience godliness; and to godliness brotherly kindness; and to brotherly kindness charity (God's love). For if these things be in you, and abound, they make you that ye shall neither be barren nor unfruitful in the knowledge of our Lord Jesus Christ. But he that lacketh these things is blind, and cannot see afar off, and hath forgotten that he was purged from his old sins. Wherefore the rather, brethren, give diligence to make your calling and election sure: for if ye do these things, ye shall never fall: for so an entrance shall be ministered unto you abundantly into the everlasting kingdom of our Lord and Saviour Jesus Christ.*

2. *1 John 1:5-7* – *This then is the message which we have heard of him, and declare unto you, that God is light, and in him is no darkness at all. If we say that we have fellowship with him, and walk in darkness, we lie, and do not the truth: but if we walk in the light, as he is in the light, we have fellowship one with another, and the blood of Jesus Christ his Son cleanseth us from all sin.*

3. *1 John 2:9-11* – *He that saith he is in the light, and hateth his brother, is in darkness even until now. He that loveth his brother abideth in the light, and there is none occasion of stumbling in him. But he that hateth his brother is in darkness, and walketh in darkness, and*

knoweth not whither he goeth, because that darkness hath blinded his eyes.

Jesus is calling us to grow up in Him by putting off the old man and putting on the new man, as this is where true and abundant life is found. Paul writes,

> *And I, brethren, could not speak unto you as unto spiritual, but as to carnal, even as unto babes in Christ. I have fed you with milk, and not with meat: for hitherto ye were not able to bear it, neither yet now are ye able. For ye are yet carnal: for whereas there is among you envying, and strife, and divisions, are ye not carnal, and walk as men?*
>
> (1 Corinthians 3:1-3)

And Peter writes,

> *Wherefore laying aside all malice, and all guile, and hypocrisies, and envies, and all evil speakings, as newborn babes, desire the sincere milk of the word, that ye may grow thereby: if so be ye have tasted that the Lord is gracious.*
>
> (1 Peter 2:1-3)

As we feed on the Word of God and renew our minds to the Word of His truth, we grow in Christ *(1 Corinthians 3:1-3; 1 Peter 2:1-2; Romans 12:1-2; Ephesians 4:17-24; Colossians 3:10)*. Jesus said in *Matthew 12:34*, *"...Out of the abundance of the heart the mouth speaketh."* And in *Matthew 12:37*, *"For by thy words thou shalt be justified, and by thy words thou shalt be condemned."* These sayings are very powerful and reveal two things:

1. The heart and tongue are connected.
2. Life and death are in the power of the tongue.

> *A man's belly shall be satisfied with the fruit of his mouth; and with the increase of his lips shall he be filled. Death and life are in the power of the tongue: and they that love it shall eat the fruit thereof.*
>
> (Proverbs 18:20-21)

This is why it is important to use our tongues to renew our minds to the holy Scriptures regarding the new man in Christ. As we speak aloud the holy Scriptures, they enter into our *inmost mind* and through the power of His Holy Spirit remove any hindering force that is keeping the new man in Christ from becoming a reality within us *(Hebrews 4:12-14)*. Below are three passages of Scripture revealing the importance of circumcising the heart in order to reveal the true nature of Christ:

1. ***Romans 2:25-29*** – *(NKJV)* – *For circumcision is indeed profitable if you keep the law; but if you are a breaker of the law, your circumcision has become uncircumcision. Therefore, if an uncircumcised man keeps the righteous requirements of the law, will not his uncircumcision be counted as circumcision? And will not the physically uncircumcised, if he fulfills the law, judge you who, even with your written code and circumcision, are a transgressor of the law? For he is not a Jew who is one outwardly, nor is circumcision that which is outward in the flesh; but he is a Jew who is one inwardly; and circumcision is that of the heart, in the Spirit, not in the letter; whose praise is not from men but from God.*

2. **Galatians 5:6** – *For in Jesus Christ neither circumcision availeth any thing, nor uncircumcision; but faith which worketh by love.*
3. **Galatians 6:15** – *For in Christ Jesus neither circumcision availeth any thing nor uncircumcision, but a new creature.*

As a history lesson, circumcision began when God made covenant with Abraham, the father of Israel *(Genesis 17:9-14)*. God commanded that Abraham and his seed be circumcised as a seal of the Old Covenant. The seal of the New Covenant is the circumcision of the heart in order to walk in the new man in Christ or the hidden man of the heart—faith which works by love *(Romans 2:28-29; Galatians 5:6, 6:15; 1 Peter 1:3-5)*. Paul writes,

> *For we are his workmanship, created in Christ Jesus unto good works, which God hath before ordained that we should walk in them. Wherefore remember, that ye being in time past Gentiles in the flesh, who are called Uncircumcision by that which is called the Circumcision in the flesh made by hands; that at that time ye were without Christ, being aliens from the commonwealth of Israel, and strangers from the covenants of promise, having no hope, and without God in the world: but now in Christ Jesus ye who sometimes were far off are made nigh by the blood of Christ. For he is our peace, who hath made both one, and hath broken down the middle wall of partition between us; having abolished in his flesh the enmity, even the law of commandments contained in ordinances; for to make in himself of twain (two) one new man, so making peace; and that he might reconcile both unto God in one body by the cross, having slain the enmity thereby: and came and preached peace to you which were afar off, and to them that were nigh. For through him we both have access by one Spirit unto the Father. Now therefore ye are no more strangers and foreigners, but fellow citizens with the saints, and of the household of God; and are built upon the foundation of the apostles and prophets, Jesus Christ himself being the chief corner stone; in whom all the building fitly framed together groweth unto an holy temple in the Lord: in whom ye also are builded together for an habitation of God through the Spirit.*
>
> (Ephesians 2:10-22)

This is a very powerful passage of Scripture as it reveals that only through Christ and His cross can true circumcision be made, bringing forth the true nature of Christ, the new man, as Paul writes in *Colossians 2:9-12,*

> *For in him dwelleth all the fulness of the Godhead bodily. And ye are complete in him, which is the head of all principality and power: in whom also ye are circumcised with the circumcision made without hands, in putting off the body of the sins of the flesh by the circumcision of Christ: buried with him in baptism, wherein also ye are risen with him through the faith of the operation of God, who hath raised him from the dead.*

In *Deuteronomy 30:1-20,* Moses declares to the children of Israel,

> *...And the LORD thy God will bring thee into the land which thy fathers possessed, and thou shalt possess it; and he will do thee good, and multiply thee above thy fathers. And the LORD thy God will circumcise thine heart, and the heart of thy seed, to love the LORD thy God with all thine heart, and with all thy soul, that thou mayest live...*

Circumcision of the heart is the key to living out of God's love and therefore experiencing abundant life in Christ! The Lord said in *Deuteronomy 10:16 – Circumcise therefore the foreskin of your heart, and be no more stiffnecked."* The foreskin of our heart is the flesh, carnality, the old man and its protective coverings. As I shared in **My Story – Part Two - Volume 1**, the Lord removed a protective covering from my heart by His Word and by the power of His Spirit. Here is a brief summary of what happened:

> After about fifteen years of walking with the Lord, He revealed to me that my defense mechanisms, the carnal protective covering and ingrained carnal beliefs and mindsets (e.g., argumentativeness, anger, protecting my right to be right), were keeping me from being hurt, because of my own deep-seated fears and insecurities. However, it was also keeping me from growing into His image and bearing the fruit of the Spirit, the life-giving attributes of His nature. He began teaching me how to die to those carnal defense mechanisms by renewing my mind to the new man in Christ and releasing my fears, hurts, pains, etc., to Him, trusting in His love for me in every area of my life. As an example, a peach seed is protected by its pit. The pit must be removed in order for the seed, when planted into good ground, to grow into its destiny of being a mature peach tree producing fruit. So too I was <u>not</u> able to grow spiritually until the carnal protective covering within me was removed and the ingrained carnal beliefs and mindsets were flushed out through the renewal process. Please see **My Story – Part Two - Volume 1** for details.

Below are Scriptures relating to living out of God's love:

1. **Matthew 5:43-48** – *Jesus said, "Ye have heard that it hath been said, 'Thou shalt love thy neighbour, and hate thine enemy.' But I say unto you, Love your enemies, bless them that curse you, do good to them that hate you, and pray for them which despitefully use you, and persecute you; that ye may be the children of your Father which is in heaven: for he maketh his sun to rise on the evil and on the good, and sendeth rain on the just and on the unjust. For if ye love them which love you, what reward have ye? Do not even the publicans the same? And if ye salute your brethren only, what do ye more than others? Do not even the publicans so? Be ye therefore perfect, even as your Father which is in heaven is perfect."*

References:

Proverbs 10:12 – Hatred stirreth up strifes: but love covereth all sins. **Proverbs 17:9** – *He that covereth a transgression seeketh love; but he that repeateth a matter separateth friends.* **Matthew 22:35-40** – *Then one of them, which was a lawyer, asked him a question, tempting him, and saying, "Master, which is the great commandment in the law?" Jesus said unto him, "Thou shalt love the Lord thy God with all thy heart, and with all thy soul, and with all thy mind. This is the first and great commandment. And the second is like unto it, thou shalt love thy neighbour as thyself. On these two commandments hang all the law and the prophets."* **John 14:15-18, 21-24** – *Jesus said, "If ye love me, keep my commandments. And I will pray the Father, and he shall give you another Comforter, that he may abide with you for ever; even the Spirit of truth; whom the world cannot receive, because it seeth him not, neither knoweth him; for he dwelleth with you, and shall be in you. I will not leave you comfortless: I will come to you. He that hath my commandments, and keepeth them, he it is that loveth me: and he that loveth me shall be loved of my Father, and I will love him, and will manifest myself to him." Judas saith unto him, not Iscariot, "Lord, how is it that thou wilt manifest thyself to us, and not unto the world?" Jesus answered and said unto him, "If a man love me, he* *will keep my words: and my Father will love him, and we will come unto him, and make our abode with him. He that loveth me not keepeth not my sayings: and the word which ye hear is not mine, but the Father's which sent me."* **John 15:8-14** *— Jesus said, "Herein is my Father glorified, that ye bear much fruit; so shall ye be my disciples. As the Father hath loved me, so have I loved you: continue ye in my love. If ye keep my commandments, ye shall abide in my love; even as I have kept my Father's commandments, and abide in his love. These things have I spoken unto you, that my joy might remain in you, and that your joy might be full. This is my commandment, that ye love one another, as I have loved you. Greater love hath no man than this, that a man lay down his life for his friends. Ye are my friends, if ye do whatsoever I command you."* **1 Corinthians 16:14** *— Let all your things be done with charity (God's love). (True love for Christ and for others is when we can sincerely proclaim as Paul did in* **Galatians 2:20** *— "I am crucified with Christ: nevertheless I live; yet not I, but Christ liveth in me: and the life which I now live in the flesh I live by the faith of the Son of God, who loved me, and gave himself for me.").* **Galatians 5:22-25** *— But the fruit of the Spirit is love, joy, peace, longsuffering, gentleness, goodness, faith, meekness, temperance: against such there is no law. And they that are Christ's have crucified the flesh with the affections and lusts. If we live in the Spirit, let us also walk in the Spirit.* **Ephesians 5:1-2** *— Be ye therefore followers of God, as dear children; and walk in love, as Christ also hath loved us, and hath given himself for us an offering and a sacrifice to God for a sweetsmelling savour.* **Philippians 1:9-11** *— and this I pray, that your love may abound yet more and more in knowledge and in all judgment; that ye may approve things that are excellent; that ye may be sincere and without offence till the day of Christ; being filled with the fruits of righteousness, which are by Jesus Christ, unto the glory and praise of God.* **Philippians 2:1-3** *— If there be therefore any consolation in Christ, if any comfort of love, if any fellowship of the Spirit, if any bowels (inward affection) and mercies, fulfil ye my joy, that ye be likeminded, having the same love, being of one accord, of one mind. Let nothing be done through strife or vainglory; but in lowliness of mind let each esteem other better than themselves.* **1 Timothy 4:12** *— Let no man despise thy youth; but be thou an example of the believers, in word, in conversation (behavior), in charity (God's love), in spirit, in faith, in purity.* **1 Peter 1:22-25** *— Seeing ye have purified your souls in obeying the truth through the Spirit unto unfeigned love of the brethren, see that ye love one another with a pure heart fervently: being born again, not of corruptible seed, but of incorruptible, by the word of God, which liveth and abideth for ever. For all flesh is as grass, and all the glory of man as the flower of grass. The grass withereth, and the flower thereof falleth away: but the word of the Lord endureth for ever. And this is the word which by the gospel is preached unto you.* **1 Peter 4:8** *— And above all things have fervent charity (God's love) among yourselves: for charity (God's love) shall cover the multitude of sins."* **1 John 3:11-16** *— For this is the message that ye heard from the beginning, that we should love one another. Not as Cain, who was of that wicked one, and slew his brother. And wherefore slew he him? Because his own works were evil, and his brother's righteous. Marvel not, my brethren, if the world hate you. We know that we have passed from death unto life, because we love the brethren. He that loveth not his brother abideth in death. Whosoever hateth his brother is a murderer: and ye know that no murderer hath eternal life abiding in him. Hereby perceive we the love of God, because he laid down his life for us: and we ought to lay down our lives for the brethren.* **1 John 4:7-21** *— Beloved, let us love one another: for love is of God; and every one that loveth is born of God, and knoweth God. He that loveth not knoweth not God; for God is love. In this was manifested the love of God toward us, because that God sent his only begotten Son into the world, that we might live through him. Herein is love, not that we loved God, but that he loved us, and sent his Son to be the propitiation for our sins. Beloved, if God so loved us, we ought also to love one another. No man hath seen God at any time. If we love one another, God dwelleth in us, and his love is perfected in us. Hereby know we that we dwell in him, and he in us, because he hath given us of his Spirit. And we have seen and do testify that the Father sent the Son to be the Saviour of the world. Whosoever shall confess that Jesus is the Son of God, God dwelleth in him, and he in God. And we have known and believed the love that God hath to us.*

God is love; and he that dwelleth in love dwelleth in God, and God in him. Herein is our love made perfect, that we may have boldness in the day of judgment: because as he is, so are we in this world. There is no fear in love; but perfect love casteth out fear: because fear hath torment. He that feareth is not made perfect in love. We love him, because he first loved us. If a man say, I love God, and hateth his brother, he is a liar: for he that loveth not his brother whom he hath seen, how can he love God whom he hath not seen? And this commandment have we from him, that he who loveth God love his brother also.

2. ***Ephesians 3:14-21*** – *Paul said, "For this cause I bow my knees unto the Father of our Lord Jesus Christ, of whom the whole family in heaven and earth is named, that he would grant you, according to the riches of his glory, to be strengthened with might by his Spirit in the inner man; that Christ may dwell in your hearts by faith; that ye, being rooted and grounded in love, may be able to comprehend with all saints what is the breadth, and length, and depth, and height; and to know the love of Christ, which passeth knowledge, that ye might be filled with all the fullness of God. Now unto him that is able to do exceeding abundantly above all that we ask or think, according to the power that worketh in us, unto him be glory in the church by Christ Jesus throughout all ages, world without end. Amen."* (The power that works in a believer is determined by the maturity level of the born-again creation within).

Reference:
Proverbs 20:27 – *The spirit of man is the candle of the LORD, searching all the inward parts of the belly.*

Please refer to **Note 14b** for additional information and Scriptures relating to the goodness of God within born-again believers.

Please refer to **Notes 24a**, **24b**, **29a**, **29b**, **29c**, **30**, **32a**, and **32b** for additional information and/or Scriptures relating to God's love.

Note 28 Summary:

Notes 28a, **28b**, and **28c** are the character traits and behavior patterns of the new man in Christ. These character traits develop over time as we become rooted and grounded in Him, in the same way a fruit tree bears fruit as it becomes deeply rooted in the earth (*Ephesians 3:14-21*; *Colossians 2:6-7*). In *Galatians 5:22-23*, Paul tells us what "fruit" will be seen in those who choose to grow and mature in Christ, by putting on the new man: love, joy, peace, longsuffering, gentleness, goodness, faith, meekness, and temperance – against such there is no law! These fruits, the attributes of God's nature, are not something we have to make happen; it is the manifestation of the new man. Let's look at each fruit and its Greek meaning:

KJV	Greek Word and Meaning
- love	*agape* – love, i.e. affection or benevolence; specially (plural) a love-feast.
- joy	*chara* – cheerfulness, i.e. calm delight:–gladness, x greatly, (be exceeding) joy(ful, -fully, -fulness, -ous).
- peace	*eirene* – (to join); peace (literally or figuratively); by implication, prosperity:– one, peace, quietness, rest.
- longsuffering	*makrothymia* – longanimity, i.e. (objectively) forbearance or (subjectively)

	fortitude:—longsuffering, patience.
- gentleness	*chrestotes* – usefulness, i.e. morally, excellence (in character or demeanor):–gentleness, good(-ness), kindness.
- goodness	*agathosyne* – goodness, i.e. virtue or beneficence:–goodness.
- faith	*pistis* – fidelity, faithfulness, i.e. the character of one who can be relied on. *(Thayer's Greek Lexicon).*
- meekness	*praotes* – gentleness, by implication, humility:–meekness.
- temperance	*egkrateia* – self-control, (the virtue of one who masters his desires and passions, especially his sensual appetites). *(Thayer's Greek Lexicon).*

In looking at these character traits of the new man, I think it is important to look again at an excerpt from **Note 4a:**

<u>new man</u>

This new man is the born-again creation within. In *John 14:30*, Jesus said to His disciples, *"…for the prince of this world cometh, and hath nothing in me."* Jesus did not have the carnal nature residing within Him as He was not born of a corruptible seed (the seed of Adam), but of an incorruptible seed, by the Holy Spirit and the power of the Most High *(Luke 1:35)*. As we become born again, by an incorruptible seed, the Word of God, we too have the nature of Christ residing within us *(1 Peter 1:22-25)*. As we, the church, choose to allow that incorruptible seed to grow and mature through the renewal process, our carnal nature loses its strength and therefore Satan, the prince of this world, loses his authority in our lives.

<u>foundation</u>

Inspired by the Holy Spirit, Jesus used His holy apostles and prophets to pen His God-breathed Words of truth within the pages of the Bible *(2 Peter 1:17-21; 2 Timothy 3:16-17 – AMPCE)*. We are His temple and God *(Yahweh-Shammah)* dwells within us and He will never leave us nor forsake us *(1 Corinthians 3:16, 6:19-20; 2 Corinthians 6:16; Luke 17:20-21; Hebrews 13:5)*! It is essential that we allow the Holy Spirit to dig deep into the core of our very being, by the Word of God, to remove ungodly mindsets/beliefs, judgments, etc., that are tied to the carnal sin nature, the old man *(Hebrews 4:12)*. As Jesus instructed us,

> *Whosoever cometh to me, and heareth my sayings, and doeth them, I will shew you to whom he is like: he is like a man which built an house, and digged deep, and laid the foundation on a rock: and when the flood arose, the stream beat vehemently upon that house, and could not shake it: for it was founded upon a rock. But he that heareth, and doeth not, is like a man that without a foundation built an house upon the earth; against which the stream did beat vehemently, and immediately it fell; and the ruin of that house was great.*
>
> (Luke 6:47-49)

Now let's look at the following passage of Scripture,

> *When Jesus came into the region of Caesarea Philippi, He asked his disciples, saying, "Whom do men say that I, the Son of Man, am?" So they said, "Some say John the Baptist, some Elijah, and others Jeremiah or one of the prophets." He said to them, "But who do you say that I am?" Simon Peter answered and said, "You are the Christ, the Son of the living God."*

Jesus answered and said to him, "Blessed are you, Simon Barjonah, for flesh and blood has not revealed this to you, but my Father who is in heaven. And I also say to you that you are Peter, and on this <u>rock</u> I will build My church, and the gates of Hades shall not prevail against it."

(Matthew 16:13-18, NKJV)

The word "rock" in both *Matthew 16:18* and *Luke 6:48* in the Greek is *petra* meaning "a (mass of) rock (literally or figuratively):–rock." Its meaning in the Thayer's Greek Lexicon is "metaphorically, <u>a man like a rock, by reason of his firmness and strength of soul</u>: Matthew 16:18." Peter was one of the Lord's apostles and through the revelations contained in the Scriptures written by Peter and the other apostles (i.e., Matthew, Mark, Luke, John, Paul), the church, the body of Christ, is built. Through the firmness and strength of the revelation of who Christ is within each individual member of the body of Christ, the gates of hell cannot prevail against her! This firmness and strength of soul is usually attained through resistance. Let's read *1 Timothy 4:7-8* in order to get a better understanding of this. *"But refuse profane and old wives' fables, and exercise thyself rather unto godliness. For bodily exercise profiteth little: but godliness is profitable unto all things, having promise of the life that now is, and of that which is to come."* The word "exercise" in *1 Timothy 4:7* in the Greek is *gymnazo*. Its meaning in the Thayer's Greek Lexicon is "to exercise vigorously in any way, either in body or the mind: of one who strives earnestly to become godly, 1 Timothy 4:7." God's desire for every member of the body of Christ is to grow in godliness, or in the new man in Christ (e.g., righteousness, holiness, love, joy, perseverance). In order to do this, let's think of someone who uses weights in resistance or strength training. This type of exercise causes muscles to contract against external pressure resulting in a greater strength and firmness. In the same way, spiritually, as we equip ourselves with His Word by renewing our minds to it and "exercise" godly attributes against the pressures and trials of life, we begin to grow strong and firm in who we are in Christ (the new man). I believe this helps to better understand *Acts 14:22* – *"Confirming the souls of the disciples, and exhorting them to continue in the faith, and that we must through much tribulation enter into the kingdom of God."*

In closing, I thought it would be enlightening to look at some Scriptures in the Old Testament concerning the benefits of behaving wisely. The main passage of Scripture I would like to focus on is found in *1 Samuel 18:5, 14-15*:

> *And David went out whithersoever Saul sent him, and behaved himself wisely: and Saul set him over the men of war, and he was accepted in the sight of all the people, and also in the sight of Saul's servants. And David behaved himself wisely in all his ways; and the LORD was with him. Wherefore when Saul saw that he behaved himself very wisely, he was afraid of him.*

The Hebrew word for "<u>behaved himself wisely</u>" is *sakal* meaning "… intelligent:–consider, expert, instruct, <u>prosper</u>, (deal) prudent(-ly), (give) skill(-ful), <u>have good success</u>, teach, (have, make to) understand(-ing), wisdom, (be, behave self, consider, make) wise(-ly), <u>guide wittingly</u>." This same Hebrew word *sakal* is found in *Joshua 1:1-8* when the Lord directed Joshua, after Moses' death, on how to prepare himself to lead the children of Israel into the promised land. In following the Lord's command, Joshua would prosper (*sakal*) and have good success (*sakal*):

> *Only be thou strong and very courageous, that thou mayest observe to do according to all*

the law, which Moses my servant commanded thee: turn not from it to the right hand or to the left, that thou mayest prosper (sakal) whithersoever thou goest. This book of the law shall not depart out of thy mouth; but thou shalt meditate therein day and night, that thou mayest observe to do according to all that is written therein: for then thou shalt make thy way prosperous, and then thou shalt have good success (sakal).

The key to obtaining this was by renewing his heart and mind to the truth of God's Word.

Below are additional Scriptures where the Hebrew word *sakal* is used where underlined:

Psalm 32:8 – <u>I will instruct</u> thee and teach thee in the way which thou shalt go: I will guide thee with mine eye. Psalm 36:3 – The words of his mouth are iniquity and deceit: he hath left off <u>to be wise</u>, and to do good. Psalm 53:2 – God looked down from heaven upon the children of men, to see if there were <u>any that did understand</u>, that did seek God. Psalm 101:1-2 – [A Psalm of David.] I will sing of mercy and judgment: unto thee, O LORD, will I sing. <u>I will behave myself wisely in a perfect way</u>. O when wilt thou come unto me? I will walk within my house with a perfect heart. Psalm 119:99 – <u>I have more understanding</u> than all my teachers: for thy testimonies are my meditation. Proverbs 10:19 – In the multitude of words there wanteth not sin: but he that refraineth his lips is <u>wise</u>. Proverbs 15:24 – The way of life is above <u>to the wise</u>, that he may depart from hell beneath. Proverbs 16:20, 23 – He that handleth a matter <u>wisely</u> shall find good: and who trusteth in the LORD, happy is he. The heart of the wise <u>teacheth</u> his mouth, and addeth learning to his lips. Proverbs 19:14 – House and riches are the inheritance of fathers: <u>and a prudent</u> wife is from the LORD. Jeremiah 9:23-24 – Thus saith the LORD, "Let not the wise man glory in his wisdom, neither let the mighty man glory in his might, let not the rich man glory in his riches: but let him that glorieth glory <u>in this, that he understandeth</u> and knoweth me, that I am the LORD which exercise lovingkindness, judgment, and righteousness, in the earth: for in these things I delight," saith the LORD.

We too will prosper and have good success as we choose to put off the old man and be renewed in the *spirit of our minds,* and put on the new man in Christ proving what is that good, acceptable, and perfect will of God *(Ephesians 4:22-24; Romans 12:1-2)*. In doing this, we will become more Christlike in character and nature, operating out of the light of the knowledge of the glory of God *(2 Corinthians 4:6-7)*. Hallelujah!!

29(a) *Your* love has been poured out in *my heart* through *Your* Holy Spirit Who has been given to *me*. (Romans 5:5-AMPCE)

Let's look at this passage of Scripture in the King James Version: *"…the love of God is <u>shed abroad</u> in our hearts by the Holy Ghost which is given unto us."* The Greek word for "shed abroad" is *ekcheo* meaning "to pour forth; figuratively, to bestow:–gush (pour) out…" There are two passages of Scripture that I would like to share as it relates to this subject matter:

The first Scripture is *John 7:38-39* where Jesus said,

He that believeth on me, as the scripture hath said, out of his belly shall flow rivers of living water. (But this spake he of the Spirit, which they that believe on him should receive: for the Holy Ghost was not yet given; because that Jesus was not yet glorified.)

In order to enjoy the flow of His living water, it is necessary that we yield to Him any earthly thing that He reveals to us that is hindering the flow of His Spirit (e.g., prejudice, sexual immorality, hardness of heart, religion, judgments, hatred). Just as the Lord revealed to the Samaritan woman at Jacob's well her deep need that she was trying to satisfy through men (five husbands and currently living with a man who was not her husband). Jesus is faithful to reveal to us those things that are hindering the flow of His living water (His Spirit) from truly permeating every part of our being in order to bring fulfillment and refreshing to us *(John 4:1-29)*.

The second Scripture is *Ephesians 3:14-21* where Paul writes,

> *For this cause I bow my knees unto the Father of our Lord Jesus Christ, of whom the whole family in heaven and earth is named, that he would grant you, according to the riches of his glory, to be strengthened with might by his Spirit in the inner man; that Christ may dwell in your hearts by faith; that ye, being rooted and grounded in love, may be able to comprehend with all saints what is the breadth, and length, and depth, and height; and to know the love of Christ, which passeth knowledge, that ye might be filled with all the fulness of God. Now unto him that is able to do exceeding abundantly above all that we ask or think, according to the power that worketh in us, unto him be glory in the church by Christ Jesus throughout all ages, world without end. Amen.*

God's love is stronger than any force in heaven or on earth. His love has been shed abroad in our hearts by His Holy Spirit who lives in us. His love is contained within the incorruptible seed of His Word that gives birth to the new creation in Christ within every believer *(1 Peter 1:23-2:3)*. As this new creation in Christ grows within us so does the love of God. In *Mark 4:1-32*, Jesus talks about sowing the Word of God in different types of heart grounds. He talks about the seed being sown on stony ground where the believer is not rooted in the love of God and therefore falls away during times of adversity. He talks about the seed being sown among thorns where the cares of this world, deceitfulness of riches, and the lust of other things choke the word and it becomes unfruitful. Then the Lord talks about the seed sown on good ground (an honest and good heart) such as a believer who hears the Word, receives it, and brings forth fruit with patience, some thirtyfold, some sixty, and some a hundred *(Luke 8:15)*. Then Jesus said,

> *So is the kingdom of God, as if a man should cast seed into the ground; and should sleep, and rise night and day, and the seed should spring and grow up, he knoweth not how. For the earth bringeth forth fruit of herself; first the blade, then the ear, after that the full corn in the ear. But when the fruit is brought forth, immediately he putteth in the sickle, because the harvest is come." And he said, "Whereunto shall we liken the kingdom of God? Or with what comparison shall we compare it? It is like a grain of mustard seed, which, when it is sown in the earth, is less than all the seeds that be in the earth: but when it is sown, it groweth up, and becometh greater than all herbs, and shooteth out great branches; so that the fowls of the air may lodge under the shadow of it.*

(Mark 4:26-32)

In order to live out of the love of God, it is essential that we allow His Words to do a cleansing within our hearts from all that would defile (or pollute) our heart ground *(Galatians 5:22-23; Matthew 15:10-20; Ephesians 5:25-27)*. The Lord uses His written Word and He also speaks on the inside of us to reveal things that are hindering the growth of the incorruptible seed or the life-giving flow of His Spirit.

We are God's creation, who created all things by Jesus Christ *(Ephesians 3:9)*. This creation was distorted after Adam and Eve ate of the tree of the knowledge of good and evil. God has come in the Person of Jesus Christ to restore us back to His original intent, found in the new man in Christ. Only our Creator knows how to satisfy us, His creation, and God through Jesus Christ has made it possible to come into the depths of our being through His Holy Spirit to satisfy the deep longings of our hearts, bringing security where there is insecurity and bringing hope to our hopelessness. Apart from Christ, we look for fulfillment and/or completion through His created (e.g., male, female) or through what the world has to offer (e.g., false glamour, deceitfulness of riches, and the craving and passionate desire for other things, fame, fortune). False religions, traditions of men, deception, wrong mindsets, demonic influences, etc., block the flow of His love from becoming a reality within us. When His Spirit comes to make His abode within our hearts, and as we continue to yield to Him, He reveals to us the reality of His love for us and we become confident and secure in Him, freeing us from our own self-centeredness and insecurities. Christ has come to set us free from sin and to bring healing to our wounded hearts.

Below are Scriptures relating God's love:

1. ***Matthew 24:3-13*** – *And as he sat upon the mount of Olives, the disciples came unto him privately, saying, "Tell us, when shall these things be? And what shall be the sign of thy coming, and of the end of the world?" Jesus answered and said unto them, "Take heed that no man deceive you. For many shall come in my name, saying, 'I am Christ;' and shall deceive many. And ye shall hear of wars and rumours of wars: see that ye be not troubled: for all these things must come to pass, but the end is not yet. For nation shall rise against nation, and kingdom against kingdom: and there shall be famines, and pestilences, and earthquakes, in divers (various) places. All these are the beginning of sorrows. Then shall they deliver you up to be afflicted, and shall kill you: and ye shall be hated of all nations for my name's sake. And then shall many be offended, and shall betray one another, and shall hate one another. And many false prophets shall rise, and shall deceive many. And because iniquity shall abound, the love of many shall wax cold. But he that shall endure unto the end, the same shall be saved."*

Reference:
Proverbs 14:14 – *The backslider in heart shall be filled with his own ways: and a good man shall be satisfied from himself.*

2. ***Galatians 5:1-6*** – *Stand fast therefore in the liberty wherewith Christ hath made us free, and be not entangled again with the yoke of bondage. Behold, I Paul say unto you, that if ye be circumcised, Christ shall profit you nothing. For I testify again to every man that is circumcised, that he is a debtor to do the whole law. Christ is become of no effect unto you, whosoever of you are justified by the law; ye are fallen from grace. For we through the Spirit wait for the hope of righteousness by faith. For in Jesus Christ neither circumcision availeth any thing, nor uncircumcision; but faith which worketh by love.*

References:
Romans 2:28-29 – *For he is not a Jew, which is one outwardly; neither is that circumcision, which is*

outward in the flesh: but he is a Jew, which is one inwardly; and circumcision is that of the heart, in the spirit, and not in the letter; whose praise is not of men, but of God. **Ephesians 6:23** – *Peace be to the brethren,* <u>and love with faith</u>, *from God the Father and the Lord Jesus Christ.* **1 Thessalonians 3:12-13** *– And the Lord make you to increase and abound in love one toward another, and toward all men, even as we do toward you: to the end he may stablish your hearts unblameable in holiness before God, even our Father, at the coming of our Lord Jesus Christ with all his saints.* **1 Timothy 1:1-7, 12-14** *– Paul, an apostle of Jesus Christ by the commandment of God our Saviour, and Lord Jesus Christ, which is our hope; unto Timothy, my own son in the faith: Grace, mercy, and peace, from God our Father and Jesus Christ our Lord. As I besought thee to abide still at Ephesus, when I went into Macedonia, that thou mightest charge some that they teach no other doctrine, neither give heed to fables and endless genealogies, which minister questions, rather than godly edifying which is in faith: so do. Now the end of the commandment is charity (God's love) out of a pure heart, and of a good conscience, and of faith unfeigned (sincere): from which some having swerved have turned aside unto vain jangling (empty talk); desiring to be teachers of the law; understanding neither what they say, nor whereof they affirm. And I thank Christ Jesus our Lord, who hath enabled me, for that he counted me faithful, putting me into the ministry; who was before a blasphemer, and a persecutor, and injurious: but I obtained mercy, because I did it ignorantly in unbelief. And the grace of our Lord was exceeding abundant with faith and love which is in Christ Jesus.* **Hebrews 9:13-14** *– For if the blood of bulls and of goats, and the ashes of an heifer sprinkling the unclean, sanctifieth to the purifying of the flesh: how much more shall the blood of Christ, who through the eternal Spirit offered himself without spot to God, purge your conscience from dead works to serve the living God?*

Below are Scriptures relating to God working in us:

Ephesians 5:25-27 *– Husbands, love your wives, even as Christ also loved the church, and gave himself for it; that he might sanctify and cleanse it with the washing of water by the word, that he might present it to himself a glorious church, not having spot, or wrinkle, or any such thing; but that it should be holy and without blemish.*

References:
Philippians 1:1-6 *– Paul and Timotheus, the servants of Jesus Christ, to all the saints in Christ Jesus which are at Philippi, with the bishops and deacons: Grace be unto you, and peace, from God our Father, and from the Lord Jesus Christ. I thank my God upon every remembrance of you, always in every prayer of mine for you all making request with joy, for your fellowship in the gospel from the first day unto now; being confident of this very thing, that he which hath begun a good work in you will perform it until the day of Jesus Christ.* **Philippians 2:12-13** *– Wherefore, my beloved, as ye have always obeyed, not as in my presence only, but now much more in my absence, work out your own salvation with fear and trembling. For it is God which worketh in you both to will and to do of his good pleasure.* **2 Thessalonians 3:1-5** *– Finally, brethren, pray for us, that the word of the Lord may have free course, and be glorified, even as it is with you: and that we may be delivered from unreasonable and wicked men: for all men have not faith. But the Lord is faithful, who shall stablish you, and keep you from evil. And we have confidence in the Lord touching you, that ye both do and will do the things which we command you. And the Lord direct your hearts into the love of God, and into the patient waiting for Christ.*

Please refer to **Notes 24a**, **24b**, **28c**, **29b**, **29c**, **30**, **32a**, and **32b** for additional information and/or Scriptures relating to God's love.

When we keep God's Word, holding it as the highest value in our lives, we are displaying our love for Christ. Jesus said,

> *"If ye love me, keep my commandments. He that hath my commandments, and keepeth them, he it is that loveth me: and he that loveth me shall be loved of my Father, and I will love him, and will manifest myself to him." Judas saith unto him, not Iscariot, "Lord, how is it that thou wilt manifest thyself unto us, and not unto the world?" Jesus answered and said unto him, "If a man love me, he will keep my words: and my Father will love him, and we will come unto him, and make our abode with him. He that loveth me not keepeth not my sayings: and the word which ye hear is not mine, but the Father's which sent me."*
>
> (John 14:15, 21-24)

Jesus also said,

> *Lay not up for yourselves treasures upon earth, where moth and rust doth corrupt, and where thieves break through and steal: but lay up for yourselves treasures in heaven, where neither moth nor rust doth corrupt, and where thieves do not break through nor steal: for where your treasure is, there will your heart be also.*
>
> (Matthew 6:19-21)

You cannot separate Jesus Christ from His Word as it is written in *John 1:1-3, 14*:

> *In the beginning was the Word, and the Word was with God, and the Word was God. The same was in the beginning with God. All things were made by him; and without him was not any thing made that was made. And the Word was made flesh, and dwelt among us, (and we beheld his glory, the glory as of the only begotten of the Father,) full of grace and truth.*

The word "Word" in the Greek is *logos*. Its meaning in the Thayer's Greek Lexicon "denotes the essential Word of God, i.e. the personal (hypostatic) wisdom and power in union with God, his minister in the creation and government of the universe, the cause of all the world's life both physical and ethical, which for the procurement of man's salvation put on human nature in the person of Jesus the Messiah and shone forth conspicuously from his words and deeds." Jesus said,

> *"Not every one that saith unto me, 'Lord, Lord,' shall enter into the kingdom of heaven; but he that doeth the will of my Father which is in heaven. Many will say to me in that day, 'Lord, Lord, have we not prophesied in thy name? And in thy name have cast out devils? And in thy name done many wonderful works?' And then will I profess unto them, I never knew you: depart from me, ye that work iniquity. Therefore <u>whosoever heareth these sayings of mine, and doeth them, I will liken him unto a wise man, which built his house upon a rock</u>."*
>
> (Matthew 7:21-24)

This is a very powerful passage of Scripture. First, the word "sayings" is the same Greek word *logos*. Second, just think, the Creator of the universe, came down from Heaven and gave Himself for mankind. Through the power of His Holy Spirit, He worked miracles, walked on water, raised the dead, and did many other things that if all were accounted for, one by one, even the world itself could not contain the books that would be written *(John 21:25)*. This same Jesus has made it possible for us to build our house upon a rock, revelation knowledge of Christ within our own souls, through not only being a hearer of His Word but a doer also, causing our lives to take on a whole new meaning of life and joy *(John 10:10; Romans 14:17)*! To those who love Him by keeping or treasuring His Word, the Lord Jesus Christ and God the Father makes their residence within and forever changes their lives through regeneration and transformation *(John 14:23; Titus 3:3-6; Romans 12:1-2)*.

As an example of how we should treasure the Word of God, let's look at Shadrach, Meshach, and Abednego who by the request of Daniel to King Nebuchadnezzar were set over the affairs of the province of Babylon *(Daniel 2:49)*. *Daniel 3:1-30* gives the account of these three young men who chose not to serve Nebuchadnezzar's gods nor fall down and worship the golden image that King Nebuchadnezzar had set up. The king gave proclamation to all peoples, nations, and languages that at what time they heard all kinds of music playing that they should fall down and worship the golden image that he had set up. He also said that whoever did not fall down and worship would be cast into a burning fiery furnace. Therefore, when all the people heard the sound of all kinds of music, all the peoples, nations, and languages fell down and worshipped the golden image. However, Shadrach, Meshach, and Abednego, honoring the Lord God by not putting other gods before Him, did not succumb to the "peer pressure," what the king or others may have thought of them, nor the fear of being thrown into the fiery furnace. When King Nebuchadnezzar was told that these three men did not worship the golden image, the king was full of rage and had them brought before him. He said,

> *Is it true, O Shadrach, Meshach, and Abednego, do not ye serve my gods, nor worship the golden image which I have set up? Now if ye be ready that at what time ye hear the sound of the cornet, flute, harp, sackbut, psaltery, and dulcimer, and all kinds of musick, ye fall down and worship the image which I have made; well: but if ye worship not, ye shall be cast the same hour into the midst of a burning fiery furnace; and who is that God that shall deliver you out of my hands?*
>
> (Daniel 3:14-15)

The three young men responded with,

> *O Nebuchadnezzar, we are not careful to answer thee in this matter. If it be so, our God whom we serve is able to deliver us from the burning fiery furnace, and he will deliver us out of thine hand, O king. But if not, be it known unto thee, O king, that we will not serve thy gods, nor worship the golden image which thou hast set up.*
>
> (Daniel 3:16-18)

These three young men were wholeheartedly committed to their God! They knew that their God was well able to deliver them from the fiery furnace but regardless, even if the Lord chose not to deliver them, they would not serve the king's gods nor worship the golden image. Again, they are an example of how we should treasure our relationship with our Lord and Savior, Jesus Christ.

The story continues:

Then was Nebuchadnezzar full of fury, and the form of his visage (face) was changed against Shadrach, Meshach, and Abednego: therefore he spake, and commanded that they should heat the furnace one seven times more that it was wont (usually) to be heated. And he commanded the most mighty men that were in his army to bind Shadrach, Meshach, and Abednego, and to cast them into the burning fiery furnace. Then these men were bound in their coats, their hosen, and their hats, and their other garments, and were cast into the midst of the burning fiery furnace. Therefore because the king's commandment was urgent, and the furnace exceeding hot, the flame of the fire slew (killed) those men that took up Shadrach, Meshach, and Abednego. And these three men, Shadrach, Meshach, and Abednego, fell down bound into the midst of the burning fiery furnace. Then Nebuchadnezzar the king was astonied (astonished), and rose up in haste, and spake, and said unto his counsellors, "Did not we cast three men bound into the midst of the fire?" they answered and said unto the king, "True, O King." He answered and said, "Lo, I see four men loose, walking in the midst of the fire, and they have no hurt; and the form of the fourth is like the Son of God." Then Nebuchadnezzar came near to the mouth of the burning fiery furnace, and spake, and said, "Shadrach, Meshach, and Abednego, ye servants of the most high God, come forth, and come hither (here)." Then Shadrach, Meshach, and Abednego, came forth of the midst of the fire. And the princes, governors, and captains, and the king's counsellors, being gathered together, saw these men, upon whose bodies the fire had no power, nor was an hair of their head singed, neither were their coats changed, nor the smell of fire had passed on them. Then Nebuchadnezzar spake, and said, "Blessed be the God of Shadrach, Meshach, and Abednego, who hath sent his angel, and delivered his servants that trusted in him, and have changed the king's word, and yielded their bodies, that they might not serve nor worship any god, except their own God."

(Daniel 3:19-28)

Just as Shadrach, Meshach, and Abednego were not harmed in the fiery furnace, God desires to do such a work in our own hearts and minds through the purification and sanctification of His Word *(Malachi 3:2-3; Titus 3:4-7)*. As we allow God's Word to have its way in us, it will begin to purify, refine, and remove all the ingrained carnal beliefs and mindsets or toxic waste (e.g., rebellion, pride, evil thoughts, fears). So, when we are faced with the fiery trials of life, we will not be singed or harmed, knowing Jesus is with us. Our bodies may be destroyed, but our true self, our inner man, will not be harmed *(Hebrews 12:25-29; 1 Peter 4:12-19)*!

As Shadrach, Meshach, and Abednego said,

If it be so, our God whom we serve is able to deliver us from the burning fiery furnace, and he will deliver us out of thine hand, O king. But if not, be it known unto thee, O king, that we will not serve thy gods, nor worship the golden image which thou hast set up.

(Daniel 3:17-18)

We need to settle this in our own hearts and minds as well, to stand with Christ in the good times and in the times of fiery trials. Just as John writes,

And I heard a loud voice saying in heaven, "Now is come salvation, and strength, and the kingdom of our God, and the power of his Christ: for the accuser of our brethren is cast down, which accused them before our God day and night. And they overcame him by the blood of the Lamb, and by the word of their testimony; and they loved not their lives unto the death."

(Revelation 12:10-11)

The Old Testament saints, Abraham, Moses, Sarah, Deborah, David, Daniel, Shadrach, Meshach, and Abednego, etc., did not have the Spirit of the living God dwelling on the inside of them as we do. God is calling us to a higher and more glorious standard. It is only through the born-again creation that we can truly walk in the love of Christ. It is essential that we grow and mature in Christ in order to walk as He walked.

So, let us cultivate our relationship with the Lord and repent of anything less than wholehearted worship and service toward Him. He is the one true and living God who displayed His love for us by sending His only begotten Son, Jesus Christ, into the world that we might "live" in Him. If God so loved us to give His only Son so that we have the amazing privilege to live in Him, we should love Him wholeheartedly and love one another as Jesus commanded, even as He has loved us *(Acts 17:28; John 15:12; 1 John 4:9-11)*. It is written in *1 John 4:20-21,*

If a man say, I love God, and hateth his brother, he is a liar: for he that loveth not his brother whom he hath seen, how can he love God whom he hath not seen? And this commandment have we from him, that he who loveth God love his brother also.

You cannot separate Christ from His church as Christ said in *Matthew 25:31-46, "...Verily I say unto you, inasmuch as ye have done it unto one of the least of these my brethren, ye have done it unto me."* Jesus also said in *John 15:13 – "Greater love hath no man than this, that a man lay down his life for his friends."* In this, Jesus is asking us to die to our carnal nature which blocks His love from flowing from our hearts to others:

1. **Romans 13:8** – *Owe no man any thing, but to love one another: for he that loveth another hath fulfilled the law.*
2. **Galatians 2:20** – *Paul said, "I am crucified with Christ: nevertheless I live; yet not I, but Christ liveth in me: and the life which I now live in the flesh I live by the faith of the Son of God, who loved me, and gave himself for me."*
3. **Galatians 5:24** – *And they that are Christ's have crucified the flesh with the affections and lusts.*

In *Matthew 22:36*, one of the Pharisees who was a lawyer asked Jesus, *"Master, which is the great commandment in the law?"* Jesus said to him,

Thou shalt love the Lord thy God with all thy heart, and with all thy soul, and with all thy mind. This is the first and great commandment. And the second is like unto it, thou, shalt love thy neighbour as thyself. On these two commandments hang all the law and the prophets.

(Matthew 22:37-40)

Paul writes,

> *And I, brethren could not speak unto you as unto spiritual, but as unto carnal, even as unto babes in Christ. I have fed you with milk, and not with meat: for hitherto ye were not able to bear it, neither yet now are ye able. For ye are yet carnal: for whereas there is among you envying, and strife, and divisions, are ye not carnal, and walk as men?*
>
> (1 Corinthians 3:1-3)

This passage of Scripture reveals that as long as we are babes in Christ we cannot truly walk in the love of God. The Lord is calling us to put on the new man, to put on Christ, for in this new creation dwells the wisdom, power, and love of God *(Romans 13:14; 2 Corinthians 3:17-18; Ephesians 4:20-24; 1 Peter 3:4; Galatians 3:27; James 1:21-25; Romans 5:5)*. This treasure is contained in our hearts, in these earthen vessels *(2 Corinthians 4:6-11)*!

Below are Scriptures relating to treasuring God's Word and loving others:

1. ***Psalm 91:14-16*** *— God said, "Because he hath set his love upon me, therefore will I deliver him: I will set him on high, because he hath known my name. He shall call upon me, and I will answer him: I will be with him in trouble; I will deliver him, and honour him. With long life will I satisfy him, and shew him my salvation.*

Reference:
John 15:7-13 *— Jesus said, "If ye abide in me, and my words abide in you, ye shall ask what ye will, and it shall be done unto you. Herein is my Father glorified, that ye bear much fruit; so shall ye be my disciples. As the Father hath loved me, so have I loved you: continue ye in my love. If ye keep my commandments, ye shall abide in my love; even as I have kept my Father's commandments, and abide in his love. These things have I spoken unto you, that my joy might remain in you, and that your joy might be full. This is my commandment, that ye love one another, as I have loved you. Greater love hath no man that this, that a man lay down his life for his friends."*

2. ***1 Thessalonians 4:9-12*** *— But as touching brotherly love ye need not that I write unto you: for ye yourselves are taught of God to love one another. And indeed ye do it toward all the brethren which are in all Macedonia: but we beseech you, brethren, that ye increase more and more, and that ye study to be quiet, and to do your own business, and to work with your own hands, as we commanded you; that ye may walk honestly toward them that are without (those who are not Christians), and that ye may have lack of nothing.*

References:
Romans 12:10 *— Be kindly affectionate one to another with brotherly love; in honour preferring one another.* ***Romans 13:8-14*** *— Owe no man anything, but to love one another: for he that loveth another hath fulfilled the law. For this, 'Thou shalt not commit adultery,' 'Thou shalt not kill,' 'Thou shalt not steal,' 'Thou shalt not bear false witness,' 'Thou shalt not covet;' and if there be any other commandment, it is briefly comprehended in this saying, namely, 'Thou shalt love thy neighbour as thyself.'* <u>*Love worketh no ill to his neighbour: therefore love is the fulfilling of the law.*</u> *And that, knowing the time, that now it is high time to awake out of sleep: for now is our salvation nearer than when we believed. The night is far spent, the day is at hand: let us therefore cast off the works of darkness, and let us put on the armour of light. Let us walk*

honestly, as in the day; not in rioting and drunkenness, not in chambering and wantonness, not in strife and envying. But put ye on the Lord Jesus Christ, and make not provision for the flesh, to fulfil the lusts thereof. **Galatians 5:13-16** – *For, brethren, ye have been called unto liberty; only use not liberty for an occasion to the flesh, but by love serve one another. For all the law is fulfilled in one word, even in this; "Thou shalt love thy neighbour as thyself." But if ye bite and devour one another, take heed that ye be not consumed one of another. This I say then, walk in the Spirit, and ye shall not fulfil the lust of the flesh.* **Galatians 6:1-3** – *Brethren, if a man be overtaken in a fault, ye which are spiritual, restore such an one in the spirit of meekness; considering thyself, lest thou also be tempted. Bear ye one another's burdens, and so fulfil the law of Christ. For if a man think himself to be something, when he is nothing, he deceiveth himself.* **1 Thessalonians 3:12-13** – *And the Lord make you to increase and abound in love one toward another, and toward all men, even as we do toward you: to the end he may stablish your hearts unblameable in holiness before God, even our Father, at the coming of our Lord Jesus Christ with all his saints.* **James 2:8-11** – *If ye fulfil the royal law according to the scripture, "Thou shalt love thy neighbour as thyself," ye do well. But if ye have respect to persons (show partiality), ye commit sin, and are convinced of the law as transgressors. For whosoever shall keep the whole law, and yet offend in one point, he is guilty of all. For he that said, "Do not commit adultery," said also, "Do not kill." Now if thou commit no adultery, yet if thou kill, thou art become a transgressor of the law.* **1 Peter 1:22-25** – *Seeing ye have purified your souls in obeying the truth through the Spirit unto unfeigned (sincere) love of the brethren, see that ye love one another with a pure heart fervently: being born again, not of corruptible seed, but of incorruptible, by the word of God, which liveth and abideth for ever. For all flesh is as grass, and all the glory of man as the flower of grass. The grass withereth, and the flower thereof falleth away: but the word of the Lord endureth for ever. And this is the word which by the gospel is preached unto you.* **1 John 2:3-11, 15-17** – *And hereby we do know that we know him, if we keep his commandments. He that saith, I know him, and keepeth not his commandments, is a liar, and the truth is not in him. But whoso keepeth his word, in him verily is the love of God perfected: hereby know we that we are in him. He that saith he abideth in him ought himself also so to walk, even as he walked. Brethren, I write no new commandment unto you, but an old commandment which ye had from the beginning. The old commandment is the word which ye have heard from the beginning. Again, a new commandment I write unto you, which thing is true in him and in you: because the darkness is past, and the true light now shineth. He that saith he is in the light, and hateth his brother, is in darkness even until now. He that loveth his brother abideth in the light, and there is none occasion of stumbling in him. But he that hateth his brother is in darkness, and walketh in darkness, and knoweth not whither he goeth, because that darkness hath blinded his eyes. Love not the world, neither the things that are in the world. If any man love the world, the love of the Father is not in him. For all that is in the world, the lust of the flesh, and the lust of the eyes, and the pride of life, is not of the Father, but is of the world. And the world passeth away, and the lust thereof: but he that doeth the will of God abideth for ever.* **1 John 3:23-24** – *And this is his commandment, that we should believe on the name of his Son Jesus Christ, and love one another, as he gave us commandment. And he that keepeth his commandments dwelleth in him, and he in him. And hereby we know that he abideth in us, by the Spirit which he hath given us.* **1 John 4:8-21** – *He that loveth not knoweth not God; for God is love. In this was manifested the love of God toward us, because that God sent his only begotten Son into the world, that we might live through him. Herein is love, not that we loved God, but that he loved us, and sent his Son to be the propitiation for our sins. Beloved, if God so loved us, we ought also to love one another. No man hath seen God at any time. If we love one another, God dwelleth in us, and his love is perfected in us. Hereby know we that we dwell in him, and he in us, because he hath given us of his Spirit. And we have seen and do testify that the Father sent the Son to be the Saviour of the world. Whosoever shall confess that Jesus is the Son of God, God dwelleth in him, and he in God. And we have known and believed the love that God hath to us. God is love; and he that dwelleth in love dwelleth in*

God, and God in him. Herein is our love made perfect, that we may have boldness in the day of judgment: because as he is, so are we in this world. There is no fear in love; but perfect love casteth out fear: because fear hath torment. He that feareth is not made perfect love. We love him, because he first loved us. If a man say, "I love God," and hateth his brother, he is a liar: for he that loveth not his brother whom he hath seen, how can he love God whom he hath not seen? And this commandment have we from him, that he who loveth God love his brother also.

Please refer to **Notes 24a**, **24b**, **28c**, **29a**, **29c**, **30**, **32a**, and **32b** for additional information and/or Scriptures relating to God's love.

29(c) *I yield to Your love,* which springs from a pure heart and a good (clear) conscience and sincere (unfeigned) faith. (1 Timothy 1:5-AMPCE)

This passage of Scripture is found in *1 Timothy 1:5* which reads in the King James Version – *"Now the end of the commandment is charity (God's love) out of a pure heart, and of a good conscience, and of faith unfeigned (sincere)."* In order to yield to God's love, it is essential for us to yield to Him our sinful nature and to release to Him our fears (e.g., anxieties, cares, worries, unforgiveness, offenses, control, our own self-centeredness), allowing Him to cleanse us from defilement (pollutants) and to bring healing to our wounded hearts (please refer to **Note 9** and ***A Personal Prayer Journal – From your heart to His – Details and Instructions - Volume 1***). This is certainly a process as Peter describes,

> *...according as his divine power hath given unto us all things that pertain unto life and godliness, through the knowledge of him that hath called us to glory and virtue: whereby are given unto us exceeding great and precious promises: that by these ye might be partakers of the divine nature, having escaped the corruption that is in the world through lust. And beside this, giving all diligence, add to your faith virtue; and to virtue knowledge; and to knowledge temperance; and to temperance patience; and to patience godliness; and to godliness brotherly kindness; and to brotherly kindness charity (God's love). For if these things be in you, and abound, they make you that ye shall neither be barren nor unfruitful in the knowledge of our Lord Jesus Christ. But he that lacketh these things is blind; and cannot see afar off, and hath forgotten that he was purged from his old sins.*
>
> (2 Peter 1:1-9)

As Paul said in *Acts 24:16*, *"And herein do I <u>exercise</u> myself, to have always a conscience void of offence toward God, and toward men."* It is important for us to exercise – train or strive – to always have a conscience void of offence toward God and toward men. We need to line ourselves up with what God thinks is just and right rather than what our flesh thinks is just and right based on how we think or feel! In order to do this, it is essential that we renew the *spirit of our minds* to the truth of God's Word. In *Acts 24:16*, the word "exercise" in the Greek is *askeo* and is used only once in the New Testament and means "to elaborate, i.e. (figuratively) train (by implication, strive):–exercise." Paul also writes,

> *But refuse profane and old wives' fables, and <u>exercise</u> thyself rather unto <u>godliness</u>. For bodily exercise profiteth little: but godliness is profitable unto all things, having promise of the life that now is, and of that which is to come.*
>
> (1 Timothy 4:7-8)

In *verse 7*, the word "exercise" in the Greek is *gymnazo* and means "to practise naked (in the games), i.e. train (figuratively):–exercise." Its meaning in the Thayer's Greek Lexicon is "to exercise vigorously, in any way, either the body or the mind, of one who strives earnestly to become godly, 1 Timothy 4:7." When giving this definition, the Thayer's Greek Lexicon refers to *Hebrews 5:14* which reads – *"But strong meat belongeth to them that are of full age, <u>even those who by reason of use have their senses exercised to discern both good and evil</u>."* I believe the Greek meaning "to practice naked (in the game), i.e. train" is referring to stripping off all hindrances of the old man in order to fully engage in the task of growing in Christ! In reading the above passage of Scripture *(Hebrews 5:14)*, I'm reminded of the following passage where Paul writes:

> *And I, brethren, could not speak unto you as unto spiritual, but as unto carnal, even as unto babes in Christ. I have fed you with milk, and not with meat: for hitherto ye were not able to bear it, neither yet now are ye able. For ye are yet carnal: for whereas there is among you envying, and strife, and divisions, are ye not carnal, and walk as men?*
>
> (1 Corinthians 3:1-3)

The Lord is calling us to become deeply rooted in Him through partaking of the strong meat of the Word. The Greek word for "godliness" is *eusebeia* meaning "piety; specially, the gospel scheme:– godliness, <u>holiness</u>." Paul writes,

> *But you did not so learn Christ! Assuming that you have really heard Him and been taught by Him, as [all] Truth is in Jesus [embodied and personified in Him], strip yourselves of your former nature [put off and discard your old unrenewed self] which characterized your previous manner of life and becomes corrupt through lusts and desires that spring from delusion; and be constantly renewed in the spirit of your mind [having a fresh mental and spiritual attitude], and put on the new nature (the regenerate self) created in God's image, [Godlike] in true righteousness and holiness.*
>
> (Ephesians 4:20-24, AMPCE)

Our new nature (the new man or hidden man of the heart) is where true godliness (true righteousness and holiness) is produced and in the sight of God is of great price *(1 Peter 3:4)*. It is in yielding to the nurture and development of this new creation within us that His love springs forth!

Let's look again at what I shared earlier in **Note 28c**,

> Circumcision of the heart is the key to living out of God's love and therefore experiencing abundant life in Christ! The Lord said in *Deuteronomy 10:16 – "Circumcise therefore the foreskin of your heart, and be no more stiffnecked."* The foreskin of our heart is the flesh, carnality—the old man and its protective coverings. As I shared in ***My Story – Part Two - Volume 1***, the Lord removed a protective covering from my heart by His Word and by the power of His Spirit. Here is a brief summary of what happened: After about fifteen years of walking with the Lord, He revealed to me that my defense mechanisms, the carnal protective covering and ingrained carnal mindsets (e.g., argumentativeness, anger, protecting my right to be right), were keeping me from being hurt, because of my own deep-seated fears and insecurities. However, it was also keeping me from growing into His image and bearing the fruit of the Spirit, the life-giving attributes of

His nature. He began teaching me how to die to those carnal defense mechanisms by renewing my mind to the new man in Christ and releasing my fears, hurts, pains, etc., to Him, trusting in His love for me in every area of my life. As an example, a peach seed is protected by its pit. The pit must be removed in order for the seed, when planted into good ground, to grow into its destiny of being a mature peach tree producing fruit. So too I was <u>not</u> able to grow spiritually until the carnal protective covering within me was removed and the ingrained carnal beliefs and mindsets were flushed out through the renewal process. Please see *My Story – Part Two - Volume 1* for details.

Below are Scriptures relating to purity of heart and mind:

1. ***Proverbs 15:26*** – *The thoughts of the wicked are an abomination to the LORD: but the words of the pure are pleasant words.*

References:
*Psalm 12:6 – the words of the LORD are pure words: as silver tried in a furnace of earth, purified seven times. **Psalm 19:14** – Let the words of my mouth, and the meditation of my heart, be acceptable in thy sight, O LORD, my strength, and my redeemer. **Psalm 119:9** – Wherewithal shall a young man cleanse his way? By taking heed thereto according to thy word. **Proverbs 30:5** – Every word of God is pure: he is a shield unto them that put their trust in him. **Romans 12:9** – Let love be without dissimulation (hypocrisy). Abhor what is evil; cleave to that which is good. **Ephesians 5:25-32** – Husbands, love your wives, even as Christ also loved the church, and gave himself for it; that he might sanctify and cleanse it with the washing of water by the word, that he might present it to himself a glorious church, not having spot, or wrinkle, or any such thing; but that it should be holy and without blemish. So ought men to love their wives as their own bodies. He that loveth his wife loveth himself. For no man ever yet hated his own flesh; but nourisheth and cherisheth it, even as the Lord the church: for we are members of his body, of his flesh, and of his bones. For this cause shall a man leave his father and mother, and shall be joined unto his wife, and they two shall be one flesh. This is a great mystery: but I speak of Christ and the church. (The word of God cleanses and purifies our hearts and minds). **2 Timothy 2:22** – Flee also youthful lusts: but follow righteousness, faith, charity (God's love), peace, with them that call on the Lord out of a pure heart. **Titus 1:15-16** – Unto the pure all things are pure: but unto them that are defiled and unbelieving is nothing pure; but even their mind and conscience is defiled. They profess that they know God; but in works they deny him, being abominable, and disobedient, and unto every good work reprobate (castaway/rejected). **1 John 3:19-24** – And hereby we know that we are of the truth, and shall assure our hearts before him. For if our heart condemn us, God is greater than our heart, and knoweth all things. Beloved, if our heart condemn us not, then have we confidence toward God. And whatsoever we ask, we receive of him, because we keep his commandments, and do those things that are pleasing in his sight. And this is his commandment, that we should believe on the name of his Son Jesus Christ, and love one another, as he gave us commandment. And he that keepeth his commandments dwelleth in him, and he in him. And hereby we know that he abideth in us, by the Spirit which he hath given us.*

2. ***2 Corinthians 1:12*** – *For our rejoicing is this, the testimony of our conscience, that in simplicity and godly sincerity, not with fleshly wisdom, but by the grace of God, we have had our conversation (behavior) in the world, and more abundantly to you-ward (toward you).*

References:
Isaiah 57:19-21 – "I create the fruit of the lips; Peace, peace to him that is far off, and to him that is near,"

*saith the LORD; "and I will heal him." But the wicked are like the troubled sea, when it cannot rest, whose waters cast up mire and dirt. "There is no peace," saith my God, "to the wicked." **Matthew 12:34-37** – Jesus said, "O generation of vipers, how can ye, being evil, speak good things? For out of the abundance of the heart the mouth speaketh. A good man out of the good treasure of the heart bringeth forth good things: and an evil man out of the evil treasure bringeth forth evil things. But I say unto you, that every idle word that men shall speak, they shall give account thereof in the day of judgment. For by thy words thou shalt be justified, and by thy words thou shalt be condemned." **2 Corinthians 10:3-6** – For though we walk in the flesh, we do not war after the flesh: (for the weapons of our warfare are not carnal, but mighty through God to the pulling down of strong holds;) casting down imaginations, and every high thing that exalteth itself against the knowledge of God, and bringing into captivity every thought to the obedience of Christ; and having in a readiness to revenge all disobedience, when your obedience is fulfilled. **1 Timothy 1:18-19** – This charge I commit unto thee, son Timothy, according to the prophecies which went before on thee, that thou by them mightest war a good warfare; holding faith, and a good conscience; which some having put away concerning faith have made shipwreck. **1 Timothy 3:8-9** – Likewise must the deacons be grave (honorable), not doubletongued, not given to much wine, not greedy of filthy lucre (money); holding the mystery of the faith in a pure conscience. **Hebrews 10:22** – Let us draw near with a true heart in full assurance of faith, having our hearts sprinkled from an evil conscience,… **Hebrews 12:1-2** – Wherefore seeing we also are compassed about with so great a cloud of witnesses, let us lay aside every weight, and the sin which doth so easily beset us, and let us run with patience the race that is set before us, looking unto Jesus the author and finisher of our faith… **James 1:5-8** – If any of you lack wisdom, let him ask of God, that giveth to all men liberally, and upbraideth not; and it shall be given him. But let him ask in faith, nothing wavering. For he that wavereth is like a wave of the sea driven with the wind and tossed. For let not that man think that he shall receive any thing of the Lord. A double minded man is unstable in all his ways. **James 3:8-18** – But the tongue can no man tame; it is an unruly evil, full of deadly poison. Therewith bless we God, even the Father; and therewith curse we men, which are made after the similitude (likeness) of God. Out of the same mouth proceedeth blessing and cursing. My brethren, these things ought not so to be. Doth a fountain send forth at the same place sweet water and bitter? Can the fig tree, my brethren, bear olive berries? Either a vine, figs? So can no fountain both yield salt water and fresh. Who is a wise man and endued with knowledge among you? Let him shew out of a good conversation (behavior) his works with meekness of wisdom. But if ye have bitter envying and strife in your hearts, glory not, and lie not against the truth. This wisdom descendeth not from above, but is earthly, sensual, devilish. For where envying and strife is, there is confusion and every evil work. But the wisdom that is from above is first pure, then peaceable, gentle, and easy to be intreated, full of mercy and good fruits, without partiality, and without hypocrisy. And the fruit of righteousness is sown in peace of them that make peace. **James 4:7-8** – Submit yourselves therefore to God. Resist the devil, and he will flee from you. Draw nigh (near) to God, and he will draw nigh (near) to you. Cleanse your hands, ye sinners; and purify your hearts, ye double minded.*

Please refer to **Notes 24a**, **24b**, **28c**, **29a**, **29b**, **30**, **32a**, and **32b** for additional information and Scriptures relating to God's love.

Please refer to **Note 41** for additional information and/or Scriptures relating to a your conscience.

30. *So now, I put on love...*

- *Your* love *in me* endures long and is patient and kind.
- *Your* love *in me* rejoices in the truth.
- *Your* love *in me* bears all things. *It is a safe place for others.*
- *Your love in me* is ever ready to believe the best of every person. Its hopes are fadeless under all circumstances.
- *Your love in me* endures everything [without weakening].
- *Your love in me* never fails. (1 Corinthians 13:4-AMPCE, 13:6-7, 13:7-8-AMPCE) *(Ref.: Colossians 3:14)*

This is what springs forth from a pure heart, a good clear conscience, and sincere faith; the very essence of our Lord Jesus Christ through His Holy Spirit, rivers of living water, flowing forth from the heart of born-again believers *(John 7:38-39)*. The end result of His love flowing out of the heart of man is that *"His love never fails!"* For the first twenty years of my walk with the Lord, when I would read in *Galatians 5:22-23* about the fruit of the Spirit or *Colossians 3:12-17* about the behavior of the new man, I would become perplexed. I could not see how to produce that fruit or behavior in my own life, especially at home, even though I spent much time in God's Word and desired to be obedient to Him in every area of my life! I remember hearing a pastor share about the fruit of the Spirit and he compared it to a fruit-bearing tree. He said that the tree doesn't have to force the fruit to come out, the fruit just comes forth because of the maturity of the tree. I didn't understand why the fruit of the Spirit was not evident in my own life, I just had to continue to trust God with this dilemma as it would cause frustration within me if I meditated on it too long. As I share in *My Story – Part Two - Volume 1*, there was a protective covering within me that came from a deep-seated root of rebellion. It was blocking the flow of the wellspring of living water and keeping the born-again creation, my true self, from becoming a reality within me. Once that protective covering was removed, through a radical change of mind, I could see the fruit of the Spirit operating in my life! This radical change of mind is what Paul calls "washing of regeneration" in *Titus 3:5*, a spiritual renovation that took place in my mind, by renewing the *spirit of my mind* to the born-again creation within by using the *Personalized Scripture Guide - Volume 1*. Now I can attest to what the pastor shared; it is not something I try to make happen, it just happens and has been life changing for me! The rivers of living water, His Holy Spirit within, is essential to draw from when presented with difficult situations in life and in order to enjoy life's journey while here on earth *(John 7:37-39)*. Most importantly, it enables us to be witnesses unto Christ and His glory *(Acts 1:8)*. I give God much thanks for this treasure that He has given to us in our earthen vessels – *Christ in you, the hope of glory (2 Corinthians 4:6-7, Colossians 1:27)*!

I recommend reading the book *Sparkling Gems from the Greek* by Rick Renner in order to gain a better understanding of *1 Corinthians 13* and many other Scriptures in the New Testament.

Please refer to **Notes 24a, 24b, 28c, 29a, 29b, 29c, 32a,** and **32b** for additional information and/or Scriptures relating to God's love.

31. When I was a child, I talked like a child, I thought like a child, I reasoned like a child; now that I have become a (wo)man, I am done with childish ways and have put them aside, *so...*
  - *Your* love *in me is* not envious nor boils over with jealousy.
  - *Your love in me* is not boastful or vainglorious.
  - *Your love in me* does not display itself haughtily.
  - *Your love in me* is not conceited (arrogant and inflated with pride).
  - *Your love in me* is not rude (unmannerly) and does not act unbecomingly.
  - *Your* love *in me* does not insist on its own rights or its own way, for it is not self-seeking.
  - *Your love in me* is not easily provoked [*it is not* overly sensitive *nor* easily angered].
  - *Your love in me* thinks no evil. It takes no account of the evil done to it [it pays no attention to a suffered wrong].
  - *Your love in me* does not rejoice in inquity (*in justice and unrighteousness*), but rejoices in the truth. (1 Corinthians 13:11, 4, 5-AMPCE, 13:5-AMP, 13:5-6)

It's important to understand what is not God's love! These actions are part of our carnal nature, the old man, and when living out of ingrained carnal mindsets, our soul can be like a spoiled child! When we are self-centered and things do not go our way we may become touchy, fretful, or resentful, act rude, or insist on our own rights or our own way. When someone receives something that we desire we may become envious or jealous. Also, when we think we have arrived or think that we are God's gift to humanity, we can become conceited, arrogant, and inflated with pride, even rude. We are not to rejoice in our carnal attitudes or actions but rather in our true self, the new man in Christ (*Ephesians 4:20-24*). Paul writes,

> *And I, brethren could not speak unto you as unto spiritual, but as unto carnal, even as unto babes in Christ. I have fed you with milk, and not with meat: for hitherto ye were not able to bear it, neither yet now are ye able. For ye are yet carnal: for whereas there is among you envying, and strife, and divisions, are ye not carnal, and walk as men?*
>
> (1 Corinthians 3:1-3)

Someone who is a babe in Christ behaves in much the same way as someone who is not born again because he or she is not spiritually mature enough to walk in the ways of Christ. The way to overcome these behavior patterns and mindsets is to continue to grow in Christ through prayer and submission to Him. Put off the old man by being real (honest) with the Lord, feeding on the sincere milk of the Word of God, and continuing to renew the *spirit of your mind* or your *inmost mind* to the truth of His Word concerning the new man in Christ (*1 Peter 2:3; Ephesians 4:22-24*). Producing the fruit of the Spirit in one's life takes time, so be patient with yourself and consistent in your walk with the Lord (*Luke 8:11-15; Galatians 5:22-24*). As an example, I had been walking with the Lord for twenty years before a protective covering was removed from within me that was keeping me bound to many aspects of the old man and keeping me from growing in Christ. As soon as the covering was removed, I said to the Lord, "This is it! This is what everybody is looking for! How can I help others get here?" **Character Development in Christ** is the answer to my prayer! Mature believers may be tempted to act out of these behaviors at one time or another, but because of their maturity in Christ, are well aware that these behaviors are coming from the carnal nature and are quick to reject them (*2 Corinthians 10:3-6*).

There is a difference between the tender, innocent heart of a child and childish behavior as listed above. Young children have a tender, innocent heart and believe most anything they are told. Unfortunately, after years of living in a fallen world and internalizing life's dynamics through fear and/or through woundings of the heart (i.e., pain and suffering), their hearts can become hardened and in turn they can become very insecure and/or prideful. This is where God wants to restore purity of heart and mind back to His children. In the two passages of Scripture below, Jesus is referring to what I believe to be the importance of born-again believers having a tender, innocent heart and believing the Words of their heavenly Father, regardless of circumstances (*2 Corinthians 4:18*):

1. *Matthew 18:1-4 – At the same time came the disciples unto Jesus, saying, "Who is the greatest in the kingdom of heaven?" And Jesus called a little child unto him, and set him in the midst of them, and said, "Verily I say unto you, except ye be converted, and become as little children, ye shall not enter into the kingdom of heaven. Whosoever therefore shall humble himself as this little child, the same is greatest in the kingdom of heaven."*
2. *Matthew 19:13-14 – Then were there brought unto him little children, that he should put his hands on them, and pray: and the disciples rebuked them. But Jesus said, "Suffer little children, and forbid them not, to come unto me: for of such is the kingdom of heaven."*

As we continue to press forward in the things of God, living and operating out of His kingdom becomes more of a reality within us. Through our Lord and Savior's final sacrifice of Himself, He took on the impact of fallen humanity and by His blood and through the power of His Holy Spirit we can walk in newness of life through purity of heart.

Below are Scriptures relating to innocence:

Psalm 26:6-7 – <u>I will wash my hands in innocency</u>: so will I compass thine altar, O LORD: that I may publish with the voice of thanksgiving, and tell of all thy wonderous works.

References:
Daniel 6:22 – (Concerning Daniel and the Lions' Den) *– Daniel said, "My God hath sent his angel, and hath shut the lions' mouths, that they have not hurt me: forasmuch as before him innocency (purity) was found in me; and also before thee, O king, have I done no hurt."* **1 Corinthians 14:20 –** *Brethren, be not children in understanding: howbeit in malice be ye children, but in understanding be men.* **1 Thessalonians 3:12-13 –** *And the Lord make you to increase and abound in love one toward another, and toward all men, even as we do toward you: to the end he may stablish your hearts unblameable in holiness before God, even our Father, at the coming of our Lord Jesus Christ with all his saints.*

32(a) Faith, hope, love abide, these three; but the greatest of these is love. *I* eagerly pursue and seek to acquire [this] love – *I* [make it *my* aim, *my* great quest]. (1 Corinthians 13:13-14:1-AMPCE)

The Lord helped me to see, in my own life, the importance of walking in faith, hope, and His unconditional love rather than control, expectations (especially the ones I placed on my husband), and conditional love based on whether my expectations were met!

Let's look at these three spiritual attributes and why love is greater. The word "greatest" in the Greek is *meizon* meaning "larger (literally or figuratively, specially, in age):–elder, greater(-est), more." In *Galatians 5:6* – Paul said, *"For in Jesus Christ neither circumcision availeth any thing, nor uncircumcision; but faith which worketh by love."* Faith and hope go hand in hand as it is written in *Hebrews 11:1* – *"Now faith is the substance of things hoped for, the evidence of things not seen."* Faith and hope operating within the love of God, that is shed abroad in the heart of the mature believer, is what brings the things of heaven to us, producing abundant life *(Romans 5:1-5; John 10:10)*. His eternal purpose is at work within us in order for us to become deeply rooted and grounded in His love, His divine nature, and then are we truly able to live by faith and abound in hope *(Ephesians 3:17; Colossians 2:7; Romans 15:13)*. He is able to do exceeding abundantly above all that we ask or think, according to the power that works in us *(Ephesians 3:20)*. To Him be glory forever and ever! God is love and God and His Word are One—you cannot separate the two *(1 John 4:16; John 1:1,14)*. His Word produces faith and He is the God of hope *(Romans 10:17, 15:13)*.

Paul writes,

> *Whereof I am made a minister, according to the dispensation of God which is given to me for you, to fulfil the word of God; even the mystery which hath been hid from ages and from generations, but now is made manifest to his saints: to whom God would make known what is the riches of the glory of this mystery among the Gentiles; which is Christ in you, the hope of glory.*

(Colossians 1:25-27)

He also writes,

> *For God, who commanded the light to shine out of darkness, hath shined in our hearts, to give the light of the knowledge of the glory of God in the face of Jesus Christ. But we have this treasure in earthen vessels, that the excellency of the power may be of God, and not of us.*

(2 Corinthians 4:6-7)

These two passages of Scripture are very powerful as they reveal to us that the Creator of the universe, Love Himself, desires to dwell within our hearts by the power of His Spirit. His desire is to reveal Christ in us in order for us to put on the new man *(Ephesians 4:24; Colossians 3:10; 1 Peter 3:4; Romans 1:17; Galatians 2:20)*. This is abundant life and there is nothing this world has to offer that can compare! Our part is to renew the *spirit of our minds* to the truth of God's Word especially concerning the new man in Christ in order for us to tap into this divine treasure, which is Christ *(2 Corinthians 4:7)*! I believe Paul had a revelation of this when he wrote,

> *[For my determined purpose is] that I may know Him [that I may progressively become more deeply and intimately acquainted with Him, perceiving and recognizing and understanding the wonders of His Person more strongly and more clearly], and that I may in that same way come to know the power outflowing from His resurrection [which it exerts over believers], and that I may so share His sufferings as to be continually transformed [in spirit into His likeness even] to His death, [in the hope] that if possible I may attain to the [spiritual and moral] resurrection [that lifts me] out from among the dead [even while in the body]. Not that I have now attained [this ideal], or have already been made perfect, but I press on to lay hold of (grasp) and make my own, that for which Christ Jesus (the Messiah) has laid hold*

of me and made me His own. I do not consider, brethren, that I have captured and made it my own [yet]; but one thing I do [it is my one aspiration]: forgetting what lies behind and straining forward to what lies ahead, I press on toward the goal to win the [supreme and heavenly] prize to which God in Christ Jesus is calling us upward.

(Philippians 3:10-14, AMPCE)

Below are Scriptures relating to faith, hope, and love:

1. *2 Timothy 2:22* – *Flee also youthful lusts: but follow righteousness, faith, charity (God's love), peace, with them that call on the Lord out of a pure heart.*

References:

John 13:34-35 – *Jesus said, "A new commandment I give unto you, that ye love one another; as I have loved you, that ye also love one another. By this shall all men know that ye are my disciples, if ye have love one to another." 2 Corinthians 4:3-4* – *But if our gospel be hid, it is hid to them that are lost: in whom the god of this world (Satan) hath blinded the minds of them which believe not, lest the light of the glorious gospel of Christ, who is the image of God, should shine unto them. 1 Thessalonians 1:3-4* – *Remembering without ceasing your work of faith, and labour of love, and patience of hope in our Lord Jesus Christ, in the sight of God and our Father; knowing, brethren beloved, your election of God. 1 Thessalonians 5:6-9* – *Therefore let us not sleep, as do others; but let us watch and be sober. For they that sleep sleep in the night; and they that be drunken are drunken in the night. But let us, who are of the day, be sober, putting on the breastplate of faith and love; and for an helmet, the hope of salvation. For God hath not appointed us to wrath, but to obtain salvation by our Lord Jesus Christ. 2 Thessalonians 1:3-4* – *We are bound to thank God always for you, brethren, as it is meet (befitting), because that your faith groweth exceedingly, and the charity (God's love) of every one of you all toward each other aboundeth; so that we ourselves glory in you in the churches of God for your patience and faith in all your persecutions and tribulation that ye endure. Hebrews 10:22-24* – *Let us draw near with a true heart in full assurance of faith, having our hearts sprinkled from an evil conscience, and our bodies washed with pure water. Let us hold fast the profession of our faith without wavering; (for he is faithful that promised;) and let us consider one another to provoke unto love and to good works. Hebrews 11:6* – *But without faith it is impossible to please him: for he that cometh to God must believe that he is, and that he is a rewarder of them that diligently seek him. 1 John 1:1-5* – *That which was from the beginning, which we have heard, which we have seen with our eyes, which we have looked upon, and our hands have handled, of the Word of life; (for the life was manifested, and we have seen it, and bear witness, and shew unto you that eternal life, which was with the Father, and was manifested unto us;) that which we have seen and heard declare we unto you, that ye also may have fellowship with us: and truly our fellowship is with the Father, and with his Son Jesus Christ. And these things write we unto you, that your joy may be full. This then is the message which we have heard of him, and declare unto you, that God is light, and in him is no darkness at all. 1 John 5:4* – *For whatsoever is born of God overcometh the world: and this is the victory that overcometh the world, even our faith. 2 Peter 1:1-11* – *Simon Peter, a servant and an apostle of Jesus Christ, to them that have obtained like precious faith with us through the righteousness of God and our Saviour Jesus Christ: Grace and peace be multiplied unto you through the knowledge of God, and of Jesus our Lord, according as his divine power hath given unto us all things that pertain unto life and godliness, through the knowledge of him that hath called us to glory and virtue: whereby are given unto us exceeding great and precious promises: that by these ye might be partakers of the divine nature, having escaped the corruption that is in the world through lust. And beside this, giving all diligence, add to your faith virtue; and to virtue knowledge; and to knowledge temperance; and to temperance patience;*

and to patience godliness; and to godliness brotherly kindness; and to brotherly kindness charity (God's love). For if these things be in you, and abound, they make you that ye shall neither be barren nor unfruitful in the knowledge of our Lord Jesus Christ. But he that lacketh these things is blind, and cannot see afar off, and hath forgotten that he was purged from his old sins. Wherefore the rather, brethren, give diligence to make your calling and election sure: for if ye do these things, ye shall never fall: for so an entrance shall be ministered unto you abundantly into the everlasting kingdom of our Lord and Saviour Jesus Christ.

2. ***2 Corinthians 4:17-18*** *(AMPCE) – For our light, momentary affliction (this slight distress of the passing hour) is ever more and more abundantly preparing and producing and achieving for us an everlasting weight of glory [beyond all measure, excessively surpassing all comparisons and all calculations, a vast and transcendent glory and blessedness never to cease!], since we consider and look not to the things that are seen but to the things that are unseen; for the things that are visible are temporal (brief and fleeting), but the things that are invisible are deathless and everlasting.*

References:
Romans 8:24-25 *– For we are saved by hope: but hope that is seen is not hope: for what a man seeth, why doeth he yet hope for? But if we hope for that we see not, then do we with patience wait for it.* ***Romans 10:17*** *– so then faith cometh by hearing, and hearing by the word of God.* ***Romans 15:4-6, 13*** *– For whatsoever things were written aforetime were written for our learning, that we through patience and comfort of the scriptures might have hope. Now the God of patience and consolation grant you to be likeminded one toward another according to Christ Jesus: that ye may with one mind and one mouth glorify God, even the Father of our Lord Jesus Christ. Now the God of hope fill you with all joy and peace in believing, that ye may abound in hope, through the power of the Holy Ghost.* ***Galatians 3:11*** *– But that no man is justified by the law in the sight of God, it is evident: for, the just shall live by faith. (See Galatians 5:6.)*

Please refer to **Notes 24a, 24b, 28c, 29a, 29b, 29c, 30,** and **32b** for additional information and/or Scriptures relating to God's love.

32(b) Love does no wrong to one's neighbor [it never hurts anybody]. <u>Therefore love meets all the requirements and is the fulfilling of the Law.</u> (Romans 13:10-AMPCE)

Let's look at *Romans 13:8-10* in the King James Version,

> *Owe no one any thing, but to love one another: for he that loveth another has fulfilled the law. For this, 'Thou shalt not commit adultery,' 'Thou shalt not kill,' 'Thou shalt not steal,' 'Thou shall not bear false witness,' 'Thou shall not covet;' and if there be any other commandment, it is briefly comprehended in this saying, namely, 'Thou shalt love your neighbor as yourself.' <u>Love worketh no ill to his neighbor: therefore love is the fulfilling of the law.</u>*

Let's look a little closer at this passage of Scripture where underlined.

Love worketh no ill to his neighbor: Therefore love is the fulfilling of the law. The Greek word for "ill" is *kakos* meaning "…i.e. (subjectively) depraved, or (objectively) injurious:–bad, evil, harm, ill, noisome, wicked." A person operating in the love of God or the new man in Christ does not commit adultery, does not murder, does not steal, does not bear false witness, does not covet, etc. This is why it is so important to nurture, develop, and support the born-again creation within, for it is only through our true self that we can love others well. This is very powerful and why Paul, after addressing what God's love is and the importance of it in *1 Corinthians 13*, said in *1 Corinthians 14:1 (AMPCE)* – *"Eagerly pursue and seek to acquire [this] love [make it your aim, your great quest]…"* God's love operating in us is the fulfilling of the law! Let's look back at *Joshua 1:1-8* to see God's directive to Joshua when he was called by Him, after Moses' death, to fulfill His promise to divide to the children of Israel, as an inheritance, the land which He swore to their fathers to give them.

> *Now after the death of Moses the servant of the LORD it came to pass, that the LORD spake unto Joshua the son of Nun, Moses' minister, saying, "Moses my servant is dead; now therefore arise, go over this Jordan, thou, and all this people, unto the land which I do give to them, even to the children of Israel. Every place that the sole of your foot shall tread upon, that have I given unto you, as I said unto Moses. From the wilderness and this Lebanon even unto the great river, the river Euphrates, all the land of the Hittites, and unto the great sea toward the going down of the sun, shall be your coast. There shall not any man be able to stand before thee all the days of thy life: as I was with Moses, so I will be with thee: I will not fail thee, nor forsake thee. Be strong and of a good courage: for unto this people shalt thou divide for an inheritance the land, which I sware unto their fathers to give them. Only be thou strong and very courageous, that thou mayest observe to do according to all the law, which Moses my servant commanded thee: turn not from it to the right hand or to the left, that thou mayest prosper whithersoever thou goest. This book of the law shall not depart out of thy mouth; but thou shalt meditate therein day and night, that thou mayest observe to do according to all that is written therein: for then thou shalt make thy way prosperous, and then thou shalt have good success."*

As I shared in detail in **Note 28 Summary**, the Hebrew word for "success" is *sakal* meaning "… intelligent:–consider, expert, instruct, prosper, (deal) prudent(-ly), (give) skill(-ful), have good success, teach, (have, make to) understand(-ing), wisdom, (be, behave self, consider, make) wise(-ly), guide wittingly." Let's look at *1 Samuel 18:5* where this Hebrew word *sakal* is also found: *"And David went out whithersoever Saul sent him, and behaved himself wisely (sakal): and Saul set him over the men of war, and he was accepted in the sight of all the people, and also in the sight of Saul's servants."* Scripture states that this man, David, was a man after God's own heart and was the apple of God's eye or cherished above all *(1 Samuel 13:13-14; Acts 13:22; Psalm 17:8)*. As we choose to make the love of God our aim and great quest by putting on the new man, we too will fulfill the law and walk in God's wisdom and light!

Jesus said in *John 14:15, 23* – *"If ye love me, keep my commandments. If a man love me, he will keep my words: and my Father will love him, and we will come unto him, and make our abode with him."* Paul writes,

> *But as it is written, "Eye hath not seen, nor ear heard, neither have entered into the heart of man, the things which God hath prepared for them that love him." But God hath revealed them unto us by his Spirit: for the Spirit searcheth all things, yea, the deep things of God. For what man knoweth the things of a man, save the spirit of man which is in him? Even so the things of God knoweth no man, but the Spirit of God. Now we have received, not the*

spirit of the world, but the spirit which is of God; that we might know the things that are freely given to us of God.

(1 Corinthians 2:9-12)

This goes along with a prayer that Paul prayed in *Ephesians 3:14-21*. Leading up to this prayer in *Ephesians 3:1-11*, Paul said that he was called by God to preach to the Gentiles (people who are not Jews) the unsearchable riches of Christ. To make all men know the fellowship of this mystery which has been hid in God who created all things by Jesus Christ: to the intent that now the principalities and powers in heavenly places might be known by the church the manifold wisdom of God, according to the eternal purpose which God purposed in Christ. Then he begins his prayer in *Ephesians 3:14-21*,

> *For this cause I bow my knees unto the Father of our Lord Jesus Christ, of whom the whole family in heaven and earth is named, that he would grant you, according to the riches of his glory, to be strengthened with might by his Spirit in the inner man; that Christ may dwell in your hearts by faith; that ye, being rooted and grounded in love, may be able to comprehend with all saints what is the breadth, and length, and depth, and height; and to know the love of Christ, which passeth knowledge, that ye might be filled with all the fulness of God. Now unto him that is able to do exceeding abundantly above all that we ask or think, according to the power that worketh in us, unto him be glory in the church by Christ Jesus throughout all ages, world without end. Amen.*

The word "power" in the Greek is *dynamis* meaning "<u>force</u> (literally or figuratively); specially, <u>miraculous power</u> (usually by implication, a miracle itself):—ability, abundance, meaning, <u>might</u>(-ily, -y, -y deed), (worker of) miracle(-s), <u>power</u>, <u>strength</u>, violence, mighty (wonderful) work." This Greek word *dynamis* is where we get the word dynamite. It is used 120 times in the King James Version including *2 Peter 1:3* – "*according to his divine <u>power</u> hath given unto us all things that pertain unto life and godliness, through the knowledge of him that hath called us to glory and virtue.*" This power resides within His divine nature—love, and changes the very character and nature within the hearts and minds of born-again believers! When this takes place, these believers meet the requirements of the law and therefore fulfill the law. When we choose to crucify our flesh of the affections and lusts by renewing the *spirit of our minds* or the *inmost mind* to the truth of who we are in Christ, submitting to His will, the maturity springing forth from this incorruptible seed will be evident in our lives *(1 Peter 1:23)*. We must always remember, according to the following two passages of Scripture, that holy men of God were moved by His Holy Spirit to write God-breathed Words contained in every Scripture verse in the Bible in order to reveal Himself to the hearts and minds of His children and to transform their lives:

1. ***2 Timothy 3:16-17*** *– All scripture is given by inspiration (divinely breathed) of God, and is profitable for doctrine, for reproof, for correction, for instruction in righteousness: that the man of God may be perfect, throughly furnished unto all good works.*

2. ***2 Peter 1:19-21*** *– We have also a more sure word of prophecy; whereunto ye do well that ye take heed, as unto a light that shineth in a dark place, until the day dawn, and the day star arise in your hearts: knowing this first, that no prophecy of the scripture is of any private interpretation. For the prophecy came not in old time by the will of man: but holy men of God spake as they were moved by the Holy Ghost.*

Therefore, let's purpose to keep our focus on Christ and continue to feed on His Word in order to strengthen and support the born-again creation within, our true selves, giving glory to God.

Below are Scriptures relating to walking in the light of His Word:

Psalm 19:7-11 – The law of the LORD is perfect, converting the soul: the testimony of the LORD is sure, making wise the simple. The statutes of the LORD are right, rejoicing the heart: the commandment of the LORD is pure, enlightening the eyes. The fear of the LORD is clean, enduring for ever: the judgments of the LORD are true and righteous altogether. More to be desired are they than gold, yea, than much fine gold: sweeter also than honey and the honeycomb. Moreover by them is thy servant warned: and in keeping of them is great reward.

References:

*Psalm 111:10 – The fear of the LORD is the beginning of wisdom: a good understanding have all they that do his commandments: his praise endureth for ever. **Psalm 119:16, 72, 105, 165-168** – I will delight myself in thy statutes: I will not forget thy word. The law of thy mouth is better unto me than thousands of gold and silver. Thy word is a lamp unto my feet, and a light unto my path. Great peace have they which love thy law: and nothing shall offend them. LORD, I have hoped for thy salvation, and done thy commandments. My soul hath kept thy testimonies; and I love them exceedingly. I have kept thy precepts and thy testimonies: for all my ways are before thee. **Proverbs 15:16-17** – Better is little with the fear of the LORD than great treasure and trouble therewith. Better is a dinner of herbs where love is, than a stalled ox and hatred therewith. **Proverbs 16:7** – When a man's ways please the LORD, he maketh even his enemies to be at peace with him. **Proverbs 19:16, 21** – He that keepeth (or attends to) the commandment keepeth (or guards) his own soul… There are many devices (plans) in a man's heart; nevertheless the counsel of the LORD, that shall stand. **Proverbs 21:23** – Whoso keepeth (or guards) his mouth and his tongue keepeth (or guards) his soul from troubles. **Isaiah 51:7** – The LORD said, "Hearken unto me, ye that know righteousness, the people in whose heart is my law; fear ye not the reproach of men neither be ye afraid of their revilings." **Isaiah 64:4** – For since the beginning of the world men have not heard, nor perceived by the ear, neither hath the eye seen, O God, beside thee, what he hath prepared for him that waiteth for him (see 1 Corinthians 2:4-16). **Matthew 25:31-40** – Jesus said, "When the Son of man shall come in his glory, and all the holy angels with him, then shall he sit upon the throne of his glory: and before him shall be gathered all nations: and he shall separate them one from another, as a shepherd divideth his sheep from the goats: and he shall set the sheep on his right hand, but the goats on the left. Then shall the King say unto them on his right hand, 'Come, ye blessed of my Father, inherit the kingdom prepared for you from the foundation of the world: for I was an hungered, and ye gave me meat (food): I was thirsty, and ye gave me drink: I was a stranger, and ye took me in: naked, and ye clothed me: I was sick, and ye visited me: I was in prison, and ye came unto me.' Then shall the righteous answer him, saying, 'Lord, when saw thee an hungered, and fed thee? Or thirsty, and gave thee drink? When saw we thee a stranger, and took thee in? Or naked, and clothed thee? Or when saw we thee sick, or in prison, and came unto thee?' And the King shall answer and say unto them, 'Verily I say unto you, Inasmuch as ye have done it unto one of the least of these my brethren, ye have done it unto me.'" **Revelation 22:12-15** – Jesus said, "And, behold, I come quickly; and my reward is with me, to give every man according as his work shall be. I am Alpha and Omega, the beginning and the end, the first and the last. Blessed are they that do his commandments, that they may have right to the tree of life, and may enter in through the gates into the city. For without are dogs, and sorcerers, and whoremongers, and murderers, and idolaters, and whosoever loveth and maketh a lie."*

Here are additional Scriptures relating to walking in the light of His Word: Deuteronomy 30:10-

16 (Romans 10:4-10); Matthew 5:17-30, 7:21-29; John 13:34-35; Colossians 1:9-23; 1 Timothy 4:7-11, 6:10-16; 1 John 5:1-5.

Please refer to **Notes 24a, 24b, 28c, 29a, 29b, 29c, 30,** and **32a** for additional information and/or Scriptures relating to God's love.

Please refer to **Notes 29c** and **41** for information and Scriptures relating to your conscience.

33(a) *I never return evil for evil or insult for insult (scolding, tongue-lashing, berating), but on the contrary blessing [praying for their welfare, happiness, and protection, and truly pitying and loving them]. For know that to this I have been called, that I may myself inherit a blessing [from God—that I may obtain a blessing as an heir, bringing welfare and happiness and protection].* (1 Peter 3:9-AMPCE)

This is the love of God and the wisdom of God in action—maturity in Christ—by putting on the new man! There is no way that someone living out of their carnal nature can function this way as the carnal nature protects and justifies itself against wrongdoings. Our born-again spiritual nature has nothing to protect, for the old man is dead and the born-again believer's life and security is hidden in Christ *(Colossians 3:1-3)*! It is important to remember that when we become born again, our citizenship is in Heaven *(Philippians 3:20)*. God's Word, through the power of His Holy Spirit, reveals His life, His love, His wisdom within us and thereby we are able to live by faith and not by sight. Paul writes,

> *For our light, momentary affliction (this slight distress of the passing hour) is ever more and more abundantly preparing and producing and achieving for us an everlasting weight of glory [beyond all measure, excessively surpassing all comparisons and all calculations, a vast and transcendent glory and blessedness never to cease!], Since we consider and look not to the things that are seen but to the things that are unseen; for the things that are visible are temporal (brief and fleeting), but the things that are invisible are deathless and everlasting.*
> (2 Corinthians 4:17-18, AMPCE)

We do not wrestle with flesh and blood but against principalities, powers, rulers of the darkness of this world, and against spiritual wickedness in high places *(Ephesians 6:10-12)*. Paul also writes,

> *And I, brethren, could not speak unto you as unto spiritual, but as unto carnal, even as unto babes in Christ. I have fed you with milk, and not with meat: for hitherto ye were not able to bear it, neither yet now are ye able. For ye are yet carnal: for whereas there is among you envying, and strife, and divisions, are ye not carnal, and walk as men?*
> (1 Corinthians 3:1-3)

Growth is a process and we will continue to grow in Christ until we leave this earth! Jesus said,

> *Therefore all things whatsoever ye would that men should do to you, do ye even so to them: for this is the law and the prophets. Enter ye in at the strait gate: for wide is the gate, and*

broad is the way, that leadeth to destruction, and many there be which go in thereat: because strait is the gate, and narrow is the way, which leadeth unto life, and few there be that find it.

(Matthew 7:12-14)

God is calling us to grow up in Christ by putting on the new man created after God in righteousness and true holiness. This is the strait gate and the narrow way that leads to life! It is in this posture that we are able to see clearly through the light of His Word how to treat others. Jesus also said,

But I say unto you, love your enemies, bless them that curse you, do good to them that hate you, and pray for them which despitefully use you, and persecute you; that ye may be the children of your Father which is in heaven: for he maketh his sun to rise on the evil and on the good, and sendeth rain on the just and on the unjust. For if ye love them which love you, what reward have ye? Do not even the publicans the same? And if ye salute your brethren only, what do ye more than others? Do not even the publicans so? Be ye therefore perfect, even as your Father which is in heaven is perfect.

(Matthew 5:44-48)

Isaiah 55:7-11 reveals the key to walking in the realm of heaven,

Let the wicked forsake his way, and the unrighteous man his thoughts: and let him return unto the LORD, and he will have mercy upon him; and to our God, for he will abundantly pardon. "For my thoughts are not your thoughts, neither are your ways my ways," saith the LORD. "For as the heavens are higher than the earth, so are my ways higher than your ways, and my thoughts than your thoughts. For as the rain cometh down, and the snow from heaven, and returneth not thither, but watereth the earth, and maketh it bring forth and bud, that it may give seed to the sower, and bread to the eater: so shall my word be that goeth forth out of my mouth: it shall not return unto me void, but it shall accomplish that which I please, and it shall prosper in the thing whereto I sent it."

This was spoken before Jesus died for our sins. We now, literally, have this treasure within us which is *Christ, the hope of glory,* in whom are hid all the treasures of wisdom and knowledge *(2 Corinthians 4:6-11; Colossians 1:26-27; Colossians 2:2-3).* We have the Creator of the universe living on the inside of us through the power of His Spirit so that we can love and honor others well. Jesus said in *Matthew 25:40 – "… Inasmuch as ye have done it unto one of the least of these my brethren, ye have done it unto me."* As His Words become firmly fixed and established within us, His love, His wisdom, His peace, and His grace reigns in our hearts and minds. Again, as He said in *Isaiah 55:8-9, "For my thoughts are not your thoughts, neither are your ways my ways," saith the LORD. "For as the heavens are higher than the earth, so are my ways higher than your ways, and my thoughts than your thoughts."* As His ways become our ways and His thoughts become our thoughts, we won't pay any attention to a suffered wrong, as our security and trust rest in Someone greater than ourselves. Jesus is our example. He walked this earth in the love of God and the wisdom of God among His adversaries, who were for the most part, the scribes (teachers of the law) and the Pharisees (religious leaders). When the scribes and Pharisees tried to tempt Jesus, in order to bring a charge against Him or come against Him based on His actions, He would always challenge them with the truth of God's Word and would always leave them speechless. For example,

And the scribes and Pharisees brought unto him a woman taken in adultery; and when they had set her in the midst, they say unto him, "Master, this woman was taken in adultery, in the very act. Now Moses in the law commanded us, that such should be stoned: but what sayest thou?" This they said, tempting him, that they might have to accuse him. But Jesus stooped down, and with his finger wrote on the ground, as though he heard them not. So when they continued asking him, he lifted up himself, and said unto them, "He that is without sin among you, let him first cast a stone at her." And again he stooped down, and wrote on the ground. And they which heard it, being convicted by their own conscience, went out one by one, beginning at the eldest, even unto the last: and Jesus was left alone, and the woman standing in the midst. When Jesus had lifted up himself, and saw none but the woman, he said unto her, "Woman, where are those thine accusers? Hath no man condemned thee?" She said, "No man, Lord." And Jesus said unto her, "Neither do I condemn thee: go, and sin no more."

(John 8:3-11)

This was the love of God and the wisdom of God in operation. The love of God brought forgiveness to the woman caught in adultery and the wisdom of God convicted the conscience of the scribes and Pharisees who thought to stone her. Another example,

And he was teaching in one of the synagogues on the sabbath. And, behold, there was a woman which had a spirit of infirmity eighteen years, and was bowed together, and could in no wise lift up herself. And when Jesus saw her, he called her to him, and said unto her, "Woman, thou art loosed from thine infirmity." And he laid his hands on her: and immediately she was made straight, and glorified God. And the ruler of the synagogue answered with indignation, because that Jesus had healed on the sabbath day, and said unto the people, "There are six days in which men ought to work: in them therefore come and be healed, and not on the sabbath day." The Lord then answered him, and said, "Thou hypocrite, doth not each one of you on the sabbath loose his ox or his ass from the stall, and lead him away to watering? And ought not this woman, being a daughter of Abraham, whom Satan hath bound, lo, these eighteen years, be loosed from this bond on the sabbath day?" And when he had said these things, all his adversaries were ashamed: and all the people rejoiced for all the glorious things that were done by him.

(Luke 13:10-17)

Again, the love of God and the wisdom of God were in operation here. The love of God brought healing to the woman on the sabbath day and the wisdom of God brought conviction to His adversaries.

Below are Scriptures relating to godly behavior:

1. ***Psalm 133:1-3*** *– Behold, how good and how pleasant it is for brethren to dwell together in unity! It is like the precious ointment upon the head, that ran down upon the beard, even Aaron's beard: that went down to the skirts of his garments; as the dew of Hermon, and as the dew that descended upon the mountains of Zion: for there the LORD commanded the blessing, even life for evermore.* (Let us choose to dwell united in Christ)!

References:

Psalm 119:165 – *Great peace have they which love thy law: and nothing shall offend them.* **Proverbs 13:10, 14** – *Only by pride cometh contention: but with the well advised is wisdom. The law of the wise is a fountain of life to depart from the snares of death.* **Proverbs 18:19** – *A brother offended is harder to be won than a strong city: and their contentions are like the bars of a castle.* **Matthew 5:38-39** – *Jesus said, "Ye have heard that it hath been said, 'An eye for an eye, and a tooth for a tooth:' but I say unto you, that ye resist not evil: but whosoever shall smite thee on thy right cheek, turn to him the other also."* **Galatians 6:7-10** – *Be not deceived; God is not mocked: for whatsoever a man soweth, that shall he also reap. For he that soweth to his flesh shall of the flesh reap corruption; but he that soweth to the Spirit shall of the Spirit reap life everlasting. And let us not be weary in well doing: for in due season we shall reap, if we faint not. As we have therefore opportunity, let us do good unto all men, especially unto them who are of the household of faith.* **Ephesians 4:26-27, 29-32** – *Be ye angry, and sin not: let not the sun go down upon your wrath: neither give place to the devil. Let no corrupt communication proceed out of your mouth, but that which is good to the use of edifying, that it may minister grace unto the hearers. And grieve not the holy Spirit of God, whereby ye are sealed unto the day of redemption. Let all bitterness, and wrath, and anger, and clamour, and evil speaking, be put away from you, with all malice: and be ye kind one to another, tenderhearted, forgiving one another, even as God for Christ's sake hath forgiven you.* **Colossians 4:5-6** – *Walk in wisdom toward them that are without, redeeming the time. Let your speech be alway with grace, seasoned with salt, that ye may know how ye ought to answer every man.* **1 Thessalonians 5:14-15** – *Now we exhort you, brethren, warn them that are unruly, comfort the feebleminded, support the weak, be patient toward all men. See that none render evil for evil unto any man; but ever follow that which is good, both among yourselves, and to all men.* **Titus 3:1-2** – *Put them in mind to be subject to principalities and powers, to obey magistrates, to be ready to every good work, to speak evil of no man, to be no brawlers, but gentle, shewing all meekness unto all men.* **Hebrews 6:10-12** – *For God is not unrighteous to forget your work and labour of love, which ye have shewed toward his name, in that ye have ministered to the saints, and do minister. And we desire that every one of you do shew the same diligence to the full assurance of hope unto the end: that ye be not slothful, but followers of them who through faith and patience inherit the promises.* **1 Peter 2:1-3, 11-16** – *Wherefore laying aside all malice, and all guile, and hypocrisies, and envies, and all evil speakings, as newborn babes, desire the sincere milk of the word, that ye may grow thereby: if so be ye have tasted that the Lord is gracious. Dearly beloved, I beseech you as strangers and pilgrims, abstain from fleshly lusts, which war against the soul; having your conversation (behavior) honest among the Gentiles: that, whereas they speak against you as evildoers, they may by your good works, which they shall behold, glorify God in the day of visitation. Submit yourselves to every ordinance of man for the Lord's sake: whether it be to the king, as supreme; or unto governors, as unto them that are sent by him for the punishment of evildoers, and for the praise of them that do well. For so is the will of God, that with well doing ye may put to silence the ignorance of foolish men: as free, and not using your liberty for a cloke of maliciousness, but as the servants of God.*

2. **Proverbs 25:21-22** – *If thine enemy be hungry, give him bread to eat; and if he be thirsty, give him water to drink: for thou shalt heap coals of fire upon his head, and the LORD shall reward thee.*

References:
Leviticus 19:18 – *"Thou shalt not avenge (take vengeance), nor bear any grudge against the children of thy people, but thou shalt love thy neighbor as thyself: I am the LORD."* **Deuteronomy 32:35** – *The LORD said, "To me belongeth vengeance, and recompense; their foot shall slide in due time: for the day of their calamity is at hand, and the things that shall come upon them make haste."* **Psalm 34:17** – *The righteous cry, and the LORD heareth, and delivereth them out of all their troubles.* **Psalm 37:27** – *Depart from evil, and do good; and dwell forevermore.* **Psalm 112:5-8** – *A good man sheweth favour, and lendeth: he will*

guide his affairs with discretion. Surely he shall not be moved for ever: the righteous shall be in everlasting remembrance. He shall not be afraid of evil tidings: his heart is fixed, trusting in the LORD. His heart is established, he shall not be afraid, until he see his desire upon his enemies. **Proverbs 16:20** – *He that handleth a matter wisely shall find good: and whoso trusteth in the LORD, happy is he.* **Proverbs 20:22** – *Say not thou, " I will recompense evil;" but wait on the LORD, and he shall save thee.* **Proverbs 24:29** – *Say not, "I will do so to him as he hath done to me: I will render to the man according to his work."* **Romans 12:14-21** – *Bless them which persecute you: bless, and curse not. Rejoice with them that do rejoice, and weep with them that weep. Be of the same mind one toward another. Mind not high things, but condescend to men of low estate (humbleness of mind). Be not wise in your own conceits. Recompense to no man evil for evil. Provide things honest in the sight of all men. If it be possible, as much as lieth in you, live peaceably with all men. Dearly beloved, avenge not yourselves, but rather give place unto wrath: for it is written, "Vengeance is mine; I will repay," saith the Lord. Therefore if thine enemy hunger, feed him; if he thirst, give him drink: for in so doing thou shalt heap coals of fire on his head. Be not overcome of evil, but overcome evil with good.* **Hebrews 10:30** – *For we know him that hath said, "Vengeance belongeth unto me, I will recompense," saith the Lord. And again, "The Lord shall judge his people."* **James 4:10-12** – *Humble yourselves in the sight of the Lord, and he shall lift you up. Speak not evil one of another, brethren. He that speaketh evil of his brother, and judgeth his brother, speaketh evil of the law, and judgeth the law: but if thou judge the law, thou art not a doer of the law, but a judge. There is one lawgiver, who is able to save and to destroy: who art thou that judgest another?*

3. **Proverbs 11:17** – *The merciful man doeth good to his own soul: but he that is cruel troubleth his own flesh.*

References:
Matthew 5:7 – *Jesus said, "Blessed are the merciful for they shall obtain mercy."* **Mark 11:24-26** – *Jesus said, "What things soever ye desire, when ye pray, believe that ye receive them, and ye shall have them. And when ye stand praying, forgive, if ye have ought against any: that your Father also which is in heaven may forgive you your trespasses. But if ye do not forgive, neither will your Father which is in heaven forgive your trespasses."*

33(b) *For I want to* enjoy life and see good days [good—whether apparent or not], *so,* I keep *my* tongue free from evil and *my* lips from guile (treachery, deceit). James 3:2 reads, ...If any man offend not in word, the same is a perfect man *(fully developed in character)*..." (1 Peter 3:10-AMPCE)

Let's look at *James 3:2* in the King James Version – *"For in many things we offend all. If any man offend not in word, the same is a perfect man, and able also to bridle the whole body."* The word "offend" in the Greek is *ptaio* meaning "to trip, i.e. (figuratively) to err, sin, fail (of salvation):—fall, offend, stumble." Its meaning in the Thayer's Greek Lexicon is "to sin in word or speech." The word "perfect" in the Greek is <u>*teleios*</u> meaning "complete (in various applications of labor, growth, mental and moral character, etc.); completeness:—of full age, man, perfect." Its meaning in the Thayer's Greek Lexicon is "of mind and character, one who has reached the proper height of virtue and integrity in an absolute sense, of God: Matthew 5:48; James 3:2." *(Matthew 5:48 reads, "Be ye therefore perfect, even as your Father which is in heaven is perfect.")* This is a man or a woman who lives out of the hidden man of the heart, the new man. It is the root word for perfectness found in *Colossians 3:10-14* where Paul tells us to put on the new man which is renewed in knowledge after the image of Him that created him. In this passage of Scripture, he specifically tells us what to put on in order to walk in the new man and in *verse 14* he said, *"And above all these things put on charity (God's love), which is the bond of <u>perfectness</u>."* The word "perfectness" in the Greek is *teleiotes* from the root word *teleios* above and its meaning in the Thayer's Greek Lexicon is "moral and spiritual perfection." The word "bridle" in the Greek is *chalinagogeo* meaning "to be a bit-leader, i.e. to curb (figuratively):–bridle." Its meaning in the Thayer's Greek Lexicon is "to lead by a bridle, to guide, to bridle, hold in check, restrain." As it is written, the tongue is connected to the heart, and therefore guides our lives. Let's continue with *James 3:3-18*:

> *Behold, we put bits in the horses' mouths, that they may obey us; and we turn about their whole body. Behold also the ships, which though they be so great, and are driven of fierce winds, yet are they turned about with a very small helm (rudder), whithersoever the governor (helmsman) listeth (impulse). Even so the tongue is a little member, and boasteth great things. Behold, how great a matter a little fire kindleth! And the tongue is a fire, a world of iniquity: so is the tongue among our members, that it defileth the whole body, and setteth on fire the course of nature; and it is set on fire of hell. For every kind of beasts, and of birds, and of serpents, and of things in the sea, is tamed, and hath been tamed of mankind: but the tongue can no man tame; it is an unruly evil, full of deadly poison. Therewith bless we God, even the Father; and therewith curse we men, which are made after the similitude of God. Out of the same mouth proceedeth blessing and cursing. My brethren, these things ought not so to be. Doth a fountain send forth at the same place sweet water and bitter? Can the fig tree, my brethren, bear olive berries? Either a vine, figs? So can no fountain both yield salt water and fresh. Who is a wise man endued with knowledge among you? Let him shew out of a good conversation (behavior) his works with meekness of wisdom. But if ye have bitter envying and strife in your hearts, glory not, and lie not against the truth. This wisdom descendeth not from above, but is earthly, sensual, devilish. For where envying and strife is, there is confusion and every evil work. But the wisdom that is from above is first pure, then peaceable, gentle, and easy to be intreated, full of mercy and good fruits, without partiality, and without hypocrisy. And the fruit of righteousness is sown in peace of them that make peace.*

James uses the analogy of a fruit-bearing tree and a fruit-bearing vine when comparing the heart as a fountain of water and its spigot, the tongue. I believe he is saying here that it is the seed that determines what type of fruit a tree or a vine will produce, and in the same way, if we are living out of the old man (the corruptible seed) or if we are living out of the new man (the incorruptible seed) determines if sweet or bitter water flows from our mouth *(1 Peter 1:23)*.

In going a little deeper into this subject matter, let's look at the following passage of Scripture:

> *A man's belly shall be satisfied with the fruit of his mouth; and with the increase of his lips shall he be filled. <u>Death and life are in the power of the tongue</u>: and they that love it shall eat the fruit thereof.*

> (Proverbs 18:20-21)

Let's think about that for a moment. *Death and life are in the power of the tongue.* Jesus said in *Matthew 12:34* that out of the abundance of the heart the mouth speaks. He is saying here that there is a connection between the heart and the tongue; the tongue is the expression of the heart and reveals our maturity in Christ or lack thereof. Therefore, we have a huge role to play in our destiny and who we are as believers. We are responsible for our own heart and apart from Christ, the heart is deceitful above all things and desperately wicked *(Jeremiah 17:9)*. This is why it is important for us to speak aloud the Word of God! It is written in *Psalm 45:1 – "…My tongue is the pen of a ready writer."* And in *Proverbs 3:3-4 – "Let not mercy and truth forsake thee: bind them about thy neck; write them upon the table of thine heart: so shalt thou find favour and good understanding in the sight of God and man."* Only the Word of God by the power of His Holy Spirit can circumcise the heart and, in turn, tame the tongue *(Deuteronomy 30:6; Colossians 2:9-11)*. The Word of God is living and powerful and sharper than any two-edged sword. It reveals within us what is soulish and what is spiritual and it is a discerner of our thoughts and intentions *(Hebrews 4:12)*. Only His Word within us sheds light on any underlying motives, hidden agendas, and/or secret sins and brings us to a deeper level of repentance by changing us at a heart level. So allow the Word of God to go deep within by speaking aloud the Word, <u>receiving it as your own</u>, in order to bring a deeper connection to God and a life filled with His light, truth, and wisdom! This will cause our speech to be more in line with His will and purpose – *Proverbs 16:23 – "The heart of the wise teacheth his mouth, and addeth learning to his lips."*

Below are Scriptures relating to the words we speak:

Psalm 15:1-5 – [A Psalm of David.] LORD, who shall abide in thy tabernacle? Who shall dwell in thy holy hill? He that walketh uprightly, and worketh righteousness, and speaketh the truth in his heart. He that backbiteth not with his tongue, nor doeth evil to his neighbor, nor taketh up a reproach against his neighbour. In whose eyes a vile person is contemned; but he honoureth them that fear the LORD. He that sweareth to his own hurt, and changeth not. He that putteth not out his money to usury, nor taketh reward against the innocent. He that doeth these things shall never be moved.

References:
Psalm 17:3 – Thou hast proved mine heart; thou hast visited me in the night; thou hast tried me, and shalt find nothing; I am purposed that my mouth shall not transgress. **Psalm 19:14** *– Let the words of my mouth, and the meditation of my heart, be acceptable in thy sight, O LORD, my strength, and my redeemer.* **Psalm 34:11-15** *– Come, ye children, hearken unto me: I will teach you the fear of the LORD. What man is he that desireth life, and loveth many days, that he may see good? Keep thy tongue from evil, and thy lips from speaking guile. Depart from evil, and do good; seek peace, and pursue it. The eyes of the LORD are upon the righteous, and his ears are open unto their cry.* **Psalm 37:30-31** *– The mouth of the righteous speaketh wisdom, and his tongue talketh of judgment. The law of his God is in his heart; none of his steps shall slide.* **Psalm 106:32-33** *– They angered him (Moses) also at the waters of strife, so that it went ill with Moses for their sakes: because they provoked his spirit, so that he spake unadvisedly with his lips. (See Numbers 20:1-12).* **Psalm 141:3** *– Set a watch, O LORD, before my mouth; keep the door of my lips.* **Proverbs 10:6, 11, 19, 31-32** *– Blessings are upon the head of the just: but violence covereth the mouth of the wicked. The mouth of a righteous man is a well of life: but violence covereth the mouth of the wicked. In the multitude of words there wanteth not sin (sin is not lacking): but he that refraineth his lips is wise. The mouth of the just bringeth forth wisdom… The lips of the righteous know what is acceptable: but the mouth of the wicked speaketh frowardness.* **Proverbs 12:14, 19** *– A man shall be satisfied with good by the fruit of his mouth and the recompense of a man's hands shall be rendered unto him. The lip of truth shall be established for ever: but a lying tongue is but for a moment.* **Proverbs 13:3, 14** *– He that keepeth his mouth keepeth his life: but he that openeth wide his lips shall have destruction. The law of the wise is a fountain of life, to depart from the snares of death.* **Proverbs 15:1-2, 4, 7, 24** *– A soft answer turneth away wrath: but*

grievous words stir up anger. The tongue of the wise useth knowledge aright: but the mouth of fools poureth out foolishness. A wholesome tongue is a tree of life: but perverseness therein is a breach in the spirit. The lips of the wise disperse knowledge: but the heart of the foolish doeth not so. The way of life is above to the wise, that he may depart from hell beneath. **Proverbs 16:23, 29-30** – The heart of the wise teacheth his mouth, and addeth learning to his lips. A violent man enticeth his neighbour, and leadeth him into the way that is not good. He shutteth his eyes to devise froward things: moving his lips he bringeth evil to pass. **Proverbs 17:20, 27-28** – He that hath a froward heart findeth no good: and he that hath a perverse tongue falleth into mischief. He that hath knowledge spareth his words: and a man of understanding is of an excellent spirit. Even a fool, when he holdeth his peace, is counted wise: and he that shutteth his lips is esteemed a man of understanding. **Proverbs 18:4, 7** – The words of a man's mouth are as deep waters, and the wellspring of wisdom as a flowing brook. A fool's mouth is his destruction, and his lips are the snare of his soul. **Proverbs 19:8** – He that getteth wisdom loveth his own soul: he that keepeth understanding shall find good. **Proverbs 20:15** – There is gold, and a multitude of rubies: but the lips of knowledge are a precious jewel. **Proverbs 21:23** – Whoso keepeth his mouth and his tongue keepeth his soul from troubles. **Proverbs 25:15** – By long forbearing is a prince persuaded, and a soft tongue breaketh the bone. **Proverbs 26:20-21** – Where no wood is, there the fire goeth out: so where there is no talebearer, the strife ceaseth. As coals are to burning coals, and wood to fire; so is a contentious man to kindle strife. **Proverbs 29:11, 20** – A fool uttereth all his mind: but a wise man keepeth it in till afterwards. Seest thou a man that is hasty in his words? There is more hope of a fool than him. **Ecclesiastes 2:13** – Then I saw that wisdom excelleth folly, as far as light excelleth darkness. **Ecclesiastes 10:12** – The words of a wise man's mouth are gracious; but the lips of a fool will swallow up himself. **Matthew 12:34-37** – Jesus said, "O generation of vipers, how can ye, being evil, speak good things? For out of the abundance of the heart the mouth speaketh. A good man out of the good treasure of the heart bringeth forth good things: and an evil man out of the evil treasure bringeth forth evil things. But I say unto you, that every idle word that men shall speak, they shall give account thereof in the day of judgment. For by thy words thou shalt be justified, and by thy words thou shalt be condemned. **2 Corinthians 10:3-5** – For though we walk in the flesh, we do not war after the flesh: (For the weapons of our warfare are not carnal, but mighty through God to the pulling down of strong holds;) casting down imaginations, and every high thing that exalteth itself against the knowledge of God, and bringing into captivity every thought to the obedience of Christ. **Ephesians 4:29** – Let no corrupt communication proceed out of your mouth, but that which is good to the use of edifying, that it may minister grace unto the hearers. **2 Timothy 2:15-16** – Study to shew thyself approved unto God, a workman that needeth not to be ashamed, rightly dividing the word of truth. But shun profane and vain babblings: for they will increase unto more ungodliness. **James 1:26** – If any man among you seem to be religious, and bridleth not his tongue, but deceiveth his own heart, this man's religion is vain (profitless).

33(c) *I choose to be* quick to hear [a careful, thoughtful listener], slow to speak [a speaker of carefully chosen words and], slow to anger [patient, reflective, forgiving]; for the [resentful, deep-seated] anger of man does not produce the righteousness of God... (James 1:19-20-AMP)

Below are Scriptures relating to being slow to speak:

Proverbs 14:29 – He that is slow to wrath is of great understanding: but he that is hasty of spirit exalteth folly.

References:

Proverbs 15:28 – The heart of the righteous studieth how to answer: but the mouth of the wicked poureth out evil things. Proverbs 16:32 – He that is slow to anger is better than the mighty; and he that ruleth his spirit than he that taketh a city. Ecclesiastes 5:2-3 – Be not rash with thy mouth, and let not thine heart be hasty to utter any thing before God: for God is in heaven, and thou upon earth: therefore let thy words be few. For a dream cometh through the multitude of business; and a fool's voice is known by multitude of words.

34(a) *I let* nothing be done through strife or vainglory *(self-conceit)*; but in lowliness of mind *I* esteem others better than *myself. I* look out not only for *my* own interests, but also for the interests of others. *I am genuinely interested in the welfare of others. I seek to advance the interest of Jesus Christ and not my own.* (Philippians 2:3, 2:4-NKJV) *(Ref.: Philippians 2:20-21)*

The word "strife" in the Greek is *eritheia* meaning "<u>faction</u>:–contention(-ious) strife." Its meaning in the Thayer's Greek Lexicon is "…a desire to put oneself forward, a partisan and factious spirit…" The word "vainglory" in the Greek is *kenodoxia* meaning "empty glorying, i.e. <u>self-conceit</u>:– vain-glory." Its meaning in the Thayer's Greek Lexicon is "vain-glory, groundless self-esteem, empty pride." This word is used only once in the New Testament and comes from the Greek word *kenodoxos* meaning "vainly glorifying, i.e. self-conceited:–desirous of vain-glory." Its meaning in the Thayer's Greek Lexicon is "glorying without reason, conceited, vain-glorious, eager for empty glory." This Greek word is used only once in the New Testament and is found in *Galatians 5:26 – "Let us not be desirous of <u>vain glory</u>, provoking one another, envying one another."* Now, let's look at a passage of Scripture that reveals the difference between earthly, sensual, devilish wisdom and the wisdom that comes from above:

> *But if ye have bitter envying and strife* (Greek word – *eritheia* see definition above) *in your hearts, glory not, and lie not against the truth. This wisdom descendeth not from above, but is earthly, sensual, devilish. For where envying and strife is, there is confusion and every evil work. But the wisdom that is from above is first pure, then peaceable, gentle, and easy to be intreated, full of mercy and good fruits, without partiality, and without hypocrisy. And the fruit of righteousness is sown in peace of them that make peace.*
>
> (James 3:14-18)

True righteousness and holiness comes only from the new man in Christ and the fruit of righteousness is love, joy, peace, longsuffering, gentleness, goodness, faith, meekness, temperance: against such there is no law *(Ephesians 4:22-24; Galatians 5:22-26)*. When we are <u>secure and complete in Christ</u> and operating in the mind of Christ, our motivation is no longer about serving ourselves but instead giving of ourselves to others for this is the Lord's nature. It is written in *Proverbs 14:14 – "The backslider in heart shall be filled with his own ways: and a good man shall be satisfied from himself."* For example, a wife who has found her security in Christ, no longer looks to her husband to meet her emotional/soulish needs, but instead looks toward the welfare of her husband and her children. The hidden man of the heart is compelled by the love of Christ to serve and to minister to them bringing peace and joy to the home. We become outwardly focused towards the welfare of others as our security and wholeness is found in Christ by being rooted in Him and thereby tapping into the wellspring of life flowing from within *(Ephesians 3:17; Colossians 2:7; John 7:37-38)*. In summary, when we are rooted in pride, we are self-centered, easily angered, and inwardly focused because of our own insecurities. When we are rooted in God's love, we are God-centered producing the fruits of righteousness, trusting in His love and faithfulness in our lives, and genuinely interested in the welfare of others *(Galatians 5:22-26)*. Let's look at two passages of Scripture that help us to see why this is so important:

1. **Matthew 25:31-45** – Jesus said, "…*Verily I say unto you, inasmuch as ye have done it unto one of the least of these my brethren, ye have done it unto me.*"
2. **1 Corinthians 12:13-27** – Paul said, "*For by one Spirit are we all baptized into one body, whether we be Jews or Gentiles, whether we be bond or free; and have been all made to drink into one Spirit. For the body is not one member, but many. If the foot shall say, 'Because I am not the hand, I am not of the body;' is it therefore not of the body? And if the ear shall say, 'Because I am not the eye, I am not of the body;' is it therefore not of the body? If the whole body were an eye, where were the hearing? If the whole were hearing, where were the smelling? But now hath God set the members every one of them in the body, as it hath pleased him. And if they were all one member, where were the body? But now are they many members, yet but one body. And the eye cannot say unto the hand, 'I have no need of thee:' nor again the head to the feet, 'I have no need of you.' Nay, much more those members of the body, which seem to be more feeble, are necessary: and those members of the body, which we think to be less honourable, upon these we bestow more abundant honour; and our uncomely parts have more abundant comeliness. For our comely parts have no need: but God hath tempered the body together, having given more abundant honour to that part which lacked: that there should be no schism in the body; but that the members should have the same care one for another. And whether one member suffer, all the members suffer with it; or one member be honoured, all the members rejoice with it. Now ye are the body of Christ, and members in particular.*"

Below are Scriptures relating to walking in lowliness of mind and its reflection toward others:

1. **Psalm 41:1-2** – *Blessed is he that considereth the poor: the LORD will deliver him in time of trouble. The LORD will preserve him, and keep him alive; and he shall be blessed upon the earth: and thou wilt not deliver him unto the will of his enemies.*

References:
Proverbs 14:31 – *He that oppresseth the poor reproacheth his Maker: but he that honoureth him hath mercy on the poor.* **Proverbs 19:17** – *He that hath pity upon the poor lendeth unto the LORD; and that which he hath given will he pay him again.* **Proverbs 28:27** – *He that giveth unto the poor shall not lack: but he that hideth his eyes shall have many curse.*

2. **Romans 15:1-6** – *We then that are strong ought to bear the infirmities of the weak, and not to please ourselves. Let every one of us please his neighbour for his good to edification. For even Christ pleased not himself; but, as it is written, "The reproaches of them that reproached thee fell on me." For whatsoever things were written aforetime were written for our learning, that we through patience and comfort of the scriptures might have hope. Now the God of patience and consolation grant you to be likeminded one toward another according to Christ Jesus: that ye may with one mind and one mouth glorify God, even the Father of our Lord Jesus Christ.*

References:
Proverbs 27:2 – *Let another man praise thee, and not thine own mouth; a stranger, and not thine own*

lips. **Romans 12:9-16** *(NKJV) – Let love be without hypocrisy. Abhor what is evil. Cling to what is good. Be kindly affectionate to one another with brotherly love, in honor giving preference to one another; not lagging in diligence, fervent in spirit, serving the Lord; rejoicing in hope, patient in tribulation, continuing steadfastly in prayer; distributing to the needs of the saints, given to hospitality. Bless those who persecute you; bless and do not curse. Rejoice with those who rejoice, and weep with those who weep. Be of the same mind toward one another. Do not set your mind on high things, but associate with the humble. Do not be wise in your own opinion.* **1 Corinthians 10:24, 31-33** *– Let no man seek his own, but every man another's wealth. Whether therefore ye eat, or drink, or whatsoever ye do, do all to the glory of God. Give none offence, neither to the Jews, nor to the Gentiles, nor to the church of God: even as I please all men in all things, not seeking mine own profit, but the profit of many, that they may be saved.* (Paul is not talking here of being a man pleaser which is rooted in fear but on the contrary being rooted in the love of Christ in order to be a light and a blessing to all men and in so doing winning many to Christ). **1 Corinthians 13:1-8** *– …God's love doth not behave itself unseemly, seeketh not her own, is not easily provoked, thinketh no evil…* **2 Corinthians 9:6-8** *– But this I say, He which soweth sparingly shall reap also sparingly; and he which soweth bountifully shall reap also bountifully. Every man according as he purposeth in his heart, so let him give; not grudgingly, or of necessity: for God loveth a cheerful giver. And God is able to make all grace abound toward you; that ye, always having all sufficiency in all things, may abound to every good work.* **Galatians 5:13-26** *– For, brethren, ye have been called unto liberty; only use not liberty for an occasion to the flesh, but by love serve one another. For all the law is fulfilled in one word, even in this; "Thou shalt love thy neighbour as thyself." But if ye bite and devour one another, take heed that ye be not consumed one of another. This I say then, Walk in the Spirit, and ye shall not fulfil the lust of the flesh…* **Galatians 6:1-10** *– Brethren, if a man be overtaken in a fault, ye which are spiritual, restore such an one in the spirit of meekness; considering thyself, lest thou also be tempted. Bear ye one another's burdens, and so fulfil the law of Christ. For if a man think himself to be something, when he is nothing, he deceiveth himself. But let every man prove his own work, and then shall he have rejoicing in himself alone, and not in another. For every man shall bear his own burden. Let him that is taught in the word communicate unto him that teacheth in all good things. Be not deceived; God is not mocked: for whatsoever a man soweth, that shall he also reap. For he that soweth to his flesh shall of the flesh reap corruption; but he that soweth to the Spirit shall of the Spirit reap life everlasting. And let us not be weary in well doing: for in due season we shall reap, if we faint not. As we have therefore opportunity, let us do good unto all men, especially unto them who are of the household of faith.* **Ephesians 4:1-6, 29-32** *– Paul said, "I therefore, the prisoner of the Lord, beseech you that ye walk worthy of the vocation wherewith ye are called, with all lowliness and meekness, with longsuffering, forbearing one another in love; endeavoring to keep the unity of the Spirit in the bond of peace. There is one body, and one Spirit, even as ye are called in one hope of your calling; one Lord, one faith, one baptism, one God and Father of all, who is above all, and through all, and in you all. Let no corrupt communication proceed out of your mouth, but that which is good to the use of edifying, that it may minister grace unto the hearers. And grieve not the holy Spirit of God, whereby ye are sealed unto the day of redemption. Let all bitterness, and wrath, and anger, and clamour, and evil speaking, be put away from you, with all malice: and be ye kind one to another, tenderhearted, forgiving one another, even as God for Christ's sake hath forgiven you."* **Colossians 1:3-5** *– We give thanks to God and the Father of our Lord Jesus Christ, praying always for you, since we heard of your faith in Christ Jesus, and of the love which ye have to all the saints, for the hope which is laid up for you in heaven, whereof ye heard before in the word of the truth of the gospel.* **1 Thessalonians 1:2-4** *– We give thanks to God always for you all, making mention of you in our prayers; remembering without ceasing your work of faith, and labour of love, and patience of hope in our Lord Jesus Christ, in the sight of God and our Father; knowing, brethren beloved, your election of God.* **Hebrews 6:10-12** *– For God is not unrighteous to forget your work and labour of love, which ye have shewed toward his name, in that ye have* *ministered to the saints, and do minister. And we desire that every one of you do shew the same diligence to the full assurance of hope unto the end: that ye be not slothful, but followers of them who through faith and patience inherit the promises. **1 Peter 5:5** – Likewise, ye younger, submit yourselves unto the elder. Yea, all of you be subject one to another, and be clothed with humility: for God resisteth the proud, and giveth grace to the humble. **3 John 1:11** – Beloved, follow not that which is evil, but that which is good. He that doeth good is of God: but he that doeth evil hath not seen God.*

Please refer to **Notes 5c** and **35** for additional information and Scriptures relating to humility.

34(b) *I* do all things without murmurings and disputings: that *I* may be blameless and harmless, *a child* of God, without rebuke, in the midst of a crooked and perverse nation, among whom *I* shine as *a light* in the world; holding forth the word of life. (Philippians 2:14-16)

Let's first look at the words blameless and harmless, and then we will look at the words murmurings and disputings. The word "blameless" in the Greek is *amemptos*. Its meaning in the Thayer's Greek Lexicon is "blameless, deserving no censure, free from fault or defect." The word "harmless" in the Greek is *akeraios*. Its meaning in the Thayer's Greek Lexicon is "**a. unmixed, pure,** as wine, metals, **b.** of the mind, **without admixture of evil, free from guile, innocent, simple:** Matthew 10:16; Romans 16:19; Philippians 2:15..." Right before this passage of Scripture, Paul writes,

> *Wherefore, my beloved, as ye have always obeyed, not as in my presence only, but now much more in my absence, work out your own salvation with fear and trembling. For it is God which worketh in you both to will and to do of his good pleasure.*
>
> (Philippians 2:12-13)

This reveals a very important fact that as dross is removed from silver, the Lord, through our submission to Him, by the Word of His grace and the power of His Spirit, <u>works</u> in us to remove ingrained carnal core beliefs and mindsets, impurities of the flesh, strongholds, etc., that are keeping His image from being seen within us *(Acts 20:32; Hebrews 4:12-13; 2 Corinthians 3:17-18)*. The word "murmurings" in the Greek is *goggysmos* meaning "a grumbling:–grudging, murmuring." Its meaning in the Thayer's Greek Lexicon is "...without querulous discontent, without murmurings, i.e. with a cheerful and willing mind, Philippians 2:14; 1 Peter 4:9." The word "disputings" in the Greek is *dialogismos*. Its meaning in the Thayer's Greek Lexicon is "a deliberating, questioning, about what is true: Luke 24:38; when in reference to what ought to be done, hesitation, doubting: Philippians 2:14." Rather than murmuring and disputing, the Lord is calling us, as born-again believers, to surrender our lives to Him and renew our minds to the truth of His Word in order to walk in this life with a cheerful and willing mind concerning His will for our lives without hesitating or doubting *(Romans 12:1-2; Ephesians 4:22-24)*. It is important to note that when someone habitually grumbles, finds fault, and complains, it could be coming from a root of bitterness. It is written,

> *Follow peace with all men, and holiness (the new man in Christ), without which no man shall see the Lord: looking diligently lest any man fail of the grace of God; lest any root of bitterness springing up trouble you, and thereby many be defiled...*
>
> (Hebrews 12:14-16)

Galatians 5:4 is a reference to *"looking diligently lest any man fail of the grace of God,"* in the above passage of Scripture. Before we look at *Galatians 5:4*, let's first look at *Galatians 4:19-23, 28-5:3* to get the full context of what Paul is saying here:

> *My little children, of whom I travail in birth again until Christ be formed in you, I desire to be present with you now, and to change my voice; for I stand in doubt of you. Tell me, ye that desire to be under the law, do ye not hear the law? For it is written, that Abraham had two sons, the one by a bondwoman, the other by a freewoman. But he who was of the bondwoman was born after the flesh; but he of the freewoman was by promise. Now we, brethren, as Isaac was, are the children of promise. But as then he that was born after the flesh persecuted him that was born after the Spirit, even so it is now. Nevertheless, what saith the scripture? "Cast out the bondwoman and her son: for the son of the bondwoman shall not be heir with the son of the freewoman." So then, brethren, we are not children of the bondwoman, but of the free. Stand fast therefore in the liberty wherewith Christ hath made us free, and be not entangled again with the yoke of bondage. Behold, I Paul say unto you, that if ye be circumcised, Christ shall profit you nothing. For I testify again to every man that is circumcised, that he is a debtor to do the whole law.*

Paul is telling us that we have been born from above and are no longer slaves to our carnality. He then writes in *Galatians 5:4*, *"Christ is become of no effect unto you, whosoever of you are justified by the law; ye are fallen from grace."* There is no way that we can keep the whole law! Thank God Jesus did it for us. Our part is to keep Christ first place in our hearts and minds, and to put on the new man. It is only through yielding to the born-again creation that we can overcome the works of the flesh. If you feel you may have a root of bitterness (e.g., holding grudges, grumbling, doubting others motives), it is important to repent before God and ask for His forgiveness and forgive yourself as well. Also consider confessing this to a mature believer in Christ where you can receive prayer (*James 5:16*). As sons and daughters of the freewoman, we are called to live out of the new man, the born-again creation within – *"And the effect of righteousness will be peace [internal and external], and the result of righteousness will be quietness and confident trust forever"* – *Isaiah 32:17 (AMPCE)*. This new man comes through circumcision made without hands, by putting off the sinful deeds of the flesh, our carnality, through the circumcision of the heart in order to reveal the true nature of Christ, as noted in the following two passages of Scripture:

1. ***Romans 2:28-29*** – *For he is not a Jew, which is one outwardly; neither is that circumcision, which is outward in the flesh: but he is a Jew, which is one inwardly; and circumcision is that of the heart, in the spirit, and not in the letter; whose praise is not of men, but of God.*
2. ***Colossians 2:11-12*** – *In whom also ye are circumcised with the circumcision made without hands, in putting off the body of the sins of the flesh by the circumcision of Christ: buried with him in baptism, wherein also ye are risen with him through the faith of the operation of God, who hath raised him from the dead.*

Are you also aware that when we grumble, complain, and/or harm another we are doing this against God? Here are some examples:

1. In the Old Testament, when the children of Israel were being delivered from Egypt, they witnessed many miraculous acts by the Lord through the hand of Moses. However, while

in the wilderness and hungry they began to murmur and complain to Moses and Aaron. And they said to the children of Israel,

"And in the morning, then ye shall see the glory of the LORD; for that he heareth your murmurings against the LORD: and what are we, that ye murmur against us?" And Moses said, "This shall be, when the LORD shall give you in the evening flesh to eat, and in the morning bread to the full; <u>for that the LORD heareth your murmurings which ye murmur against him: and what are we? Your murmurings are not against us, but against the LORD.</u>"

(Exodus 16:7-8)

The children of Israel chose to murmur and complain rather than to give thanks, trust the Lord, and stay focused on the truth. It would have been well for them to have said, "If God delivered us out of Egypt through miraculous acts and even parted the Red Sea, how much more is He able and willing to provide food for us."

2. Let's look at *Acts 9:3-5* at the exchange Jesus had with Saul (now Paul) who was persecuting His people: And as he (Saul) journeyed, he came near Damascus: and suddenly there shined round about him a light from heaven: and he fell to the earth, and heard a voice saying unto him, *"Saul, Saul, why persecutest thou me?"* And he said, *"Who art thou, Lord?"* And the Lord said, *"I am Jesus whom thou persecutest."*

Therefore, let's be mindful that whatever we do or say to one of God's beloved we are doing it to Him!

We are a light when we are truly thankful and others see us living out of the goodness of God and the grace of God—righteousness, peace, and joy *(Luke 17:20-21; Romans 14:17)*. Paul writes in *1 Thessalonians 5:18, "In every thing give thanks: for this is the will of God in Christ Jesus concerning you."* In order to be a light and a true example of Christlikeness, the fruit of the Spirit must be evident in our lives as Paul writes,

For all the law is fulfilled in one word, even in this; 'Thou shalt love thy neighbour as thyself.' But if ye bite and devour one another, take heed that ye be not consumed one of another. This I say then, Walk in the Spirit, and ye shall not fulfil the lust of the flesh. For the flesh lusteth against the Spirit, and the Spirit against the flesh: and these are contrary the one to the other: so that ye cannot do the things that ye would. But if ye be led of the Spirit, ye are not under the law. Now the works of the flesh are manifest, which are these; adultery, fornication, uncleanness, lasciviousness, idolatry, witchcraft, hatred, variance (contentions), emulations (jealousy), wrath, strife, seditions (dissension), heresies, envyings, murders, drunkenness, revellings, and such like: of the which I tell you before, as I have also told you in time past, that they which do such things shall not inherit the kingdom of God. <u>But the fruit of the Spirit is love, joy, peace, longsuffering, gentleness, goodness, faith, meekness, temperance: against such there is no law. And they that are Christ's have crucified the flesh with the affections and lusts. If we live in the Spirit, let us also walk in the Spirit. Let us not be desirous of vain glory, provoking one another, envying one another.</u>

(Galatians 5:14-26)

We are to shine as lights in this world (i.e., our home, our workplace, community gatherings with friends and family, the marketplace). In *1 Thessalonians 5:5*, Paul writes, *"Ye are all the children of light, and the children of the day: we are not of the night, nor of darkness.* He also writes in *Ephesians 5:8-10*, *"For ye were sometimes darkness, but now are ye light in the Lord: walk as children of light: (For the fruit of the Spirit is in all goodness and righteousness and truth;) proving what is acceptable unto the Lord."* The fruit of the Spirit is the manifestation of walking in the new man, so let's purpose to yield to those things that are acceptable to God, allowing the light of His Word to be seen by all through a renewed and cheerful mind.

Below are Scriptures relating to shining as a light in the world:

1. ***Proverbs 4:11, 18-27*** *– I have taught thee in the way of wisdom; I have led thee in right paths. But the path of the just is as the shining light, that shineth more and more unto the perfect day. The way of the wicked is as darkness: they know not at what they stumble. My son, attend to my words; incline thine ear unto my sayings. Let them not depart from thine eyes; keep them in the midst of thine heart. For they are life unto those that find them, and health to all their flesh. Keep thy heart with all diligence; for out of it are the issues of life. Put away from thee a froward mouth, and perverse lips put far from thee. Let thine eyes look right on, and let thine eyelids look straight before thee. Ponder the path of thy feet, and let all thy ways be established. Turn not to the right hand nor to the left: remove thy foot from evil.*

References:
Psalm 16:11 *– Thou wilt shew me the path of life: in thy presence is fulness of joy; at thy right hand there are pleasures for evermore.* ***Proverbs 12:28*** *– In the way of righteousness is life; and in the pathway thereof there is no death.* ***Ecclesiastes 2:13*** *– Then I saw that wisdom excelleth folly, as far as light excelleth darkness.* ***Matthew 5:14-16*** *– Jesus said, "Ye are the light of the world. A city that is set on a hill cannot be hid. Neither do men light a candle, and put it under a bushel, but on a candlestick; and it giveth light unto all that are in the house. Let your light so shine before men, that they may see your good works, and glorify your Father which is in heaven."* ***Matthew 10:16*** *– Jesus said, "Behold, I send you forth as sheep in the midst of wolves: be ye therefore wise as serpents, and harmless as doves."*

2. ***Matthew 25:40*** *– Jesus said "And the King (Jesus) shall answer and say unto them, 'Verily I say unto you, inasmuch as ye have done it unto one of the least of these my brethren, ye have done it unto me.'"*

References:
Luke 14:12-14 *(NIV) – Then Jesus said to his host, "When you give a luncheon or dinner, do not invite your friends, your brothers or sisters, your relatives, or your rich neighbors; if you do, they may invite you back and so you will be repaid. But when you give a banquet, invite the poor, the crippled, the lame, the blind, and you will be blessed. Although they cannot repay you, you will be repaid at the resurrection of the righteous."* ***1 Corinthians 8:12*** *– But when ye sin so against the brethren, and wound their weak conscience, ye sin against Christ.* ***James 4:11-17*** *– Speak not evil one of another, brethren. He that speaketh evil of his brother, and judgeth his brother, speaketh evil of the law, and judgeth the law: but if thou judge the law, thou art not a doer of the law, but a judge. There is one lawgiver, who is able to save and to destroy: who art thou that judgest another? Go to now, ye that say, "To day or to morrow we will go into such a city, and continue there a year, and buy and sell, and get gain:" whereas ye know not what shall be on the morrow. For what is your life? It is even a vapour, that appeareth for a little time, and then vanisheth away.*

*For that ye ought to say, "if the Lord will, we shall live, and do this, or that." But now ye rejoice in your boastings: all such rejoicing is evil. Therefore, to him that knoweth to do good, and doeth it not, to him it is sin. **1 Peter 4:9** (NASB)– Be hospitable to one another without complaint.*

3. ***Hebrews 13:20-21*** *– Now the God of peace, that brought again from the dead our Lord Jesus, that great shepherd of the sheep, through the blood of the everlasting covenant, make you perfect (complete) in every good work to do his will, working in you that which is wellpleasing in his sight, through Jesus Christ; to whom be glory for ever and ever.*

References:
2 Peter 1:17-21 *– Peter said, "For he received from God the Father honour and glory, when there came such a voice to him from the excellent glory, 'This is my beloved Son, in whom I am well pleased.' And this voice which came from heaven we heard, when we were with him in the holy mount. We have also a more sure word of prophecy; whereunto ye do well that ye take heed, as unto a light that shineth in a dark place, until the day dawn, and the day star arise in your hearts: knowing this first, that no prophecy of the scripture is of any private interpretation. For the prophecy came not in old time by the will of man: but holy men of God spake as they were moved by the Holy Ghost." **Revelation 22:16** – I Jesus have sent mine angel to testify unto you these things in the churches. I am the root and the offspring of David, and the bright and morning star.*

Please refer to **Note 5b** for additional information and Scriptures relating to the light of His Word.

Please refer to **Note 23b** for a greater understanding of innocence and an example of someone in the Old Testament who walked in true innocence before God and man.

---

35. *I* let this same attitude and purpose and [humble] mind be in *me* which was in Christ Jesus: *I* [let *You* be *my* example in humility]. (Philippians 2:5-AMPCE)

The Lord's example of humility is this: In order to fulfill the will of His heavenly Father, even though He was One with God and is God—the image of the invisible God, He took upon Himself the form of a servant and was made in the likeness of men (*John 6:38, 10:30, 1:1, 14; Colossians 1:15*). He continued to humble Himself and became obedient unto death, even the death of the cross (*Philippians 2:5-8*). This is true humility and we are called to walk in that same mindset as we choose to put off the old man, our carnal nature, and put on the new man in Christ (*Philippians 2:5-7; Romans 12:1-2; Galatians 3:27; Ephesians 4:21-24; Colossians 3:10-14*). Because Jesus Christ walked in total obedience to His heavenly Father, even unto death, God highly exalted Him and gave Him a name above every name that at the name of Jesus every knee shall bow and every tongue shall confess that He is Lord (*Romans 14:11; Philippians 2:9-11*). After the Lord's resurrection and before He was taken up to Heaven, He told His disciples in *Matthew 28:18, "All power is given unto me in heaven and earth."* It is essential for us as born-again believers to serve God with reverence and godly fear, by allowing His will to be done in our lives, as it is the instruction of wisdom and produces within us true humility (*Proverbs 15:33; James 3:13-18; Hebrews 12:28-29*). It is also important to understand, based on *Proverbs 15:33*, before honor is humility. As it is written in *Hebrews 5:7-10*, Jesus, Himself, while

He walked this earth served his heavenly Father with reverence and godly fear:

Who in the days of his flesh, when he had offered up prayers and supplications with strong crying and tears unto him that was able to save him from death, and was heard in that he feared; though he were a Son, yet learned he obedience by the things which he suffered; and being made perfect, he became the author of eternal salvation unto all them that obey him; called of God an high priest after the order of Melchisedec.

(Hebrews 5:7-10)

We are to walk as Christ walked:

Forasmuch then as Christ hath suffered for us in the flesh, arm yourselves likewise with the same mind: for he that hath suffered in the flesh hath ceased from sin; that he no longer should live the rest of his time in the flesh to the lusts of men, but to the will of God.

(1 Peter 4:1-2)

Many people believe that humility is a sign of weakness; this is far from the truth! As it is written in *James 3:13*, humility is the proper attribute of true wisdom:

Who is there among you who is wise and intelligent? Then let him by his noble living show forth his [good] works with the [unobtrusive] humility [which is the proper attribute] of true wisdom.

(James 3:13, AMPCE)

This wisdom is found in those who operate in the mind of Christ! Paul said in *1 Corinthians 1:24*, Christ is the power of God and the wisdom of God. Let's look at King Solomon who was the son of David. Solomon loved the Lord and in *1 Kings 3:3-4*, Solomon went to Gibeon to sacrifice there and he offered a thousand burnt offerings on that altar. And in *verses 5-10*:

<u>*In Gibeon the LORD appeared to Solomon in a dream by night: and God said, "Ask what I shall give thee.*</u>*" And Solomon said, "Thou hast shewed unto thy servant David my father great mercy, according as he walked before thee in truth, and in righteousness, and in uprightness of heart with thee; and thou hast kept for him this great kindness, that thou hast given him a son to sit on his throne, as it is this day. And now, O LORD my God, thou hast made thy servant king instead of David my father: and I am but a little child: I know not how to go out or come in. And thy servant is in the midst of thy people which thou hast chosen, a great people, that cannot be numbered nor counted for multitude. <u>Give therefore thy servant an understanding heart to judge thy people, that I may discern between good and bad: for who is able to judge this thy so great a people?' And the speech pleased the Lord, that Solomon had asked this thing</u>."*

In *verses 11-15* God said to him,

Because thou hast asked this thing, and hast not asked for thyself long life; neither hast asked riches for thyself, nor hast asked the life of thine enemies; but hast asked for thyself understanding to discern judgment; behold, I have done according to thy words: lo, I have given thee a wise and an understanding heart; so that there was none like thee before thee, neither after thee shall any arise like unto thee. And I have also given thee that which thou hast not asked, both riches, and honour: so that there shall not be any among the kings like unto thee all thy days. And if thou wilt walk in my ways, to keep my statutes and commandments, as thy father David did walk, then I will lengthen thy days. And Solomon awoke; and, behold, it was a dream.

And now let's look at *1 Kings 4:29-34*:

<u>*And God gave Solomon wisdom and understanding exceedingly much, and largeness of heart, even as the sand that is on the sea shore.*</u> *And Solomon's wisdom excelled the wisdom of all the children of the east country, and all the wisdom of Egypt. For he was wiser than all men; than Ethan the Ezrahite, and Heman, and Chalcol, and Darda, the sons of Mahol: and his fame was in all nations round about. And he spake three thousand proverbs: and his songs were a thousand and five. And he spake of trees, from the cedar tree that is in Lebanon even unto the hyssop that springeth out of the wall: he spake also of beasts, and of fowl, and of creeping things, and of fishes. And there came of all people to hear the wisdom of Solomon, from all kings of the earth, which had heard of his wisdom.*

Notice again in *1 Kings 3:3-4* what moved God to grant Solomon such wisdom: Solomon loved God and went to Gibeon to sacrifice there and he offered a thousand burnt offerings on that altar. In the Old Testament, God required animal sacrifices to cover the sins of His people. In the New Testament, where Jesus became the final sacrifice for our sin, He no longer requires animal sacrifices *(Hebrews 10:1-17)*. It now pleases God for born-again believers to offer themselves to Him as "a living sacrifice" and to not be conformed to this world but be transformed by the renewing of their minds *(Romans 12:1-2)*. Jesus' disciples came to Him saying,

"Who is the greatest in the kingdom of heaven?" And Jesus called a little child unto him, and set him in the midst of them, and said, "Verily I say unto you, except ye be converted, and become as little children, ye shall not enter into the kingdom of heaven. Whosoever therefore shall humble himself as this little child, the same is greatest in the kingdom of heaven."

(Matthew 18:1-4)

As we choose to humble ourselves, allowing His Word to change us into His image, we tap into His hidden treasure of wisdom and knowledge *(Colossians 2:3)*. This goes exceedingly beyond anything this life has to offer as Paul writes,

But we all, with open face beholding as in a glass the glory of the Lord, are changed into the same image from glory to glory, even as by the Spirit of the Lord. For God, who commanded the light to shine out of darkness, hath shined in our hearts, to give the light of the knowledge of the glory of God in the face of Jesus Christ. But we have this treasure in earthen vessels, that the excellency of the power may be of God, and not of us. For our light affliction, which is but for a moment, worketh for us a far more exceeding and eternal weight of glory; while we look not at the things which are seen, but at the things which are not seen: for the things which are seen are temporal; but the things which are not seen are eternal.

(2 Corinthians 3:18, 4:6-7, 17-18)

Paul writes,

Unto me, who am less than the least of all saints, is this grace given, that I should preach among the Gentiles the unsearchable riches of Christ; and to make all men see what is the fellowship of the mystery, which from the beginning of the world hath been hid in God, who created all things by Jesus Christ: to the intent that now unto the principalities and powers in heavenly places might be known by the church the manifold wisdom of God, according to the eternal purpose which he purposed in Christ Jesus our Lord: in whom we have boldness and access with confidence by the faith of him. Wherefore I desire that ye faint not at my tribulations for you, which is your glory.

(Ephesians 3:8-13)

Now let's look at *1 Kings 10:1-8*:

And when the queen of Sheba heard of the fame of Solomon concerning the name of the LORD, she came to prove him with hard questions. And she came to Jerusalem with a very great train, with camels that bare spices, and very much gold, and precious stones: and when she was come to Solomon, she communed with him of all that was in her heart. And Solomon told her all her questions: there was not any thing hid from the king, which he told her not. And when the queen of Sheba had seen all Solomon's wisdom, and the house that he had built, and the meat of his table, and the sitting of his servants, and the attendance of his ministers, and their apparel, and his cupbearers, and his ascent by which he went up unto the house of the LORD; there was no more spirit in her. And she said to the king, "It was a true report that I heard in mine own land of thy acts and of thy wisdom. Howbeit I believed not the words, until I came, and mine eyes had seen it: and, behold, the half was not told me: thy wisdom and prosperity exceedeth the fame which I heard. Happy are thy men, happy are these thy servants, which stand continually before thee, and that hear thy wisdom."

Again, in *1 Kings 4:29-31*, "*God gave Solomon wisdom and understanding exceedingly much, and largeness of heart, even as the sand that is on the sea shore. And Solomon's wisdom excelled the wisdom of all the children of the east country, and all the wisdom of Egypt. For he was wiser than all men.*" In *1 Kings 3:12*, God told Solomon that there has not been anyone like him who was before him, nor shall after him shall any arise like him. Therefore, the only one that could arise after Solomon who was greater than him in wisdom and understanding would be Christ—the wisdom of God and the power of God *(1 Corinthians 1:24)*! Jesus said in *Matthew 12:42*,

The queen of the south shall rise up in the judgment with this generation, and shall condemn it: for she came from the uttermost parts of the earth to hear the wisdom of Solomon; and, behold, a greater than Solomon is here.

In closing, Paul writes, "*To whom God would make known what is the riches of the glory of this mystery among the Gentiles; which is Christ in you, the hope of glory*" *(Colossians 1:27)*. We have One who is greater than Solomon's wisdom living on the inside of us (Christ) and we have the mind of Christ! God desires to do so much in and through His people:

But as it is written, 'Eye hath not seen, nor ear heard, neither have entered into the heart of

man, the things which God hath prepared for them that love him.' But God hath revealed them unto us by his Spirit: for the Spirit searcheth all things, yea, the deep things of God. For what man knoweth the things of a man, save the spirit of man which is in him? Even so the things of God knoweth no man, but the Spirit of God. Now we have received, not the spirit of the world, but the spirit which is of God; that we might know the things that are freely given to us of God.

(1 Corinthians 2:9-12)

Hallelujah! Therefore, let us lay aside every weight and the sin which so easily besets us and let us run with patience the race set before us, looking unto Jesus the author and the finisher of our faith… *(Hebrews 12:1-4).*

Below are Scriptures relating to obedience and the fear of the Lord (which go hand in hand):

Matthew 26:39 *– And he (Jesus) went a little further, and fell on his face, and prayed, saying, "O my Father, if it be possible, let this cup pass from me: nevertheless, not as I will, but as thou wilt.*

References:
Deuteronomy 4:4-6 *– Moses said, "But ye that did cleave unto the LORD your God are alive every one of you this day. Behold, I have taught you statutes and judgments, even as the LORD my God commanded me, that ye should do so in the land whither ye go to possess it. Keep therefore and do them; for this is your wisdom and your understanding in the sight of the nations, which shall hear all these statutes, and say, 'Surely this great nation is a wise and understanding people.'"* ***Job 28:28*** *– And unto man he (God) said, "Behold, the fear of the Lord, that is wisdom; and to depart from evil is understanding."* ***Psalm 111:10*** *– The fear of the LORD is the beginning of wisdom: a good understanding have all they that do his commandments: his praise endureth forever.* ***Proverbs 1:7*** *– The fear of the LORD is the beginning of knowledge: but fools despise wisdom and instruction.* ***Proverbs 22:4*** *– By humility and the fear of the LORD are riches, and honour, and life.* ***Ecclesiastes 12:13-14*** *– Let us hear the conclusion of the whole matter: Fear God, and keep his commandments: for this is the whole duty of man. For God shall bring every work into judgment, with every secret thing, whether it be good, or whether it be evil.*

Below are Scriptures relating to the wisdom of God:

Proverbs 1:20-23, 33 *– Wisdom crieth without; she uttereth her voice in the streets: she crieth in the chief place of concourse, in the openings of the gates: in the city she uttereth her words, saying, "How long, ye simple ones, will ye love simplicity? And the scorners delight in their scorning, and fools hate knowledge? Turn you at my reproof: behold, I will pour out my spirit unto you, I will make known my words unto you. But whoso hearkeneth unto me shall dwell safely, and shall be quiet from fear of evil."*

References:
Proverbs 3:13-24, 35 *– Happy is the man that findeth wisdom, and the man that getteth understanding. For the merchandise of it is better than the merchandise of silver, and the gain thereof than fine gold. She is more precious than rubies: and all the things thou canst desire are not to be compared unto her. Length of days is in her right hand; and in her left hand riches and honour. Her ways are ways of pleasantness and all her paths are peace. She is a tree of life to them that lay hold upon her: and happy is every one that retaineth her. The LORD by wisdom hath founded the earth; by understanding hath he established the heavens. By*

his knowledge the depths are broken up, and the clouds drop down the dew. My son, let not them depart from thine eyes: keep sound wisdom and discretion: so shall they be life unto thy soul, and grace to thy neck. Then shalt thou walk in thy way safely, and thy foot shall not stumble. When thou liest down, thou shalt not be afraid: yea, thou shalt lie down, and thy sleep shall be sweet. The wise shall inherit glory: but shame shall be the promotion of fools. **Proverbs 4:5-13** – *Get wisdom, get understanding: forget it not; neither decline from the words of my mouth. Forsake her not, and she shall preserve thee: love her, and she shall keep thee. Wisdom is the principal thing; therefore get wisdom: and with all thy getting get understanding. Exalt her, and she shall promote thee: she shall bring thee to honour, when thou doest embrace her. She shall give to thine head an ornament of grace: a crown of glory shall she deliver to thee. Hear, O my son, and receive my sayings; and the years of thy life shall be many. I have taught thee in the way of wisdom; I have led thee in right paths. When thou goest, thy steps shall not be straitened; and when thou runnest, thou shalt not stumble. Take fast hold of instruction; let her not go: keep her; for she is thy life.* **Proverbs 7:1-4** – *My son, keep my words, and lay up my commandments with thee. Keep my commandments, and live; and my law as the apple of thine eye. Bind them upon thy fingers, write them upon the table of thine heart. Say unto wisdom, "Thou art my sister;" and call understanding thy kinswoman (friend).* **Proverbs 8:1-11, 17-23** – *Doth not wisdom cry? And understanding put forth her voice? She standeth in the top of high places, by the way in the places of the paths. She crieth at the gates, at the entry of the city, at the coming in at the doors. Unto you, O men, I call; and my voice is to the sons of man. O ye simple, understand wisdom: and, ye fools, be ye of an understanding heart. Hear; for I will speak of excellent things; and the opening of my lips shall be right things. For my mouth shall speak truth; and wickedness is an abomination to my lips. All the words of my mouth are in righteousness; there is nothing froward or perverse in them. They are all plain to him that understandeth, and right to them that find knowledge. Receive my instruction, and not silver; and knowledge rather than choice gold. For wisdom is better than rubies; and all the things that may be desired are not to be compared to it. I love them that love me; and those that seek me early shall find me. Riches and honour are with me; yea, durable riches and righteousness. My fruit is better than gold, yea, than fine gold; and my revenue than choice silver. I lead in the way of righteousness, in the midst of the paths of judgment: that I may cause those that love me to inherit substance; and I will fill their treasures. The LORD possessed me in the beginning of his way, before his works of old. I was set up from everlasting, from the beginning, or ever the earth was.* **Proverbs 16:16** – *How much better is it to get wisdom than gold! And to get understanding rather to be chosen than silver!* **Ecclesiastes 7:19** – *Wisdom strengtheneth the wise more than ten mighty men which are in the city.* **Ecclesiastes 9:13-18** – *This wisdom have I seen also under the sun, and it seemed great unto me: There was a little city, and few men within it; and there came a great king against it, and besieged it, and built great bulwarks against it: now there was found in it a poor wise man, and he by his wisdom delivered the city; yet no man remembered that same poor man. Then said I, "Wisdom is better than strength: nevertheless, the poor man's wisdom is despised, and his words are not heard. The words of wise men are heard in quiet more than the cry of him that ruleth among fools. Wisdom is better than weapons of war: but one sinner destroyeth much good."* **1 Corinthians 1:20-25** – *Where is the wise? Where is the scribe? Where is the disputer of this world? Hath not God made foolish the wisdom of this world? For after that in the wisdom of God the world by wisdom knew not God, it pleased God by the foolishness of preaching to save them that believe. For the Jews require a sign, and the Greeks seek after wisdom: but we preach Christ crucified, unto the Jews a stumbling block, and unto the Greeks foolishness; but unto them which are called, both Jews and Greeks, Christ the power of God, and the wisdom of God. Because the foolishness of God is wiser than men; and the weakness of God is stronger than men.* **Colossians 2:1-3** – *For I would that ye knew what great conflict I have for you, and for them at Laodicea, and for as many as have not seen my face in the flesh; that their hearts might be comforted, being knit together in love, and unto all riches of the full assurance of understanding, to the acknowledgement of the mystery of God, and* *of the Father, and of Christ; in whom are hid all the treasures of wisdom and knowledge.*

Below are Scriptures relating to the importance of renewing our minds to the mind of Christ:

Psalm 92:5 – O LORD, how great are thy works! And thy thoughts are very deep.

References:
Isaiah 40:12-14 – Who hath measured the waters in the hollow of his hand, and meted out the heaven with the span, and comprehended the dust of the earth in a measure, and weighed the mountains in scales, and the hills in a balance? Who hath directed the Spirit of the LORD, or being his counsellor hath taught him? With whom took he counsel, and who instructed him, and taught him in the path of judgment, and taught him knowledge, and shewed him the way of understanding? **Jeremiah 6:16** *– Thus saith the LORD, "Stand ye in the ways, and see, and ask for the old paths, where is the good way, and walk therein, and ye shall find rest for your souls." But they said, "We will not walk therein."* **Matthew 11:28-30** *– Jesus said, "Come unto me, all ye that labour and are heavy laden, and I will give you rest. Take my yoke upon you, and learn of me; for I am meek and lowly in heart: and ye shall find rest unto your souls. For my yoke is easy, and my burden is light.* **Luke 6:46-49** *– Jesus said, "And why call ye me, Lord, Lord, and do not the things which I say? Whosoever cometh to me, and heareth my sayings, and doeth them, I will shew you to whom he is like: he is like a man which built an house, and digged deep, and laid the foundation on a rock: and when the flood arose, the stream beat vehemently upon that house, and could not shake it: for it was founded upon a rock. But he that heareth, and doeth not, is like a man that without a foundation built an house upon the earth; against which the stream did beat vehemently, and immediately it fell; and the ruin of that house was great."* **Romans 11:33-36** *– O the depth of the riches both of the wisdom and knowledge of God! How unsearchable are his judgments, and his ways past finding out! For who hath known the mind of the Lord? Or who hath been his counsellor? Or who hath first given to him, and it shall be recompensed unto him again? For of him, and through him, and to him, are all things: to whom be glory forever. Amen.* **Romans 12:1-2, 16** *– I beseech you therefore, brethren, by the mercies of God, that ye present your bodies a living sacrifice, holy, acceptable unto God, which is your reasonable service. And be not conformed to this world: but be ye transformed by the renewing of your mind, that ye may prove what is that good, and acceptable, and perfect, will of God. Be of the same mind one toward another. Mind not high things, but condescend to men of low estate. Be not wise in your own conceits.* **Romans 15:5-6** *– Now the God of patience and consolation grant you to be likeminded one toward another according to Christ Jesus: that ye may with one mind and one mouth glorify God, even the Father of our Lord Jesus Christ.* **1 Corinthians 1:10** *– Now I beseech you, brethren, by the name of our Lord Jesus Christ, that ye all speak the same thing, and that there be no divisions among you; but that ye be perfectly joined together in the same mind and in the same judgment.* **1 Corinthians 2:6-16** *– Howbeit we speak wisdom among them that are perfect: yet not the wisdom of this world, nor of the princes of this world, that come to nought (nothing): but we speak the wisdom of God in a mystery, even the hidden wisdom, which God ordained before the world unto our glory: which none of the princes of this world knew: for had they known it, they would not have crucified the Lord of glory. But as it is written, "Eye hath not seen, nor ear heard, neither have entered into the heart of man, the things which God hath prepared for them that love him." But God hath revealed them unto us by his Spirit: for the Spirit searcheth all things, yea, the deep things of God. For what man knoweth the things of a man, save the spirit of man which is in him? Even so the things of God knoweth no man, but the Spirit of God. Now we have received, not the spirit of the world, but the spirit which is of God; that we might know the things that are freely given to us of God. Which things also we speak, not in the words which man's wisdom teacheth, but which the Holy Ghost teacheth; comparing spiritual things with spiritual. But*

the natural man receiveth not the things of the Spirit of God: for they are foolishness unto him: neither can he know them, because they are spiritually discerned. But he that is spiritual judgeth all things, yet he himself is judged of no man. For who hath known the mind of the Lord, that he may instruct him? But we have the mind of Christ. **2 Corinthians 3:17-18** *– Now the Lord is that Spirit: and where the Spirit of the Lord is, there is liberty. But we all, with open face beholding as in a glass the glory of the Lord, are changed into the same image from glory to glory, even as by the Spirit of the Lord.* **2 Corinthians 13:11** *– Finally, brethren, farewell. Be perfect (complete), be of good comfort, be of one mind, live in peace; and the God of love and peace shall be with you.* **Ephesians 4:9-24** *– ...He that descended is the same also that ascended up far above all heavens, that he might fill all things.) and he gave some, apostles; and some, prophets; and some, evangelists; and some, pastors and teachers; for the perfecting of the saints, for the work of the ministry, for the edifying of the body of Christ: till we all come in the unity of the faith, and of the knowledge of the Son of God, unto a perfect man, unto the measure of the stature of the fulness of Christ: that we henceforth be no more children, tossed to and fro, and carried about with every wind of doctrine, by the sleight of men, and cunning craftiness, whereby they lie in wait to deceive; but speaking the truth in love, may grow up into him in all things, which is the head, even Christ: from whom the whole body fitly joined together and compacted by that which every joint supplieth, according to the effectual working in the measure of every part, maketh increase of the body unto the edifying of itself in love. This I say therefore, and testify in the Lord, that ye henceforth walk not as other Gentiles walk, in the vanity of their mind, having the understanding darkened, being alienated from the life of God through the ignorance that is in them, because of the blindness of their heart.: who being past feeling have given themselves over unto lasciviousness, to work all uncleanness with greediness. But ye have not so learned Christ; if so be that ye have heard him and have been taught by him, as the truth is in Jesus: that ye put off concerning the former conversation (behavior) the old man, which is corrupt according to the deceitful lusts; and be renewed in the spirit of your mind; and that ye put on the new man, which after God is created in righteousness and true holiness.* **Colossians 3:8-11** *– But now ye also put off all these; anger, wrath, malice, blasphemy, filthy communication out of your mouth. Lie not one to another, seeing that ye have put off the old man with his deeds; and have put on the new man, which is renewed in knowledge after the image of him that created him:...* **James 1:23-25** *– For if any be a hearer of the word, and not a doer, he is like unto a man beholding his natural face in a glass: for he beholdeth himself, and goeth his way, and straightway forgetteth what manner of man he was. But whoso looketh into the perfect law of liberty, and continueth therein, he being not a forgetful hearer, but a doer of the work, this man shall be blessed in his deed.* **1 Peter 2:20-25** *– ...For even hereunto were ye called: because Christ also suffered for us, leaving us an example, that ye should follow his steps:...* **1 John 2:5** *– But whoso keepeth his word, in him verily is the love of God perfected: hereby know we that we are in him. He that saith he abideth in him ought himself also so to walk, even as he walked.*

Please refer to **Notes 36a** and **37b** for additional information and Scriptures relating to this subject matter.

Please refer to **Notes 5c** and **34a** for additional information and Scriptures relating to humility.

36(a) [For my determined purpose is] that I may know *You* [that I may progressively become more deeply and intimately acquainted with *You*, perceiving and recognizing and understanding the wonders of *Your* Person more strongly and more clearly], and that I may in that same way come to know the power outflowing from *Your* resurrection [which it exerts over believers], (Philippians 3:10-AMPCE)

The word "know" in the Greek is *ginosko*. Its meaning in the Thayer's Greek Lexicon is "to become acquainted with, to know, is employed in the N. T. of the knowledge of God and Christ, and of the things relating to them or proceeding from them; ...his consummate kindness toward us, and the benefits redounding to us from fellowship with him..." This is revelation knowledge of the One and True living God in the Person of Jesus Christ revealed through the power of His Holy Spirit to those who have a genuine intimate relationship with Him. In *John 8:31-32*, Jesus said to the Jews that believed in Him – *"If ye continue in my word, then are ye my disciples indeed; and ye shall know the truth, and the truth shall make you free."* The word "know" here is the same Greek word *ginosko* as defined above. Let's look at *Matthew 16:13-18*:

> *When Jesus came into the coasts of Caesarea Philippi, he asked his disciples, saying, "Whom do men say that I the Son of man am?" and they said, "Some say that thou art John the Baptist: some, Elias (Elijah); and others, Jeremias (Jeremiah), or one of the prophets." He saith unto them, "But whom say ye that I am?" And Simon Peter answered and said, "Thou art the Christ, the Son of the living God." And Jesus answered and said unto him, "Blessed art thou, Simon Barjona: for flesh and blood hath not revealed it unto thee, but my Father which is in heaven. And I say also unto thee, that thou art Peter, and upon this rock I will build my church; and the gates of hell shall not prevail against it."*

The word "rock" in the Greek is *petra* meaning "a (mass of) rock (literally or figuratively):–rock." Its meaning in the Thayer's Greek Lexicon is "metaphorically, a man like a rock, by reason of his firmness and strength of soul: Matthew 16:18." I believe this rock that Jesus is referring to is revelation knowledge of Him revealed in the hearts and minds of born-again believers who seek to know Him. Upon this rock of revelation knowledge the gates of hell will not prevail! This goes along with what Jesus said in *Matthew 7:21-27*,

> *Not every one that saith unto me, "Lord, Lord," shall enter into the kingdom of heaven; but he that doeth the will of my Father which is in heaven. Many will say to me in that day, "Lord, Lord, have we not prophesied in thy name? And in thy name have cast out devils? And in thy name done many wonderful works?" And then will I profess unto them, "I never knew you: depart from me, ye that work iniquity." Therefore whosoever heareth these sayings of mine, and doeth them, I will liken him unto a wise man, which built his house upon a rock: and the rain descended, and the floods came, and the winds blew, and beat upon that house; and it fell not: for it was founded upon a rock. And every one that heareth these sayings of mine, and doeth them not, shall be likened unto a foolish man, which built his house upon the sand: and the rain descended, and the floods came, and the winds blew, and beat upon that house; and it fell: and great was the fall of it.*

The following passage of Scripture is also very important when relating to this subject matter:

Simon Peter, a servant and an apostle of Jesus Christ, to them that have obtained like precious faith with us through the righteousness of God and our Saviour Jesus Christ: grace and peace be multiplied unto you through the knowledge of God, and of Jesus our Lord, according as his divine power hath given unto us all things that pertain unto life and godliness, through the knowledge of him that hath called us to glory and virtue: whereby are given unto us exceeding great and precious promises: that by these ye might be partakers of the divine nature, having escaped the corruption that is in the world through lust. And beside this, giving all diligence, add to your faith virtue; and to virtue knowledge; and to knowledge temperance; and to temperance patience; and to patience godliness; and to godliness brotherly kindness; and to brotherly kindness charity (God's love). For if these things be in you, and abound, they make you that ye shall neither be barren nor unfruitful in the knowledge of our Lord Jesus Christ. But he that lacketh these things is blind, and cannot see afar off, and hath forgotten the he was purged from his old sins. Wherefore the rather, brethren, give diligence to make your calling and election sure: for if ye do these things, ye shall never fall: for so an entrance shall be ministered unto you abundantly into the everlasting kingdom of our Lord and Saviour Jesus Christ.

(2 Peter 1:1-11)

The word "knowledge" in *verse 8* in the Greek is *epignosis* and ultimately comes from the root word *ginosko*. The definition for *epignosis* in the Thayer's Greek Lexicon is "precise and correct knowledge used in the N. T. of the knowledge of things ethical and divine: absolute, Philippians 1:9; Colossians 3:10; Romans 10:2… of Christ, i.e., the true knowledge of Christ's nature, dignity, benefits: Ephesians 4:13; 2 Peter 1:8; 2 Peter 2:20." Let's look again at *verses 5-8*,

And beside this, giving all diligence, add to your faith virtue; and to virtue knowledge; and to knowledge temperance; and to temperance patience; and to patience godliness; and to godliness brotherly kindness; and to brotherly kindness charity (God's love). For if these things be in you, and abound, they make you that ye shall neither be barren nor unfruitful in the knowledge of our Lord Jesus Christ.

As a citizen of Heaven, it is essential to build upon these godly attributes in order to walk in newness of life and to be fruitful in the knowledge of our Lord and Savior Jesus Christ!

Jesus said,

The thief cometh not, but for to steal, and to kill, and to destroy: I am come that they might have life, and that they might have it more abundantly. I am the good shepherd: the good shepherd giveth his life for the sheep. I am the good shepherd, and know my sheep, and am known of mine.

(John 10:10-11, 14)

In *verse 10*, the word "life" in the Greek is *zoe*. Its meaning in the Thayer's Greek Lexicon is "**life real and genuine, vita quae sola vita nominanda** (Cicero, de sen. 21, 77), **a life active and vigorous, devoted to God, blessed, the portion even in this world of those who put their trust in Christ, but after the resurrection to be consummated by new accessions (among them a more perfect body), and to last forever**… to be obtained in fellowship with Christ." And in *verse 14*, the word "known" is the same Greek word *ginosko*. Jesus said in *John 17:3*, *"And this is life eternal, that they might know thee the only true God, and Jesus Christ, whom thou hast sent."* The word "known" here in the Greek is also *ginosko*. Eternal life is birthed into the heart and mind of the born-again believer through knowing Christ and functioning in the mind of Christ. This eternal life, the abundant life that only resides in Christ Jesus, springs forth from the wellspring of living water (His Holy Spirit) that resides within the born-again believer *(John 7:38-39)*. We must understand that no matter how successful we are in this present life, nothing compares with the inherent life that comes only through an intimate relationship with Him and living out of the new man as Paul writes,

> *Though I might also have confidence in the flesh. If any other man thinketh that he hath whereof he might trust in the flesh, I more: circumcised the eighth day, of the stock of Israel, of the tribe of Benjamin, an Hebrew of the Hebrews; as touching the law, a Pharisee; concerning zeal, persecuting the church; touching the righteousness which is in the law, blameless. But what things were gain to me, those I counted loss for Christ. Yea doubtless, and I count all things but loss for the excellency of the knowledge of Christ Jesus my Lord: for whom I have suffered the loss of all things, and do count them but dung, that I may win Christ, and be found in him, not having mine own righteousness, which is of the law, but that which is through the faith of Christ, the righteousness which is of God by faith: that I may know (Greek = ginosko) him, and the power of his resurrection, and the fellowship of his sufferings, being made conformable unto his death; if by any means I might attain unto the resurrection of the dead. Not as though I had already attained, either were already perfect: but I follow after, if that I may apprehend that for which also I am apprehended of Christ Jesus. Brethren, I count not myself to have apprehended: but this one thing I do, forgetting those things which are behind, and reaching forth unto those things which are before, I press toward the mark for the prize of the high calling of God in Christ Jesus. Let us therefore, as many as be perfect, be thus minded: and if in any thing ye be otherwise minded, God shall reveal even this unto you.*
>
> (Philippians 3:4-15)

Below are Scriptures relating to seeking God:

2 Chronicles 26:5 — *And he sought God in the days of Zechariah, who had understanding in the visions of God: and as long as he sought the LORD, God made him to prosper.*

References:
Ezra 8:22 — *For I was ashamed to require of the king a band of soldiers and horsemen to help us against the enemy in the way: because we had spoken unto the king, saying, "The hand of our God is upon all them for good that seek him; but his power and his wrath is against all them that forsake him."* *Psalm 27:4-5* — *One thing have I desired of the LORD, that will I seek after; that I may dwell in the house of the LORD all the days of my life, to behold the beauty of the LORD, and to enquire in his temple. For in the time of trouble he shall hide me in his pavilion: in the secret of his tabernacle shall he hide me; he shall set me up upon a rock.* *Psalm 40:16* — *Let all those that seek thee rejoice and be glad in thee: let such as love thy salvation say continually, "The LORD be magnified."* *Proverbs 19:20-21* — *Hear counsel, and receive instruction, that thou mayest be wise in thy latter end. There are many devices in a man's heart; nevertheless the counsel of the LORD, that shall stand.* *Jeremiah 9:23-24* — *Thus saith the LORD, "Let not the wise man glory in his wisdom, neither let the mighty man glory in his might, let not the rich man glory in his riches: but let*

*him that glorieth glory in this, that he understandeth and knoweth me, that I am the LORD which exercise lovingkindness, judgment, and righteousness, in the earth: for in these things I delight," saith the LORD. **Matthew 6:28-34** (NKJV) – Jesus said, "So why do you worry about clothing? Consider the lilies of the field, how they grow: they neither toil nor spin; and yet I say to you that even Solomon in all his glory was not arrayed like one of these. Now if God so clothes the grass of the field, which today is, and tomorrow is thrown into the oven, will He not much more clothe you, O you of little faith? Therefore, do not worry, saying, 'What shall we eat?' or 'What shall we drink?' or 'What shall we wear?' For after all these things the Gentiles seek. For your heavenly Father knows that you need all these things. But seek first the kingdom of God and His righteousness, and all these things shall be added to you. Therefore do not worry about tomorrow, for tomorrow will worry about its own things. Sufficient for the day is its own trouble." **Luke 10:38-42** – Now it came to pass, as they went, that he (Jesus) entered into a certain village: and a certain woman named Martha received him into her house. And she had a sister called Mary, which also sat at Jesus' feet, and heard his word. But Martha was cumbered about much serving, and came to him, and said, "Lord, dost thou not care that my sister hath left me to serve alone? Bid her therefore that she help me." And Jesus answered and said unto her, "Martha, Martha, you are worried and troubled about many things. But one thing is needful: and Mary hath chosen that good part, which shall not be taken away from her." **2 Peter 1:16-21** – For we have not followed cunningly devised fables, when we made known unto you the power and coming of our Lord Jesus Christ, but were eyewitnesses of his majesty. For he received from God the Father honour and glory, when there came such a voice to him from the excellent glory, "This is my beloved Son, in whom I am well pleased." And this voice which came from heaven we heard, when we were with him in the holy mount. We have also a more sure word of prophecy; whereunto ye do well that ye take heed, as unto a light that shineth in a dark place, until the day dawn, and the day star arise in your hearts: knowing this first, that no prophecy of the scripture is of any private interpretation. For the prophecy came not in old time by the will of man: but holy men of God spake as they were moved by the Holy Ghost. **1 John 2:3-6** – And hereby we do know that we know him, if we keep his commandments. He that saith, "I know him, and keepeth not his commandments," is a liar, and the truth is not in him. But whoso keepeth his word, in him verily is the love of God perfected: hereby know we that we are in him. He that saith he abideth in him ought himself also so to walk, even as he walked. **1 John 5:20** – And we know that the Son of God is come, and hath given us an understanding, that we may know (Greek = ginosko) him that is true, and we are in him that is true, even in his Son Jesus Christ. This is the true God, and eternal life.*

Please refer to **Note 17a** for additional Scriptures relating to seeking God.

Please refer to **Notes 27b, 28a, 28b, and 28c** relating to the new spiritual self, the new man.

> **36(b)** and that I may so share *Your* sufferings as to be continually transformed [in spirit into *Your* likeness even] to *Your* death, [in the hope] that if possible I may attain to the [spiritual and moral] resurrection [that lifts me] out from among the dead [even while in my body]. (Philippians 3:10-11-AMPCE)

As we continue to yield ourselves to Christ and seek Him, we become more and more like Him! This occurs as Paul writes in *Titus 3:4-8*:

> *But after that the kindness and love of God our Saviour toward man appeared, not by works of righteousness which we have done, but according to his mercy he saved us, by the washing*

of regeneration, and renewing of the Holy Ghost; which he shed on us abundantly through Jesus Christ our Saviour; that being justified by his grace, we should be made heirs according to the hope of eternal life. This is a faithful saying, and these things I will that thou affirm constantly, that they which have believed in God might be careful to maintain good works. These things are good and profitable unto men.

The word "regeneration" in the Greek is *paliggenesia*. Its meaning in the Thayer's Greek Lexicon is "new birth, reproduction, renewal, recreation; hence, 'moral renovation, regeneration, the production of a new life consecrated to God, a radical change of mind for the better.' Commonly, however, the word denotes the restoration of a thing to its pristine state, its renovation, as the renewal or restoration of life after death." Obtaining this pristine state is walking in the new man, the born-again creation within. I believe Paul best describes this outcome when he writes,

For God, who commanded the light to shine out of darkness, hath shined in our hearts, to give the light of the knowledge of the glory of God in the face of Jesus Christ. But we have this treasure in earthen vessels, that the excellency of the power may be of God, and not of us. We are troubled on every side, yet not distressed; we are perplexed, but not in despair; persecuted, but not forsaken; cast down, but not destroyed; always bearing about in the body the dying of the Lord Jesus, that the life also of Jesus might be made manifest in our body. For we which live are always delivered unto death for Jesus' sake, that the life also of Jesus might be made manifest in our mortal flesh. So then death worketh in us, but life in you. We having the same spirit of faith, according as it is written, 'I believed, and therefore have I spoken;' we also believe, and therefore speak; knowing that he which raised up the Lord Jesus shall raise up us also by Jesus, and shall present us with you. For all things are for your sakes, that the abundant grace might through the thanksgiving of many redound to the glory of God. For which cause we faint not; but though our outward man perish, yet the inward man is renewed day by day. For our light affliction, which is but for a moment, worketh for us a far more exceeding and eternal weight of glory; while we look not at the things which are seen, but at the things which are not seen: for the things which are seen are temporal (temporary); but the things which are not seen are eternal.

(2 Corinthians 4:6-18)

Below are Scriptures relating to entering into Christ's sufferings:

Hebrews 12:1-4 *— Wherefore seeing we also are compassed about with so great a cloud of witnesses, let us lay aside every weight, and the sin which doth so easily beset us, and let us run with patience the race that is set before us, looking unto Jesus the author and finisher of our faith; who for the joy that was set before him endured the cross, despising the shame, and is set down at the right hand of the throne of God. For consider him that endured such contradiction of sinners against himself, lest you be wearied and faint in your minds. Ye have not yet resisted unto blood, striving against sin.*

References:
Luke 22:41-44 *— and he (Jesus) was withdrawn from them (his disciples) about a stone's cast, and kneeled down, and prayed, saying, "Father, if thou be willing, remove this cup from me: nevertheless, not my will, but thine, be done." And there appeared an angel unto him from heaven, strengthening him. And being in an agony he prayed more earnestly: and his sweat was as it were great drops of blood falling down to*

the ground. ***Acts 5:34-35, 38-42*** – *Then stood there up one in the council, a Pharisee, named Gamaliel, a doctor of the law, had in reputation among all the people, and commanded to put the apostles forth a little space; and said unto them, "Ye men of Israel, take heed to yourselves what ye intend to do as touching these men… And now I say unto you, Refrain from these men, and let them alone: for if this counsel or this work be of men it will come to naught (nothing): but if it be of God, ye cannot overthrow it; lest haply ye be found even to fight against God." And to him they agreed: and when they had called the apostles, and beaten them, they commanded that they should not speak in the name of Jesus, and let them go. And they departed from the presence of the council, rejoicing that they were counted worthy to suffer shame for his name. And daily in the temple, and in every house, they ceased not to teach and preach Jesus Christ. **Acts 14:22** – Confirming the souls of the disciples, and exhorting them to continue in the faith, and that we must through much tribulation enter into the kingdom of God. **Romans 5:1-5** – Therefore being justified by faith, we have peace with God through our Lord Jesus Christ: by whom also we have access by faith into this grace wherein we stand, and rejoice in hope of the glory of God. And not only so, but we glory in tribulations also: knowing that tribulation worketh patience; and patience, experience; and experience, hope: and hope maketh not ashamed; because the love of God is shed abroad in our hearts by the Holy Ghost which is given to us. **Romans 8:15-19** – For ye have not received the spirit of bondage again to fear; but ye have received the Spirit of adoption, whereby we cry, "Abba, Father." The Spirit itself beareth witness with our spirit, that we are the children of God: and if children, then heirs; heirs of God, and joint-heirs with Christ; if so be that we suffer with him, that we may be also glorified together. For I reckon that the sufferings of this present time are not worthy to be compared with the glory which shall be revealed in us. For the earnest expectation of the creature waiteth for the manifestation of the sons of God. **1 Corinthians 9:24-27** – Know ye not that they which run in a race run all, but one receiveth the prize? So run, that ye may obtain. And every man that striveth for the mastery is temperate in all things. Now they do it to obtain a corruptible crown; but we an incorruptible. I therefore so run, not as uncertainly; so fight I, not as one that beateth the air: but I keep under my body, and bring it into subjection: lest that by any means, when I have preached to others, I myself should be a castaway. **2 Timothy 2:11-13** – It is a faithful saying: For if we be dead with him, we shall also live with him: if we suffer, we shall also reign with him: if we deny him, he also will deny us: if we believe not, yet he abideth faithful: he cannot deny himself. **James 1:1-4, 12-18** – James, a servant of God and of the Lord Jesus Christ, to the twelve tribes which are scattered abroad, greeting. My brethren, count it all joy when ye fall into divers temptations; knowing this, that the trying of your faith worketh patience. But let patience have her perfect work, that ye may be perfect and entire, wanting nothing. Blessed is the man that endureth temptation: for when he is tried, he shall receive the crown of life, which the Lord hath promised to them that love him. Let no man say when he is tempted, "I am tempted of God": for God cannot be tempted with evil, neither tempteth he any man: but every man is tempted, when he is drawn away of his own lust, and enticed. Then when lust hath conceived, it bringeth forth sin: and sin, when it is finished, bringeth forth death. Do not err, my beloved brethren. Every good gift and every perfect gift is from above, and cometh down from the Father of lights, with whom is no variableness, neither shadow of turning. Of his own will begat he us with the word of truth, that we should be a kind of firstfruits of his creatures. **James 5:10-11** – Take, my brethren, the prophets, who have spoken in the name of the Lord, for an example of suffering affliction, and of patience. Behold, we count them happy which endure. Ye have heard of the patience of Job, and have seen the end of the Lord; that the Lord is very pitiful, and of tender mercy. **1 Peter 4:12-19** – Beloved, think it not strange concerning the fiery trial which is to try you, as though some strange thing happened unto you: but rejoice, inasmuch as ye are partakers of Christ's sufferings; that, when his glory shall be revealed, ye may be glad also with exceeding joy. If ye be reproached for the name of Christ, happy are ye; for the spirit of glory and of God resteth upon you: on their part he is evil spoken of, but on your part, he is glorified. But let none of you suffer as a murderer, or as a thief, or as an evildoer, or as a busybody in other men's matters. Yet if any* *man suffer as a Christian, let him not be ashamed; but let him glorify God on this behalf. For the time is come that judgment must begin at the house of God: and if it first begin at us, what shall the end be of them that obey not the gospel of God? And if the righteous scarcely be saved, where shall the ungodly and the sinner appear? Wherefore let them that suffer according to the will of God commit the keeping of their souls to him in well doing, as unto a faithful Creator. **1 Peter 5:8-11** — Be sober, be vigilant; because your adversary the devil, as a roaring lion, walketh about, seeking whom he may devour: whom resist stedfast in the faith, knowing that the same afflictions are accomplished in your brethren that are in the world. But the God of all grace, who hath called us unto his eternal glory by Christ Jesus, after that ye have suffered a while, make you perfect, stablish, strengthen, settle you. To him be glory and dominion for ever and ever. Amen.*

Please refer to **Notes 39** and **41** for additional information and Scriptures relating to entering into Christ's sufferings.

37(a) *For* I have been crucified with Christ; it is no longer I who live, but Christ lives in me; (Galatians 2:20-NKJV)

Paul writes,

> *For I through the law am dead to the law, that I might live unto God. I am crucified with Christ: nevertheless, I live; yet not I, but Christ liveth in me: and the life which I now live in the flesh I live by the faith of the Son of God, who loved me, and gave himself for me. I do not frustrate the grace of God: for if righteousness come by the law, then Christ is dead in vain.*
>
> (Galatians 2:19-21)

There are two laws that govern the hearts and minds of every man and woman on the face of this earth:

1. The law of sin and death *(Romans 8:1-2)*. This law originates from the first man, Adam. In *Genesis 2:16-17*, God commanded Adam saying, "*Of every tree of the garden thou mayest freely eat: but of the tree of the knowledge of good and evil, thou shalt not eat of it: for in the day that thou eatest thereof thou shalt surely die.*" Adam disobeyed God's command by eating of the tree of the knowledge of good and evil *(Genesis 3:1-7)*. At that moment death began operating in Adam and Eve as they were no longer living out of God's nature but living out of a sinful fallen nature. Their firstborn son, Cain, was a murderer. They became rulers of their own destiny, as they were no longer governed by the life-giving flow of God's Spirit but by their own human carnality. They became individuals who by their own self-centered means would try to fulfill their own needs, desires, hopes, and dreams. Satan uses this sinful fallen nature in man and woman to whisper lies and deceptive thoughts that, when entertained, can cause a spiral effect within to a place of darkness and despair. This law governs those who have not yet been born again as the carnal nature is the only nature that resides within them. This nature serves sin in order to gratify the lusts and desires of the flesh. Babes in Christ also struggle with this because the carnal nature, or the old man, is so ingrained within them and it takes time for the renewal and growth process of the

new man to take effect *(Romans 12:1-2; Ephesians 4:22-24)*. Unfortunately, this is why some fall away from the faith because they have not endured long enough to see the fruit of the born-again creation, as we enter the kingdom of God through much tribulation *(Mark 4:14-32; Acts 14:22)*. Let's see how great the devastation of the law of sin and death became:

> *And God saw that the wickedness of man was great in the earth, and that every imagination of the thoughts of his heart was only evil continually. And it repented the LORD that he had made man on the earth, and it grieved him at his heart. And the LORD said, "I will destroy man whom I have created from the face of the earth; both man, and beast, and the creeping thing, and the fowls of the air; for it repenteth me that I have made them." But Noah found grace in the eyes of the LORD.*
>
> (Genesis 6:5-8)

Thank God for Noah or we would not be here! The law of God given by Moses intensified sin within us, showing us just how miserable we are in our carnality. Paul writes,

> *For when we were in the flesh, the motions of sins, which were by the law, did work in our members to bring forth fruit unto death. But now we are delivered from the law, that being dead wherein we were held; that we should serve in newness of spirit, and not in the oldness of the letter. What shall we say then? Is the law sin? God forbid. Nay, I had not known sin, but by the law: for I had not known lust, except the law had said, "Thou shalt not covet." But sin, taking occasion by the commandment, wrought in me all manner of concupiscence (desire for what is forbidden, lust). For without the law sin was dead. For I was alive without the law once: but when the commandment came, sin revived, and I died. And the commandment, which was ordained to life, I found to be unto death. For sin, taking occasion by the commandment, deceived me, and by it slew me. Wherefore the law is holy, and the commandment holy, and just, and good. Was then that which is good made death unto me? God forbid, But sin, that it might appear sin, working death in me by that which is good; that sin by the commandment might become exceeding sinful. For we know that the law is spiritual: but I am carnal, sold under sin.*
>
> (Romans 7:5-14)

2. The law of the Spirit of life in Christ Jesus *(Romans 8:1-2)*. This law overcomes the law of sin and death by lifting us up and out of the body of sin, causing us to mount up with wings as eagles soaring above the challenges and complexities of human life *(Isaiah 40:28-31)*. The law of the Spirit of life in Christ Jesus is what gives life to the new nature within the born-again believer in Christ. The key to operating out of this new life is found in the following passage of Scripture where Paul writes,

> *...put off concerning the former conversation (behavior) the old man, which is corrupt according to the deceitful lusts; and be renewed in the spirit of your mind; and that ye put on the new man, which after God is created in righteousness and true holiness.*
>
> (Ephesians 4:21-24)

300

Only by putting off the old man and putting on the new man, through the renewal process, can we truly walk in true righteousness and holiness. For the *spirit of the mind* or the *inmost mind* is the life source, the power source, the energy source of the mind. It gives life, power, and energy to the internal beliefs concerning who we are and causes those internal beliefs to operate automatically (see *Understanding Its Importance - Volume 1* for details). God has called us to crucify the old man (our carnal sinful nature) that keeps us bound to the law of sin and death and to put on the new man in Christ that lifts us up and out of our sinful nature to the abundant life in Him! Below are two Scripture references that go along with this subject matter:

1. **Romans 6:3-13, 18-23** – *Know ye not, that so many of us as were baptized into Jesus Christ were baptized into his death? Therefore, we are buried with him by baptism into death: that like as Christ was raised up from the dead by the glory of the Father, even so we also should walk in newness of life. For if we have been planted together in the likeness of his death, we shall be also in the likeness of his resurrection: knowing this, that our old man is crucified with him, that the body of sin might be destroyed, that henceforth we should not serve sin. For he that is dead is freed from sin. Now if we be dead with Christ, we believe that we shall also live with him: knowing that Christ being raised from the dead dieth no more; death hath no more dominion over him. For in that he died, he died unto sin once: but in that he liveth, he liveth unto God. Likewise reckon ye also yourselves to be dead indeed unto sin, but alive unto God through Jesus Christ our Lord. Let not sin therefore reign in your mortal body, that ye should obey it in the lusts thereof. Neither yield ye your members as instruments of unrighteousness unto sin: but yield yourselves unto God, as those that are alive from the dead, and your members as instruments of righteousness unto God. Being then made free from sin, ye became the servants of righteousness. I speak after the manner of men because of the infirmity of your flesh: for as ye have yielded your members servants to uncleanness and to iniquity unto iniquity; even so now yield your members servants to righteousness unto holiness. For when ye were the servants of sin, ye were free from righteousness. What fruit had ye then in those things whereof ye are now ashamed? For the end of those things is death. But now being made free from sin, and become servants of God, ye have your fruit unto holiness, and the end everlasting life. For the wages of sin is death; but the gift of God is eternal life through Jesus Christ our Lord.*

2. **Romans 7:22-8:8** – *For I delight in the law of God after the inward man: but I see another law in my members, warring against the law of my mind, and bringing me into captivity to the law of sin which is in my members. O wretched man that I am! Who shall deliver me from the body of this death? I thank God through Jesus Christ our Lord. So then with the mind I myself serve the law of God; but with the flesh the law of sin. There is therefore now no condemnation to them which are in Christ Jesus, who walk not after the flesh, but after the Spirit. For the law of the Spirit of life in Christ Jesus hath made me free from the law of sin and death. For what the law could not do, in that it was weak through the flesh, God sending his own Son in the likeness of sinful flesh, and for sin, condemned sin in the flesh: that the righteousness of the law might be fulfilled in us, who walk not after the flesh, but after the Spirit. For they that are after the flesh do mind the things of the flesh; but they that are after the Spirit the things of the Spirit. For to be carnally minded is death; but to be spiritually minded is life and peace. Because the carnal mind is enmity (hostile) against God: for it is not subject to the law of God, neither indeed can be. So then, they that are in the flesh cannot please God.*

Let's look at a portion of the above Scripture reference again,

For the law of the Spirit of life in Christ Jesus hath made me free from the law of sin and death. For what the law could not do, in that it was weak through the flesh, God sending his own Son in the likeness of sinful flesh, and for sin, condemned sin in the flesh.

(Romans 8:2-3)

In other words, Paul had crucified the old man (or carnal nature) within him and was living out of his born-again spirit man, his true self, who lives by faith in the Son of God! This, my friend, is the victory that overcomes the world, even our faith *(1 John 5:4)*! Paul said it best when he wrote,

But God forbid that I should glory, save in the cross of our Lord Jesus Christ, by whom the world is crucified unto me, and I unto the world. For in Christ Jesus neither circumcision availeth anything, nor uncircumcision, but a new creature. And as many as walk according to this rule, peace be on them, and mercy, and upon the Israel of God.

(Galatians 6:14-16)

As discussed earlier about the law of sin and death, Paul said in *2 Corinthians 4:4* that the god of this world (Satan) has blinded the minds of those who believe not lest the glorious light of the gospel of Christ, who is the image of God, should shine unto them. He also said in *Ephesians 2:2-5* that in times past we all walked according to the course of this world, according to the prince of the power of the air, the spirit that now works in the children of disobedience, fulfilling the desires of the flesh and of the mind; and were by nature the children of wrath, even as others. Our carnal nature loves the world and the things of the world, but John writes,

Love not the world, neither the things that are in the world. If any man love the world, the love of the Father is not in him. For all that is in the world, the lust of the flesh, and the lust of the eyes, and the pride of life, is not of the Father, but is of the world. And the world passeth away, and the lust thereof: but he that doeth the will of God abideth for ever.

(1 John 2:15-17)

In *Matthew 4:1-10*, when Jesus was tempted by the devil in the wilderness, Satan tempted Him with three things: the lust of the flesh (*"turn the stones into bread"*), the lust of the eyes (*"showing Jesus all of the kingdoms of the world and their glory. And Satan said, 'All these things will I give you if you will fall down and worship me'"*), and the pride of life (*"if you are the Son of God jump off this pinnacle of the temple and the angels will bear you up"*). Each time Satan tempted Jesus, Jesus would respond with *"It is written…!"* This is our example on how to deal with Satan and his temptations. We need to realize how important the Word of God is in our own personal lives! Jesus said in *Matthew 24:35 – "Heaven and earth shall pass away, but my words shall not pass away."* This is why it is so important to renew our minds to the truth of God's Word as the battleground between good and evil, light and dark, truth and error is in the mind. The first Adam is of the earth and the last Adam is from Heaven. God loves us so much that He gave His only Son to do what the first Adam failed to do *(John 3:16; 1 Corinthians 15:45-49)*! This is why it is essential to set our affections on things above and not on the things of the earth for as far as this world is concerned, we have died and our new real life is hidden with Christ in God *(Colossians 3:1-4)*.

In lieu of all of this, it is important to understand that Satan wants to keep us ignorant of the reality of God living on the inside of us and walking in that reality. God had an amazing plan for His offspring, Adam and Eve, who were created in His image (and that included us), but Satan came and offered them another way, tempting them with what God told them not to partake of and therefore sin and death entered into their lives and into ours, cutting off the plan of God for their lives and ours. God sent Jesus who was sinless in order to redeem mankind back to Himself. Satan again tried to thwart God's plan for Jesus and if he had succeeded, for us as well. Satan offered Jesus the kingdoms of this world and their glory if He would worship him. It's amazing how deceived Satan is. He was offering the kingdoms of this world and their glory to the Creator of the universe! Jesus is all God and all man; the human part of Jesus, who was tempted in all points as we are, yet without sin, continued to live out of the truth of God's Word *(Hebrews 4:15)*. God's plan prevailed for Jesus! Jesus suffered greatly but His reward was great! After He was raised from the dead, He told His disciples in *Matthew 28:18 – "All power is given unto me in heaven and in earth."* In closing, Paul writes,

> *And being found in fashion as a man, he humbled himself, and became obedient unto death, even the death of the cross. Wherefore God also hath highly exalted him, and given him a name which is above every name: that at the name of Jesus every knee should bow, of things in heaven, and things in earth, and things under the earth; and that every tongue should confess that Jesus Christ is Lord, to the glory of God the Father. Wherefore, my beloved, as ye have always obeyed, not as in my presence only, but now much more in my absence, work out your own salvation with fear and trembling. For it is God which worketh in you both to will and to do of his good pleasure.*
>
> (Philippians 2:8-13)

God is at work within us both to will and to do His good pleasure and we too will be rewarded if we overcome in this life by crucifying the old man and living unto God through the new man in Christ *(Revelation 22:12)*!

Paul said in *1 Timothy 4:7-8, "But refuse profane and old wives' fables, and exercise thyself rather unto godliness. For bodily exercise profiteth little: but godliness is profitable unto all things, having promise of the life that now is, and of that which is to come."* Continue looking unto Jesus, the Author and the Finisher of your faith and do not allow Satan to steal God's best from you:

1. *1 Corinthians 2:9-10 – But as it is written, "Eye hath not seen, nor ear heard, neither have entered into the heart of man, the things which God hath prepared for them that love him." But God hath revealed them unto us by his Spirit: for the Spirit searcheth all things, yea, the deep things of God.*
2. *Ephesians 3:20-21 – Now unto him that is able to do exceeding abundantly above all that we ask or think, according to the power that worketh in us, unto him be glory in the church by Christ Jesus throughout all ages, world without end. Amen.*

Below are Scriptures relating to overcoming:

Revelation 2:7 – He that hath an ear, let him hear what the Spirit saith unto the churches; "To him that overcometh will I give to eat of the tree of life, which is in the midst of the paradise of God."

References:
John 16:33 – Jesus said, "These things I have spoken unto you, that in me ye might have peace. In the

*world ye shall have tribulation: but be of good cheer; I have overcome the world." **Romans 12:21** – Be not overcome of evil, but overcome evil with good. **Hebrews 11:35** – …and others were tortured, not accepting deliverance; that they might obtain a better resurrection. **2 Peter 2:20** – For if after they have escaped the pollutions of the world through the knowledge of the Lord and Saviour Jesus Christ, they are again entangled therein, and overcome, the latter end is worse with them than the beginning. 1 **John 2:13-14** – …I write unto you, young men, because ye have overcome the wicked one… I have written unto you, young men, because ye are strong, and the word of God abideth in you, and ye have overcome the wicked one. **1 John 4:4** – ye are of God, little children, and have overcome them: because greater is he that is in you, than he that is in the world. **1 John 5:4-5** – For whatsoever is born of God overcometh the world: and this is the victory that overcometh the world, even our faith. Who is he that overcometh the world, but he that believeth that Jesus is the Son of God? **Revelation 2:11, 17, 26-29** – He that hath an ear, let him hear what the Spirit saith unto the churches; "He that overcometh shall not be hurt of the second death." He that hath an ear, let him hear what the Spirit saith unto the churches; "To him that overcometh will I give to eat of the hidden manna, and will give him a white stone, and in the stone a new name written, which no man knoweth saving he that receiveth it. And he that overcometh, and keepeth my works unto the end, to him will I give power over the nations: and he shall rule them with a rod of iron; as the vessels of a potter shall they be broken to shivers: even as I received of my Father. And I will give him the morning star." He that hath an ear, let him hear what the Spirit saith unto the churches. **Revelation 3:5, 12** – "He that overcometh, the same shall be clothed in white raiment (clothing); and I will not blot out his name out of the book of life, but I will confess his name before my Father, and before his angels. Him that overcometh will I make a pillar in the temple of my God, and he shall go no more out: and I will write upon him the name of my God, and the name of the city of my God, which is new Jerusalem, which cometh down out of heaven from my God: and I will write upon him my new name." **Revelation 12:10-11** – And I heard a loud voice saying in heaven, "Now is come salvation, and strength, and the kingdom of our God, and the power of his Christ: for the accuser of our brethren (Satan) is cast down, which accused them before our God day and night. And they overcame him by the blood of the Lamb, and by the word of their testimony; and they loved not their lives unto the death. **Revelation 21:7-8** – He that overcometh shall inherit all things; and I will be his God, and he shall be my son. But the fearful, and unbelieving, and the abominable, and murderers, and whoremongers, and sorcerers, and idolaters, and all liars, shall have their part in the lake which burneth with fire and brimstone: which is the second death.*

Below are Scriptures relating to crucifying the flesh:

1. ***Galatians 3:10-14, 26-29*** – *For as many as are of the works of the law are under the curse: for it is written, "Cursed is everyone that continueth not in all things which are written in the book of the law to do them." But that no man is justified by the law in the sight of God, it is evident: for, "The just shall live by faith." And the law is not of faith: but, the man that doeth them shall live in them. Christ hath redeemed us from the curse of the law, being made a curse for us: for it is written, "Cursed is every one that hangeth on a tree": that the blessing of Abraham might come on the Gentiles through Jesus Christ; that we might receive the promise of the Spirit through faith. For ye are all the children of God by faith in Christ Jesus. For as many of you as have been baptized into Christ have put on Christ. There is neither Jew nor Greek, there is neither bond nor free, there is neither male nor female: for ye are all one in Christ Jesus. And if ye be Christ's, then are ye Abraham's seed, and heirs according to the promise.*

2. ***Philippians 1:21*** – *Paul said, "For to me to live is Christ, and to die is gain."*

References:

Matthew 16:24-27 – *Then said Jesus unto his disciples, "If any man will come after me, let him deny himself, and take up his cross, and follow me. For whosoever will save his life shall lose it: and whosoever will lose his life for my sake shall find it. For what is a man profited, if he shall gain the whole world, and lose his own soul? Or what shall a man give in exchange for his soul? For the Son of man shall come in the glory of his Father with his angels; and then he shall reward every man according to his works."* **Acts 20:22-24** – *Paul said, "And now, behold, I go bound in the spirit unto Jerusalem, not knowing the things that shall befall me there: save that the Holy Ghost witnesseth in every city, saying that bonds and afflictions abide me. But none of these things move me, neither count I my life dear unto myself, so that I might finish my course with joy, and the ministry, which I have received of the Lord Jesus, to testify the gospel of the grace of God.* ***Romans 6:16-18*** – *Know ye not, that to whom ye yield yourselves servants to obey, his servants ye are to whom ye obey; whether of sin unto death, or of obedience unto righteousness? But God be thanked, that ye were the servants of sin, but, ye have obeyed from the heart that form of doctrine which was delivered you. Being then made free from sin, ye became the servants of righteousness.* ***Romans 8:16-19*** – *The Spirit itself beareth witness with our spirit, that we are the children of God: and if children, then heirs; heirs of God, and joint-heirs with Christ; if so be that we suffer with him, that we may be also glorified together. For I reckon that the sufferings of this present time are not worthy to be compared with the glory which shall be revealed in us. For the earnest expectation of the creature waiteth for the manifestations of the sons of God.* ***1 Corinthians 15:31*** – *Paul said, "…I die daily."* ***Galatians 5:24-26*** – *And they that are Christ's have crucified the flesh with the affections and lusts. If we live in the Spirit, let us also walk in the Spirit. Let us not be desirous of vain glory, provoking one another, envying one another.* ***Colossians 3:1-7*** – *If ye then be risen with Christ, seek those things which are above, where Christ sitteth on the right hand of God. Set your affection on things above, not on things on the earth. For ye are dead, and your life is hid with Christ in God. When Christ, who is our life, shall appear, then shall ye also appear with him in glory. Mortify therefore your members which are upon the earth…* ***Philippians 3:7-9*** – *But what things were gain to me, those I counted loss for Christ. Yea doubtless, and I count all things but loss for the excellency of the knowledge of Christ Jesus my Lord: for whom I have suffered the loss of all things, and do count them but dung, that I may win Christ, and be found in him, not having mine own righteousness, which is of the law, but that which is through the faith of Christ, the righteousness which is of God by faith.* ***1 Peter 4:1-5*** – *Forasmuch then as Christ hath suffered for us in the flesh, arm yourselves likewise with the same mind: for he that hath suffered in the flesh hath ceased from sin; that he no longer should live the rest of his time in the flesh to the lust of men, but to the will of God. For the time past of our life may suffice us to have wrought the will of the Gentiles, when we walked in lasciviousness, lusts, excess of wine, revellings, banquetings, and abominable idolatries: wherein they think it strange that ye run not with them to the same excess of riot, speaking evil of you: who shall give account to him that is ready to judge the quick (living) and the dead.*

37(b) and the life which I now live in the flesh I live by faith in the Son of God, who loved me and gave Himself for me. (Galatians 2:20-NKJV)

Living by faith is living out of the new man in Christ, the born-again creation within! Faith is the strength of the new man and faith comes by hearing the Word of God *(Romans 10:17)*. It is written in *Hebrews 11:1, "Now faith is the substance of things hoped for, the evidence of things not seen."* The word "substance" in the Greek is *hypostasis*. Its meaning in the Thayer's Greek Lexicon is "that which has foundation, is firm; hence, steadfastness of mind, firmness, courage, resolution – confidence, firm trust, assurance." Let's look at the following passage of Scripture:

Now in the fourth watch of the night Jesus went to them, walking on the sea. And when the disciples saw Him walking on the sea, they were troubled, saying, "it is a spirit"; and they cried out for fear. But straightway Jesus spake unto them, saying, "Be of good cheer; it is I; be not afraid." And Peter answered Him and said, "Lord, if it be thou, bid me come unto thee on the water." And he said, "Come." And when Peter was come down out of the ship, he walked on the water, to go to Jesus. But when he saw the wind boisterous, he was afraid; and beginning to sink, he cried, saying, "Lord, save me." And immediately Jesus stretched forth his hand, and caught him, and said unto him, "O thou of little faith, wherefore didst thou doubt?"

(Matthew 14:25-31)

Jesus spoke the word "come" to Peter and that word "come" became the substance upon which Peter could walk on the water. As long as Peter stayed focused on Christ, he literally walked on the water. But as soon as he began to focus on the gusting winds and storm he became fearful and began to sink. The Lord immediately stretched out His hand and caught him and said to him. *"O you of little faith, why did you doubt?"* As we mature in Christ and grow in faith, we are able to face challenging circumstances through the <u>substance</u> of faith operating within us. We grow in faith by being a hearer and a doer of His Word. Jesus said in *Luke 6:47-49* that whoever comes to Him and hears His sayings and does them, he is like a man building a house, who <u>dug deep</u> and laid the foundation on the rock. I believe He is referring to a man who continues to allow the Word of God to take precedence over his own carnal thought processes (e.g., prejudices, judgments, pain, fears, unforgiveness) allowing the Word of God to bring revealed knowledge of his true identity in Christ at his core, circumcising his heart *(Hebrews 4:12-13; Romans 2:29; Colossians 2:11)*. To those who choose to allow God's Word to operate in them in this manner, when the storms of life come, they will be able to stand through the strength of "knowing" Christ *(Matthew 16:13-18)*. To those who choose not to allow the Word of God to operate within them in this manner, Jesus said they would be like a man who built his house on sand (i.e., temporary, emotional based, unregenerate mindsets where there is no depth) and apart from the mercies of Christ, when the storms of life come, they will not be able to stand. My husband was a homebuilder and understood that the foundation of a house is the strength of the house; without a good foundation a house cannot stand. Jesus desires for us to be more than conquerors in this life and faith is the victory that overcomes *(1 John 5:4)*! Let's look at *James 1:22-25*:

But be ye doers of the word, and not hearers only, deceiving your own selves. For if any be a hearer of the word, and not a doer, he is like unto a man beholding his natural face in a glass: for he beholdeth himself, and goeth his way, and straightway forgetteth what manner of man he was. But whoso looketh into the perfect law of liberty, and continueth therein, he being not a forgetful hearer, but a doer of the work, this man shall be blessed in his deed.

Another passage of Scripture that goes along with this is *2 Corinthians 3:18 – But we all, with open face beholding as in a glass (mirror) the glory of the Lord, are changed into the same image from glory to glory, even as by the Spirit of the Lord.* Putting on the new man, being a hearer and a doer of the Word of God, is how we are transformed into His image! Paul writes,

Therefore we do not become discouraged (utterly spiritless, exhausted, and wearied out through fear). Though our outer man is [progressively] decaying and wasting away, yet our inner self is being [progressively] renewed day after day. For our light, momentary affliction

(this slight distress of the passing hour) is ever more and more abundantly preparing and producing and achieving for us an everlasting weight of glory [beyond all measure, excessively surpassing all comparisons and all calculations, a vast and transcendent glory and blessedness never to cease!], since we consider and look not to the things that are seen but to the things that are unseen; for the things that are visible are temporal (brief and fleeting), but the things that are invisible are deathless and everlasting.

(2 Corinthians 4:16-18, AMPCE)

Please refer to **Notes 3b, 11,** and **12** for additional information and Scriptures relating to faith.

38(a) Whatever *I* do [no matter what it is] in word or deed, *I* do everything in the name of the Lord Jesus and in [dependence upon] His Person, giving praise to God the Father through Him. *I obey those who are in authority over me,* not only when their eyes are on *me* as pleasers of men, but in simplicity of purpose [with all my heart] because of my reverence for *You, Lord,* and as a sincere expression of *my* devotion to *You.* So, whatever may be *my* task, I work at it heartily (from the soul), as [something done] for the Lord and not for men, knowing [with all certainty] that it is from the Lord [and not from men] that *I* will receive the inheritance which is *my* [real] reward. [The One Whom] *I'm* actually serving [is] the Lord Christ (the Messiah). For he who deals wrongfully will [reap the fruit of his folly and] be punished for his wrongdoing. (Colossians 3:17, 22-25-AMPCE) *(Ref.: Titus 3:1-2)*

This is true devotion and reverence to Christ! Whatever we do, in word or deed, should be done as unto Him. We, as Christians, should stand out above all others concerning our character and work ethics as we <u>truly serve Christ</u> from our hearts no matter what position we hold in the work place, in the home, in school, etc. Regardless of others (e.g., the customers, employers, husbands, wives, teachers, peers) faith or attitudes, our devotion and reverence toward Christ should cause us to shine in dark places, <u>not becoming offended or lashing out with ungodly attitudes but glorifying God in all</u> that we do or say. I can testify to how God exalts those who choose to humble themselves before Him through their devotion and reverence. In 1974, at the age of seventeen, I was hired at AT&T. From 1974 up until 1984, I was a clerical secretary. In 1983, when I asked the Lord to come back into my life, I began to immerse myself in His Word, renewing my mind to the truth of His Word and giving myself over to much prayer and fasting. Every waking moment outside of work I was either reading the Bible, praying, fasting, going to church, listening to teaching tapes, or serving at the church. The only thing that I was crying out for was wisdom and understanding. Other than that, I was seeking the Lord with my whole heart and soul and being obedient to Him. He began to bless me with wisdom to do my work with excellence and during that time, from 1983 to 1986, I received two promotions both in management positions and on two separate occasions I received a Professional Performer's Award and a Team Award. Promotion comes from God, He exalts those who humble themselves and He humbles those who exalt themselves – *Psalm 75:6-7 – "For promotion cometh neither from the east, nor from the west, nor from the south. But God is the judge: he putteth down one, and setteth up another."*

Paul reiterates this command to the Church at Ephesus when addressing servants:

307

Servants, be obedient to them that are your masters according to the flesh, with fear and trembling, in singleness of your heart, as unto Christ; not with eyeservice, as men pleasers; but as the servants of Christ, doing the will of God from the heart; with good will doing service, as to the Lord, and not to men: knowing that whatsoever good thing any man doeth, the same shall he receive of the Lord, whether he be bond or free.

(Ephesians 6:5-8)

Jesus addressed his disciples in *Mark 10:42-45,*

Ye know that they which are accounted to rule over the Gentiles exercise lordship over them; and their great ones exercise authority upon them. But so shall it not be among you: but whosoever will be great among you, shall be your minister: and whosoever of you will be the chiefest, shall be servant of all. For even the Son of man came not to be ministered unto, but to minister, and to give his life a ransom for many.

Let's look at Daniel in the Old Testament as an example of one saint that had an excellent spirit and excelled in all that he did because of his devotion and reverence toward God. Let's begin with *Daniel 6:1-5:*

It pleased Darius to set over the kingdom an hundred and twenty princes, which should be over the whole kingdom; and over these three presidents; of whom Daniel was first: that the princes might give accounts unto them, and the king should have no damage. Then this Daniel was preferred above the presidents and princes, because an excellent spirit was in him; and the king thought to set him over the whole realm. Then the presidents and princes sought to find occasion against Daniel concerning the kingdom; but they could find none occasion nor fault; for as much as he was faithful, neither was there any error or fault found in him. Then said these men, "We shall not find any occasion against this Daniel, except we find it against him concerning the law of his God."

Then these presidents and princes came together and went to King Darius and said,

All the presidents of the kingdom, the governors, and the princes, the counsellors, and the captains, have consulted together to establish a royal statute, and to make a firm decree, that whosoever shall ask a petition of any God or man for thirty days, save of thee, O king, he shall be cast into the den of lions. Now, O king, establish the decree, and sign the writing, that it be not changed, according to the law of the Medes and Persians, which altereth not.

(Daniel 6:7-8)

The king signed the written decree. Now when Daniel knew that the writing had been signed, *"He went into his house; and his windows being open in his chamber toward Jerusalem, he kneeled upon his knees three times a day, and prayed, and gave thanks before his God, as he did aforetime" Daniel 6:10.* Daniel was not going to compromise or shrink with fear because a law had been made to keep him from praying to his God! In his heart, the law of God superseded the law of man. He had built his life on the truths of God's Word and therefore was not moved by the storm brewing against him *(Luke 6:47-48).* These men came together and found Daniel praying and making supplication before his God. They approached the king, reminding him of what he had just signed into law and informed him that Daniel had disregarded this law by continuing to make his petition three times a day before his God *(Daniel 6:12-13)*. When the king heard these words, he was displeased with himself for signing the decree and tried to deliver Daniel, but these men reminded the king of the law of the Medes and Persians that any decree which the king establishes cannot be changed *(Daniel 6:14-15)*. Now let's read *Daniel 6:16-23*:

> *Then the king commanded, and they brought Daniel, and cast him into the den of lions. Now the king spake and said unto Daniel, "Thy God whom thou servest continually, he will deliver thee." And a stone was brought, and laid upon the mouth of the den; and the king sealed it with his own signet, and with the signet of his lords; that the purpose might not be changed concerning Daniel. Then the king went to his palace, and passed the night fasting: neither were instruments of musick (music) brought before him: and his sleep went from him. Then the king arose very early in the morning, and went in haste unto the den of lions. And when he came to the den, he cried with a lamentable voice unto Daniel: and the king spake and said to Daniel, "O Daniel, servant of the living God, is thy God, whom thou servest continually, able to deliver thee from the lions?" Then said Daniel unto the king, "O king, live for ever. My God hath sent his angel, and hath shut the lions' mouths, that they have not hurt me: forasmuch as before him innocency was found in me; and also before thee, O king, have I done no hurt." Then was the king exceeding glad for him, and commanded that they should take Daniel up out of the den. So Daniel was taken up out of the den, and no manner of hurt was found upon him, because he believed in his God.*

This is an example of the kind of faith that moves mountains and brings protection and blessing! Jesus Christ is the same yesterday, today, and forever *(Hebrews 13:8)*. God never changes *(Malachi 3:6)*! God's Word is the final authority in heaven and in earth. Jesus said in *Matthew 24:35*, "*Heaven and earth shall pass away, but my words shall not pass away.*" In *Psalm 138:2*, David said to the Lord, "*I will worship toward thy holy temple, and praise thy name for thy lovingkindness and for thy truth: for thou hast magnified thy word above all thy name.*" I believe Daniel had this same revelation in his heart and mind, that regardless of any decree that a king establishes, the Word of God supersedes that decree. If we truly believe in God, we will serve Him continually and our dedication to Him will be reflected in every aspect of our lives (e.g., our behavior, works ethics, integrity).

Let's look at *James 2:14-26 (NASB)*:

> *What use is it, my brethren, if someone says he has faith but he has no works? Can that faith save him? If a brother or sister is without clothing and in need of daily food, and one of you says to them, "Go in peace, be warmed and be filled," and yet you do not give them what is necessary for their body, what use is that? Even so faith, if it has no works, is dead, being by itself. But some may well say, "You have faith and I have works; show me your faith without the works, and I will show you my faith by my works." You believe that God is one. You do well; the demons also believe, and shudder. But are you willing to recognize, you foolish fellow, that faith without works is useless? Was not Abraham our father justified by works when he offered up Isaac his son on the altar? You see that faith was working with his works, and as a result of the works, faith was perfected; and the Scripture was fulfilled which says, "AND ABRAHAM BELIEVED GOD, AND IT WAS RECKONED TO HIM AS RIGHTEOUSNESS," and he was called the friend of God. You see that a man is justified*

by works and not by faith alone. In the same way, was not Rahab the harlot also justified by works when she received the messengers and sent them out by another way? For just as the body without the spirit is dead, so also faith without works is dead.

We need to do more than just "believe" that Jesus is the Son of God and died for our sins; we need to be devoted with reverential fear to the One who gave His life for us! Because Daniel devoted his life to God, we see the wisdom and protection from the Lord which is an outward manifestation of the inheritance that is promised to all those who love Him. We'll find out what happened to those men that had King Darius sign that decree in **Note 38b**.

Below are Scriptures relating to the importance of work ethics:

1. ***Proverbs 12:14*** *– A man shall be satisfied with good by the fruit of his mouth: and the recompence of a man's hands shall be rendered unto him.*

Reference:
Galatians 6:7-9 *– Be not deceived; God is not mocked: for whatsoever a man soweth, that shall he also reap. For he that soweth to his flesh shall of the flesh reap corruption; but he that soweth to the Spirit shall of the Spirit reap life everlasting. And let us not be weary in well doing: for in due season we shall reap, if we faint not.*

2. ***Proverbs 16:3*** *(AMPCE) – Roll your works upon the Lord [commit and trust them wholly to Him; He will cause your thoughts to become agreeable to His will, and] so shall your plans be established and succeed.*

3. ***Proverbs 19:15*** *– Slothfulness (laziness) casteth into a deep sleep; and an idle soul shall suffer hunger.*

References:
Proverbs 6:6-11 *(NASB) – Go to the ant, O sluggard (lazy), observe her ways and be wise, which, having no chief, officer or ruler, prepares her food in the summer and gathers her provision in the harvest. How long will you lie down, O sluggard? When will you arise from your sleep? "A little sleep, a little slumber, a little folding of the hands to rest" — your poverty will come in like a vagabond and your need like an armed man.* ***Proverbs 12:24*** *(NASB) – The hand of the diligent will rule, but the slack hand will be put to forced labor.* ***Proverbs 13:4, 11*** *(NASB) – The soul of the sluggard craves and gets nothing, but the soul of the diligent is made fat. Wealth obtained by fraud dwindles, but the one who gathers by labor increases it.* ***Proverbs 15:19*** *– The way of the slothful man is as an hedge of thorns: but the way of the righteous is made plain.* ***Proverbs 18:9*** *– He also that is slothful in his work is brother to him that is a great waster.* ***Proverbs 22:29*** *– Seest thou a man diligent in his business? He shall stand before kings; he shall not stand before mean men.* ***Proverbs 24:30-34*** *– I went by the field of the slothful, and by the vineyard of the man void of understanding; and, lo, it was all grown over with thorns, and nettles had covered the face thereof, and the stone wall thereof was broken down. Then I saw, and considered it well: I looked upon it, and received instruction. Yet a little sleep, a little slumber, a little folding of the hands to sleep: so shall thy poverty come as one that travelleth; and thy want as an armed man.* ***Proverbs 26:14*** *– As the door turneth upon his hinges, so doth the slothful upon his bed.* ***Romans 12:10-13*** *– Be kindly affectioned one to another with brotherly love; in honour preferring one another; not slothful in business; fervent in spirit; serving the Lord; rejoicing in hope; patient in tribulation; continuing instant in prayer; distributing to the necessity of saints;*

given to hospitality. **1 Thessalonians 4:10-12** – *…but we beseech you, brethren, that ye increase more and more; and that ye study to be quiet, and to do your own business, and to work with your own hands, as we commanded you; that ye may walk honestly toward them that are without, and that ye may have lack of nothing.*

4. **1 Corinthians 10:31** *(NASB) – Whether, then, you eat or drink or whatever you do, do all to the glory of God.*

Reference:
1 Peter 4:11 – If any man speak, let him speak as the oracles of God; if any man minister, let him do it as of the ability which God giveth: that God in all things may be glorified through Jesus Christ, to whom be praise and dominion for ever and ever. Amen.

Please read *Matthew 25:14-30* concerning the importance of using our God-given talents.

38(b) And [with God] there is no partiality [no matter what a person's position may be… (Colossians 3:25-AMPCE)

Let's look at *Colossians 3:25* in the King James Version – *"But he that doeth wrong shall receive for the wrong which he hath done: and there is no respect of persons."* "Respect of persons" in the Greek is *prosopolempsia* meaning "partiality, i.e. favoritism:–respect of persons." Its meaning in the Thayer's Greek Lexicon is **respect of persons, partiality,** the fault of one who when called on to give judgment has respect to the outward circumstances of men and not to their intrinsic merits, and so prefers, as the more worthy, one who is rich, high-born, or powerful, to another who is destitute of such gifts." God is not like this! His judgment is perfect as He looks at the thoughts and intents of the heart of man not on his outward worth or appearance. An example of this is when God told Samuel that He had found someone to be the next king to replace King Saul, who would be one of Jesse's sons, David. The Lord told Samuel to take a heifer and say, "I am come to sacrifice to the Lord" and to call Jesse to the sacrifice as well. So in *1 Samuel 16:4-7*:

> *And Samuel did that which the LORD spake, and came to Bethlehem. And the elders of the town trembled at his coming, and said, "Comest thou peaceably?" And he said, "Peaceably: I am come to sacrifice unto the LORD: sanctify yourselves, and come with me to the sacrifice." And he sanctified Jesse and his sons, and called them to the sacrifice.* <u>*And it came to pass, when they were come, that he looked on Eliab, and said, "Surely the LORD'S anointed is before him." But the LORD said unto Samuel, "Look not on his countenance, or on the height of his stature; because I have refused him: for the LORD seeth not as man seeth; for man looketh on the outward appearance, but the LORD looketh on the heart."*</u>

Also, as noted in **Note 38a**, let's find out what happened to those men that had King Darius sign the decree that caused Daniel to be put into the lions' den, as there are consequences to sowing foolishness and harm:

> <u>*And the king commanded, and they brought those men which had accused Daniel, and they cast them into the den of lions, them, their children, and their wives; and the lions*</u>

had the mastery of them, and brake all their bones in pieces or ever they came at the bottom of the den. Then king Darius wrote unto all people, nations, and languages, that dwell in all the earth; "Peace be multiplied unto you. I make a decree, that in every dominion of my kingdom men tremble and fear before the God of Daniel: for he is the living God, and stedfast for ever, and his kingdom that which shall not be destroyed, and his dominion shall be even unto the end. He delivereth and rescueth, and he worketh signs and wonders in heaven and in earth, who hath delivered Daniel from the power of the lions." So this Daniel prospered in the reign of Darius, and in the reign of Cyrus the Persian

(Daniel 6:24-28)

These men chose to act out of their feelings of jealousy and hatred by setting a trap for Daniel in order to destroy him, but because of Daniel's devotion and reverence toward God he was saved from the lions. Why didn't God protect these men, along with their families, who were cast into the same den of lions, as He protected Daniel? Is it because He loved Daniel more than those men and their families? No! God so loved the world that He gave His only begotten Son, Jesus. His love for all of us runs deep *(John 3:16).* God's promises protect the obedient. Daniel chose to honor God with his life and to dwell in the secret place of the Most High and God protected him:

He that dwelleth in the secret place of the most High shall abide under the shadow of the Almighty. I will say of the LORD, "He is my refuge and my fortress: my God; in him will I trust." Surely, he shall deliver thee from the snare of the fowler, and from the noisome pestilence. He shall cover thee with his feathers, and under his wings shalt thou trust: his truth shall be thy shield and buckler. Thou shalt not be afraid for the terror by night; nor for the arrow that flieth by day; nor for the pestilence that walketh in darkness; nor for the destruction that wasteth in noonday. A thousand shall fall at thy side, and ten thousand at thy right hand; but it shall not come nigh thee. Only with thine eyes shalt thou behold and see the reward of the wicked. Because thou hast made the LORD, which is my refuge, even the most High, thy habitation; there shall no evil befall thee, neither shall any plague come nigh thy dwelling. For he shall give his angels charge over thee, to keep thee in all thy ways. They shall bear thee up in their hands, lest thou dash thy foot against a stone. Thou shalt tread upon the lion and adder: the young lion and the dragon shalt thou trample under feet. "Because he hath set his love upon me, therefore will I deliver him: I will set him on high, because he hath known my name. He shall call upon me, and I will answer him: I will be with him in trouble; I will deliver him, and honour him. With long life will I satisfy him, and shew him my salvation."

(Psalm 91:1-16)

God looks on the heart and because of what Jesus did on the cross, God has made it possible for "whosoever will" to walk in newness of life by living out of the "hidden man of the heart," the new man in Christ. He wills for all of His children to surrender their lives to Him and to grow in Christ. As we continue to grow and mature in the Lord our carnality loses its strength in our lives, and therefore, no longer identifies us. God is calling us to build our lives upon Christ who is our true foundation and life source *(Luke 6:47-49).*

Below are Scriptures relating to impartiality:

Exodus 23:8 (NASB) – You shall not take a bribe, for a bribe blinds the clear-sighted and subverts the cause of the just.

References:
***Deuteronomy 16:19** (NASB) – You shall not distort justice; you shall not be partial, and you shall not take a bribe, for a bribe blinds the eyes of the wise and perverts the words of the righteous.* **2 Samuel 23:3** *(NASB) – David said, "The God of Israel said, the Rock of Israel spoke to me, 'He who rules over men righteously, who rules in the fear of God, is as the light of the morning when the sun rises, a morning without clouds, when the tender grass springs out of the earth, through sunshine after rain.'"* **Romans 2:4-11** *(NASB) – Or do you think lightly of the riches of His kindness and tolerance and patience, not knowing that the kindness of God leads you to repentance? But because of your stubbornness and unrepentant heart you are storing up wrath for yourself in the day of wrath and revelation of the righteous judgment of God, who WILL RENDER TO EACH PERSON ACCORDING TO HIS DEEDS: to those who by perseverance in doing good seek for glory and honor and immortality, eternal life; but to those who are selfishly ambitious and do not obey the truth, but obey unrighteousness, wrath and indignation. There will be tribulation and distress for every soul of man who does evil, of the Jew first and also of the Greek, but glory and honor and peace to everyone who does good, to the Jew first and also to the Greek. For there is not partiality with God.*
Ephesians 6:5-9 *– Servants, be obedient to them that are your masters according to the flesh, with fear and trembling, in singleness of your heart, as unto Christ; not with eyeservice, as menpleasers; but as the servants of Christ, doing the will of God from the heart; with good will doing service, as to the Lord, and not to men: knowing that whatsoever good thing any man doeth, the same shall he receive of the Lord, whether he be bond or free. And, ye masters, do the same things unto them, forbearing threatening: knowing that your Master also is in heaven; neither is there respect of persons with him.* **1 Peter 1:17-19** *(NASB) – If you address as Father the One who impartially judges according to each one's work, conduct yourselves in fear during the time of your stay on earth; knowing that you were not redeemed with perishable things like silver or gold from your futile way of life inherited from your forefathers, but with precious blood, as of a lamb unblemished and spotless, the blood of Christ.*

Please refer to **Note 20b** for additional information and Scriptures relating this subject matter.

---

39. *I am submissive to those who are in authority over me* with all [proper] respect, not only to those who are kind and considerate and reasonable, but also to those who are surly (overbearing, unjust, and crooked). For one is regarded favorably if, as in the sight of God, he endures the pain of unjust suffering. [After all] what kind of glory [is there in it] if, when *I* do wrong and are punished for it, *I* take it patiently? But if *I* bear patiently with suffering [which results] when *I* do right and that is undeserved, it is acceptable and pleasing to God. For even to this *I have been* called [it is inseparable from *my* vocation]. For Christ also suffered for *me*, leaving *me* [His personal] example, so that *I* should follow in His footsteps. He was guilty of no sin, neither was deceit (guile) ever found on His lips. When He was reviled and insulted, He did not revile or offer insult in return; [when] He was abused and suffered, He made no threats [of vengeance]; but He trusted [Himself and everything] to *His heavenly Father* Who judges *righteously.* (1 Peter 2:18-23-AMPCE) *(Ref.: Titus 3:1-2; 1 Peter 2:23)*

Let's look at *1 Peter 2:18* in the King James Version – *"Servants, be subject to your masters with all fear; not only to the good and gentle, but also to the froward."* The word "fear" in the Greek is *phobos*. Its meaning in the Thayer's Greek Lexicon is "reverence, respect (for authority, rank, dignity)." The word "froward" in the Greek is *skolios* meaning "warped, i.e. winding; figuratively, perverse, crooked, froward, untoward." Its meaning in the Thayer's Greek Lexicon is "unfair, surly, forward." Submission to authority is very important. We, as Christians, are called to be a light and witnesses unto Christ to those who live in darkness. Unregenerate souls need to see Christ in us. You may be the only reflection of Christ they see. Your Christlike character (e.g., integrity, excellent work ethics, humbleness of mind, kind nature) is the light others need to see. When they behold this type of character, their hearts may be open to hear your testimony. It is also important to understand that the law of Christ always supercedes the law of man. Therefore, God is not calling you to compromise His truth, which has become a reality in your heart, in order to submit to a directive from your superior that is contrary to it (e.g., doing something that goes against your conscience). An example of this is found in Daniel's life, **Note 38a**, and also in the story of Shadrach, Meshach, and Abednego, **Note 29b**. This level of following in Christ's footsteps not only refers to relationships between employer/employee, husband/wife, master/servant, but goes above and beyond as we trust God in every situation and circumstance of life and in every relationship we have *(Ephesians 5:21)*. Putting on Christ or the new man is how we walk in victory in this life! How can we fulfill the commandments of Jesus to love our enemies, bless those that curse us, do good to those that hate us, and pray for those who despitefully use us and/or persecute us except by living out of the born-again creation within *(Matthew 5:44-48)*. Why would suffering for doing right be pleasing and acceptable to God? I believe it is because He sees His Son, Jesus, in the hearts and minds of His sons and daughters who choose to trust themselves to Him who judges righteously, rather than to be vengeful through bitterness or anger. Paul writes,

> *Therefore, if you have been raised up with Christ, keep seeking the things above, where Christ is, seated at the right hand of God. Set your mind on the things above, not on the things that are on earth. For you have died and your life is hidden with Christ in God.*
> (Colossians 3:1-3, NASB)

This is very important as we, as sons and daughters of the Most High God, choose to crucify the old man, our carnality, and put on Christ. As we do this, we do not get offended when we are treated unfairly and if we do, it is important that we take our pain to the One who suffered for us leaving us His example that we should follow in His footsteps. It is written in *Psalm 119:165*, *"Great peace have they which love thy law: and nothing shall offend them."* He has called us not to live out of our feelings and emotions based on what we think is right, but to live out of the finished work of Christ in whom we live and move and have our being *(Acts 17:28)*. We dwell in the secret place of the Most High, and therefore, we release any hurts and offenses to the Lord and trust Him with the outcome because we know that God is faithful. Remember, vengeance belongs to God, He will repay *(Romans 12:19; Hebrews 10:30-31)*. When we choose to renew the *spirit of our minds* to the truth of God's Word and pour out our pain to Him instead of taking it out on the one who caused it, the wisdom of God and the peace of God prevails in every situation and circumstance of life (e.g., He may move in your heart to go to the one who offended you and share your heart. He may bring peace upon you to the point where you are free from the offense without speaking a word to anyone. He may reveal a core belief, judgment, or insecurity that is at work in your own heart and mind that caused that act to become an offense). He is faithful! It is also important to take time to praise Him!

Let's look at *James 3:11-18 (NASB)*:

Does a fountain send out from the same opening both fresh and bitter water? Can a fig tree, my brethren, produce olives, or a vine produce figs? Nor can salt water produce fresh. Who among you is wise and understanding? Let him show by his good behavior his deeds in the gentleness of wisdom. But if you have bitter jealousy and selfish ambition in your heart, do not be arrogant and so lie against the truth. This wisdom is not that which comes down from above, but is earthly, natural, demonic. For where jealously and selfish ambition exist, there is disorder and every evil thing. <u>*But the wisdom from above is first pure, then peaceable, gentle, reasonable, full of mercy and good fruits, unwavering, without hypocrisy. And the seed whose fruit is righteousness is sown in peace by those who make peace.*</u>

God wants us to operate and function out of the mind of Christ from which flows the wisdom and power of God. James is saying here that there are two types of wisdom and they cannot flow in the same vessel, just as salt water and fresh water cannot flow in the same spring. If we belong to Christ, He has called us to live in Him and not in the world. Understandably, as we are growing in Him, at times, we still think and act as those that are worldly and through this growth process, God's grace helps us through it (*1 Corinthians 3:1-3*). But ultimately, we are called to bear His image and His likeness, not being conformed to this world but transformed by the renewing of our minds (*Romans 12:1-2; Ephesians 4:20-24; Colossians 3:10*). Regardless of the circumstances or the consequences of life, His will is for us to operate and function out of the mind of Christ (*1 Corinthians 2:14-16; Philippians 2:1-13*). Shadrach, Meshach, Abednego, and Daniel, who were not born again, are perfect examples of men whose devotion and reverence toward God pleased Him. How much more through the shed blood of Jesus Christ should we please Him! Remember what Jesus said about John the Baptist in *Matthew 11:11, "Verily I say unto you, among them that are born of women there hath not risen a greater than John the Baptist: notwithstanding he that is least in the kingdom of heaven is greater than he."* In other words, these godly men and so many other godly men and women mentioned in the Old Testament such as Abraham, Sarah, Moses, David, Samuel, Deborah, etc., who had great faith, are not to be compared to the one who is least in the kingdom of heaven, as this one is born again because the greater One resides in him through the incorruptible seed (*John 3:1-8; 1 Peter 1:22-25*).

I would also like to note concerning a wife's submission to her husband, Peter writes in *1 Peter 2:21-3:1 (AMPCE),*

For even to this were you called [it is inseparable from your vocation]. For Christ also suffered for you, leaving you [His personal] example, so that you should follow in His footsteps. He was guilty of no sin, neither was deceit (guile) ever found on His lips. <u>*When He was reviled and insulted, He did not revile or offer insult in return; [when] He was abused and suffered, He made no threats [of vengeance]; but He trusted [Himself and everything] to Him Who judges fairly (righteously).*</u> *He personally bore our sins in his [own] body on the tree [as on an altar and offered Himself on it], that we might die (cease to exist) to sin and live to righteousness. By his wounds you have been healed. For you were going astray like [so many] sheep, but now you have come back to the Shepherd and Guardian (the Bishop) of your souls.* <u>*In like manner, you married women, be submissive to your own husbands...*</u>

The sufferings of Christ was relating to His submission to His heavenly Father when going to the cross. Then Peter goes on to write in *1 Peter 3:1 (AMPCE)* – *"In like manner, you married women, be submissive to your own husbands..."* This is very important and spoke volumes to me after years of struggling with submitting to God's will in crucifying my flesh in my marriage! Please refer to ***My Story – Part Two - Volume 1*** where I share my struggle as it relates to submission and **Note 44a** where I share the revelation the Lord shared with me concerning the importance of it.

Let's close with words of encouragement from the following passage of Scripture:

> *Therefore, we do not lose heart. Though outwardly we are wasting away, yet inwardly we are being renewed day by day. For our light and momentary troubles are achieving for us an eternal glory that far outweighs them all. So we fix our eyes not on what is seen, but on what is unseen, since what is seen is temporary, but what is unseen is eternal.*
>
> (2 Corinthians 4:16-18, NIV)

Below are Scriptures relating to entering into Christ's sufferings:

1. ***Psalm 33:18-22*** – *Behold, the eye of the LORD is upon them that fear him, upon them that hope in his mercy; to deliver their soul from death, and to keep them alive in famine. Our soul waiteth for the LORD: he is our help and our shield. For our heart shall rejoice in him, because we have trusted in his holy name. Let thy mercy, O LORD, be upon us, according as we hope in thee.*

References:
Proverbs 27:1 *(NIV)* – *Do not boast about tomorrow, for you do not know what a day may bring.*
Revelation 1:9 – *I John, who also am your brother, and companion in tribulation, and in the kingdom and patience of Jesus Christ...* ***Revelation 12:10-11*** – *...And they overcame him by the blood of the Lamb, and by the word of their testimony; and they loved not their lives unto the death.*

2. ***Isaiah 51:7*** *(NIV)* – *Hear me, you who know what is right, you people who have taken my instruction to heart: do not fear the reproach of mere mortals or be terrified by their insults.*

References:
Romans 12:14 – *Bless them which persecute you: bless, and curse not.* ***Romans 13:12-14*** – *The night is far spent, the day is at hand: let us therefore cast off the works of darkness, and let us put on the armour of light. Let us walk honestly, as in the day; not in rioting and drunkenness, not in chambering and wantonness, not in strife and envying. But put ye on the Lord Jesus Christ, and make not provision for the flesh, to fulfil the lusts thereof.* ***1 Corinthians 4:11-16*** – *Paul said, "... being reviled, we bless; being persecuted, we suffer it: being defamed, we intreat: we are made as the filth of the world, and are the offscouring of all things unto this day. I write not these things to shame you, but as my beloved sons I warn you. For though ye have ten thousand instructors in Christ, yet have ye not many fathers: for in Christ Jesus I have begotten you through the gospel. Wherefore I beseech you, be ye followers of me."* ***1 Corinthians 6:19-20*** – *What? Know ye not that your body is the temple of the Holy Ghost which is in you, which ye have of God, and ye are not your own? For ye are bought with a price: therefore, glorify God in your body, and in your spirit, which are God's.* ***Ephesians 6:11-20*** – *Put on the whole armour of God, that ye may be able to stand against the wiles of the devil. For we wrestle not against flesh and blood, but against principalities, against powers, against the rulers of the darkness of this world, against spiritual wickedness in high places. Wherefore take unto you the whole armour of God, that ye may be able to withstand in the evil day, and having done all, to stand...*

1 John 2:6 – He that saith he abideth in him ought himself also so to walk, even as he walked.

3. **1 Timothy 6:1-2** – *Let as many servants as are under the yoke count their own masters worthy of all honour, that the name of God and his doctrine be not blasphemed. And they that have believing masters, let them not despise them, because they are brethren; but rather do them service, because they are faithful and beloved, partakers of the benefit. These things teach and exhort.*

References:
1 Corinthians 9:19 – For though I be free from all men, yet have I made myself servant unto all, that I might gain the more. **2 Corinthians 4:5** – For we preach not ourselves, but Christ Jesus the Lord; and ourselves your servants for Jesus' sake. **Ephesians 6:5-8** – Servants, be obedient to them that are your masters according to the flesh, with fear and trembling, in singleness of your heart, as unto Christ; not with eyeservice, as men pleasers; but as the servants of Christ, doing the will of God from the heart; with good will doing service, as to the Lord, and not to men: knowing that whatsoever good thing any man doeth, the same shall he receive of the Lord, whether he be bond or free. **Colossians 3:22** – Servants, obey in all things your masters according to the flesh; not with eyeservice, as men pleasers; but in singleness of heart fearing God. **Titus 2:7-10** – In all things shewing thyself a pattern of good works: in doctrine shewing uncorruptness (incorruptibleness, purity of doctrine), gravity (honesty) and sincerity (genuineness), sound speech, that cannot be condemned; that he that is of the contrary part may be ashamed, having no evil thing to say of you. Exhort servants to be obedient unto their own masters, and to please them well in all things; not answering again; not purloining, but shewing all good fidelity; that they may adorn the doctrine of God our Saviour in all things.

4. **Hebrews 10:30-31** – *For we know him that hath said, "Vengeance belongeth unto me, I will recompense (repay)," saith the Lord. And again, "The Lord shall judge his people." It is a fearful thing to fall into the hands of the living God.*

References:
Deuteronomy 32:35 *(NASB)* – Vengeance is Mine, and retribution, in due time their foot will slip; for the day of their calamity is near, and the impending things are hastening upon them." **Romans 12:19-20** *(NASB)* – Never take your own revenge, beloved, but leave room for the wrath of God, for it is written, "VENGEANCE IS MINE, I WILL REPAY," says the Lord. "BUT IF YOUR ENEMY IS HUNGRY, FEED HIM, AND IF HE IS THIRSTY, GIVE HIM A DRINK; FOR IN SO DOING YOU WILL HEAP BURNING COALS ON HIS HEAD." Do not be overcome by evil, but overcome evil with good.

Please refer to **Notes 14a**, **40**, **44a**, and **44b** for more information and Scriptures relating to this subject matter.

Please refer to **Notes 36b** and **41** for additional information and Scriptures relating to entering into Christ's sufferings.

---

40. *Father, today, I trust myself and everything to You who judges righteously. (Ref.: 1 Peter 2:23)*

This is the key to not returning evil for evil or insult for insult and is cultivated through relationship with our Lord and our heavenly Father. When we are focused on Him, there is an assurance that He is our covering and protector. We, as born-again believers, have an assurance that our steps are ordered of the Lord and that the Lord is the true Judge and will judge righteously and without partiality *(Psalm 37:23)*. He is our Protector, our Comforter, our Helper, our Advocate, our constant Companion, our Counselor, our life, and the length of our days. In order to stay focused on Him, trusting Him with our lives, it is essential to guard our hearts with all diligence for out of it flows the issues of life *(Proverbs 4:23)*. The born-again creation, the hidden man of the heart, grows and becomes strengthened in us day by day as we renew our minds to His Word and enjoy His presence through praise, worship, and prayer (see **Note 9**). Let's look at the following passage of Scripture:

> *Incline your ear and hear the words of the wise, and apply your heart to my knowledge; for it is a pleasant thing if you keep them within you; let them all be fixed upon your lips, so that your trust may be in the LORD; I have instructed you today, even you.*
>
> (Proverbs 22:17-19, NKJV)

The words "them within thee" in Hebrew is *beten* meaning "from an unused root probably meaning to be hollow; the belly, especially the womb; also, the bosom or body of anything…" As the born-again creation grows "within" us our security in Him grows stronger and stronger and therefore the cares, fears, frustrations, and tribulations of this life begin to lose their power over us. I want to encourage you to trust in His wisdom, in His mercy, in His goodness, in His strength, in His care for you. He has your best interest at heart! Trusting in the LORD is the key to true submission. The Lord is calling us to a new life! A life where we do not look on those things that are seen which are temporary but to those things which are not seen the eternal things of God *(2 Corinthians 4:18)*. This occurs as our inner man grows stronger in Him.

Below are Scriptures relating to trusting in the living God.

1. ***Daniel 3:28-30*** *— Then Nebuchadnezzar spake, and said, "Blessed be the God of Shadrach, Meshach, and Abednego, who hath sent his angel, and delivered his servants that trusted in him, and have changed the king's word, and yielded their bodies, that they might not serve nor worship any god, except their own God. Therefore I make a decree, That every people, nation, and language, which speak anything amiss against the God of Shadrach, Meshach, and Abednego, shall be cut in pieces, and their houses shall be made a dunghill: because there is no other God that can deliver after this sort. Then the king promoted Shadrach, Meshach, and Abednego, in the province of Babylon.*

References:
*Psalm 1:1-6 — Blessed is the man that walketh not in the counsel of the ungodly, nor standeth in the way of sinners, nor sitteth in the seat of the scornful. But his delight is in the law of the LORD; and in his law doeth he meditate day and night. And he shall be like a tree planted by the rivers of water, that bringeth forth his fruit in his season; his leaf also shall not wither; and whatsoever he doeth shall prosper. The ungodly are not so: but are like the chaff which the wind driveth away. Therefore, the ungodly shall not stand in the judgment, nor sinners in the congregation of the righteous. For the LORD knoweth the way of the righteous: but the way of the ungodly shall perish. **Psalm 2:12** — …Blessed are all they that put their trust in him. Psalm 31:19-24 — Oh how great is thy goodness, which thou hast laid up for them that fear thee; which thou hast wrought for them that trust in thee before the sons of men! Thou shalt hide them in the secret of thy*

presence from the pride of man: thou shalt keep them secretly in a pavilion from the strife of tongues. Blessed be the LORD: for he hath shewed me his marvelous kindness in a strong city. For I said in my haste, "I am cut off from before thine eyes:" nevertheless thou heardest the voice of my supplications when I cried unto thee. O love the LORD, all ye his saints: for the LORD preserveth the faithful, and plentifully rewardeth the proud doer. Be of good courage, and he shall strengthen your heart, all ye that hope in the LORD. **Psalm 32:10** *– Many sorrows shall be to the wicked: but he that trusteth in the LORD, mercy shall compass him about.* **Psalm 34:8, 19** *– O taste and see that the LORD is good: blessed is the man that trusteth in him. Many are the afflictions of the righteous: but the LORD delivereth him out of them all.* **Psalm 37:3-9** *– Trust in the LORD, and do good; so shalt thou dwell in the land, and verily thou shalt be fed. Delight thyself also in the LORD; and he shall give thee the desires of thine heart. Commit thy way unto the LORD; trust also in him; and he shall bring it to pass. And he shall bring forth thy righteousness as the light, and thy judgment as the noonday. Rest in the LORD, and wait patiently for him: fret not thyself because of him who prospereth in his way, because of the man who bringeth wicked devices to pass. Cease from anger, and forsake wrath: fret not thyself in any wise to do evil. For evildoers shall be cut off: but those that wait upon the LORD, they shall inherit the earth.* **Psalm 57:7** *– My heart is fixed, O God, my heart is fixed: I will sing and give praise.* **Psalm 64:10** *– The righteous shall be glad in the LORD, and shall trust in him; and all the upright in heart shall glory.* (Remember, true righteousness and holiness only comes from the new man – Ephesians 4-22-24). **Psalm 84:12** *– O LORD of hosts, blessed is the man that trusteth in thee.* **Psalm 91:1-16** *– He that dwelleth in the secret place of the most High shall abide under the shadow of the Almighty. I will say of the LORD, 'He is my refuge and my fortress: my God; in him will I trust.' Surely, he shall deliver thee from the snare of the fowler, and from the noisome pestilence. He shall cover thee with his feathers, and under his wings shalt thou trust: his truth shall be thy shield and buckler. Thou shalt not be afraid for the terror by night; nor for the arrow that flieth by day; nor for the pestilence that walketh in darkness; nor for the destruction that wasteth in noonday. A thousand shall fall at thy side, and ten thousand at thy right hand; but it shall not come nigh thee. Only with thine eyes shalt thou behold and see the reward of the wicked. Because thou hast made the LORD, which is my refuge, even the most High, thy habitation; there shall no evil befall thee, neither shall any plague come nigh thy dwelling. For he shall give his angels charge over thee, to keep thee in all thy ways. They shall bear thee up in their hands, lest thou dash thy foot against a stone. Thou shalt tread upon the lion and adder: the young lion and the dragon shalt thou trample under feet. 'Because he hath set his love upon me, therefore will I deliver him: I will set him on high, because he hath know my name. He shall call upon me, and I will answer him: I will be with him in trouble; I will deliver him, and honour him. With long life will I satisfy him, and shew him my salvation.'* **Psalm 112:5-8** *– …He shall not be afraid of evil tidings: his heart is fixed, trusting in the LORD. His heart is established, he shall not be afraid, until he see his desire upon his enemies.* **Proverbs 16:20** *– He that handleth a matter wisely shall find good: and whoso trusteth in the LORD, happy is he.* **Proverbs 29:25** *– The fear of man bringeth a snare: but whoso putteth his trust in the LORD shall be safe.* **Isaiah 26:3-4** *(NKJV) – You will keep him in perfect peace, whose mind is stayed on You, because he trusts in You. Trust in the LORD forever, for in YAH, the LORD, is everlasting strength.* **Jeremiah 17:7-8** *– Blessed is the man that trusteth in the LORD, and whose hope the LORD is. For he shall be as a tree planted by the waters, and that spreadeth out her roots by the river, and shall not see when heat cometh, but her leaf shall be green; and shall not be careful in the year of drought, neither shall cease from yielding fruit.* **1 Timothy 4:10** *(NASB) – For it is for this we labor and strive, because we have fixed our hope on the living God, who is the Savior of all men, especially of believers.*

2. **Romans 8:31-39** *– What shall we then say to these things? If God be for us, who can be against us? He that spared not his own Son, but delivered him up for us all, how shall he not with him also freely*

319

give us all things? Who shall lay any thing to the charge of God's elect? It is God that justifieth. Who is he that condemneth? It is Christ that died, yea rather, that is risen again, who is even at the right hand of God, who also maketh intercession for us. Who shall separate us from the love of Christ? Shall tribulation, or distress, or persecution, or famine, or nakedness, or peril, or sword? As it is written, "For thy sake we are killed all the day long; we are accounted as sheep for the slaughter." Nay, in all these things we are more than conquerors through him that loved us. For I am persuaded, that neither death, nor life, nor angels, nor principalities, nor powers, nor things present, nor things to come, nor height, nor depth, nor any other creature, shall be able to separate us from the love of God, which is in Christ Jesus our Lord.

Please refer to **Note 6b, 12, 14a, 39, 44a, 44b** for further information and Scriptures relating to this subject matter.

---

41. [*I* see to it that] *my* conscience is entirely clear (unimpaired), so that, when *I am* falsely accused as *an evildoer*, those who threaten *me* abusively and revile *my* right behavior in Christ may come to be ashamed [of slandering *my* good *life*]. For [it is] better to suffer [unjustly] for doing right, if that should be God's will, than to suffer [justly] for doing wrong. For Christ [the Messiah Himself] died for sins once for all, the Righteous for the unrighteous (the Just for the unjust, the Innocent for the guilty), that He might bring us to God. In His human body He was put to death, but He was made alive *by the Spirit.* (1 Peter 3:16-18-AMPCE) *(Ref.: 1 Peter 3:18)*

Let's look at *1 Peter 3:13-18* in the King James Version in order to get the full context of what Peter is saying here:

And who is he that will harm you, if ye be followers of that which is good? But and if ye suffer for righteousness' sake, happy are ye: and be not afraid of their terror, neither be troubled; <u>but sanctify the Lord God in your hearts</u>: and be ready always to give an answer to every man that asketh you a reason of the hope that is in you with meekness and fear: <u>having a good conscience</u>; that, whereas they speak evil of you, as of evildoers, they may be ashamed that falsely accuse your good conversation (behavior) in Christ. For it is better, if the will of God be so, that ye suffer for well doing, than for evil doing. For Christ also hath once suffered for sins, the just for the unjust, that he might bring us to God, being put to death in the flesh, but quickened (made alive) by the spirit.

The key to walking in this kind of faith is found in *verse 15 – "But sanctify the Lord God in your hearts."* The word "sanctify" in the Greek is *hagiazo*. Its meaning in the Vine's Expository Dictionary is "the acknowledgement of the Lordship of Christ."[1] It is only through this acknowledgement that, by the grace of God, we can genuinely walk in godly sincerity through singleness of mind and heart *(2 Corinthians 1:12; Hebrews 13:18)*. The Greek word for "conscience" is *syneidesis* and the definition in the Vine's Expository Dictionary is "lit., 'a knowing with' (*sun*, 'with,' *oida*, 'to know'), i.e., a co-knowledge (with oneself), the witness borne to one's conduct by conscience, that faculty by which we apprehend the will of God, as that which is designed to govern our lives."[2] Jesus said,

The light of the body is the eye: if therefore thine eye be single, thy whole body shall be full of light. But if thine eye be evil, thy whole body shall be full of darkness. If therefore the light that is in thee be darkness, how great is that darkness!

(Matthew 6:22-23)

The word "eye" in the Greek is *ophthalmos*. Its meaning in the Vine's Expository Dictionary is "singleness of motive."[3] His Word strengthens a weak conscience and brings calm to an overactive one.

Paul writes,

Therefore, if you have been raised up with Christ, keep seeking the things above, where Christ is, seated at the right hand of God. Set your mind on the things above, not on the things that are on earth. For you have died and your life is hidden with Christ in God.

(Colossians 3:1-3, NASB)

As we renew our minds by setting them on things above, the light of His Word becomes a reality within us *(2 Corinthians 4:18)*. God is calling us to put to death the deeds of the flesh, the old man or false self, and to live in His righteousness and holiness, the new man or true self. Therefore, if our single motive is Christ and His will for our lives, we will seek to live righteous and holy before Him. Paul also writes in *Acts 24:16, "And herein do I exercise myself, to have always a conscience void of offence toward God, and toward men."* The word "exercise" in the Greek is *askeo* and is used only once in the New Testament. Its meaning in the Vine's Expository Dictionary – "signifies to form by art, to adorn, to work up raw material with skill; hence, in general, to take pains, endeavor, exercise by training or discipline, with a view to a conscience void of offence."[4] A pure conscience is formed by adorning ourselves with the doctrine of Christ and allowing His "living" Word to work in us both to will and to do of His good pleasure *(Philippians 2:12-13; Hebrews 4:12-13)*. An example of this is found in the following passage of Scripture:

Then Daniel spoke to the king, "O king, live forever! My God sent His angel and shut the lions' mouths and they have not harmed me, inasmuch as I was found innocent before Him; and also toward you, O king, I have committed no crime."

(Daniel 6:21-22, NASB)

Just as Daniel walked in innocence before God and others, how much more should we as born-again believers *(Romans 8:11)*! Daniel is also a good example of someone who suffered unjustly for doing right and God was with him to deliver him from death. The Hebrew word for "innocence" or "innocency" in the KJV is *zakuw (Aramaic)* meaning "purity–innocence." As we choose to surrender our lives to Christ, in submission to His Word, the power of His Holy Spirit will cleanse us from all pollutants of the flesh and restore purity or innocence to our conscience. In *Matthew 18:1-2*, the disciples came to Jesus and asked Him, "Who is the greatest in the kingdom of heaven?" Then Jesus called a little child to Him, and set him in the midst of them and said,

Verily I say unto you, Except ye be converted, and become as little children, ye shall not enter into the kingdom of heaven. Whosoever therefore shall humble himself as this little child, the same is greatest in the kingdom of heaven.

(Matthew 18:3-4)

The word "converted" in the Greek is *strepho*. Its meaning in the Thayer's Greek Lexicon is "absolutely and tropically, to turn oneself namely, from one's course of conduct, i.e. to change one's mind." Paul writes in *1 Corinthians 14:20 – "Brethren, be not children in understanding: howbeit in malice be ye children, but in understanding be men."* In *2 Corinthians 7:2*, Paul is an example; his innocence was restored before God and others. He wrote, *"Receive us; we have wronged no man, we have corrupted no man, we have defrauded no man."* Before Paul had a revelation of Christ, on the road to Damascus, he was chief in persecuting the church. However, through the revelations of Christ and the blood of Christ, Paul's conscience was cleansed from his past sins and therefore in good conscience he could make that statement *(Hebrews 9:14)*. We need to line ourselves up with what God thinks is just and right rather than what we "think or feel" is just and right based on our carnality! As we become deeply rooted in His love, finding our security in Him, we can stand in the midst of false accusations and hatred from those who revile or persecute us wrongfully.

Paul writes,

> *But refuse profane and old wives' fables, and exercise thyself rather unto godliness. For bodily exercise profiteth little: but godliness is profitable unto all things, having promise of the life that now is, and of that which is to come.*
>
> (1 Timothy 4:7-8)

The word "exercise" in the Greek is *gymnazo*. Its meaning in the Vine's Expository Dictionary – "primarily signifies to exercise naked (from gumnos, naked); then, generally, to exercise, to train the body or mind (Eng., gymnastic), with a view of godliness."[5] When using exercise in this context, I believe we must stay focused on training the mind without any hindrances as is written in the following two passages of Scripture:

1. ***Hebrews 12:1-2** (NASB) – Therefore, since we have so great a cloud of witnesses surrounding us, let us also lay aside every encumbrance and the sin which so easily entangles us, and let us run with endurance the race that is set before us, fixing our eyes on Jesus, the author and perfecter of faith, who for the joy set before Him endured the cross, despising the shame, and has sat down at the right hand of the throne of God.*
2. ***1 Peter 1:13-16** – Wherefore gird up the loins of your mind, be sober, and hope to the end for the grace that is to be brought unto you at the revelation of Jesus Christ; as obedient children, not fashioning yourselves according to the former lusts in your ignorance: but as he which hath called you is holy, so be ye holy in all manner of conversation (behavior); because it is written, "Be ye holy; for I am holy."*

The Greek word for "godliness" in *1 Timothy 4:7-8* is *eusebeia*. Its meaning in the Vine's Expository Dictionary is "from *eu*, well, and *sebomai*, to be devout, denotes that piety which, characterized by a Godward attitude, does that which is well-pleasing to Him."[6] Let's look at the following passage of Scripture:

> *But you did not so learn Christ! Assuming that you have really heard Him and been taught by Him, as [all] Truth is in Jesus [embodied and personified in Him], strip yourselves of your former nature [put off and discard your old unrenewed self] which characterized your previous manner of life and becomes corrupt through lusts and desires that spring from*

delusion; and be constantly renewed in the spirit of your mind [having a fresh mental and spiritual attitude], and put on the new nature (the regenerate self) created in God's image, [Godlike] in true righteousness and holiness.

(Ephesians 4:20-24, AMPCE)

Our new nature (the new man or our true self) is where godliness is produced (true righteousness and holiness) and in the sight of God is of great price *(1 Peter 3:4)*. It is by yielding to the nurturing and development of this new creation, bringing cleansing and purity to our conscience, that God's love and genuine faith springs forth! This is what is well-pleasing to Him *(Romans 12:1-2; Ephesians 5:8-10)*!

I have found in my own personal life since the *spirit of my mind* or my *inmost mind* has been renewed and is continuing to be renewed to the born-again creation within, my own conscience has been strengthened in areas where it was weak (easily hurt or offended) and tempered in areas where it was overactive (fear-based guilt). To learn more about the conscience, I recommend reading *Conscience: What It Is, How to Train It, and Loving Those Who Differ* by Andrew David Naselli and J. D. Crowley. In Chapter 2, they take the 30 Scripture references relating to the conscience and explain each in one or two sentences. I also recommend reading *The Vanishing Conscience – Drawing the Line in a No-Fault, Guilt-Free World* by John MacArthur, Jr. The following is an excerpt from his book:

> The conscience reacts to the convictions of the mind and therefore can be encouraged and sharpened in accordance with God's Word. The wise Christian wants to master biblical truth so that the conscience is completely informed and judges right because it is responding to God's Word. A regular diet of Scripture will strengthen a weak conscience or restrain an overactive one. Conversely, error, human wisdom, and wrong moral influences filling the mind will corrupt or cripple the conscience.
>
> In other words, the conscience functions like a skylight, not a light bulb. It lets light into the soul; it does not produce its own. Its effectiveness is determined by the amount of pure light we expose it to, and by how clean we keep it. Cover it or put it in total darkness and it ceases to function. That's why the apostle Paul spoke of the importance of a clear conscience (1 Tim. 3:9) and warned against anything that would defile or muddy the conscience (1 Cor. 8:7; Tit. 1:15).
>
> Or, to switch metaphors, our conscience is like the nerve endings in our fingertips. Its sensitivity to external stimuli can be damaged by the buildup of callouses or even wounded so badly as to be virtually impervious to any feeling. Paul also wrote of the dangers of a calloused conscience (1Cor. 8:10), a wounded conscience (v. 12), and a seared conscience (1 Tim. 4:2). (MacArthur, 1995, page 39).[7]

Below are Scriptures relating to entering into Christ's sufferings:

Matthew 10:37-39 *– Jesus said, "He that loveth father or mother more than me is not worthy of me: and he that loveth son or daughter more than me is not worthy of me. And he that taketh not his cross, and followeth after me, is not worthy of me. He that findeth his life shall lose it: and he that loseth his life for my sake shall find it."*

References:
Proverbs 16:2, 25 *– All the ways of a man are clean in his own eyes; but the LORD weigheth the spirits.*

*There is a way that seemeth right unto a man, but the end thereof is death. **Proverbs 21:2** – Every way of a man is right in his own eyes: but the LORD pondereth the hearts. **Matthew 16:24-27** – Then said Jesus unto his disciples, "If any man will come after me, let him deny himself, and take up his cross, and follow me. For whosoever will save his life shall lose it: and whosoever will lose his life for my sake shall find it. For what is a man profited, if he shall gain the whole world, and lose his own soul? Or what shall a man give in exchange for his soul? For the Son of man shall come in the glory of his Father with his angels; and then he shall reward every man according to his works." **Luke 9:23** – Jesus said, "If any man will come after me, let him deny himself, and take up his cross daily, and follow me." **Philippians 3:8-11** (NASB) – More than that, I count all things to be loss in view of the surpassing value of knowing Christ Jesus my Lord, for whom I have suffered the loss of all things, and count them but rubbish so that I may gain Christ, and may be found in Him, not having a righteousness of my own derived from the Law, but that which is through faith in Christ, the righteousness which comes from God on the basis of faith, that I may know Him and the power of His resurrection and the fellowship of His sufferings, being conformed to His death; in order that I may attain to the resurrection from the dead. **2 Timothy 3:12** – Yea, and all that will live godly in Christ Jesus shall suffer persecution. **Hebrews 13:8** – Jesus Christ the same yesterday, and to day, and for ever.*

Below are Scriptures relating to our conscience and its cleansing from the guilt of sin:

1. ***Romans 5:6-21*** *– For when we were yet without strength, in due time Christ died for the ungodly. For scarcely for a righteous man will one die: yet peradventure for a good man some would even dare to die. But God commendeth his love toward us, in that, while we were yet sinners, Christ died for us. Much more then, being now justified by his blood, we shall be saved from wrath through him. For if, when we were enemies, we were reconciled to God by the death of his Son, much more, being reconciled, we shall be saved by his life. And not only so, but we also joy in God through our Lord Jesus Christ, by whom we have now received the atonement. Wherefore, as by one man (Adam) sin entered into the world, and death by sin; and so death passed upon all men, for that all have sinned: (For until the law sin was in the world: but sin is not imputed when there is no law. Nevertheless death reigned from Adam to Moses, even over them that had not sinned after the similitude (likeness) of Adam's transgression, who is the figure of him that was to come. But not as the offence, so also is the free gift. For if through the offence of one (Adam) many be dead, much more the grace of God, and the gift by grace, which is by one man, Jesus Christ, hath abounded unto many. And not as it was by one that sinned, so is the gift: for the judgment was by one to condemnation, but the free gift is of many offences unto justification. For if by one man's offence death reigned by one; much more they which receive abundance of grace and of the gift of righteousness shall reign in life by one, Jesus Christ.) Therefore, as by the offence of one judgment came upon all men to condemnation; even so by the righteousness of one the free gift came upon all men unto justification of life. For as by one man's disobedience many were made sinners, so by the obedience of one shall many be made righteous. Moreover, the law entered, that the offence might abound. But where sin abounded, grace did much more abound: that as sin hath reigned unto death, even so might grace reign through righteousness unto eternal life by Jesus Christ our Lord.*

References:
Ephesians 5:25-27 *– Husbands, love your wives, even as Christ also loved the church, and gave himself for it; that he might sanctify and cleanse it with the washing of water by the word, that he might present it to himself a glorious church, not having spot, or wrinkle, or any such thing; but that it should be holy and without blemish. **Hebrews 9:6-14** – Now when these things were thus ordained, the priests went always into the first tabernacle, accomplishing the service of God. But into the second went the high priest alone once*

every year, not without blood, which he offered for himself, and for the errors of the people: the Holy Ghost this signifying, that the way into the holiest of all was not yet made manifest, while as the first tabernacle was yet standing: which was a figure for the time then present, in which were offered both gifts and sacrifices, that could not make him that did the service perfect, as pertaining to the conscience; which stood only in meats and drinks, and divers washings, and carnal ordinances, imposed on them until the time of reformation. But Christ being come an high priest of good things to come, by a greater and more perfect tabernacle, not made with hands, that is to say, not of this building; neither by the blood of goats and calves, but by his own blood he entered in once into the holy place, having obtained eternal redemption for us. For if the blood of bulls and of goats, and the ashes of an heifer sprinkling the unclean, sanctifieth to the purifying of the flesh: how much more shall the blood of Christ, who through the eternal Spirit offered himself without spot to God, purge your conscience from dead works to serve the living God? **Hebrews 10:22** *– Let us draw near with a true heart in full assurance of faith, having our hearts sprinkled from an evil conscience, and our bodies washed with pure water.* **1 John 1:7-9** *– But if we walk in the light, as he is in the light, we have fellowship one with another, and the blood of Jesus Christ his Son cleanseth us from all sin. If we say that we have no sin, we deceive ourselves, and the truth is not in us. If we confess our sins, he is faithful and just to forgive us our sins, and to cleanse us from all unrighteousness.* (Please read *Hebrews 10:1-22*, as only the blood of Jesus can cleanse and purify our conscience from the guilt of sin)!

2. **Romans 13:1-5** *(NASB) – Every person is to be in subjection to the governing authorities. For there is no authority except from God, and those which exist are established by God. Therefore whoever resists authority has opposed the ordinance of God; and they who have opposed will receive condemnation upon themselves. For rulers are not a cause of fear for good behavior, but for evil. Do you want to have no fear of authority? Do what is good and you will have praise from the same; for it is a minister of God to you for good. But if you do what is evil, be afraid; for it does not bear the sword for nothing; for it is a minister of God, an avenger who brings wrath on the one who practices evil. Therefore, it is necessary to be in subjection, not only because of wrath, but also for conscience' sake.*

References:

2 Corinthians 1:12 *– For our rejoicing is this, the testimony of our conscience, that in simplicity and godly sincerity, not with fleshly wisdom, but by the grace of God, we have had our conversation (behavior) in the world, and more abundantly to you-ward.* **1 Timothy 1:5-11, 18-20** *– Paul said, "Now the end of the commandment is charity (God's love) out of a pure heart, and of a good conscience, and of faith unfeigned: from which some having swerved have turned aside unto vain jangling (empty talk); desiring to be teachers of the law; understanding neither what they say, nor whereof they affirm. But we know that the law is good, if a man use if lawfully; knowing this, that the law is not made for a righteous man, but for the lawless and disobedient, for the ungodly and for sinners, for unholy and profane, for murderers of fathers and murderers of mothers, for manslayers, for whoremongers, for them that defile themselves with mankind, for menstealers, for liars, for perjured persons, and if there be any other thing that is contrary to sound doctrine; according to the glorious gospel of the blessed God which was committed to my trust. This charge I commit unto thee, son Timothy, according to the prophecies which went before on thee, that thou by them mightest war a good warfare; holding faith, and a good conscience; which some having put away concerning faith have made shipwreck..."* **1 Timothy 3:9** *– Holding the mystery of the faith in a pure conscience.* **1 Timothy 4:1-3** *– Now the Spirit speaketh expressly, that in the latter times some shall depart from the faith, giving heed to seducing spirits, and doctrines of devils; speaking lies in hypocrisy; having their conscience seared with a hot iron...* **2 Timothy 1:3** *(NASB) – I thank God, whom I serve with a clear conscience the way my forefathers did...* **Titus 1:15-16** *– Unto the pure all things are pure: but unto them* *that are defiled and unbelieving is nothing pure; but even their mind and conscience is defiled. They profess that they know God; but in works they deny him, being abominable, disobedient, and unto every good work reprobate.* **Hebrews 13:18** – *Pray for us: for we trust we have a good conscience, in all things willing to live honestly.*

Below are Scriptures relating to submission through singleness of mind and heart in Christ:

Proverbs 28:5 – *Evil men understand not judgment: but they that seek the LORD understand all things.*

References:
2 Timothy 2:3-7 (NASB) – *Suffer hardship with me, as a good soldier of Christ Jesus. No soldier in active service entangles himself in the affairs of everyday life, so that he may please the one who enlisted him as a soldier. Also if anyone competes as an athlete, he does not win the prize unless he competes according to the rules. The hard-working farmer ought to be the first to receive his share of the crops. Consider what I say, for the Lord will give you understanding in everything.* **Ephesians 6:5-8** – *Servants, be obedient to them that are your masters according to the flesh, with fear and trembling, in singleness of your heart, as unto Christ; not with eyeservice, as men pleasers; but as the servants of Christ, doing the will of God from the heart; with good will doing service, as to the Lord, and not to men: knowing that whatsoever good thing any man doeth, the same shall he receive of the Lord, whether he be bond or free.* **Colossians 3:22** – *Servants, obey in all things your masters according to the flesh; not with eyeservice, as menpleasers; but in singleness of heart, fearing God.* **1 Timothy 4:12** – *Let no man despise thy youth; but be thou an example of the believers, in word, in conversation (behavior), in charity (God's love), in spirit, in faith, in purity.* **1 Peter 3:1-4** – *Likewise, ye wives, be in subjection to your own husbands; that, if any obey not the word, they also may without the word be won by the conversation (behavior) of the wives; while they behold your chaste (pure) conversation (behavior) coupled with fear. Whose adorning let it not be that outward adorning of plaiting the hair, and of wearing of gold, or of putting on of apparel; but let it be the hidden man of the heart, in that which is not corruptible, even the ornament of a meek and quiet spirit, which is in the sight of God of great price.*

Please refer to **Note 29c** for additional information and Scriptures relating to your conscience.

Please refer to **Notes 36b** and **39** for additional information and Scriptures relating to entering into Christ's sufferings.

---

42. So, since Christ suffered in the flesh for *me*, I arm *myself* with the same thought and purpose [patiently to suffer rather than fail to please God]. For whoever has suffered in the flesh [having the mind of Christ] is done with [intentional] sin [has stopped pleasing himself and the world, and pleases God], so *I* can no longer spend the rest of my natural life living by [*my*] human appetites and desires, but [*I live*] for what God wills. (1 Peter 4:1-2-AMPCE)

This is referring to putting to death or crucifying the deeds of the flesh, the old man or false self and living out of the born-again creation in Christ, the new man or true self. Paul had this revelation as he wrote,

I am crucified with Christ: nevertheless, I live; yet not I, but Christ liveth in me: and the life which I now live in the flesh I live by the faith of the Son of God, who loved me, and gave himself for me. I do not frustrate the grace of God: for if righteousness come by the law, then Christ is dead in vain.

(Galatians 2:20-21)

Paul writes in *Galatians 5:18*, *"But if ye be led of the Spirit, ye are not under the law."* He then, describes in *verses 19-23*, the works of the flesh and the fruit of the Spirit and in *verses 24-25* he writes, *"And they that are Christ's have crucified the flesh with the affections and lusts. If we live in the Spirit, let us also walk in the Spirit."* The key to walking in the Spirit is to be transformed by the renewing of our minds or the renovation of our minds *(Romans 12:1-2; Ephesians 4:22-24; Colossians 3:10-14)*. In so doing, His wisdom and knowledge that abides within us will direct us day by day. Paul sums it up in *Titus 2:11-14*:

For the grace of God that bringeth salvation hath appeared to all men, teaching us that, denying ungodliness and worldly lusts, we should live soberly, righteously, and godly, in this present world; looking for that blessed hope, and the glorious appearing of the great God and our Saviour Jesus Christ; who gave himself for us, that he might redeem us from all iniquity, and purify unto himself a peculiar people, zealous of good works.

Below are Scriptures relating to putting off the old man and putting on the new man:

Matthew 7:13-14 – Jesus said, *"Enter ye in at the strait gate: for wide is the gate, and broad is the way, that leadeth to destruction, and many there be which go in thereat: because strait is the gate, and narrow is the way, which leadeth unto life, and few there be that find it."* (The word "narrow" in the Greek is *thlibo* meaning "to crowd (literally or figuratively)–afflict, narrow, throng, suffer tribulation, trouble." Tribulation is the way in which we enter into the kingdom. This is why in *Acts 14:22*, Paul exhorts the disciples to continue in the faith, and that we must through much tribulation enter into the kingdom of God. Unfortunately, compared to all the people on the face of this earth, there are few in this life who truly choose to press into Christ during trials and tribulation, and to walk this life through faith in Him. Choose to be one of them! He is the way, the truth, and the life – *Matthew 13:1-8, 18-23; John 14:6*. It is only through knowing Him and being deeply rooted in His love that we can truly enjoy the abundant life which is righteousness, peace, and joy in the Holy Ghost – *Ephesians 3:17-19; Romans 14:17*).

References:
Proverbs 4:20-27 *(NASB)* – *My son, give attention to my words; incline your ear to my sayings. Do not let them depart from your sight; keep them in the midst of your heart. For they are life to those who find them and health to all their body. Watch over your heart with all diligence, for from it flow the springs of life. Put away form you a deceitful mouth and put devious speech far from you. Let your eyes look directly ahead and let your gaze be fixed straight in front of you. Watch the path of your feet and all your ways will be established. Do not turn to the right nor to the left; turn your foot from evil.* ***John 17:1-3*** *– These words spake Jesus, and lifted up his eyes to heaven, and said, "Father, the hour is come; glorify thy Son, that thy Son also may glorify thee: as thou hast given him power over all flesh, that he should give eternal life to as many as thou hast given him. And this is life eternal, that they might know thee the only true God, and Jesus Christ, whom thou hast sent.* ***Romans 12:1-2*** *– I beseech you therefore, brethren, by the mercies of God,*

that ye present your bodies a living sacrifice, holy, acceptable unto God, which is your reasonable service. And be not conformed to this world: but be ye transformed by the renewing of your mind, that ye may prove what is that good, and acceptable, and perfect, will of God. **2 Corinthians 3:17-18** *– Now the Lord is that Spirit: and where the Spirit of the Lord is, there is liberty. But we all, with open face beholding as in a glass the glory of the Lord, are changed into the same image from glory to glory, even as by the Spirit of the Lord.* **2 Corinthians 5:14-21** *– For the love of Christ constraineth (compels) us; because we thus judge, that if one died for all, then were all dead: and that he died for all, that they which live should not henceforth live unto themselves, but unto him which died for them, and rose again. Wherefore henceforth know we no man after the flesh: yea, though we have known Christ after the flesh, yet now henceforth know we him no more. Therefore if any man be in Christ, he is a new creature: old things are passed away; behold, all things are become new. And all things are of God, who hath reconciled us to himself by Jesus Christ, and hath given to us the ministry of reconciliation; to wit, that God was in Christ, reconciling the world unto himself, not imputing their trespasses unto them; and hath committed unto us the word of reconciliation. Now then we are ambassadors for Christ, as though God did beseech you by us: we pray you in Christ's stead, be ye reconciled to God. For he hath made him to be sin for us, who knew no sin; that we might be made the righteousness of God in him.* **Galatians 5:19-26** *– Now the works of the flesh are manifest, which are these; adultery, fornication, uncleanness, lasciviousness, idolatry, witchcraft, hatred, variance, emulations, wrath, strife, seditions, heresies, envyings, murders, drunkenness, revellings, and such like: of the which I tell you before, as I have also told you in time past, that they which do such things shall not inherit the kingdom of God. But the fruit of the Spirit is love, joy, peace, longsuffering, gentleness, goodness, faith, meekness, temperance: against such there is no law. And they that are Christ's have crucified the flesh with the affections and lusts. If we live in the Spirit, let us also walk in the Spirit. Let us not be desirous of vain glory, provoking one another, envying one another.* **Ephesians 4:20-24** *– But ye have not so learned Christ; if so be that ye have heard him, and have been taught by him, as the truth is in Jesus: that ye put off concerning the former conversation (behavior) the old man, which is corrupt according to the deceitful lusts; and be renewed in the spirit of your mind; and that ye put on the new man, which after God is created in righteousness and true holiness.* **Ephesians 5:8-10** *– For ye were sometimes darkness, but now are ye light in the LORD: walk as children of light: (for the fruit of the Spirit is in all goodness and righteousness and truth;) proving what is acceptable unto the Lord.* **Colossians 3:5-10** *– Mortify therefore your members which are upon the earth; fornication, uncleanness, inordinate affection, evil concupiscence, and coveteousness, which is idolatry: for which things' sake the wrath of God cometh on the children of disobedience: in the which ye also walked some time, when ye lived in them. But now ye also put off all these; anger, wrath, malice, blasphemy, filthy communication out of your mouth. Lie not one to another, seeing that ye have put off the old man with his deeds; and have put on the new man, which is renewed in knowledge after the image of him that created him.* **Hebrews 11:24-26** *– By faith Moses, when he was come to years, refused to be called the son of Pharaoh's daughter; choosing rather to suffer affliction with the people of God, than to enjoy the pleasures of sin for a season; esteeming the reproach of Christ greater riches than the treasures in Egypt: for he had respect unto the recompence of the reward.* **Hebrews 12:3-11** *– For consider him that endured such contradiction of sinners against himself, lest ye be wearied and faint in your minds. Ye have not yet resisted unto blood, striving against sin. And ye have forgotten the exhortation which speaketh unto you as unto children, "My son, despise not thou the chastening of the Lord, nor faint when thou art rebuked of him: for whom the Lord loveth he chasteneth, and scourgeth every son whom he receiveth." If ye endure chastening, God dealeth with you as with sons; for what son is he whom the father chasteneth not? But if ye be without chastisement, whereof all are partakers, then are ye bastards, and not sons. Furthermore, we have had fathers of our flesh which corrected us, and we gave them reverence: shall we not much rather be in subjection unto the Father of spirits, and live? For they verily for a few days chastened us after their own pleasure; but he for our profit, that we might be partakers* *of his holiness. Now no chastening for the present seemeth to be joyous, but grievous: nevertheless afterward it yieldeth the peaceable fruit of righteousness unto them which are exercised thereby. **James 1:13-18, 27** – Let no man say when he is tempted, "I am tempted of God": for God cannot be tempted with evil, neither tempteth he any man: but every man is tempted, when he is drawn away of his own lust, and enticed. Then when lust hath conceived, it bringeth forth sin: and sin, when it is finished, bringeth forth death. Do not err, my beloved brethren. Every good gift and every perfect gift is from above, and cometh down form the Father of lights, with whom is not variableness, neither shadow of turning. Of his own will begat us with the word of truth, that we should be a kind of first fruits of his creatures. Pure religion and undefiled before God and the Father is this, to visit the fatherless and widows in their affliction, and to keep himself unspotted from the world. **1 John 5:20** – And we know that the Son of God is come, and hath given us an understanding, that we may know him that is true, and we are in him that is true, even in his Son Jesus Christ. This is the true God, and eternal life. **Jude 1:21** – Keep yourselves in the love of God, looking for the mercy of our Lord Jesus Christ unto eternal life.*

Below are Scriptures relating to Christ, the power of God and the wisdom of God:

***1 Corinthians 1:18-31** (NKJV) – For the message of the cross is foolishness to those who are perishing, but to us who are being saved it is the power of God. For it is written: "I will destroy the wisdom of the wise, and bring to nothing the understanding of the prudent." Where is the wise? Where is the scribe? Where is the disputer of this age? Has not God made foolish the wisdom of this world? For since, in the wisdom of God, the world through wisdom did not know God, it pleased God through the foolishness of the message preached to save those who believe. For Jews request a sign, and Greeks seek after wisdom; but we preach Christ crucified, to the Jews a stumbling block and to the Greeks foolishness, but to those who are called, both Jews and Greeks, Christ the power of God and the wisdom of God. Because the foolishness of God is wiser than men, and the weakness of God is stronger than men. For you see your calling, brethren, that not many wise according to the flesh, not many mighty, not many noble, are called. But God has chosen the foolish things of the world to put to shame the wise, and God has chosen the weak things of the world to put to shame the things which are mighty; and the base things of the world and the things which are despised God has chosen, and the things which are not, to bring to nothing the things that are, that no flesh should glory in His presence. But of Him you are in Christ Jesus, who became for us wisdom from God—and righteousness and sanctification and redemption—that, as it is written, "He who glories, let him glory in the LORD."*

References:
Proverbs 3:13-24, 35 *(NKJV) – Happy is the man who finds wisdom, and the man who gains understanding; for her proceeds are better than the profits of silver, and her gain than fine gold. She is more precious than rubies, and all the things you may desire cannot compare with her. Length of days is in her right hand, in her left hand riches and honor. Her ways are ways of pleasantness, and all her paths are peace. She is a tree of life to those who take hold of her, and happy are all who retain her. The LORD by wisdom founded the earth; by understanding He established the heavens; by His knowledge the depths were broken up, and clouds drop down the dew. My son, let them not depart from your eyes—keep sound wisdom and discretion; so they will be life to your soul and grace to your neck. Then you will walk safely in your way, and your foot will not stumble. When you lie down, you will not be afraid; yes, you will lie down and your sleep will be sweet. The wise shall inherit glory, but shame shall be the legacy of fools.* **1 Corinthians 2:6-16** *(NKJV) – However, we speak wisdom among those who are mature, yet not the wisdom of this age, nor of the rulers of this age, who are coming to nothing. But we speak the wisdom of God in a mystery, the hidden wisdom which God ordained before the ages for our glory, which none of the rulers of this age knew; for had*

they known, they would not have crucified the Lord of glory. But as it is written: "Eye has not seen, nor ear heard, nor have entered into the heart of man the things which God has prepared for those who love Him." But God has revealed them to us through His Spirit. For the Spirit searches all things, yes, the deep things of God. For what man knows the things of a man except the spirit of the man which is in him? Even so no one knows the things of God except the Spirit of God. Now we have received, not the spirit of the world, but the Spirit who is from God, that we might know the things that have been freely given to us by God. These things we also speak, not in words which man's wisdom teaches but which the Holy Spirit teaches, comparing spiritual things with spiritual. But the natural man does not receive the things of the Spirit of God, for they are foolishness to him; nor can he know them, because they are spiritually discerned. But he who is spiritual judges all things, yet he himself is rightly judged by no one. For "who has known the mind of the LORD that he may instruct Him?" But we have the mind of Christ. **2 Corinthians 4:6-11** *– For God, who commanded the light to shine out of darkness, hath shined in our hearts, to give the light of the knowledge of the glory of God in the face of Jesus Christ. But we have this treasure in earthen vessels, that the excellency of the power may be of God, and not of us. We are troubled on every side, yet not distressed; we are perplexed, but not in despair; persecuted, but not forsaken; cast down, but not destroyed; always bearing about in the body the dying of the Lord Jesus, that the life also of Jesus might be made manifest in our body. For we which live are always delivered unto death for Jesus' sake, that the life also of Jesus might be made manifest in our mortal flesh.* **Philippians 4:10-13** *– But I rejoiced in the Lord greatly, that now at the last your care of me hath flourished again; wherein ye were also careful, but ye lacked opportunity. Not that I speak in respect of want: for I have learned, in whatsoever state I am, therewith to be content. I know both how to be abased, and I know how to abound: everywhere and in all things I am instructed both to be full and to be hungry, both to abound and to suffer need.* <u>*I can do all things through Christ which strengtheneth me.*</u>

Please refer to **Notes 17a**, **17b**, **27a**, and **27b** for further information and additional Scriptures relating to this subject matter.

---

43. *I also choose to* let *my character* be without covetousness; and *I am* content with such things as *I* have: for *You have* said, "I will never leave *you*, nor forsake *you*." So that *I* may boldly say, "The Lord is my helper, and I will not fear what man shall do unto me." (Hebrews 13:5-6)

The phrase "be without covetousness" in the Greek is *aphilargyros* and means "unavaricious:– without covetousness, not greedy of filthy lucre." Its meaning in the Thayer's Greek Lexicon is "not loving money, not avaricios *(an extreme desire to get or keep wealth)."* Paul writes,

> *But godliness with contentment is great gain. For we brought nothing into this world, and it is certain we can carry nothing out. And having food and raiment (clothing) let us be therewith content. But they that will be rich fall into temptation and a snare, and into many foolish and hurtful lusts, which drown men in destruction and perdition. For the love of money is the root of all evil: which while some coveted after, they have erred from the faith, and pierced themselves through with many sorrows. But thou, O man of God, flee these things; and follow after righteousness, godliness, faith, love, patience, meekness. Fight the good fight of faith, lay hold on eternal life, whereunto thou art also called, and hast professed a good profession before many witnesses.*

330

Let's look a little closer at *verse 10, "For the love of money is the root of all evil: which while some coveted after, they have erred from the faith…"* Paul did not say that money is the root of all evil, he said the "love of money" is the root of all evil. The "love of money" becomes a god to those, who in this life, crave and desire it more than anything else. They make money, fame, or riches their aim and great quest, revealing self-centeredness, rather than making the reality of the love of God their aim and great quest, revealing God-centeredness *(1 Corinthians 14:1 – AMPCE)*. In *Matthew 6:19-34*, Jesus reveals His will for us concerning what our aim and quest in this life should be:

Lay not up for yourselves treasures upon earth, where moth and rust doth corrupt, and where thieves break through and steal: but lay up for yourselves treasures in heaven, where neither moth nor rust doth corrupt, and where thieves do not break through nor steal: for where your treasure is, there will your heart be also. The light of the body is the eye: if therefore thine eye be single, thy whole body shall be full of light. But if thine eye be evil, thy whole body shall be full of darkness. If therefore the light that is in thee be darkness, how great is that darkness! No man can serve two masters: for either he will hate the one, and love the other; or else he will hold to the one, and despise the other. Ye cannot serve God and mammon. Therefore I say unto you, take no thought for your life, what ye shall eat, or what ye shall drink; nor yet for your body, what ye shall put on. Is not the life more than meat, and the body than raiment? Behold the fowls of the air: for they sow not, neither do they reap, nor gather into barns; yet your heavenly Father feedeth them. Are ye not much better than they? Which of you by taking thought can add one cubit unto his stature? And why take ye thought for raiment? Consider the lilies of the field, how they grow; they toil not, neither do they spin: and yet I say unto you, that even Solomon in all his glory was not arrayed like one of these. Wherefore, if God so clothe the grass of the field, which to day is, and to morrow is cast into the oven, shall he not much more clothe you, O ye of little faith? Therefore, take no thought, saying, 'What shall we eat?' or, 'What shall we drink?' or, 'wherewithal shall we be clothed?' (For after all these things do the Gentiles seek:) for your heavenly Father knoweth that ye have need of all these things. But seek ye first the kingdom of God, and his righteousness; and all these things shall be added unto you. Take therefore no thought for the morrow: for the morrow shall take thought for the things of itself. Sufficient unto the day is the evil thereof.

In the following passage of Scripture, Jesus spoke a parable to the crowd after someone from the crowd said to Him,

"Master, speak to my brother, that he divide the inheritance with me." And he said unto him, "Man, who made me a judge or a divider over you?" And he said unto them, "Take heed, and beware of covetousness: for a man's life consisteth not in the abundance of the things which he possesseth."

(Luke 12:13-15)

Below is the parable Jesus spoke:

The ground of a certain rich man brought forth plentifully: and he thought within himself,

331

saying, "What shall I do, because I have no room where to bestow my fruits?" And he said, "This will I do: I will pull down my barns, and build greater; and there will I bestow all my fruits and my goods. And I will say to my soul, 'Soul, thou hast much goods laid up for many years; take thine ease, eat, drink, and be merry.' But God said unto him, "Thou fool, this night thy soul shall be required of thee: then whose shall those things be, which thou hast provided?" So is he that layeth up treasure for himself, and is not rich toward God.

(Luke 12:16-21)

Notice that the rich man was more focused on this temporary life, taking care of himself and providing pleasure for his own soul. He was blinded to the fact that this life is as a vapor and that true riches and abundant life abide with God in the eternal *(James 4:14; Luke 16:11; John 10:10, 17:3)*! He was self-centered rather than God-centered and therefore continued to store up more and more riches for himself which was a very serious mistake. When his soul was required of him, how did those stored up riches help him? Please read the parable Jesus spoke in *Luke 16:1-17* to better understand the importance of being a good steward of wealth. God has not called us to be hoarders but to be cheerful givers *(2 Corinthians 9:6-9)*! Paul admonishes those that are rich in this world with the following:

Charge them that are rich in this world, that they be not highminded, nor trust in uncertain riches, but in the living God, who giveth us richly all things to enjoy; that they do good, that they be rich in good works, ready to distribute, willing to communicate (share with others); laying up in store for themselves a good foundation against the time to come, that they may lay hold on eternal life.

(1 Timothy 6:17-19)

Also, it is important to understand that God has no problem with prospering His people. Let's look at three passages of Scripture that help establish this:

1. **Deuteronomy 8:18** – Moses said to the children of Israel before they entered into the promised land, *"But thou shalt remember the LORD thy God: for it is he that giveth thee power to get wealth, that he may establish his covenant which he sware unto thy fathers, as it is this day."*
2. **Psalm 75:6-7** – *For promotion cometh neither from the east, nor from the west, nor from the south. But God is the judge: he putteth down one, and setteth up another.*
3. **Proverbs 10:22** – *The blessing of the LORD, it maketh rich, and he addeth no sorrow with it.*

In the Old Testament, there are several examples of men who God exalted to a place of great wealth (e.g., Abraham, Isaac, Jacob, Joseph, David). The key was their focus was on God and not on their riches. Our true happiness comes from knowing Him and living out of the wellspring of life springing forth from our hearts *(Jeremiah 9:23-24; Isaiah 12:2-3; John 7:37-39)*.

Now, let's look again at *Luke 12:15* where Jesus said, *"Take heed, and beware of covetousness: for a man's life consisteth not in the abundance of the things which he possesseth."* Jesus said in *John 17:3 (NASB)* – *"This is eternal life, that they may know You, the only true God, and Jesus Christ whom You have sent."* I believe Jesus is saying in these two passages of Scripture, that a man's life consists not in the abundance of the things which he possesses, but rather in knowing the only true God and Jesus Christ wherein lies the wellspring of eternal life and the hidden treasures of wisdom and knowledge *(John 7:37-39;*

Colossians 2:2-3). In *Luke 12:15* and *John 17:3*, the word "life" in the Greek is *zoe* and is used over 130 times in the New Testament, King James Version. It is defined in the Vine's Expository Dictionary as "is used in the N. T. of life as a principle, life in the absolute sense, life as God has it, that which the Father has in Himself, and which He gave to the Incarnate Son to have in Himself, John 5:26, and which the Son manifested in the world, 1 John 1:2. From this life man has become alienated in consequence of the Fall, Eph. 4:18, and of this life men become partakers through faith in the Lord Jesus Christ, John 3:15, who becomes its Author to all such as trust in Him, Acts 3:15, and who is therefore said to be 'the life' of the believer, Col. 3:4, for the life that He gives He maintains, John 6:35, 63. Eternal life is the present actual possession of the believer because of his relationship with Christ, John 5:24; 1 John 3:14, and that it will one day extend its domain to the sphere of the body is assured by the Resurrection of Christ, 2 Cor. 5:4 and 2 Tim. I:10. <u>This life is not merely a principle of power and mobility, however, for it has moral associations which are inseparable from it, as of holiness and righteousness</u>. Death and sin, life and holiness, are frequently contrasted in the Scriptures."[1] True righteousness and holiness can only be found in the born-again creation, the new man *(Ephesians 4:22-24)*. Eternal life is birthed into the hearts and minds of born-again believers through the maturity of knowing Christ and walking in the mind of Christ. This eternal life, the abundant life that resides only in Christ, springs forth from the wellspring of living water that abides within our hearts *(John 7:37-39)*. We must understand that no matter how successful we are in this present life, if we are not God-centered, making His love our aim and great quest, in the end, our successes in life profits us nothing *(1 Corinthians 13:1-3; 1 Corinthians 14:1 – AMPCE; Matthew 7:13-14)*.

As mentioned earlier, it is important to note, when the foolish rich man died, he was not able to take with him the riches he had accumulated in this life. However, when born-again believers, who have built their lives on being faithful hearers and doers of God's Word, pass from this life to the next, their works follow them *(Revelations 14:13)*.

In closing, let's look again at *Hebrews 13:5-6*, and focus on *"for he hath said, 'I will never leave thee, nor forsake thee.' So that we may boldly say, 'The Lord is my helper, and I will not fear what man shall do unto me.'"* First, I believe it is important to establish a very important fact, "God does not lie." Let's look at three passages of Scripture that confirm this:

1. *Numbers 23:19 – <u>God is not a man, that he should lie</u>; neither the son of man, that he should repent: hath he said, and shall he not do it? <u>Or hath he spoken, and shall he not make it good</u>?*
2. *Titus 1:1-3 – Paul, a servant of God, and an apostle of Jesus Christ, according to the faith of God's elect, and the acknowledging of the truth which is after godliness; in hope of eternal life, <u>which God, that cannot lie, promised before the world began</u>...*
3. *Hebrews 6:17-18 – Wherein God, willing more abundantly to shew unto the heirs of promise the immutability of his counsel, confirmed it by an oath: that by two immutable (unchangeable) things, <u>in which it was impossible for God to lie</u>, we might have a strong consolation, who have fled for refuge to lay hold upon the hope set before us: which hope we have as an anchor of the soul, both sure and steadfast...*

So when He says, *"I will never leave you, nor forsake you,"* He means it! If we truly believe this we can boldly say, *"The Lord is my helper, and I will not fear what man shall do unto me."* After coming back to the Lord in 1983, the times I felt confident that He was with me was when "I felt" I was doing everything right (e.g., fasting, praying, reading His Word, abstaining from fleshly lusts). On the other hand, the times when I struggled with wrong behavior, attitudes, eating habits, or a lack of prayer, thanksgiving, and fasting, "I thought" He was mad at me, and therefore, withholding His love and presence from me. In other words, I felt like I had to do everything right in order for Him to be with me and to help me. However, since February 2003 when the protective covering was removed from me, I have truly felt His presence in me and with me (Please refer to *My Story – Part Two - Volume 1*). When Jonathan and Jessica were young during homeschool, or when we would be outside playing ball, "I knew" He was with us. When I clean house, "I know" He is with me. When I go to the grocery store, "I know" He is with me. The joy of being set free from legalism and walking in the new man, drawing from His living water on a continual basis, makes life worth living!

Below are Scriptures relating to wealth in the Lord:

1. *Psalm 1:1-6 – Blessed is the man that walketh not in the counsel of the ungodly, nor standeth in the way of sinners, nor sitteth in the seat of the scornful. But his delight is in the law of the LORD; and in his law doeth he meditate day and night. And he shall be like a tree planted by the rivers of water, that bringeth forth his fruit in his season; his leaf also shall not wither; and whatsoever he doeth shall prosper. The ungodly are not so: but are like the chaff which the wind driveth away. Therefore, the ungodly shall not stand in the judgment, nor sinners in the congregation of the righteous. For the LORD knoweth the way of the righteous: but the way of the ungodly shall perish.*

References:
Genesis 13:1-2 – And Abram went up out of Egypt, he, and his wife, and all that he had, and Lot with him, into the south. And Abram was very rich in cattle, in silver, and in gold. Genesis 24:34-35 – And he said, "I am Abraham's servant. And the LORD hath blessed my master greatly; and he is become great: and he hath given him flocks, and herds, and silver, and gold, and menservants, and maidservants, and camels, and asses." Psalm 112:1-3 – Praise ye the Lord. Blessed is the man that feareth the LORD, that delighteth greatly in his commandments. His seed shall be mighty upon earth: the generation of the upright shall be blessed. Wealth and riches shall be in his house: and his righteousness endureth forever. Galatians 3:26-29 (NIV) – So in Christ Jesus you are all children of God through faith, for all of you who were baptized into Christ have clothed yourselves with Christ. There is neither Jew nor Gentile, neither slave nor free, nor is there male and female, for you are all one in Christ Jesus. If you belong to Christ, then you are Abraham's seed, and heirs according to the promise. 3 John 1:1-4 (NASB) – The elder to the beloved Gaius, whom I love in truth. Beloved, I pray that in all respects you may prosper and be in good health, just as your soul prospers. For I was very glad when brethren came and testified to your truth, that is, how you are walking in truth. I have no greater joy than this, to hear of my children walking in the truth.

2. *Psalm 37:16, 18-25 – A little that a righteous man hath is better than the riches of many wicked. The LORD knows the days of the upright: and their inheritance shall be for ever. They shall not be ashamed in the evil time: and in the days of famine they shall be satisfied. But the wicked shall perish, and the enemies of the LORD shall be as the fat of lambs: they shall consume; into smoke shall they consume away. The wicked borroweth, and payeth not again: but the righteous sheweth mercy, and giveth. For such as be blessed of him shall inherit the earth; and they that be cursed of him shall be cut off. The steps of a good man are ordered by the LORD: and he delighteth in his way. Though he fall, he shall not be utterly cast down: for the LORD upholdeth him with his hand. I have been young, and now am old; yet have I not seen the righteous forsaken, nor his seed begging bread.*

References:

Proverbs 3:9-10 – *Honor the LORD with thy substance, and with the firstfruits of all thine increase: so shall thy barns be filled with plenty, and thy presses shall burst out with new wine.* ***Proverbs 15:16*** – *Better is little with the fear of the LORD than great treasure and trouble therewith.* ***Proverbs 19:17*** – *He that hath pity upon the poor lendeth unto the LORD; and that which he hath given will he pay him again.* ***Acts 4:32-35 (NASB)*** – *And the congregation of those who believed were of one heart and soul; and not one of them claimed that anything belonging to him was his own, but all things were common property to them. And with great power the apostles were giving testimony to the resurrection of the Lord Jesus, and abundant grace was upon them all. For there was not a needy person among them, for all who were owners of land or houses would sell them and bring the proceeds of the sales and lay them at the apostles' feet, and they would be distributed to each as any had need.* ***Ephesians 4:28*** – *Let him that stole steal no more: but rather let him labour, working with his hands the thing which is good, that he may have to give to him that needeth.* ***Philippians 4:10-20 (NASB)*** – *Paul writes, "But I rejoiced in the Lord greatly, that now at last you have revived your concern for me; indeed, you were concerned before, but you lacked opportunity. Not that I speak from want, for I have learned to be content in whatever circumstances I am. I know how to get along with humble means, and I also know how to live in prosperity; in any and every circumstance I have learned the secret of being filled and going hungry, both of having abundance and suffering need. I can do all things through Him who strengthens me. Nevertheless, you have done well to share with me in my affliction. You yourselves also know, Philippians, that at the first preaching of the gospel, after I left Macedonia, no church shared with me in the matter of giving and receiving but you alone; for even in Thessalonica you sent a gift more than once for my needs. Not that I seek the gift itself, but I seek for the profit which increases to your account. But I have received everything in full and have an abundance; I am amply supplied, having received from Epaphroditus what you have sent, a fragrant aroma, and acceptable sacrifice, well-pleasing to God. And my God will supply all your needs according to His riches in glory in Christ Jesus. Now to our God and Father be the glory forever and ever. Amen."*

3. ***Proverbs 10:22*** – *The blessing of the LORD, it maketh rich, and he addeth no sorrow with it.*

References:

Proverbs 11:28 – *He that trusteth in his riches shall fall: but the righteous shall flourish as a branch.* ***Proverbs 13:7*** – *There is that maketh himself rich, yet hath nothing: there is that maketh himself poor, yet hath great riches.* ***Proverbs 15:27*** – *He that is greedy of gain troubleth his own house …* ***Proverbs 16:8, 16*** – *Better is a little with righteousness, than great revenues without right. How much better is it to get wisdom than gold! And to get understanding rather to be chosen than silver!* ***Proverbs 20:15*** – *There is gold, and a multitude of rubies: but the lips of knowledge are a precious jewel.* ***Proverbs 22:1, 7*** – *A good name is rather to be chosen than great riches, and loving favour rather than silver and gold. The rich ruleth over the poor, and the borrower is servant to the lender.* ***Proverbs 28:6, 20, 22*** – *Better is the poor who walks in his uprightness, than he that is perverse in his ways, though he be rich. A faithful man shall abound with blessings: but he that maketh haste to be rich shall not be innocent. He that hasteth to be rich hath an evil eye, and considereth not that poverty shall come upon him.*

4. ***Proverbs 23:20-21*** – *Be not among winebibbers; among riotous eaters of flesh: for the drunkard and the glutton shall come to poverty: and drowsiness shall clothe a man with rags.* (Temperance in all things is a virtue)!

References:

Proverbs 24:30-34 – *I went by the field of the slothful, and by the vineyard of the man void of understanding; and, lo, it was all grown over with thorns, and nettles had covered the face thereof, and the stone wall thereof was broken down. Then I saw, and considered it well: I looked upon it, and received instruction. Yet a little sleep, a little slumber, a little folding of the hands to sleep: so shall thy poverty come as one that travelleth; and thy want as an armed man.* **Ecclesiastes 2:24-26** *(NASB)* – *There is nothing better for a man than to eat and drink and tell himself that his labor is good. This also I have seen that it is from the hand of God. For who can eat and who can have enjoyment without Him? For to a person who is good in His sight He has given wisdom and knowledge and joy, while to the sinner He has given the task of gathering and collecting so that he may give to one who is good in God's sight. This too is vanity and striving after wind.* **Ecclesiastes 5:18-19** – *Behold that which I have seen: it is good and comely for one to eat and to drink, and to enjoy the good of all his labour that he taketh under the sun all the days of his life, which God giveth him: for it is his portion. Every man also to whom God hath given riches and wealth, and hath given him power to eat thereof, and to take his portion, and to rejoice in his labour; this is the gift of God.* **Ecclesiastes 12:13-14** – *Let us hear the conclusion of the whole matter: fear God, and keep his commandments: for this is the whole duty of man. For God shall bring every work into judgment, with every secret thing, whether it be good, or whether it be evil.*

5. **Ecclesiastes 7:11-12** – *Wisdom is good with an inheritance: and by it there is profit to them that see the sun. for wisdom is a defence, and money is a defence: but the excellency of knowledge is, that wisdom giveth life to them that have it.*

References:

Proverbs 18:11 – *The rich man's wealth is his strong city, and as an high wall in his own conceit.* **2 Timothy 3:1-9** *(NASB)* – *But realize this, that in the last days difficult times will come. For men will be lovers of self, lovers of money, boastful, arrogant, revilers, disobedient to parents, ungrateful, unholy, unloving, irreconcilable, malicious gossips, without self-control, brutal, haters of good, treacherous, reckless, conceited, lovers of pleasure rather than lovers of God, holding to a form of godliness, although they have denied its power; avoid such men as these. For among them are those who enter into households, and captivate weak women weighed down with sins, led on by various impulses, always learning and never able to come to the knowledge of the truth. Just as Jannes and Jambres opposed Moses, so these men also oppose the truth, men of depraved mind, rejected in regard to the faith. But they will not make further progress; for their folly will be obvious to all, just as Jannes's and Jambres's folly was also.*

Below are Scriptures relating to trusting in the living God and not in uncertain riches:

1 Timothy 6:17-19 – <u>*Charge them that are rich in this world, that they be not highminded, nor trust in uncertain riches, but in the living God, who giveth us richly all things to enjoy;*</u> *that they do good, that they be rich in good works, ready to distribute, willing to communicate (share with others); laying up in store for themselves a good foundation against the time to come, that they may lay hold on eternal life.*

References:

Mark 10:17-30 – *And when he was gone forth into the way, there came one running, and kneeled to him, and asked him, "Good Master, what shall I do that I may inherit eternal life?" And Jesus said unto him, "Why callest thou me good? There is none good but one, that is, God. Thou knowest the commandments, do not commit adultery, do no kill, do not steal, do not bear false witness, defraud not, honour thy father and mother." And he answered and said unto him, "Master, all these have I observed from my youth?" Then Jesus* *beholding him loved him, and said unto him, "One thing thou lackest: go thy way, sell whatsoever thou hast, and give to the poor, and thou shalt have treasure in heaven: and come, take up the cross, and follow me." And he was sad at that saying, and went away grieved: for he had great possessions. And Jesus looked around about, and saith unto his disciples, "How hardly shall they that have riches enter into the kingdom of God!" And the disciples were astonished at his words. But Jesus answereth again, and saith unto them, "<u>Children, how hard is it for them that trust in riches to enter into the kingdom of God</u>! It is easier for a camel to go through the eye of a needle, than for a rich man to enter into the kingdom of God." And they were astonished out of measure, saying among themselves, "Who then can be saved?" And Jesus looking upon them saith, "With men it is impossible, but not with God: for with God all things are possible." Then Peter began to say unto him, "Lo, we have left all, and have followed thee." And Jesus answered and said, "Verily I say unto you, there is no man that hath left house, or brethren, or sisters, or father, or mother, or wife, or children, or lands, for my sake, and the gospel's, but he shall receive an hundredfold now in this time, houses, and brethren, and sisters, and mothers, and children, and lands, with persecutions; and in the world to come eternal life."* **Romans 8:28-39** *– And we know that all things work together for good to them that love God, to them who are the called according to his purpose. For whom he did foreknow, he also did predestinate to be conformed to the image of his Son, that he might be the firstborn among many brethren. Moreover, whom he did predestinate, them he also called: and whom he called, them he also justified: and whom he justified, them he also glorified. What shall we then say to these things? If God be for us, who can be against us? He that spared not his own Son, but delivered him up for us all, how shall he not with him also freely give us all things? Who shall lay anything to the charge of God's elect? It is God that justifieth. Who is he that condemneth? It is Christ that died, yea rather, that is risen again, who is even at the right hand of God, who also maketh intercession for us. Who shall separate us from the love of Christ? Shall tribulation, or distress, or persecution, or famine, or nakedness, or peril, or sword? As it is written, "For thy sake we are killed all the day long; we are accounted as sheep for the slaughter." Nay, in all these things we are more than conquerors through him that loved us. For I am persuaded, that neither death, nor life, nor angels, nor principalities, nor powers, nor things present, nor things to come, nor height, nor depth, nor any other creature, shall be able to separate us from the love of God, which is in Christ Jesus our Lord.* **Acts 14:21-22** *– And when they had preached the gospel to that city, and had taught many, they returned again to Lystra, and to Iconium, and Antioch, confirming the souls of the disciples, and exhorting them to continue in the faith, and that we must through much tribulation enter into the kingdom of God.* **2 Corinthians 13:14** *– The grace of the Lord Jesus Christ, and the love of God, and the communion of the Holy Ghost, be with you all. Amen.* **Ephesians 3:14-21** *– For this cause I bow my knees unto the Father of our Lord Jesus Christ, of whom the whole family in heaven and earth is named, that he would grant you, according to the riches of his glory, to be strengthened with might by his Spirit in the inner man; that Christ may dwell in your hearts by faith; that ye, being rooted and grounded in love, may be able to comprehend with all saints what is the breadth, and length, and depth, and height; and to know the love of Christ, which passeth knowledge, that ye might be filled with all the fulness of God. Now unto him that is able to do exceeding abundantly above all that we ask or think, according to the power that worketh in us, unto him be glory in the church by Christ Jesus throughout all ages, world without end. Amen.* **Hebrews 6:11-20** *(NKJV) – And we desire that each one of you show the same diligence to the full assurance of hope until the end, that you do not become sluggish, but imitate those who through faith and patience inherit the promises. <u>For when God made a promise to Abraham, because He could swear by no one greater, He swore by Himself, saying, "Surely blessing I will bless you, and multiplying I will multiply you."</u> And so, after he had patiently endured, he obtained the promise. For men indeed swear by the greater, and an oath for confirmation is for them an end of all dispute. <u>Thus God, determining to show more abundantly to the heirs of promise the immutability of His counsel, confirmed it by an oath, that by two immutable things, in which it is impossible for God to lie, we might have strong consolation, who have fled for refuge to lay</u>*

hold of the hope set before us. This hope we have as an anchor of the soul, both sure and steadfast, and which enters the Presence behind the veil, where the forerunner has entered for us, even Jesus, having become High Priest forever according to the order of Melchizedek. (Concerning this passage of Scripture, it is important to remember that if you are Christ's, then you are Abraham's seed and heirs according to the promise – Galatians 3:29). *James 1:9-11 – Let the brother of low degree rejoice in that he is exalted: but the rich, in that he is made low: because as the flower of the grass he shall pass away. For the sun is no sooner risen with a burning heat, but it withereth the grass, and the flower thereof falleth, and the grace of the fashion of it perisheth: so also shall the rich man fade away in his ways. James 2:5 – Hearken, my beloved brethren, hath not God chosen the poor of this world rich in faith, and heirs of the kingdom which he hath promised to them that love him? 1 Peter 1:24-25 – For all flesh is as grass, and all the glory of man as the flower of grass. The grass withereth, and the flower thereof falleth away: but the word of the Lord endureth for ever. And this is the word which by the gospel is preached unto you.*

Please refer to **Note 38a** for further information and additional Scripture references relating to this subject matter.

44(a) Ephesians 5:22-24 (AMPCE) reads, "Wives, be subject (be submissive and adapt yourselves) to your own husbands as [a service] to the Lord. For the husband is head of the wife as Christ is the Head of the church, Himself the Savior of [His] body. As the church is subject to Christ, so let wives also be subject in everything to their husbands." *So, as (husband's name) wife, I am* subject to *him*, [*I subordinate and adapt myself to him*], as is right and fitting and *my proper duty in the Lord, so that even if he does not obey the Word [of God], he may be won over not by discussion but by the [godly] life in which he sees in me*. When *he* observes the pure and modest way in which I conduct *myself*, together with *my* reverence [for *him*...]. *I* let *it* not be the [merely] external adorning with [elaborate] interweaving and knotting of the hair, the wearing of jewelry, or changes of clothes; but *I let it be* the hidden man of the heart *(the new man)*, in that which is not corruptible, *even the ornament* of a meek and quiet spirit, which is in the sight of God of great price. (Colossians 3:18-AMPCE; 1 Peter 3:1-3-AMPCE, 3:4-NKJV) *(Ref.: 1 Peter 2:21-23)*

Let's look at the following subject matters in detail as outlined below:

1. *God's creation, woman.*
2. *The correlation between Adam and his bride, Eve, and Christ and His bride, the church.*
3. *Woman's worth and value.*
4. *The result of the fall of man and His redemptive intent for the church.*

1. *God's creation, woman.* Let's go back to the beginning when God created Adam in His image. Notice in the following passage of Scripture that God revealed to Adam his need for someone like him before He moved to bring it to pass:

Now the Lord God said, "It is not good (sufficient, satisfactory) that the man should be alone; I will make him a helper meet (suitable, adapted, complementary) for him." And out of the ground the Lord God formed every [wild] beast and living creature of the field and every bird of the air and brought them to Adam to see what he would call them; and whatever Adam called every living creature, that was its name. And Adam gave names to all livestock, and to the birds of the air and to every [wild] beast of the field; but for Adam there was not found a helper meet (suitable, adapted, complementary) for him.

(Genesis 2:18-20, AMPCE)

As Adam named all the creatures, I believe the reality of aloneness was made known to him, realizing that there was no one like him on the earth. It was at that point God moved to meet that need:

And the Lord God caused a deep sleep to fall upon Adam; and while he slept, He took one of his ribs or a part of his side <u>and closed up the [place with] flesh. And the rib or part of his side which the Lord God had taken from the man He built up and made into a woman, and brought her to the man</u>.

(Genesis 2:21-22, AMPCE)

Then Adam said,

"This [creature] is now bone of my bones and flesh of my flesh; she shall be called <u>Woman</u>, because she was taken out of a man. Therefore, a man shall leave his father and his mother and shall become united and cleave to his wife, and they shall become one flesh." And the man and his wife were both naked, and were not embarrassed or ashamed in each other's presence.

(Genesis 2:23-25, AMPCE)

Marriage is a great mystery as it is a picture of Christ and the church, as Paul writes in *Ephesians 5:22-33* – "*...For this cause shall a man leave his father and mother, and shall be joined unto his wife, and they two shall be one flesh. <u>This is a great mystery: but I speak concerning Christ and the church</u>.*" (Note: God united Adam and Eve. I also believe the reason they were not ashamed in each other's presence is because they were clothed in His glory. He was their covering! Notice every creature on the face of this earth is clothed from the inside out except for man. Let's look at *Luke 9:29-32 (AMPCE)*,

<u>*And as He was praying, the appearance of His countenance became altered (different), and His raiment became dazzling white [flashing with the brilliance of lightning]*</u>*. And behold, two men were conversing with Him—Moses and Elijah, who appeared in splendor and majesty and brightness and were speaking of His exit [from life], which He was about to bring to realization at Jerusalem.*

The glory and splendor within Jesus caused His clothing to become dazzling white – flashing with the brilliance of lightning. This is what I believe to be Adam and Eve's clothing before the fall!

2. *The correlation between Adam and his bride, Eve, and Christ and His bride, the church.* When God formed Adam out of the dust of the earth and breathed His glory into him—the very express image of God's nature was complete in Adam; then God put Adam to sleep in order to bring forth woman (*1 Corinthians 11:8-9, 12*). We, the church, are created in Christ Jesus, the last Adam (*1 Corinthians 15:45; Ephesians 2:10*). As Adam was put to sleep in order to bring forth woman—his bride, Jesus was put to death in order to bring forth the church—His bride. Let's look at the following two passages of

Scripture:

1. *John 19:33-34 (AMPCE) – But when they came to Jesus and they saw that He was already dead, they did not break His legs. But one of the soldiers pierced His side with a spear, and immediately blood and water came (flowed) out.*
2. *1 John 5:7-8 (AMPCE) – So there are three witnesses in heaven: the Father, the Word and the Holy Spirit, and these three are One; and there are three witnesses on the earth: the Spirit, the water, and the blood; and these three agree [are in unison; their testimony coincides].*

As relating to the Lord's bride, the church, I believe the following:

1. The *Spirit* is the power to transform our lives into the new creation in Christ *(2 Corinthians 3:18).*
2. The *water* represents the Word of God used as a cleansing agent from the effects of living out of the carnal nature and the building block of the new creation in Christ *(Ephesians 5:25-27).*
3. The power and purity of His *blood* establishes the new covenant between Christ (and those who are in Christ) and God, our new life in Him—and totally washes away our unrighteousness *(1 Corinthians 11:25; Hebrews 8, 9, 10; 1 John 1:7).*

These three witnesses on earth represent the formation of the church!

3. *Woman's worth and value.* Let's move to *Genesis 2:22 (AMPCE)* to obtain a greater understanding of this – *"And the rib or part of his side which the Lord God had taken from the man He built up and made into a woman, and brought her to the man."* The Lord showed me that His will was to give to Adam a <u>part of Himself</u> that could only be seen through woman. Therefore, He caused a deep sleep to come upon Adam and took one of his ribs <u>and closed up the place with flesh instead of it.</u> Why a rib? The Lord helped me to see this by showing me the following analogy: In order to get to our physical heart, we must go through our rib cage. With this thought in mind and from a spiritual perspective, the Father took one of Adam's ribs, an opening to an expression of His heart, and closed up the place with flesh instead of it and used it to form woman. When He brought her to Adam, He brought to Adam an expression of Himself that could only be seen through her. What a gift! So the two together were the express image of God on this earth where there was no jealousy, rivalry, envy, or competition. They were both created by the Father and they were both secure in the Father's love. The love of the Father within them was the superior rule and reign – *Genesis 5:1-2 – "This is the book of the generation of Adam. In the day that God created man, in the likeness of God made he him; male and female created he them; and blessed them, and called their name Adam, in the day when they were created."*

4. *The result of the fall of man and His redemptive intent for the church.* When Adam ate of the fruit of the tree of the knowledge of good and evil, disorder came into them and to their offspring, which includes us, where we no longer were able to function in the order that God had established. This disorder or dysfunction brought independence from God, producing pride, fear, insecurity, etc., within us causing Satan to wreak havoc in our lives. *Psalm 22:14 (AMPCE)* shows a picture of the crucifixion – *"I am poured out like water, <u>and all my bones are out of joint.</u> My heart is like wax; it is softened [with anguish] and melted down within me."* I believe that all of the Lord's bones became "out of joint" as sin came

340

into Him, reflecting the dysfunction of mankind through Adam's sin. Now that the debt for sin has been paid through the death, burial, and resurrection of Jesus Christ, the Father is bringing His body, the church, back into order and operating properly. Paul writes,

For because of Him the whole body (the church, in all its various parts), closely joined and firmly knit together by the joints and ligaments with which it is supplied, when each part [with power adapted to its need] is working properly [in all its functions], grows to full maturity, building itself up in love.

(Ephesians 4:16, AMPCE)

Let's look at the following two passages of Scripture:

1. *John 14:12 (NASB) – Jesus said, "Truly, truly, I say to you, he who believes in Me, the works that I do, he will do also; and greater works than these he will do; because I go to the Father."*
2. *Ephesians 3:10-11 – To the intent that now unto the principalities and powers in heavenly places might be known by the church the manifold wisdom of God, according to the eternal purpose which he purposed in Christ Jesus our Lord.*

We, as Christians, are called to reveal the heart of the Father to the lost and hurting. We, the church, as a picture of Christ and His bride, are all feminine in our submission to Him as the head of His body. As the church is obedient to Him, His glory is revealed and seen in and through her, declaring His manifold wisdom and goodness to a lost and hurting world. When Adam and Eve ate from the tree of the knowledge of good and evil, the Lord began to speak to them about the consequences of living independent from Him. In *Genesis 3:16 (NASB)*, He said to the woman, *"I will greatly multiply your pain in childbirth, in pain you will bring forth children; yet your desire will be for your husband, and he will rule over you."* A wife's carnal tendency is to look to her husband for identity, to meet her emotional needs, and/or to take from him his God-given authority as the head (*1 Corinthians 11:3; Ephesians 5:24*). The husband's carnal tendency is to control and to rule over his wife or to allow his wife to be the head and to follow her lead. Because of what Jesus did on the cross, as born-again believers, Christ now becomes the center of the husband and the wife and His rule is love and honor one toward the other. Marriage is a beautiful institution designed and ordained by God, with both the husband and wife having the same worth and value in Him (*Genesis 2:20-25*). Marriage is also a place where the Lord deals with our carnal tendencies, bringing sanctification to us (*Ephesians 5:22-31*).

I have learned through my own personal experience the power of submission! This is not about being a doormat to an unregenerate man or being a whimp and not standing up for what you believe. It's about living out of the hidden man of the heart, the new man, where true security resides and where wholeness and healthy boundaries are formed as we become deeply rooted in Christ and tap into the treasures of His wisdom and knowledge (*Acts 17:28; 2 Corinthians 4:6-7; Colossians 2:1-8*). Before the Lord revealed His heart to me concerning submission, I wanted to remove *1 Peter 3:1-6* from my Bible! It bothered me every time I read this portion of Scripture because as far as I was concerned submission was equivalent to weakness or feeling like a child and I wanted no part of it! Thankfully the Lord, through His longsuffering with me, helped me to see His will regarding submission by revealing the following: In *1 Peter 3* Peter begins with, *"Likewise (or in the same way), ye wives, be in subjection to your own husbands."* This Scripture caused me to look back at *1 Peter 2:18-25 (AMPCE)* to see what

Peter said in what manner I was to submit:

> [You who are] household servants, be submissive to your masters with all [proper] respect, not only to those who are kind and considerate and reasonable, but also to those who are surly (overbearing, unjust, and crooked). For one is regarded favorably (is approved, acceptable, and thankworthy) if, as in the sight of God, he endures the pain of unjust suffering. [After all] what kind of glory [is there in it] if, when you do wrong and are punished for it, you take it patiently? But if you bear patiently with suffering [which results] when you do right and that is undeserved it is acceptable and pleasing to God. *For even to this were you called [it is inseparable from your vocation]. For Christ also suffered for you, leaving you [His personal] example, so that you should follow in His footsteps. He was guilty of no sin, neither was deceit (guile) ever found on His lips. When He was reviled and insulted, He did not revile or offer insult in return; [when] He was abused and suffered, He made no threats [of vengeance];* **but He trusted [Himself and everything] to Him Who judges fairly (righteously).** He personally bore our sins in His [own] body on the tree [as on an altar and offered Himself on it], that we might die (cease to exist) to sin (the old man) and live to righteousness (the new man). By His wounds you have been healed. For you were going astray like [so many] sheep, but now you have come back to the Shepherd and Guardian (the Bishop) of your souls.

This passage of Scripture is very important and spoke volumes to me in my own marriage after years of struggling with submitting to my husband! I realized the key to submission was to trust myself and everything to my heavenly Father who judges righteously. God's truth concerning His will began to dismantle the stronghold within me that submissive women were weak. For instance, I saw my mom as a strong and independent woman. I was raised in a home where her wisdom reigned; I heard her say many times, "No man is ever going to tell me what to do!" This type of mindset was firmly fixed or established within me and therefore difficult to change. So, when my husband would act contrary to "my wisdom" (what I thought was right) or try to tell me what to do, feelings of insecurity and anger would begin to surface and I would become defensive and argumentative.

Paul writes,

> For though we walk in the flesh, we do not war after the flesh: (For the weapons of our warfare are not carnal, but mighty through God to the pulling down of strong holds;) casting down imaginations, and every high thing that exalteth itself against the knowledge of God, and bringing into captivity every thought to the obedience of Christ; and having in a readiness to revenge all disobedience, when your obedience is fulfilled.
>
> (2 Corinthians 10:3-6)

In order to break this stronghold, God led me to do three very important things:

1. Submit to the Lord's will to go to Christian counseling and also to a *Living Waters Program* in order to dispel darkness through the light of His Word and to bring healing to my heart in many areas.
2. Journal my anger, frustration, and disappointments to the Lord instead of acting out of those emotions. I was then able to communicate with a right spirit, if needed. However,

most of the time, after I journaled my anger to the Lord, I had no need to express my heart any further. I continue to do this.

3. Renew the *spirit of my mind* or *my inmost mind* to the truth of God's Word concerning the new man in Christ (Please see the ***Personalized Scripture Guide - Volume 1***). I continue to do this.

In doing these three specific things, I began putting off the old man and putting on the new man, and God, through the power of His Word, began changing the carnal core beliefs and mindsets that were so deeply ingrained within me and strongholds began to crumble. Now when Don acts contrary to what I think is right or tries to tell me what to do, the Word of God, so ingrained within me, overrides any feelings of insecurity or anger *(Psalm 18:2; Proverbs 10:29; Nahum 1:7)*. I am Christ's servant and my submission to my husband is a picture of the church's submission to Christ and goes above and beyond my husband's shortcomings and weaknesses of the flesh *(Ephesians 5:22 – "Wives, submit yourselves unto your own husbands, as unto the Lord"* – for an example see **Note 44b**). Let's look at *Proverbs 22:17-19 (NKJV) – "Incline your ear and hear the words of the wise, and apply your heart to my knowledge; for it is a pleasant thing if you keep them within you; let them all be fixed upon your lips, so that your trust may be in the LORD; I have instructed you today, even you."* The words "them within you" in Hebrew is *beten* meaning "from an unused root probably meaning to be hollow; the belly, especially the womb; also the bosom or body of anything:—belly, body, as they be born, within, womb." The Word of God is so powerful that it will change the very character and nature of the one who chooses to incline his or her ear and lips to His words of wisdom. This causes the Word of God to become ingrained within and the result is the Lord and His truth becoming his or her stronghold and strength. This is the key to true submission in the midst of unpleasant circumstances. As we continue to renew our minds to His Words of truth, our strength and security in Him will cause us to be more than conquerors in this life *(Colossians 3:16; Hebrews 4:12-13; Romans 12:1-2, 8:28-39)*.

In the process of renewing the *spirit of my mind* or *inmost mind* to the truth of God's Word, He moved upon me to write the following verses of Scripture on a sheet of notebook paper and to put it on the side of my refrigerator, which was right next to my kitchen sink. It was usually when washing dishes, that I would find myself brewing over certain things that aggravated or frustrated me. When I would look up from the sink and notice those Scriptures, I would quickly be reminded of the truth of God's Word and would immediately say, "Lord, forgive me, I give this situation to You," and the brewing would end. The two Scripture verses I am referring to are *Proverbs 21:9-AMPCE, 19*:

It is better to dwell in a corner of a housetop [on the flat oriental roof, exposed to all kinds of weather] than in a house shared with a nagging, quarrelsome, and faultfinding woman. It is better to dwell in the wilderness, than with a contentious and an angry woman.

Please refer to ***My Story – Part Two - Volume 1*** where I share detailed information about my struggle concerning submission. When we choose to renew the *spirit of our minds* to the truth of God's Word concerning the new man in Christ, and to pour our hearts out to Him instead of taking it out on others, the light of His truth, through the power of His Holy Spirit, prevails in every situation and circumstance of life.

Let's look at the following passage of Scripture:

Does a fountain send forth at the same place sweet water and bitter? Can the fig tree, my brethren, bear olive berries? Either a vine, figs? So can no fountain both yield salt water and fresh. Who is a wise man and endued with knowledge among you? Let him shew out of a good conversation (behavior) his works with meekness of wisdom. But if ye have bitter envying and strife in your hearts, glory not, and lie not against the truth. This wisdom descendeth not from above, but is earthly, sensual, devilish. For where envying and strife is, there is confusion and every evil work. But the wisdom that is from above is first pure, then peaceable, gentle, and easy to be intreated (compliant), full of mercy and good fruits, without partiality, and without hypocrisy. And the fruit of righteousness is sown in peace of them that make peace.

(James 3:11-18)

God wants us to operate and function out of the mind of Christ from which flows the wisdom and power of God. James is saying here that there are two types of wisdom and they cannot flow out of the same vessel, just as salt water and fresh water cannot flow from the same spring. If we belong to Christ, He has called us to live in Him and not in the world. We are called to bear His image and His likeness, not being conformed to this world but transformed by the renewing of our minds in order to live in the truth which is in Christ *(Romans 12:1-2; Ephesians 4:20-24)*. Regardless of our feelings, emotions, and/or circumstances of life, His desire is for us to operate and function out of the hidden man of the heart *(1 Corinthians 2:14-16; 2 Corinthians 4:18; Philippians 2:1-13; 1 Peter 3:1-4)*.

Notice what Peter wrote in *1 Peter 3:3-4* when addressing wives,

Whose adorning let it not be that outward adorning of plaiting the hair, and of wearing of gold, or of putting on of apparel; but let it be the hidden man of the heart, in that which is not corruptible, even the ornament of a meek and quiet spirit, which is in the sight of God of great price.

There is a strength and confidence that comes from living out of this new creation. *Isaiah 32:17* reads in the *AMPCE* – *"And the effect of righteousness will be peace [internal and external], and the result of righteousness will be quietness and confident trust forever."* When living and functioning out of the new man which is created in His righteousness and holiness, there is a strength and confidence in Christ that is very evident to those who are closest to you and there is no one closer to you than your family *(Ephesians 4:24)*. When your husband notices that you do not get all worked up over his shortcomings and ill responses, I guarantee you, whether you realize it or not, he takes notice and can quite frankly, at times, be amazed. If you feel you need to repent before the Lord concerning your role as a wife, a prayer of repentance is included in ***Prayers of Repentance - Volume 1***.

Below are Scriptures relating to a virtuous woman:

Proverbs 12:4 *– A virtuous woman is a crown to her husband: but she that maketh ashamed is as rottenness in his bones.*

References:
Proverbs 11:16 *– A gracious woman retaineth honor: and strong men retain riches.* ***Proverbs 31:10-31*** *– Who can find a virtuous woman? For her price is far above rubies. The heart of her husband doth safely trust*

in her, so that he shall have no need of spoil. She will do him good and not evil all the days of her life. She seeketh wool, and flax, and worketh willingly with her hands. She is like the merchants' ships; she bringeth her food from afar. She riseth also while it is yet night, and giveth meat to her household, and a portion to her maidens. She considereth a field, and buyeth it: with the fruit of her hands she planteth a vineyard. She girdeth her loins with strength, and strengtheneth her arms. She perceiveth that her merchandise is good: her candle goeth not out by night. She layeth her hands to the spindle, and her hands hold the distaff. She stretcheth out her hand to the poor; yea, she reacheth forth her hands to the needy. She is not afraid of the snow for her household: for all her household are clothed with scarlet. She maketh herself coverings of tapestry; her clothing is silk and purple. Her husband is known in the gates, when he sitteth among the elders of the land. She maketh fine linen, and selleth it, and delivereth girdles unto the merchants. Strength and honour are her clothing; and she shall rejoice in time to come. She openeth her mouth with wisdom; and in her tongue is the law of kindness. She looketh well to the ways of her household, and eateth not the bread of idleness. Her children arise up, and call her blessed; her husband also, and he praiseth her. Many daughters have done virtuously, but thou excellest them all. Favour is deceitful, and beauty is vain: but a woman that feareth the LORD, she shall be praised. Give her of the fruit of her hands; and let her own works praise her in the gates. (Does this description of a virtuous woman seem to you like an insecure or a stupid woman or a doormat to an unregenerate husband? Of course not! This woman is functioning out of the wisdom and strength of her God. How much more is God's strength and wisdom seen through born-again believers in Christ! She is full of strength, substance, and wisdom which are the true riches in Christ and is clearly seen as the hidden man of the heart, the born-again creation, grows in strength and maturity within her. A virtuous woman gains much respect from her husband and her children).

Ephesians 5:22-33 *— Wives, submit yourselves unto your own husbands, as unto the Lord. For the husband is the head of the wife, even as Christ is the head of the church: and he is the saviour of the body. Therefore, as the church is subject unto Christ, so let the wives be to their own husbands in everything. Husbands, love your wives, even as Christ also loved the church, and gave himself for it; that he might sanctify and cleanse it with the washing of water by the word, that he might present it to himself a glorious church, not having spot, or wrinkle, or any such thing; but that it should be holy and without blemish. So ought men to love their wives as their own bodies. He that loveth his wife loveth himself. For no man ever yet hated his own flesh; but nourisheth and cherisheth it, even as the Lord the church: for we are members of his body, and of his flesh, and of his bones. For this cause shall a man leave his father and mother, and shall be joined unto his wife, and they two shall be one flesh. This is a great mystery: but I speak concerning Christ and the church. Nevertheless let every one of you in particular so love his wife even as himself; and the wife see that she reverence her husband.* ***1 Timothy 5:9-15*** *— ...I will therefore that the younger women marry, bear children, guide the house, give none occasion to the adversary to speak reproachfully. For some are already turned aside after Satan.* (The phrase "guide the house" in the Greek is *oikodespoteo*. It's used only once in the New Testament and its meaning is "to be the head of (i.e. rule) a family:–guide the house." Its meaning in the Thayer's Greek Lexicon is "to be master (or head) of a house; to rule a household, manage family affairs." Based on this passage of Scripture, when a woman steps into her God given role as a wife and mother, she has been given the responsibility of managing family affairs as a homemaker in a fun loving, practical, and God-centered fashion – in honor and submission to her husband, as unto Christ, as he is her covering – *1 Corinthians 11:1-3*). ***Titus 2:1-5*** *— ...the aged women likewise, that they be in behaviour as becometh holiness, not false accusers, not given to much wine, teachers of good things; that they may teach the young women to be sober, to love their husbands, to love their children, to be discreet, chaste, keepers at home, good, obedient to their own husbands, that the word of God be not blasphemed.* (Or in other words operate and function out of the hidden man of the heart).

Please refer to **Note 14a**, **39**, **40**, and **44b** for additional information and Scriptures relating to submission.

> **44(b)** For in this manner, in former times, the holy women who trusted in God also adorned themselves, being submissive to their own husbands. It was thus that Sarah obeyed Abraham [following his guidance and acknowledging his headship over her by] calling him lord. <u>And *I am* her true daughter *because I* do right and let nothing terrify *me* [*I do* not *give* way to hysterical fears or let anxieties unnerve *me*]. *My trust is in You, Lord*</u>! (1 Peter 3:5-NKJV, 3:6-AMPCE) *(Ref: 1 Peter 2:21-23)*

When John the Baptist was born, his father, Zacharias, prophesied,

> *...To perform the mercy promised to our fathers, and to remember his holy covenant; the oath which he sware to our father Abraham, that he would grant unto us, that we being delivered out of the hand of our enemies might serve him without fear, in holiness and righteousness before him, all the days of our life. And thou, child, shalt be called the prophet of the Highest: for thou shalt go before the face of the Lord to prepare his ways; to give knowledge of salvation unto his people by the remission of their sins, through the tender mercy of our God; whereby the dayspring from on high hath visited us, to give light to them that sit in darkness and in the shadow of death, to guide our feet into the way of peace.*
>
> (Luke 1:72-79)

This prophecy was about being born again and living out of the new man or hidden man of the heart—serving Him without fear, in holiness and righteousness before Him, all the days of our lives *(Ephesians 4:22-24)*. The hidden man of the heart does not give way to hysterical fears because his or her trust, security, and confidence is in Christ! Let's look at an example of Sarai's submission to Abram's weakness:

> *Now there was a famine in the land, and Abram went down to Egypt to dwell there, for the famine was severe in the land. And it came to pass, when he was close to entering Egypt, that he said to Sarai his wife, "Indeed I know that you are a woman of beautiful countenance. Therefore, it will happen, when the Egyptians see you, that they will say, 'This is his wife'; and they will kill me, but they will let you live. Please say you are my sister, that it may be well with me for your sake, and that I may live because of you." So it was, when Abram came into Egypt, that the Egyptians saw the woman, that she was very beautiful. The princes of Pharaoh also saw her and commended her to Pharaoh. And the woman was taken to Pharaoh's house. He treated Abram well for her sake. He had sheep, oxen, male donkeys, male and female servants, female donkeys, and camels. But the LORD plagued Pharaoh and his house with great plagues because of Sarai, Abram's wife. And Pharaoh called Abram and said, "What is this you have done to me? Why did you not tell me that she was your wife? Why did you say, 'She is my sister'? I might have taken her as my wife. Now therefore, here is your wife; take her and go your way." So Pharaoh commanded his men concerning him; and they sent him away, with his wife and all that he had.*
>
> (Genesis 12:10-20, NKJV)

Notice how the Lord took care of Sarai despite Abram's weakness. He will also take care of us who choose to trust in "Him" concerning our submission to our own husband's weaknesses of the flesh *(Romans 8:28)*. However, wives take heed, it is important that we do not come into agreement with our husbands or try to convince our husbands to go along with us when it comes to going against the things of God as happened with Ananias and Sapphira. Here is the story:

> *But a certain man named Ananias, with Sapphira his wife, sold a possession, and kept back part of the price, his wife also being privy to it (aware of it), and laid it at the apostles' feet. But Peter said, "Ananias, why hath Satan filled thine heart to lie to the Holy Ghost, and to keep back part of the price of the land? Whiles it remained, was it not thine own? And after it was sold, was it not in thine own power? Why hast thou conceived this thing in thine heart? Thou hast not lied unto men, but unto God." And Ananias hearing these words fell down, and gave up the ghost: and great fear came on all them that heard these things. And the young men arose, wound him up, and carried him out, and buried him. And it was about the space of three hours after, when his wife, not knowing what was done, came in. And Peter answered unto her, "Tell me whether ye sold the land for so much?" And she said, "Yea, for so much." Then Peter said unto her, "How is it that ye have agreed together to tempt the Spirit of the Lord? Behold, the feet of them which have buried thy husband are at the door, and shall carry thee out." Then fell she down straightway at his feet, and yielded up the ghost: and the young men came in, and found her dead, and, carrying her forth, buried her by her husband.*
>
> (Acts 5:1-10)

Notice in this passage of Scripture that Peter gave Ananias' wife, Sapphira, an opportunity to tell him the truth about how much they sold their land for. Instead of telling the truth, she chose to lie to the Holy Spirit as well, and it cost her—her life.

Let's move on. As a history lesson, Sarai was chosen by God to give birth to Isaac, the son of promise. In the process of waiting, when Sarai was about seventy-four and Abram was eighty-five, she told Abram in *Genesis 16:2* – *"Behold now, the LORD hath restrained me from bearing: I pray thee, go in unto my maid (Hagar); it may be that I may obtain children by her.' And Abram hearkened to the voice of Sarai."* So, Hagar conceived and bore Abram a son and called him Ishmael. Fourteen years later, when Abram was ninety-nine years old, God appeared to him to establish His covenant. First, He changed his name from Abram to Abraham and then God said to Abraham,

> *"This is My covenant, which you shall keep, between Me and you and your descendants after you: every male among you shall be circumcised. And you shall be circumcised in the flesh of your foreskin, and it shall be the sign of the covenant between Me and you..." Then God said to Abraham, "As for Sarai your wife, you shall not call her name Sarai, but Sarah shall be her name. I will bless her, and indeed I will give you a son by her. Then I will bless her, and she shall be a mother of nations; kings of peoples will come from her." Then Abraham fell on his face and laughed, and said in his heart, "Will a child be born to a man one hundred years old? And will Sarah, who is ninety years old, bear a child?" And Abraham said to God, "Oh that Ishmael might live before you!" But God said, "No, but Sarah your wife will bear you a son, and you shall call his name Isaac; and I will establish My covenant with him for an everlasting covenant for his descendants after him."*

Sarah was ninety or ninety-one years old when she gave birth to Isaac and Abraham was one hundred years old *(Genesis 17:1-18, 21:1-3)*. This background information is important as Paul referred to this when he was addressing those who desired to be under the law of Moses rather than living in Christ, the born-again creation:

> *For it is written, that Abraham had two sons, the one by a bondmaid (Hagar), the other by a freewoman (Sarah). But he who was of the bondwoman was born after the flesh; but he of the freewoman was by promise. Which things are an allegory: for these are the two covenants; the one from the mount Sinai, which gendereth to bondage, which is Agar (Hagar). For this Agar is mount Sinai in Arabia, and answereth to Jerusalem which now is, and is in bondage with her children. But Jerusalem which is above is free, which is the mother of us all. For it is written, "Rejoice, thou barren that bearest not; break forth and cry, thou that travailest not: for the desolate hath many more children than she which hath an husband." Now we, brethren, as Isaac was, are the children of promise. But as then he that was born after the flesh persecuted him that was born after the Spirit, even so it is now. Nevertheless what saith the scripture? "Cast out the bondwoman and her son: for the son of the bondwoman shall not be heir with the son of the freewoman." So then, brethren, we are not children of the bondwoman, but of the free.*
>
> (Galatians 4:22-31)

Paul writes in *Galatians 2:21,* "*I do not frustrate the grace of God: for if righteousness come by the law, then Christ is dead in vain.*" Paul continues in *Galatians 5:6,* "*For in Jesus Christ neither circumcision availeth anything, nor uncircumcision; but faith which worketh by love.*" He then details the works of the flesh and the fruit of the Spirit being contrary or opposite one to another. Jesus gave His life for us so that we could be born again and grow in maturity in Him. Flesh and blood cannot inherit the kingdom of God, it is only the born-again creation, the new man in Christ, that can walk in newness of life *(1 Corinthians 15:50)*. The key to living out of this new nature is found in the following passage of Scripture:

> *For they that are after the flesh do mind the things of the flesh; but they that are after the Spirit the things of the Spirit. For to be carnally minded is death; but to be spiritually minded is life and peace. Because the carnal mind is enmity against God: for it is not subject to the law of God, neither indeed can be. So then they that are in the flesh cannot please God.*
>
> (Romans 8:5-8)

As sons and daughters of the freewoman, we are called to live out of the new man, the born-again creation within – "*And the effect of righteousness will be peace [internal and external], and the result of righteousness will be quietness and confident trust forever*" *(Isaiah 32:17, AMPCE)*. This new man comes through circumcision made without hands, by putting off the sinful deeds of the flesh—our carnality—through the circumcision of the heart in order to reveal the true nature of Christ, as noted in the following two passages of Scripture:

1. ***Romans 2:28-29*** *– For he is not a Jew, which is one outwardly; neither is that circumcision,*

which is outward in the flesh: but he is a Jew, which is one inwardly; and circumcision is that of the heart, in the spirit, and not in the letter; whose praise is not of men, but of God.

2. **Colossians 2:11-12** – *In whom also ye are circumcised with the circumcision made without hands, in putting off the body of the sins of the flesh by the circumcision of Christ: buried with him in baptism, wherein also ye are risen with him through the faith of the operation of God, who hath raised him from the dead.*

Please refer to **Note 14a, 39, 40, and 44a** for additional information relating to this subject matter.

Please refer to **Note 28c** and **34b** for additional information and Scriptures relating to circumcision.

---

45. Proverbs 21:9 (AMPCE) and 19 reads, "It is better to dwell in a corner of the housetop [on he flat oriental roof, exposed to all kinds of weather] than in a house shared with a <u>nagging, quarrelsome, and faultfinding woman.</u> *It is* better to dwell in the wilderness, than with a contentious and an angry woman." *(Continue to) help me see my faults and to examine my own heart so that I may be an example of Your character and nature to my family. I desire to be an example of the true bride of Christ, by allowing You to sanctify and wash me with the water of Your Word. Let Your Word that I am speaking, which is alive and full of power, go into the deepest parts of my nature to expose, sift, analyze, and judge the very thoughts and purposes of my heart. (Ref.: 2 Corinthians 13:5; Ephesians 5:25-26; Hebrews 4:12)*

As I shared in **Note 44a**, these are the verses of Scripture that I wrote down on a sheet of notebook paper and put on the side of my refrigerator which was right next to the kitchen sink. It was usually when washing dishes, that I would find myself brewing over certain things that aggravated or frustrated me. When I would look up from the sink and notice those verses, I would quickly be reminded of the truth of God's Word and would immediately say, "Lord, forgive me, I give this situation to You," and the brewing would end. I give God much praise for His grace and truth! Peter writes,

> *Seeing ye have purified your souls in obeying the truth through the Spirit unto unfeigned love of the brethren, see that ye love one another with a pure heart fervently: being born again, not of corruptible seed, but of incorruptible, by the word of God, which liveth and abideth for ever. For all flesh is as grass, and all the glory of man as the flower of grass. The grass withereth, and the flower thereof falleth away: but the word of the Lord endureth for ever. And this is the word which by the gospel is preached to you. Wherefore laying aside all malice, and all guile, and hypocrisies, and envies, and all evil speakings, as newborn babes, desire the sincere milk of the word, that ye may grow thereby: if so be ye have tasted that the Lord is gracious.*
>
> (1 Peter 1:22-2:3)

God is calling us to put off the old man and to put on the new man in Christ, which produces the fruit of the Spirit, as Paul explains in *Galatians 5:22-24* – *"But the fruit of the Spirit is love, joy, peace, longsuffering, gentleness, goodness, faith meekness, temperance: against such there is no law. And they that are Christ's have crucified the flesh with the affections and lusts."* As we do this, we will grow in His righteousness. Wife, your husband is your head and your protector but that does not give him the right to be overbearing, hard, a dictating tyrant, etc. It is essential that you find your security and strength in the Lord. If your husband does not obey the Word of God, your relationship with the Lord and living out of the hidden man of the heart is crucial in possibly winning him over to Christ and His Lordship. God has <u>not</u> called you to be his preacher, his conscience, or his mother. God has called you to have a relationship with Him and to grow in grace and truth in your inner man. By doing this, you will find your security and strength in Christ. Trust God with your husband and allow the joy of the Lord, the strength of the Lord, and the peace of God to be your rule and guide. Choose to focus on the good things about your husband and cast down the imaginations that would cause you to be bitter or resentful toward him. Take your fears and insecurities to the Lord and continue to renew the *spirit of your mind* or *your inmost mind* to the new man or your true self. Just as God made every tree grow from the ground and the baby to grow inside the mother's womb, He is faithful to cause the new creation to grow within you *(Genesis 2:9; Psalm 139:13-16; 1 Peter 2:2-3)*. Here is a story about a rich young ruler who came to Jesus:

> *Now behold, one came and said to Him, "Good Teacher, what good thing shall I do that I may have eternal life?" So He said to him, "Why do you call Me good? No one is good but One, that is, God. But if you want to enter into life, keep the commandments." He said to Him, "Which ones?" Jesus said, "You shall not murder, you shall not commit adultery, you shall not steal, you shall not bear false witness, honor your father and your mother, and you shall love your neighbor as yourself." The young man said to Him, "All these things I have kept from my youth. What do I still lack?" Jesus said to him, "If you want to be perfect, go, sell what you have and give to the poor, and you will have treasure in heaven; and come, follow Me." But when the young man heard that saying, he went away sorrowful, for he had great possessions. Then Jesus said to His disciples, "Assuredly, I say to you that it is hard for a rich man to enter the kingdom of heaven. And again I say to you, it is easier for a camel to go through the eye of a needle than for a rich man to enter the kingdom of God." When His disciples heard it, they were greatly astonished, saying, "Who then can be saved?" But Jesus looked at them and said to them, "With men this is impossible, but with God all things are possible."*

(Matthew 19:16-26, NKJV)

Be encouraged that nothing is too hard for the Lord concerning your husband, your loved ones, and/or yourself as revealed in the following passage of Scripture:

> *Now Abraham and Sarah were old and well stricken in age; and it ceased to be with Sarah after the manner of women. Therefore, Sarah laughed within herself, saying, "After I am waxed old shall I have pleasure, my lord being old also?" And the LORD said unto Abraham, "Wherefore did Sarah laugh, saying, 'Shall I of a surety bear a child, which am old?' <u>Is anything too hard for the LORD</u>? At the appointed time I will return unto thee, according to the time of life, and Sarah shall have a son."*

(Genesis 18:11-14)

Be assured that it is God's will for you and your household to be saved and to live and function out of the new man in Christ. Just as He brought forth Isaac, the son of promise, from Sarah who was passed the age of childbearing, and brought forth Jesus from the "virgin" Mary, He is faithful to bring forth the new man, the born-again creation, in us as we choose to renew the *spirit of our minds* to His truths and surrender to His Lordship! Again, if you feel the need to repent before the Lord concerning your role as a wife, a prayer of repentance is included in ***Prayers of Repentance - Volume 1***.

Below are Scriptures relating to the importance of operating in God's wisdom:

1. ***Psalm 37:8-11*** *– Cease from anger, and forsake wrath: fret not thyself in any wise to do evil. For evildoers shall be cut off: but those that wait upon the LORD, they shall inherit the earth. For yet a little while, and the wicked shall not be: yea, thou shalt diligently consider his place, and it shall not be. But the meek shall inherit the earth; and shall delight themselves in the abundance of peace.*

References:
Proverbs 14:1-2 *– Every wise woman buildeth her house: but the foolish plucketh it down with her hands. He that walketh in his uprightness feareth the LORD: but he that is perverse in his ways despiseth him.* ***Proverbs 15:1, 17*** *– A soft answer turneth away wrath: but grievous words stir up anger. Better is a dinner of herbs where love is, than a stalled ox and hatred therewith.* ***Proverbs 17:1*** *– Better is a dry morsel, and quietness therewith, than an house full of sacrifices with strife.* ***Proverbs 18:6*** *– A fool's lips enter into contention, and his mouth calleth for strokes.* ***Proverbs 19:13*** *– ... the contentions of a wife are a continual dropping.* ***Proverbs 25:24*** *– It is better to dwell in the corner of the housetop, than with a brawling (contentious) woman and in a wide house.* ***Proverbs 27:15*** *– A continual dropping in a very rainy day and a contentious woman are alike.* ***Matthew 5:5*** *– Blessed are the meek: for they shall inherit the earth.* ***Luke 6:46-49*** *– Jesus said, "And why call ye me, 'Lord, Lord,' and do not the things which I say? Whosoever cometh to me, and heareth my sayings, and doeth them, I will shew you to whom he is like: he is like a man which built an house, and digged deep, and laid the foundation on a rock: and when the flood arose, the stream beat vehemently upon that house, and could not shake it: for it was founded upon a rock. But he that heareth, and doeth not, is like a man that without a foundation built an house upon the earth; against which the stream did beat vehemently, and immediately it fell; and the ruin of that house was great."* ***Romans 7:23-25*** *– But I see another law in my members, warring against the law of my mind, and bringing me into captivity to the law of sin which is in my members. O wretched man that I am! Who shall deliver me from this body of death? I thank God through Jesus Christ our Lord. So then with the mind I myself serve the law of God; but with the flesh the law of sin.*

2. ***Proverbs 18:20-21*** *– A man's belly shall be satisfied with the fruit of his mouth; and with the increase of his lips shall he be filled. Death and life are in the power of the tongue: and they that love it shall eat the fruit thereof.*

References:
Proverbs 11:11-14 *– By the blessing of the upright the city is exalted: but it is overthrown by the mouth of the wicked. He that is void of wisdom despiseth his neighbour: but a man of understanding holdeth his peace. A talebearer revealeth secrets: but he that is of a faithful spirit concealeth the matter. Where no counsel is, the people fail: but in the multitude of counsellors there is safety.* ***James 1:26-27*** *– If any man among you seem to be religious, and bridleth not his tongue, but deceiveth his own heart, this man's religion is vain. Pure religion and undefiled before God and the Father is this, to visit the fatherless and widows in their affliction, and to keep himself unspotted from the world.* ***James 3:3-18*** *– Behold, we put bits in the horses' mouths, that they may obey us; and we turn about their whole body. Behold also the ships, which though they be so great, and are driven of fierce winds, yet are they turned about with a very small helm (rudder), whithersoever the governor (helmsman) listeth (impulse). Even so the tongue is a little member, and boasteth*

great things. Behold, how great a matter a little fire kindleth! And the tongue is a fire, a world of iniquity: so is the tongue among our members, that it defileth the whole body, and setteth on fire the course of nature; and it is set on fire of hell. For every kind of beasts, and of birds, and of serpents, and of things in the sea, is tamed, and hath been tamed of mankind: but the tongue can no man tame; it is an unruly evil, full of deadly poison. Therewith bless we God, even the Father; and therewith curse we men, which are made after the similitude of God. Out of the same mouth proceedeth blessing and cursing. My brethren, these things ought not so to be. Doth a fountain send forth at the same place sweet water and bitter? Can a fig tree, my brethren, bear olive berries? Either a vine, figs? So can no fountain both yield salt water and fresh. Who is a wise man endued with knowledge among you? Let him shew out of a good conversation (behavior) his works with meekness of wisdom. But if ye have bitter envying and strife in your hearts, glory not, and lie not against the truth. This wisdom descendeth not from above, but is earthly, sensual, devilish. For where envying and strife is, there is confusion and every evil work. But the wisdom that is from above is first pure, then peaceable, gentle, and easy to be intreated, full of mercy and good fruits, without partiality, and without hypocrisy. And the fruit of righteousness is sown in peace of them that make peace.

---

46. *I thank You that (husband's name) loves me, as You, Lord, loved the church and gave Yourself up for her, so that You might sanctify her, having cleansed her by the washing of water with the Word, that You might present the church to Yourself in glorious splendor, without spot or wrinkle or any such things [that she might be holy and faultless]. Even so, my husband loves me as [being in a sense] his own body. He who loves his own wife loves himself. For no man ever hated his own flesh, but nourishes and carefully protects and cherishes it, as Christ does the church. (Husband's name) is [affectionate and sympathetic with me]; he is not harsh or bitter or resentful toward me. He lives considerately with [me], with an intelligent recognition [of the marriage relation], honoring me as [physically] the weaker, but [realizing that we] are joint heirs of the grace (God's unmerited favor) of life, in order that our prayers may not be hindered and cut off. [Otherwise we cannot pray effectively]. (Ephesians 5:25-29-AMPCE; Colossians 3:19-AMPCE; 1 Peter 3:7-AMPCE)*

Your husband may not love you as Christ loves the church. Your husband may not be affectionate or sympathetic toward you. He may not understand that you are both "joint" heirs of the grace of God's unmerited favor of life. If this is the case, he needs to see your patience and strength in Christ by living out of the hidden man of the heart (please refer to **Notes 44a** and **45**). As you declare words of faith and forgiveness over your husband, during your own prayer time, you are releasing the grace and truth of God in his life and are able to see above and beyond his own weaknesses and shortcomings (*John 1:14*). In doing this, you are operating in the same manner as your heavenly Father and as faithful Abraham,

Therefore it is of faith, that it might be by grace; to the end the promise might be sure to all the seed; not to that only which is of the law, but to that also which is of the faith of Abraham; who is the father of us all, (as it is written, "I have made thee a father of many nations,") before him whom he (Abraham) believed, even God, who quickeneth (makes alive) the dead, and calleth those things which be not as though they were. Who against hope believed in hope, that he might become the father of many nations, according to that which was spoken, "So shall thy seed (offspring) be." And being not weak in faith, he

*considered not his own body now dead, when he was about an hundred years old, neither
yet the deadness of Sara's womb: he staggered not at the promise of God through unbelief;
but was strong in faith, giving glory to God; and being fully persuaded that, what he had
promised, he was able also to perform. And therefore it was imputed to him for righteousness.
Now it was not written for his sake alone, that it was imputed to him; but for us also, to
whom it shall be imputed, if we believe on him that raised up Jesus our Lord from the dead;
who was delivered for our offences, and was raised again for our justification.*

(Romans 4:16-25)

Be encouraged, for all of the promises of God in Christ are Yes, and in Him Amen *(2 Corinthians 1:20)*!

---

47. As <u>*(wife's name)*</u> husband, *I love her as You, Lord,* loved the church and gave *Yourself* up for her, so that *You* might sanctify her, having cleansed her by the washing of water with the Word, that *You* might present the church to *Yourself* in glorious splendor, without spot or wrinkle or any such things [that she might be holy and faultless]. Even so *I* love <u>*(wife's name)*</u> as [being in a sense] *my* own *body. For* he who loves his own wife loves himself. For no man ever hated his own flesh, but nourishes and carefully protects and cherishes it, as Christ does the church. *I am* [affectionate and sympathetic with *her*] and *I am* not harsh or bitter or resentful toward *her. I* live considerately with <u>*(wife's name)*</u>, with an intelligent recognition [of the marriage relation], honoring *her* as [physically] the weaker, <u>but [realizing that *we*] are joint heirs of the grace (God's unmerited favor) of life, in order that *our* prayers may not be hindered and cut off.</u> [Otherwise we cannot pray effectively].
(Ephesians 5:25-29-AMPCE; Colossians 3:19-AMPCE; 1 Peter 3:7-AMPCE)

God's will for the husband is to love his wife as Christ loved the church and gave Himself for her. Christ's love for His bride, the church, is unconditional and the same should be true for a husband's love for his wife in all her weaknesses and insecurities. The key is loving her with Christ's love in you. The word "love" in the Greek is *agapao*. Its meaning in the Thayer's Greek Lexicon is "to love, to be full of good-will and to exhibit the same: Luke 7:47; 1 John 4:7; with the accusative of the person, to have a preference for, wish well to, regard the welfare of: Matthew 5:43, 19:19; Luke 7:5; John 11:5; Romans 13:8; 2 Corinthians 11:11, 12:15; Galatians 5:14; Ephesians 5:25, 28; 1 Peter 1:22." It is the root word for *agape* described in **Notes 28c, 29a, 29b, 29c, 30, 31, 32a,** and **32b.** I highly recommend that husbands read each of these notes along with **Notes 33a, 33b, 33c,** and **34a.** It is essential for you, as a husband, to "give yourself" to Christ in order to truly have a revelation of His love for you; it is only then that you can truly love your wife well. When this happens, your wife will internalize your love within herself producing security, safety, and a sense of well-being. When your wife sees that you have her best interest at heart she will gladly submit to your lead and when there needs to be correction or trust in your leadership, she will respond in a place of security and well-being. Let's look at a very important portion of the main Scripture reference:

*'So ought men to love their wives as their own bodies. He that loveth his wife loveth himself.
For no man ever yet hated his own flesh; but nourisheth and cherisheth it, <u>even as the Lord
the church</u>: for we are members of his body, of his flesh, and of his bones.*

(Ephesians 5:28-30)

353

It is important to understand that if you do not love your wife, in essence, you do not love yourself. The Lord wants to get to the root of any self-hatred, judgments, bitterness, resentment, insecurities, etc., working on the inside of you, keeping you bound to the old man and from truly loving your wife the way Christ loves His bride, the church. Let's look at the following passage of Scripture:

> *Then one of them, which was a lawyer, asked him a question, tempting him, and saying, "Master, which is the great commandment in the law?" Jesus said unto him, "Thou shalt love the Lord thy God with all thy heart, and with all thy soul, and with all thy mind. This is the first and great commandment. And the second is like unto it, Thou shalt love thy neighbour as thyself. On these two commandments hang all the law and the prophets."*
>
> (Matthew 22:35-40)

The Greek word for "love" is the same Greek word concerning a husband's love for his wife – *agapao* as defined above.

Below is a revelation the Lord gave to me of the husband's headship and covering over his wife as it relates to Adam and Eve and their partaking of the fruit from the tree of the knowledge of good and evil:

First, let's read *Genesis 2:7-9, 15-18,*

> *And the LORD God formed man of the dust of the ground, and breathed into his nostrils the breath of life; and man became a living soul. And the LORD God planted a garden eastward in Eden; and there he put the man whom he had formed. And out of the ground made the LORD God to grow every tree that is pleasant to the sight, and good for food; the tree of life also in the midst of the garden, and the tree of knowledge of good and evil. And the LORD God took the man, and put him into the garden of Eden to dress it and to keep it. And the LORD God commanded the man, saying, "Of every tree of the garden thou mayest freely eat: but of the tree of the knowledge of good and evil, thou shalt not eat of it: for in the day that thou eatest thereof thou shalt surely die." And the LORD God said, "It is not good that the man should be alone; I will make him an help meet (aid:–help) for him."*

Notice that before Eve was created the Lord commanded Adam not to eat from the tree of the knowledge of good and evil and the consequences if he did. Now let's read *Genesis 3:1-7,*

> *Now the serpent was more subtle (cunning) than any beast of the field which the LORD God had made. And he said unto the woman, "Yea, hath God said, ye shall not eat of every tree of the garden?" And the woman said unto the serpent, "We may eat of the fruit of the trees of the garden: but of the fruit of the tree which is in the midst of the garden, God hath said, 'Ye shall not eat of it, neither shall ye touch it, lest you die.'" And the serpent said unto the woman, "Ye shall not surely die: for God doth know that in the day ye eat thereof, then your eyes shall be opened, and ye shall be as gods, knowing good and evil." And when the woman saw that the tree was good for food, and that it was pleasant to the eyes, and a tree to be desired to make one wise, she took of the fruit thereof, and did eat, and gave also unto her husband with her; and he did eat. And the eyes of them both were opened, and they knew that they were naked; and they sewed fig leaves together, and made themselves aprons.*

354

Notice the eyes of them both were opened after Adam ate of the fruit, not after Eve ate of the fruit. Adam was Eve's covering and protector which included the consequences of eating from the tree of the knowledge of good and evil. She was covered and protected as long as he was obedient to do what God had commanded him in *Genesis 2:16-17 – "Of every tree of the garden thou mayest freely eat: but of the tree of the knowledge of good and evil, thou shalt not eat of it: for in the day that thou eatest thereof thou shalt surely die."* The moment Adam ate of the fruit, the eyes of them both were opened and they knew that they were naked. God has not changed His mind concerning the man's role as a husband and the woman's role as a wife *(Malachi 3:6)*. As your wife and children's covering and protector, it is essential to surrender to the Lordship of Jesus Christ through humbleness of mind and heart. The Lord will help you be the husband and father He has called you to be. This union is truly a mystery concerning Christ and His church *(Ephesians 5:32)*.

Below is a paragraph from **Note 18b** that I believe is very important for us to understand:

In the following passage of Scripture, God commanded Adam:

"Of every tree of the garden thou mayest freely eat: but of the tree of the knowledge of good and evil, thou shalt not eat of it: for in the day that thou eatest thereof thou shalt surely die." And the LORD God said, "It is not good that the man should be alone; I will make him an help meet for him."

(Genesis 2:16-18)

God commanded Adam not Eve! The moment Eve ate of the fruit, before she gave the fruit to Adam, her eyes were not opened – *Genesis 3:6-7 – "...she took of the fruit thereof and did eat, and gave also unto her husband with her; and he did eat. And the eyes of them both were opened, and they knew that they were naked..."* Adam was Eve's covering and protector against Satan's craftiness and as long as he chose not to eat of that fruit, Eve was covered. Also, we must remember that the life of the flesh is in the blood which comes from the seed of man *(Leviticus 17:11)*. The man's seed or sperm gives life to the egg within the woman. Woman then becomes the carrier of that life within her. Before Adam ate of the fruit of the knowledge of the tree of good and evil his seed was pure and incorruptible. At that point, Adam's offspring, born after him, would not have been tainted by sin and death! However, after Adam ate of the fruit his seed became impure and corruptible and we are the product of that seed. Mary became the carrier of Jesus Christ, the last Adam, who was the Son of God because the seed that impregnated her was pure and incorruptible as it came from the power of the Most High God. In the same way, if only Eve had partaken of the fruit of the tree of the knowledge of good and evil, and not Adam, Adam's pure and incorruptible seed would have produced pure and holy offspring. Therefore, I believe, if Eve alone had partaken of the forbidden fruit there would not have been life altering consequences *(1 Corinthians 15:45; Luke 1:30-35)*. What God intended in the beginning for mankind is still His plan!

Jesus Christ came that we might have life and that more abundantly! Christ has redeemed us, but we are not exempt from Satan's craftiness to keep us from God's best by detouring us to what we think, in our wisdom, will bring us life *(Ephesians*

6:10-12). Remember, Eve was in a perfect environment and she was deceived. How much more can we be deceived and drawn away from God's best by Satan's craftiness! As Paul said in *2 Corinthians 11:3, AMPCE, "But [now] I am fearful, lest that even as the serpent beguiled Eve by his cunning, so your minds may be corrupted and seduced from wholehearted and sincere and pure devotion to Christ."* Through a twisted lie, Satan (the serpent) deceived Eve to rebel against God's will in the hopes that when she offered the fruit to Adam he would also partake. In Adam's disobedience, Satan's desire was achieved causing both Adam and Eve and their seed after them to operate and function out of a carnal nature—independent from God, produced by a corruptible seed *(Isaiah 14:12-15; Genesis 3:1-4)*. This is why the law given by Moses could not make us perfect, because of this carnal nature. This is why Jesus came in order for a spiritual circumcision to take place within our hearts to strip away the whole corrupt flesh life (our carnal nature) from within us so that we can walk in an entirely new nature, His divine nature within—the born-again creation or hidden man of the heart, our true selves!

Husbands, it is important to cultivate a relationship with your heavenly Father though prayer, worship, and renewing your mind to His truths, especially concerning the new man, in order to walk in newness of life and to hear His voice concerning your role as the head of your wife and household. It is important for you to stand in the truth for that is where true masculine strength resides. Also as stated in **Note 44a**:

When Adam and Eve ate from the tree of the knowledge of good and evil, the Lord began to speak to them about the consequences of living independent from Him. In *Genesis 3:16 (NASB)*, He said to the woman, *"I will greatly multiply your pain in childbirth, in pain you will bring forth children; yet your desire will be for your husband, and he will rule over you."* A wife's carnal tendency is to look to her husband for identity, to meet her emotional needs, and/or to take from him his God-given authority as the head *(1 Corinthians 11:3; Ephesians 5:24)*. The husband's carnal tendency is to control and to rule over his wife or to allow his wife to be the head and to follow her lead. Because of what Jesus did on the cross, as born-again believers, Christ now becomes the center of the husband and the wife and His rule is love and honor one toward the other. Marriage is a beautiful institution designed and ordained by God, with both the husband and the wife having the same worth and value in Him *(Genesis 2:20-25)*. Marriage is also a place where the Lord deals with our carnal tendencies, bringing sanctification to us *(Ephesians 5:22-31)*.

Husband, you are the head of your wife, but it does not give you the right to be overbearing, hard, a dictating tyrant, etc., as this type of behavior reveals a stronghold of perfection which is rooted in pride and also reveals insecurity and possibly self-hatred. This is why it is important to have a genuine relationship with the Lord and to talk to Him, preferably journaling your heart to Him concerning issues of the heart along with speaking "life-giving" Scriptures over your wife during your prayer time (please see **Note 9** and *A Personal Prayer Journal – From your heart to His – Part Three - Volume 1*).

You are your wife's covering and protector and God is her Father. Trust God with your wife and allow the joy of the Lord, the strength of the Lord, and the peace of God to be your rule and guide. Choose to focus on the good things about your wife and cast down the imaginations that would cause you to be bitter or resentful toward her. Take your fears and insecurities to the Lord and continue to renew the *spirit of your mind* or *inmost mind* to the new man or your true self (please refer to the ***Personalized Scripture Guide - Volume 1***). Just as God made every tree grow from the ground and the baby to grow inside the mother's womb, He is faithful to cause the new creation to grow within you (*Genesis 2:9; Psalm 139:13-16; 1 Peter 2:2-3*). God is well able to open your wife's eyes to her own faults instead of you continually pointing them out to her as He has not called you to be her father or her preacher, but an example of Christ! There is nothing wrong with speaking the truth in love, but certainly not out of anger, pain, or frustration. If anger and bitterness is surfacing toward your wife, again, I recommend you journal your heart to the Lord concerning your pain, disappointment, frustration, etc. I want to also encourage you to seek out an accountability partner, one who is mature in Christ, who can help you work through any difficult areas of your life. Acting out of anger and pain with sarcastic jesters, a sign of being bitter and resentful, can be as a sharp sword toward your wife and is very hurtful to her and grievous to the Lord. If you do act out of anger or bitterness toward your wife, it is important to ask her to forgive you and to ask the Lord to forgive you as well. The definition for sarcasm is "a sharp and often satirical or ironic utterance designed to cut or give pain."[1] God desires for you to operate out of the born-again creation within, not out of your carnal nature. Remember how God used Moses? Scripture says in *Numbers 12:3 – Now the man Moses was very meek, above all the men which were upon the face of the earth.* The word "meek" in Hebrew is *anav* meaning "depressed (figuratively), in mind (gentle) or circumstances (needy, especially saintly):– humble, lowly, meek." And Jesus said in *Matthew 11:29, "Take my yoke upon you, and learn of me; for I am meek and lowly in heart: and ye shall find rest for your souls."* The word "meek" in the Greek is *praos* meaning "gentle, i.e. humble:–meek." This Greek word is the root word for the fruit of the Spirit, "meekness," found in *Galatians 5:22-23*. The word "meekness" in the Greek is *praotes* meaning "gentleness, by implication, humility:–meekness." This reveals someone who is able to repress outbursts of anger and to control himself in the midst of injurious accusations as his strength of character produces patience and forbearance, a product of the fruit of meekness. Again, God desires for you to operate out of the born-again creation within, not out of your carnal nature—being conformed to the image of Jesus Christ *(Romans 8:29).* I want to encourage you to cultivate the fruits of the Spirit within your own heart and mind *(Galatians 5:22-23).* If you feel the need to repent before the Lord concerning your role as a husband, a prayer of repentance is included in ***Prayers of Repentance - Volume 1***.

Below are Scriptures relating to the tongue:

Psalm 57:4 – My soul is among lions: and I lie even among them that are set on fire, even the sons of men, whose teeth are spears and arrows, and their tongue a sharp sword.

References:
Psalm 37:30-31 – The mouth of the righteous speaketh wisdom, and his tongue talketh of judgment. The law of his God is in his heart; none of his steps shall slide. **Psalm 64:2-5** *– Hide me from the secret counsel of the wicked; from the insurrection of the workers of iniquity: who whet (sharpen) their tongue like a sword, and bend their bows to shoot their arrows, even bitter words: that they may shoot in secret at the perfect: suddenly do they shoot at him, and fear not. They encourage themselves in an evil matter: they commune of laying snares privily; they say, "Who shall see them?"* **Proverbs 4:20-27** *– My son, attend to my words; incline thine ear unto my sayings. Let them not depart from thine eyes; keep them in the midst of thine heart.*

For they are life unto those that find them, and health to all their flesh. Keep thy heart with all diligence; for out of it are the issues of life. Put away from thee a froward mouth, and perverse lips put far from thee. Let thine eyes look right on, and let thine eyelids look straight before thee. Ponder the path of thy feet, and let all thy ways be established. Turn not to the right hand nor to the left: remove thy foot from evil. **Proverbs 12:18** – *There is that speaketh like the piercings of a sword: but the tongue of the wise is health.* **Proverbs 16:27** – *An ungodly man diggeth up evil: and in his lips there is as a burning fire.* **James 1:26-27** – *If any man among you seem to be religious, and bridleth not his tongue, but deceiveth his own heart, this man's religion is vain (useless). Pure religion and undefiled before God and the Father is this, to visit the fatherless and widows in their affliction, and to keep himself unspotted from the world.* **James 3:3-18** – *Behold, we put bits in the horses' mouths, that they may obey us; and we turn about their whole body. Behold also the ships, which though they be so great, and are driven of fierce winds, yet are they turned about with a very small helm (rudder), whithersoever the governor (helmsman) listeth (impulse). Even so the tongue is a little member, and boasteth great things. Behold, how great a matter a little fire kindleth! And the tongue is a fire, a world of iniquity: so is the tongue among our members, that it defileth the whole body, and setteth on fire the course of nature; and it is set on fire of hell. For every kind of beasts, and of birds, and of serpents, and of things in the sea, is tamed, and hath been tamed of mankind: but the tongue can no man tame; it is an unruly evil, full of deadly poison. Therewith bless we God, even the Father; and therewith curse we men, which are made after the similitude of God. Out of the same mouth proceedeth blessing and cursing. My brethren, these things ought not so to be. Doth a fountain send forth at the same place sweet water and bitter? Can a fig tree, my brethren, bear olive berries? Either a vine, figs? So can no fountain both yield salt water and fresh. Who is a wise man endued with knowledge among you? Let him shew out of a good conversation (behavior) his works with meekness of wisdom. But if ye have bitter envying and strife in your hearts, glory not, and lie not against the truth. This wisdom descendeth not from above, but is earthly, sensual, devilish. For where envying and strife is, there is confusion and every evil work. But the wisdom that is from above is first pure, then peaceable, gentle, and easy to be intreated, full of mercy and good fruits, without partiality, and without hypocrisy. And the fruit of righteousness is sown in peace of them that make peace.*

Below are Scriptures relating to the importance of submitting to His will:

1. ***Psalm 128:1-6*** *(NKJV)* – *Blessed is every one who fears the LORD, who walks in His ways. When you eat the labor of your hands, you shall be happy, and it shall be well with you. Your wife shall be like a fruitful vine in the very heart of your house, your children like olive plants all around your table. Behold, thus shall the man be blessed who fears the LORD. The LORD bless you out of Zion, and may you see the good of Jerusalem all the days of your life. Yes, may you see your children's children. Peace be upon Israel!*

Reference:
Ecclesiastes 12:13-14 – *Let us hear the conclusion of the whole matter: fear God, and keep his commandments: for this is the whole duty of man. For God shall bring every work into judgment, with every secret thing, whether it be good, or whether it be evil.*

2. ***Matthew 25:31-40*** – *Jesus said, "When the Son of man shall come in his glory, and all the holy angels with him, then shall he sit upon the throne of his glory: and before him shall be gathered all nations: and he shall separate them one from another, as a shepherd divideth his sheep from the goats: and he shall set the sheep on his right hand, but the goats on the left. Then shall the King say unto them on his right hand, 'Come, ye blessed of my Father, inherit the kingdom prepared for you from the foundation*

of the world: for I was an hungered, and ye gave me meat (food): I was thirsty, and ye gave me drink: I was a stranger, and ye took me in: naked, and ye clothed me: I was sick, and ye visited me: I was in prison, and ye came unto me.' Then shall the righteous answer him, saying, 'Lord, when saw we thee an hungered, and fed thee? Or thirsty, and gave thee drink? When saw we thee a stranger, and took thee in? Or naked, and clothed thee? Or when saw we thee sick, or in prison, and came unto thee?' And the King shall answer and say unto them, 'Verily I say unto you, inasmuch as ye did it unto one of the least of these my brethren, ye have done it unto me.'"

References:

Luke 6:46-49 – Jesus said, "And why call ye me, 'Lord, Lord,' and do not the things which I say? Whosoever cometh to me, and heareth my sayings, and doeth them, I will shew you to whom he is like: he is like a man which built an house, <u>*and digged deep,*</u> *and laid the foundation on a rock: and when the flood arose, the stream beat vehemently upon that house, and could not shake it: for it was founded upon a rock. But he that heareth, and doeth not, is like a man that without a foundation built an house upon the earth; against which the stream did beat vehemently, and immediately it fell; and the ruin of that house was great* [digging deep, is allowing the Lord into the depths of our carnality (e.g., self-hatred, judgments, selfishness, bitterness, resentment, partiality, pride) and removing it, through repentance and cleansing in order for Him to be the true source of our security and wholeness]. *Ephesians 4:31-32 – Let all bitterness, and wrath, and anger, and clamour, and evil speaking, be put away from you, with all malice: and be ye kind one to another, tenderhearted, forgiving one another, even as God for Christ's sake hath forgiven you.*

2 Timothy 2:22-26 (NKJV) – Flee also youthful lusts; but pursue righteousness, faith, love, peace with those who call on the Lord out of a pure heart. But avoid foolish and ignorant disputes, knowing that they generate strife. And a servant of the Lord must not quarrel but be gentle to all, able to teach, patient, in humility correcting those who are in opposition, if God perhaps will grant them repentance, so that they may know the truth, and that they may come to their senses and escape the snare of the devil, having been taken captive by him at his will. Titus 3:1-2 – Put them in mind to be subject to principalities and powers, to obey magistrates, to be ready to every good work, to speak evil of no man, to be no brawlers, but gentle, shewing all meekness unto all men.

3. *1 Peter 3:7 – Likewise, ye husbands, dwell with them (wives) according to knowledge, giving honour unto the wife, as unto the weaker vessel, and as being heirs together of the grace of life; that your prayers be not hindered.*

Reference:

Matthew 5:22-24 – "But I (Jesus) say unto you, That whosoever is angry with his brother without a cause shall be in danger of the judgment: and whosoever shall say to his brother, 'Raca,' shall be in danger of the council: but whosoever shall say, 'Thou fool,' shall be in danger of hell fire. Therefore, if thou bring thy gift to the altar, and there rememberest that thy brother hath ought against thee; leave there thy gift before the altar, and go thy way; first be reconciled to thy brother, and then come and offer thy gift." (How much more your wife).

---

48. *I thank You that* <u>*(wife's name)*</u> *is* subject *to* me, *she* [subordinates *and* adapts herself *to* me], *as is right and fitting and* her *proper duty in the Lord. As the church is subject to Christ, so* <u>*(wife's name)*</u> *is* subject *to* me *in everything.* (Colossians 3:18-AMPCE; Ephesians 5:24-AMPCE)

Your wife may not be subject to you, as her proper duty in the Lord, as she may be very insecure in her own personhood and a babe in Christ. If this is the case, she needs to see your patience and strength in Christ through words of encouragement. As you declare words of faith over your wife, during your own prayer time, you are releasing the grace and truth of God in her life and are able to see above and beyond her own weaknesses and shortcomings *(John 1:14)*. In doing this, <u>you are operating in the same manner as your heavenly Father</u> and as faithful Abraham,

> *Therefore it is of faith, that it might be by grace; to the end the promise might be sure to all the seed; not to that only which is of the law, but to that also which is of the faith of Abraham; who is the father of us all, <u>(as it is written, "I have made thee a father of many nations,") before him whom he (Abraham) believed, even God, who quickeneth (makes alive) the dead, and calleth those things which be not as though they were.</u> Who against hope believed in hope, that he might become the father of many nations, according to that which was spoken, "So shall thy seed (offspring) be." And being not weak in faith, he considered not his own body now dead, when he was about an hundred years old, neither yet the deadness of Sara's womb: he staggered not at the promise of God through unbelief; but was strong in faith, giving glory to God; and being fully persuaded that, what he had promised, he was able also to perform. And therefore it was imputed to him for righteousness. Now it was not written for his sake alone, that it was imputed to him; but for us also, to whom it shall be imputed, if we believe on him that raised up Jesus our Lord from the dead; who was delivered for our offences, and was raised again for our justification.*
>
> (Romans 4:16-25)

Be encouraged for all of the promises of God in Christ are Yes, and in Him Amen *(2 Corinthians 1:20)*!

---

49. *I thank You that* <u>(mom or dad's name)</u> *and I* do no irritate and provoke *our child*/children to anger *we* [do not exasperate *him/her*/them to resentment]. *We are* [not hard on *him/her*/them or harass *him/her*/them], lest *he/she*/they become(s) discouraged and sullen and morose and feel(s) inferior and frustrated. *We* [do not break *his/her*/their spirit], but *we* rear *him/her*/them [tenderly] in the training and discipline and the counsel and admonition of the Lord. (Ephesians 6:4-AMPCE; Colossians 3:21-AMPCE; Ephesians 6:4-AMPCE)

In this portion of Scripture, the King James Version reads as follows:

- *Ephesians 6:4 – And, ye fathers, provoke not your children to wrath: but bring them up in the nurture and admonition of the Lord.*
- *Colossians 3:21 – Fathers, provoke not your children to anger, lest they be discouraged.*

In *Colossians 3:21*, the Amplified Version includes, *[do not break their spirit.]*. There are three passages of Scripture found in the book of Proverbs that mention a broken or wounded spirit:

1. *Proverbs 15:13 – A merry heart maketh a cheerful countenance: but by sorrow of the heart the spirit is broken.*

2. *Proverbs 17:22 – A merry heart doeth good like a medicine: but a broken spirit drieth the bones.*

3. *Proverbs 18:14 – The spirit of a man will sustain his infirmity; but a wounded spirit who can bear?*

The Hebrew word for "broken" and "wounded" in these three passages of Scripture is *naka* meaning "smitten, i.e. (figuratively) afflicted:—broken, stricken, wounded." Parents who harass and/or are hard on their child(ren) (e.g., belittling them, slapping them around, yelling and screaming at them) can truly wound them internally and cause them to suffer with low self-esteem, feelings of insignificance and unimportance, and hardness of heart. This brokenness and woundedness will carry into their adult life where only Christ can bring healing to their wounded heart.

Children are very special to the Lord and are mentioned over 1,370 times in the Old Testament. Therefore, raising children in the nurture and admonition of the Lord is very important. Let's look at *Genesis 18:16-19*:

> *And the men rose up from thence, and looked toward Sodom: and Abraham went with them to bring them on the way. And the LORD said, "Shall I hide from Abraham that thing which I do; seeing that Abraham shall surely become a great and mighty nation, and all the nations of the earth shall be blessed in him? <u>For I know him, that he will command his children and his household after him, and they shall keep the way of the LORD</u>, to do justice and judgment; that the LORD may bring upon Abraham that which he hath spoken of him."*

Abraham had a great reverence for His God and God knew that Abraham would teach and train his children in that same manner, to keep the ways of the Lord! Joshua also said,

> *Now therefore fear the LORD, and serve him in sincerity and in truth: and put away the gods which your fathers served on the other side of the flood, and in Egypt; and serve ye the LORD. And if it seem evil unto you to serve the LORD, choose you this day whom ye will serve; whether the gods which your fathers served that were on the other side of the flood, or the gods of the Amorites, in whose land ye dwell: but <u>as for me and my house, we will serve the LORD</u>.*
>
> (Joshua 24:14-15)

Moses instructed the children of Israel with the following:

> *Hear, O Israel: The Lord our God is one Lord [the only Lord]. And you shall love the Lord your God with all your [mind and] heart and with your entire being and with all your might. <u>And these words which I am commanding you this day shall be [first] in your [own] minds and hearts; [then] you shall whet and sharpen them so as to make them penetrate, and teach and impress them diligently upon the [minds and] hearts of your children, and shall talk of them when you sit in your house and when you walk by the way, and when you lie down and when you rise up</u>. And you shall bind them as a sign upon your hand, and they shall be as frontlets (forehead bands) between your eyes. And you shall write them upon the doorposts of your house and on your gates...*

Proverbs 22:6 reads – *Train up a child in the way he should go: and when he is old, he will not depart from it.* Children internalize mom and dad's behavior (good or bad). Therefore, the most important thing parents can do for themselves and for their child(ren) is to put off the old man and put on the new man in Christ. Mom and Dad, this is done through repentance before a holy God, being real with Him about your own pain and shortcomings, and renewing the *spirit of your mind* or your *inmost mind* to the truth of His Word. This paints a picture within a child's heart of the power of submission to the One who has all authority *(Matthew 28:18)*.

Planting and watering seeds from God's Word concerning your child(ren)'s character in Christ and understanding the nature of God is the foundation for receiving their true inheritance. It is important that this begin when they are young and their hearts are tender. When you as a parent see ungodly behavior (e.g., disobedience, selfishness, hurtful ways, disrespect, laziness), correct it quickly and lovingly and continue to reinforce the truth of God's Word into their lives in practical ways. The most important thing for parents to remember is to operate in patience, love, and consistency toward their child(ren). Once a child reaches puberty, mindsets and behavior patterns have been set within them and, if need be, it will then take an act of God to turn them around. Below is part of **My Story – Part Two - Volume 1**, where I share important direction and insight the Lord revealed to me when I cried out to Him to help me concerning my anger issues toward my children:

> During times of frustration, usually when I was upset with something Don had said or done, or just because I was ill and didn't want to be bothered, I would lash out in anger toward Jonathan and/or Jessica when they would do the least little thing that aggravated me. I never beat them, but I would raise my voice at them in an angry tone, and I could see how my behavior hurt their feelings. I would feel terrible after I acted out and would ask them to forgive me. Afterwards, I would pour my heart out to the Lord, through journaling, and would ask Him to forgive me as well. On one occasion during a time of fasting and prayer, when Jonathan was five years old and Jessica was three, the Lord spoke to my heart concerning this issue. He impressed upon me to initiate a family meeting anytime I acted out of anger toward my children. The Lord impressed upon me that He wanted me to confess my faults to Jonathan and to Jessica 'in front of their daddy' and to tell them that what I did was not right and to ask them to forgive me and to also ask Don to forgive me. That was very humbling for me, because I didn't want Don to know! I was concerned that he would get upset with me and make me feel even worse than I already felt. However, because of my reverence for the Lord, I did what He instructed me to do. I knew that even though I was fearful to do it, there would be safety in it, because I was humbling myself by following His instructions. As His Word says in *1 Peter 5:5* and in *James 4:6,* "*God resists the proud, but gives grace to the humble.*"

These family meetings proved to be very rewarding. Don was gracious and blessed my humility and honesty, and after I confessed my faults to Jonathan and Jessica and asked them to forgive me, they would always say, *"You're forgiven Mommy."* During this time, we would ask Jonathan and Jessica if there was anything that was bothering them or hurting them? On several occasions, they would open up their little hearts and share, and where applicable, we would ask them to forgive us. Don also used this time to confess areas of weakness and faults, and at the end of the meeting we would pray. It turned into a very fruitful time for all of us! In the beginning, it seemed I would have to call a family meeting at least once every other week, but as time went on the family meetings grew less and less. I believe in doing this, it helped to remove the hurt produced by my tongue from Jonathan and Jessica *(James 3:8)*.

About a year had passed and one day while thinking about these family meetings, the Lord spoke to me and said, "In having these family meetings, you are painting a picture in Jonathan and Jessica's hearts of humility, accountability, and submission." It was so exciting to hear this from the Lord, but at the same time sobering. Exciting, because I know how powerful these three character traits are when operating in a person's life. Sobering, as I realized the awesome responsibility of being a parent and how our actions and behavior patterns paint pictures, good or bad, in the hearts and minds of our children. There may still be things that Jonathan and/or Jessica may have been hurt by or internalized during their formative years from significant others (i.e., me, their dad, their teachers, or peers) where they may need healing and to forgive. If so, I'm confident that the Lord, through their own relationship with Him, will be faithful to reveal them.

Again, children are very special to the Lord and we should treat them as such as they are not insignificant or menial. Jesus made this very clear to His disciples in the following two passages of Scripture:

1. ***Matthew 18:1-7 (NASB)*** – *At that time the disciples came to Jesus and said, "Who then is greatest in the kingdom of heaven?" And He called a child to Himself and set him before them, and said, "Truly I say to you, unless you are converted and become like children, you will not enter the kingdom of heaven. Whoever then humbles himself as this child, he is the greatest in the kingdom of heaven. And whoever receives one such child in My name receives Me; but whoever causes one of these little ones who believe in Me to stumble, it would be better for him to have a heavy millstone hung around his neck, and to be drowned in the depth of the sea. Woe to the world because of its stumbling blocks! For it is inevitable that stumbling blocks come; but woe to that man through whom the stumbling block comes!"*

2. ***Mark 10:13-16*** – *And they brought young children to him, that he should touch them: and his disciples rebuked those that brought them. But when Jesus saw it, he was much displeased, and said unto them, "Suffer (Permit) the little children to come unto me, and forbid them not: for of such is the kingdom of God. Verily I say unto you, whosoever shall not receive the kingdom of God as a little child, he shall not enter therein." And he took them up in his arms, put his hands upon them, and blessed them.*

Let's look at the importance of correcting our children. Below are two passages of Scripture concerning the rod of correction:

1. ***Proverbs 23:13-14 (NKJV)*** – *Do not withhold correction from a child, for if you beat him with a rod, he will not die. You shall beat him with a rod, and deliver his soul from hell.*

2. ***Proverbs 29:15, 17 (NKJV)*** – *The rod and rebuke give wisdom, but a child left to himself*

brings shame to his mother. Correct your son, and he will give you rest; yes, he will give delight to your soul.

Children should not be left to themselves to figure out who they are and the true meaning of life. This can lead them to living out of a foolish heart when they reach puberty, as with me. Because I lived out of a foolish heart, I caused much pain and sorrow for my parents and it did not go well with me. My parents were Christians and they taught my sister and me manners and right from wrong, but they did not raise us in the nurture and admonition of the Lord as they were babes in Christ. Please refer to **My Story Part One - Volume 1** for details. It is also important to correct children in the proper way and if they need a good spanking with a rod (paddle), it is important to do so. The word "rod" in the Hebrew is *shebet* meaning "a scion, i.e. (literally) a stick (for punishing, writing, fighting, ruling, walking, etc.) or (figuratively) a clan:—x correction, dart, rod, sceptre, staff, tribe." The Word of God should be the parent's main measuring stick in correcting their children. David said in *Psalm 23:4 – "Yea, though I walk through the valley of the shadow of death, I will fear no evil: for thou art with me; thy rod and thy staff they comfort me."* The Lord's rod and staff, used for guidance and protection, comforted David in his time of trouble. It is written in *Hebrews 12:11 – Now no chastening for the present seemeth to be joyous, but grievous: nevertheless afterward it yieldeth the peaceable fruit of righteousness unto them which are exercised thereby.* The word "chastening" in the Greek is *paideia* meaning "tutorage, i.e. education or training; by implication, disciplinary correction:—chastening, chastisement, instruction, nurture." This Greek word *paideia* is used in *Ephesians 6:4* where Paul instructs fathers not to provoke their children to wrath: but bring them up in the nurture (*paideia*) and admonition of the Lord. As I shared in the beginning of this Note, this passage of Scripture brings us back to Abraham and his relationship with God. Let's look again at *Genesis 18:16-19*:

> *And the men rose up from thence, and looked toward Sodom: and Abraham went with them to bring them on the way. And the LORD said, "Shall I hide from Abraham that thing which I do; seeing that Abraham shall surely become a great and mighty nation, and all the nations of the earth shall be blessed in him? For I know him, that he will command his children and his household after him, and they shall keep the way of the LORD, to do justice and judgment; that the LORD may bring upon Abraham that which he hath spoken of him."*

Abraham had a great reverence for His God and God knew that Abraham would teach and train his children to keep the ways of the Lord! He is calling us to do the same. If we are in Christ, we are God's representatives to our children. Allow the born-again creation within to grow and mature so you can be a true example of God's goodness and mercy, and able to teach and correct your children in the ways of the Lord. Below is a sample concerning the "rod of correction" from the book, *65 Promises From God for your Child, Powerful Prayers for Supernatural Results*. I recommend using this book during your time with the Lord as you offer up prayers for your children:

Foolishness Removed

Foolishness is bound up in the heart of a child; the
rod of correction will drive it far from him
– Proverbs 22:15

Most Bible promises are given with conditions. This verse in Proverbs is a prime example. In order for foolishness to be driven from the hearts of our children, we must be willing to wield "the rod of correction"—but what is that rod? Is it just physical punishment for shortcomings? That may certainly be part of it. As the adage goes, "Spare the rod and spoil the child." (See Proverbs 23:14.)

Sometimes, though, a rod can represent words—especially words spoken with authority. A good example is Isaiah 11:4, a prophecy that the Messiah would "strike the earth with the rod of His mouth." (See also Proverbs 14:3.) Jesus certainly was no easygoing preacher; He exposed hypocrisy, sin, and rebellion whenever He preached.

Those who love God welcome His words of correction, for they keep us from the contaminating influence of a foolish world. In the end our children will love us also, if we are careful to discipline them this way—correcting wrong behavior and leading them in the path of wisdom. David, in his famed Twenty-Third Psalm, told the Shepherd-God, "Your rod and Your staff, they comfort me" (v. 4). Similarly, the "rod of correction" wielded by loving parents should also be a "comfort" to any child—for their words point the way to a life that pleases God.

Prayer Declaration

Lord God, how foolish this world is with its ungodly agendas and its refusal to surrender to the truth. Your Word says that even the "thought of foolishness is sin" (Prov. 24:9, KJV). I repent of it all. I ask You to cleanse me and my child of all worldly influence. I recognize that "foolishness is bound up in the heart" of my child because of an inherited fallen nature. But Your Word can remove it and drive it far from him/her. I pray that _____ will not succumb to the foolishness of the carnal nature but will instead embrace the wisdom of God and receive a new nature. I make a commitment to lovingly discipline my child when it is needed so that the "rod of my mouth" will lead him/her in the way of truth and bring comfort to my child, now and forevermore. In the name of Jesus, amen (let it be so)! (Shreve, 2013, page 53).[1]

If you feel the need to repent before the Lord concerning your role as a parent, a prayer of repentance is included in ***Prayers of Repentance - Volume 1***.

Below are Scriptures relating to correcting our children:

Proverbs 22:15 *— Foolishness is bound in the heart of a child; but the rod of correction will drive it far from him.*

References:
Proverbs 3:11-12 *— My son, despise not the chastening of the LORD; neither be weary of his correction: for whom the LORD loveth he correcteth; even as a father the son in whom he delighteth.* ***Proverbs 13:24*** *— He that spareth his rod hateth his son: but he that loveth him chasteneth him betimes.* ***Proverbs 15:5, 10, 20, 31-33*** *(NASB) — A fool rejects his father's discipline, but he who regards reproof is sensible. Grievous punishment is for him who forsakes the way; he who hates reproof will die. A wise son makes a father glad, but a foolish man despises his mother. He whose ear listens to the life-giving reproof will dwell among the wise. He who neglects discipline despises himself, but he who listens to reproof acquires understanding. The*

fear of the Lord is the instruction for wisdom, and before honor comes humility. ***Proverbs 17:21, 25 (NIV)*** *– To have a fool for a child brings grief; there is no joy for the parent of a godless fool. A foolish son brings grief to his father and bitterness to the mother who bore him.* ***Proverbs 19:13, 18*** *– A foolish son is the calamity of his father. Chasten thy son while there is hope, and let not thy soul spare for his crying.* ***Hebrews 12:3-11*** *– For consider him that endured such contradiction of sinners against himself, lest ye be wearied and faint in your minds. Ye have not yet resisted unto blood, striving against sin. And ye have forgotten the exhortation which speaketh unto you as unto children, "My son, despise not thou the chastening of the Lord, nor faint when thou art rebuked of him: for whom the Lord loveth he chasteneth, and scourgeth every son whom he receiveth." If ye endure chastening, God dealeth with you as with sons; for what son is he whom the father chasteneth not? But if ye be without chastisement, whereof all are partakers, then are ye bastards (illegitimate), and not sons. Furthermore we have had fathers of our flesh which corrected us, and we gave them reverence: shall we not much rather be in subjection unto the Father of spirits, and live? For they verily for a few days chastened us after their own pleasure; but he for our profit, that we might be partakers of his holiness. Now no chastening for the present seemeth to be joyous, but grievous: nevertheless afterward it yieldeth the peaceable fruit of righteousness unto them which are exercised thereby.*

Below are Scriptures relating to the importance of laying up His Words in your mind and heart and teaching them to your children:

Deuteronomy 11:16-21 *(AMPCE) – Take heed to yourselves, lest your [minds and] hearts be deceived and you turn aside and serve other gods and worship them, and the Lord's anger be kindled against you, and He shut up the heavens so that there will be no rain and the land will not yield its fruit, and you perish quickly off the good land which the Lord gives you. Therefore you shall lay up these My words in your [minds and] hearts and in your [entire] being, and bind them for a sign upon your hands and as forehead bands between your eyes. And you shall teach them to your children, speaking of them when you sit in your house and when you walk along the road, when you lie down and when you rise up. And you shall write them upon the doorposts of your house and on your gates, that your days and the days of your children may be multiplied in the land which the Lord swore to your fathers to give them, as long as the heavens are above the earth.*

References:
Deuteronomy 4:9-10 *– Only take heed to thyself, and keep thy soul diligently, lest thou forget the things which thine eyes have seen, and lest they depart from thy heart all the days of thy life: but teach them thy sons, and thy sons' sons; specially the day that thou stoodest before the LORD thy God in Horeb, when the LORD said unto me, "Gather me the people together, and I will make them hear my words, that they may learn to fear me all the days that they shall live upon the earth, and that they may teach their children."* ***Deuteronomy 32:46-47*** *– Moses said to the children of Israel, "Set your hearts unto all the words which I testify among you this day, which ye shall command your children to observe to do, all the words of this law. For it is not a vain thing for you; because it is your life: and through this thing ye shall prolong your days in the land, whither ye go over Jordan to possess it."* ***1 Chronicles 28:8*** *– Now therefore in the sight of all Israel the congregation of the LORD, and in the audience of our God, keep and seek for all the commandments of the LORD your God: that ye may possess this good land, and leave it for an inheritance for your children after you for ever.* ***Psalm 102:28*** *– The children of thy servants shall continue, and their seed shall be established before thee.* ***Psalm 127:3*** *– Lo, children are an heritage of the LORD: and the fruit of the womb is his reward.* ***Psalm 147:11-13*** *– The LORD taketh pleasure in them that fear him, in those that hope in his mercy. Praise the LORD, O Jerusalem; praise thy God, O Zion. For he hath strengthened the bars of thy gates; he hath blessed thy children within thee.* ***Proverbs 11:21*** *– Though hand join in hand, the wicked*

shall not be unpunished: but the seed (children) of the righteous shall be delivered. **Jeremiah 32:36-41** – *And now therefore thus saith the LORD, the God of Israel, "…And they shall be my people, and I will be their God: and I will give them one heart, and one way, that they may fear me for ever, for the good of them, and of their children after them: and I will make an everlasting covenant with them, that I will not turn away from them, to do them good; but I will put my fear in their hearts, that they shall not depart from me. Yea, I will rejoice over them to do them good and I will plant them in this land assuredly with my whole heart and with my whole soul."* **Malachi 4:4-6** – *Thus saith the LORD of hosts, "Remember ye the law of Moses my servant, which I commanded unto him in Horeb for all Israel, with the statutes and judgments. Behold, I will send you Elijah the prophet before the coming of the great and dreadful day of the LORD: and he shall turn the heart of the fathers to the children, and the heart of the children to their fathers, lest I come and smite the earth with a curse."* **2 Timothy 1:3-5** *(NASB)* – *I thank God, whom I serve with a clear conscience the way my forefathers did, as I constantly remember you in my prayers night and day, longing to see you, even as I recall your tears, so that I may be filled with joy. For I am mindful of the sincere faith within you, which first dwelt in your grandmother Lois and your mother Eunice, and I am sure that it is in you as well.* **2 Timothy 3:14-17** *(NASB)* – *You, however, continue in the things you have learned and become convinced of, knowing from whom you have learned them, and that from childhood you have known the sacred writings which are able to give you the wisdom that leads to salvation through faith which is in Christ Jesus. All Scripture is inspired by God and profitable for teaching, for reproof, for correction, for training in righteousness; so that the man of God may be adequate, equipped for every good work.*

Below are Scriptures relating to God's heart toward the fatherless:

Exodus 22:22 – *Ye shall not afflict any widow, or fatherless child.*

References:
Deuteronomy 10:17-18 – *For the LORD your God is God of gods, and Lord of lords, a great God, a mighty, and a terrible, which regardeth not persons, nor taketh reward: he doth execute the judgment of the fatherless and widow, and loveth the stranger, in giving him food and raiment (clothing).* **Deuteronomy 27:19** *(NIV)* – *Cursed is anyone who withholds justice from the foreigner, the fatherless or the widow. Then all the people shall say, "Amen!"* **Psalm 10:14** *(NIV)* – *But you, God, see the trouble of the afflicted; you consider their grief and take it in hand. The victims commit themselves to you; you are the helper of the fatherless.* **Psalm 68:4-5** – *Sing unto God, sing praises to his name: extol him that rideth upon the heavens by his name JAH, and rejoice before him. A father of the fatherless, and a judge (advocate) of the widows, is God in his holy habitation.* **Psalm 82:3** – *Defend the poor and fatherless: do justice to the afflicted and needy.* **Psalm 146:9-10** – *The LORD preserveth the strangers; he relieveth the fatherless and widow: but the way of the wicked he turneth upside down. The LORD shall reign for ever, even thy God, O Zion, unto all generations. Praise ye the LORD.* **Proverbs 23:10-11** – *Remove not the old landmark; and enter not into the fields of the fatherless: for their redeemer is mighty; he shall plead their cause with thee.* **James 1:27** – *Pure religion and undefiled before God is this, To visit the fatherless and widows in their affliction, and to keep himself unspotted from the world.*

50. *I thank You that (child(ren)'s name(s)) obey(s) (mom or dad's name) and me in the Lord [as His representatives], for this is just and right and it is pleasing to You. (Child(ren)'s name(s)) honor(s) (esteem(s) and value(s) as precious) his/her/their father and his/her/their mother—this is the first commandment with a promise—that all may be well with him/her/them and that he/she/they may live long on the earth. (Ephesians 6:1-3-AMPCE) (Ref.: Colossians 3:20)*

Parents are the only two people on the face of this earth that were created by God to love their child(ren) unconditionally. No one can experience a parent's love for their child(ren) unless you are one. It runs deep! Unfortunately, due to the fall of man, that love has become compromised for many of us because of selfish desires and/or woundings and pain in our own hearts. It is God's intent for children to know Him at a very young age, to be taught and raised in the ways of the Lord. Let's look at the following passage of Scripture:

> *Hear, O my son, and receive my sayings; and the years of thy life shall be many. I have taught thee in the way of wisdom; I have led thee in right paths. When thou goest, thy steps shall not be straightened; and when thou runnest, thou shalt not stumble. Take fast hold of instruction; let her not go: keep her; for she is thy life. Enter not into the path of the wicked, and go not in the way of evil men. Avoid it, pass not by it, turn from it, and pass away.*
>
> (Proverbs 4:10-15)

According to this passage of Scripture and many others, it is for the child's good to be raised in the nurture and admonition of the Lord. In order to do this, the truth of God's Word must first become a reality in our own hearts and minds, otherwise it can become legalistic and possibly foster a rebellious spirit within our children *(Deuteronomy 6:4-15, AMPCE; Romans 8:15)*. If you are reading this material, I believe you are raising or desire to raise your child(ren) in the ways of the Lord. If you truly love them, you will seek God and form a relationship with Him and deal with your own heart issues in order to be a better parent. God's love for children is evident throughout Scripture. Let's look at *Mark 10:13-16*:

> *And they brought young children to him, that he should touch them: and his disciples rebuked those that brought them. But when Jesus saw it, he was much displeased, and said unto them, "Suffer (Permit) the little children to come unto me, and forbid them not: for of such is the kingdom of God. Verily I say unto you, Whosoever, shall not receive the kingdom of God as a little child, he shall not enter therein." And he took them up in his arms, put his hands upon them, and blessed them.*

It is important to God for children to honor their father and their mother as He gives that command with a promise—*"That all may be well with them and that they may live long on the earth"* (*Ephesians 6:1-3*). A child's responsibility is to honor their parents and to obey them as God's representatives; in doing so, the child honors the Lord. If we, as parents, put God first place in our lives and honor Him by putting off the old man, our carnal nature, and putting on the new man in Christ, His wisdom and understanding will flow through us to help us raise our children well. When children see their parents sincerely walking humbly before God in His love and His truth, and are disciplined accordingly, I sincerely believe that they will truly honor and respect their parents. If we, as parents, do our part in raising our children in the nurture and admonition of the Lord, the Lord is faithful to keep them. If they should stray from Him when they become young adults, I believe He will be faithful to bring them back to Him *(Proverbs 22:6)*. If you feel the need to repent before the Lord concerning your role as a parent, a prayer of repentance is included in ***Prayers of Repentance - Volume 1***.

Below are Scriptures relating to the importance of children obeying their parents:

1. ***Proverbs 10:1 (NIV)*** – *The proverbs of Solomon: A wise son brings joy to his father, but a foolish son brings grief to his mother.*

References:
Proverbs 13:1, 18 – *A wise son heareth his father's instruction: but a scorner heareth not rebuke. Poverty and shame shall be to him that refuseth instruction: but he that regardeth reproof shall be honoured.* ***Proverbs 15:5*** – *A fool despiseth his father's instruction: but he that regardeth reproof is prudent.* ***Proverbs 19:26-27 (NKJV)*** – *He who mistreats his father and chases away his mother is a son who causes shame and brings reproach. Cease listening to instruction, my son, and you will stray from the words of knowledge.* ***Proverbs 20:20*** – *Whoso curseth his father or his mother, his lamp shall be put out in obscure darkness.* ***Proverbs 23:22, 24-25 (NASB)*** – *Listen to your father who begot you, and do not despise your mother when she is old. The father of the righteous will greatly rejoice, and he who sires a wise son will be glad in him. Let your father and your mother be glad, and let her rejoice who gave birth to you.* ***Proverbs 30:17 (NKJV)*** – *The eye that mocks his father, and scorns obedience to his mother, the ravens of the valley will pick it out, and the young eagles will eat it.* (Or in other words it will not go well with you)! ***Mark 7:9-13 (NASB)*** – *Jesus said to the Pharisees and scribes, "You are experts at setting aside the commandment of God in order to keep your tradition. For Moses said, 'HONOR YOUR FATHER AND YOUR MOTHER'; and, 'HE WHO SPEAKS EVIL, OF FATHER OR MOTHER, IS TO BE PUT TO DEATH'; but you say, 'If a man says to his father or his mother, whatever I have that would help you is Corban (that is to say, given to God),' you no longer permit him to do anything for his father or his mother; thus invalidating the word of God by your tradition which you have handed down; and you do many things such as that."* (Adult children no longer have to obey their father or mother, but they should always honor and respect them and value their wisdom. The word "honor" in the Greek is *timao* meaning "to prize, i.e. fix a valuation upon; by implication, to revere:–honor, value."). ***Colossians 3:20*** – *Children, obey your parents in all things: for this is well pleasing unto the Lord.*

2. ***Proverbs 20:11*** – *Even a child is known by his doings, whether his work be pure, and whether it be right.*

3. ***Proverbs 22:28*** – *Remove not the ancient landmark, which thy fathers have set.*

Reference:
Job 12:12 – *With the ancient is wisdom; and in length of days understanding.*

4. ***2 Timothy 2:22*** – *Flee also youthful lusts: but follow righteousness, faith, charity (God's love), peace, with them that call on the Lord out of a pure heart.*

SUPPORT AND HELP

Ministry	Resources Available
Desert Stream Ministries 706 Main Street Grandview, MO 64030	Provides help for Christians struggling with aspects of the old man or false self, regarding sexual and relational issues. Through biblical wisdom, godly support, and the power of prayer, they help Christians identify root issues of the old man and to stand in Christ as their hope and source of healing (i.e., the *Living Waters Program* as I shared in ***My Story – Part Two***). Contact: Visit www.desertstream.org/group to find a *Living Waters Program* near you.
His Wonderful Works P.O. Box 81943 Conyers, GA 30013	Non-licensed Christian counseling and healing prayers – seeking the Lord's presence and power to meet our deepest needs for healing and wholeness. Contact: Visit www.hiswonderfulworks.com and go to Contact. Also, please go to Resources for additional support/help.
Restored Hope Network P.O. Box 64588 Colorado Springs, CO 80962	An interdenominational membership governed network dedicated to restoring hope to those bound to the old man through sexual and relational sin. Contact: Visit restoredhopenetwork.org and go to Find Help for support/help.

SUGGESTED READING

Bevere, John. *Breaking Intimidation* (Lake Mary, Florida: Charisma House, 1995).

Frangipane, Francis. *The Power of One Christlike Life* (New Kensington, Pennsylvania: Whitaker House, 2000).

MacArthur, John. *The Vanishing Conscience* (Nashville, Tennessee: Nelson Books, 1995).

Meyer, Joyce. *Battleground of the Mind* (New York, New York: Warner Faith, 1995).

Missler, Chuck and Nancy. *Be Ye Transformed* (Coeur d'Alene, Idaho: King's High Way Ministries, 1996).

Naselli, David and J.D. Crowley. *Conscience: What It Is, How to Train It, and Loving Those Who Differ* (Wheaton, Illinois: Crossway, 2016).

Payne, Leanne. *The Broken Image* (Grand Rapids, Michigan: Hamewith Books, 1996).

Payne, Leanne. *The Healing Presence* (Grand Rapids, Michigan: Hamewith Books, 1995).

Perkins, Bill. *When Good Men Get Angry* (Carol Stream, Illinois: Tyndale House Publishers, Inc., 2009).

Renner, Rick. *Sparkling Gems From the Greek* (Tulsa, Oklahoma: Teach All Nations, 2003).

Shreve, Mike. *65 Promises from God for your Child – Powerful Prayers for Supernatural Results* (Lake Mary, Florida: Charisma House, 2013).

Thomas, W. Ian. *The Indwelling Life of Christ: All of Him in All of Me* (Colorado Springs, Colorado: Multnomah Books, 2006).

ENDNOTES

Note 1

1. Payne, L. (1996). The Broken Image. Grand Rapids, Michigan: Hamewith Books. Page 125.

2. *God of Creation* by Moody Institute of Science, publication date 1945, archive.org, usage: creativecommons.org/publicdomain/mark 1.0.

3. *God of Creation* by Moody Institute of Science, publication date 1945, archive.org, usage: creativecommons.org/publicdomain/mark 1.0.

Note 3

1. *God of Creation* by Moody Institute of Science, publication date 1945, archive.org, usage: creativecommons.org/publicdomain/mark 1.0.

Note 7

1. "Abba". Vine's Expository Dictionary of Old and New Testament Words, Copyright © 1981 by Fleming H. Revell Company. All rights reserved. Page 9.

Note 13

1. "ingrained." Oxford Dictionary of English. © 2020 MobiSystems, Inc.

Note 23

1. Be Ye Transformed, Chuck and Nancy Missler, © Copyright 1996 by Nancy Missler, Thirteenth printing, April, 2016, Published by The King's High Way Ministries, Inc., Coeur d'Alene ID 83816. All rights reserved. Page 216.

Note 27

1. "deep-seated." © 2012 Merriam-Webster, Inc. (15 June 2019).

Note 41

1. "sanctify." Vine's Expository Dictionary of Old and New Testament Words. Copyright © 1981 by Fleming H. Revell Company. All rights reserved. Page 318.

2. "conscience." Vine's Expository Dictionary of Old and New Testament Words. Copyright © 1981 by Fleming H. Revell Company. All rights reserved. Page 228.

3. "eye." Vine's Expository Dictionary of Old and New Testament Words. Copyright © 1981 by Fleming H. Revell Company. All rights reserved. Page 64.

4. "exercise." Vine's Expository Dictionary of Old and New Testament Words. Copyright © 1981 by Fleming H. Revell Company. All rights reserved. Page 59.

5. "exercise." Vine's Expository Dictionary of Old and New Testament Words. Copyright © 1981 by Fleming H. Revell Company. All rights reserved. Page 59.

6. "godliness." Vine's Expository Dictionary of Old and New Testament Words. Copyright ©

1981 by Fleming H. Revell Company. All rights reserved. Page 162.

7. The Vanishing Conscience. Copyright © 1995 by John F. MacArthur, Jr.. Published by Nelson Books, a Division of Thomas Nelson Publishers. All rights reserved. Page 39.

Note 43

1. "life." Vine's Expository Dictionary of Old and New Testament Words. Copyright © 1981 by Fleming H. Revell Company. All rights reserved. Page 336.

Note 47

1. "sarcasm." © 2019 Meriam-Webster, Inc. (15 June 2019).

Note 49

1. 65 Promises From God for your Child, Powerful Prayers for Supernatural Results. Copyright © 2013 by Mike Shreve. Published by Charisma House. 600 Rinehart Road, Lake Mary, Florida 32746. All rights reserved. Page 53, 54.

SUBJECT INDEX

Men of faith who were not moved by the circumstances of life	6b
The new man, our true identity (including the fruit of the Spirit and walking in humility)	2a, 2b, 3b, 4b, 5a, 5c, 5d, 6b, 7a, 8a, 8d, 9, 10a, 11, 12, 13b, 14a, 14b, 15b, 16a, 17a, 17b, 18a, 18b, 19b, 20a, 20b, 21a, 21b, 22a, 22b, 23a, 23b, 23c, 25b, 26b, 27a, 27b, 28a, 28b, 28c, 29a, 29b, 29c, 30, 31, 32b, 33a, 33b, 34a, 34b, 35, 36a, 36b, 37a, 37b, 38a, 39, 40, 41, 42, 43, 44a, 44b, 45, 46, 49, 50
The old man, the carnal nature (including walking in pride)	2b, 5a, 5c, 6b, 8a, 8d, 9, 11, 12, 13b, 14b, 15a, 15b, 16a, 17a, 17b, 18a, 18b, 20a, 20b, 21a, 21b, 22b, 23c, 25b, 27a, 27b, 28a, 28c, 29a, 29b, 29c, 30, 31, 32b, 33a 33c, 34a, 34b, 35, 37a, 37b, 38b, 41, 42, 43, 45, 47
Our free will, the power of choice	14b, 24b
Our heavenly Father	2b, 7a, 7b, 7c, 9, 20b, 25b, 26a, 26b, 38a, 38b, 39, 40
Our heart ground (including pollutants/defilement/tongue)	2b, 5a, 15b, 16a, 17b, 22b, 23c, 29a, 29c, 30, 31, 33b, 33c, 41
Parents	27a, 34a, 49, 50
The peace of God	5d, 8a, 8b, 8d, 10a
Prayer and intercession for loved ones and the lost (*including a prayer to be born again)	1b*, 17b, 24b
Renewing our minds (including setting our affections on things above and transformation)	3b, 5b, 7b, 7c, 8a, 8b, 8d, 10a, 10b, 11, 12, 13b, 17a, 17b, 18a, 21b, 23c, 25b, 26b, 27a, 27b, 28a, 28b, 8c, 29a, 29b, 29c, 35, 36b, 37a, 39, 40, 41, 42, 43, 44a, 49, 50

SCRIPTURE INDEX
BY SUBJECT MATTER
(Includes all Scriptures in the study notes highlighted in bold-faced type)

"CHRISTY MORGAN'S CHARACTER DEVELOPMENT IN CHRIST
IS AN "OFF THE CHARTS" RESOURCE TO HELP BRING BREAKTHROUGH
FOR EVERY BORN-AGAIN BELIEVER..."
—**Deanne "Dee" Barnes**, Founder, His Wonderful Works, Inc., CEO, Evans Tool & Die, Inc.

"IT IS IMPORTANT THAT CHRISTIANS BUILD A SCRIPTURE BASED FOUNDATION SO THAT
OUR FAITH IS UNSHAKEABLE. WAY TOO OFTEN BELIEVERS ARE TOLD TO READ THE BIBLE.
MANY HAVE TRIED AND FAILED HAVING HAD NO DIRECTION IN THEIR STUDIES.
THE SCRIPTURE GUIDE STUDY NOTES, THIS SUPPLEMENTAL BOOK FOR CHARACTER
DEVELOPMENT IN CHRIST, PROVIDES A PRACTICAL, SCRIPTURAL GUIDE TO BUILDING
A BIBLICAL FOUNDATION. THE NOTES WALK YOU THROUGH THE SCRIPTURES
THAT BRING HEALING AND MATURITY IN CHRIST."
—**Eddie Mason**, Senior Pastor, Southside Christian Fellowship Church

Available on Amazon!

Made in the USA
Columbia, SC
19 June 2023

18007395R00224